ER,
E THE
OW

17. MAR. 1975

Wages and Labour Economics

644

Wages and Labour Economics

J. M. Jackson

Senior Lecturer in Economics,
University of Dundee

McGRAW-HILL

London · New York · Toronto · Sydney
Mexico · Johannesburg · Panama · Singapore

Published by

McGRAW-HILL Publishing Company Limited

MAIDENHEAD · BERKSHIRE · ENGLAND

07 094130 0

792,118

PRINTED AND BOUND IN GREAT BRITAIN

Preface

As a teacher of labour economics, I have long felt the need for a British textbook in this field. There are numerous American textbooks, but, admirable as these may be in many respects, the British student requires one that will treat the economics of labour within the institutional framework of his own country.

This book is aimed primarily at university students in their first or second year. Although I have, for the most part, fully explained in Part 1 the theoretical techniques used, I would hope that most students coming to this book would already have completed an elementary course in economic theory, and would be pursuing further studies in theoretical economics alongside their study of labour economics. The emphasis throughout is on the economics of labour, and on the problems that arise because labour is a scarce productive resource which needs to be allocated in such a way as to make the best use of the available supply. However, institutional matters, such as trade union organization and the law relating to trade unions, are introduced because one cannot expect to understand fully how wages are determined or labour allocated between jobs without some knowledge of the institutional framework. There are many institutional aspects of the labour market that would have been more fully and very differently treated if I had been interested in these for their own sake.

There are inevitably omissions, and also areas where the treatment is less detailed than some readers might like. A full treatment of all the topics raised here would require several volumes. It must be understood that this is no more than an introduction to labour economics, and the student who wishes to specialize in this field will need to refer to the many more specialized works dealing with limited areas of the subject. I shall be content if this introduction serves to interest him in this aspect of economics and to assist him in his further studies. Although I have written with the needs of the university student in mind, I hope, nevertheless, that this book will prove helpful to students in other higher educational establishments, and even the general reader.

While time has not permitted me to submit my manuscript to my colleagues in the Department of Economics in Dundee, I have benefitted from frequent discussion with them (and also the students of the department) on many of the topics covered.

J. M. Jackson

TABLE OF CONTENTS

1. Introduction

Labour: a scarce resource

All economic problems involve scarcity and choice: the productive resources needed to bring about the satisfaction of our many and varied wants are scarce, and we therefore have to make choices about how we will use them. One of these scarce resources is human labour. Most of us would like to have more money to spend on the goods and services that are available to us on the market. Many of us could, perhaps, earn more money by working overtime or by taking a second job. There are limits to this, however. We all need a minimum amount of rest if we are to remain fit for work; moreover, unless we are living at a very low standard, we want a certain amount of leisure. Thus, there is a limit to the amount of time any person is prepared to work. There is also a limit to the number of people who are seeking work at any given time. In recent years, planners in Britain have foreseen the possibility of a shortage of labour limiting the rate of growth that can be achieved.

Shortages of particular skills. It may be necessary, therefore, to try to induce a larger proportion of the population to enter the labour market, for example, by encouraging more married women to remain at work or to return to work after their children have grown up. But it is not only the total number of workers that is important; shortages of particular kinds of labour may be just as important.

In many underdeveloped countries, there may be plenty of unskilled labourers seeking work. Even if everyone appears to have a job, there may still be disguised unemployment, for instance, a family farm may give work to more men than are required to run it efficiently. If some of these men could be found other jobs, those remaining on the farm might still be able to maintain the previous level of output. In the process of development, men should be persuaded, or compelled, to leave the farms (where they have been making no real contribution to production) and take jobs in factories. As the factories are built, there would then be plenty of

A*

1

men to fill some of the jobs that are created. There would be no shortage of unskilled labourers to sweep the factory floor or to fetch and carry away materials and finished goods. There may even be a reasonably adequate number of men who could be trained for semiskilled jobs as machine operators and so on. It is unlikely, however, that there would be enough skilled mechanics in the native population to service the machines in the factories and keep them operating, so underdeveloped countries may have to rely, to a large extent, upon expatriate labour to fill a good many of the more highly skilled jobs.

In the more advanced countries, a very different situation may exist. Although shortages of skilled labour may arise, and certainly there may be a shortage of a particular skill, it is also possible that, with rising educational standards and the growing aspirations of the majority of citizens, there will be a shortage of people willing to undertake some of the least skilled and least pleasant jobs. Something of this kind has been occurring in Britain. There has, it is true, been an influx of immigrants who have often been prepared to take the jobs that British workers try to avoid, but this may not be an ideal solution. In the long run, it is one which may create as many problems as it solves.[1] For the moment, it is enough to recognize the possibility of a shortage of unskilled as well as of skilled labour.

Labour, then, is a scarce resource and it is therefore necessary to try to ensure that the best use is made of the available supply.

Man in the economy

Labour is not the only scarce factor of production. The other productive resources, land and capital, are also in short supply, and it is therefore necessary to make the most effective use of these, too. It is important not to lose sight of the fact that in a book such as this we are limiting our study somewhat arbitrarily to one particular aspect of the much wider problem of efficient resource allocation.

It is also essential to realize that labour is different from the other productive factors. Land and capital are both inanimate resources which are to be used for the benefit of man, while men, on the other hand, are not merely agents of production, but also the ultimate end of all productive activity. Production is intended to bring about the satisfaction of human wants – in large measure, the wants of those same men who make an essential contribution to the process of production. A free society, in which all men are regarded as

2

equal, cannot view the problem of how to allocate labour in exactly the same light as one in which the majority of workers are slaves. Regard for the dignity and fundamental rights of the worker may necessitate some regulation of the conditions under which people may work. Wages may have a role to play in getting men to take those jobs which society, in a sense, deems the most important. In so far as this is the case,[2] there may be theoretical arguments which suggest that there should be as little interference as possible with the free working of the labour market. For most men, however, a wage is their only source of income, and some measure of interference with the market mechanism may be necessary in order to ensure that all workers have enough to live on.

Non-market incomes. In addition to minimum wage legislation, there are other measures to help ensure that people are adequately provided for, even when their earnings are too low to permit them to enjoy a decent standard of living. Family allowances help those with heavier than average family responsibilities. National Insurance provides a large number of people with a minimum basic income during periods of sickness or unemployment, and on retirement or during widowhood.[3] Supplementary pensions and allowances are available to those in need and who are not eligible for National Insurance benefits or who, in the absence of any other income, cannot manage on these benefits.[4] Today, the economist recognizes that such interferences with the market mechanism may be necessary in order to fulfil the policy objectives which society sets itself. The labour economist must accept such objectives as part of the data with which he deals. It may be recalled, however, that society did not always display such concern for all its members, nor were economists prepared to admit that such policy objectives could be taken as given and independent of their analysis of the working of the economy.[5]

The plan of the book

The treatment of the subject falls into four main parts. Part 1 is devoted to the economist's theoretical analysis of wage determination. It traces the evolution of wages theory and then considers in more detail the modern analysis of wage determination, including the share of wages in the national income. Part 2 looks at more practical aspects of wages, including such topics as what workers actually earn, the methods by which they are paid, and the importance of fringe benefits. Part 3 is concerned with organized labour

3

and collective bargaining, and Part 4 is devoted to the role of the Government in the labour market.

NOTES

1. The fresh problems created may be social rather than strictly economic. Second generation Indians and Pakistanis in this country, that is, the children of the original immigrants, may not be content to accept the narrow range of unskilled jobs that their parents did. Therefore, unless immigration continues, a time comes when we again have to face the original problem of finding people to take the less pleasant and less skilled jobs, or else the second generation Asians are forced into those jobs by discrimination against them in more skilled fields. If this happens, we have the seeds of racial unrest well and truly sown.

2. The effectiveness of wages as a mechanism for allocating labour may, it will be seen later, prove to be less than many economists have believed.

3. Under the National Insurance scheme, permanent pensions are paid to widows only if they are over the age of fifty, either when they are widowed or when they cease to have dependent children.

4. Supplementary benefits are paid only after a means test.

5. Some of the Classical economists argued that no good came from interfering with the market mechanism, and that a free market economy was *morally* right. Some of the implications of Classical economic theory for the labourer are considered in chapter 2.

Part 1
Wage Theory

2. Changing approaches to wage theory

The Classical school

The purpose of this chapter is not so much to give a detailed account of how earlier generations of economists have analysed the way in which wages are determined, as to try and give some indication of their general approach to this topic and their attitude towards the labouring class. There is little real economic analysis prior to the publication of Adam Smith's *The Wealth of Nations* in 1776, and it is therefore unnecessary to take this brief discussion of the attitude of economists to wage theory back beyond this date. Two main ideas dominated the thinking of the Classical school on wage theory, the Malthusian *principle of population* and the concept of the *wages fund*. Malthus argued that when wages rose more children would survive because of better nutrition and that the population would increase. As the population rose, it would be impossible for food production to keep pace. Malthus believed that the population might double every 25 years if unchecked, a potential eightfold increase in a century. Because of the scarcity of good land and the tendency towards diminishing returns, food production would increase more slowly – perhaps in the arithmetical progression 1:2:3:4 over the course of the century. If this were so, in the same period, the population would tend to increase twice as rapidly as the supply of food, so that food would become scarcer and prices would rise. Money wages might rise, but not enough to offset the rise in prices. Real wages would fall, and there would be increased hunger and malnutrition, fewer children would survive, and the tendency for population to increase would thus be checked.

The wages fund doctrine asserted that there was a fixed sum available for the support of labour. Wages were paid out of this fund, and if, for any reason, employers paid more to one group of workers than hitherto, there would be less available to pay to

7

others. This would mean that they would either have to employ fewer workers or pay some lower wages than before. A trade union might be able to secure higher wages for its members, but, in the last resort, it would be at the expense of other workers, not the employers.

The Classical economists firmly believed that wages tended to oscillate around their natural level, the subsistence level.[1] Any attempt to interfere with the working of supply and demand in the labour market was regarded as useless and even positively harmful. Yet while the Classical theories were pessimistic, they were at the same time comforting for the employing classes. If it was impossible to improve the lot of the masses, if any attempt to do so were liable to reduce everyone to the lowest level, why should they worry?[2]

The Poor Law. Some writers of the Classical school were opposed to the provisions of the Poor Law for the relief of those who could not find work or were unfit for work. Malthus believed that the Poor Law was worse than useless:

> ... the poor laws of England tend to depress the general conditions of the poor ... to increase population without increasing the food for its support ... the quantity of provisions consumed in workhouses upon a part of society that in general cannot be considered as the most valuable part, diminishes the shares that could otherwise belong to more industrious and worthy members.[3]

Malthus would not admit that some, at least, of the poor were victims of circumstances and not just suffering the consequences of their own idleness or improvidence. There were, however, other writers of the school who showed more sympathy with the lot of the poor. M'Culloch, for example, dealing with the impotent poor, said, 'there does not seem to be much room for doubt as to the policy, as well as the humanity, of giving them a legal claim to relief'.[4] M'Culloch was perhaps not only more humane than Malthus, but also more realistic, for he showed an awareness of the true alternative implicit in the line taken by Malthus. Even if the possibility of relief may, in some people, reduce the incentive to thrift, 'whatever may have been the faults of individuals, it would be abhorrent to all the feelings of humanity to allow them to suffer the extremity of want'[5] and to die in the street.

Relative wages. The Classical economists were aware that wages varied between occupations and, although their main concern was to explain the general level of labourers' wages and how the shares of wages, profits, and rents in the national product changed with

8

population growth, they gave some attention to these variations. A great deal of their analysis of differentials is still valid today. Smith and others, for example, realized that wages might have to be higher in jobs that were unpleasant or dangerous than in those that were pleasant or safe. The acquisition of skill meant an apprenticeship or period of training during which earnings would be low, and the sacrifice that this entailed needed to be rewarded by the prospect of higher earnings when qualified.

The most significant contribution to the understanding of wage differentials made by the Classical school came from Cairnes, who introduced the concept of *non-competing groups*.[6] It was generally accepted that, subject to such qualifications as those made above, wages tended towards equality in all occupations. Cairnes, however, pointed out that different jobs call for different degrees of skill, that not everyone has the natural abilities required of a skilled worker. The man who lacks the necessary abilities cannot take a skilled job, however much he is attracted by the higher wages. Workers therefore form non-competing groups. Among unskilled labourers, wages will tend towards equality. If this were not so, workers would flock to the better paid jobs and refuse to take the lower paid ones. A similar tendency would be at work at higher levels of skill. However, a differential may persist between each level of skill because workers cannot compete for jobs in a group demanding greater abilities than they possess.

The Neo-Classical approach

Gradually, the approach to the theory of wages changed. The later writers of the Classical school abandoned the concept of the wages fund, though they continued to cling to the Malthusian principle of population. It is with Marshall,[7] however, that we get a clear recognition of the fact that the worker is paid out of a flow of revenue from the sale of the goods he has helped to produce and not out of a fixed fund. If employing more men would increase this flow of revenue sufficiently, the employer would seek to hire more labour. Nevertheless, the attitude of economists in the late nineteenth and early twentieth century towards the trade unions remained hostile. They still believed that the power of the trade unions to raise the real wages of their members was strictly limited. The employers' demand for labour was dependent upon its marginal productivity, and since marginal productivity fell as more men were employed, an increase in wages must lead to a fall in employment. Trade unions might gain higher wages for their members in a particular trade, but fewer would be employed. The men who could no longer find employment in their old occupation would seek other work. If they were to do so, it would only be as a result of wages in other fields being lowered. So, although Marshall and his successors had a theory based upon very different assumptions from the Classical school, the implications for trade unionism were not greatly different.[8]

Monopsony in the labour market. Marshallian theory was refined and elaborated in the early 1930s by the publication of two books on imperfect competition.[9] The application of these new theories to the labour market showed that profit-maximizing firms might not be equating the marginal product of labour to the wage paid, but to the marginal cost of employing another man. This would be higher than the wage if the employer were forced to raise wages when he wanted to attract more labour. If trade union action were to force the wage up, it did not follow that fewer men would be employed. Because the employer would now, within limits, be able to get as much labour as he wished at the going rate, the wage would equal the marginal cost of employing an extra man. As long as the wage did not exceed the original marginal productivity of labour, it would still pay the employer to hire at least as many men as before.[10]

The Keynesian revolution

Where the Classical school had concentrated their attention on the general level of wages and the share of wages in the national income, Marshall and his successors had been more concerned with the wages paid in a particular industry or occupation. The work of Keynes[11] brought about important changes in emphasis, especially in matters relating to wages and unemployment. The neo-Classical writers had argued that firms would employ extra men so long as the amount added to the wage bill was less than the increase in the value of total output. Falling marginal productivity meant that a rise in wages would cause a fall in the numbers employed. Subject to some qualification regarding the case of monopsony just mentioned, this is true at the level of partial equilibrium analysis. If all other product and factor prices remain unchanged, as do consumer tastes, a rise in the wages paid by one firm or industry will lead to a lower level of employment in that firm or industry. The trouble was that some economists had been too ready to apply these same arguments to the labour market as a whole. It had been argued that

10

if there were unemployment the remedy was to cut wages. But while it is true that if a single firm is able to lower wages, it will, *ceteris paribus*, find it profitable to employ more men, when there is a general cut in wage rates, the *ceteris paribus* assumption is inappropriate. There will be less money in the hands of the general public to spend, and most firms will find their product demand curves (and hence their marginal productivity curves for labour) shifted.

In the long run, however, the revolution engendered by Keynes brought the unions under fire on another score. By the end of the Second World War, most governments had accepted Keynesian ideas and were committed to the maintenance of full employment. With full employment, the bargaining power of the trade unions was enhanced, and they were blamed for causing cost-push inflation.[12] To prevent such inflation, governments in many countries have tried to devise some kind of wages or incomes policy to ensure that money incomes, especially wages, do not rise faster than the supply of goods and services on which these incomes are to be spent.

The attitude of the economist

It may seem that economists have a built-in suspicion of trade unionism. Even though economic theory has undergone radical changes over the years, it seems impossible for economists to cast aside for long the old idea that if trade unions are not useless they are harmful. In the past, some of these suspicions were based upon faulty assumptions and analysis. It remains to be seen whether future work will confirm the assumptions and reasoning of the present generation of economists or show them also to be false.

The present situation is, however, different in many important respects from the situation envisaged by the Classical and neo-Classical writers. They failed to appreciate the need for the workers to organize in their own defence. Without such organization, they could not hope to secure decent wages and conditions of employment. While it would be wrong to argue that the trade unions do not still have a useful role to play, they are no longer the champions of the underdog in the same way they once were. That situation has been transformed by the realization of the goal of full employment.

It is well for the labour economist to remember that these mistakes have been made in the past, and that his own analysis today is fallible. He should remember, too, that the Trade Union movement is made up of men and women with memories of conditions that were very different from those of today, and that it is unrealistic to ignore

11

these memories. In the field of labour economics, perhaps more than in any other branch of the subject, we are dealing with ordinary men of flesh and blood; men with aspirations; men with ideas of what is right and wrong. At times, it may be convenient and even necessary to construct theoretical models in which we make use of something very close to an *economic man*, but such models can never be more than the starting point of a realistic analysis. Modern economists have been apt to stress the ethical neutrality of their subject, and there is much to be said in favour of so doing. In labour economics, it would be wrong to push this idea too far. We should certainly not go to the extreme of supposing that ethical ideas are irrelevant to economic behaviour, or maintain that such ideas have no place in the determination of economic policy. Instead, we should recognize that such ideas are an essential part of the economic scene we are studying and take full account of them.

NOTES

1. It should be added that Ricardo admitted that the natural wage was not one which allowed the worker a bare subsistence. Subsistence, in practice, was determined partly by convention, and he believed that a British worker would not marry and have a family if he could only afford to live in a mud hut on a diet of potatoes. Malthus, too, recognized that the lowering of the birth rate through later marriage could prevent the excessive growth of population.
2. While this was one reaction to the Classical theories, there was another. The same theories formed the basis for much of Marx's thinking, though the Marxian policy implications were very different.
3. T. R. Malthus, *Essay on the Principle of Population*, London, 1798.
4. J. R. M'Culloch, *Principles of Political Economy*, Edinburgh, 1825.
5. Ibid., part III, section VII.
6. J. E. Cairnes, *Some Leading Principles of Political Economy*, London, 1874.
7. A. Marshall, *Principles of Economics* 1st edn, Macmillan, London, 1890.
8. See A. Marshall, *Elements of the Economics of Industry*, 3rd edn, Macmillan, London, 1899, for a fuller treatment of the factors limiting the power of the trade unions to raise wages.
9. J. V. Robinson, *The Economics of Imperfect Competition*, Macmillan, London, 1933; E. H. Chamberlain, *The Theory of Monopolistic Competition*, Harvard U.P., Cambridge, Mass., 1933.
10. But see chapter 5 for the necessary qualifications.
11. J. M. Keynes, *General Theory of Employment, Interest and Money*, Macmillan, London, 1936.
12. Keynes himself dealt with the role of the unions and inflation in *How to Pay for the War*, Macmillan, London, 1940.

3. The supply of labour

The quantity of labour

The factor of production, labour, cannot be measured in terms of a single dimension. In some of our models it may be more convenient to speak of fewer men being employed, but this is only one way of varying the quantity of labour employed. A firm that wanted to increase (or decrease) its output might decide, if it thought the increase (decrease) in output would only last for a short time, to rely upon overtime (short-time) working. If the demand were expected to remain at a higher (lower) level for some considerable period, it might prefer to engage more workers (dismiss some workers). There may be circumstances where it is preferable to vary the number of workers employed and others where it is preferable to vary the hours each works. For the moment, the essential point is that the supply of labour is to be measured in manhours rather than just the number of workers.

There are other dimensions to the labour supply, though it is not easy to introduce these into any practical measurement. The amount of work which a man accomplishes in the course of an hour may vary within quite wide limits. It is, for example, well known that the introduction of some kind of payment by result scheme may lead to increased production. When the worker is given the opportunity of earning more by working harder, he may be prepared to make a greater effort than when his pay is unrelated to the effort he makes.[1] The men employed on a particular job may not be equally efficient. In theoretical models, we may assume that the supply of labour is homogeneous, but this is rarely the case in practice. There are some workers who are very good at their job and some who are on the margin of employability. While the intensity of effort and the efficiency of the worker are important, we must freely admit that we cannot readily incorporate them into our measurement of the supply of labour.

All these factors are relevant when we are considering the supply

13

of labour for any particular kind of job. If people worked longer, if more people could be employed, if people worked harder or became more efficient, we could speak of the supply of labour as having been increased, in some sense. When we are considering the supply of labour to the economy as a whole, it is necessary to take account of a further factor. There is a variety of jobs to be done, some of them calling for particular aptitudes or acquired skills. The productivity of the whole labour force will depend not only upon such factors as its size, the willingness to work, the general level of intelligence and education, and so on, but also upon whether the labour force contains the right mixture of abilities and skills in relation to the demand for them.

The supply of labour by the individual

We must now ask how much labour the individual worker is prepared to supply. We assume that the worker is free to decide not only whether he will work or not, but also exactly how long he will work.

Marshall's analysis of the supply of labour was based on the assumption that the individual would try to equate the utility derived from an hour's earnings with the disutility of another hour's work. This analysis was not entirely satisfactory, for a change in the wage rate has two effects, an income effect and a substitution effect. If the wage rate is increased, a man earns more for the marginal hour worked, and it is tempting to argue that this will induce him to work for a longer period. In this case, however, money is not an adequate measure of marginal utility. When wages rise, a man is better off, and an increment of income may have less significance for him. Although he may be earning more for an extra hour worked, these extra earnings may mean less to him than the original wage rate *at the margin*. The qualification that the marginal utility of money is constant, emphasized by Marshall in his treatment of consumer surplus, inevitably breaks down when we consider the impact of a wage change on a man who is entirely dependent upon what he earns by selling his labour. Or, in other words, with a higher wage rate a man is better off and can afford to 'purchase' more leisure. It is therefore preferable to base our analysis of the supply of labour upon the more modern indifference curve technique.

In Fig. 3.1, the indifference curves, I_1, I_2, I_3, show combinations of earnings and leisure. Combinations on any indifference curve are equally satisfactory to the worker. A curve lying above and to the

14

right of another shows combinations that are regarded as giving more satisfaction than combinations on the other.[2] On the indifference map we superimpose a wage line; this shows the combinations

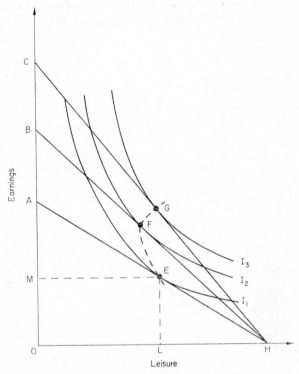

Fig. 3.1. The supply of labour by the individual.

of income and leisure which the worker can achieve when the wage rate is given. This is a straight line with the slope representing the wage rate. The worker seeks to maximize his satisfaction by reaching the highest possible indifference curve. This, of course, means reaching the point where the wage line is tangential to an indifference curve.

Where the wage rate is given by the slope of the line HA, the worker is in equilibrium at the point E on curve I_1. He will work for a period LH and take OL leisure, and his earnings will be LE (= OM). At higher wage rates represented by slopes of HB, HC, the individual is in equilibrium at points F, G, on curves I_2, I_3 respectively. If we join the points E, F, G, and the many similar

15

points we could obtain on other wage lines, we get a *wage-leisure curve* EFG.[3] In the case shown in Fig. 3.1, it will be seen that the amount of labour supplied at first increases with the wage rate, but after a certain point more leisure is taken as the wage rate rises. Thus, we would find the individual's labour supply curve becoming backward sloping above a certain wage rate, as in Fig. 3.2.

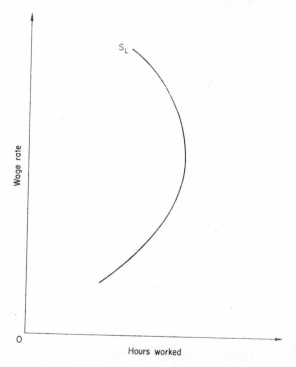

Fig. 3.2. The individual's labour supply curve.

There is no theoretical reason why the individual's labour supply curve should take this particular shape. The curve might have a positive slope throughout its length, or a negative slope throughout.[4] In practice, however, we would expect that a time would come when an increase in the wage rate would lead to the individual supplying less labour than before. A man values both income and leisure. It is not surprising, therefore, that as wages rise the worker should choose to take part of the benefit in the form of greater leisure and part in the form of increased income.

Income and Subsitution Effects. The effect of a wage change can be split into an income and a substitution effect. The substitution effect

16

arises because leisure becomes dearer when the wage rate rises. By taking an hour of leisure, the worker is sacrificing more potential income than he did before the wage rise. The substitution effect will tend to induce him to substitute work for leisure. A rise in wages also makes the worker better off if he still works the same hours. If leisure is a normal commodity, the worker will choose more of it when he becomes better off. We would see an income effect in its pure form if, for example, a worker acquired an unearned income, perhaps through a legacy. In such an event, he might well work fewer hours although no change in the wage rate had taken place.

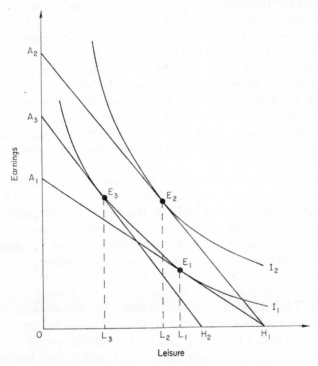

Fig. 3.3. Income and substitution effects of a change in the wage rate.

The income effect is clearly working in the opposite direction to the substitution effect, and may easily be more important than it. In demand theory, it is accepted that there are inferior goods, the demand for which declines as income rises. The possibility of a Giffen good is also recognized, where the income effect may predominate over the substitution effect, thus reversing the normal law of demand. The Giffen good is little more than a theoretical

17

possibility in most economies, because one rarely finds that a sufficient proportion of income is spent on any one commodity for the income effect to outweigh the substitution effect. When we are considering wages and the supply of labour, the position is very different. Wages are people's main source of income and the income effect of a wage change is bound to be large.

A diagrammatic demonstration of the income and substitution effect is given in Fig. 3.3. When the wage rate is given by the slope of H_1A_1, the individual is in equilibrium at E_1. If the wage rate rises so that the wage line becomes H_1A_2, his equilibrium position becomes the point E_2. If, however, the increase in the wage rate were to be accompanied by the imposition of a polltax amounting to A_2A_3, the individual would now be in equilibrium at E_3, which lies on the same indifference curve as that passing through E_1.[5]

The movement from E_1 to E_3 is the substitution effect. It is the movement that occurs when the wage rate rises, but a polltax is imposed which leaves the individual no better off than before. If no polltax is imposed, the income effect operates, and this is shown as the movement from E_3 to E_2. In the case drawn, the income effect is less than the substitution effect. If it were greater, E_2 would lie to the right of E_1.

Overtime. If overtime is paid at a higher rate than normal hours, a pure substitution effect may be observed. In Fig. 3.4, the normal wage rate is given by the slope of the line HA_1. The individual would be in equilibrium at the point E_1. He works for a period HL_1. If overtime rates are now introduced for hours of work in excess of HL_1, the individual now has the opportunity of moving to some point on the line E_1A_2, such as E_2. Because the worker only gets the benefit of the higher rate of pay after he has worked a certain number of hours, there is no income effect. The higher rate is only paid for the marginal hours worked, and will always induce him to work longer than if all work is paid at the ordinary rate.

In practice, workers are not free to choose exactly how long they will work at a given wage rate. A job may carry a wage of £15 for a 40 hour week. A man is expected to work for the 40 hours or not at all. If he wants more leisure, he may occasionally take an unauthorized holiday, but he cannot do this too often if he is to keep his job.

All that the individual can decide, therefore, is whether he would prefer to work for 40 hours in return for a £15 wage or try to get some other job which might, let us assume, pay £14·25 for a 38 hour week. Even this choice may not be available to him, because the working week may be more or less the same in most jobs. If it

18

varies, it may well be that the job with shorter hours, which he would prefer, is not one for which he is qualified. He may, of course, prefer to work for more than the standard hours. If the firm is busy and

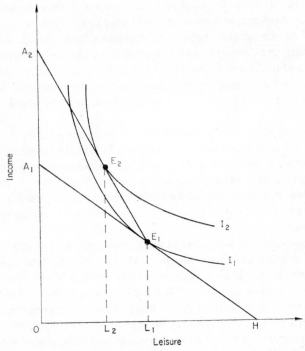

Fig. 3.4. The worker's reaction to overtime rates market.

looking for men to work overtime, he may be able to decide just how much overtime he will work, and reach his true equilibrium point. But when trade is slack, firms may not be offering overtime. So it is quite possible that the individual worker will simply have to accept the standard working week, which may be longer or shorter than he would like.

Although the individual may not be free to choose exactly how long he will work, the preferences of the workers are not without effect. If most men would prefer a shorter working week, it may be possible for them, through their trade union, to secure this. If we look at what has happened over a long period of years, it is evident that hours worked have been greatly reduced. Before the Second World War, a working week of 48 hours was not uncommon, whereas a 5 day week of 40 hours is now fairly usual.[6]

The total supply of labour

The Classical economists included in their study of the supply of labour the factors governing the size of the population itself. Such a study today would need to be a very different one from the simple theory of Malthus. Population trends are far more complex than Malthus supposed, and account would have to be taken of migration as well as the natural increase or decrease of population. For the most part, the economist today is content to take the population as given, and to discuss the supply of labour in terms of the proportion of the population entering the labour market, the hours each individual is prepared to work, the readiness to acquire particular skills, and so on.

We have seen already that there is a good chance that a rise in wages will lead individuals to take more leisure. We must now ask whether a rise in wages will induce more people to enter the labour market in search of employment, or fewer. A moment's reflection will show that there are reasons why either result is possible, that, at any given moment of time, there may be factors working in both directions.

If wages are very low, a rise in wages may easily lead to a reduction in the amount of labour supplied. Married women who found it necessary to work to supplement their husbands' earnings may choose to remain at home. When wages are low, children may be sent to work at the earliest opportunity. As the community becomes more prosperous, children may be kept at school longer, and more young people may be sent to the university and other places of higher education. The labour force is reduced. On the other hand, as wages reach still higher levels, and as technology advances, it may become possible for more married women to remain at work, or to return to work after their children reach a certain age.[7]

All that we can say is that when wages rise there are some factors at work which will bring more people into the labour market and some which will reduce the number seeking work. Either may predominate. It may well be that, as wages rise from a low level, some people can afford to withdraw from the labour market. Above a certain level, some people may be tempted back into the labour market and the supply curve may take on a positive slope again. Beyond a still higher level, there may be a very limited effect, bringing more people into the labour market while increasing the numbers who remain later at school, so that the total labour supply is reduced. Thus, the labour supply curve may take the form shown in Fig. 3.5, though many variations on this shape are possible. Pure theory can tell us very little about the total supply of labour. If we want to know what will happen when wages rise, we must study the conditions under which people live, their social attitudes, and so on.

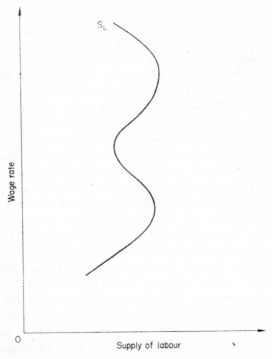

Fig. 3.5. Possible shape of a labour supply curve.

The economist is, in practice, more likely to be concerned with the supply of labour to a firm, an industry, an occupation, or even a fairly wide geographical area, rather than the whole country. The supply of labour to any one of these regions will depend upon such factors as the initial endowment of population, the way in which individual workers and groups of workers react to changes in wages, but there is another important consideration. If there is a general increase in wages throughout a country, this may well meet with a limited response. Very few additional workers may be attracted into the labour market; indeed, we have seen that in some circumstances the opposite result may occur. If, however, one firm (or industry, or occupation, or region) offers higher wages while other firms (or industries, or occupations, or regions) continue to pay the same wages as before, the differential will tend to attract

21

workers to the unit offering higher pay. This is not to say that the effect of the differential will necessarily be great. In the real world, the impact of wages differential may be greatly reduced by inertia and ignorance. But we can be sure that a five per cent increase in the wages offered by one economic unit (whatever that unit may be) will meet with a proportionately greater response than a five per cent increase in wages throughout the country.

Supply of labour to a firm. The responsiveness of the supply of labour to a change in the wage rate is normally measured by the elasticity of supply, the proportionate change in the quantity of labour supplied divided by the proportionate change in the wage rate. The elasticity of the labour supply curve facing a firm will depend upon, among other factors, the size of the firm. As we shall see later, in this context, what matters is the size of the firm's labour force in relation to the local labour market, rather than any absolute measure of size or size in relation to the product market. If the firm is fairly small, it may find that the supply of labour is relatively elastic; a small increase in wages offered as compared to other firms will lead to a significant increase in its supply of labour. In the limiting case of perfect competition among employers, we assume that the firm is so small that it can secure as much labour as it requires at the going wage rate. At the other end of the scale, the firm that dominates the local labour market will find that supply is relatively inelastic. Since it dominates the labour market, there is little labour to be drawn from other firms, and it must rely almost entirely on any increase in the total quantity of labour supplied in the area and, perhaps, on drawing some labour from further afield.

Supply to an industry or occupation. It is important to distinguish between the supply of labour to an industry and the supply to an occupation. Sometimes, an industry will employ mainly workers with a particular type of skill, for example, coalmining, which gives employment mainly to colliers. On the other hand, the many varied branches of the engineering and shipbuilding industries – to say nothing of a good many other industries – give employment to men in a variety of trades including fitters, turners, welders, electricians, storekeepers, drivers, and so on.

Typically, then, we may think of an industry employing men with many different skills. If one industry raises the wages it pays, say, electricians, the differential is likely to attract some electricians from other industries. The supply of electricians to any particular industry is likely to be more elastic than the supply of electricians in general. The supply of electricians, or any other skilled trade that calls for a

22

lengthy period of training, is bound to be inelastic in the short run, although higher pay may serve to attract some electricians to continue to work as such when they might have retired or perhaps taken some other kind of job. More electricians can be trained *in time*, but it is a slow process. Even a big increase in the number of youths starting apprenticeships will, at the end of five years, if that is the period of training, only have a small impact on total supply. For instance, if the working life of a qualified craftsman is normally from 21 to 65, then we would expect that each year just over 2 per cent of the qualified craftsmen would retire to be replaced by the newly qualified apprentices. Thus, a 20 per cent increase in the number of lads starting apprenticeships (itself an unrealistically large increase) would only lead, after a time lag of 5 years, to an increase in the total supply of $\frac{1}{2}$ per cent.

Regional labour supply. If wages are higher in one region than another, a movement of labour might be expected to result from the differential. In practice, such movement is limited. Workers may be ignorant of opportunities in other parts of the country, they may be reluctant to break their ties with their home areas, and they may be deterred by the difficulty of finding accommodation in the new region. Moving also involves costs – the cost of moving furniture, and, for the houseowner, the legal fees involved in buying and selling a house. One would only expect a differential in wages to lead to a movement of labour from one part of the country if it were sufficient to outweigh the costs of movement.

Nevertheless, it is clear that at the present time there is a substantial movement of labour to the Midlands and the South-east. It would be wrong, however, to attribute this solely to higher wages. Regions may be attractive in themselves, for instance, a lot of people may prefer to live near London rather than in the provinces. Apart from this factor, the regions with low unemployment may attract people who are having difficulty in finding a job. Wages may be higher in the South-east, but this may be a minor factor in the movement of labour that is taking place: the better employment opportunities might exercise almost as strong a pull, even without a differential.

NOTES

1. This is not to deny that it is possible, with good management and generous time rates of wages, to achieve a high level of productivity without a direct link between output and pay.

2. Any reader unfamiliar with the nature and properties of indifference curves should consult one of the many textbooks which use this technique as the basis of the theory of demand.

3. Corresponding to the price-consumption curve in demand theory.

4. In the long run, there is a limit to the number of hours a week a man can work: he must have some rest. If the curve has a negative slope throughout, it will cut the abscisse at a point representing the maximum working week that can be maintained regularly. If the curve is positively inclined, it must become vertical when this maximum working week is reached.

5. The amount of the polltax is assumed to be such that a wage line having the same slope as H_1A_1 is tangential to the same indifference curve as that passing through E_1. With the wage line, H_2A_3, OH_2 represents the maximum leisure that the individual can enjoy. Even if he does not want to earn income for himself, he must work for the period H_1H_2 in order to earn enough to pay the polltax.

6. The standard working week has declined more than actual hours worked, with the result that more hours are paid at overtime rates. Nevertheless, more leisure is enjoyed now than before the war.

7. High wages may enable a family to buy the many domestic appliances that are on the market today, and make it easy for the married woman to go out to work. At a period when such appliances did not exist, a high wage would not have had the same effect of drawing married women into the labour market. Such changes in technology over a long period involve a shift in the supply curve. Over a long period we cannot assume that we are moving along one supply curve.

4. The demand for labour: 1. Perfect competition

The assumptions of the model

In this chapter, we consider the perfectly competitive labour market. We must therefore begin by setting out the necessary assumptions for the existence of a perfectly competitive labour market. The first is that there should be a large number of employers and employees, and no collusion between the individuals on either side of the market. The numbers on both sides of the market must be so large that no individual employer or employee can, by altering the quantity of labour he demands or supplies, have any significant effect on the total demand or supply. Second, we must assume that the supply of labour is homogeneous, and also that workers have no cause to prefer one employer rather than another. It is also convenient to make certain additional assumptions. Initially, at least, we may neglect the fact that an employer will normally require different kinds of labour.[1] We assume that there is perfect knowledge, and that there are no costs if a man changes his job.

In a perfectly competitive labour market, the individual has to take the wage rate as given. The employer only hires a small part of a homogeneous labour force. If he wants to hire another man, he can do so and this additional demand for labour will go unnoticed in the market. The fact that he hires another man will have no influence on the market wage rate. Similarly, the individual worker cannot influence the wage rate. The market will not notice whether an individual decides to enter the labour market or to withdraw from it altogether, let alone whether he works another hour more or less.

If an employer can hire as many men as he wishes at the going wage rate, there is no reason why he should consider paying more than this. He will also find that he cannot pay less, for, if he did so, nobody would work for him. There will be no reason why workers

B

should prefer to work for him, and they will not do so if they are aware of what other employers are paying.

In the first simple model, we shall also assume that a firm is selling its product in a perfectly competitive market. This means that the firm will be able to dispose of any output it cares to produce at the prevailing market price. In later models, we shall relax this assumption and take account of the fact that a firm may be selling in an imperfect market. In all cases, it is assumed that the firm seeks to maximize money profits.

The simple model

With some few exceptions, the demand for labour is a derived demand.[2] A farmer will employ a man because he helps to increase the output of the farm; a manufacturing firm will employ men in its factories because their services are necessary to the production of the goods the firm hopes to sell. The demand for labour will therefore depend, in the main, on the contribution labour makes to production and on the demand for the product itself. It is not enough, however, to say that the demand for labour is in some way a function of its productivity. We must look more closely at the nature of this relationship.

The law of variable proportions. If we are asking how many men will be employed, we must assume that the other factors of production are used in fixed quantities.[3] We cannot expect that output will increase in proportion to the increase in the quantity of the variable factor. After a point at least, to employ more of the variable factor will lead to a less than proportionate increase in output.

Let us take, as an example, the cultivation of a fixed area of land. The area may really be too big for one man to cultivate. If this is so, output will be more than doubled by employing a second man.[4] For some time, another man employed may make a bigger addition to output than his predecessor.[5] However, the law of variable proportions (sometimes called the 'law of diminishing returns') tells us that a point must come when each additional man will add less and less to output.

Table 4.1 shows how the total output of a farm might vary as the labour force is increased from 1 to 10. The first column shows the number of men employed and the second the total product. The third column shows the average product, that is, the total product divided by the number of men employed. The fourth column shows the marginal product. We shall define the marginal product of the fourth man employed as the difference between the total output when 4 men are employed and the total output when 3 men are employed. As this marginal product is strictly the difference in the

Table 4.1

Production on a fixed area of land

Number of men employed	Total product	Average product	Marginal product	Wage bill	Profit
		(all measured in bushels of corn)			
1	11	11·0		13	−2
			14		
2	25	12·5		26	−1
			17		
3	42	14·0		39	3
			20		
4	62	15·5		52	10
			18		
5	80	16·0		65	15
			16		
6	96	16·0		78	18
			13		
7	109	15·6		91	18
			9		
8	118	14·8		104	14
			4		
9	122	13·6		117	5
			−2		
10	120	12·0		130	−10

output resulting from the employment of 1 man more *or* less, it is shown in the table between the rows showing the other variables. For the present, we are assuming that the firm is selling in a perfectly competitive market at a fixed price. It is buying labour in a perfectly competitive market, at a fixed price, and we can conveniently measure our product in physical units and convert the wage into these same units.

We may look a little more closely at the relationship between the average and marginal product columns. We see that the marginal product is increasing at first. It is with the fifth man that the marginal product begins to diminish. The average product only shows a decline with the employment of the seventh man. The maximum average product occurs, according to the table, with 5 or 6 men employed. At these levels of employment, the average and marginal products are equal.

There is, of course, no reason why the labour force of the farm should only be increased in steps of 1 man. The unit of labour is the manhour. There is no reason why, for example, the farmer should not hire 5 full-time workers and 1 half-time worker, which is a labour force of $5\frac{1}{2}$ men. If $5\frac{1}{2}$ men were employed, we would find that the output was perhaps 88·5 bushels of corn.[6] The average product would be roughly 16·1. In other words, the average product rises a little between the twin maxima shown in the table. We will always find that the maximum average product occurs at roughly the point where the average and marginal products are equal. The smaller we make the increments of labour, the closer we get to the rule that average product is maximized when the average and marginal products are equal.[7]

We also show in Table 4.1 the total wage bill, assuming this to be 13 bushels of corn per man, and the resulting level of profit. We see that the maximum profit occurs when 6 or 7 men are employed, and the wage is equal to the marginal product of labour. It is easy enough to see why this should be. If the marginal product is greater than the wage, it means that an extra man increases output by more than the amount he adds to the wage bill. Since the wage is given, for the individual employer, and the marginal productivity of labour is falling, a point must be reached when the wage equals the marginal product. If another man were now employed, the marginal product would fall below the wage. The amount of extra output resulting from the employment of an extra man would be less than the amount he added to the wage bill, and profits would be reduced.[8]

It should now be clear that the lower the wage, the more men it will pay the farmer to hire. If the reader cares to refer back to the figures in Table 4.1, but substitutes a wage rate of 9 bushels instead of 13, he will see that maximum profits occur with 7 or 8 men, and that the marginal product shown between the seventh and eighth man is 9 bushels. So we have the general rule that the number of men employed will be such as to equate the marginal product of labour to the wage rate. This rule will be modified later. For the moment, we will add two important qualifications. The first is that the employer cannot, except temporarily, afford to pay a wage that is greater than the maximum average product. The second qualification is that the marginal productivity must be falling at the point of where it equals the wage. It is clear from Table 4.1 that profits are not maximized at the point where marginal productivity is equal to the wage, but rising.[9]

Diagrammatic treatment. The kind of data presented in Table 4.1 could equally well have been shown in the form of a diagram similar to Fig. 4.1. If the reader plots the data in Table 4.1, the

28

total, average, and marginal product curves will all be rather disjointed. If, however, we assume that the quantity of labour can be varied continuously (as, in fact, it can), we will get the kind of smooth curve shown in Fig. 4.1.

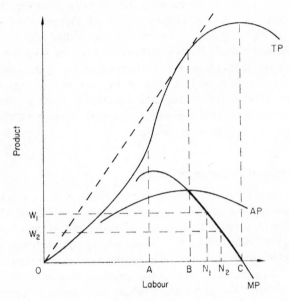

Fig. 4.1.
TP = Total product   MP = Marginal product   AP = Average product

As more labour is employed, up to the quantity OA, the marginal product increases, and the total product curve becomes steadily steeper. After OA, the marginal product of labour gradually falls off and the total product curve becomes less steep. We have seen already, from Table 4.1, that the average product continues to increase after the marginal product begins to fall. It does so until, with employment at OB, marginal and average products are equal. At this point, the average product reaches its maximum value and then begins to fall. When the level of employment reaches OC, marginal productivity is zero, and thereafter becomes negative, a result which might occur, for example, if so many men were employed that they simply got in each other's way. At this level of employment, the total product curve reaches its maximum and thereafter declines.

These relationships hold between all total, average, and marginal

29

curves. It does not matter whether we are dealing with cost or product curves, with net or gross product curves, or using value or physical units.

If the wage is fixed at OW_1, the employer will maximize his profits by engaging the quantity of labour ON_1. If the wage falls to OW_2, it will pay the employer to increase the quantity of labour hired to ON_2. Thus, the heavily shaded section of the marginal product curve is, in fact, the demand curve of the individual firm for labour. We have seen already that the firm cannot, in the long run, afford to pay a wage that exceeds the maximum average product of labour. Neither will a firm that is seeking to maximize profits employ labour beyond the point where the marginal product reaches zero: to do so would involve a negative marginal product which would reduce profits, even at a zero wage.

The marginal revenue product

If a firm is selling in a perfectly competitive product market, the curve showing the marginal physical product of labour will also show, with a suitable adjustment of scale, the marginal revenue product. The same will be true of the average physical and revenue products. We must, however, consider the case where a firm is selling in a less than perfectly competitive product market. This is quite compatible with the firm buying labour in a perfectly competitive market. A firm might, for example, have a monopoly of some product, based perhaps on patent protection. If this were, say, in the engineering field, there is no reason why the kind of labour employed should not be similar to that employed in a good many other engineering enterprises. Although the firm would not compete with other engineering firms in the market for its product, it would compete with them in the same market for labour.

If the firm is selling in an imperfectly competitive product market, it means that the price of the product will be influenced by the firm's output. If the firm produces more, it will have to lower the price of the product in order to dispose of the increased output. If a firm employs 10 men instead of 9, it may cause output to rise from 100 articles to 110. The marginal physical product is 10 articles. If the firm could sell as much as it liked at a price of 50p an article, the marginal revenue product would equal the marginal physical product times the price of the product. If, however, it has to lower price below 50p to sell 110 articles instead of 100, the marginal revenue product, the amount by which total revenue is increased,

30

will be less than £5 ($10 \times 50p$). Suppose that 110 articles can only be sold at a price of $47\frac{1}{2}p$. 100 articles sold at a price of $50p$ brought in a revenue of $5000p$. 110 articles sold at $47\frac{1}{2}p$ each bring in a total of $5225p$. The marginal revenue product is $225p$. Another way of calculating the marginal revenue product is to say that the additional 10 articles sell for $47\frac{1}{2}p$ each, a total of $475p$, from which one must deduct the loss of $2\frac{1}{2}p$ on each of 100 articles that could otherwise have sold for $50p$ each, a total of $250p$, making a net increase in revenue of $225p$.

The profit-maximizing employer is clearly interested in the revenue he derives from selling the additional output when he employs more men. It does not matter how great the marginal physical product may be, he will not employ an extra man if the wage that that man is paid is more than the marginal revenue product, the amount by which his employment increases the firm's sales revenue. We shall normally, therefore, use the marginal (and average) revenue product curves, rather than the physical product curves.[10]

Gross and net productivity

The assumption that there is only one variable factor of production is unrealistic, and must now be relaxed. There will always be a fixed *plant* with which the variable factors of production are combined, whether it consists of the farmer's land or a factory building equipped with large heavy machines. If an additional man is employed on a farm, the farmer will have to make use of greater quantities of some other productive resources also. With an extra man, it may become possible to spread a greater quantity of fertilizer, or plant a greater quantity of seed. If so, the resulting increase in output when an extra man is employed is due, in part, to his employment, in part, to the use of more fertilizer or seed. Similarly, if an additional man is employed on the production line in a factory, it may be necessary to use more raw materials and, perhaps, to increase the quantity of other kinds of labour employed, such as storekeepers, maintenance staff, and so on. Again, the resulting increase in output is partly attributable to the employment of that additional man, partly to the employment of increased quantities of other factors.

Let us consider the case where there are just two variable factors, labour and raw materials. Output can be increased, at least within limits, by using more of the one factor or the other. If more labour is employed, it may be possible to increase output without using

31

more raw materials because with more labour management could insist upon more careful working, thus reducing the wastage of raw materials.[11] When working with valuable raw materials, it may pay to be lavish with the input of labour, and workers may be instructed to take great care to eliminate waste. If materials are cheap and labour is dear, the management will tolerate some waste of raw materials in order to get a higher output per manhour.

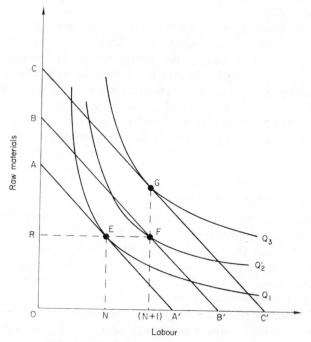

Fig. 4.2 The derivation of marginal net product.

If the price ratio of the two factors is known, and also the amount of money the firm is prepared to spend on purchases of the two variable factors, we can discover just how they will be combined. In Fig. 4.2, we have an isoproduct map. The curves Q_1, Q_2, and Q_3 show the combinations of the two factors that can be used to secure successively larger outputs of the product.[12] The slope of an outlay line, like AA′, shows the combinations of the two factors which may be purchased with a fixed sum, the slope depending on the ratio of the two factor prices.

As with indifference curves, an infinite number of isoproduct curves may be drawn. The greatest output for a given expenditure

32

on the variable factors of production is achieved when the outlay line is tangential to an isoproduct curve.

If the firm spends on the variable factors the sum represented by the outlay line AA', it will employ the two factors in the proportions indicated by the point E. It will use a quantity R of raw materials and N of labour. If it were to employ $(N+1)$ units of labour, in combination with R of raw materials, output would increase from Q_1 to Q_2. The difference in output, (Q_2-Q_1), is the simple marginal physical productivity of labour that we considered in the earlier part of this chapter. The point F, however, can never be an equilibrium point. The slope of the outlay line BB' is not equal to the marginal rate of substitution between the factors (i.e., the slope of the isoproduct curve). It can be seen by looking at Fig. 4.2 that the line BB' will be tangential to an isoproduct curve representing a greater output than Q_2.

If $(N+1)$ units of labour were to be used in the productive process, it would have to be in combination with a different amount of raw materials, at some point, such as G, where the outlay line CC' is tangential to the isoproduct curve for an output Q_3. The question we now have to decide is how much of this increase in output is to be attributed to labour and how much to the employment of more raw materials.

For the moment, we may assume that the product is sold in a perfectly competitive market. The employment of one more unit brings about an increase in sales revenue of (Q_3-Q_1) times the price of product. This is the marginal gross revenue product of labour.[13] If the employer has to decide whether it is worth while employing the $(N+1)$th man, he will have to ask himself whether the marginal gross revenue product exceeds the wage of the extra man plus the cost of the additional raw materials. Alternatively, we can define the marginal net product of labour as (Q_3-Q_1) times price of product $-\Delta R$ times price of raw materials.

The curves. The two pairs of average and marginal curves are shown in Fig. 4.3. In drawing the gross productivity curves, we assume that the firm always operates at an equilibrium point, such as E or G in Fig. 4.2, and never at a point such as F in the same figure. The *average gross product curve* (AGRP) simply shows the value of total output divided by the number of men employed. The *average net revenue product curve* shows the value of total output less total payments to the other factors of production divided by the number of men employed. We have seen already that the *marginal gross revenue product curve* (MGRP) shows the total increase in the value

B*

of output when an extra unit of labour is employed, while the *marginal net revenue product curve* (MNRP) shows this increase minus the increased cost of the cooperating factors. The two net

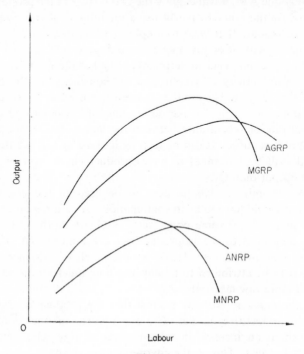

Fig. 4.3.

AGRP = Average Gross Revenue Product
MGRP = Marginal Gross Revenue Product
ANRP = Average Net Revenue Product
MNRP = Marginal Net Revenue Product

product curves must clearly lie below the two gross product curves. Both average product curves have their maximum value where they are cut by the corresponding marginal curves. There is no reason why the two average curves should have maximum values with the same quantity of labour employed.

We have seen that a firm will be willing to employ an extra man so long as the wage the man is paid is less than his marginal net revenue product. Therefore, the marginal net revenue product curve is the individual firm's demand curve for labour.

In our simple model, we saw that a firm could not continue for long if the wage were greater than the average product of labour.

34

A similar qualification must be made now that we are using a rather more sophisticated model. In the long run, the firm's demand curve for labour is the falling portion of the marginal net revenue product curve beyond its intersection with the average net revenue product curve.

Net productivity and normal profits. To understand this fully, we must look at the relationship of the net productivity curves to normal profit. In perfect competition, we assume that there is some minimum profit that a firm must earn if it is to remain in a particular line of business. The pressure of competition will ensure that the marginal firms earn no more than this normal profit. If profits for the marginal firms are greater, it will be an inducement to new firms to enter the industry; if they are less, some marginal firms will leave the industry. The normal profit is generally included as a fixed cost item in drawing the average cost curve of the firm. In our present analysis, the normal profit is one of the deductions to be made in respect of the payments for the factors of production cooperating with labour when calculating the average net product.

It follows, then, that if the wage is equal to the average net product of labour, the wage bill absorbs the whole of the revenue that is left after making the necessary payments to the other factors of production, including the payment of the normal profit. If the wage were greater than this, there would be insufficient revenue to make all the necessary payments to the other factors. The firm could continue, in the short run, because profits can be squeezed. If the situation is more than temporary, however, it will look for a more profitable line of business or else close down.

If the wage is less than the average net revenue product of labour, it means that after paying the wage bill the revenue left is more than enough to pay the cooperating factors, the excess being a supernormal profit. Intramarginal firms, that have some special advantage, may normally be in this position. For the marginal firms in an industry, it can be only a temporary situation. If supernormal profits are being earned, new firms will enter the industry. This will increase total output and prices of products will fall, and this will mean that the revenue product curves for all firms are lowered. This will go on until the marginal firm is paying a wage that is just equal to its average net product. Since profit-maximization requires the wage to be equal to the marginal net revenue product also, it follows that it can only be operating at the point where the two curves intersect, that is, at the point where the average net revenue product is at its maximum value.[14]

The industry's demand for labour

In a perfectly competitive labour market, the firm takes the wage rate as given and decides how many men it is worth while employing. We must now turn our attention to the labour market as a whole, to see how the wage level is determined. We know that each firm will employ more men as the wage rate falls. It follows, therefore, that the market demand curve, obtained by aggregating the demands of all the firms at each wage level, will also have a negative slope. On the diagram (Fig. 4.4), we can superimpose the labour supply curve on the demand curve, and the wage rate will be determined where supply and demand are equal.

If S_L and D_L are the supply and demand curves, the wage rate will be fixed at the level OW_1 and a total of ON_1 men will be employed. Individual firms confronted with the wage rate OW_1 will decide how many men to employ. In Fig. 4.4, the righthand side of the diagram shows the industry's supply and demand curves and the lefthand side shows the productivity curves for a representative firm. The individual firm shown would employ On_1 men at the wage OW_1. At this position, the firm and industry would be in full equilibrium, the firm making only a normal profit.[15]

If the supply curve were S'_L, the wage level would be OW_2, total employment would be ON_2, and the representative firm would employ On_2 men.

In this situation, however, there would not be full equilibrium. Some firms, at least, would find the wage below the average net revenue product and be earning supernormal profits. New firms would be attracted to the industry, and this would tend to shift the demand curve for labour to the right. If we could assume that the product price remained unchanged, the entry of new firms would cease when the wage had risen to OW_1 and the marginal firms were making normal profits. This assumption, however, is unrealistic. As new firms enter the industry, the price of the product will fall. This will limit the shift of the industry's demand curve to the right and lower the firms' productivity curves. Thus, an equilibrium position will be reached with a wage somewhere between OW_1 and OW_2 when the supply curve is S'_L.

The long and short period. The preceding analysis has been primarily a short period one. With a given number of firms in the industry, their demand for labour can be obtained by aggregating the demands, at each wage, of the individual firms. We must now look briefly at the long period demand curve for labour.

In the long run, the marginal firms in an industry must be making only a normal profit. The demand for labour will, in fact, depend in large measure upon the relative efficiencies of different firms. There are two cases that we need to look at. In the first, we make the unrealistic assumption that all firms have the same maximum average net product of labour.[16] If, in this case, we take the product price as given, the demand for labour can be regarded as perfectly elastic. More and more firms could be established, increasing the demand for labour indefinitely at a wage equal to the maximum average net revenue product of labour. The second case we need to consider is where some firms are able to achieve a higher maximum average net revenue productivity than others. The firms capable of achieving the highest productivity will normally be established first in an industry. If the demand for the product increases, firms which are, in some sense, less well placed to produce in this industry will establish themselves. Or they might establish themselves if, for example, the wage rate fell. At a lower wage rate, it would become possible for these firms to cover their minimum average costs. Better placed firms would find it profitable to expand beyond their optimum size and would earn supernormal profits. If, then, the product price is given, a fall in wages will enable more firms to cover their minimum costs. There will be some firms that operate at the point where the wage is equal to the maximum average net revenue product; intra-marginal firms will produce beyond this point. But it will be possible to discover what firms can operate at each wage level and how many men they will employ. We can obtain the demand curve of the industry for labour in the long run.

Where firms have the same maximum average net revenue product, the demand curve is horizontal; where some firms have different levels of productivity, a fall in wages enables more firms to cover their costs, so the long-run demand curve for labour of the industry is negatively inclined. In both cases, the intersection with the supply curve determines the wage.

Wage determination with a variable product price

We have argued that the firm's demand curve for labour is given by the curve showing the marginal net revenue product of labour. In obtaining the curve of marginal net revenue productivity, we can make allowance for the effect of changes in the firm's output when it is selling in an imperfectly competitive market. There are, how-ever, other changes in product price which cannot be disposed of by assuming that they are allowed for in drawing the marginal net revenue product curve. Let us take the situation where the firm is selling its product in a perfectly competitive market. Let us suppose that the firm and industry start from a position of full equilibrium. Then, the supply of labour increases. What happens?

It would seem obvious that the labour supply and demand curves for the market as a whole intersect at a lower wage. Each firm will

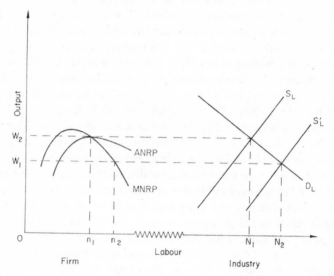

Fig. 4.4 The industry's demand curve for labour.

employ more men, up to the point where the new and lower wage equals the marginal net revenue product of labour. In fact, the marginal net revenue product curve was drawn on the assumption that there was a fixed product price, and that this would not be influenced by any change *in the firm's own output*. This is reasonable, but when the supply of labour increases, there is a tendency for *all firms* to employ more labour and to increase output. This will cause the price of the product to fall and therefore lower the marginal revenue product curves of individual firms and shift the market demand curve for labour to the left. This will limit the increase in the quantity of labour demanded when the supply increases.[17]

We need a rather more refined technique if we are to introduce the price of the product as a variable into our model. In Fig. 4.4, we draw a single demand curve for labour, on the assumption that there was a given product price.[18] If the product price were different,

38

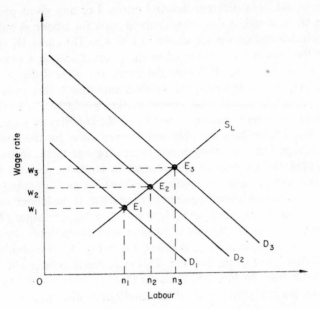

Fig. 4.5. The labour market with undetermined product price.

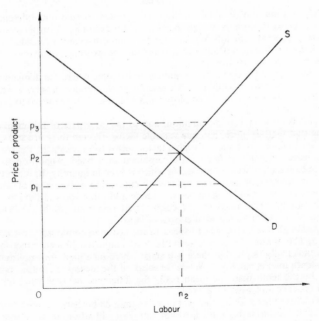

Fig. 4.6. Determination of product price.

there would be a different demand curve. For any given product price, there would be a different demand curve for labour. A number of such demand curves are shown in Fig. 4.5. The curve D_1 represents the demand for labour when the product sells at a price p_1, and so on. The point E_1 would determine the wage if the product price were p_1. If, however, the product sold at a higher price, p_3, the equilibrium point in the labour market would be E_3. Until we know the product price, we do not know the equilibrium wage.

In Fig. 4.6, we have a supply and demand curve for the product. This is a perfectly ordinary curve, except for one thing. Instead of measuring the quantity of the product in terms of physical units (kilogrammes of sugar, or number of tables), we measure it in terms of the quantity of labour required to produce it. If the labour supply curve is sloping upward, as S_L in Fig. 4.5, a bigger output of the product can only be supplied if a higher price is obtained, since the higher labour costs must be covered. From Fig. 4.6, we obtain the equilibrium price of the product. This is assumed to be p_2. We can then refer back to Fig. 4.5, knowing that we must use the labour demand curve D_2, and read off the equilibrium wage w_2.

NOTES

1. The assumption of homogeneity was intended to rule out differences of efficiency between workers of a given category, for example, all carpenters would be equally good at their job. We now further limit ourselves to considering only one kind of worker, and take no account of the existence of many different trades, even within one workshop.

2. The demand for domestic servants is an example where the demand is not derived. The servant is employed because he or she renders a service which is valued for its own sake by the employer, not because he or she helps to produce something which can be sold.

3. This is an unrealistic assumption, and in the later part of this chapter we assume that there is more than one variable factor, though there are still one or more fixed factors. If a single variable factor seems too unrealistic, the reader is free to assume that two factors are combined in a fixed proportion to each other in conjunction with a third factor which is fixed in quantity. If, for example, a variable number of men are employed in cultivating a fixed area of land, he can think of each man bringing his own spade and other tools to the job.

4. If this happens, it means, of course, that one man would do better to concentrate his efforts on a smaller area of land.

5. Although it is convenient to speak of the last man employed, we are really thinking about what the output would be *if* we employed 10 men rather than 9. We do not really imply that there is a stage where nine men *are* employed and *then* a tenth man is employed. When we speak of the increase in output brought about by the tenth man, we mean really the difference between what ten men would produce and what nine would.

6. Total product with $5\frac{1}{2}$ men will be more than 88 bushels. Because marginal productivity is diminishing, the eleventh half-man will add more to output than the twelfth.

7. If the marginal product is greater than the average product, the marginal product must be pulling the average up: if it is less, it will be pulling it down. If it is equal to the average product, it does neither. If the marginal product is greater than the average product but falling, it will pull the average product up until the two are equal. When it falls further, it will become less than the average product and begin to pull the average product down. If q = total product and n = number of men employed, and $q = f(n)$ it follows that $d/dn(q/n) = \{f'(n) - f(n)\}/n$. For the maximum value of average product, q/n, we put this = 0, from which it follows that $f'(n) = f(n)/n = q/n$.

8. There will be a true point of maximum profit when the number employed is somewhere between 6 and 7. The line of argument is similar to that relating to the point of maximum average product coinciding with the point where marginal and average products are equal. If profits, $P = f(n) - wn$ where n is the number of men and w the wage rate, $dP/dn = f'(n) - w$ which, for maximum profits = 0, and this clearly occurs when $f'(n) = w$.

9. The mathematician will recognize that such a point is one of minimum profits or maximum loss.

10. In most situations, it will not be necessary to consider whether the firm is selling under conditions of perfect or imperfect competition. The marginal revenue product curve will always slope downwards from left to right, but will do so more steeply under imperfect competition when the price has to be lowered to allow a greater output to be sold.

11. There are obvious limits. If there are no wasted materials, no amount of greater care can help. To increase output, more raw materials have to be used. For a given output, there is a minimum raw material input, and at this level an isoproduct curve in Fig. 4.2 would become horizontal. Similarly, there may be a minimum input of labour and the isoproduct curves would become vertical at the appropriate limit.

12. These isoproduct curves have much in common with the indifference curves encountered in the previous chapter. Whereas an indifference curve joins points which the consumer regards as equally satisfactory, and points on one curve can merely be said to be better or worse than points on another, we can attach to isoproduct curves a cardinal value. They show the combinations of factors required to produce a specific level of output. The isoproduct map is a reflection of technical possibilities that are available to a producer at a given time.

13. If the product market is not competitive, we simply substitute the increase in total revenue for $(Q_3 - Q_1) \times$ price of product. It will, of course, be smaller.

14. This is fundamentally the same argument as that which states that the firm in perfect competition operates at the point where average costs are minimized.

15. In Fig. 4.4, the industry's demand curve for labour is shown rising above the wage equal to the firm's maximum ANRP. This may be justified in two ways. First, not all firms are identical and, at such wages, a demand for labour might come from firms with higher maximum ANRP than the representative firm shown. Second, our representative firm will employ men at such wages in the short run.

16. It is not neccessarily true that the firms are identical and achieve this maximum ANRP at the same level of employment.

17. In the theory of the firm, it is assumed that the marginal cost curve is the supply curve of the firm, and the market supply curve may be obtained by aggregating the supply curves of individual firms. Again, if demand increases, all firms tend to increase output, and the increased demand for factors of production could put up their prices and so shift the firms' marginal cost curves. If we assume that a particular industry uses only a small proportion of the supply of any factor of production, this effect is avoided. But it is not so easy to make a similar assumption to get rid of the problem we are now considering.

18. If there is imperfect competition in the product market, the influence *of the firm's own output* on price is allowed for in the marginal revenue product curve. However, in this case, too, there is also the effect of a general change in output by all firms to be considered, as well as the effect of changes in the firm's output when the price and output of other firms are given. This more complex problem is not pursued further here. The reader is referred for a fuller discussion of the whole question of wage determination with a variable product price to J. M. Jackson, 'A diagrammatic analysis of wage determination with a variable product price', *Scottish Journal of Political Economy*, 1964. The mathematically inclined reader will realize that there is no problem of defining equilibrium conditions in terms of an appropriate set of simultaneous equations. The problem is to present the analysis diagrammatically for the non-mathematician.

5. The demand for labour : 2. Imperfect competition

It is now necessary to consider the demand for labour in a labour market that is imperfectly competitive. As in the case of the market for some product, imperfections may be found on either the demand side, or the supply side of the market, or both. Whether we are concerned with a product market or the labour market, it is easy enough to construct a model to show what happens when there is imperfection on one side or the other of the market. We shall consider first the situation where there is monopsony in the labour market, and then the case of a trade union exercising a monopolistic control. We can then turn to the rather special case of discriminating monopsony. Finally, we may take a brief look at the much more difficult question of imperfections on both sides of the labour market.

Monopsony in the labour market

In the analysis of wage determination in a perfectly competitive labour market, it was possible to assume that the individual firm would neglect any slight influence it might have on the prevailing wage rate by employing more or fewer men, and simply decide how many workers it was most profitable to employ at the going rate. If, however, there is a single firm employing labour of a certain kind, it is unreasonable to suppose that this firm can neglect the effect of changes in its demand for labour on the wage rate. If the firm employs more labour, it will mean an increase in the total demand for labour and, therefore, a rise in the wage rate.

Monopsony means, strictly speaking, that there is a single buyer. In a perfectly competitive labour market, there must be many employers. Often, however, there will not be the very large number of employers required to create a perfectly competitive market, nor the single employer that is necessary for monopsony, in the strict sense. There may be a few employers, and this will mean that each one represents a significant proportion of the total demand for labour. This being so, any change in the firm's demand for labour will have a significant effect on the market demand and therefore on the wage rate in the market.

The marginal labour cost. We have seen that the employer in a perfectly competitive labour market will employ labour up to the point where the marginal net revenue product of labour is equal to the wage rate. The reason for this is that profits are increased so long as the employment of an extra man adds more to the value of output than to the wage bill. Under perfect competition, the wage rate represents the addition to the wage bill when an extra man is employed. Under conditions of monopsony, this is no longer the case. If a firm employs more men, it will find it necessary to raise wages in order to call forth the required supply. Since, under normal circumstances, the same wage is paid to all workers, this means that the wage bill will rise by more than the wages of the marginal man or men. It will also rise by the amount of additional payments to those already employed.

The point may be clarified by a simple numerical example. Suppose a firm is employing 10 men at a wage of £15 a week. The total wage bill is £150. If an employer could engage an eleventh man at the same wage, the wage bill would increase to £165. Under monopsony, however, the employer can only obtain an eleventh worker if he offers a higher wage. Suppose that the wage must rise to £16 a week to get the eleventh man: the total wage bill will rise to £176. This is an increase of £26.[1] It is this increase in the total wage bill, not just his wage of £16, that must be offset by the increase in output, if it is to be worth while to employ the eleventh man.

We have, then, the basic rule: an employer will employ men up to the point where the marginal net revenue product of labour is just equal to the marginal labour cost, that is, the increase in the total wage bill when one more man is employed.[2]

The equilibrium of the firm under monopsony is illustrated diagrammatically in Fig. 5.1. The curve S_L is the labour supply curve, or average labour cost curve, and shows the wage that must be paid in order to attract any given number of workers. The curve MLC shows the marginal labour cost or the amount by which the wage bill rises when an extra man is employed. Thus, to attract ON men, the wage offered must be NW. NR shows the addition to the wage bill when ON men are employed instead of (ON−1). The point

44

R is the point at which the marginal labour cost and marginal net revenue product are equal, and therefore ON men will be employed. NP is the average net revenue product of ON men. In the case illustrated, the wage is less than the average net revenue product of labour. For each man employed, the employer derives a profit of WP: in other words, the supernormal profits of the firm total ABPW.[3]

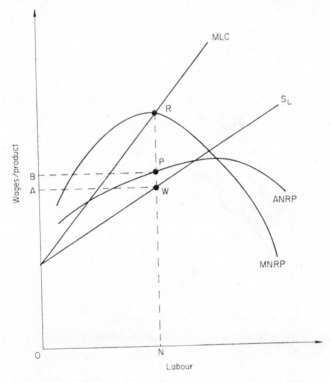

Fig. 5.1. Monopsony in the labour market, with abnormal profits.

Equilibrium of the industry. If the firm that finds itself in a monopsonistic position in the labour market also has an element of monopoly power in the product market, a position such as that shown in Fig. 5.1 may be quite stable. The profit ABPW is the firm's monopoly revenue. There is no reason, however, why monopsony in the labour market need imply monopoly in the product market: the two could, of course, go together. If a firm had a monopoly of some product, it would naturally be a monopsonist in the market

45

for any kind of labour that was required only in the manufacture of this one product. On the other hand, a monopolist may often employ labour that also helps to make other products, and so, in the labour market, he has to compete with employers who are, in fact, producing in other industries. Again, there is the case of a firm which may dominate the local market for labour, though it may be

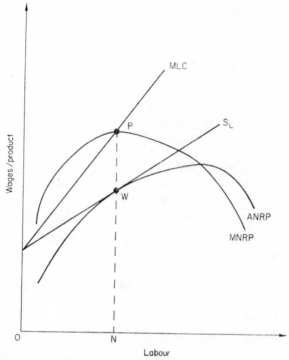

Fig. 5.2. Monopsony in the labour market, after elimination of abnormal profits.

selling its product in competition with other firms, perhaps in different parts of the country, who buy labour in different labour markets.

We must now look a little more closely at the case of the firm which has a degree of monopsony power in the labour market, but is selling its products in a market which is competitive. The market for the product may be perfectly competitive, or there may be a fairly large number of firms making differentiated products with freedom of entry. Even under the latter conditions, there will be a tendency for abnormal profits to be competed away as new firms enter the

46

industry. If we make the heroic assumption that all firms are identical with regard to their cost and sales curves, equilibrium will occur when all firms are earning a normal profit, and each firm will reach an equilibrium position similar to that shown in Fig. 5.2. To maximize profits, labour is employed up to the point where the marginal labour cost is equal to the marginal net revenue product of labour. If, however, all abnormal profits are competed away by the entry of new firms, the wage must also equal the average net revenue product of labour. This occurs when the labour supply curve is tangential to the average net revenue product curve vertically below the intersection of the marginal labour cost and marginal net revenue product curves.[4]

If firms are initially in equilibrium, in a position such as that shown in Fig. 5.1, the fact that they are earning abnormal profits will be an inducement to new firms to enter the industry. Under such conditions, the sales of each firm will tend to fall at any given price, and this will lower the revenue product curves of all firms until all are in equilibrium at a position such as that shown in Fig. 5.2. There will then be no further incentive for new firms to enter the industry, and the industry, as well as the individual firms, will be in equilibrium.

If the heroic assumption about the identical labour supply and productivity curves is relaxed, only the marginal firm or firms will be earning normal profits, as in Fig. 5.2, with wages equal to average product. Some firms may enjoy an advantage of some kind in either the labour or the product market and be earning a supernormal profit, even when the industry is in full equilibrium. Because the marginal firm is only earning a normal profit, there is no incentive for new firms to enter the industry. The newcomers would presumably have to face greater difficulties than the marginal firms; the supernormal profits of the intramarginal firms are irrelevant.

Trade Union monopoly

It would be quite possible to construct a model to show how wages would be determined in a market where the workers are organized in a trade union which monopolizes the supply of labour and employers are entirely unorganized. The demand for labour would be determined in the manner described in the previous chapter. The trade union would have to decide what wage it preferred to fix, knowing that the employers would then decide how many men they were going to employ at that wage.

The difficulty about this kind of approach is that it is usually based upon the maximization of some variable. It is, for example, assumed that the firm normally tries to maximize profits. This is not an unreasonable first approximation. Firms are in business to earn profits, and while they may not always maximize profits in the short run, there would have to be some very good reason for a firm's refusing to take an opportunity to add to its profits. It might be put off by the degree of risk involved, or by the effort involved for the top management, but it would not neglect the opportunity because it was uninterested in profit. Those in charge may be motivated as much by the idea of building up an industrial empire as by the enjoyment of money profits. Nevertheless, such profits are a useful means to this end. If the profits are retained, they help to finance expansion, while good distributed profits facilitate the raising of new capital issues for expansion.

In the case of the trade unions, it is not so easy to point to an obvious variable to maximize, even as a first approximation. It is not realistic, for example, to suppose that union leaders think seriously in terms of trying to maximize the total wage bill received by their members.[5] Apart from this, the case of a trade union facing a large number of unorganized employers is quite unrealistic under presentday conditions.[6] In our discussion of trade union monopoly, therefore, we shall limit ourselves to the impact of trade union action in enforcing a minimum wage, without asking how it decides upon that wage.

Competition among employers. When there is competition among employers and the individual employer has to take the market wage as given, the action of the trade union in enforcing a minimum wage does not alter the analysis of the firm's behaviour in any way. Whether the wage is determined by supply and demand in the labour market or by the decision of the trade union, the individual firm will employ labour up to the point where that wage is equal to the marginal net revenue product.[7]

If the minimum wage is fixed above the level previously prevailing, each firm will tend to employ fewer workers. Employment will contract to the point where the wage equals the marginal net revenue product. Firms which may have been earning only a normal profit, with the wage also equal to the maximum average net revenue product (with a wage OW_1 in Fig. 4.4, page 38, for example), will now find profits are less than normal. In the long run, some firms will be forced out of the industry. Those which remain may be firms with greater labour productivity than those marginal firms

48

which have been forced out. Alternatively, if firms are identical, the exodus of some will mean that total output falls and product prices rise, raising the labour productivity curves until a new industry equilibrium is reached with all firms earning normal profits, and with wages equal to the maximum average net product of labour.

Monopsony in the labour market. Where the labour market is monopolistic, there is a possibility that a trade union can impose a minimum wage which is above that previously prevailing without the level of employment being reduced. We must now consider this possibility.[8]

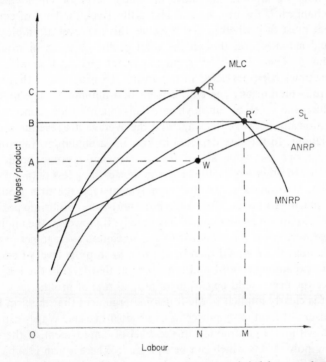

Fig. 5.3. Imposition of minimum wage in monopsonistic labour market.

The situation prevailing in the absence of trade union action is shown in Fig. 5.3, with ON men employed at a wage NW. The marginal cost of employing an extra man is equal to NR which is also the marginal net revenue product of labour. If the trade union now enforces a minimum wage of NR, it will still pay the firm best to employ ON men. Previously, the last man employed added to the wage bill exactly the same amount as he added to the value of

49

the firm's output. With the enforcement of the minimum wage of NR by the trade union, the ONth man employed still adds the same amount to the wage bill as he did before, and it is just worth while employing him. All that has altered is that it is now necessary to pay the wage NR, however many men are employed, whereas, before, ON men could be employed at a wage of only NW. Clearly, the result of enforcing a minimum wage of NR is to reduce the monopoly revenue of the firm by the area AWRC or ON . WR.

If the minimum wage is equal to the original marginal net revenue product of labour, the most profitable level of employment is unchanged. If the new wage is above this level, the level of employment must fall, whereas if it is below this the level of employment could actually rise, though the total profits of the firm would be reduced. There is, however, an important qualification which has sometimes been neglected in presenting the proposition that where there is monopsony the enforcement of a minimum wage need not reduce the level of employment. This qualification concerns the relationship between the wage and the average net revenue product of labour. In the case depicted in Fig. 5.3, a minimum wage of NR would put the wage above the average net revenue product of labour. In other words, the firm would be earning less than a normal profit. With a wage NR and employment ON, the firm would be minimizing its losses. This would be a short-run equilibrium position, but it could not be maintained indefinitely. If, however, the minimum wage were set at a level equal to the maximum average net product of labour, there would then be nothing to stop the level of employment expanding to OM and remaining at that level in the long run, since the firm would be earning a normal rate of profit.

It is clearly implicit in the foregoing argument that the firm has a measure of monopoly power in its product market. Wages can only rise, without a contraction in the level of employment, if there are monopoly profits which can be squeezed. Where a firm is subject to competition in the product market, and is in the kind of situation depicted in Fig. 5.2, any increase in the wage rate must mean that profits are reduced below normal. A situation is created, therefore, which cannot be one of long-run equilibrium. The marginal firms will leave the industry, until a situation is reached where the wage equals the maximum average net revenue product, as in Fig. 5.3. It may well be that each firm now employs more men than it did before, but because some firms have left the industry the level of employment will have fallen.[9]

Discriminating monopsony

In dealing with monopsonistic conditions, it has hitherto been assumed that the supply of labour can be regarded as coming from a single source. Even though each worker had his own individual supply price, in the sense of the minimum price that would induce him to supply his labour, it may be impossible for the employer to pay one worker less than another. The employer would clearly maximize his profits if he could pay each worker only his supply price. With such perfect discrimination, the employer would have to pay a higher wage to attract another worker into his employ, but he would pay this wage only to the marginal worker engaged, and he would continue to pay all those previously employed their supply prices. The wage paid to the marginal man would represent the marginal cost of employing that man, and that wage would be equated to the marginal net revenue product of labour. Equilibrium would occur where the labour supply curve cut the marginal net revenue product curve. The situation would differ from the normal competitive situation in that each man was paid a different wage.

There are two main reasons why an employer is unlikely to be able to exercise such perfect discrimination. First, it might be too difficult for him to bargain individually with a large number of workers. Second, although workers may have their own supply prices, in the sense that there is a certain wage the offer of which would just induce them to work, they may be unwilling to work at these supply prices if they know others are being paid more. For instance, a man who would be willing to work for £12 a week seeks a job at a factory where he knows some men are getting £14 a week for the kind of job he wants. When interviewed, he would naturally ask for the £14 and not reveal that he would really be willing to work for £2 a week less.

In certain circumstances, it may be possible to distinguish between two distinct groups in the labour force, and to pay different wages to the two groups, even though their efficiency is the same. It may, for example, be possible to pay women less than men for doing the same work. This is the kind of situation which we must now consider.

In Fig. 5.4, two labour supplies are depicted, the supply of women workers being indicated by the curve AS_w and the supply of men workers by the curve BS_m. At any wage above OA, there will be a certain number of women workers entering the labour market, but there will be no men working until the wage reaches OB. If men and women were paid the same wage, the curve AS_{m+w}, with its discontinuity at the wage OB, would be the supply curve. The employer may, however, find that he need not pay men and women workers the same wage, and, given the possibility of discriminating, he may find that it pays him to do so. Even though the total level of

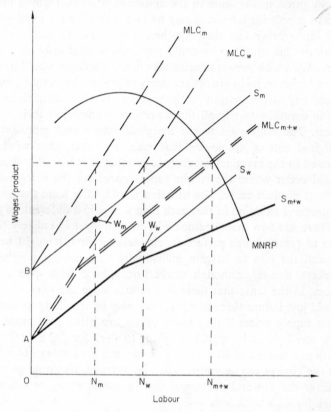

Fig. 5.4. Discriminating monopsony in the labour market.

employment may be unaffected by the fact that he can discriminate, he may be able to increase his profits by adjusting the proportions of men and women in his labour force so as to keep his wage bill to the minimum.

The essential condition for minimizing his wage bill for a given total labour force is that the marginal labour cost of employing another man is equal to that of employing another woman. If employing another man adds more to the wage bill than another woman, it will pay the employer to substitute one or more women workers for one or more men, and vice versa. Nevertheless, it may seem strange at first sight to some readers that it can pay an employer to take on men when women workers are still available at a lower wage. A simple numerical example will help to explain this paradox. Suppose 10 women are employed at a wage of £9 a week, but an eleventh woman may only be obtained if the wage is raised to £10 a week. Although the eleventh woman is paid £10, she adds more than this to the total wage bill, because another £1 has to be paid to each of the 10 already employed. It therefore costs the employer £20 to take on the eleventh woman, and he would therefore be indifferent as to whether he took her at £10 a week or a man at £20 a week.

We may now return to Fig. 5.4 and the diagrammatic exposition of wage determination with discriminating monopsony. The curves MLC_m and MLC_w are the curves showing the marginal cost of employing another man or woman; they are derived from the two separate supply curves in the ordinary way. The curve MLC_{m+w} is obtained by the horizontal summation of the two curves. Consider the point C on this curve. This point corresponds to a level of employment ON_{m+w}, and when this number of workers is made up of ON_m men and ON_w women, the additional cost of employing either an extra man or woman is the same and equal to NC. The intersection of this curve with the MNRP curve determines the most profitable level of employment and also the most profitable distribution of the labour force between men and women. The ON_m men will be paid a wage of N_mW_m and the ON_w women a wage of N_wW_w.[10]

Next, we must look at the case where the men have formed a trade union and are imposing a minimum wage, while the women remain unorganized and are prepared to accept the wage necessary to attract the marginal worker. The situation is depicted in Fig. 5.5. The curve S_w shows the supply of women workers and MLC_w the amount the marginal worker adds to the wage bill. OW_m is the minimum wage for men workers fixed by the trade union. The employer will take on women workers to the point where the marginal labour cost equals the wage paid to the men (which will also be the marginal labour cost of employing another man). In Fig. 5.5, ON represents the total level of employment; ON_w women are employed and N_wN men.

Bilateral monopoly

Finally, we must look at the case of bilateral monopoly in the labour market. This is the typical case. On the supply side, the position is dominated by the existence of trade unions which bargain on behalf of their members, while on the demand side there may be a single large employer or an association of employers formed to bargain with the trade unions. The traditional view of economists has been that the outcome of bilateral monopoly is indeterminate, but there have been attempts to arrive at a determinate solution,

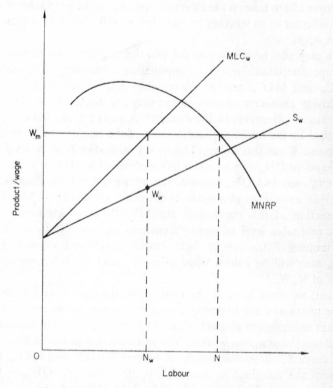

Fig. 5.5. Discriminating monopsony with a trade union.

some of which are of general application and some of which are concerned specifically with collective bargaining in the labour market. We shall deal mainly with one of the latter approaches.[11]

In his attempt to develop Hicks' theory of bargaining, Turner assumed that it was necessary for a theory to take account of both trade union demands for higher wages and employers' demands for lower wages. In the conditions that have prevailed since the end of the Second World War, employers' demands to lower wages are virtually unheard of, and we may therefore concentrate on an explanation of what happens when a union makes a claim for higher wages. A trade union will normally prefer to secure a higher wage for its members. In pressing its claim for a pay increase, however, it has to remember that it may fail, or succeed only after a strike which brings hardship and loss to its members. A strike of any length involves a certain amount of hardship and loss to the union members, but there will be some wage increase which makes it just worth while suffering these. The higher the wage that is gained, the longer will be the strike it is worth while incurring in order to get that wage. Therefore, if we plot the union's *claim curve*, plotting the length of strike along the abscisse against the wage that makes it just worth while, we would expect the curve to be positively inclined – that is rising from left to right.

This will be true, at least over part of the length of the curve. We would expect, however, that increments of income show diminishing marginal utility. The typical union member will attach very great importance to a 50p pay increase which makes all the difference between relative comfort and difficulty trying to make ends meet. Another 50p on top of this would, of course, be very welcome but, nevertheless, makes a decidedly smaller addition to the worker's total satisfaction. On the other hand, the worker may not feel that a very short strike involves very great hardship, but as a strike drags on each day's lost pay assumes a greater significance. The marginal disutility of striking increases with the length of the strike. For both these reasons, therefore, the claim curve will not merely slope upwards from left to right, but the slope will steadily increase. In other words, the longer the strike being considered, the bigger is the increase in wages needed to offset a given prolongation of the strike.

Probably, the claim curve should be drawn as finally bending back. This implies that, at some point, a further increase in wages ceases to be a benefit. This is a real possibility, and was envisaged in Hicks's original formulation of the theory of bargaining. A higher wage is only an unequivocal gain to the workers, so long as the level of employment is assumed not to fall. If a higher wage leads to falling employment, as it must after some point, then the gains of some workers from higher pay must be set against the losses of those who become unemployed or are forced to seek other jobs which may be less well paid or less attractive in some other way. The union leaders (or to some extent the members themselves) may, at some point, be forced to think in these terms, even though their thinking may not be as precise and quantitative as the model suggests.

On the employer's side, a higher wage is seen as a disutility. He is seeking to avoid paying it, and therefore the higher the wage in question, the longer the strike that it is worth while to incur in trying to prevent the increase. His *concession curve* also slopes upward from left to right, but with a diminishing slope. As each increment to the existing wage becomes of greater significance to him, he finds a greater and greater prolongation of the stoppage worth while, rather than give in. There is a final level at which the concession curve flattens out, for, at some wage, the business will become totally unprofitable and the employer would prefer to close down permanently rather than pay the wage being asked.

Given the characteristics of the two curves, there will be a point at which they intersect; under appropriate assumptions, the wage will be determined at this point of intersection. The critical assumption is that both sides to the bargaining know exactly what is in the mind of the other. The employers must know exactly what length of strike the union considers worth while in order to get a certain wage, and the union must know exactly how long the employers are prepared to hold out rather than concede this wage.

It is not unreasonable to suppose that the parties to collective bargaining pay some regard to the gain or loss resulting from a wage increase, and try to balance this in some way against the losses resulting from a strike. They will also try, as far as possible, to put themselves in the position of their opponents and try to guess what they will do. Nevertheless, the theory fails in three important respects. First, men do not always behave rationally. A strike may occur when there is very little prospect of gaining anything, let alone enough to offset the loss and hardship brought about by striking.[12]

Second, the theory overemphasizes the short-term gains and losses to the exclusion of longer-term considerations. In particular, Shackle[13] emphasizes the importance of 'loss of face'. This is not merely a matter of foolish pride. In certain circumstances, to make a concession might be worth while in the short run, but, if it led to the party being regarded as a weak bargainer, it might lead to losses on future occasions.

The last, and perhaps the most serious, criticism is that this theory does not really describe the bargaining process at all. If the one side does not know exactly what the other feels, the risk of conflict is very real. If the employer, for example, underestimates the willingness of the union to fight for higher pay, he may decide it is worth holding out against a claim when it would really be better for him to concede what is demanded. The same is true if the union under-estimates the resistance of employers. Moreover, it is not merely a case that one party may have a mistaken idea of what the attitude of the other party is. There is in any bargaining process a deliberate element of bluff. Initially, at least, one party will appear to take a tough line in the hope that the other side will accept this attitude at its face value, but, generally, it will be willing to make some concessions if the bluff is called. A theory of bargaining based on perfect knowledge is sadly deficient. Moreover, it is wrong to think in terms of some increase over and above the current wage. Initially, the union asks for £1 and the employers offer 50p increase. Immediately two figures other than the initial wage have to be considered.

This kind of approach to the theory of bargaining does not appear, therefore, to be particularly useful. Nevertheless, it does serve to concentrate our attention on some of the essential factors in the process of wage determination. The two sides must give some attention to the gains they are seeking, and to the costs involved in a failure to agree. If we do not regard this type of theory as offering a satisfactory explanation of wage determination under collective bargaining, we must either accept the traditional view that there can be no determinate theory of bilateral monopoly, and be satisfied with a theory that merely defines the limits within which a settlement is possible,[14] or we must look for a much more complex explanation of the bargaining process.

Attempts have been made to formulate such theories.[15] The general approach of some of these theories will be outlined here, but no attempt will be made to go into great detail. Suppose that a trade union has made a claim for increased pay and the employers have made a counter offer. Will the union accept the offer made by the employers or will it continue to press its original claim? If it can press its original claim with success, it stands to achieve certain gains for its members resulting from the higher level of wages compared with the employers' offer. If, however, it fails in its claim, it will lose for its members the gains represented by the employers' offer as compared with a conflict situation (a strike with no pay). When the union has to decide between continuing to press its original claim or making some concession, or between continuing to press for something substantially better than they have been offered or accepting the employers' offer, they do not know whether they are going to succeed in getting what they want or whether they will precipitate a conflict. The benefits of successfully pressing the

C

claim for the higher wage and the loss from refusing to accept the employers' offer must both be weighted, in some way, by their relative probabilities. In the same way, the employers will be trying to decide whether they should stick to the offer they have made or make an improvement upon it.

There is no reason why, when bargaining begins, there should be any obvious level of wage at which agreement should be reached. This type of theory does not produce a neat pair of curves which intersect at a point of equilibrium, nor do they produce a consistent set of simultaneous equations with equality between the number of equations and unknowns. During the process of bargaining, however, changes occur in the expectations of the two sides. They begin to get a clearer idea of what is in the mind of their opponents. At first, the union might have reckoned that the risk of conflict was fairly slight, if they held out for an improvement on the employers' original offer. When the employers make a revised offer, the risk of conflict, if the union continues to hold out, will be increased, and the union negotiators will recognize this. As the union recognizes this and lowers its demands, the employers also come to see that the risk of conflict, if they try to keep too close to their original offer, is increasing. What this type of theory does, therefore, is to set up conditions which must be satisfied in the equilibrium position, but which are achieved by movements in the important parameters: the equilibrium conditions do not define an equilibrium situation which is known from the beginning. Indeed, we cannot suppose that in a bargaining process there is a unique solution that is going to be reached. The way in which the vital parameters shift could, for example, depend in large measure upon the psychological characteristics of the two teams of negotiators.

Although economists are attempting to use this and other approaches[16] in order to provide a theory of bargaining, it remains to be seen whether the attempt will be of any real value to the economist. The process of bargaining is a fascinating field for study, and a legitimate one, but not necessarily for the economist. Psychologists clearly have an interest in the way people react in a bargaining situation. The economist is only interested in so far as an understanding of the bargaining process helps him to understand, or perhaps predict, the outcome. Bargaining as such is not his proper field of study.

NOTES

1. This figure can be calculated as follows: the marginal man employed receives £16 and to this we add the extra £1 a week paid to each of the original 10 workers.

2. This, of course, is the general rule. In perfect competition, the wage equals the marginal labour cost.

3. It will be recalled that the average net revenue product of labour is calculated after deducting from the total product all necessary payments to other factors, including normal profit. Therefore, a situation such as that in Fig. 5.1, where the wage is less than the average net revenue product, means that after paying wages there is more than enough left to pay the other factors and there is an abnormal profit.

4. Some students may wonder whether the double condition requires the labour supply curve to be tangential to the average net product curve. The reader with even a slight acquaintance with the differential calculus should have no difficulty in proving that the satisfaction of the two conditions does require tangency. For the non-mathematician, this necessity can be demonstrated as follows. Suppose the average product curve were to cut the supply curve, showing the wage, from below. There would be two points at which the wage equalled the average product of labour, but neither of these could be a point of profit-maximization. At either of these points, there would be no abnormal profit, but any level of employment between these two points would involve an average product greater than the wage and the earning of supernormal profits. Neither point, at which the wage equalled the average product, could be a point of maximum profit with the marginal labour cost equal to the marginal product. If, on the other hand, the supply curve is tangential to the average product curve, the point of tangency is one of maximum profit. At this point, normal profits are earned. To either side, the wage is greater than average product and, therefore, there are losses made (less than normal profit).

5. Models of this kind have, however, been used in economic theory. See, for example, J. T. Dunlop, *Wage Determination under Trade Unions*, Blackwell, Oxford, 1950.

6. The opposite case, dealt with earlier in this chapter, of a monopsonistic employer dealing with a large number of unorganized workers, is by no means impossible.

7. We could, in fact, say that with a minimum wage enforced by trade union action, the wage is still determined by the intersection of the market supply and demand curves. The labour supply curve will now be horizontal over the first part of its length. No labour will be forthcoming below the minimum wage, and the market supply will be perfectly elastic at this wage. At some point, it may become necessary to offer more than the minimum wage to increase the quantity of labour supplied. If the demand curve cuts the supply curve on this rising section, where the wage is above the minimum fixed by the union, the action of the union in fixing the minimum is pointless. Presumably, the union would fix a minimum *above* the equilibrium wage of the competitive labour market.

8. The argument which follows will, of course, apply equally to the case where a minimum wage is imposed by law rather than by trade union action.

9. The process of adjustment will be complex. As firms leave the industry, output falls and the product price rises. The revenue product curves of labour to the firm rise, enabling an equilibrium to be reached where the wage is equal to the maximum average net revenue product.

10. At this point, it should be made clear that the curve MLC_{m+w} is not the marginal labour cost curve corresponding to the aggregated supply curve AS_{m+w}. The marginal labour cost curve corresponding to this curve, which would be the supply curve in the absence of discrimination, would follow the

59

MLC$_w$ curve to a point vertically above the discontinuity in the supply curve, and would then drop vertically to the MLC$_{m+w}$ curve and follow that. If the intersection of the MNRP curve with the MLC$_{m+w}$ curve occurs beyond the point where this vertical drop would occur, the level of employment is unaffected by discrimination.

11. The argument presented here is based upon that of J. R. Hicks in his *Theory of Wages*, Macmillan, London, 1932, chapter 7. This theory was developed by Turner in an article in vol. 1 of the *Review of Economic Studies* (the approach of which is used by J. K. Eastham in his *Graphical Economics*, English U.P., London, 1960). This account also draws on the comments of G. L. S. Shackle in his contribution to J. T. Dunlop, ed., *The Theory of Wage Determination*, Macmillan, London, 1964.

12. The strike of Dundee busmen in the late summer of 1968 may be cited as a case in point. Agreement had been reached between the busmen and the corporation for an increase in pay coupled with certain changes affecting productivity. The agreement was vetoed by the Government under powers assumed in connection with its incomes policy. The immediate result of the veto was a strike, although this clearly had little prospect of achieving anything. The strikers could hardly have expected the Corporation to break the law by ignoring the Government veto, and, in this particular case, the strike action could scarcely be expected to influence the Government.

13. Loc. cit.

14. For an example of this approach, see A. C. Pigou, *The Economics of Welfare*, Macmillan, London, 4th end, 1932. Pigou argues that there is a *range of indeterminateness* determined by the minimum the employers will always offer (because at any lower wage they would lose opportunities for profitable production because labour was not forthcoming on the desired scale) and the maximum the unions would ask (because above a certain level of wages there would be too much unemployment). Both sides also have their *sticking points*. There is a minimum below which the trade unions will not go, and a maximum above which the employers will not go. If the union's sticking point is below the employers', there is a *range of practical bargains* within which a solution may be found. If the union's sticking point is higher than the employers', a conflict is inevitable.

15. See the sources already quoted, and A. Coddington, *Theories of the Bargaining Process*, Allen and Unwin, London, 1968.

16. Games theory, for example, may be used in a theory of bargaining. One could approach the problem as a zero-sum game, if employment, output, and price were all fixed, and a higher wage merely squeezed the employers' profits. If, however, all these are free to vary, and particularly if there is scope in the long run for substituting capital for labour, the game becomes a non-zero-sum one.

6. The optimum allocation of labour

The need for economy

Economic problems have their origins in the existence of scarce resources which are capable of alternative uses. Labour is one of these scarce resources, and it is therefore necessary to try to ensure that labour is used to the best advantage. There are two aspects to this task. First, it is necessary to use the available labour supply efficiently. This means that we should not employ five men to do a job that could equally well be done by three or four. In later parts of this book, it will be necessary to return to this aspect. For the remainder of this chapter, however, we will be concerned with the second aspect of the problem of making the best use of labour: the allocative aspect.

The best allocation of labour. Labour is essential in some way or other to the production of all goods and services. The question that arises, therefore, is how to secure the production of the combination of goods and services that will best meet the needs of society. The decisions which have to be taken about how many men are to be employed in farming, how many in making motor cars, how many in different services, and so on, are all clearly part of a very much wider and more fundamental process of decision-making. It is part of the wider group of decisions involving the allocation of *all* scarce resources. The discussion of the optimum allocation of labour is therefore greatly simplified. It is nevertheless worth while. In the first place, the subject with which we are primarily concerned is labour, and in discussing any more general topic it must be with special reference to labour. Second, it may be much easier for many readers to follow an argument couched in terms of one variable factor of production rather than in terms of many, as would be necessary for a full consideration of the conditions for the achievement of a welfare optimum.

Any assessment of what constitutes an optimum allocation of labour must start from some kind of value judgement about the ends of economic activity. We should not automatically equate the good of society with the wishes of the individual consumer. A good many economists, from Adam Smith onwards, have argued that it is best to leave the allocation of scarce resources to be determined by the free working of the market mechanism: this may be true under certain conditions. However, the free market may not produce ideal results, for example, if monopolists are left free to exploit the consumer. Even when the working of the market mechanism is not distorted by monopoly or other imperfections, to say that an ideal allocation of resources results implies that we accept a particular set of value judgements. It implies that we consider the primary purpose of economic activity to be the satisfaction of the wants of individual members of society, that individuals are the best judges of their own interests, and that we are prepared to accept the income distribution that emerges from the free play of market forces.

Some qualifications. Few people would accept these value judgements today without considerable qualification. Society as a whole may have certain objectives quite separate from those of individuals, even though the great majority of individuals are in sympathy with them. The defence of a country against external aggression, the maintenance of law and order, and the administration of justice within its boundaries are services which cannot be provided through the working of the market mechanism; the government must use its authority to provide them. In peacetime, it may be sufficient to levy taxes to pay for these services, and labour and other resources will be attracted to this public sector through the ordinary working of the market mechanism. The market mechanism can be left to function freely to determine what goods are produced in the sectors producing consumer goods and investment goods for business enterprises.

In wartime, however, the primary aim of prosecuting the war may call for severe curtailment of freedom in the private sector. It may be necessary to resort to the direction of labour and other similar controls. Or again, in communist countries, the expansion of the countries' future productive capacity may be given priority over the satisfaction of the consumers' present wants. There may therefore be reluctance by governments to place much reliance on the working of the market mechanism.

In the remainder of this chapter, we shall be concerned with the efficacy of the market mechanism in allocating labour with a view to satisfying individual wants. This is not to deny the importance of society's collective wants, but rather to show that even in meeting this limited objective the case for a completely free market is valid only when certain conditions are satisfied.

The perfectly competitive optimum

We have seen in chapter 4 that in a perfectly competitive labour market an employer will take on labour to the point where the wage he pays is equal to the marginal net revenue product of labour. For the purposes of the present chapter, it is convenient to simplify the analysis and to assume that labour is the only variable factor and to refer to the marginal revenue product. If there is also perfect competition in the product market, the price the firm receives for its product may be assumed to be independent of the quantity it markets. In other words, it will not have to lower the price to dispose of the greater quantity produced when more labour is engaged. The marginal revenue product of labour is therefore equal to the marginal physical product times the price of the product.

There is no reason to suppose that the existence of competition in the labour market need be associated with competition in the product market. Either market may be competitive, while the other has an element of monopoly on one side or the other. It is possible, for example, for a firm to be subject to fairly intense competition in the market for its product. It may be selling its product in competition with firms all over the country. It may, however, have chosen a location away from the main centres of industry and be the only employer of importance in the local labour market. An engineering firm, on the other hand, may have developed some special line of production in which it enjoys a near-monopoly. It may nevertheless be located in one of the main centres of the engineering industry and be competing for labour with many firms making different products.

If there were no specific skills, or at least no skills that were specific to one industry, and no barriers to mobility arising from the location of expanding industries in one area and declining industries in another, we would expect the wages of a given grade of labour to be the same in all occupations. Unless there were marked differences in other conditions of employment, a man would not work in one industry if he knew he could get a higher wage in another. In each industry, if there were everywhere perfect competition in labour and rod uct markets, the wage would equal the value of the marginal physical product of labour. It follows, therefore, that since the wage is everywhere the same, the value of the marginal product of labour must be the same in every industry. We can express this in the equation:

$$MPP_a.P_a = W_a = W_b = MPP_b.P_b \ldots$$
$$\therefore MPP_a.P_a = MPP_b.P_b,$$

where MPP refers to marginal physical product, P to the price of product, W to the wage, and the subscripts to particular industries.

If we ignore the difficulties raised by commodities which are purchased only rarely, or which do not permit marginal adjustments of the quantity purchased, we may accept the prices paid for commodities as reflecting the value placed by each consumer on his marginal purchase of each commodity. It follows, therefore, that under conditions of universal perfect competition the consumer's valuation of the product of the marginal unit of labour is the same in all industries. If the consumers were to value the product of an additional unit of labour in one industry more highly than the product of an additional unit of labour in another, it means that they would prefer to see a unit of labour transferred from the industry where its marginal product is low to the one where it is high. Consumers would benefit from such a transfer of labour, until such time as the marginal products were equal. Once the point is reached where the values of the marginal products are equal, there is nothing to be gained by any further transfer of labour. To continue the transfer would be to transfer labour from an industry where a certain value was placed on the product of the unit transferred to an industry where a lower value was placed on its product. The situation created would be similar to the original one, except that the relative position of the two industries would be reversed.

We have therefore established that, when there is perfect competition in both labour and product markets, the value of the marginal product of labour is the same in all industries, and the combination of goods produced is that which is most highly prized by the consumers. Any transfer of labour from one industry to another would reduce consumer satisfaction. It is in this sense that the situation resulting under conditions of perfect competition in labour and product markets can be described as optimal.[1]

Before considering conditions where perfect competition is not present in one of the markets, it should be noted that two forces would operate as labour was moved from an industry where its marginal product was low to one where it was high. Both of these forces would tend to bring about equality of the marginal products in the two industries. First, marginal physical products in the two industries will change. As labour leaves the industry where the value of its marginal product is low, there will be a tendency for marginal physical productivity to increase (law of variable proportions). Similarly, in the other industry, the marginal physical product will tend to fall. At constant product prices, this would tend to bring the values of the marginal products closer together, and ultimately to the point of equality. People might prefer a unit of labour to be used to produce 10 apples rather than 8 pears. When a point has been reached where another unit of labour only raises apple production by 9, whereas a unit taken away from pear production will lower output by 9, the consumers may now feel the transfer has gone far enough. They may regard 9 apples or 9 pears as yielding equal satisfaction.

The second factor is the change that will take place in the relative product prices. As more labour is transferred to one industry, output increases and the price falls. In the other industry, output is falling and so price rises. This clearly reinforces the effect of the transfer of labour on marginal physical product in bringing about equality of the value of the marginal physical products. In the example above, as labour is transferred from the production of pears to the production of apples, we find not only that each successive unit transferred involves the gain of fewer apples for the loss of more pears, but each apple gained becomes less highly prized by the consumers and each pear lost more highly prized.

Monopoly in the product market

The firm which is seeking to maximize its profits will always equate the cost of employing an extra man with his marginal revenue product. So long as the labour market remains perfectly competitive, the going wage rate will represent the cost of employing an extra man, and will therefore be equated with the marginal revenue product. It is only in the special case, where there is also perfect competition in the product market, that this will also equal the value of the marginal physical product of labour. We must now turn to the case where the labour market is perfectly competitive, but where monopolistic elements are to be found in one or more of the product markets.

C*

It was explained in chapter 4 that the firm which is a monopolist in the product market has to lower the price of its product in order to sell the greater output when more men are employed. The additional revenue obtained is therefore less than the marginal physical product of labour multiplied by the price received for the product. It is smaller by the amount of the necessary reduction in price times the output of the smaller labour force.

Because the labour market is still perfectly competitive, the same wage will be paid in all industries, even though some products are sold in monopolistic markets. If we write MRP for the marginal revenue product, we get the following equation, corresponding to the one we derived in the previous section:

$$MRP_a = W_a = W_b = MRP_a,$$
$$\therefore \quad MRP_a = MRP_b.$$

Let us suppose that industry A is perfectly competitive, but that industry B is monopolistic. It follows that:

$$MRP_a = MPP_a.P_a, \tag{6.1}$$

$$MRP_b < MPP_b.P_b. \tag{6.2}$$

Since the two marginal revenue products are equal, it follows finally that:

$$MPP_a.P_a < MPP_b.P_b.$$

It is always the value of the marginal physical product of labour that represents the consumer's valuation of the output of the marginal unit of labour. The marginal revenue product is only relevant to the employer in calculating his profits. The final equation means, therefore, that the consumers place a higher valuation on the product of a marginal unit of labour in the monopolized industry as opposed to the competitive industry. They would prefer to sacrifice the output of industry A that would result from transferring a unit of labour to industry B, in order to have the increased output of industry B. However, the transfer of labour does not take place because, although this would be in the interests of the consumers, it would not pay the monopolist to increase his labour force and expand output. Monopoly in the product market therefore distorts the optimum allocation of labour. Or it might be more accurate to say that the misallocation of labour is merely one facet of mis-allocation of resources resulting from the existence of monopoly.

The imperfect labour market

It is now necessary to look at those cases where it is the labour market that is imperfect. Here, we have to consider two cases. First, the situation where there is perfect competition in the product markets, but the supply of labour is under the control of a trade union, is one of monopoly in the labour market. Second, the case where there is monopsony in the labour market, where a single employer dominates the market.

Trade union monopoly. In practice, the monopoly powers of the trade unions generally spring from the existence of specific skills and the power of the unions to regulate apprenticeship. The profit-maximizing firm will not employ labour beyond the point where the wage equals the marginal net revenue product of labour.[2] Since the marginal net revenue product curve is falling, higher wages mean fewer men will be employed. If there are a large number of people seeking work, wages will tend to fall. If, however, the union can limit the number of men acquiring a particular skill, it will avoid having too many men looking for work and so be able to keep the wage level relatively high. This kind of policy has been adopted in the past not only by the craft unions, but also by some of the professional bodies.

If a job is relatively unskilled, and it is fairly easy for men to take up this job, it will be more difficult for a trade union to exercise effective control over wages. This is why the craft unions were able to exert a significant influence on the wages of their members at a time when unions of unskilled and semiskilled workers were ineffective. Nevertheless, it is possible for unions of unskilled workers to have an impact on wage levels. An employer may find it easy enough to replace any workman who leaves: there may be a pool of unemployed workers waiting to fill any vacancies that occur. If, however, a strike is called in some factory, or in some industry, it may be impossible for an employer, or employers, to find replacements for the whole of the striking labour force. Even if replacements were available on the required scale, few employers could contemplate carrying on production with an entirely new labour force.[3]

For the purposes of our theoretical exposition, it will be more convenient to continue to assume that there are no specific skills required for different industries or occupations. Under such conditions, it might seem unlikely that a trade union could have very much power to influence wage levels. A union could, however, raise the wage level of its members if, for example, it were granted a legal monopoly of employment in some particular sphere. A similar result could occur if entry to some occupation were limited by custom.

Let us suppose that industry A is representative of all industries where no trade unions exist and industry B is one industry where a trade union forces wages above the competitive level. In each industry, firms will employ labour up to the point where the wage equals the value of the marginal physical product.[4] We can represent this state of affairs by the following equations:

$$W_a = MPP_a.P_a, \tag{6.3}$$
$$W_b = MPP_b.P_b, \tag{6.4}$$
$$W_b > W_a. \tag{6.5}$$

It follows, of course, that $MPP_a.P_a < MPP_b.P_b$. The product of the marginal unit of labour employed in industry B is more highly prized than the product of that same unit of labour in industry A. There is a misallocation of resources of the same kind as resulted from the existence of monopoly in the product market; this was because of the desire of the monopolist firm to maximize its profits. In this case, it is the result of the trade union in industry B setting a higher wage for its members than is paid to similar workers in industries where there is no such trade union action.

The assumption that has so far been made is that a trade union has been established in a particular industry and has been able to regulate the level of wages in that industry. One may also envisage a situation where trade unionism is the order of the day, and the supply of labour to all industries is controlled by a trade union or trade unions. It should, however, be apparent from the foregoing argument that the divergence from the optimum allocation of labour is the result of wage levels being different in different industries. It does not matter whether this difference arises because some industries have a competitive supply of labour while others have the labour supply dominated by a trade union, or because the trade unions in some industries feel themselves to be in a stronger position than others, and so able to get higher wages for their members.

It follows, therefore, that we do not need to consider separately the case where there are different unions with different degrees of control over the wages of their members. However, the case where trade union action forces the wage in all industries to a common level, above that which would prevail in a competitive labour market, does call for special attention.

The equilibrium of the perfectly competitive labour market is shown in Fig. 4.4. The industry is in equilibrium when the wage level is at W_1, and firms in the industry are in equilibrium when the

68

wage is equal to the maximum average net product of labour (assuming all firms are identical). There is no reason why this diagram should not be reinterpreted as referring to the labour market as a whole.[5] The lefthand curves represent the position of

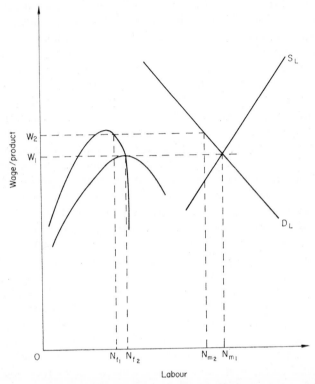

Fig. 6.1. Equilibrium of the firm and industry.

the firm, no matter what industry it is in, and the righthand curves represent the labour market as a whole. For convenience, a similar diagram is reproduced as Fig. 6.1.

What we have to examine is the effect of a trade union being formed and imposing a wage rate above the equilibrium level W_1. Suppose the wage is forced to a level W_2. It is tempting to argue that in the short-run employment in the industry would contract from N_m to N_{m_1} and the number of men employed by each firm would contract from N_f to N_{f_1}. Two points must be made, however. First, the situation is not one of long-run equilibrium, because firms would be earning less than normal profits. Second, an increase in *all* wages must have macroeconomic effects via the propensity to consume.

Because firms are not making a normal profit, there will be an exodus of firms from all industries. With a contraction of output, the price of products will rise and therefore the revenue product curves will rise. This will also mean a shift in the demand curve for labour and a new equilibrium position will be reached where W_2 is now the maximum average net revenue product of labour.

This, however, is neglecting the macroeconomic effect. The initial effect of the higher wage level is to reduce profits. Employment is also reduced, but we do not know whether aggregate wages will be reduced or increased. This depends upon the elasticity of the demand curve for labour. If the demand for labour is inelastic, and an increase in wages leads to a less than proportionate decrease in the numbers employed, the total wage bill will be increased: if the demand for labour is elastic and a rise in wages leads to a more than proportionate decrease in employment, the wage bill will be reduced.

If the demand for labour is elastic, and the rise in the wage rate leads to a fall in aggregate wages, there must be a fall in the total demand for goods and services, for there is nothing to offset the fall in profits. If, however, the demand for labour is inelastic, a rise in wages leads to an increase in the total wage bill. This, in itself, cannot entirely offset the fall in profits. Profits must fall by more than the increase in the wage bill, because the level of activity has fallen and there is more than a simple transfer of income from profits to wages. Nevertheless, wage-earners are likely to spend a greater proportion of income than the recipients of profits. This will tend to offset the fall in the aggregate demand for goods and services that might otherwise have resulted from a fall in total incomes. Indeed, it may more than offset it. This could mean that the final result of an increase in the wage rate could be an increased level of aggregate demand for goods and services, leading to an increase in employment. This would mean that, in the final equilibrium situation, the curves in Fig. 6.1 would need to be completely redrawn.

Can we say whether the action of a trade union in forcing up the general level of wages is good or bad? It does not create an easily demonstrable divergence from the optimum allocation of resources, as in the other cases discussed. We cannot say that the consumers would prefer more labour to be employed in one industry and less in another. It would be tempting to say that if the enforcement of the higher wage led to a curtailment of employment it would be a bad thing. It would mean that workers were idle when, as individuals, they would be willing to work for a wage equal to, or even below, the level being enforced, and people would be willing to buy the additional output these workers helped to produce. If higher wages seriously discouraged investment and caused widespread unemployment, we might well regard this as undesirable. But if higher wages were accompanied by only a small rise in unemployment, some workers could be regarded as benefiting at the expense of others. To say whether this was good or bad would be to make a value judgement – and it would be a more difficult one to make, or, at least, one where different people would be more likely to disagree. If, on the other hand, the level of employment were to increase, as is just possible, there might be widespread agreement that the change was beneficial.

It must not be imagined, however, that a rise in wages, even when it would lead to increased employment, is the only way of achieving this end. There are other and, perhaps, surer means to this end. Government can, by monetary or fiscal policy, take steps to ensure that full employment is reached. Moreover, it may be quite sure that a policy of reducing taxation while maintaining expenditure will lead to increased employment. While it is *possible* that a higher wage rate will have this effect, it is by no means *certain*: the probability may, indeed, be that it will reduce employment. If this would be the result of a higher wage level being enforced by trade unions, it would still be possible for the Government to bring the economy back to full employment by using these other weapons it has in its armoury. Some years ago, Professor Hicks referred to the economy being on the *labour standard*. By this, he meant that the trade union determined the level of wages, and the Government took the necessary steps to maintain full employment, if necessary increasing the monetary circulation and allowing the price level in the country to rise.[6]

It may seem that if all wages are raised to the same level, the existence of trade unions does not distort the allocation of resources. It is true that it does not create a *distortion* in the same way that raising wages in only one industry would. The very word distortion implies a change for the worse, and we have seen that it is not easy to say that the total effect of changes resulting from the enforcement of higher wages is harmful. It must not be thought, however, that all industries would be equally affected. We have seen already that there would be possible effects on employment, on the distribution of income, and on the average propensity to consume. All of these changes could carry with them some change in the pattern of

71

demand. If a greater proportion of the total national income goes to wage-earners as a result of an increase in wages, there will be a shift of demand, from goods demanded by the recipients of profits to goods demanded by wage-earners.

Again, if we relax the assumption that all firms are identical, and allow instead that there may be different revenue product curves, it follows that the impact of a wage increase will be different in different industries. The level of employment will contract most in those industries where the demand for labour is most elastic: where the demand is inelastic there will be comparatively little decrease in the numbers employed.

Although there is this change in the pattern of output, we cannot say that it is a change for the better or worse. The kind of optimum we considered in the earlier cases is essentially static. It is concerned with the best allocation of labour in relation to a given situation. If there is a major change in employment and income distribution, an entirely new situation is created, and the allocation of resources must be judged in relation to that new situation.

Monopsony and the allocation of labour. At this point, it is necessary to return to this kind of narrow concept of the optimum allocation of labour, and to see how it is affected when the employers are able to exercise a degree of monopsony power. It will be recalled from chapter 5 that under monopsony the employer needs to raise the wage in order to attract more labour, and that his wage bill therefore rises by more than the wage paid to the marginal man.

To facilitate the analysis, let us assume that one employer is important enough to possess monopsony power in the labour market, but that other employers are relatively small and have to accept the going wage. If employer A is the monopsonist, his equilibrium position may be represented by the equation:

$$MPP_a . P_a = MLC_a > W.$$

For other firms, of which B is representative, the position is one where:

$$MPP_b . P_b = W$$

(Note that perfect competition is assumed in product markets, and that the same wage prevails for all firms. This is because we assume a common labour market in which most employers are small, but A is the one firm large enough to find that its demand for labour has a significant effect on the wage that has to be paid. If this seems difficult to reconcile with the assumption of all product markets

72

being perfectly competitive, the difficulty may be resolved by assuming that the market for A's product is made perfectly competitive by the availability of supplies of imported goods.)

It follows from the two foregoing equations, that the marginal product of labour in firm A is higher than in firm B ($MPP_a.P_a > MPP_b.P_b$). The consumers would prefer the output of A to expand at the expense of B, but this is not profitable to B because of the degree of monopsony power possessed.

The real world

The argument of this chapter has been that, with the possible exception of trade union action which secures a uniform increase in all wages, monopolistic elements on either side of the labour market lead to a distortion of the optimum allocation of labour. In the real world, however, some elements of monopoly are inevitable, while others, like trade unionism, are so firmly established that it would be unrealistic to think of eliminating them. Under these circumstances, it becomes necessary to ask whether we should try to eliminate all monopolistic elements, where this is possible. Will the elimination of some elements of monopoly always lead to an improved allocation of resources? Or is it possible that in a world where some elements of monopoly are inevitable the introduction of others will improve rather than worsen the allocation of resources?

There are two possibilities. The first is that monopolistic elements may have a cumulative effect: the more monopolistic the elements, the greater the distortion of the allocation of resources. The second is that some monopolistic elements in a situation may help to counteract the effects of others, and perhaps even represent the deliberate use of *countervailing power*.

Cumulative impact. In order to see how the impact of monopoly elements on the allocation of labour may be cumulative, let us take the case in which a firm is in a monopolistic position in the product market, and in a monopsonistic position in the labour market. For firm A in such a position, we know that it will equate its marginal revenue product (which is less than the value of the marginal physical product) to the marginal labour cost (which, in turn, is greater than the wage rate).

$$MPP_a.P_a > MRP_a = MLC_a > W.$$

If other firms are selling in competitive markets, and competing with firm A for labour, but are too small to have any monopsony power,

73

the position of firm B, representative of these others, will be:

$$MPP_b.P_b = W.$$

It is apparent from these equations that there are two factors at work, both tending to make

$$MPP_a.P_a > MPP_b.P_b.$$

In the competitive sector, the wage is equal to the value of the marginal physical product of labour, and, because the wage is everywhere the same, the value of the marginal physical product of labour is everywhere the same; this is the optimal situation. In the case of the firm combining monopsony power, a departure from the optimum occurs because the employer looks at the marginal labour cost rather than the wage on the one hand, and at the marginal revenue product rather than the value of the marginal physical product on the other. These effects are cumulative, and a better allocation of labour would result if either were eliminated. Consumers would prefer the output of firm A to be expanded at the expense of competitive firms like B. The elimination of either the monopoly or the monopsony power of firm A would lead to such an increase in output and would therefore represent a preferred use of the community's scarce supply of labour.

Countervailing impact. It is important to remember the assumptions we made in reaching this conclusion. We have one firm with both monopoly and monopsony power. Elsewhere, the economy is perfectly competitive. Under such assumptions, we can say confidently that it will be beneficial to eliminate either the firm's monopoly power or its monopsony power, or both. The position is much more difficult if monopoly elements are widespread. Is it then desirable to try to eliminate a particular monopoly element, or to prevent a single additional monopoly element being introduced? If, for example, trade unionism is common in many industries, but is non-existent (or at least weak and ineffective) in others, the extension of effective unionism to the latter group could certainly be regarded as an extension of monopolistic elements in the economy, but it would be rash to argue that it would lead to a worsening of the allocation of resources.

Even if it could be shown that any element of monopoly contributed to a misallocation of resources, it would not inevitably follow that a case was established for its elimination. The concept of an optimum allocation of resources in welfare economics is a limited and relative one. We have been looking at the achievement of the

74

welfare optimum in a very simplified form. But whether we look at the more complex models of welfare economics which take account of many variables, or whether we look at the allocation of labour in a very simplified model, we are making use of a concept which tries to steer clear of value judgements. The welfare optimum is achieved subject to certain conditions, including the distribution of income. Given these conditions, one may reach an optimum position where

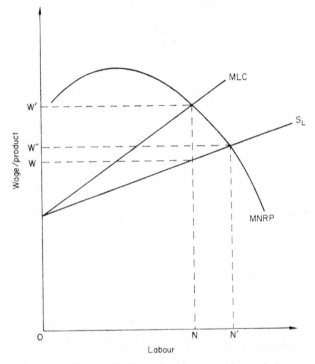

Fig. 6.2 Welfare implications of raising wages in one industry.

it can be shown that no person may be made better off without somebody else being made worse off.

The distribution of income, however, is something which many people, including trade unionists, may feel ought to be changed. If trade union action in forcing up wages in certain industries is the only way of bringing about a desired redistribution of income, most people will judge such action to be good. The theoretical concept of the optimum allocation of resources may be relatively unimportant in most people's minds compared with the distribution of income.

It can, however, be shown that the introduction of an additional monopoly element may, in certain circumstances at least, be beneficial. The additional monopoly element may, in fact, bring the situation closer to the optimum allocation of labour. We may look at the situation where monopsony has existed in the labour market, and a trade union has been formed. This situation is illustrated in Fig. 6.2. When there is only monopsony in the labour market, the employer will take on ON men at a wage OW, for this is the level of employment at which the additional cost resulting from the employment of an extra man equals his marginal net revenue product. If the trade union enforces a wage level of OW', the level of employment will remain at ON and there will be a transfer of WW'.ON from profits to wages. If the wage level were set by the union at some intermediate level, such as OW'', the level of employment would increase to ON'. We have seen already that the effect of monopsony is to reduce the output of the firm concerned below the optimum, and this increase in output would represent a better allocation of resources.

At this stage, two points must be made. First, it must be stressed that it is only possible for the employer to continue to pay a higher wage in the long run if he had previously been earning monopoly profits. Second, although the introduction of the minimum wage as a result of trade union action may improve the allocation of labour, it may not achieve the optimum allocation. There are three reasons for this. First, the true optimum can only be reached if there is already perfect competition elsewhere. Second, even if this condition holds, the optimum cannot be reached if the firm concerned is itself a monopolist, and still exercising a measure of monopoly power in the product market. Third, it is possible that the trade union action may have forced the wage of its members in the employ of this particular firm above the general level, with the result that the wage level itself causes a misallocation of resources.

Let us look at this last point in more detail. In developing the argument that monopsony causes a misallocation of resources, we assumed that there was a single firm which had a large enough demand for labour to have a significant influence on the wage it had to pay, but it was competing for labour with a large number of small firms who accepted the going wage rate. The wage OW in Fig. 6.2 would thus represent the general level of wages paid in all firms. It is only possible, therefore, to reach the optimum allocation of labour if trade union action does not force the wage level too far above OW. (The reader may be inclined to think, at first, that the optimum allocation can only be reached if the union does not

76

force the wage above OW. There would, of course, be no point in the union doing this. If, however, the wage is set below OW', the monopsonistic firm is going to employ more men. An increase in the labour supply will only be forthcoming if the wage level rises in all firms. Only if the wage in this particular enterprise is kept artificially high in relation to that in other firms is there a distortion of the optimum allocation of labour.)[7]

The difficulty of making judgements. From what has been said, it appears that while universal perfect competition might be expected to lead to an optimum allocation of resources, and that the existence of monopolistic elements leads to a misallocation, it does not follow that in every situation it is desirable to eliminate a particular monopoly element. (Strictly speaking, we cannot even say that perfect competition leads to an optimum allocation of resources. It does so, provided an entrepreneur has to meet all the costs incurred by a project, and also reaps the benefits. If he disregards the costs that his project implies for others, or the benefits it confers on others without yielding him a return, the optimum allocation of resources will still not be achieved.) We have seen that it is possible for two monopolistic elements to have a cumulative effect in bringing about misallocation, and also that one monopolistic element may help to counteract the misallocative effect of another.

It is therefore often difficult to make really firm judgements about the effects of monopolies and restrictive practices, whether in product or factor markets. It may be quite impossible to do so on strictly economic grounds. If necessary, we should not be afraid of introducing value judgements in order to enable us to decide whether a change is good or bad. Some economists would like to make the subject a positive science and to steer clear of normative pronouncements. Usually, this is a counsel of perfection in their textbooks, for none of them observe this approach in practice. However, the economist who attempted to do so could rarely have anything useful to say on the important economic issues of the day. What matters is that, if value judgements have to be introduced, they should be made explicit.

This is particularly true in the field of labour economics. We must not forget that the relative nature of the optimum allocation of resources as seen by the theorist and the effect of making minor adjustments, which bring the economy a little nearer to or a little further away from that optimum, may be insignificant beside changes which involve, perhaps, a major shift in income distribution and move the optimum at the same time. We could, for example, be in

77

an optimal situation and, then, as the result of increasing union power, wages rise and the workers receive a larger share of the national income. The new situation may, however, be non-optimal in the theoretical sense. If, however, we regard the shift in the distribution of income as desirable, and the use of trade union power as the only way of achieving this shift, then we may regard the new situation as preferable, notwithstanding the fact that labour is not allocated optimally. Trade unions may, of course, abuse their power. While we might regard the results of growing union power as generally desirable, we might still want to eliminate some of the abuses, abuses which might well involve a misallocation of resources. For example, if a particular union were severely restricting the entry of apprentices to a craft in order to keep wages at an artificially high level, we might try to devise appropriate countermeasures. But we would not say that trade unions, generally, are monopolistic and must be abolished because they cause a misallocation of labour.

The allocative role of wages

In all the discussion so far in this chapter, it has been assumed that labour is homogeneous, and that there is either a common wage level or else the wage paid for those doing some particular job is kept high artificially. In fact, labour is not homogeneous. There are at least three important ways in which one kind of labour differs from another. First, jobs may call for different inborn abilities on the part of those called upon to perform them. Some may require physical strength, others manual dexterity, and others intelligence. Second, some jobs call for a higher level of education than others, and entry to these jobs will not be open to those who have not received the appropriate level of education, whatever their inborn abilities. Finally, a job may require specific training, and it can only be performed by the worker who has acquired the specialized knowledge and skills that are relevant to it.

It is necessary to look briefly at wage differentials, from two points of view. First, it is necessary to offer a theoretical explanation of differentials and, second, we must look at the role of wage differentials in the allocation of labour between jobs.

The theory of wage differentials. We may begin with a relatively simple model. Let us assume that there are several readily recognized grades of labour. We need not think solely in terms of one grade being superior to another; what matters is that they are different. We might think of labourers who require strength, artisans who need manual skill, and managers who need a high level of intelligence. How will the wages of each group be determined, and what kind of relationship will be established between the three groups?

We must treat each group as a separate factor of production. If we suppose that the worker possesses the abilities required for only one kind of job, the picture is a very simple one. For each kind of labour, there will be an appropriate supply curve, and for each kind of labour there will be a demand curve. The demand curve will be derived in the manner already described in chapters 4 and 5. If the labour markets are competitive, each type of labour will be employed within the firm in such quantities that its wage is equal to its marginal revenue product.

There is also the question of the proportions in which the different grades of labour are employed. We saw in chapter 4 that labour and raw materials would be employed in such proportions that the marginal rate of substitution between them would equal the price ratio. This is merely a special case of a general rule: a firm which is maximizing profits must ensure that the ratio of any two factor prices is equal to the marginal rate of substitution between them. In so far as there are possibilities of substituting one type of labour for another, this rule must hold good for different kinds of labour, as well as for labour and other variable factors of production.

We are accustomed to think of the wages of labourers being low by comparison with those of skilled craftsmen, which, in turn, are well below the salaries commanded by managers. We are almost inclined to think of this as something so natural as to require little or no explanation. A craftsman may say that he 'ought to get something extra for his skill'. He does, it is true, have to serve an apprenticeship during which his earnings are low, and might be unwilling to do so unless there were the prospect of compensation from higher earnings later on. The size of the differential, in the past at least, has been far greater than would be needed to compensate for low earnings during apprenticeship. Is there any reason why the kind of dexterity required of the craftsman should command a higher reward than the physical strength required of the labourer? From the economist's point of view, there is no reason at all. It is merely a matter of supply and demand.

Wages are high where supply is small in relation to demand, and low where supply is relatively abundant. It is wrong to speak, as many students do, of there being a great demand for the services of skilled craftsmen. This may sometimes be true, but all we can be sure of is that in our experience there is a greater demand for their services *relative to the available supply*. In other words, the supply and demand curves intersect at a higher wage level. In a world which calls for manual skills and intelligence rather than sheer brawn, the man who has nothing to offer but his strength will be poorly paid. If, for some strange reason, dexterity and intelligence became far commoner in the working population than they are, and physical strength less common, or if for some equally strange reason the demand for workers with greater strength increased, we might find the present pattern of differentials reversed.

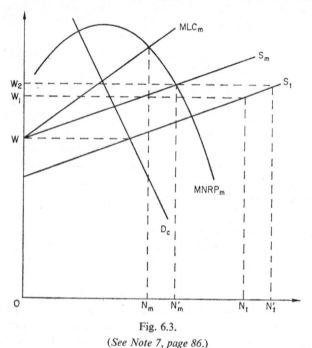

Fig. 6.3.
(*See Note 7, page 86.*)

There are other factors helping to explain the differentials which exist between jobs. The supply of labour capable of undertaking many of the more skilled jobs has been limited, in the past especially, by lack of education and training. If the necessary education or training for a job is costly, the supply of labour will be limited to those who have the necessary inborn abilities and the good fortune to choose parents who can afford the costs involved in education and training. This factor tends to widen the differentials between skilled and unskilled workers. Differentials may also emerge between workers of roughly comparable abilities, but in different occupations.
80

There are several possible explanations for this state of affairs. It will suffice to mention two. The demand for workers in two occupations may change. At one time, they may have received the same rate of pay, but if the demand for one increases and for the other diminishes, wages will tend to rise in the one case and fall in the other. A differential will emerge. This might be expected to attract workers to the job where demand has increased and wages risen. This might well happen, if the jobs were semiskilled, required little or no retraining, so that there was a real chance of a man moving from one to the other. If, however, we are considering, say, two skilled crafts for which a four year apprenticeship is necessary, the position is very different. The wage differential may attract more young men to the one craft and discourage some from entering the other. It will be four years before this has any impact at all on the supply of qualified craftsmen and, perhaps, it will then be only a small impact in relation to the change in demand. For this reason, workers in an occupation for which the demand has increased may, for a long time, continue to earn wages above the level that is necessary to keep them in that employment. These extra earnings over what is needed to keep them in the job are in the nature of a quasirent.[8]

Differences between the wages of workers of comparable skills may also occur because the position of trade unions (or professional associations) are stronger in some fields than others. This difference in strength may arise because some unions are able to get a higher proportion of the workers enrolled as members, or because they are able to get legal sanction for some of their rules, or because, in some situations (for example, where monopoly exists), the employers may be better able to afford concessions.

Differentials exist, in the first place, because jobs call for different abilities. The differences in inborn abilities are reinforced by differences in opportunities for education and training. Further differences emerge because specific skills have to be acquired and the supply of labour can only adjust slowly, and because of differing degrees of union success in trying to secure higher wages. The tendency for wages to be equal, even for workers of a given level of skill, is therefore approximate at the most.

We must now turn to another question. Do these differences attract labour to jobs that need to be done, or are they simply curious anomalies?

Differentials exist not only between jobs, but also between workers doing similar jobs in different parts of the country. Such differentials can be explained in terms of differences in supply and demand relationships in the different areas, but this still leaves an explanation necessary of why workers do not leave an area where pay in a particular job is low and seek employment in an area where it is high. There is no single answer to this question. Part of the answer may be that workers are ignorant of the opportunities open to them in other parts of the country, or they may prefer to stay where they are, even at a lower wage than they could get by moving. It has long been recognized that, even under free competition, the tendency is for the net advantages of different employments (and similarly of employment in different areas) to be equalized. Thus, a man may prefer to remain in a pleasant environment (whether this is interpreted in terms of the natural or social conditions) rather than seek higher pay. Again, moving home may involve certain costs. It would be worth moving only if wages were sufficiently higher in the new area to give a reasonable rate of return on the investment – that is, if the discounted value of expected additional earnings exceed the cost of moving. But even if a man were willing to consider a move, the wage differential were sufficient to make this attractive, he could not move if it were not possible for him to raise the money required for the removal.

The mechanism of allocation. There are many economists and others who believe that if an industry is expanding it will offer higher wages in order to secure the additional labour it requires. They believe that, if firms in the expanding industry offer wages sufficiently above the levels being paid by other industries, they will succeed in attracting labour away from these other industries. The underlying assumption is that workers will sooner or later respond to the offer of higher wages.

In the perfectly competitive model, no wage differentials could persist so long as there were no barriers to the movement of labour from one job to another. As soon as wages rose in one industry compared with others, there would be a transfer of labour on a considerable scale. Marginal productivity would fall in the expanding industry and rise in the industries that were losing labour. Very quickly, a new equilibrium would be established with the same wage continuing to be paid throughout industry, but with the labour force reallocated to meet changing demands. In a frictionless world, differentials would be transitory.

The real world is not one of perfect competition. Quite apart from the presence of monopoly elements, there are a good many frictions present which render competition less than perfect and

82

which modify the responses of both employers and labour compared with the theoretical model. The worker is not completely free to move from a job in a declining industry to one in an expanding industry. Barriers may be created by the existence of specific skills. Even where a man may be competent to take another job, or where the time needed to train for a semiskilled job is quite short, he may be reluctant to move. For example, he may be unsure what the prospects in the new job are. It is all very well thinking that a man would change his job if he knew he could get, say 25p a week more by doing so. He might be able to do so, but unless he *knows* that he can he will not change jobs. There is, in fact, remarkably little known about earnings in different jobs. Complicated systems of bonus payment, the opportunities for overtime working, and so on, make it very difficult for a man to have a clear idea of what his prospects would be if he moved to another job. Similarly, a man might be quite capable of doing some other job, but he may not feel confident about his ability. He may feel that he is happy in his present job, that he gets on well with his workmates and his bosses, and he might well wonder whether he would fit into a new set-up as well as he does into his present one.

All of these are reasons why a man might continue in one job rather than take another job which is going, is within his abilities, and which offers a higher rate of pay. Jaques has suggested that workers will feel reasonably satisfied if their pay is within 5 per cent of the general level for workers of comparable skill. Within the range of a 5 to 10 per cent underpayment by comparison with similar workers, there is likely to be a lowering of morale; when the differential goes beyond this level morale is not only seriously affected, but there is an increasing tendency for workers to look for other jobs.[9]

This suggests that labour responds only sluggishly to monetary inducements to change jobs. Indeed, the advocates of differentials as a means of reallocating labour are inconsistent. If differentials were really effective in bringing about a reallocation of labour, they would only need to be small. If differentials need to be large, it suggests that they may not be a very efficient allocator, and that it might be preferable to look for an alternative mechanism.

Wages do tend to be higher in expanding industries and lower in declining ones, and there is a constant reallocation of labour taking place between the two groups of industries. This does not necessarily mean that the existence of the wage differentials plays any important part in securing the reallocation of labour, though it may play some. It could, for example, be argued that the reallocation of labour between industries is brought about by the differences in job opportunities and security. A man may not look for another job when he is getting 10 per cent less than he could earn, did he but know, and was prepared to take the risks associated with changing jobs. However, if he becomes redundant, or even sees the threat of redundancy, he will look for a new job. Moreover, he is likely to look for a job in one of the industries he sees to be relatively prosperous and expanding rather than with another firm in his old industry. The fact that industries are prosperous and expanding will allow them to pay comparatively high wages, but the level of these wages may be unimportant in attracting labour. What matters is that men who are out of work, or perhaps see the danger of being out of work, learn that these expanding industries have jobs to offer, and believe they will enjoy greater security in these industries. The younger, more adaptable workers, in particular, are likely to respond to this kind of incentive.[10]

It is doubtful, therefore, whether big differentials are necessary to bring about a reallocation of labour. Of course, it is important that an industry which wants to expand should offer wages comparable to those offered by other industries for similar work. Industries under private enterprise will only expand if it is profitable, and if they expand they will certainly be in a position to offer as good a level of pay as most employers. There is a danger, however, that a public enterprise may think it ought to expand, yet continue to offer pay which is below the general level for a given level of work. It is no use the Government expecting to fill all the vacancies for nurses and teachers, if it is offering them a lower level of pay than people of equivalent abilities can get elsewhere. On the other hand, even if the Government were to raise the pay of nurses and teachers to comparability with pay in other professions (assuming they have, in fact, been paying less), it might still be impossible to recruit enough nurses and teachers to fill all vacancies. The demand for workers of this level may be so great that there is bound to be difficulty in recruiting enough people in every occupation. This is especially so in the public sector, where requirements may be determined in a rather arbitrary manner and without reference to any economic calculation of the value of product of the labour in question. In such cases, it may be quite useless to try to increase recruitment by raising wages much above the general level for a given type of work. Such an increase will have only a very limited effect on recruitment. The only real solution is to accept the inevitable shortage of suitably qualified workers and to devise new techniques which will reduce the demand for labour. Is it possible in teaching, for example, to substitute capital for labour? If we cannot recruit enough teachers to reduce classes to what is now considered the desirable size, might it be possible to make greater use of such aids as television, tape recorders, and so on, and thus enable the teachers to cope with larger numbers, perhaps radically altering the whole approach to teaching?

Trade unions make great use of the concept of fair relativities or comparability in making their wage claims. This concept can be abused; it certainly ought not to mean that the whole wage structure becomes frozen. There is, however, no real economic argument against the idea that there ought to be common level of pay for all who are doing work at a common level. If trade unions succeed in establishing such a common level of pay, it need not prevent the reallocation of labour between expanding and declining industries. The more effective the unions are in ensuring that wages in declining industries keep pace with wages in expanding industries, the more rapidly will these industries decline. They will not be able to meet the rising wage bill, redundancies will come earlier, and, if it is true that it is the men who become redundant, or are faced with a real threat of redundancy, who are prepared to look for other jobs, the whole process of readjustment will be speeded up. It would be argued that by ensuring that wages rise steadily throughout the economy, and not faster in the expanding industries, the unions assisted rather than hindered the reallocation of labour between industries.

NOTES

1. The situation is optimal in relation to the prevailing income distribution. One might wish to change the income distribution even if this meant creating a situation which was non-optimal.

2. It is here assumed that the firm is not also a monopsonist in the labour market.

3. What this really means is that, in an advanced economy, so-called unskilled work often calls for a higher degree of ability and knowledge than we sometimes suppose.

4. We again assume that all product markets are competitive, and there is no monopsony in the labour market.

5. Since we are now considering firms making different products, firms cannot be identical in all respects. We may, however, assume that they have the same net revenue product curves for labour. Since we are measuring the revenue product on one axis against labour on the other, the nature of the physical product of the firm is irrelevant.

6. If prices rise as the Government endeavours to maintain full employment in the face of rising wages, part, at least, of the increase in money wages is

offset, and real wages rise more slowly, if at all. This point is further discussed in chapter 7.

7. The process of wage determination in the situation under consideration might be represented in the terms shown in Fig. 6.3. We construct a supply curve S_t showing the total supply of labour to the market at different wage levels, and a demand curve D_c showing the demand for labour of the small competitive firms at different wage levels (by aggregating their individual marginal revenue product curves). The wage level clearly cannot be less than OW, and at this wage the small firms would take all the labour that was supplied. The monopsonistic firm can obtain a supply of labour by offering a wage above OW. The higher the wage, the less labour is demanded by the other firms and the more is offered by workers. Thus, the horizontal distance between the S_t and the D_c curves gives the supply of labour at wages above OW to the monopsonistic firm S_m. (This, in fact, is the supply curve drawn in Fig. 6.2.) Under monopsonistic conditions, the firm employs labour up to the point where the MLC curve corresponding to S_m cuts its MNRP curve. If the formation of a trade union led to the imposition of a wage OW_2 instead of OW_1, employment in the monopsonistic firm would increase. This would result partly from an increase in the total supply of labour and partly from the release of labour by other firms at the higher wage. It is when the wage is fixed at OW_2, equal to the marginal net revenue product of labour in the monopsonistic firm, *and* in such a manner that supply and demand in the labour market are equal, that the achievement of the optimum allocation of labour is possible.

8. One could conveniently measure this rent element in terms of the difference between one group's wage and that of most groups of workers of comparable skill.

9. For a fuller discussion, see E. Jaques, *Equitable Payment*, Heinemann, London, 1961.

10. For a fuller discussion of this line of argument, see (a) J. R. Crossley's contribution to *Wage Structure in Theory and Practice*, E. M. Hugh-Jones, ed., North Holland Publishing Co., Amsterdam, 1966; (b) OECD, *Wages and Labour Mobility*, Paris, 1965; and (c) J. M. Jackson, 'Wages: Just Reward or Efficient Allocator', *British Journal of Industrial Relations*, Vol. J, No. 3, November, 1967.

7. The share of wages in the national income

The limitations of wage theory

The type of wage theory which we have been studying can help us a great deal in our understanding of the wage structures of the real world and the implications of certain developments. It can help us to see what is likely to happen if there should be a change in the demand for some product, with a resultant change in the demand for labour employed in producing that product, or if there is some technological advance which substitutes capital for labour in the production of a commodity, or if the supply of workers capable of accepting more skilled or more responsible jobs is increased by changes in educational policy which give greater equality of opportunity. The mistake of some of the critics of the traditional wage theory is to suppose that there is a settled body of wage theory, whereas all economic theory is really an apparatus which the economist applies to the problems confronting him.[1]

Nevertheless, it must be admitted that the usual type of wage theory has its limitations. Normally, it is part of a more general theory of factor prices, and is a piece of partial equilibrium analysis. It can explain what happens in one particular labour market, on the assumption that other things remain the same. It can tell us quite a lot about the wage structure and the relationship between different wage rates, but it does not really explain the general level of wages or why wage incomes constitute 75 per cent of the national income rather than 50 per cent or 90 per cent. There is a need in modern economic theory for a genuine theory of distribution. While some attempts have been made to tackle this weakness, there has not, as yet, been much success, and there is at present nothing comparable to that of the Classical economists.

The general level of wages

It may be felt by some people that there is no need for a theoretical explanation of the general level of wages. Wage theory explains the determination of particular wage rates in the relevant labour markets. The assumptions of the theoretical models of the labour market may be criticized, but it is at least true that wage rates are determined in separate labour markets. For instance, employers and unions in the textile industry get together and bargain separately from employers and unions in the engineering industry. Thus, the general level of wages is merely a statistical abstraction and, like the general level of prices, it is difficult to measure, though it is common enough to measure changes in the level by means of an index number.

While it may be true that wage-bargaining takes place separately, in the sense that negotiators from one industry meet entirely on their own, it is not true to say that they conduct their negotiations without reference to the outcome of bargaining in other industries or to factors that are common to most industries. The idea of fair relativity or comparability in wages for men doing work that is believed to be of the same level commands a fair measure of support among trade unionists, and implies a measure of interrelationship between different wage rates. Similarly, the general level of economic activity is bound to be a factor influencing the outcome of nearly all wage-bargaining. In this sense, the general level of wages is not just a statistical abstraction describing the outcome of a number of entirely unrelated wage bargains. There are factors influencing the outcome of most bargains, and therefore influencing the general level of wages, so it is not inappropriate to study the general level of wages as such.

On closer examination, it will be seen that the general level of wages is to be explained very largely in terms of macroeconomics, along with the determination of employment, rather than in terms of the supply of and demand for labour. To try to construct something in the nature of a demand curve for and a supply curve of labour as a whole would be unsatisfactory, because the level of wages would itself influence the aggregate demand for goods and therefore, indirectly, the demand for labour. This effect can be ignored when we are dealing with one particular labour market, but not when we are dealing with the market for all labour.

A Keynesian model. It is possible to construct a fairly simple Keynesian model of the economy in which the general level of wages features. In this model, we might include the following nine variables:

Y = income or output
C = consumption
I = investment
w = wage rate
N = employment
π = profits
r = marginal efficiency of capital
i = rate of interest
M = quantity of money.

We may begin by stating two identities or definitions:

$$Y = C + I. \tag{7.1}$$
$$Y = w.N + \pi. \tag{7.2}$$

The quantity of money may be determined, at will, by the monetary authorities, so we may write:

$$M = \overline{M}, \tag{7.3}$$

where $\overline{M}$ represents the quantity of money the authorities decide to create. The remaining equations in the system either describe the way in which people behave or conditions which must be satisfied in equilibrium. Consumption is a function of income, and the level of income is dependent upon the number of men employed (the production function).

$$C = C(Y) \tag{7.4}$$
$$Y = Y(N) \tag{7.5}$$

According to Keynes, the marginal efficiency of capital, or what we might loosely call the 'return on an investment', tended to diminish as more investment took place, because the more profitable investments were undertaken first. This means the marginal efficiency of capital is a function of investment, and investment would, according to Keynes, be pushed to the point where the marginal efficiency of capital is equal to the rate of interest paid on borrowed funds.

$$r = r(I). \tag{7.6}$$
$$r = i. \tag{7.7}$$

Keynes held that the demand for money depended upon the rate of interest the speculative demand) and the level of income (transactions and precautionary demand).

$$M = M(i, Y) \tag{7.8}$$

D

Finally, Keynes argued that the wage rate would be determined by the marginal productivity of labour. Keynes accepted that there was a measure of rigidity in money wages, but, under competition, employers would employ labour to the point where wages equalled marginal productivity. Moreover, although money wages might rarely, if ever, fall, real wages could fall without a reduction in the supply of labour if prices rose.

$$\frac{dY}{dN} = w. \tag{7.9}$$

It is possible to use a model of this kind to try to discover what is likely to happen to the wage level if the Government increases the supply of money. One may argue that this is likely to lower the rate of interest and therefore lead to an increase in investment. This, in turn, has a multiplier effect on income, which means more men must be employed. Equation (7.9) tells us that this implies a fall in the level of real wages.[2]

Real wages and economic expansion. Keynes argued that real wages fell as employment increased. The view was once widely held that real wages fell during periods of economic expansion and rose during depression. During depression, many workers suffered through unemployment, but those who remained employed benefited because prices fell, while money wages remained unchanged. If we look at the postwar period, however, it will be seen that in Britain real wages have tended to increase fairly steadily, except, perhaps, during the period of the 'wage freeze' in the second half of 1966. This does not necessarily disprove the Keynesian model. This model is static, and takes no account of the fact that in the real world productivity is increasing steadily, and that this would be associated with a steady increase in wages at a constant level of employment. When there is this upward trend in wages, the fall in real wages associated with increased employment in the static model may become a mere slowing down of the rate of increase that would otherwise have occurred.

Enough has been said to indicate that the general level of wages is closely tied up with the general state of the economy, and to warn the reader of the dangers of too narrow a specialization within economics.

The share of wages in the national product

The marginal analysis of wage determination, outlined in earlier

90

chapters, is part of a more general theory of factor prices. It is at its best in explaining why a particular wage, or any other factor price, is fixed at a particular level when all conditions are assumed to be given except the supply of and demand for the factor in question. That is, it is essentially a partial equilibrium analysis. It is not entirely satisfactory in explaining why the national product is distributed in a particular way between wages, profits, interest, and rent. It has been used by some economists to try to explain the more general pattern of distribution, and other writers have sought alternative explanations. In this section, five approaches will be considered: (a) the use of marginal analysis, (b) the attempt to relate distribution to trade union bargaining power, (c) to the degree of monopoly, (d) to the different propensities to consume of different groups, and (e) an approach which views distribution as the outcome of an intergroup conflict which may be fought in the market place or in the political arena.

Marginal analysis. Sir Denis Robertson has attempted to use marginal analysis to answer the questions about what happens to the relative and absolute shares of wages in the national product if, for example, its supply is increased when the quantity of capital is held constant.[3] Robertson's approach may be summarized as follows. If the quantity of labour is increased, total product will increase, the marginal product of capital is likely to be increased, the reward of capital (which under perfect competition will equal the value of its marginal product) will increase, and therefore the absolute share of profits in the national income will rise.[4] What is not so obvious is what happens to the absolute share of labour, and what happens to the relative shares.

The marginal product of labour will, of course, fall. Whether the total wage bill will fall or not depends upon the elasticity of the demand curve for labour. The absolute share of labour may fall or, if the demand for labour is elastic, it may increase. If the demand for labour is sufficiently elastic, the relative, as well as the absolute, share of labour may increase. To determine the direction of change (if any) in relative shares, the elasticity of substitution is introduced. The elasticity of substitution of labour for capital is defined as the ratio which the proportionate change in the ratio of labour to capital bears to the consequent proportionate change in the ratio of the marginal productivity of labour to the marginal productivity of capital. Labour's share will increase if the elasticity of substitution is greater than unity.

This type of argument is not entirely satisfactory. Robertson makes the implicit assumption that the total product is exhausted if each factor is paid the value of its marginal product. This will hold if the production function (relating output to the inputs of the factors of production) is linear homogeneous. Once we consider a situation where the production function does not satisfy this condition, there is no reason why (taking the opposite case to Robertson) the marginal product of labour should increase because it has more capital at its disposal. Total product, and therefore the average product of labour, will increase. However, there is no reason why, with more capital, the marginal product of labour should not decline more rapidly, so that when the same quantity of labour is employed as before the marginal product is lower. (This, under conditions of competition, might lead to a fall in the wage rate with capital accumulation and increasing general prosperity – a result that may seem unlikely, but cannot be disregarded in a theoretical analysis.)

Attempts have been made to analyse economic growth using a particular type of production function, the Cobb-Douglas. This takes the form:

$$P = K^\alpha L^\beta,$$

where P is product, K is the quantity of capital, and L is the quantity of labour.[5] In the special case where $\beta = 1-\alpha$, the function is linear homogeneous, and gives constant returns to scale and the total product is exhausted when each factor is paid its marginal product.

If $P = K^\alpha L^{1-\alpha}$, we have the two marginal products:

$$\frac{dP}{dK} = \alpha K^{\alpha-1} L^{1-\alpha} \text{ and } \frac{dP}{dL} = (1-\alpha)L^{-\alpha}K^\alpha.$$

If we multiply each of these marginal products by the quantity of the factor employed, the total shares of each factor will be $\alpha(K^\alpha L^{1-\alpha})$ and $(1-\alpha)L^{1-\alpha}K^\alpha$. In other words, if the production function is of this kind, the total product will always be shared between profits and wages in the ratio $\alpha/1-\alpha$, regardless of the proportions in which the factors are combined. If, therefore, the quantity of capital available to assist the labour force increases, as is to be expected in an advanced economy, the marginal product of labour will increase,

$$\frac{dP}{dL} = (1-\alpha)L^{\alpha-}K^\alpha$$

and K^α increases with an increase in K, but relative shares are

92

unaffected. Since relative shares are unchanged and the total product has increased, it follows that the absolute shares have both increased.

Union bargaining power. An article by Phelps Brown and Hart showed that major shifts in the share of wages in the national income could be linked to factors which might be expected to produce a change in the bargaining power of trade unions.[6] Their analysis defines wages in a narrow sense, as the earnings of 'operatives' as opposed to the salaries of 'staff', a distinction which is primarily social and has no real meaning in economic theory. The proportion of wage-earners in the occupied population is tending to fall as more workers become recognized as staff. The proportion of wages in the national income tends to fall as a result. The statistics collected by Phelps Brown and Hart showed that the trend was for wages to fall proportionately to the fall in the proportion of wage-earners in the occupied population. To illustrate this trend by a simple example, if wage-earners constituted 80 per cent of the occupied population and wages comprised 40 per cent of the national income, a fall in the proportion of wage-earners to 75 per cent of the occupied population would be accompanied by a fall in the share of wages to $37\frac{1}{2}$ per cent of the national income. Such a trend implies that the average wage remains relatively constant at a level equal to half the national income per head of occupied persons.

Although the share of wages tended to fall in proportion to the falling proportion of wage-earners for a period, there were occasions when it increased or decreased sharply. The average wage rose as a proportion of the average income of the whole occupied population. Thereafter, the share of wages again fell for a period proportionately to the falling proportion of wage-earners. It was, in other words, following a higher or lower trend than before, corresponding to the change in the relationship between the average wage and the average earnings of all the population. These changes could be shown to occur on occasions when one might expect the bargaining power of the trade unions to have changed. The share of wages in the national income rose in 1870–72 and in 1888–89, and it fell in 1903–05 and in 1926–28. The first two occasions were periods of 'exceptional trade union growth and initiative', while 1903–05 'falls in the shadow of the Taff Vale decision . . . and that of 1926–28 falls after the collapse of the General Strike'. On the other hand, there was a collapse of union power in 1879, and a period of belligerence in 1909–13, but neither was associated with a change in the share of wages in the national income.[7] It seemed to Phelps Brown and Hart that some additional factor was involved.

The additional factor that had to be taken into account was whether the market environment in which firms found themselves was 'hard' or 'soft'. A soft market situation means that a firm will be able to raise prices if unions press for higher wages, or be able to maintain prices at the current level if it proves possible to lower wages. If the market situation is hard, a firm cannot pass the cost of a wage increase onto the consumer in higher prices, and, if wages fall, it is forced to lower its prices.

An increase in union bargaining power may occur when the market situation is hard. In such a case, it will be able to get higher wages from the employers by the exercise of its increased bargaining power, and firms will have to hold their prices steady. Real wages rise and wage-earners receive a larger share of the national income. If the market situation is soft, however, the firm will concede wage increases, but will also raise prices. The increase in real wages and, therefore, any change in the share of wages in the national income, is reduced if not eliminated.

Similarly, union bargaining power may be reduced and wages fall. If the market is hard and firms have to lower prices, wage-earners are cushioned from the worst effects of lower wages and the share of wages in the national income may be little changed. If, however, the market is soft and firms can maintain prices when wages fall, there will be a lowering of real wages and of the share of wages in the national income.[8]

Can trade unions influence wages? Economists have long been interested in the question as to whether trade unions can increase the real wages of their members or increase the share of the national income going to labour. The question has been tackled by empirical methods, of which the one adopted by Phelps Brown and Hart is an example, and by purely theoretical techniques. The Classical economists believed that little could be gained by trade union action. They believed there was a limited fund out of which wages were paid. Trade union activity might get a larger share of the wages fund for one group of workers, but only at the expense of lower wages or unemployment for others. Marshall's supply and demand analysis, with the demand for labour related to marginal productivity, again suggested that trade unions could negotiate higher wages for their members, but would inevitably reduce employment in the trade concerned, and might lower other wage rates by increasing the supply of labour to non-unionized jobs. Only when the marginal

94

analysis was refined to cover imperfect markets was it seen that there were some cases, at least, where a higher wage need not lead to a fall in the level of employment.

The opportunities for securing an increase in a particular occupation can, of course, be shown to be greatest when, for example, the demand for both labour and the product is inelastic, and when wage costs are a comparatively small part of the total. It is, however, desirable that we should try to confirm any ideas we have about trade unions securing benefits either for particular groups of workers or for the wage-earners as a whole by empirical studies. The shifts in the distribution of income which Phelps Brown and Hart showed to be linked to changes in union power (as well as to other factors) are a useful indicator of the effectiveness of trade unionism. There are other empirical approaches which may be used. Two call for note. It is possible to try to compare wage rates, or changes in wage rates, in an occupation or, perhaps, a fairly large sector of employment at times of union strength and weakness, or one may try to make comparisons between industries or occupations which differ in the degree of unionization. The former method has been used by Ozanne.[9]

Ozanne chose to study wage movements in a particular sector at different periods. He rejected interindustry comparisons because he believed that too many other factors influenced wage rates in different industries for it to be possible to isolate the influence of union bargaining power. He rejected studying the share of wages in the national income for the same reason, though it must be emphasized that one of the most important of the other factors influencing the shares of wages in the national income, the proportion of wage-earners in the population, was taken fully into account by Phelps Brown and Hart.

In his study, Ozanne chose a period of comparatively stable prices in the interwar period, when trade unionism in the United States was weak, and the postwar period of gently rising prices, when the trade unions were stronger. The periods differ to some extent in their characteristics. The postwar period was one of mild inflation, and this might have been expected to work against the trade unions. In the years before the Second World War, inflationary periods had generally been associated with declining real wages. Money wages rose, but tended to lag behind prices. The fact that, in the postwar period of mild inflation and strong unions, real wages rose and, compared with the interwar period, the manual workers fared better relative to other groups, suggests very strongly that the unions were proving effective. (It is, of course, difficult to offer rigorous proof of such a proposition. This would involve proving that there could be no other factor responsible for the more favourable trends in wages, and it is very difficult to prove a negative proposition.)

Different propensities to consume. It is also possible to look at the share of wages in the national income in quite a different light. For example, it may be related to the propensity to consume of the wage-earning section of the community compared with that of other sections of the community.[10] The starting point for this analysis, a theoretical one, is that the marginal propensity and average propensity to consume of the wage-earning class is likely to be greater than that of those whose incomes are in the form of profits, rent, or interest. There are individual exceptions, for some people with property incomes may be quite poor, but as a general rule this assumption is true. The propensity to consume falls as income rises, and, in the advanced countries, those deriving incomes from property are wealthy as compared with the wage-earner.[11]

For a simple model, one assumes that there are just two sections of the community, wage-earners and profit-receivers. Other groups, and the possibility that a person may fall into both categories, may be ignored. The wage-earners have a high propensity to consume, the profit-receivers a low one. The amount that will be consumed out of a given national income will therefore depend upon the way income is distributed between wages and profits. The greater the proportion taken by wages, the higher will be the level of consumption. If we assume the level of investment to be determined already, we can see the relevance of the comparative propensities to consume to the establishment of equilibrium in the economy. Savings must equal investment, and there may be only one distribution of income that is compatible with this condition.[12]

If the share of wages is too high, plans for consumption and investment will be incompatible: they will exceed the capacities of the economy. Such a situation is inflationary, and prices would rise, though these might be prevented, at least partially, in an open economy by additional imports. These imports would make good the gap between demand and home capacity. In so far as prices rise, profits are likely to increase and the distribution of income will be changed in favour of profit-receivers. If wage-earners accept this, equilibrium may be reached. Provided, then, that wage-earners are prepared to accept the loss of real income through rising prices, the differences in the propensities to consume could be regarded as an important factor in determining the distribution of income. If,

96

however, powerful trade unions are able to secure wage increases when prices rise, equilibrium would be unobtainable. Under such conditions, the Government would have to take other steps to combat inflation. It could try lowering both propensities to consume by taxation, or try to limit the level of investment. However, it could no longer be said that the differences in propensities to consume was the important factor in determining the distribution of income.

The degree of monopoly. The attempt by Kalecki to analyse the distribution of income in terms of the degree of monopoly[13] must not be thought of as a rival theory to that of Kaldor. It is an alternative theory in the sense that it looks at the process in a somewhat different light, and at a different aspect of the process. We must accept the fact that any theory is bound to involve simplification, and that it is quite possible for each of several theories to add to our understanding of a situation, with no one theory telling us all we need to know.

The rule of profit-maximization indicates that, under conditions of perfect competition, firms will endeavour to equate price to marginal cost. It is worth their while to expand output so long as price is above average cost. The monopolist, on the other hand, equates marginal cost to marginal revenue, which is less than price. It is not surprising, therefore, that economists have taken the divergence between price and marginal cost to be a sign of the existence of monopoly, and also a measure of the degree of monopoly. In his model, Kalecki defines k as the ratio of a firm's (or industry's) sales revenue to prime costs (wages[14] plus the cost of bought-in materials).

Before going any further, two important points must be made. Kalecki takes k to be dependent upon the degree of monopoly. The higher the value of k, the greater is the degree of monopoly. This is identifying prime, or variable costs, with marginal costs. Moreover, his variables W and M stand for the aggregate wage bill and the aggregate value of bought-in materials. A divergence between the value of the firm's output and the total prime costs is not necessarily an indication that monopoly is present. Such a situation would be bound to occur even in a normal equilibrium situation under perfect competition. Under perfect competition, the firm equates price to marginal cost, and the marginal firm must be making only a normal profit, so that price also equals average cost. The situation is shown in Fig. 7.1. The firm is in equilibrium when selling output OQ at a price OP. P'Q (= OP) is greater than average variable cost QC.

The ratio P'Q/QC is, in fact, Kalecki's k.[15] It follows that k does not depend solely upon the degree of monopoly, in any meaningful sense, but also upon the relative importance of fixed costs to prime costs.

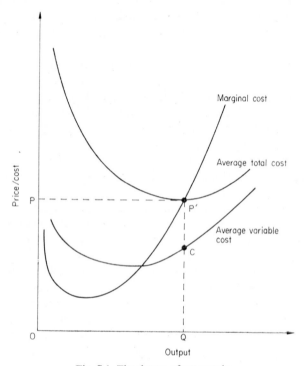

Fig. 7.1. The degree of monopoly.

The second point to be made is that even the divergence between price and marginal cost, in the strict sense, is not necessarily a good indication of the degree of monopoly in any ordinary meaning of the word. It might be better to refer to it as indicating the degree of monopoly power. Some people, at least, may prefer to think of a complete monopoly existing, where only one firm is making a product which is quite distinct, where it has no competitors making what is obviously a rival product. Nevertheless, the demand for that product may be highly elastic. The more elastic is the demand for the product, the closer will be the price to marginal cost. The power of the monopolist to exploit the situation is limited. It may, of course, be argued that the firm, in such a case, does not possess a high degree of monopoly because it is subject to strong competition

98

from a great variety of other goods. This is quite true, and the point that needs to be emphasized is that we must interpret the degree of monopoly in this special sense, and not necessarily expect it to coincide with a measurement of the degree of monopoly in terms of such indicators as the concentration of production of an identifiable product on the three largest firms.

Bearing these qualifications in mind, we may return to examine the Kalecki model. It can easily be shown that:

$$\text{Profits} + \text{overheads} = (k-1)(W+M).$$

The share of wages in the total product, w, is, of course,

$$\frac{W}{W + \text{profits} + \text{overheads} + M,}$$

and it follows that:

$$w = \frac{W}{W + (k-1)(W+M).}$$

If we now put j for the ratio of material costs to wages (M/W), we get:

$$w = \frac{W}{1 + (k-1)(1+j).}$$

The share of wages in the product of the firm or industry can then be related to the two variables, k and j, that is, to the ratio of total product to prime cost and the ratio of material to wage costs. Kalecki extends the argument from the firm to the industry and to the whole economy. The first of the two ratios he identifies, perhaps not too accurately, with the degree of monopoly.

The theory is tautological. All that Kalecki has done is to re-arrange an expression for the share of wages in the product of industry in such a way as to include two ratios, one of which is closely linked with the degree of monopoly. This explains nothing. Nevertheless, this is not to say that the theory is valueless. It focuses our attention on the ratios k and j, and, if we can then discover how they are likely to behave in particular situations, we have the makings of a causal explanation of the distribution of the national income. Kalecki, for example, was particularly interested in the way in which the share of wages varied during the trade cycle. He suggests that the degree of monopoly tends to increase during depression, tending to reduce the share of wages in the national income: there is, however, a relative fall in raw material costs and this works in the opposite direction.

Interesting as such theories are, the labour economist must concentrate on theories which seek to explain the actual process of distribution, to explain how the representatives of labour, and other groups in the economy, make the relevant decisions, and how these interact.

Distribution and group conflict

The distribution of the national income can be regarded as the outcome of a process in which different groups strive to increase their shares at the expense of others. In this sense, therefore, a conflict of interests exists between the members of different groups. In his study of this process, Marchal distinguishes between active and passive groups.[16] Some groups are in a position to try to increase their share of the national income, or to maintain their present share in the face of circumstances which threaten to reduce it. Other groups are unable to play any important part in influencing the pattern of distribution. At times, they may do well, but when circumstances are adverse they are unable to defend their interests.

Marchal also suggests that it may be a mistake to think in terms of a primary distribution of income determined by market forces, which is then subject to redistribution through fiscal and social policies. A group may try to increase its share of the national income through the use of its bargaining power in the market or through political lobbying. Trade unions, for example, may try to get higher wages or to secure greater social benefits for their members. This possibility may be more important in a country like France where social benefits, particularly family allowances, are on a much more generous scale than in Britain. British trade unions have relied primarily upon securing higher wages in order to promote the interests of their members. Yet we should not disregard entirely the possibility that some sections of British society will seek to promote their economic interests through political lobbying rather than the use of market power. This will be apparent when we consider the possible groupings in the British economy, whether they are active or passive, and if active how they go about promoting their interests.

Groups and their characteristics. We may take *wage- and salary-earners* as the first of our groups. There is little point in differentiating them at a time when white collar unions are becoming more active, and, what is more, linking themselves much more closely to the TUC and the unions of manual workers. There is little doubt that this group is one of the most active in the economy. As we have said already, it relies mainly on the use of its bargaining power with the employers to secure higher money wages for its members, though it may also use political pressure to secure some marginal benefits for the workers. The Labour Party may, for example, try to protect the real incomes of members by seeking legislation to control rents and so prevent workers having to pay a high price for accommodation at a time of scarcity.

The second group consists of *shareholders*. Shareholders, as such are weakly organized, many have only minimal holdings in any enterprise and do not take an active part in the affairs of their companies. They are, however, served by management. Those in control of companies may want to expand, and will want to ensure that if it becomes necessary to make a capital issue the public will be willing to subscribe. This they can do only if the companies can show a reasonably good record of profits earned and dividends distributed. To this extent, those who receive dividends can be regarded as an active group in the distribution process, even if only by proxy.

Third, there are the *farmers*. In so far as they are small and are predominantly price-takers in the market, it might seem appropriate to regard them as a passive group. British farmers, however, enjoy the benefit of guarantees from the Government about the price of certain produce. If the market price falls short of the guarantee, the Government will make good the difference. If the farmers merely accepted whatever guarantees the Government cared to offer, they would indeed be a passive group; the farming lobby, however, is both active and influential. The group should therefore be treated as active.[17]

Fourth, we may treat as a single class those people who depend upon rents and fixed interest securities and call them *rentiers*. This class is likely to be weak, both in terms of bargaining power in the market and in terms of political influence, and is therefore mainly a passive group. It is true, as already noted, that there may be times when the market favours the *rentiers*. For example, in the absence of rent controls and with the shortage of housing that has existed since the war, the owners of domestic property could expect a period of prosperity. To enjoy prosperity because the market is favourable is quite compatible with passivity. This group is not in the same position as, say, the trade unions, which may continue to gain higher wages even when unemployment is increasing. Moreover, the fact that they have been powerless to resist the imposition of rent controls itself suggests that the *rentiers* are not an important political lobby.

Finally, come the *social beneficiaries*. These are chiefly the people on National Insurance benefits or supplementary benefits. People drawing pensions from their former employment come under the *rentier* heading, and, as such, they do not form part of a socially cohesive and active group. To some extent, the same may be said of social beneficiaries. This statement needs some qualification, however. There are signs that the social beneficiaries, or some sub-groups, at least, are becoming more cohesive and active. For some time, retirement pensioners have formed associations which have actively compaigned for improved pensions. It is clearly possible for state retirement pensioners to associate and campaign for better pensions in a way which is impossible for people drawing private pensions. The essential difference is that private pensions are fixed: workers may try to get better pension facilities as a fringe benefit, but once retired their pensions cannot be altered. The state pensions are financed in an entirely different manner, and adjustments are possible. In addition, two other powerful lobbies have been formed, the Child Poverty Action Group and the Disablement Income Group. These pressure groups are not so much organizations of the people directly concerned, as organizations of people, including outsiders, who see the problems of others and campaign on their behalf.

The first of these pressure groups has done much to increase the community's awareness of the problem of poverty among the lower-paid workers, especially where there are three or more children. It would not be unreasonable to give the group a substantial measure of credit for the increases in Family Allowances made during 1968. The Disablement Income Group has had less success. Its target is to get the Government to provide an adequate income for all disabled persons.[18] The important point, for the moment, is that we cannot regard the social beneficiaries as being an entirely passive group, even if only by proxy, they are fairly active.

The model in action. No complete theory of the distribution of the national income has been worked out on the basis of this kind of model, and it is by no means certain that such a theory is possible. Nevertheless, this kind of model provides a framework which the economist can use to try to discover the consequences of certain changes within the system. Suppose, for example, the economy is fairly stable, with prices level or only rising gently, with the balance of payment in equilibrium, and a state of full employment. Suppose that in such a situation the trade unions press for higher wages to try to improve the lot of the wage- and salary-earners. What are the likely consequences?

We will assume that the wage claims are granted, even if not in full. The wage bill of the country will be increased. Management might put up prices in order to maintain the level of profits. Farmers might lobby the Government to try to get increases in guaranteed prices to offset the higher labour costs facing them. It remains to consider, however, what happens to the incomes of the other two groups, the *rentiers* and the social beneficiaries. It seems probable that there will be no immediate effect on the income of the former. This group would, of course, be hit by the rise in the cost of living, but being passive could do nothing about it. At a later stage, the *rentiers* might be affected indirectly: the rise in wages might lead to an increased demand for houses to rent, and give landlords bigger incomes, unless the continued operation of rent controls prevented this. Social beneficiaries would also be hit by the rising cost of living, and it is probable that, before too long, pressure would be put on the Government to increase benefits proportionately.

Let us try to examine the impact of a 10 per cent increase in wages on the economy. In Table 7.1, we show the situation before the wage increase occurs. The first column shows the contribution of the various groups to the national product. Social beneficiaries and the Government contribute nothing. The whole product is attributed to the factors of production comprising the first four groups. The second column shows the taxes paid. The social beneficiaries are assumed to pay nothing. The Government, of course, receives these taxes. In the third column, we show social benefits paid out and received. The final column shows the share of the national product over which each group has command after paying taxes and receiving social benefits. The Government share is what it spends on goods and services, as distinct from transfer payments, like social benefits.

In Table 7.2, we look at the position after a 10 per cent increase in wages. Taxes paid by workers are assumed to increase proportionately. It is assumed that management and farmers succeed in increasing prices just enough to maintain their money profits. It is assumed that this table is drawn up before social benefits have been increased. The value of the national product has increased by 7½ per cent, but, since the initial situation was one of full employment, we assume that there is no real increase. If social benefits are increased by $7\frac{1}{2}$ per cent (or about 0·6 in absolute terms), social beneficiaries have the same real income and share of the national

Table 7.1

Distribution of national product before wage claim

	Factor income		Tax*		Social benefits		Disposable income
Wages	75	—	15			=	60
Farmers	5	—	2			=	3
Profits	10	—	4			=	6
Rents	10	—	4			=	6
Social benefits					$7\frac{1}{2}$	=	$7\frac{1}{2}$
Government		+	25	—	$7\frac{1}{2}$	=	$17\frac{1}{2}$

*In both this, and Table 7.2, it is assumed 20 per cent of wages go in tax and 40 per cent of farmers' incomes, profits, and rents.

Table 7.2

Distribution of national product after wage claim

	Factor income		Tax		Social benefits		Disposable income
Wages	$82\frac{1}{2}$	—	$16\frac{1}{2}$			=	66
Farmers	5	—	2			=	3
Profits	10	—	4			=	6
Rents	10	—	4			=	6
Social benefits					$7\frac{1}{2}$	=	$7\frac{1}{2}$
Government		+	$26\frac{1}{2}$	—	$7\frac{1}{2}$	=	19

product as before. Farmers, shareholders, *rentiers*, and the Government will all have a smaller share of the product and a smaller real income than before. The management of industrial firms and the farmers may try to anticipate the effect of the rise in prices on the real value of their profits and try to make bigger adjustments in order to maintain their real incomes. In so far as they succeed in doing so, the burden thrown on the Government and the *rentiers* is so much the greater.

We may assume that the Government would not readily curtail its real level of expenditure. The situation shown by Table 7.2 could not therefore last for long. Taxes would have to be increased and part of the gains of the workers would be lost through extra taxation. The Government might well have to raise taxation by more than was necessary to restore its command over real resources. There might also be other difficulties. The rise in home prices might lead to loss of exports and to balance of payments difficulties. There would be some shift in the distribution of income in favour of wage-earners, and we have seen already that their propensity to consume is higher than that of those depending mainly on property incomes. This means consumption would increase, and, with a given level of investment, there would be inflationary pressure.

It will be clear by now that the share of the wage- and salary-earners in the economy can increase only to the extent that other groups can be squeezed, especially the passive *rentiers* group. Moreover, it will be seen that the attempt to increase the share of the wage- and salary-earners may create difficulties in other directions. This kind of problem will be dealt with in more detail when we look at incomes policy in chapter 16.

NOTES

1. An example of this critical attitude towards wage theory is to be found in B. Wootton, *The Social Foundation of Wage Policy*, Unwin University Books, London, 1955.

2. It is assumed, in this treatment of the subject, that the reader is familiar with the main outlines of the Keynesian theory of employment. The conclusions presented here follow from the characteristics usually assumed for the various functions, and not from the very formal relationships stated in the text.

3. See *Lectures on Economic Principles*, part II, chapter II, Collins Fontana Library, London, 1963.

4. For simplicity, a two factor model is considered. Robertson refers to labour and non-labour as his two factors.

5. The function may sometimes be written $P = AK^a L^\beta$, but the constant A can be eliminated by choosing suitable units for measuring the two factors.

6. E. H. Phelps Brown and P. E. Hart, 'The Share of Wages in the National Income', *Economic Journal*, LXII, 1952. See also E. H. Phelps Brown and Margaret H. Browne, *A Century of Pay*, Macmillan, London, 1968 where this approach is further developed.

7. Of course, the share of wages continued to fall with the declining proportion of wage-earners.

8. In the postwar period, wages rarely if ever have fallen. We could, however, regard as equivalent to a fall, a situation in which wages fail to rise as rapidly as the national product.

9. R. Ozanne, 'The impact of unions on wage differentials and income distribution', *Quarterly Journal of Economics*, LXIII, 1959.

10. This kind of approach has been developed by N. Kaldor, 'Alternative Theories of Distribution' in *Essays on Value and Distribution*, Duckworth, London, 1960.

11. There may be many small property incomes, perhaps going to people who are mainly dependent on wages. These, however, account for only a small

part of the total of property incomes. The bulk of such incomes go to individuals with large incomes, and so the propensity to consume out of property incomes is low.

12. There may be many distributions compatible with equilibrium at less than full employment, but only one that is compatible with full employment equilibrium. If the level of investment is high, and the propensity to consume of profit-receivers high, there may be no equilibrium distribution.

13. For a full treatment of this approach, see M. Kalecki, *Theory of Economic Dynamics*, Allen and Unwin, London, 1954, Part 1.

14. This refers to the wages of direct labour. Salaries are included in overheads.

15. Strictly speaking, Kalecki's definition of k is in terms of aggregates, and could therefore be written $OQ.P'Q/QC.OQ$, in which case, OQ cancels out and we are left with $P'Q/QC$.

16. For a fuller treatment, see J. Marchal, 'Wage Theory and Social Groups', in J. T. Dunlop, ed., *The Theory of Wage Determination*, Macmillan, London, 1964.

17. Continental farmers do not enjoy such guarantees. They tend, instead, to be protected by tariffs, and may campaign at times for greater protection. This means that, like British farmers, they are active in our sense.

18. 'Disabled' means those who are permanently unfit for work as the result of illness or injury. The DIG wants to get them an income bigger than the present National Insurance sickness benefit, which may be enough to tide many people over a short period of illness, but as a permanent income, is inadequate. They also want this income to be paid to disabled persons who fall outside the National Insurance scheme, such as housewives.

Part 2

Wages in practice

8. What workers earn

In this chapter, we shall look briefly at the actual levels of earnings of workers in Britain at the present time. Any such account must relate to some particular moment of time, with perhaps some reference to changes which have taken place in recent years. The student of labour economics must try to keep himself well informed about current wage levels and structures. He should therefore know where to look for the kind of information that will enable him to keep the picture given in this chapter up to date. One of the best sources of labour statistics is the monthly *Employment and Productivity Gazette* (formerly the *Ministry of Labour Gazette*). Much of the information contained in the *Gazette*, together with some additional data, is reproduced in the quarterly *Statistics on incomes, prices, employment, and production*. In April and October of each year, the Department of Employment and Productivity makes a survey of the average earnings of manual workers in industry. It also makes a regular survey of the earnings of white collar workers. On rare occasions, the latest being 1960, there is a survey of the distribution of earnings. This is particularly useful, for, while it is interesting to know, for example, that the average worker earns over £20 a week, there are occasions when it is much more important to know what proportion of workers are earning less than, say, two-thirds of the average wage.

Earnings of manual workers, April 1968

Table 8.1 shows the earnings of manual workers for each group in the Standard Industrial Classification in the first week in April 1968. The average earnings of adult male workers was £22 5s, and in manufacturing industry the average was £22 16s. The same table shows the average hours worked in April 1968 and the percentage increase in earnings over April 1960. Finally, the table shows hourly earnings in April 1968 and the percentage increase over 1960.

Table 8.1

Earnings and hours of work, adult male manual workers, April 1968

SIC	Weekly earnings	Per cent increase over Apl 1960	Hours worked	Hourly earnings	Per cent increase over Apl 1960
Food, drink and tobacco	425s	61	47·2	108d	68
Chemicals and allied industries	468s	63	46·0	122d	69
Metal manufacture	466s	44	45·3	123d	52
Engineering and electrical goods	444s	53	45·1	118d	57
Shipbuilding and marine engineering	466s	59	46·0	122d	69
Vehicles	520s	47	43·9	142d	59
Metal goods not elsewhere specified	445s	53	45·8	117d	58
Textiles	407s	58	46·1	106d	66
Leather, leather goods and fur	391s	56	45·5	103d	58
Clothing and footwear	386s	54	47·7	111d	63
Bricks, pottery, glass, cement, etc.	451s	58	45·6	113d	64
Timber, furniture, etc.	429s	59	46·0	113d	64
Paper, printing, and publishing	522s	59	46·5	136d	64
Other manufacturing industries	457s	57	45·6	118d	64
All manufacturing industries	457s	52	45·6	120d	60
Mining and quarrying (exc. coal)	434s	61	51·0	102d	58
Construction	446s	68	47·6	113d	74
Gas, electricity and water	404s	61	43·4	112d	75
Transport and communications (exc. railway, etc.)	459s	62	49·6	111d	71
Certain miscellaneous services	382s	59	44·8	102d	70
Public administration	347s	58	43·8	95d	70
All the above	445s	59	46·2	116d	65

Source: *Employment and Productivity Gazette,* August 1968 and *Statistics on Incomes, Prices, Employment and Production*, No. 25, June 1968. (Subsequently quoted as *Gazette* and *Statistics*).

Note: Earnings figures have been rounded to nearest whole number.

It must be remembered that the figures relate to earnings, rather than to basic wage rates. They are, therefore, the result of a variety of factors. An industry may have high earnings because it pays high basic rates, because it offers ample opportunities to earn bonuses under payment by results schemes, or because a great deal of overtime is worked. One of the questions we would like to be able to answer is whether the differentials between industries are increasing or decreasing. The changes between 1960 and 1968 in weekly and hourly earnings shown in Table 8.1 enable us to make a rather tentative attempt to answer this question, but the evidence is far from clear.

For what it is worth, there is some slight evidence for a narrowing of the interindustry differentials. This implies that the industries with less than average earnings should show an above the average increase over 1960. This is fairly well borne out for hourly earnings. Six of the industry groups with above average earnings show less than average increases between 1960 and 1968, while seven with less than average earnings show above average increases. In the case of weekly earnings, the pattern is not so clear cut. Whereas for hourly earnings 13 out of 20 industry groups conformed to the pattern of narrowing interindustry differentials, this is the case with only seven groups for total weekly earnings. Four show low earnings combined with a high rate of increase and three high earnings combined with a low rate of increase. In the case of weekly earnings, there are six groups which show an opposing tendency (high earnings, fast increase, and vice versa), and another seven groups with either earnings or rates of increase corresponding closely to the average. Nevertheless, a closer examination will show some little additional evidence for the thesis that the differentials are narrowing. Two groups, engineering and miscellaneous metal industries, both have average earnings combined with a low rate of increase. In 1960, both these industries had above average earnings, and it may be argued that a less than average rate of increase has served to bring them into line with the average. One of the two groups with both high weekly earnings and a high rate of increase, transport, has less than average hourly earnings.

One would expect that, where an industry offers low wages, difficulties over recruitment would be likely to arise. Sooner or later, unless the industry is in steady decline, firms may find they are forced to raise wages in order to maintain the recruitment of enough workers of the right calibre. This may well have been happening in transport. In April 1968, weekly earnings were about 13s above the average, but hourly earnings were still below the average (despite a 71 per cent increase over 1960), and the hours of work were the longest for any of the industrial groups.

The lower paid industries. It is worth stopping to notice which are the lowest paid industry groups, and especially those where low weekly earnings are combined with a less than average rate of increase. The four industries in this situation are textiles, leather, clothing, and public administration. Both the leather and clothing industries also show less than average increases in hourly earnings. In textiles, the increase in hourly earnings was barely above the average, but in public administration it was well above, at 70 per cent. On the other hand, this is the industry with the shortest hours worked. In fact, public administration shows the lowest weekly earnings, the lowest hourly earnings, and the lowest number of hours worked.

One would expect some variation in average earnings between industries. The four referred to here, however, all have earnings which are substantially below the general average. The best paid of the four, textiles, has weekly earnings that are only about 90 per cent of the average, while in public administration earnings are less than 80 per cent of the average. Attention may also be drawn to two other industries where the earnings are well below the average, public utilities (gas, water, and electricity) and miscellaneous services (laundries, dry cleaning, motor repairs, shoe repairs). These, however, were at least keeping up with the general rate of increase (miscellaneous services) or catching up (gas, water, and electricity).

The non-manufacturing sector. A closer examination of the data in Table 8.1 will show that any reduction of interindustry differentials that has taken place since 1960 has been the result of a relative improvement of the position of workers in the non-manufacturing sectors. The average increase in hourly earnings was 65 per cent between 1960 and 1968, but only three manufacturing industries showed significantly greater increases. One, food remains a comparatively lowly paid industry, while the two better paid industries, getting big increases in hourly earnings, were chemicals and shipbuilding. On the other hand, five of the six non-manufacturing industries showed increases of 70 to 75 per cent in their hourly earnings.

All the non-manufacturing industries have hourly earnings below the general average, and four have weekly earnings that are below the average. It would seem that workers in these industries are dissatisfied with their comparatively low earnings and are being

112

successful in trying to get the situation redressed. In the two cases where weekly pay is lowest, and where the increase in weekly earnings has not exceeded the average, the hours worked are low. It seems, therefore, that rates of pay have increased, but reduced hours have kept down the size of the final pay packet. We might expect, however, the pressure for improvements in this sector to continue, and for important changes to occur over the next few years.

Basic rates and earnings

The changes that take place from time to time in earnings are the result of changes in basic rates, overtime opportunities, and opportunities for payment by results bonuses. Table 8.2 shows the changes which have taken place in the period April 1960 to April 1968 in basic weekly and basic hourly rates of pay for adult male manual workers, as well as in their earnings and in the earnings of salaried workers. The change in the retail price index is also given, and the change in the purchasing power of the basic wage and actual earnings have been worked out.

It will be seen immediately that for manual workers there was a markedly greater increase in the basic hourly rate than in the basic weekly rate. Hourly rates increased, in fact, about 10 per cent more than the weekly rates, indicating a corresponding reduction in the normal working week for which the basic weekly wage is paid. Details given by the Department of Employment and Productivity show a reduction in the working week from 43·7 hours in 1960 to 40·5 hours in April 1968.[1]

It is also apparent that weekly earnings for manual workers have increased more rapidly than even the basic hourly rates. This means that there have either been additional opportunities for increasing earnings through overtime or through payment by result bonuses. There is certainly some evidence to suggest that additional overtime earnings have been possible. The figures just quoted suggest a lowering of the normal working week, on average, by 3·2 hours. If anything, the relative changes in weekly and hourly basic rates suggests that this is an understatement. But the actual average number of hours worked by adult male manual workers declined between April 1960 and April 1968 by only 1·8 hours, from 48·0 hours to 46·2 hours. Payment by results may have accounted for some of the additional earnings, but clearly more hours were qualifying for payment at the higher rates applicable to overtime.

Table 8.2

Changes in basic weekly and hourly wage rates of adult male manual workers and earnings of adult male manual and salaried workers, April 1960 to April 1968

	Index number Apl 1968 Apl 1960 = 100	Index number of purchasing power Apl 1968 Apl 1960 = 100
Manual workers		
Basic weekly rates	138	105
Basic hourly rates	154	117
Weekly earnings	158	120
Salaried workers		
Earnings	154	117
Prices		
Index of retail prices	132	Not applicable

Sources: *Statistics*, no. 25 and *Gazette*, April 1968.

Salaried earnings increased at roughly the same rate as basic weekly rates, so that in terms of actual earnings, the salaried workers lost some ground in the period 1960 to 1968.

The gap between basic rates and actual earnings is a very big one. This is illustrated by Table 8.3, which takes the basic weekly wage rate for selected categories of workers and compares this rate with the average weekly earnings for the SIC order to which the selected workers belong. It will be seen from this table that the basic rate for skilled men even may be little more than half the average actual earnings (and this figure will be influenced by the lower earnings of unskilled men).

Regional variations in earnings

From economic theory, one would expect to find that wages for any given type of labour tended towards equality within a particular labour market. Should we regard the United Kingdom as forming one market for labour, or does it comprise many local markets, with the possibility that wages for a certain kind of labour may be at a different level in each of these markets? This is a question that can only be answered by looking at the facts of the situation. If the United Kingdom formed one perfect labour market, the offer of a higher rate for a job in one part of the country than in another would lead to workers flocking to the area offering the higher pay.

Table 8.3

Comparison of some typical weekly wage rates for adult male manual workers with average earnings, April 1968

Category of worker	Basic weekly rate	Average earnings of adult males in whole of SIC group
Agricultural workers (Wages Board minimum)	231s	317s*
Coalmining,		
underground worker, minimum	278s	458s*
surface worker, minimum	258s	
Baking, lowest rated workers, London	190s	
Cocoa, chocolate, and sugar confectionery, JIC minimum	216s	425s
Tobacco manufacture, minimum	244s	
Heavy chemicals, JIC firms,		
labourers	236s	467s
Drug and fine chemicals, highest rated		
workers, London	249s	
Engineering,		
fitters, London	258s	444s
labourers, London	217s	
Shipbuilding, skilled workers	257s	466s
Vehicle building,		
craftsmen, London	283s	520s
labourers, London	240s	
Road passenger transport, LTE Central drivers on maximum	326s	459s

*Earnings in October 1967.
Source: *Gazette*, April 1968 and *Statistics*, no. 25.
All figures rounded to nearest whole shilling.

The supply of labour between regions would be readjusted, in relation to demand, until wages were again equal.

We know that in practice this is not so. There are a good many factors which prevent workers from moving into the areas offering the highest rates of pay. At least three important barriers to movement exist. First, workers may have only very imperfect knowledge of the opportunities existing in other parts of the country, they may even be ignorant of the true extent of opportunities open to them in their home towns. On balance, such ignorance is probably a barrier to mobility of labour.[2] Second, workers may be reluctant to move away from their home area: they may not wish to break the ties with their families and friends, and to make a new life in a strange environment. Third, even if they are willing to consider a move, there may be practical difficulties. For instance, a move may be costly, even though, in certain circumstances, a man moving from an area of high unemployment may get some help from the Government. Or, if a man is paying a low rent for a council house, he may know that if he moves, say, to London he will not get a council house for a long time, and meanwhile will have to pay a very high rent for such accommodation as he can find. A man leaving a privately rented house subject to rent control may be in a similar position. A man owning his own house may incur very substantial costs in selling and buying if he moves to another job.

It is not surprising, therefore, that there is a marked variation in earnings from one part of the country to another. A number of factors help to explain the particular pattern that emerges. First, the industrial structure of one region is different from that of another. One region may have an unduly large share of the relatively more poorly paid industries, which would tend to lower the level of earnings in such a region. Second, areas with relatively high unemployment may, on average, offer little opportunity for overtime working, so that the level of average earnings is kept low. Third, there are differences in the level of hourly earnings between regions, even when overtime is disregarded: a given amount of work in a particular industry will earn a higher wage in one region than another.

Table 8.4 shows the average weekly earnings of adult male workers in industry in April 1967, and the increase in earnings at that date over April 1960.

Table 8.4

Average weekly earnings by region, adult male manual workers, April 1967

Region	Weekly earnings, Apl 1967	Per cent increase, Apl 1960–Apl 1967
London and south-eastern	432s	46
Eastern and southern	412s	45
South-western	383s	49
Midlands	421s	42
Yorkshire and Humberside	392s	41
North-western	401s	48
Northern	401s	48
Scotland	394s	52
Wales	408s	43
Northern Ireland	351s	53

Source: *Statistics*, no. 22.
All earnings figures rounded to nearest shilling.

116

Variations within an industry. The overall average weekly earnings were highest in London and the South-east, the lowest in Northern Ireland. There was a difference of 81s between the two regions, earnings in London being 23 per cent higher than those in Northern Ireland. In particular industries, the variation may be greater than this. In textiles, average earnings in London were 418s. In the North-west, one of the traditional centres of the industry, they were 353s, and in Scotland 340s. In Northern Ireland, they were only 318s. London earnings in textiles, therefore, were 100s or 31 per cent above those in Northern Ireland.

By contrast, the chemical industry shows a very much smaller variation in earnings between regions. The highest level of earnings was found in the East and South (460s) and the lowest (397s) in the Midlands. The range was only 63s or 15 per cent.

The changing pattern. It will be apparent from Table 8.4 that the differences in regional earnings are tending to diminish. There is a high negative correlation ($r = -0.675$) between the level of earnings in April 1967 and the increase between 1960 and 1967. Even the non-statistician will have little difficulty in seeing that, in general, the regions with a high level of earnings have had the smaller increases in earnings, while the regions of low pay have had bigger than average increases. This is tending to make the distribution of earnings by region much less uneven.[3]

The distribution of earnings

So far, the discussion has centred on the earnings of adult male manual workers, and has extended to the variations in average earnings from industry to industry and from region to region. In the later sections of the chapter, it will be necessary to look at the earnings of other groups of workers. The earnings of women and young people must be examined as well as those of adult men, and the earnings of white collar workers as well as those of manual workers. Before embarking on this wider examination of earnings, however, it remains to consider the distribution of earnings among adult male manual workers. Unfortunately, data on this subject are limited. Because of the cost, the Ministry of Employment and Productivity only undertakes a survey of the distribution of earnings at fairly long and irregular intervals. It is unlikely, however, that the pattern of distribution changes rapidly and the picture given by the last Ministry survey, which was made in 1960, is probably not very different from the picture that would be revealed by a survey undertaken today.

Table 8.5 gives details of the average weekly earnings by range of income for October 1960. At the time of the survey, the average wage was roughly £14 10s a week, or the midpoint of the £13–£16 range. Ten per cent of workers covered by the survey (the coverage is the same as for the earnings surveys undertaken each April and October) had average earnings of less than £10 a week, £10 a week representing just over two-thirds of the average weekly earnings. Less than half of 1 per cent were earning less than £7 a week, which is just under half the average weekly earnings. Only 6½ per cent earned £22 a week or over, that is roughly 50 per cent or more above the average, and only a little over 1 per cent earned more than £28 a week or double the average.

Table 8.5

Distribution of weekly earnings of adult male manual workers in industry, October 1960

Range of earnings	Percentage workers in range
Under £7	0·4
£7 and under £10	9·6
£10 and under £13	28·1
£13 and under £16	28·3
£16 and under £19	17·9
£19 and under £22	9·2
£22 and under £25	3·9
£25 and under £28	1·5
£28 and under £35	0·8
£35 and over	0·3

Source: *Statistics*, no. 15. The table has been simplified by reducing the number of income ranges.

By April 1968, average earnings had risen to £22 5s a week. If the pattern of distribution is roughly the same, this means that about 10 per cent of all workers are earning less than £15 a week, and perhaps 1 man in 200 is still earning less than £11 a week. At the other end of the scale, 6½ per cent may be earning £33 a week or more and 1 per cent earning £44 a week or more.

Before leaving this subject, a word of caution is necessary. The earnings inquiries relate to a single pay day in the month in question. On the whole, the average earnings revealed for the whole of industry and for individual industries and regions are probably quite reliable. We can probably accept also the distribution as being typical: there is no reason to think that the choice of any other pay day would reveal a markedly more or less egalitarian distribution of earnings. What must not be supposed, however, is that the table tells us how many men *regularly* have earnings in a particular range. There can be a fairly wide swing in an individual's earnings from week to week, especially where payments by results schemes are in operation. A man whose earnings are high one week may be low the next, while a man with low earnings the first week may have high earnings the second. In both weeks, these men would feature in the distribution of earnings surveys as cases of high or low wages, whereas their average earnings over a fairly long period might both conform to the average. The table may, therefore, exaggerate the spread of earnings.

Some of the workers included in the survey may be part-time workers or on short time. Short time is usually present in some degree except, perhaps, at the height of a boom, and its effects should not be excluded from any survey of the distribution of earnings. Part-time work, however, is a matter of choice. Part-timers may include, for example, men who have retired from full-time work and wish to work for a limited period for the sake of companionship and to supplement their pensions. To include them in the distribution survey clearly distorts the picture.

Women and young people

Table 8.6 compares the average weekly earnings of men with those of youths and boys, women, and girls. The most striking feature of the table is the fact that the average weekly earnings of women are roughly half those of men; this difference can be explained by a number of factors. There is a measure of discrimination, in the sense that women are paid less than men for the same work. More important is the fact that men and women only rarely do the same work. Women, for example, have few, if any, opportunities to serve apprenticeships and enter the skilled crafts. They are, therefore, employed mainly in semiskilled and unskilled work. They are less well organized than male workers, and are often employed in large numbers in industries where wages are low and women form a large proportion of the labour force.

The difference between the earnings of men and women is substantially less if measured on an hourly basis rather than on a weekly

Table 8.6

Average weekly earnings and hours of work of manual workers, April 1968

	Weekly earnings	Percentage increase of weekly earnings over Oct. 1959	Hours worked	Hourly earnings
Men (over 21)	445s	55	46·2	116d
Youths and Boys (under 21)	215s	83	42·1	61d
Women (over 18)	219s	56	38·4	68d
Girls (under 18)	151s	68	38·9	47d

Source: *Gazette*, August 1968.
Note: The data refer to full-time workers only.

one. Women typically work shorter hours than men, so that, while their weekly earnings are 49 per cent of men's earnings, their hourly earnings amount to 59 per cent of men's.

Table 8.6 also shows the changes in weekly earnings over the period from October 1959 to April 1968. The weekly earnings of men rose over this period by 55 per cent and those of women by 56 per cent. There is obviously no significance to be attached to the marginally faster increase in women's earnings. The earnings of youths and boys, however, increased by 83 per cent and those of girls by 68 per cent. This clearly indicates that there are factors at work increasing the earnings of young people relative to those of adult workers.

Table 8.7

Average monthly earnings of administrative, technical, and clerical workers, October 1967

	Men	Women
Monthly paid	£137	£60
Weekly paid*	£91	£46
All	£121	£51

Source: *Statistics*, no. 25.

*The weekly earnings have been multiplied by 52 and divided by 12 to obtain the monthly earnings from the weekly figure quoted in the *Statistics*. This is the reverse of the Department of Employment and Productivity's procedure for converting monthly earnings to weekly.

White collar workers

Table 8.7 shows the average monthly earnings for administrative, technical, and clerical workers in October 1967. The difference in earnings between men and women is roughly the same as for manual workers. In both instances, it is found that men earn about twice as much as women. In the white collar field, in fact, men paid monthly tend to earn rather more than twice as much as monthly paid women.

It seems likely that there are fewer formal barriers to the admission of women to the more highly skilled white collar jobs than there are to their admission to skilled manual crafts. It may be virtually impossible for a woman to qualify as a skilled craftsman, but, in theory, there is no reason why she should not reach the higher ranks in management or in a professional field. Nevertheless, the differential between men and women is as great in white collar as in the manual employment. Again, there are several explanations. In many cases, women are not given the education or training to prepare them for the higher grade jobs. The average earnings of women in white collar employment may be brought down by large numbers of relatively lowly paid shorthand typists. Even where women are able to get jobs that might lead to the higher reaches of white collar employment, they may find they are denied promotion. Many women work for a few years only. If they give up their jobs after a few years, either on marriage or when they start a family, it is natural that they may not have advanced very far up the ladder of promotion. A large number of women remaining in employment for only a limited period must serve to depress the average earnings of women. This is especially so in the white collar area, because salaried workers, in general, may expect earnings to rise with age and experience to a much greater extent than manual workers, who may reach their peak earnings quite early in their careers. Finally, employers may be reluctant to promote women workers to higher paid jobs. This may be the result of prejudice, or there may be valid reasons for it. (It may be feared, for example, that a woman may be promoted, just be beginning to be useful in her new post, and then leave to get married; or that a married woman remaining at work may be less reliable than a man because of the demands of her family.) But whatever the cause, women may be passed over for promotion in favour of a man who is not quite so able, and thus women's earnings are depressed.

The range of earnings for men in white collar jobs appears to be less than in manual employments. Taking the manufacturing

E

industry groups of the SIC, the average weekly earnings of manual workers in the highest paid, paper, printing, and publishing, were 32 per cent higher than in the lowest paid, leather goods and fur. For white collar employments, the highest paid industry group (chemicals) was only paid 19 per cent more than the lowest (metal manufacture).[4]

It is only possible to speculate as to the explanation for this. Two factors seem likely to have an important bearing on the spread of earnings. The first is that there is probably much greater scope for the white collar worker to move from one industry to another. A man may acquire a certain measure of expertise in his particular job, but the administrative, technical, or clerical worker will nevertheless find that his basic skills are fairly readily adaptable to employment in another industry. If a greater degree of mobility is possible, because skills are not specific to one industry,[5] we would expect differentials to be less. White collar workers will be less influenced by the factors affecting the prosperity of the industry, and more by factors affecting their particular occupation.

This is not likely to be the full explanation, however. Trade union influences may also be at work. White collar workers are, in general, less effectively organized than manual workers. Not all manual workers, however, enjoy the same strength of trade union organization. What matters, probably, is not so much the fact that on average manual workers are more strongly organized than white collar workers, but that there is more variability in the degree of organization by industry among manual workers. Average earnings in newspaper and periodical printing and publishing are over £29·50 a week, as a result of very strong trade union organization which is determined to make the most of its opportunities to exploit the situation. Organization in many branches of the textile industry is weak, partly because of the predominance of women workers. Such weak organization, combined with a weak market for the product, and the concentration of the industry in areas of relatively high unemployment would lead to markedly low wages. It is therefore easy to see how the variation in union strength among manual workers and the greater mobility of the white collar worker leads to bigger interindustry differentials in the case of manual workers.

NOTES

1. The index of normal hours is for all manual workers, not just adult males in the sectors covered by the six-monthly earnings surveys. Moreover, the 1960 figure is the average for the year and not the April figure. These factors account

for the reduction being less than would be indicated from the relative changes in weekly and hourly rates.

2. This will be the case if ignorance means that workers tend to under-estimate the opportunities available in another part of the country. If, however, they had exaggerated ideas about the more favourable opportunities that existed elsewhere, ignorance would encourage rather than hinder mobility.

3. For the statistician, it is worth noting that the standard deviation of the earnings pattern shown in Table 8.4, and by a comparable table for 1960, are both equal to £19, although between these dates the mean weekly earnings rose from 270s to 400s. (These calculations attach equal weight to each observation and take no account of the numbers employed in each region.)

4. If we look at the more detail figures for Minimum List Headings, we find that the ratio of earnings in the highest to lowest paid industry is 1·3:1 for white collar jobs and 1·7:1 for manual.

5. A skill may not be specific to an industry, but it is still specific. An accountant or shorthand typist might be equally at home in almost any industry, but each has a specific skill, in the sense that the one cannot do the other's job.

9. Methods of wage payment

Reference has been made in chapter 8 to the difference between what men actually earn and their basic rates of pay. There are two main methods of payment in British industry: workers may be paid according to the length of time they work, or according to the amount they produce, with the possibility of some combination of the two methods. For most workers, there is a basic time rate of pay. Many manual workers, however, are on payment by results (PBR), and their earnings under piecework, or other PBR schemes, may be far greater than their basic time rates.

There are several factors that explain the gap between the basic time rates negotiated by collective bargaining and the amount men actually earn. Employers may sometimes pay time rates that are higher than the minimum or basic rates negotiated. Overtime rates may supplement earnings. Not only are men paid more because they have worked longer hours, they are paid a premium for the hours of overtime. Hours worked beyond the normal length of the working week may be paid as time and a quarter or time and a half, with perhaps double time for Sunday work. The overtime premium may be paid for working beyond the normal day or on Sunday, even when total hours worked are not in excess of the normal week. Nearly all manual workers, and many of the lower grade white collar workers, are paid overtime, but in the higher ranks of the white collar workers a man may be expected to work whatever hours are necessary in return for the appropriate salary.

Overtime is not the most important factor in explaining the gap between basic rates and earnings, and nor are such special payments as are given to shift workers in recompense for the inconvenience of this type of work. The most important factor is payment by results. Often, PBR schemes have been introduced to provide an incentive for the workers to increase their output, but in many instances the real purpose would seem to be that of raising wages to a reasonable level when the basic rates negotiated are unrealistically low. Equally,

125

much overtime may not be a genuine necessity in the face of some emergency, but a device to enable men to supplement their earnings. In such cases, the chance to work overtime is more or less guaranteed, and the employer must make sure that all workers have an opportunity to a reasonable share of it.

Payment by results are clearly an important element in our wage structure and call for closer examination. For the most part, they have been ignored in the theoretical models of wage determination. These tacitly assume a time rate method of wage payment, a simple rate of so much per hour, day, week, or month, as the case may be. The models take no account of the possibility that a man's productivity is not fixed, but may vary according to the degree to which he shares the benefits of any increased output.

The main methods of payment

So far, we have distinguished between the payment of a fixed rate per unit of time and some kind of system that links a worker's pay to his output. A great variety of such schemes exists, even if, as for the moment, we confine ourselves to systems relating the pay of the individual worker to his output during a particular week. We may divide these schemes into three main categories, those where the rate of pay is directly proportional to the worker's output, those where pay increases less than proportionately to output, and those where pay increases more than proportionately to output.

The simple piece rate system is an example of the first type, where pay increases in direct proportion to output. A price is fixed for a job. The job may consist of making some article, whether it is a finished product or a component to be used in some later stage of manufacture, or packaging some article. If there are many different tasks to be done, there will be a price for each, and a man may be paid at the appropriate rate for each job. The important thing is that pay is proportional to effort. If the rate for a particular task is 5p per unit of output, a man will get £20 if he completes 400 units of output in a week; if he completes 416, then he will get £20·80, and so on. If the basic time rate for the job is £15 a week, however, he will never be paid less than this. If his output were only 285 units, the piecework payment would be only £14·25, but in this case he would be given the minimum time rate of £15. A man who is frequently having to fall back on the basic time rate because his output is low would not normally be retained in the job. Piece rates and other PBR schemes are normally arranged so that the average
126

worker can achieve a level of output that will give him a level of earnings that is significantly above the time rate for the job. The minimum time rate also gives a guaranteed level of earnings if the flow of work is interrupted through no fault of the worker. In this case, he may get the time rate for the period of enforced idleness plus the piece rate for production achieved.

Sometimes, no piece rate is fixed, but the worker is allowed a certain time to complete a job. If he completes the task in less than the time allowed, he will be paid a bonus. The bonus payment may be a payment, at the normal time rate, for the whole or part of the 'time saved', that is the difference between the time allowed for the job and the time actually taken. This system is particularly useful for the designing of premium bonus schemes, the name usually given to some of the arrangements whereby the worker's pay increases with his output, but less than proportionately. In the case where he is paid for the whole of the time saved, the system is, in fact, identical to the ordinary piecework system. Pay is in direct proportion to output.

Suppose, for example, a man is paid $50p$ an hour. The time allowed for a job is an hour. If he does the job in three-quarters of an hour, he is paid $37\frac{1}{2}p$ for the time actually taken over the job plus $12\frac{1}{2}p$ for the time saved, making $50p$ in all. In total, he gets $50p$ for the job, and this remains true whatever the time taken, subject to his receiving $50p$ an hour minimum if he takes more than the hour allowed over the job. If he completes two jobs in an hour, he will be paid £1, double the pay of somebody who simply keeps to the time allowed.

Premium bonus systems. Mention has already been made of the existence of schemes, usually referred to as 'premium bonus systems', whereby a worker's earnings increase with his output, but less than proportionately. A variety of such schemes has been evolved, and it is unnecessary to go into the details of all. It is sufficient to look at one such scheme in order to see the essential characteristic. Under the Halsey scheme, a certain time is allowed for each job and the worker is paid for the time he takes plus a proportion of the time saved. Thus, for each job completed, a man is paid $\{TT + x(TA - TT\}.H$, where H = pay per unit of time, TT = time taken, TA = time allowed, and x = proportion of time saved for which payment is made. Most of these systems are of American origin, and the Halsey formula was introduced into Britain by the firm of G. and J. Weir. In this instance, payment was made for half the time saved, and is known in this country as the Halsey-Weir system.

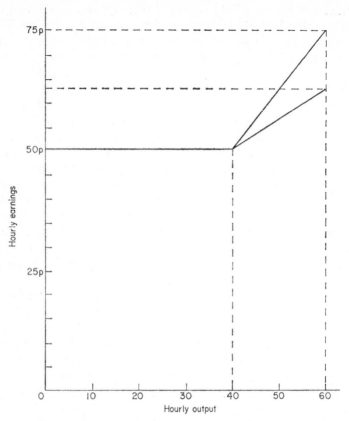

Fig. 9.1. Earnings under simple piece rates and Halsey-Weir System.

We may see what happens to a worker's earnings if we consider an example where he is on a time rate of 50p an hour and his output increases over a range of 40 to 60 articles an hour, assuming a time allowed of $1\frac{1}{2}$ minutes an article. (Any output below 40 articles an hour will carry the minimum payment of 50p an hour.) When his output reaches 50, he has produced an output for which the time allowed is 75 minutes. He will be paid for the 60 minutes he has been working plus $7\frac{1}{2}$ minutes or half of the 15 minutes he has saved compared with the time allowed. Similarly, when his output reaches 60 articles an hour he is paid for 75 minutes work in all. In Fig. 9.1, a comparison is made of hourly earnings in such a case under the Halsey-Weir system and with a simple piece rate system or system where payment is made for time taken plus the whole of the time saved. The effect of the Halsey-Weir variant is, clearly, to limit the

128

level of earnings of the worker compared with the simple piece rate system.

Incentive piece rates. Incentive piece rates are, in a sense, the opposite of the premium bonus systems. These schemes are designed to give a very strong incentive to the worker to increase his output, and involve a more than proportionate increase in earnings as a man's output rises. This kind of scheme has never been popular in Britain, but it has been used in the United States, where it operates without a guaranteed minimum hourly rate. At relatively low levels of output, the piece rate itself is low; when output reaches what is considered a reasonable standard, the rate increases; it may increase again as certain higher norms are passed.

Such a scheme can be regarded as providing both a carrot and a stick. For a man who can achieve a high level of output, there will be good earnings, because he will enjoy a high *rate* as well: the man with a very low output will simply be paid for what he produces at a low rate per unit and will have a very small paypacket. The man with a low output will be under strong pressure to increase that output or find another job.

The case for payment by results

Payment by results is intended to offer the worker an incentive to increase his output. It is worth while offering such an incentive, only if certain conditions hold. The level of output achieved by the worker should be easily measurable; he should be free to increase his rate of working in order to secure higher earnings; moreover, the quantity of output should be more important than quality. Each of these points needs to be considered in turn.

If the level of output cannot be easily measured, payment by results schemes are likely to be a cause of dispute. Not only should the level of output be measurable in itself, it should be readily measurable in relation to the normal period of payment, which for most manual workers is the week. Let us compare two situations. In the first, a man may produce, let us say, 200 articles a week. These are easily counted and, if he is paid 10*p* each on a simple piecework system, his earnings are £20. If he leaves an article unfinished, it does not affect his earnings to any significant degree: 10*p* in £20 is neither here nor there. It would be quite different if a man were only able to make, say, 10 articles a week and was offered a piece rate of £2 per article. What happens if he completes 9 articles during the week and has one unfinished? If he is paid £18, he will be seriously underpaid if the tenth article is nearly completed, while if paid £20 he would be seriously overpaid if it were only just started. To try to estimate what proportion of the work on the tenth article had been done would be difficult, and a source of argument. Although the work done could be easily measured over a long enough period, it would not be easily measurable within the span of the normal working week for which the worker is paid. Of course, if a man were paid for the jobs completed in any given week, what he lost one week he would gain the next, but this would introduce an element of uncertainty into his earnings, which might be regarded as undesirable.

An incentive to increase output can only be effective if a man is free to adjust his rate of work. A worker who has all the tools and materials to hand, and is left to get on with the job at his own rate, may feel it is worth his while to make an extra effort if by doing so he can increase his earnings. If, however, his job consists of performing certain operations on a product as it moves along the production line, he is powerless to work at any other rate than that determined by the line. If he cannot complete the required operations on one article before the next reaches him, he will disrupt the work of the whole production line and he will probably be sacked. If he can do the job more quickly than is strictly necessary, he will not be able to increase his output, but will merely have time to spare between completing one set of operations and starting the next. In such circumstances, there can be no real incentive in piecework and similar schemes, and payment by results is often introduced in such cases with a view to bringing earnings up to an acceptable level when time rates are artificially low.[1]

There is a danger that if workers are encouraged to speed up their work the quality will suffer. With any product, a minimum quality must be maintained, and inspection systems may be introduced to ensure that it is maintained. Subject to that minimum, however, a firm may prefer to see *more* goods produced, rather than the *quality* of a smaller output improved. So payment by results may be appropriate for a wide range of mass-produced goods (subject to the two qualifications already considered), but not in the production of high quality goods. Payment by results will also be inappropriate in most maintenance and repair work. Here, the work done may be very difficult to measure. A fault in a piece of machinery may be remedied quickly, but the time that will be taken to identify the fault may be quite unpredictable: it may be spotted quickly or it may only be diagnosed after every other possible source of the trouble has been

130

eliminated. Moreover, many forms of repair and maintenance work must be properly done or there may be danger to life or property. One does not want poor quality work done on a car because some kind of incentive payment scheme has encouraged the mechanics to rush the job. Thus, in this kind of field, PBR is ruled out, both by the difficulty of measurement and by the need for high quality.

PBR and labour costs. So far, we have seen that PBR schemes may afford the worker an incentive to increase his output. Rates are normally fixed so that an average worker can, with a higher level of output than when on time rates, earn at least 25 per cent more. From the workers' point of view, the logic of PBR is obvious. It remains to examine the advantages of such schemes from the employer's point of view.

One possibility is that the introduction of incentive methods of payment will lower the labour cost per unit of output. An example will make this clear. Suppose that when a worker is paid a time rate of 50p an hour he makes 10 articles in the course of an hour's work. The labour cost is 5p a unit. If the piece rate is set at 5p an hour, then the labour cost will remain unchanged, and the full benefit of any increase in productivity will go to the worker. If, on the other hand, a piece rate is set at, say, $4\frac{1}{2}p$, then the labour cost is lowered, but the worker will still be able to increase his earnings if he can produce more than 11 articles an hour. Alternatively, if the Halsey-Weir system of payment were in operation, any increase in output beyond 10 per hour, with the same rate of 50p an hour, would lead both to increased earnings on the part of the worker and falling labour cost per unit of output for the employer. Thus, if the worker increased his output to 12 units per hour his earnings per hour would increase from 50p to 55p and the labour cost per unit would fall from 5p to $4\frac{1}{2}p$.

The employer, however, may still benefit from incentive methods of payment if output per man is increased, even if there is no reduction in the labour cost per unit of output. Suppose, for example, a simple piece rate is introduced which is equal to the average labour cost per unit when payment is on a time basis. Because output per man is increased, the output of a given stock of capital equipment is increased and the overhead costs per unit of output are lowered. (The incentive piece rates, which involve increasing labour cost as the worker's output rises, are intended to bring about such savings, where overheads are a high proportion of total costs and labour costs are relatively unimportant.)

In this connection, it is important to keep in mind the fact that

131

the life of machinery may be dictated by osbolesence rather than physical deterioration. If machines have a life which is fixed in terms of years, rather than a capability of producing a total of so many units of output, there is a clear reduction in capital costs per unit of output if men can be encouraged to increase their output per unit of time. Such an increase in output per unit of time means that during its lifetime the total output of the machine will be increased and its cost spread over this larger output.[2]

Some disadvantages of payment by results

If payment by results succeeds in inducing workers to increase their hourly output and there is a saving in cost, the case for the introduction of an appropriate scheme would seem to be strong. Two qualifications must be made, however. The introduction of a PBR scheme may lead to cost savings following increased output, but it does not follow that such a scheme is the only way of achieving a satisfactory level of output and costs. While many managers believe that such schemes are one of the best ways of securing increased output (and they may certainly be one of the simplest), there are others who believe that it is possible to achieve equally good results under a system of time rates, through efficient management and good industrial relations.[3]

Although PBR may provide an incentive to the worker to increase his output, there may be incidental disadvantages, and full account must be taken of these in deciding whether to introduce a PBR scheme or not.

Variability of earnings. One of the most serious problems associated with payment by results is the element of variability introduced into the workers' earnings. The introduction of any piece rate scheme, or a scheme which gives some kind of bonus for increased output, will cause differences in the earnings of a worker from week to week; it will also introduce differences between workers. Both kinds of variation in earnings must be considered.

The earnings of an individual worker will vary from week to week for a number of reasons. He may not work as hard one week as he does another. This may not, in itself, lead to a very wide variation in earnings except in special circumstances. In some industries, for example, mining, there is a tradition that workers make an extra effort in the weeks before Christmas or the summer holidays in order to earn the extra money they require at these times. A man may not be employed all the time on the same work. Some jobs may offer greater scope for increasing earnings than others.[4] Work may be held up from time to time through no fault of the worker and during such holdups he has to rely on his basic time rate.

While some workers may find it convenient to be able to make an extra effort and boost their earnings at certain times of the year, in general, it is undesirable that earnings should fluctuate from week to week. A steady income is, in many ways, preferable to one that fluctuates, even though the latter may, on average, be just as high. The pattern of consumption associated with a steady income is often very different from that associated with a fluctuating income which reaches the same average level. It is much easier for a household to budget for certain kinds of purchase when its income is known than when it is fluctuating. A man with a steady income of £1250 a year is able to borrow up to £3000, or even more, from a building society in order to buy his own house. If a man's income is fluctuating between £18 and £30 a week, a building society is likely to take the lower figure as the wage this man can rely on and, on this basis, lend him only £2000, or a little over.[5] Thus, the man with fluctuating earnings may find greater difficulty in obtaining a loan to buy a house. He may also tend to allocate for the normal expenses of living a sum related to what he can be sure of bringing home at the end of any week. He may keep his regular commitments relatively small, and, in the weeks when his earnings are high, the money may be spent without too much thought, perhaps even irresponsibly. (Of course, a value judgement is being made here, but in this kind of field such judgements are difficult to avoid. It is preferable that we should make them and do so explicitly, rather than try to avoid areas where we are likely to be forced into making such judgements.)

Anomalies under PBR. The introduction of payment by results leads to differences in earnings between workers. It may seem, at first sight, that there is a great deal to be said in favour of a system that rewards workers according to their output. Workers are rarely of equal efficiency, and it would appear both reasonable and equitable to adjust rewards in such a way as to mirror the relative efficiency of different individuals. Piece rates, and other incentive systems, go some way towards achieving this end, though, in practice, the range of output and earnings among workers on a particular job tends to be fairly narrow. Some kind of output norm appears to emerge. Some earn a little more and others a little less, but workers who try to earn a lot more than the majority are regarded by their fellows with disfavour, while those who would earn a lot less are probably regarded as unsuitable by the management and sacked. Nor should this be thought of as simply the result of restrictive practices. There is, after all, a limit to the output the average worker can be expected to maintain day after day, week after week, for years on end. It may be quite reasonable for a group of workers to seek protection against a newcomer, who, perhaps, does not intend to stay long in the job, and who seeks very high earnings by maintaining a level of output that is only possible for a limited period. The danger that such a performance over a limited period will be used as evidence that they are slacking, or that the rates are fixed too generously, is very real.

While, within limits, payment by results may adjust the pay of men on one particular job in such a way as to reflect relative abilities, it does not follow that it does the same when we look at things in a wider light. Rate setting is not an exact science and mistakes can be made. There may even be deliberate attempts to mislead those responsible for setting the rates for different jobs. We must see how such mistakes may occur, and then look at the consequences.

A piece rate for a job, or the time allowed for a job, may be set 'tight' or 'loose'. If the rate is tight, the average worker will not be able to secure a reasonable level of earnings, even when his output has been improved appreciably in comparison with his performance under time rates. Similarly, a loose rate is one where a worker can obtain very high earnings, or alternatively reach the kind of earnings level expected without undue effort (perhaps with little or no increase of output over his performance on time rates). If a PBR scheme is to be introduced, there is clearly a danger that workers on the job will go slow to try to influence the rate to be set. It is important, therefore, that firms introducing PBR schemes should have an efficient works study department that will be able to make independent estimates of the rates of production that are possible.

Even if major errors are avoided, some rates will inevitably be set tighter than the average and others looser. This means that a man's earnings will depend not only on the level of output he is capable of, but also upon the particular job he has to do. Robertson has shown the extent of the variations in earnings that take place in engineering plants, not only between members of different trades, but between men in the same trade, although employed in different parts of the plant.[6] An even more serious anomaly may occur in the differences in earnings between men on PBR and those on time rates. In some instances, men may be engaged on work at time rates because a particular job calls for an emphasis on quality rather than quantity of output. There will therefore be cases where it is the best

134

workers who are put on such work, but they may find as a result that they lose financially for undertaking very responsible work. They may be paid the very low basic time wage which is common in so many industries, and is, perhaps, only half or two-thirds of the average earnings of men on PBR.[7]

In engineering, there is a special case in the toolroom. Here, highly skilled craftsmen make the jigs and tools that will be employed by semiskilled production workers in other parts of the factory. The level of production of the factory is dependent upon the efficiency of the men in the toolroom. A mistake in a jig on the part of a toolroom worker could mean that the whole output of a man on the production line was useless. This is clearly a job where accuracy is vital and must not under any circumstances be sacrificed to quantity. The basic time rate, however, of a skilled engineering craftsman is likely to be far less than the earnings level normally achieved by even a semiskilled man. A possible remedy in this kind of case is to give the toolroom men a bonus based not on *their individual outputs*, but on the *output of the factory*.

There is a similar danger that foremen and other supervisors, who are necessarily on time rates, may earn less than those they are supervising and who may be on PBR. The only satisfactory answer to this anomaly is to fix the time rate for supervisory staff at a sufficiently high level to maintain an adequate differential. To introduce a bonus based on the output of those they supervise would be unsatisfactory, because it could give the supervisors an incentive to try to force the pace of work unreasonably.

Collective bonuses. It has been assumed in this chapter that payment by results means that the pay of the worker is related to his output. The only exception has been the reference to the case of the toolroom workers, where, in order to supplement low basic time rates, a bonus may be paid that depends upon the output of the factory as a whole. However, there are also instances of bonuses being paid that are determined by the output of a small group of workers in some section of the plant. The case for such an arrangement must now be considered, together with the serious difficulties that may arise.

Such a group bonus scheme might have a number of minor advantages. It would only be necessary to keep a check on the total output of the group rather than the separate output of each member. A more important consideration is supervision: it may be felt that all payment by results schemes reduce the need for supervision. If a man slacks, his output will be reduced and his earnings suffer, so that the same standard of supervision is not needed to ensure that the worker remains on the job and does not waste time. In a group bonus scheme, the need for supervision might be even less. A member of the group who slacked would not only cause his own earnings to fall, but would also bring about a reduction in the earnings of other members of the group. The theory is that other members of the group would not be prepared to tolerate this and would, in effect, supervise each other.

While the logic of the argument is simple enough, in practice, there are other considerations. The group will not be a contented and efficient unit if there is any suspicion that one member is not pulling his weight. The troubles that could arise over the presence of a passenger in the team may far outweigh any expected benefits from the replacement of formal supervision by the informal supervision of each member of the group by all the others. The problem is not simply that of the deliberate slacker: the operation of a group bonus scheme will give rise to difficulties about the placing of any worker whose output is a little below the norm, including learners.[8]

Some alternative methods of payment

There are in existence a number of alternative to the use of simple time rates or the straightforward payment by results schemes that have so far been considered. Among the other possibilities that must be considered briefly are:

1. Merit-rating.
2. Incremental scales.
3. Measured daywork.
4. Scanlon and similar type plans.
5. Profit-sharing.

Merit-rating. Merit-rating is defined as 'an attempt to assess the real value of an employee to his firm', and the 'resultant merit rates are payments made in excess of the recognized base rates as a reward for the personal merit of the particular workers to whom they apply'.[9] Before a merit-rating scheme is introduced, the cooperation of the workers needs to be obtained, and this means that they must be given full information about the scheme as a first step. The workers must see that the basic rates agreed by collective bargaining will remain in force, and that the merit-rating scheme will give all workers an opportunity to secure something over and above these minima.

The scheme operates by assessing the work of an employee under

136

different headings. For a manual worker, the factors to be rated may include quality of work, speed of work, attendance and punctuality, initiative, care of tools and materials, and perhaps some others, though it is best to keep the list reasonably short. For a supervisor, there would be a different list of factors to be rated, including such things as leadership, knowledge of the job, versatility, willingness to accept responsibility, new ideas and suggestions, and so on.

Unlike the simple PBR schemes, merit-rating manages to get away from the undue emphasis on quantity of output and to take account not only of quality, but also of other factors which determine the value of the employee to the firm, such as regularity of attendance. Under a merit-rating scheme, it would be possible to ensure that a man who, because he is a good worker, is put on a special job where quality is important is not penalized: under simple PBR schemes it is only the men who are on jobs where quantity is more important that have the chance to increase their earnings.

Merit-rating schemes may not be all that easy to operate, however. Weights have to be given for the different factors to be taken into account. Let us assume that four factors only are taken into account: quality of work, speed of work, attendance and punctuality, and care of tools and materials. If 1000 points are allocated overall, are 250 to be given for each quality, or are some considered more important than others? In this case, it may be decided to allocate the following weights:

Quality	400
Speed	350
Attendance	150
Care of tools	100
	1000

Even where two people agree about the relative importance of the different factors, they might differ considerably when it comes to trying to give a quantitative expression of their priorities.

There are also difficulties in rating the individual under each of the selected headings. One may try to define performance by certain adjectives and to give a percentage of the maximum points for each. Thus, one might define a worker's performance as 'excellent', 'very good', 'good', 'satisfactory', 'poor', and give 100, 80, 60, 40, or 20 per cent of the maximum points respectively. Any attempt to make use of a more continuous rating system is almost certainly giving a spurious suggestion of accuracy to the proceedings. Even with a limited range of adjectives defining performance, there will be differences of opinion. It is unlikely that one rater will grade a man as poor and another as excellent, but two raters might easily differ over whether a man was excellent or very good. The fact that there is no objective measure of ability means that difficulties and disputes can very easily arise.

When the worker has been rated, it is still necessary to relate any bonus he is paid to this rating. The method adopted might be to set up a series of ranges of ratings and to pay a specified percentage bonus to all workers rated within a particular range. This might be done as follows:

Rating	Bonus
0–249	nil
250–499	15%
500–749	30%
750 and over	45%

This means that a worker rated at, say, 650 would receive a rate of pay that was 30 per cent above the basic rate. The bonus may reach as high a maximum as the firm cares to establish, the number of separate ranges may be varied, and the payment of bonus may begin with as low a rating as the firm considers worth while. If there is a rating 'unsatisfactory' (meaning marginally so) and 'poor' (meaning decidedly unsatisfactory), the bonus may sometimes start with a rating that is certainly below 'satisfactory' and perhaps even between 'poor' and 'satisfactory'. If too many people are excluded from the bonus, the result may be to discourage them, whereas if they get a small bonus they may well strive to increase it at the next rating.

Incremental scales. Incremental scales generally apply only to white collar workers. They are to be found in such fields as banking, teaching, the civil service, and local government employment. In much of industry and commerce, true incremental scales are not operated, but an employee's salary may be reviewed annually and any increment based upon what he is considered to be worth. The latter procedure may seem, in some ways, rather similar to the merit-rating schemes we have been considering, but there is no need for the same formality in having points for specified factors, because the numbers involved are so much smaller.

The idea of incremental scales is that they reflect the increasing value of the worker to the enterprise with growing experience. A

138

newly engaged worker will find that there is a limited range of tasks he can undertake. As his knowledge of the job increases and his experience grows he can undertake more difficult tasks, and accept a greater measure of responsibility. He may be allowed, after a time, to make certain decisions himself rather than refer them to his immediate superior; to take decisions on behalf of his superior when the latter is absent; to play a more constructive part in long-term planning.

Of course, the extent to which a worker can play this greater role within the enterprise, as his experience increases, depends upon the individual. The weakness of a formal incremental salary scale is that one man may show great ability and take on considerable responsibility, while another may perform his required functions indifferently and be able to take on little responsibility. If both have served for the same period, they may be paid the same. There is, therefore, a strong argument for the system of an annual review of salaries, or at least for introducing into any incremental salary scheme efficiency bars (at which a man may be held unless his work is satisfactory) and for advancing more rapidly the man of real ability.

From the worker's point of view, the great merit of the incremental scale is that it is pleasant to look forward to the annual increment of salary, and, for the younger man, these increments go a long way to help him maintain his standard of living as his family grows. The value of the manual worker to the enterprise does not increase in the same way with experience, and it might be hard to justify its extension to them. On the other hand, the desire to see one's income steadily rising applies equally to manual workers and is undoubtedly a factor in the pressure for annual wage increases.

Measured daywork. The introduction of piecework, or other incentive methods of payments, has often led to increased output. Some writers have suggested, however, that this is due to the preparations made before such schemes are introduced, including work study, and that the use of incentive methods of payment are not really essential to getting the increased output. The use of work study and similar methods, and the setting of appropriate standards of performance, achieve the same results; this is what is attempted by measured daywork. The weakness is that there is no incentive to the worker, and if it becomes difficult to discipline the man who fails to achieve the prescribed standards, the results are not likely to be good.

Scanlon type plans and profit-sharing. Both of these types of scheme provide for linking payment to the overall performance of the factory.[10] Profit-sharing may take the form of cash payments to workers at appropriate intervals, or it may involve giving them shares in the enterprise representing retained profits. Only the former can really be considered here as any kind of alternative to incentive methods of payment.

In the case of profit-sharing, the income of the worker is linked in some way to the overall success of the enterprise as measured by the profits earned. The Scanlon plan, on the other hand, places its emphasis on sharing with the worker the benefits of cost reduction, and especially of labour costs. The scheme is, in fact, an incentive to the workers to contribute to the lowering of labour costs. The obvious objection to profit-sharing is that the results achieved may be poor, despite improved performance by the workers. Changing demand conditions may mean low prices or reduced order books, with consequent low profits; yet workers may have increased their productivity and feel that they are entitled to some reward. The Scanlon plan may give the workers benefits from lowered labour costs (perhaps the result of increased productivity), but this could come at a time when demand conditions have led to low profits or even losses.

It is clear, then, that no ideal system of payment exists. There is, perhaps, a lot to be said in favour of the simple time rate, provided management can succeed in achieving a reasonable level of output. It is important, too, that as far as possible workers' pay in one enterprise should keep in line with what is paid in similar enterprises, and that there should also be a measure of comparability between jobs of roughly the same level. There is increasing evidence that workers themselves expect this, and this is the subject to which we turn in chapter 11.

NOTES

1. For a fuller discussion of this topic, see D. J. Robertson, *Factory Wage Structures and National Agreements*, Cambridge U.P., 1960.

2. Even if the life of the machine were fixed in terms of a capacity to produce so many units of output, incentive payment schemes could still be worth while, even in cases where no reduction in labour cost occurred. If workers are encouraged to increase their hourly rate of output, fewer machines are needed initially, though they will be worn out sooner. Although the total expenditures required to maintain a given level of output over a very long period might be the same, the *present discounted* value of the total expenditure would be reduced.

3. See, for a full development of this argument, W. Brown, *Piecework Abandoned*, Heinemann, London, 1962.

4. This point is considered again in relation to differences between workers.

140

5. The policy of building societies is to lend up to $2\frac{1}{2}$ or 3 times a persons salary, but it will disregard overtime and bonus earnings that may not continue to be earned in the future.

6. W. Brown, op. cit.

7. Where there is only a little work of this kind, the position may not be too bad if the firm can find an older man for the job who is no longer able to keep going at the normal pace if on payment by results, but who can be relied upon to do a first-class job if allowed to do it in his own time.

8. The objections raised here relate, of course, to the case where several people form a group in which each is doing the same job. In the case of workers who form a team, in which each member has his separate task, it may be quite sensible to operate a group bonus scheme. Indeed, in such a case, one can measure only the output of the team and not that of individual members.

9. N. C. Hunt, *Methods of Wage Payment in British Industry*, Pitman, London, 1951, chapter XII.

10. For a discussion of some of the implications of these types of scheme, and references to the very considerable literature on the subject, see R. B. McKersie, 'Wage Payment Methods of the Future', *British Journal of Industrial Relations*, 1, 1963.

10. Fringe benefits

In the discussion so far, it has been tacitly assumed that the price of labour is simply the wage or salary that the worker is paid at the end of the week or month. Although this is undoubtedly the most important consideration from the standpoint of both the worker and the employer, it is not the only one. The worker may derive other benefits from his employment, and these will involve costs for the employer. The benefits include such things as pension and sick pay schemes at one end of the scale, and the provision of canteen and sports facilities by the firm at the other. It might be thought that all one has to do is to calculate the money value of the various benefits offered by the employer, and to take this as an indication of their worth to the worker and their cost to the employer.

In practice, the matter is more complicated. The workers may prefer the employer to pay them another million pounds in wages rather than pay the same sum into a pension scheme. The workers do not object to pensions as such, but because the benefits accrue in the future (and for younger workers a fairly remote future) they are discounted. The employer, on the other hand, may derive benefits from contributing to a pension fund rather than increasing wages. It may, for example, reduce the labour turnover where pension rights are not transferable.

In the present chapter, the main emphasis will be on pensions, sick schemes, and redundancy compensation (extending this latter to include the wider issues of job security). In addition, a brief account will be included of the National Insurance scheme, since the benefits offered under the scheme are in many ways similar to the fringe benefits offered by employers. In some countries, far more reliance is placed on the role of employers' fringe benefits in the provision of social security and less on the role of a state scheme.

Little need be said about holidays with pay, and welfare facilities. Holidays with pay obviously add to an employer's costs. If lengthening such holidays mean prolonging any summer or bank holiday

143

closures of a works, the extra cost is limited to the payment made for the period that is no longer worked. If, on the other hand, holidays are spread over the year, additional costs may be incurred in keeping records of holidays taken and the entitlement of different workers.

Of various kinds of welfare services provided, the works canteen is perhaps the most important. Its value may lie not so much in the value to the worker of any subsidies on the canteen's operation, as in the fact that its existence enables the worker to get a good meal at a reasonable cost within his limited mealbreak. Such facilities may clearly be more important in a remote factory than in a large office in the city centre, which may be surrounded by numerous restaurants where a cheap meal can be obtained.

The subsequent sections of this chapter will consider not only the nature of the various benefits and their costs, but also the extent to which British workers at present enjoy such facilities; differences between white collar and manual workers, and between the sexes, are important.

The cost of fringe benefits. Before looking in closer detail at the kind of fringe benefits provided in British industry, it is worth comparing briefly the expenditure by British firms on them with that in other countries. Data quoted by a Glasgow University study suggests that, in 1960, supplementary labour costs in Britain (i.e., expenditure on the main fringe benefits) was equal to about 14 per cent of the payroll. This compares with about 26 per cent for the United States and figures ranging from 30 per cent to 57 per cent for the countries of the Common Market.[1]

Of this relatively small expenditure on fringe benefits, compulsory National Insurance contributions, holidays with pay, and occupational pension schemes account for the greater part. On the whole, British trade unions have not been active in pressing for the provision of improved fringe benefits by firms. This may well be because of the close links between the trade unions and the Labour Party, and the attempt to provide better social security and medical care through state provision. The existence of the National Health Service, for example, means that there is no need, as in the United States, to try to persuade employers to help pay for insurance against the costs of medical care. On the other hand, state pensions are small, and there is considerable difficulty in meeting the costs that would be involved in raising them. It would therefore have been quite reasonable for unions to have pressed for improved occupational pension schemes, as well as better provision in respect of sick

144

pay, and so on, while seeking through political action to improve the existing state schemes. Whatever the reason, this has not been done on any significant scale. At the time of writing (1969), the Government has given details of a proposed new scheme for national superannuation and social insurance. A White Paper has been published (Cmnd. 3883, 1969), but so far there has been no legislation. It should be stressed that the details of state social security provisions given later in this chapter are the 1969 figures and are subject to change, and that, even if a new scheme is introduced, certain rates of benefit will remain subject to periodic adjustment. The student must learn, therefore, to look to official sources to keep such details up to date.

National Insurance

The National Insurance scheme came into operation in 1948. It offers a wide range of benefits. We shall be concerned mainly with three, retirement pensions, sickness benefit (including the special industrial injuries scheme), and unemployment benefit. We shall be concerned with the employed contributor, who is entitled to the above-mentioned benefits and the other benefits of the scheme, including maternity grant, maternity allowance (payable only to married women who elect to pay their own contributions), benefits for widows, and death grant. The self-employed and the non-employed pay different rates of contribution, related to the range of benefits to which they are entitled: neither can claim unemployment benefit, and the non-employed cannot claim sickness benefit.

The flat-rate scheme. The main benefits under the flat-rate scheme are fixed, at the time of writing (1969) at £4 10s for a single man and an allowance of £2 16s a week for a wife or other adult dependent. There are additional allowances for dependent children. These rates apply to retirement pensions, sickness and unemployment benefit, and the various benefits for widows. (In the case of the widowed mother, her personal allowance is at the normal rate of £4 10s, but there is a more generous allowance for the first child.) To obtain the full rates of benefit, an insured person must maintain an average of 50 contributions *paid or credited* a year throughout the period he is insured under the scheme (contributions are credited during periods when a man is drawing benefit). He must also have *paid* a certain minimum of contributions in order to draw any benefit. For unemployment or sickness benefit, he must pay 26 contributions before he can benefit. If he has paid 156 contributions, his entitlement to unemployment benefit is for approximately one year, and for sickness benefit indefinite. For a retirement pension, or widow's benefit of any kind for his wife, he must, again, pay 156 contributions.[2]

If a man's incapacity for work is the result of injury at work, or of an industrial disease, he will be entitled to injury benefit under the industrial injuries scheme, which is on a more generous scale. A man is entitled to benefit under this scheme for incapacity lasting up to six months, and the benefit rate is £7 5s a week, as compared with the normal £4 10s. The same allowances are paid for dependents as under sickness benefit, which a man will receive if he is still unfit for work at the end of six months.

If a man is in any way permanently disabled as a result of industrial injury or disease, he is entitled to disablement benefit. This is at the rate of £7 12s a week for 100 per cent disablement, and correspondingly lower rates, down to £1 10s 6d a week for 20 per cent disablement; the degree of disablement is assessed by a medical board. There are additional payments which may be made to those disabled in the course of employment. A special hardship allowance, of up to £3 1s, may be paid where a man is unable to return to his old job or one of comparable standard (provided the sum of disablement benefit and special hardship allowance does not exceed £7 12s a week.)[3]

If a man (or woman) is unable to work as a result of industrial injury or disease, an unemployability supplement of £4 10s is payable, together with the same allowances for dependents as under National Insurance sickness benefit. So, for the man permanently disabled by an injury received at work, the disablement benefit and special hardship allowances are additional to the scale of benefit he would receive if permanently incapacitated by any other accident or illness. Moreover, there are additional allowances which may be paid in appropriate cases. A disabled person needing constant attendance is paid a further £3 a week, or up to £6 a week in severe cases; a further exceptionally severe disablement allowance is payable where a constant attendance allowance of more than £3 is paid, and such attendance is likely to be needed permanently.[4]

It is interesting to compare the position of a married man with one child who is disabled in an accident at work with one similarly injured elsewhere. We may assume that injuries are serious enough to render the men unemployable, but not to require constant attendance. The former will draw total benefits of £16 6s (including 28s for the child), while the other will draw only £8 14s. The former represents rather more than two-thirds of the average wage at the present time, while the latter is little more than one-third. The worker injured in the factory is relatively well cared for, whereas the man who is incapacitated in some other way is not, and may, if he had no resources of his own, be forced to go to the Ministry of Social Security for supplementary benefit. Many people feel this is a serious anomaly, although it may be argued that a scheme financed primarily by the contributions of workers and employers should aim to give adequate cover against industrial injuries, whereas other risks should be a matter for individual action, in part at least.

Finally, it is necessary to note the current contributions for adults. Men pay 16s 8d a week and women 14s (if not contracted out of the graduated pension scheme) and their employees contribute 16s 11d and 14s 2d respectively. The reader is warned, however, that these rates, and the benefit rates, are adjusted from time to time and that he should try to keep up to date.

Income-related benefits. There are two separate schemes giving income related benefits under National Insurance. The first to be introduced was the graduated pension scheme, which came into operation during the financial year 1963–64. More recently, an income related supplement to sickness and unemployment benefit has been introduced.

Under the graduated pension scheme, the insured person and his employer each pay a sum equal to $4\frac{1}{4}$ per cent of the workers earnings in excess of £9 a week up to the ceiling of £18 a week. Contributions in respect of the supplement to sickness and unemployment are at the rate of $\frac{1}{2}$ per cent of earnings between £9 a week and £30 a week. In this case, too, the employer and worker both pay this amount, which the employer determines from tables supplied to him; the deduction is made along with PAYE.

Under the graduated pension scheme, a man receives an extra 6d a week pension for every £7 10s *he* has contributed. Thus, a man whose earnings have been at the ceiling of £18 a week over a working lifetime of 40 years will have paid something like £750 or more in contributions and so be entitled to an extra 50s a week pension. This would bring the total pension of a married couple to £9 16s, or rather less than half the present average earnings of manual workers. Moreover, since benefits are in proportion to contributions, benefit on this scale will not be earned until a relatively young man, who was contributing to the scheme from its introduction in the 'sixties, comes to retire. During the immediate future, the contribution of the graduated pension scheme to the improvement of pension levels will be quite small, and new arrangements have been outlined in a White Paper.[5]

The return on contributions under this scheme is poor. It is far worse than a worker would get under any private pension scheme. For combined contributions of £15 by worker *and* employer, 6d a week barely represents the annuity which could be purchased with £15. (A good guide is that a man of 65 can purchase an annuity of £10 a year for £100 cash.) For the man retiring shortly after the introduction of the scheme, the rate of benefit offers a not unreasonable return on his and his employer's contributions. The man who contributes for 40 years, however, does not benefit from any interest on the contributions. In a private pension scheme, the capital sum accumulated would probably be more than twice the amount of actual contributions as a result of interest earned by investing them. For a man contributing to a private pension scheme for 40 years, the resulting pension might be double that offered by the graduated pension scheme. The scheme was clearly introduced to help provide extra money to meet the increasing burden of the flat-rate pensions. This is indicated by the fact that, where workers are contracted out of the scheme (which is possible if the employer offers a pension scheme with at least equal benefits and proper transferability), a higher flat-rate National Insurance contribution has to be paid.

Because women may retire at 60, the graduated pension scheme gives an extra 6d for every £9 contributed by the insured worker.

The income related supplement to sickness and unemployment benefit is at the rate of one-third of average earnings between £9 and £30. Thus, a man earning £24 a week would get a supplement of £5 a week, in addition to the normal flat-rate benefits. This benefit is subject to a maximum of 85 per cent of a man's normal earnings. A man normally earning £11 5s a week would be entitled to a supplement of 15s and with his flat-rate benefits for a wife and one child he would be entitled to a total benefit of £9 6s. In this case, however, the total benefit will be limited to £9 2s 9d or 85 per cent of £11 5s. To claim the supplement, a man only needs to produce the P60 form his employer gave him at the end of the last tax year, which shows his total earnings for that year and the amount of income tax deducted under PAYE. It is this earnings figure for the previous year that is used in calculating the entitlement to benefit. Benefit is not paid for the first fortnight of sickness or unemployment, and the income related supplement is paid for six months only. It is paid both in the case of sickness and industrial injuries benefit.

148

Private pension schemes

All that most people know about pensions is that they are paid on retirement, either from a particular job or from employment altogether. Pension schemes may take a variety of forms. In some cases, a firm may simply pay a pension to former employees out of its current earnings. The danger of this kind of scheme is that, even if the worker has a contractual right to his pension, payment is dependent upon the ability of the firm to continue honouring its obligation. Where the payment is *ex gratia*, it might be discontinued if a firm were taken over. Whether contractual or *ex gratia*, pensions may have to be discontinued in the event of insolvency. The usual arrangement, therefore, is that pension schemes are funded.

It is not proposed to outline in detail the different kind of pension schemes that may be used. Even where the same broad pattern is adopted, there is scope for considerable variation in the details. Instead, therefore, an outline will be given of a scheme that satisfies the main requirements of the Inland Revenue. (Unless these conditions are satisfied, the contributions are not allowed to rank as deductions for tax purposes.)

A pension scheme should aim to provide a pension not exceeding two-thirds of a worker's final salary. For this purpose, 'final salary' is normally taken to mean the worker's average salary over his last three years of employment. Pension or other benefits amounting to two-thirds of the final salary will result from employment over a period of, perhaps, forty years. Those employed for shorter periods will receive correspondingly smaller benefits. Typically, a worker may receive a pension of one-eightieth of his salary for each year of service up to a maximum of 40, and, in addition, a lump sum equal to three times his pension. Thus, a man with a final salary of £3000 would receive a pension of £1500 plus a lump sum of £4500. If he wished, he could use this for the purchase of an annuity, and this would bring his total pension to approximately two-thirds of his final salary. If he wishes, of course, he could use the lump sum to provide an annuity for his wife to supplement any National Insurance widow's pension she would receive if he should die before her.

If we assume a man's wage or salary is constant throughout his period of employment, the calculation of the appropriate contribution rates is relatively easy. To provide a pension of £650 for a man earning £1000 a year, it will be necessary to accumulate a capital sum of approximately £6500. Over 40 years, compound interest may provide approximately half of the sum required, leaving £3250 to be provided by the actual contributions. This means roughly £80

149

per annum or 4 per cent of the salary to be paid by the employer and the worker.

Pensions are normally paid only after some minimum period of service, perhaps, 10 years. A man who does not qualify for a pension will normally be entitled, as a minimum, to the return of his own contributions. Where a worker has been with a firm for only a relatively short period, the accumulated interest on contributions will represent a smaller proportion of the final sum accumulated than it would do in the case of a man remaining with the firm for 40 years. In so far as some pensioners have had relatively short periods of qualifying service, a slightly higher rate of contribution is required than the 4 per cent just indicated.[6]

Incremental scales and inflation. The case where a man's salary is constant over his working lifetime is unrealistic. There are four main reasons for this. First, many white collar workers are on an incremental salary scale. Second, a man may have several promotions to higher grade posts in the course of his career. Third, there is an upward trend in real earnings. Fourth, there is a further rise in money earnings brought about by inflation. Earlier, it was suggested that the accumulation of compound interest on pension fund contributions would provide about half of the total capital sum required to buy the appropriate annuity, in the case where the wage or salary is constant. Where the wage or salary is rising for any or all of the four reasons given above, the position is much more complex. In his early years, a man earns a low salary, and contributions based on this salary accumulate for long periods at compound interest. As time goes on, the pension contributions increase, but the period during which they accumulate interest is declining. Under these conditions, therefore, a much higher rate than the 4 per cent suggested will be necessary in order to provide a pension of two-thirds of final salary.

The purpose of establishing a separate pension fund is to ensure that the obligations incurred can be met, regardless of the fate of the employing firm. If this end is to be achieved, it is necessary to ensure that calculations are made from time to time with a view to seeing that the sums available are keeping step with the obligations of the fund. If there are deficiencies as a result of inflation or other causes, it may be necessary to look again at the contribution rates, and employers may have to make additional capital payments.

It will be apparent that a man who is promoted late in his career will pay smaller pension contributions than one who reaches the same final level in the enterprise, but at a much earlier stage in his career.

150

According to the formula indicated, however, their pensions will be based solely on their total length of service and final salary, and their different career patterns will be ignored. In such cases, the pension a man receives will always represent the full value of his own contributions, but not necessarily the combined contributions. In effect, the employer's contributions are used, as necessary, to bring the pension the individual's contributions would have earned up to the level considered desirable, and a certain amount of cross-subsidization is involved. An employee would only get the exact equivalent of his own and the employer's contributions in exceptional cases. A small employer might, for example, find a pension scheme too complicated and take out an insurance policy on behalf of the worker. He might take out an endowment policy maturing at retiring age (thus giving additional life cover for a the man's wife in the event of his death while still employed). On a larger scale, the FSSU scheme for university teachers allows the employee to choose a policy on which he pays 5 per cent of his salary as a premium and the university pays 10 per cent. Where individual insurance policies are used in this way, the worker receives the exact equivalent of the employer's earmarked contributions.

Transferability. The transferability of pension rights is a very important subject. A man who is considering changing his job may be greatly influenced by the arrangements that may be made regarding his pension rights. We must consider three main possibilities. The first is that the worker who changes his job may not be allowed to retain or transfer his existing pension rights. In this case, he will receive back his own contributions to the pension fund and be able to make use of this money, if he so chooses, for the purchase of an annuity on retirement. He may invest the money and accumulate the interest until the time for retirement comes. On the other hand, he may have to pay some tax on the contributions refunded, these having been a permissible deduction for tax purposes when paid into the pension fund.

The second possibility is that the pension rights a man has acquired in a scheme may be frozen. If, for example, he has worked with a firm for 20 years, and has been earning an average salary of £1600 during his last 3 years, he will be entitled, under the kind of scheme we have considered earlier, to a pension of £400 plus a lump sum of £1200. He will retain his right to receive these benefits from this scheme when he reaches the normal retiring age laid down in the scheme.

The third possibility is that a capital sum will be paid to a new pension scheme on his behalf, and he will then be regarded as holding rights in the new scheme comparable to those he held in the old. In comparing the results of these different approaches, we will assume that where this kind of transfer is made, the worker is treated as having acquired rights based on the full period he has contributed to the first scheme. In our illustration, the worker on going to his new employment will, as soon as he starts work, have the same pension rights as he would have had if he had been working with the firm for 20 years. In practice, matters are not always quite as simple as this because differences in contribution rates, normal retiring age, and so on, may be slightly different. Nevertheless, a full transfer of this kind is, as we shall see, the most satisfactory arrangement for the worker.

Where a man receives back only the contributions he has paid into a pension scheme, he is clearly losing heavily: he receives no benefit from the employer's contributions on his behalf. If he is given frozen pension rights, he may still lose, in so far as these rights will be based on the salary that he was receiving at the time he changed jobs. If he had remained with the same employer for another 20 years, his salary would almost certainly have continued to increase with inflation and the upward trend in real earnings. He might also have secured promotion or continued to move upward on an incremental salary scale. Let us suppose that in his new job he reaches a final salary of £3000 after another 20 years. His pension from his second job will now be £750 plus a lump sum of £2250. He will have, in all, a pension of £1150 and a lump sum of £3450. If, however, a capital sum had been transferred, giving him credit for 20 years' service with the new firm, he would, on retirement, have been entitled to a pension of 40/80 of £3000, that is a pension of £1500 plus £4500 in cash. With full transfer, his participation in the first pension scheme acquires rights for him in the new, based on the salary he finally reaches in his new job. Frozen rights give him, in return for his contributions to the first scheme, a pension based only on the salary he had reached at the time of changing jobs.

From these illustrative figures, it is clear that a man may lose heavily if he changes jobs. The loss involved in the freezing of rights, rather than their transfer, may be significant, but it is nothing to the loss involved in the forfeiture of rights and refund of contributions. In our example, the worker might well have received back about £1300, which would accumulate to, perhaps, £2200 in 20 years, giving him an annuity of about £225, as against a pension of £500

152

and a lump sum of £1500 from frozen rights. Such a loss is clearly a deterrent to the mobility of labour and must be set against any gains from higher pay in a new job.[7]

Sick pay schemes

Sick pay schemes are simpler than pensions to understand, though there is an infinite variety of arrangements possible. Employers may provide schemes that differ in respect of the amount of sick pay, the length of qualifying service, the period for which payment is made, and so on. There may be differences in the degree of formality in the schemes. In some instances, there may be a binding contract or an agreement with the appropriate trade union to give sick pay, while in other cases payment may be entirely at the discretion of the employer. Sick pay schemes may be contributory, or the whole cost may be met by the employer.

The amount of benefit. In many schemes, an employee may be kept on full pay for at least part of the period for which he is entitled to sick pay. Full pay may, however, be subject to the deduction of National Insurance benefits, in whole or in part. For many workers, there is also the question of defining *full pay*. The income related supplement to National Insurance sickness benefit is based on average earnings in the previous tax year. The schemes operated by many employers, however, may be based on a man's basic rate. Some additional payments may be taken into account, such as additions based on merit-rating or seniority, but no account will be taken of overtime earnings or bonuses under payment by results.

A man earning the average wage of £22 5s a week and married with two children would now be entitled to total National Insurance sickness benefit of £13 12s 4d a week after the first fortnight of illness, up to a maximum period of six months. If his employer makes his wage up to his normal earnings, he will have to pay the worker a sum of £8 12s 8d. Some employers, in the past at least, have not bothered to deduct the full amount of National Insurance benefits. Smaller employers may have felt that the work was too much and, if a deduction were to be made, merely took into account the basic benefit (now £4 10s) for a single person. With the introduction of the income related supplement, however, it is probable that more employers will take the view that the full benefit received should be deducted.

If no deduction for National Insurance benefits is made, a man could be better off when sick than when in work. In practice, this may not be so, especially if failure to deduct full benefits is confined to workers whose sick pay is based upon their basic rates rather than normal earnings. In this case, the man earning £22 5s a week may find that his basic rate may be as low as £13 or £14 a week, or even a lot less. If it is £14 a week, he will (with full deduction of National Insurance benefits) get only a few shilllings from his employer, and nothing at all if his basic rate is only £13. If his basic rate is £13 and the employer deducts only the £4 10s National Insurance benefit for a single person, he will receive £8 10s from his employer, which with his total National Insurance benefit will give him £22 2s 4d, or very nearly his normal earnings. We might well find, however, that employers today will at least deduct the income related supplement as well as the basic rate for a single person. It will not be difficult to ascertain what this is because in most cases the employer will have the necessary information in his PAYE records.

In the case of white-collar workers, there is usually little gap between the basic salary and normal earnings, and the employer is likely to be committed to paying such workers a substantial sum in sick pay, even if the full amount of National Insurance benefits is deducted.

Qualifying period for benefit. The most common arrangement is that no qualifying period is necessary before a worker can draw sick pay, if he is covered at all by a sick pay scheme. Where there is a qualifying period, the most common are 6 or 12 months.[8] A higher proportion of women than men are covered by schemes that give immediate benefits, or benefit after relatively short qualifying periods. This is not so much due to any preferential treatment of women as to the fact that women (certainly in so far as covered by sick pay schemes) tend to be employed in those occupations where entitlement to benefit is given immediately or after a short period. Sixty-five per cent of those covered in professional and immediate occupations were entitled to immediate benefit, as against 38 per cent of those in skilled occupations, 22 per cent in semi-skilled occupations, and only 12 per cent in unskilled occupations.

Period of payment. According to the Ministry of Labour report on sick pay schemes, the most common period of benefit is for a period up to 13 weeks. In the case of professional occupations, however, the majority of workers are entitled to a longer period of benefit. Again, the period of entitlement diminishes with the degree of skill. Women appear to be treated more favourably, and, again, this is the result of their employment in those occupations where generous sick pay schemes exist.

154

Redundancy compensation

Redundancy compensation is not simply a matter of providing a worker who loses his job with a source of income while he is looking for another. This is the function of unemployment benefit and, in appropriate cases, supplementary benefit. Redundancy compensation is payable only in those cases where a man loses his job because the employer is forced to contract his output by falling demand, or where the demand for labour is reduced by technological advance. Two things must be done. First, we must examine the reasons for paying redundancy compensation and the consequences of doing so. Second, we must outline the existing arrangements.

The economics of redundancy compensation. In dealing with employers' pension and sick pay schemes, and with National Insurance, we have paid little attention to the case for such arrangements or the consequences of them. It would now be regarded as self-evident that a man cannot help being unemployed or sick, and that he needs an income at such times. Equally, he will normally expect to retire and, again, must provide himself with an income. National Insurance or schemes operated by employers are among the best means of achieving these ends. For the employer, they involve some cost, and we might well think of the wage as including the cost of these fringe benefits, in addition to the normal payment of the worker. In the same way, from the worker's point of view, he receives a reward for the services he renders his employer, partly in a money wage and partly in the form of a right to receive certain benefits when the need arises.

The consequences of these benefits would not appear to be far-reaching. Some people may fear that there will be increased absenteeism when workers are kept on full pay during periods of sickness, or reluctant to find a new job if they receive too generous a level of unemployment benefit. There is, however, little evidence that the unemployed are reluctant to take jobs when they are available. It is, indeed, remarkable that so many willingly continue to work, even when they might be as well off drawing supplementary benefit. There may well be increased absenteeism on the part of workers entitled to sick pay. This is not necessarily undesirable, in so far as it means that men who are not fit to work do not try to carry on because they cannot afford to take time off. Any real malingering is likely to be on a comparatively small scale.

In the case of redundancy compensation, much more complex issues are raised. For example, it is not clear whether compensation is offered because it is felt workers ought to be compensated for the losses they sustain by redundancy or to induce them to accept redundancy. It is true that the two may be linked to some extent. Workers object to redundancy, or to a technological change that may involve redundancy, because they fear they will lose as a result. Compensation for such loss may therefore induce in the workers a greater readiness to accept changes involving redundancy.

Redundancy compensation may be offered on the basis of some such formula as a week's pay for each year of service. Such a formula can only be very approximate in relating the loss of the individual worker to the amount of compensation paid. If a man has worked with a firm for 10 years, he would be entitled to 10 weeks' pay as compensation, perhaps £225 in all. If he has been with them 20 years, he would be entitled to £450 compensation. Is it really true that, in the event of redundancy, the man who has been with the firm 20 years loses more than one who has been with the firm 10 years? There is certainly some truth in the contention that the older a man is, the more difficult it may be for him to adapt to change; beyond a certain age, it may even be difficult for him to find another job. Even if the man is quite adaptable, even if he is prepared to accept a job of much lower status, he may find it difficult to persuade an employer to take him on if he is over 50. Sometimes, it is a case even of too old at 40. This, however, is a matter of age, not length of service. The man with 10 years' service may be older than the one with 20. It may be felt that the firm has, in some way, a special responsibility towards men who have given long service. While this is true, it is also true that men who recently joined the firm might have had an entitlement to substantial redundancy compensation in their former employment. By joining the firm, they have lost that entitlement. Would it not be arguable that, if a firm wants the services of workers, they should not be asked to make sacrifices by accepting employment with it? Yet this is what may well happen under typical redundancy compensation arrangements.

A man who becomes redundant may suffer in two ways. He may be out of work for a period, which may be fairly short or may be prolonged. Much will depend upon the age and abilities of the man concerned, and upon the employment opportunities in the area. The amount of compensation paid, however, will not be related to the period during which the man is out of work. The compensation payment will be the same for a man who becomes redundant and walks straight into a new job, as for one who is out of work for several months. The second way a man loses is when he cannot find new employment which makes use of the specialized skills he

156

possesses and, in consequence, his future earning capacity is reduced. But, again, the amount of compensation bears no relationship to any loss actually incurred by the worker.

The payment of redundancy compensation, while it may not reflect precisely the cost of redundancy to the individual worker, may well make technological change more acceptable. If it does secure a readier and speedier acceptance of new methods of production, it will be in the interest of the community as a whole. Where redundancy arises from falling demand, it merely softens the inevitable blow, except in so far as it encourages the workers to accept redundancy (and so release labour for alternative employment), rather than try to secure short-time working. There is, though, a danger that in certain circumstances redundancy compensation could reduce the mobility of labour. If there were a fear that a firm would be closing down, or at least discharging a proportion of its labour force, a number of workers would, in the absence of redundancy compensation, try to find other jobs before they got their notice. If, however, men were entitled to a few hundred pounds redundancy compensation, they may decide to hang on until they are given notice, in order to qualify for this compensation. Moreover, the more notice a firm gives of impending redundancy, the greater this effect may be and the less is the firm's chance of relying on the normal labour turnover to run down the labour force.

It is also necessary to ask how a firm will react to the need to pay redundancy compensation. This may be different in the case of a firm proposing to introduce labour saving methods and one facing reduced demand. To the former, redundancy compensation adds to the cost of introducing the new method of production. To this extent, it may seem that, while compensation encourages the workers to accept the new methods, it may discourage the employer from going ahead with them. Everything will depend upon how much the employer expects to gain from the new methods. There is no reason why he should be allowed to reap the whole benefit from the new method (or share the gains with the workers he retains and, perhaps, with his customers), while imposing serious losses on those who become redundant.

In the case of the firm faced with declining demand, it is possible that it may prefer to continue in production, perhaps paying fairly low wages and earning only a very small return (if any) for its shareholders, rather than incur the costs of redundancy compensation. It may be that there will be a continuing demand for the firm's

157

products, though on a much reduced scale in the long run. Ideally, the firm should contract and equip itself to meet the reduced demand as efficiently as possible, and pay reasonable wages to its workers and dividends to its shareholders. Yet it may be unable to meet the redundancy compensation, and so may struggle on, relying on the fact that it can attract some labour at low wages; it may perhaps already have written off the capital cost of its plant. Such a situation is hardly desirable. It may be avoided, however, to some extent if part, at least, of the cost of redundancy compensation is met by some kind of insurance rather than be made a direct charge on the firm's earnings. This brings us to the way in which redundancy compensation is organized in Britain at the present time.

The redundancy compensation scheme. A good many firms in Britain may have had redundancy compensation arrangements, often as a result of agreement with the trade unions, when a state scheme was introduced in 1965. While a good many larger firms may have had fairly satisfactory arrangements, a good many workers were probably without any benefit in the event of redundancy. As with pensions, it is very difficult to ensure really complete coverage without some kind of state scheme.

The Government scheme offers compensation to workers who have been with a firm for two years or more. The compensation is based on the worker's length of service and his age. Workers under the age of 18 are not entitled to benefit under the scheme; those between the ages of 18 and 21 receive half a week's pay for each year of service; a man between 21 and 40 a week's pay for each year of service; and a man over 40 a week and a half's pay for each year of service. The scheme is financed by a flat-rate contribution of 10d a week for men and 5d a week for women which is collected as part of the National Insurance stamp. This contribution is paid into the Redundancy Fund, and the greater part of the cost of compensation is then met from the Fund, although the employer has to find a proportion of the compensation himself.

Thus, a man just under 21, who has been earning £20 and has been with a firm for 2 years, would get £20 redundancy compensation. A man of 30, who has been with a firm for 12 years and has been earning £25 a week, would get £300 in compensation. Finally, a man of 50, who has been with his employer for 30 years and has been earning £22 a week, would be entitled to £990.

For men who have been with a firm for a long period, the amount of compensation may be considerable, and the worker may well feel determined to stay with the firm until he is dismissed as redundant rather than forego a useful nest egg. This may be shortsighted, in so far as he may be induced to remain with the firm rather than take an opportunity of alternative employment before he is dismissed. If he waits until he is dismissed, he may not easily find so good an opportunity, or he may even be unemployed for a longish period.

It will be seen that many of the general criticisms made earlier in this chapter apply to the scheme introduced by the Government. The compensation by length of service is, at the best, only a rough and ready measure of the loss that may be entailed for the individual by redundancy. The greater part of the cost is met from an insurance fund, so that the direct cost to the employer is thereby lessened. Any incentive to the employer to hang on to labour, if at all possible, is correspondingly reduced.

NOTES

1. See G. L. Reid and D. J. Robertson, eds., *Fringe Benefits, Labour Costs and Social Security*, Allen and Unwin, London, 1964, p. 99.

2. Widows may, subject to the contribution condition, draw a temporary benefit at an enhanced rate for the first 26 weeks of widowhood. Thereafter, a widow receives no pension if she is under 50. If she has dependent children, she is entitled to widowed mother's allowance, and a pension if she is over 50 when her children cease to be dependent.

3. A man may be assessed as 50 per cent disabled, and be drawing disablement benefit of £3 16s. Although he may be able to undertake some kind of job, the nature of his disablement may be such that it prevents him from undertaking the particular employment for which he has been trained. In this case, he could draw special hardship allowance of up to 61s a week, bringing his total benefit to £6 17s. But a man 80 per cent disabled and getting £6 1s in disablement benefit could not get more than 31s special hardship allowance.

4. Constant attendance allowance is intended to allow payment to be made to somebody who is brought in to look after the disabled person while members of the family get out for necessary business and recreation.

5. National Superannuation and Social Insurance (Cmnd. 3883, 1969).

6. The 4 per cent is purely illustrative and in no sense represents an accurate actuarial calculation.

7. A man whose salary after 20 years was £1600 might have earned an average of £1300 over the whole period and paid 5 per cent of salary in pension contributions.

8. Ministry of Labour, *Sick Pay Schemes: A Report*, London, 1964.

11. The worker in the firm

There is a tendency for economists to think, or at least to write, in terms that suggest the worker is only interested in the wage he receives in return for the services he renders to his employer. In practice, he is interested in a good many other things as well. As we have seen in the last chapter, there may be certain fringe benefits, though it is possible to regard these as some kind of deferred wage – at least in the case of such monetary benefits as pensions, sick pay schemes, and the like. The worker will also be influenced by the environment in which he is working. He will, other things being equal, prefer to work in a modern, pleasant factory rather than in an out of date factory that is dark, ill ventilated, and perhaps dangerous in its layout. He will prefer to work for a firm that is fair in its dealings with its employees, treats them as responsible beings, and consults them, at least when their interests are directly concerned.

Job satisfaction

Ideally, a worker should be able to derive satisfaction from the job he is doing. Some work is pleasant and interesting in itself, other work may tend to be monotonous and repetitive. Even where work is not in itself very attractive, a worker should still be able to feel that, however simple or boring his task may be, he is, nevertheless, making an essential contribution to the finished product. Whether he feels that he is making such a useful contribution to the finished product may depend to a large extent on how he is treated by management. He will derive no satisfaction from a simple repetitive job on the production line if he is made to feel that he is merely an extension of the machine he is operating.

However, the knowledge that the task he is performing is essential to the finished article may not be sufficient for every worker. Some will be happy enough on dull, routine work, especially if the conditions are such as to permit conversation. Workers who have no

F*

great abilities will at least derive an income from doing a simple job, a measure of satisfaction from doing a necessary job, and, perhaps, a further measure of satisfaction from the companionship that the job brings – it has been suggested that this latter factor is often the most important inducement for married women to take up employment. On the other hand, a dull repetitive task will not satisfy the worker of greater ability. The man of high intelligence will want a job where he can make use of his abilities; the able craftsman will want to use his manual skills, and not just perform the same operation again and again throughout each working day.

Selection. The adoption of adequate selection procedures is to the advantage of both management and the worker. A firm should be interested in knowing whether a man is capable of properly performing the job for which he has applied. For many jobs, a period of training may be necessary after the worker has been engaged, and it is wasteful to employ a man only to discover, perhaps halfway through the training period, that he is not up to the standard required. There are various ways of discovering the abilities of the applicant. He may have written a letter of application giving details of his previous experience, he may be asked about this at interview, or references may have been received from previous employers. Such sources have their value, but there are obvious drawbacks. A man's own account of his abilities may be biased; a reference may not be very helpful, unless prospective employer knows the former one, and knows whether he is likely to be accurate in his assessments, or whether he will be inclined to give unduly glowing references or, on the other hand, to be grudging in his recognition of merit. Because of these weaknesses, other methods of assessing suitability for a job may be employed. Various kinds of tests have been devised by psychologists, and others, to try to discover whether the worker possesses the specific abilities that are required for a particular job.

The firm will not merely be interested in ensuring that the worker possesses certain minimum qualifications. A man of great ability will be frustrated in a job that does not offer adequate scope for his ability, and this may interfere with his efficiency in the long run. Selection procedures that match the worker's ability to the requirements of the job can equally be used to ensure that a man is not employed in a job that is so much below his capabilities that he is dissatisfied, a situation that may be unprofitable to the firm as well as frustrating to the worker.

Job enlargement. The division of labour has greatly increased the productivity of labour. It has, moreover, been carried to very great

162

lengths since Adam Smith described its application to pinmaking. We have already referred to the frustration a worker may feel if employed in a job that does not offer enough scope for his abilities. Where the division of labour is carried to extreme lengths, there is a danger that the job will be frustrating for almost any worker of normal intelligence. Even where a job calls for a certain degree of skill, it may still be so circumscribed in its content as to be frustrating. Industrial psychologists have suggested that, from the worker's point of view, it would be desirable for the content of a job to be enlarged so that it matched the worker's ability. This, of course, is contrary to the trend which has been evident since the days of the Industrial Revolution, with the division of labour being carried to ever greater lengths, and the content of particular jobs more closely specified.

In the managerial field, job enlargement may be a relatively simple matter. If a senior executive has a couple of assistants, he may delegate to them such tasks as lie within their capabilities. Where the numbers are small, it may be quite easy to give a man more responsibility, if he proves that he is ready for it. It is much more difficult to see much scope for this kind of thing when very large numbers of operatives are involved. Nevertheless, there is, here, a very real problem which may well become one of increasing importance.

Promotion opportunities. The firm should try to ensure that the man it selects for a job has the right qualities. He must possess certain minimum abilities, but it would be almost as unsatisfactory to employ a man who was overqualified as one who was underqualified. When a young man joins a firm, he may be given a job which is suitable, in the light of his abilities *at the time*. In 5 or 10 years, he may be capable of work at a much higher level, and it is important that he should be given the opportunity, if possible, of performing such work. This need not mean promotion to a job defined as having higher status. An executive officer in the Civil Service, or a detective constable, may gradually be given more difficult assignments as they mature and acquire experience. This will happen long before the stage is reached where they are ready for promotion to higher executive officer or to detective sergeant.

There will be a limit to the responsibility that a man may be allowed to exercise within a named job. Take, for example, a teacher without any post of special responsibility. At first, his work may be closely supervised. As time goes on, he may prove that he can be trusted to get on with the routine work of teaching his subject

163

without any close supervision. He may be given a share of the work of teaching classes at a higher level or in years where more is at stake.[1] Nevertheless, so long as he does not hold a post of special responsibility, there is a limit to the work that can be assigned him. The overall responsibility of organizing the teaching of a subject throughout the school will rest with a teacher who is specially appointed for this purpose, and paid accordingly. Any worker has an immediate superior, and the limit to the responsibilities that can be exercised by the worker is to be found in the role of this superior. If a man shows himself capable of undertaking the same degree of responsibility as his immediate superior, the solution is for him to be promoted. The question that arises is whether there will be opportunities within the enterprise for his promotion or whether he will have to seek promotion elsewhere. In some big firms, or in the nationalized industries or the Civil Service, a man may normally expect to remain with the same organization throughout his career.[2] In other fields, like teaching, promotion may normally involve finding a job with a fresh employer, unless a promotional opportunity happens to occur at just the right time.

There is clearly no reason why the job structure of an enterprise should be such as to allow men to be promoted at just the time when they are capable of exercising the necessary degree of responsibility. Consider, for example, the job structure in university teaching. (Although legally each university is a separate employer, it is convenient to think of the opportunities over the universities as a whole.) There are four grades: professors, readers or senior lecturers,[3] lecturers, and assistant lecturers. At present, senior posts, that is, professors, readers and senior lecturers, are limited to 30 per cent of the teaching staff. We may, for practical purposes, think of just two grades, a senior grade and lecturers. (Assistant lecturers are really a probationary grade and promotion to lecturer is more or less automatic if the individual acquits himself satisfactorily.)

If we assume that all university teachers start their careers at age 25 and retire at 65, and that there is no wastage between recruitment and retirement, that all entrants to the profession are worthy of promotion to one of the senior grades, then, on average, lecturers might expect promotion at age 53. To the extent that some men were promoted earlier, a number would have to wait longer for promotion. The vital questions are: (a) At what age are most men ready for promotion to one of the senior grades? (b) How many men are suitable for any promotion? To the extent that there are men who could never expect to be promoted to a senior grade, other men will have opportunities of earlier promotion. Even so, a situation may easily develop where more men are ready for promotion than there are senior jobs for them to fill.

In stable conditions, an approach to equilibrium may be reached by trying to adjust the nature of the different jobs so as to make best use of the available supply of workers. If, in general, there are too few men capable of taking the top level jobs, the organizational structure of an enterprise or service will have to be altered so that the top men are relieved of unnecessary routine work and are able to concentrate on those tasks which use their abilities to the full. If there are plenty of men who could be promoted to a higher grade, there is less need to do this, and it may be preferable to allow the more widespread sharing of responsibility.

A particularly serious problem may arise when there is rapid expansion or contraction. Let us return to our university example, but now suppose that men may expect promotion, if at all, somewhere between the ages of 35 and 55. Suppose that over a 10-year period there has been a 10 per cent expansion of teaching staffs. This would mean, still assuming no wastage after recruitment, a 40 per cent increase in the annual rate of recruitment. During the 10 years of expansion, a 10 per cent increase may have been made in the numbers in senior posts. Even if there are no promotions below the age of 35, a good many men may have been promoted at an earlier age than would otherwise have been the case. In the immediate future, the number of retirements from senior posts will be related the original level of recruitment, whereas the numbers in the age groups where promotion is expected will be related to the 40 per cent higher level of recruitment. Promotion prospects have thus deteriorated seriously, and under such conditions morale could be low. This may be the case, even where the higher rate of recruitment is maintained. This, however, implies a continuing increase in total numbers. If there has been an attempt to expand total staff by 10 per cent over a 10-year period, recruitment thereafter may fall back to 110 per cent of the original level. In this case, the promotion prospects of staff recruited during the period of expansion would be particularly poor.

Equitable payment

Many people will be ready to accept not only the idea that a worker should be given a job commensurate with his abilities, but also the idea that pay ought to be related to the level of work undertaken.[4]

165

Although the economist may explain wages in general by supply and demand relationships, and wage differences by the varying relationships between supply and demand in particular cases, the ordinary person still believes that the man whose work involves greater skill or responsibility *ought* to be paid more. It is, of course, difficult to discover the extent to which this is a genuinely independent belief, or how far it is a rationalization of the existing situation, in which workers are paid more for skill and responsibility because those capable of acquiring the necessary skills or exercising responsibility are relatively scarce.

Elliott Jaques has devoted considerable attention to the question of what constitutes equitable payment, and has linked this study to his own approach to the distinct question of measuring the level of work. Whereas most people are content to make intuitive guesses about which jobs are comparable in skill and responsibility, or to use job evaluation which necessarily involves elements of subjective judgement, Jaques believes that in the *time span of discretion* he has a unique and objective measure.

Job evaluation. This is a process whereby the various elements of a job (different skills, acquired knowledge, responsibility, and so on) are each rated and an overall rating for the job obtained. It is a subjective process in two respects. First, although most practitioners would have little difficulty in saying that one job was more demanding than another, either in regard to manual skill or responsibility or any other element, they would have some difficulty in quantifying the difference: this is very much a matter of personal judgement. Second, the different elements in the job have to be weighted, and this, again, is a matter for judgement. There is no objective way of saying what is the relative importance of the different elements involved.

When a firm's wage or salary structure is based on job evaluation, it is usual to find certain key jobs where the rates paid by the firm are in line with the general level of payments for such jobs in the local labour market. From these key rates, a curve is drawn relating pay to the job evaluations. Where a higher rate for a job is indicated, all workers on that job will receive this rate. Where the rate indicated is lower, the rate for the job will be lowered, but workers already employed on the job will retain their present rates as personal rates.

Time span of discretion. Jaques believes that the level of work is associated with the exercise of discretion on the part of the worker. The higher the level of work, the greater is the amount of discretion the worker is given in the performance of his job. Jaques himself cites the case of a job where all elements of discretion had been removed. Women were required to watch electric light bulbs and to reject those with broken filaments. Because the response was purely automatic and no element of discretion remained, the job was unpopular, despite the unusually high wages for a job with no real responsibility. In the end, a machine was designed to take over from human operators.[5]

Jaques distinguishes between work which is marginally substandard and that which is blatantly so. It may be quite obvious to a worker's immediate superior that he is grossly incompetent, but marginally substandard work is much harder to detect, and will often only be discovered indirectly. Marginally substandard components may only be detected when they come to be used; a time study engineer's work is shown up as suspect when his services are too much in demand by those on the job (because his rates tend to be loose, or he is the subject of complaint (because his rates are too tight). It is important to remember that speed, as well as quality, may be important in the exercise of discretion. A worker who exercises his discretion by deciding to work very carefully may do a perfect job, for example, producing certain articles in the factory, but his output may be so low, as a result of the care exercised, that his performance is quite unacceptable.

Jaques defines the *time span of discretion* as the period during which marginally substandard discretion could be exercised before it would be detected by a superior.

Time span and equitable payment. Jaques further believes that there is a definite relationship between the time span of discretion and the level of equitable payment. His idea of what is equitable is based upon what people believe to be fair, and he claims that, in inquiries he has made, people give the same rate as being a fair one for a particular job they are doing, regardless of whether they are being paid this rate or some higher or lower rate. There must inevitably be doubts about the validity of this procedure. Even if the results obtained by Jaques are repeated over most of industry, there is no reason to suppose that there is necessarily a unique relationship between the time span of discretion and the level of pay that is considered equitable for different jobs. The relationship observed at any particular time may be largely a reflection of what has been usual, and imply no deeper feeling that this particular relationship is a just one.

The kind of relationship that Jaques believes he has discovered is

167

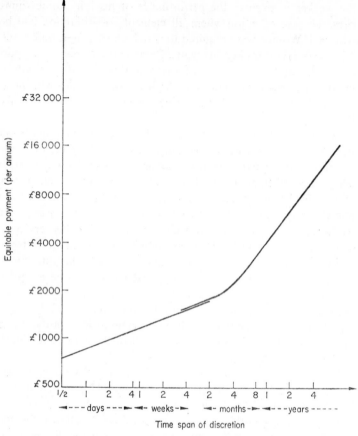

Fig. 11.1. Equitable payment and the time span of discretion.

shown in Fig. 11.1. The graph is plotted on double logarithmic
scales. The earlier part of the curve is fairly straight, indicating that
a given proportionate change in the time span of discretion is
accompanied always by the same proportionate change in the level
of pay that is felt to be fair. Over the earlier part of the range, the
doubling of the time span of discretion may be accompanied by an
increase of perhaps 10 per cent in the level of equitable pay. At
about the one-month level of discretion, there is an overlap between
two disconnected parts of the curve. This is around the level at
which a change may occur from jobs which carry overtime pay to
jobs where no special payment is made if extra hours have to be
worked, and the latter type of job carries a higher equitable level
168

of payment. Around the six-month time span, the slope of the curve increases, and from about the one year level onwards, the slope of the straight line is such that a doubling of the time span is accompanied by a doubling of the level of pay that is considered fair.[6]

Actual pay. Jaques contends that workers will be dissatisfied or uneasy if their actual pay is very different from the equitable level. It is easy enough to understand that the worker who is paid less than he considers a fair wage will feel dissatisfied. It is suggested that a level of pay 5 per cent below what is considered fair will begin to give rise to serious feelings of discontent, and that a wider difference will lead to increasingly low morale until a difference of perhaps 15 per cent will cause a fair number of workers to start looking for other jobs.

It is not so easy to see, at first, why a worker should worry if he is paid more than he regards as a fair rate for the job he is doing. If, however, the rate he is receiving is out of line with the general level of pay in the particular enterprise for the level of work, he will be aware of this, and it may cause him to feel a little uneasy. He may also feel that there is a danger that he will be asked to undertake some job where the demands are more in line with the level of pay he is receiving, but he may feel afraid that he will not be able to cope with such a job.

The ideal situation is one where there is equality between the actual level of pay, the equitable level, and a man's capacity to work. Even if the level of pay represents a fair reward for the job a man is doing, he may still feel frustrated if his capacity is such that he could undertake a more demanding job. This idea was introduced earlier in this chapter, and Jaques merely offers the time span of discretion as a suitable measure of the level of work in a particular job and in the job a man might be just capable of doing. The situation where the job is below a man's capacity is tolerable if there is a prospect of promotion in the near future. Again, it would be tolerable for a man to be paid the fair rate for his capacity, even though for a time he were engaged on a less demanding job. Finally, of course, the case where a man is getting the rate that is appropriate to the job, but his capacity is below that required, is clearly an unsatisfactory state of affairs, and will come to light in the normal course of events.

Criticisms of Jaques's ideas. The idea of the time span of discretion as a measurement of the level of work is an interesting one, and may well have practical applications. There are other aspects of Jaques's work which are valuable. He has, for example, placed considerable emphasis on the desirability of employing a man in a job that fully utilizes his abilities, and the use of earnings progression data to show the likely growth in a man's capacity over the years and the increase in his earnings that ought to accompany this growth in capacity. Nevertheless, the basic idea that the level of work is *uniquely* measured by the time span of discretion is suspect.

It is certainly arguable that, if one compares two fairly similar jobs, a longer time span of discretion implies that, in this case, one is placing a greater trust in the workman. In a sense, therefore, time span *is* a measure of the degree of responsibility. It is by no means certain that the level of work is something to be measured in a single dimension. The trust that must be placed in the worker over a short or a long period is one element, but there are surely other dimensions to the level of work? Could not two jobs have the same time span of discretion, but one involve greater physical effort than the other? Or could one job call for a greater measure of manual skill or acquired knowledge and mental skills to be used on the job, although the time span is the same? Does the seriousness of the consequences of marginally substandard work alter the intensity of responsibility, even when the time spans of discretion in different jobs vary? It may take the same time for marginally substandard work to come to light, but in one job a very slight error could carry minor financial consequences, whereas, in another, they could be great; or the cost might be measured in human lives. According to Jaques, the attraction of the time span of discretion as the measure of the level of work is that it is capable of objective determination. That may be, but if the level of work is really multidimensional, the objective measurement of one dimension alone may be more misleading than a subjective judgement based on all the dimensions. Time span measurement may therefore be useful, but it may be preferable to use it in comparing jobs in one field.

This would rule out the use of time span of discretion as the basis of an incomes policy, a proposal that has been made by Jaques, or as any kind of criterion for assessing the comparability of jobs in different fields.

The concept of equitable payment is also an uncertain one. Undoubtedly, the economist ought to take account of what people believe to be fair levels of payment. What is 'felt fair', however, may be largely determined by what is commonly paid in practice. An investigation based on a single enterprise might be unsatisfactory, in so far as most wages paid might be accepted as fair, and only those be regarded as unfair where the level of payment was lower than the general level for work of comparable skill or responsibility. If one made a survey covering many different firms in a large town, there might emerge no clear pattern of equitable payment, such as is depicted in Fig. 11.1.

The need for rational pay structures

The economist may think that all wages and salaries are determined by the interaction of the forces of supply and demand. In a sense, they are, but not in a perfectly competitive market. As we have seen, the labour market is rendered imperfect, both by frictions and by the existence of monopolistic elements on both sides of the market. There is, therefore, no reason to suppose that the market differentials are ideal, or that to set out to establish what appears to be a logical wage and salary structure is to interfere with a market mechanism that left to itself would bring about an optimum allocation of resources.

There would seem therefore to be a case for establishing differentials in a firm, which give recognition to greater skill and responsibility, and for setting up a structure which gives more or less comparable pay to workers who would be thought of as working at the same level. A rational structure would be more easily obtained if less reliance were placed on payment by results bonuses and more on time rates of pay. The time span of discretion might be used, to some extent, in establishing a rational wages and salary structure, along with schemes for job evaluation and merit rating. There is no one technique that can provide all the answers.

NOTES

1. This could mean classes taking outside examinations, though it is arguable that some earlier classes, where preparatory work is done, may in fact be more important to the final success of the pupil.

2. In the general grades of the Civil Service, however, men may be transferred from one department to another on promotion.

3. Readers are usually appointed in recognition of outstanding scholarship, whereas senior lecturers may be appointed in recognition of contributions made to a university in teaching or administration.

4. There are also related questions of what is a fair rate of pay for a given effort by the worker, and what represents a fair day's work. The student wishing to pursue these questions should read H. Behrend, 'The Effort Bargain', *Industrial and Labour Relations Review*, 10, 1957 and 'A Fair Day's Work', *Scottish Journal of Political Economy*, VIII, 1961.

5. E. Jaques, *Equitable Payment*, Heinemann, London, 1961, p. 74.

6. No great accuracy is claimed for the graph as drawn. It is based on the graph in Jaques' *Equitable Payment*, with a rough and ready adjustment for changes in wages between 1958 and 1968.

Part 3

Organized Labour

12. Trade union organization

Types of union

There are three main types of union in Britain today, the craft union, the industrial union, and the general union. The craft union, as its name implies, is intended to organize men who belong to the same craft, irrespective of the industry in which they are working. Thus, membership of the Electrical Trade Union (ETU) and the Amalgamated Engineering and Foundry Workers (AEF) is to be found in a great many different industries.

These unions, however, are no longer craft unions, in the original sense that they organized only skilled men, those who had served an apprenticeship in a particular craft. These unions may still attach a special importance to the conditions of craftsmen, but they have tended to open their membership to less highly skilled workers in the electrical and engineering industries.

Second, there are the industrial union aims at organizing all workers in one industry. One of the best examples of an industrial union is the National Union of Mineworkers (NUM). Apart from a small number of deputies and others who have their own association, no other union has a foothold in the mining industry, so, for all practical purposes, the NUM is all powerful. On the railways, the National Union of Railwaymen (NUR) also aims at organizing all grades, but, in fact, succeeds in recruiting only a minority of footplatemen and white collar workers. The majority of the former belong to the Associated Society of Locomotive Engineers and Firemen (ASLEF) and the latter to the Transport Salaried Staffs Association (TSSA).

The rivalry between ASLEF and the NUR has at times led to serious disputes on the railways. In 1955, the former was claiming higher pay for its members with the specific objective of widening the differential of the footplatemen over other railway workers. The latter, in which the other workers predominated, resisted this claim, and British Railways were in the unhappy position in which whatever

175

they did would lead to trouble. If the claim were rejected, ASLEF would strike; if they conceded the claim, the NUR would immediately put in a counter-claim to narrow the differential again, and so on. The issue was only resolved after the appointment of a court of inquiry, following strike action by ASLEF. In more recent years, there has been trouble over proposals for guards (who belong to the NUR) riding in the driver's cabin on diesel locomotives.[1]

Finally, there are the general unions, the Transport and General Workers Union (TGWU) and the National Union of General and Municipal Workers (NUMGW). These unions seek to organize workers, mostly unskilled, in a wide variety of industries. In building, for example, separate craft unions organize such craftsmen as bricklayers, woodworkers, plumbers, and so on, while the TGWU organizes the labourers. On the other hand, the TGWU has important areas where it is the predominant union. Thus, it is the main union organizing workers in municipal transport and, of course, in the docks.

Union organization

The typical union has the branch as the fundamental unit of organization. The branch tends to be a geographical unit rather than one based on the place of work: it may cover an area such as a small town, or, in a large town, there may be several. In either case, however, the branch is likely to include several establishments in which the union has members. Only in exceptional circumstances, is it likely that the branch will coincide with the workplace, for example, in coalmining, where the NUM has no interests outside mining, and where the pit probably serves as a convenient geographical unit. In printing, too, the union or 'chapel' as it is known, may coincide with a place of work.

The branch will normally have its officers, elected from among the branch membership; these will include a chairman, secretary, and treasurer, and there may be other officers and a committee. Usually, the branch officers will only work part-time at their union duties. They have to earn their living in a job, like the rank and file members, though they may sometimes be allowed some time off to attend to union business. Only in the case of a very large branch is there likely to be a full-time secretary. An exception is the National Union of Seamen (NUS) where the branch secretary is a full-time official who is in charge of the union office at a port. In this case, there would clearly be difficulties in relying on the usual lay officials

176

to run a branch, since one or more of them might be away from the country for months on end.

National level organization. The ultimate control of most unions rests with the annual conference (or, sometimes, a biennial conference). This conference is generally composed of delegates who are elected by the branches or areas. In the case of a union like the TGWU, there may be a more complicated procedure, which gives representation to the different trades or industries, as well as geographical areas. The authority of the conference extends to such matters as the amendment of the union rules. It may instruct its executive committee or officers to proceed with wage claims, though, in the last resort, the decision whether to accept or reject a settlement offered by the employers has to be left to the executive. Conference could make such a decision only in an exceptional case, where a settlement had been negotiated just at the time Conference met.

Between conferences, the affairs of the union are controlled by the executive committee and the senior full-time officials of the union, subject, in some cases, to provisions for the calling of an extraordinary delegate conference. The executive committee is composed in the main of lay members, that is, ordinary union members who are earning their living as engineers or railwaymen, and the like, rather than full-time union workers.

A key figure in most unions is the general secretary. The general secretary is elected by the membership, often for a limited period of years, but sometimes until retirement. The difference can be important: a man who is elected to serve until he is due to retire can pursue a much more independent line of action than one who has to look to the rank and file for reelection after five years. In particular, he can take a much longer-term view, having less need to concentrate on short-term results to impress his electors.

The general secretary has control of the union's full-time staff and, probably, the union journal. He has continuous access to information, and, above all, the time to keep abreast of developments. If he cannot always do as he would like, he is at least better placed than the lay members of his executive, who hold down ordinary jobs as well as carrying out their union activities. However, it would be wrong to attach too much importance to his role, for, while he is in a very powerful position to influence his executive or conference, he cannot overrule their wishes.

Intermediate levels of organization. The national level of organization is, in fact, the union as a whole and, as such, it is indispensable. Although most unions make the branch their basic unit of organization, and it is to the branch that the member belongs in the first instance, there are exceptional cases where the branch does not exist. Where numbers are very small, as in the case of the Merchant Navy and Airlines Officers Association, it may be convenient to recruit members directly into a national organization. It is, however, sometimes necessary to have an organizational level between the branch and the union at national level, and the nature of that organization will depend upon the size and character of the union.

The case for the establishment of some kind of intermediate organization arises from the fact that particular areas or districts have their own special problems. It is appropriate, therefore, that district or area committees (if necessary both) should exist to undertake negotiations about matters that are of a local interest, but extend beyond the area served by a single branch. The district or area committee would be a predominantly lay body, elected by the local union membership.

There are often full-time officers at a district or area office. These men would be called upon to undertake the work of negotiation on local issues, they would also be called in when a dispute arises at a place of work involving the interpretation, or an alleged contravention, of some local or, perhaps, national agreement. In so far as the interpretation of national agreements is concerned, any disputes arising would be dealt with by officials employed by the national office of the union. For convenience, such men would be stationed at offices throughout the country, but they would remain answerable to headquarters and the national executive, not to a local committee. If negotiation may be involved, however, it is clearly preferable that the union's full-time staff in the area should be answerable to a committee elected by union members in that area. Even if no negotiation is involved, it could be argued that it is preferable that full-time officials should be answerable directly to the men they are serving. This is ensured both by having a lay committee in charge, and insisting that full-time area officers should be elected by the area membership, in much the same way as the general secretary is elected.

We have seen already that in the case of the TGWU membership of the annual delegate conference has to ensure representation not only of different parts of the country, but of the different trades organized by the union. The union has, in fact, a dual system of organization at levels between the headquarters and the branch. As well as the usual kind of intermediate organization to serve different areas, there is a similar machinery, with its own officers, to cater for the needs of the different trade groups.

Shopfloor organization. In addition to the hierarchical branch, district and/or area, and national organization, many unions now have some kind of organization at the shopfloor level. Often, however, such an organization does not fit easily into the main organization structure of the union. The role of the shop steward is not always clearly defined, and there is a danger that, even where defined, the definition will not always be heeded.

We have seen already that a branch may include all members of the union living or working in a small or medium-sized town. It is understandable that a branch meeting does not usually attract a big attendance, most members being reluctant to go back out again after getting home from work. It is, therefore, in the interests of the unions to appoint stewards in different workplaces who are responsible for collecting the union subscriptions. In some cases, this is the only authorized function of the steward.

In many cases, however, the steward has other functions, whether they are formally recognized or not. He is the representative of the union at the shopfloor level. If there is a dispute between a worker and his immediate superior, the shop steward will be the union representative who is called upon in the first place to act on behalf of the member who thinks he has a grievance. If the shop steward cannot secure a satisfactory settlement, the normal procedure is to call in a full-time union official from the district or area office who takes the matter up at a higher level, with management. The important point is that, in almost every instance, the union rule book places severe restrictions on the powers of the shop steward. Above all, he does not have the authority to call a strike if he does not get a satisfactory answer from management. The authority to call a strike may be invested in the branch, the district, or even the national executive.

In general, the stewards do not have negotiating functions. For the most part, agreements are made at the national level, though when there is extensive use of payment by results schemes a good many issues may arise at plant level. For example, a rate per hour may be fixed for payment by results workers, but the time allowed for a particular job, and therefore the opportunities for earning bonuses, must be fixed locally, in relation to the conditions in the particular plant. In practice, shop stewards frequently take part in discussions on such matters.[2] Moreover, the shop stewards are in much closer contact with the workers on the shopfloor than any members of the official union hierarchy. There may be a shop stewards' committee which includes all the stewards of different

179

unions throughout the works. This will be a powerful body, and will be able to exert a much greater influence on the rank and file at a particular workplace than the official leadership of the union. For this reason, the shop stewards may be very much more powerful, in practice, than the union rule books would suggest. There are numerous examples of shop stewards disregarding official union policy, especially in the matter of leading unofficial strikes.

If shop stewards are sometimes troublemakers, the management may not always be blameless. A shop steward has a difficult job: although a worker in the plant, he also has to serve as a representative of his fellow workers, and this may make him unpopular with management. If management proves particularly obstructive, or even victimizes the stewards, it is obvious that most men will be reluctant to take the job, and leave it to those who want the opportunity to make trouble.

The Trade Union Congress

The Trade Union Congress is the central organization of the Trade Union movement in Britain. The majority of unions are affiliated to the TUC but by no means all. A number of associations of white collar workers have, in the past, been reluctant to affiliate, but this is something which is changing. On the other hand, some unions of manual workers remain outside the TUC and are not greatly handicapped by their non-affiliation. Compared with the central union organization in some other countries, the TUC in Britain is relatively weak. A union that disregards certain rules may be expelled, but it is unlikely to suffer seriously in consequence, so the sanction of expulsion is not all that powerful. The TUC cannot, as can its counterpart LO in Sweden, exert a strong influence on the negotiating policy of its member unions. What influence it can exert is through persuasion. The knowledge, in the period up to 1950, that most unions were prepared to give a measure of support, even though limited, to the policy of wage restraint may have persuaded some unions to moderate their demands at the time.

The annual Congress is held each autumn. It is attended by delegations representing the affiliated unions, and is, above all, a forum at which trade unionists can discuss a wide range of issues about which they feel strongly. The discussions cover the general economic situation and problems of immediate concern to workers as a whole or to particular groups, but they also extend to much wider matters including international affairs. As well as the delegations from affiliated unions, fraternal delegates from trade unions in other countries, and from the Labour Party – to which most of the British unions are also affiliated – are also present. A general council is elected, and it is the General Council of the TUC which, between Congresses, speaks on behalf of the British trade union movement as a whole.

In addition to the Congress providing trade unionists with a forum at which they can discuss matters of common concern, the TUC is a body which can speak at any time on behalf of trade unions as a whole, especially in discussions with the Government or with the Confederation of British Industry, representing employers. Although, hitherto, trade unions have fought to maintain their autonomy in all matters relating to collective bargaining, there are matters of wider concern which arise in discussions both with the Government and employers. General factory legislation, or changes in the law relating to trade unions, and so on, are clearly matters to be dealt with by the TUC rather than by individual unions. Moreover, there are many matters on which the formulation of views is not easy unless one has expert knowledge. It is usual, for example, for the TUC to make representations to the Chancellor of the Exchequer at Budget time. If such representations are to be more than ill-informed expressions of opinion, it is necessary for the TUC to find out as much as it can about the current economic situation, and, for this purpose, it has its own research staff.

There have been suggestions that the TUC should play a bigger role in the field of collective bargaining. With the introduction of an incomes policy in 1964, the TUC began to think in terms of setting up its own wage-claim vetting machinery, and has, indeed, gone some way in this direction. The machinery would depend for its efficacy entirely upon the willingness of the constituent unions to cooperate. There has so far been no suggestion of giving the TUC any more powerful sanction against recalcitrant unions than those it already possesses. Indeed, there has been no suggestion that failure to collaborate in the TUC's incomes policy machinery should carry any penalty at all. In practice, however, the machinery has not been tested, for, as we shall see, the Government has assumed gradually stronger and stronger powers as it faced one crisis after another.

Trade unions and the law
There are a number of issues which have to be considered in relation to the trade unions and the law. As a preliminary, a little must be said about the contract of employment between the worker and his

181

employer. Then, it is necessary to consider the law relating to strike action by trade unions, and, finally, to consider the legal relationships between unions and their members.

The contract of employment. In law, a contract of employment is made between the individual workman and his employer. The workman undertakes to render certain services to his employer in return for an agreed rate of remuneration. The contract need not be in writing. Any terms agreed verbally will be binding, though, in the event of a dispute, there are obvious advantages in a written contract. If the contract is a verbal one, there are bound to be arguments during a dispute over what was really agreed. Often, however, there may not even be an explicit verbal agreement. A man may be hired on the tacit understanding that he will be paid the usual rate for the job in question. If any dispute were to arise in such a case, the court would have to decide what was the usual rate: this would be a question of fact to be determined.

The contract of employment provides for notice to be given by either side to terminate it. If no agreement is made to the contrary, it will be presumed that the usual custom of the industry applies. Normally, a weekly paid man is entitled to, and required to give, a week's notice. In some cases, there has customarily been a shorter period of notice. In building, for example, a man could be given a few hour's notice, when paid on a Friday, that his services were no longer required on Monday morning, but once that deadline was passed, he would know that he would be employed for the rest of the next week. The law now requires that workers who have been in continuous employment with the same firm for two years or more are entitled to a minimum of two weeks' notice of dismissal, though no change has been made in their obligation to give notice. Workers paid by the month are normally entitled to, and required to give, at least a month's notice.

The collective bargains made by trade unions and individual employers or employers' associations are not regarded as legally enforceable contracts. Quite apart from any other consideration, the parties concerned do not intend to create a legally enforceable contract, but prefer to rely upon other sanctions, if this should be necessary. Nevertheless, in certain circumstances, the terms of the collective bargain might be regarded as part of the contract of employment. We have seen already that a man may be hired on the terms usual in the industry. If these are normally fixed by collective bargaining, any collective agreement will create an implied term in the contract of employment.

182

If the contract of employment is broken, either party can sue for damages. If a worker is not paid the wage he thinks he is entitled to, he can sue in the courts in the ordinary way. Similarly, he can sue if he is dismissed without the notice to which he is entitled. It is equally open to the employer to sue if he is harmed by a breach of contract on the part of his workers. If a worker leaves without notice, he can be sued for damages; and the employer could sue every single worker who broke his contract by strike action, though this is unlikely to be worth while for three reasons. First, it might be inconvenient and costly to sue a large number of workers, for, even if the case succeeded, it might be impracticable to recover either costs or damages. Second, any union is likely to refuse to allow a return to work while such action was pending. Third, it must be noted that, in regard to a breach of the contract of employment, the courts will only entertain an action for damages and will not order the specific enforcement of the contract.

The right to strike. Before 1825, membership of a trade union was illegal. After that date, no worker could be prosecuted for forming or joining a union, but there remained uncertainty about the legality of the action which might be taken to secure the objectives of the union. Legislation in 1875 clarified the position regarding criminal liability. No crime of conspiracy would arise unless any action taken was in itself criminal. Provided no criminal act were committed, the activities of a trade union could only be the subject of proceedings in the civil courts.

It is, of course, evident that trade unions are likely to be involved in actions which are wrongful in law. It is, for example, a tortious (wrongful) act to induce one person to break his contract with another, and the injured person has the right to institute proceedings, either against the other party to the contract (for breach of contract) or against the third party for the tort of inducing a breach of contract. Moreover, it would be more convenient for an employer to proceed against a union or union official for inducing a breach of contract instead of against each individual workman who is in breach of contract.[3] Since a strike may easily involve a breach of contract, the possibility of such actions for damages being brought against the union would constitute a serious limitation on its powers to bargain. When, therefore, the courts decided in the Taff Vale judgement at the beginning of the century that registered trade unions could be sued, Parliament subsequently passed new legislation in the Trade Disputes Act, 1906.

The 1906 Act provided that no trade union could be sued in tort (other than those arising from the use of trade union property). The immunity is a sweeping one, and undoubtedly puts the trade unions in a highly privileged position. The immunity does not apply merely to the particular tort of inducing a breach of contract, but to all wrongful actions. Thus, one could not recover damages against a trade union for a libel published in a trade union journal.[4] On the other hand, a much more limited immunity is given to trade union officials and members. They are immune from proceedings in tort where they are acting in the course of a trade dispute. So long as they act in the course of a trade dispute, they may not be sued for inducing other workers to break their contracts of employment, or for making slanderous remarks about an employer. A trade dispute might be deemed to include sympathetic strike action, but in any situation where it could be held that no trade dispute existed, individual officials and members have the same legal liabilities as anyone else.

Unions and their members. There are three matters that we must consider under this heading, the political activities of trade unions, the closed shop, and the right to expel members.

The present state of the law relating to political activities on the part of trade unions is that, if the union wishes to support candidates at local or Parliamentary elections, it must set up a special fund for this purpose, and objectors have the right to contract out of contributing. It is clearly reasonable that an institution like a trade union, which it may be argued, all workers ought to join and may be under considerable pressure to do so, should not be allowed to compel its members to contribute towards the support of a particular political party. Many people would argue that the present law is unsatisfactory, and that it would be preferable to require those wishing to pay the political levy to contract in, as was the case between 1927 and 1945.

The closed shop means, strictly speaking, that only members of a particular union may be recruited to certain jobs. The term is often wrongly applied to the more common *union shop*, where union membership is not a condition of recruitment, but, once recruited, a worker is expected to join the appropriate union within a specified period, unless already a member. There is a feeling in some quarters that the union shop (and still more the closed shop) is undesirable. Many people feel that trade unions ought to remain voluntary associations, that a man should not be denied the opportunity to earn his livelihood because he does not wish to join a union. In opposition to this view, the unions maintain that the non-unionist accepts bene-

184

fits for which union members have made sacrifices, and that he should not be allowed to get away with this. In practice, the non-unionists rarely weaken the bargaining position of the union. In those cases where a fight for the closed or union shop is likely, the union probably has already a near 100 per cent membership, and it is the small minority of non-members who arouse resentment. The issue is unlikely to arise where there is significant non-membership.

The question of the right to membership is closely linked with that of the union shop. If the worker can be refused membership, and still more important, if he can be expelled at the whim of the union, the closed or union shop carries a serious threat to the livelihood of the individual worker. The courts have tried to extend their protection, as far as possible, to union members whose interests may be threatened. The main principles which now apply may be summarized. The courts have held that a contract may exist between the union and its members, and that the wrongful expulsion of a member may be a breach of contract. This is still not a satisfactory safeguard for the man who might lose his job if wrongfully expelled. A man who is deprived of his livelihood may be in a bad position when it comes to suing the union. Even if he can get support, he may find his earning capacity greatly reduced during the months or years that may drag on before his action is heard. Nevertheless, limited protection is better than nothing. Moreover, the courts will almost certainly insist that the rules of natural justice be observed before a member is expelled. Not only must the expulsion be in accordance with the rules of the union, the courts will probably extend a measure of protection if the rules purport to give unfettered discretion to the executive. They are likely to insist that the member be notified of the complaint against him, and be given an opportunity of replying, even though this does not amount to anything approximating to the kind of fair trial that is usual in British courts. But there is no protection the courts can give a worker who is expelled from membership in accordance with the union rules and after a fair hearing, because he had, for example, refused to obey what he considered an unreasonable strike call.[5]

In place of strife. In January 1969, a White Paper was published under this title,[6] setting out government proposals for improving industrial relations. Two proposals attracted particular attention. These concerned, first, the introduction of a twenty-eight day conciliation pause in unofficial strikes, or other strikes in breach of procedural agreements, and, second, a compulsory strike ballot in major disputes involving the public interest. It would be at the discretion of the Secretary for Employment and Productivity whether or not to enforce these provisions in a particular case. If a conciliation pause were imposed, there would be machinery which could impose financial penalties on either side for attempting coercive action. Fines on workers would be enforced through attachment of wages. While workers would be liable to penalties if they struck in defiance of the conciliation pause, employers might also find that they would be required to observe certain conditions, e.g., to delay a proposed course of action that was being disputed by the workers. These proposals aroused bitter opposition from the trade unions, and in June 1969 the Government agreed not to proceed with legislation implementing them, but to rely upon the TUC to operate its own scheme.

What can the TUC do if there is an unofficial strike? It can try to put pressure on the unions whose members are concerned. If these unions do not cooperate, the only sanction is expulsion. There are disadvantages in not being affiliated to the TUC but it remains to be seen whether it is enough to force a union to act in a way it would not otherwise. If, however, the union is willing to use its influence, it remains to be seen whether this can be effective. It is true that where a closed shop exists, the ultimate threat of expulsion would be a serious one – if unions were prepared to use it.[7]

Other proposals in the White Paper relate to the extension of collective bargaining and the improvement of trade union organization. A Commission for Industrial Relations is to be set up for these purposes: the first chairman is Mr George Woodcock, formerly General Secretary of the TUC. The Commission will act mainly through persuasion, but the original proposals included a provision for compulsory arbitration where an employer refuses to take part in *bona fide* collective bargaining. When the Government dropped its proposals for quick legislation on the conciliation pause, it gave no indication of when action might be taken regarding other proposals in the White Paper which would require legislation.

Some problems of union organization

One important problem of trade union organization was touched upon earlier in this chapter. This is the role of the shop steward, who, because he is on the spot, may have much more influence with the men on the shopfloor than the official union hierarchy. The problem is aggravated by the fact that the union branch is a geographical unit which may include workers in different industries, and by the fact that most members find attendance at branch meetings inconvenient. If we could replace the present set-up, including as it does craft, industrial, and general unions, by a system which had only industrial unions, and where each major workplace was a union branch, this difficulty might be overcome. There are, however, other reasons, too, why industrial unionism might be preferable to the pattern that has emerged in Britain. Other problems that need to be considered are the recruitment of full-time officials, and the state of trade union finance.

Industrial unionism. Although workers in a particular firm or industry may be represented by several, or even by many, unions, it is rarely possible for a union to negotiate a separate agreement with the employers. It is much more usual for a single agreement to be negotiated covering all workers, or at least a single agreement to cover all manual workers. The negotiations normally take place between the representatives of the employers and the unions. The representatives on the union side may very well include at least one person from each of the unions concerned.

This gives rise to two main problems, particularly if the number of unions is large. First, negotiation itself becomes difficult if the negotiating body is too large: small committees are generally recognized as being more likely to get things done than large ones. Certainly, the larger the committee, the longer it is likely to take over any particular task. Second, if there are a dozen unions, the representative of each is likely to want to make some contribution to the discussion, and so prolong the negotiating process. The greater the multiplicity of unions, the more difficult the task of negotiating becomes.

This is true, even if the unions are agreed upon the policy to be adopted, which is not always the case. The unions may have managed to agree upon a claim for a wage increase, say, for five per cent. This does not mean, however, that there is full agreement between the different unions. Some may have the feeling that they should have tried for something more than five per cent, while others may, in fact, be prepared to settle for less. Certainly, there may be very different attitudes among the unions when faced with a counter-offer from the employers of, say, three per cent. Some may be willing enough to accept this offer, some may want to strike rather than accept less than five per cent, while others may wish to hold out for some compromise. To some extent, these difficulties may be duplicated on the employers' side.

Nor are the difficulties over once an agreement is signed. An agreement usually has to be ratified by the executives of the unions concerned, because the negotiators are not, in most instances, authorized to commit the union, or unions, finally to the terms of the settlement. If a single union is concerned, the negotiators may well be expected to know the mind of their executive; moreover, they will be pursuing their own interests throughout the negotiations. However, where there are many unions, the representative of one union may realize that he is in a minority on the union side and finally consent to some settlement that satisfies the employers and the other unions. He may later try to convince his executive that it was useless trying to get any better settlement, when all the other unions were ready to accept what was being offered, but, nevertheless, his executive may be adamant and reject the settlement.

Again, the chances of an agreement not being ratified increase with the number of unions involved. If there are real differences of opinion between the unions, and not just differences in willingness to compromise, the difficulties become all the greater. In particular, there is the danger that different unions may have conflicting ideas about the relativities that ought to exist between their members, leading to separate, leapfrogging claims.[8]

Recruitment and poaching. For the most part, where several unions organize workers in a particular industry, there is a clearly defined area from which each recruits. There will be no doubt about which union a craftsman should join, and normally there will be no difficulty about other workers either. In some cases, two unions may attempt to cater for the same group of workers. Both the NUR and ASLEF have membership among the footplatemen, the latter catering exclusively for such workers and the former seeking to organize all railwaymen. The general unions and what was originally a craft union, the AEF organize the semiskilled and unskilled workers in the engineering industry.

In some cases, two unions may achieve a measure of peaceful coexistence, catering for the same workers. In other cases, the presence of two unions has led to conflict, particularly if one has tried to increase its sphere of influence. In the docks, the majority of workers have always belonged to the TGWU, but in London (and to a much lesser extent elsewhere) there has been a second union, the National Amalgamated Stevedores and Dockers. An attempt by the latter union to extend its influence in the 1950s led to its expulsion from the TUC for contravention of the agreement prohibiting poaching of members from one union by another.[9]

Demarcation rules. The existence of several unions can create a

188

situation where, whatever the employer does, it is bound to be wrong in somebody's eyes. This kind of situation can arise when there are two or more unions with different ideas about relativities, or where two unions are claiming the right to organize the same workers. Perhaps the most common example, however, is where there are demarcation rules between different crafts. At the best, the existence of rigid lines of demarcation between crafts can be a source of difficulty and irritation; at the worst, it can create a situation where a stoppage is inevitable.

Rigid demarcation rules mean not only that certain jobs are reserved for a skilled craftsman, they also mean that all jobs are allocated to a particular craft. The existence of clearly defined and generally accepted demarcation rules can make the organization of work more difficult and add to labour costs. In the first place, not all jobs that are regarded as the preserve of skilled craftsmen really call for the services of a man who has served a long apprenticeship. A large proportion of people are probably capable of such jobs as changing a washer on a tap or renewing a fuse. Nevertheless, if such jobs have to be done on a building site or in a factory, it may be necessary to employ a fully qualified plumber or electrician. To employ such highly skilled labour, when less skilled labour might easily have been used, is unnecessarily costly.

There is a second way in which the need to employ a man of the right trade may cause difficulty or add to costs. A man capable of doing the job may be on the spot, whereas a fully qualified man, in the appropriate trade, may not and work may be held up waiting for him to arrive. The appropriate tradesman may be some distance away, and so the need to call on him may involve unproductive travelling time. Very often, a job may be of such a character that, strictly speaking, it calls for the services of several different craftsmen. An electrician may, for example, do some damage to paintwork. Often, it would be cheaper and quicker to allow him to retouch the paintwork himself rather than to wait and incur the expense of sending a painter after him. If, however, the job is such that some minor service is required from one or more craftsman before another can get on with the main task, the situation is more difficult. They may not be able to work simultaneously. The different crafts-men may not be all available at the same time. The result may be that a particular job takes a long time, because as soon as one craftsman has made his contribution, the job is left until it is convenient for the next craftsman to make his contribution. If these contributions are such that they really call for the skill of the particular craft, then these difficulties are inevitable. The task of management is to try to organize the work so that they do not add more than is necessary to the cost of production. Often, however, the preliminary work may be quite simple in character, and well within the capacity of any craftsman. In such cases, it would be very desirable for artificial barriers between crafts to be broken down. A great deal of work could be allocated to any available craftsman or to the man who was really needed for the main job.

Perhaps the most serious problem arising from demarcation rules is where changing technology results in two unions claiming the same work. With the problems we have been considering, difficulties may be created for management and costs raised, but the job at least goes on. Where two unions are claiming the work, the danger facing management is that, whichever craft it allocates to the job, the other union will call a strike, and this may, sooner or later, bring the plant to a standstill. Such problems may easily arise when one trade has traditionally been responsible for a particular job, and another has always done the work involving a particular material. If a change in technology means that a job previously done by members of union A now involves the use of material previously handled by union B, it is obvious that both unions are going to claim the work, on a different basis.

So long as there are separate crafts and demarcation rules governing the work done by members of each craft, such disputes are inevitable in a changing technology. The only solution would be to adopt an agreement that all unions should accept some independent arbitration, possibly by the TUC, and that there would be no stoppage in the meantime. Work might be allocated to both crafts pending a ruling, or to whichever had men available. In the long run, the advance of industrial unionism might help overcome the rigidity of demarcation rules, enabling labour to be employed more flexibly. Desirable as this may be, it is difficult to see the spread of industrial unionism making much progress with this particular end in mind. The more flexible use of skilled labour might be an offshoot of the growth of industrial unionism for other reasons.

Union officers and staffs. It is not always easy to distinguish between union officers and members of a union staff. In some unions, all officers are elected, and any person who is *appointed* would be regarded as a member of the staff. Some unions, however, appoint district secretaries, for example, who would certainly be regarded as officers. Not all unions would draw the line between officers and staff in exactly the same manner. For our purposes, it will be

190

sufficient if we think of the union staff as including all those employees of the union who are employed on relatively routine work. Clerks, typists, and so on, are clearly members of the union staff. There may be some posts where it is difficult to say whether a person should be treated as a member of the staff or as an officer of the union. Some of the senior employees at the head office may be undertaking work that is at a level comparable with that of men men who clearly rank as officers. If, however, this work is entirely internal union administration, there will be a sense in which their responsibilities are of a different kind from that of officers responsible for union policy and the conduct of negotiations.

No particular problems arise concerning the lower grades of union staff. If a union requires a typist, it will have to pay the usual rates, and the same for other employees. The union is in exactly the same position as any other employer.

Most union officers begin as ordinary members of the union, and have had experience working in the kind of jobs done by their rank and file members. The exceptions are the men who are, perhaps, more appropriately classified as officers, although they are in fact appointed because they have special qualifications, in more or less the same way as any member of the union staff. The payment of these full-time officers, who have risen from the rank and file of the union, may present special problems. Union officers have to carry a considerable responsibility and are, in fact, doing jobs at a level that would be very well paid in private industry. Yet their unions may be reluctant to accept salary scales that give officers very much more than the normal earnings of ordinary members. One study has shown that, in 1958, the starting salaries for full-time officers were still above the average earnings of the members they represented, but the gap had been closing since 1938, and it was possible that some officers would have had to accept a cut in salary on election or appointment to their first full-time union post.[10]

In most cases, the salary of the general secretary is high enough to allow the appointment of senior staff or specialist officers at some point in the union's salary structure and for it still to remain competitive. There are, however, instances of union's paying such senior staff salaries above those of the highest elected full-time officers.

In the long run, the unions must realize that the men of ability who would take the top jobs in the union are able to command high salaries in private firms, and that, if the rewards of union officers are squeezed too much, they will withdraw their services and go where these same services are more highly valued. If this happened, thus reducing the supply of suitable candidates for the top union offices, the unions would be faced with an increasingly serious problem.

There is reason to suppose that this might be occurring already, at least in those unions catering mainly for the less skilled workers. Over recent years, educational opportunities have been steadily improving. We may expect that, as time goes on, very few really able children will not take advantage of the educational opportunities that are offered them, and take up careers in keeping with their abilities and education. Unions catering for the unskilled workers will find fewer and fewer men and women of outstanding abilities among their members. In the past, young people who were denied educational opportunities went into unskilled jobs, educated themselves at evening classes, and worked their way up in the union movement. This source of talent will decline in the future, and unions may well have to think about radical changes in their organization. In the meantime, they cannot afford to lose potential officers by niggardliness in regard to salaries.

Trade union finance. The main source of income for a trade union is the subscriptions paid, usually weekly, by its members. In addition, some unions may charge an entrance fee to a new member, and most unions have power to make additional levies on members, if the need arises. Out of this income, a union has to meet its ordinary administrative expenses (including the salaries of officers and staff) and the benefits to which its members may be entitled. These benefits include both friendly benefits to those members who are sick or unemployed and trade benefit or strike pay to members involved in disputes.

The level of contributions and benefits varies from union to union. There has been a reluctance on the part of the unions in the postwar period to raise the subscriptions required of members in line with the rise that has been taking place generally in prices and in the costs of running the unions. Roberts has shown that, in the period from 1936 to 1950, the cost of living rose by 97 per cent, but the working expenses per head of unions by only 43 per cent. Subscriptions rose by only 9 per cent.[11] In 1950, the funds per head for all unions was under £8, a sum that is clearly inadequate to enable most unions to pay a reasonable level of strike benefit, if involved in a prolonged national stoppage involving the majority of members. In practice, of course, there have been relatively few such disputes in the postwar period. Where, for example, a general union is involved in a dispute

192

in some industry, only a proportion of its members may be involved, even though the dispute is a national one. Though funds may have increased since 1950, the basic position remains unchanged. Few unions could maintain strike pay to the whole membership for any considerable period without serious depletion of funds. Perhaps more serious, however, is the reluctance to keep subscriptions in line with current prices and costs. Good administration cannot be bought on the cheap, and any inadequacies in union administration will have serious consequences in the long run.

Collective bargaining

In most industries, voluntary collective bargaining is the main task of Joint Industrial Councils. The establishment of JICs started as a result of the recommendations of the Whitley Committee in 1917 and 1918. Since then, the number of such councils has increased, though there are still industries where voluntary collective bargaining is not firmly established, and wages councils have been set up. In some instances, however, JICs exist alongside the wages councils, and the latter often recommends a wage regulation order which merely gives statutory force to the agreement reached by the JIC. The role of the wages council in such a case is to give this statutory force to the agreement reached voluntarily by the unions and some employers, ensuring that these employers are not faced with low-wage competition from firms not belonging to the JIC. Without the knowledge that such undercutting is impossible, the firms belonging to the JIC would be less willing to make an agreement, or would insist upon a settlement at a lower wage than when they have this assurance. Where trade union organization is strong, however, firms outside the JIC are not such a serious threat, for the unions are likely to be able to force such firms to offer wages and conditions of employment at least as good as those negotiated in the JIC.

The typical pattern is for a JIC to comprise representatives of the employers and unions in the industry concerned. Usually, there is one association of employers, though occasionally there are more. Employers are normally organized in an association that has been formed within that particular industry. Thus, there is an association of employers in the engineering industry, of shipowners, or boot and shoe manufacturers, and so on. Unions, as we have already seen, are (with the exception of a few industrial unions and some highly specialized craft unions like ASLEF) likely to have members in a variety of industries, and there are also a number of different unions with membership in any one industry. All of these unions need to be represented on the JIC.

The subject matter of bargaining. The main subject matter for collective bargaining is, of course, wages. In nearly every case, the JIC is concerned with the negotiation of a national basic wage for the industry. This is a time rate for a standard working week which, today, is typically one of 40 or 42 hours. There may be separate rates to be negotiated for craftsmen and for semiskilled and unskilled workers. In some industries, the number of such rates may be small, while in others much more detailed agreements, with many separate categories, may be necessary. There are usually separate rates for women (though there is growing pressure for equal pay), and for young workers; and there may also be regional differentials.

As well as negotiating these basic rates, the JIC may also lay down certain rules governing payment by result schemes. National agreements, however, can only provide a framework within which payment by results schemes can be negotiated. Because of the variety of jobs to be done and the conditions in which they are undertaken, details of such schemes often need to be decided at the plant level. Even if payment is based on a time rate, the bonus paid will depend upon the time allowed for the completion of the job, which must be determined locally. There is, however, a danger that such schemes may be used to adjust local payments to the state of the labour market, rather than as genuine incentive schemes. It may well be that some changes in our present system of bargaining is needed. Basic rates are unrealistic, as we have seen. We should perhaps think of trying to establish a system of bargaining which negotiates realistic basic rates, and which has no place for payment by results, except where a genuine incentive is possible and desirable. This might mean more plant bargaining or, perhaps, the negotiation of agreements at a district level, possibly subject to some national agreement establishing a minimum which might be supplemented in the light of local conditions.

Often a JIC will discuss subjects other than wages: the length of the standard working week, holidays, and similar topics. In Britain, fringe benefits, such as pensions and sick pay, have formed a comparatively minor item on the agenda, mainly because the trade unions have sought, through their affiliation with the Labour Party, to provide such benefits through state schemes of social security. In countries where more reliance has been placed on the provision of such benefits directly by industry, they have been more important as a topic in collective bargaining; in the United States, the provision of insurance against the cost of medical treatment has also been important. In addition, of course, the JICs may also discuss other issues of interest to employers and workers in an industry, perhaps with a view to approaching the Government for some kind of legislation or other action: this is a use of the machinery, which exists primarily for the purpose of bargaining, for consultative purposes.

Pressures on union officers. Wage negotiations are no longer undertaken at irregular intervals, although agreements in Britain, unlike those in some other countries, are not for a specified period, but are open-ended, that is, the agreement remains in force so long as one of the parties does not revoke the agreement and make some fresh demand for negotiation. In practice in the postwar period, a wage agreement has remained in effect until the union has called for an increase in pay. Under the inflationary conditions of the postwar period, a claim from employers for a reduction of the agreed wage is unheard of, though such claims did occur in the years before the war, indeed, the threat of a reduction in pay for the miners was the cause of the General Strike in 1926. Now, the claim is always for increased pay and such claims have tended to be subimitted with increasing regularity. In the case of many manual workers, the usual procedure is for a claim to be made annually. Some white collar workers have their pay reviewed regularly, but at longer intervals.[12]

Trade union leaders may realize that there are limits to the wage increases that can be secured for their members without adverse effects on the national economy or even on employment within the industry. Such limits may be less obvious to the rank and file membership. The latter will see, for example, that a wage increase has been negotiated in a particular industry, and will see no good reason why they should not get a comparable increase. The executive of a union and the general secretary may have considerable freedom of action, but they cannot entirely ignore the expressed wishes of the rank and file. The members of the executive must submit themselves sooner or later for reelection, and, if they disregard the views of the rank and file, they may find themselves replaced by people who are more responsive and, perhaps, more militant. The general secretary, too, may have to submit himself for reelection, though less frequently. Even if he is elected for life, his powers are still not unlimited. He must work with and is answerable to the executive; if they vote for pressing a substantial wage claim, he has no choice but to take the appropriate action, no matter how unreasonable he thinks the claim to be.

In the end, it may be impossible to succeed with an unreasonable claim, and if there is a strike, the workers are worse off because they tried to get more rather than settle for what the employers offered. Union leaders may foresee this, but they may nevertheless be forced to take a tougher line in negotiations, because this is what the rank and file want.

NOTES

1. Behind this apparently childish dispute is an issue of some substance. The fear of ASLEF is that there is a danger of guards being recruited as drivers, and thus weakening the position of ASLEF in organizing footplatemen. With the diesel locomotives, there is no longer the clear line of recruitment from cleaner to fireman to driver as there was in the days of steam.

2. Ideally, these matters should not be the subject of bargaining. The time allowed for a particular job ought to be fixed by the works study department with provision for modification if it proves unsatisfactory. Bargaining over this kind of matter can lead to a chaotic earnings structure.

3. Breach of contract occurs if the workers withdraw their labour without giving the period of notice that is legally required. There may be some doubt as to whether a notice to strike would, in fact, constitute a proper notice to terminate employment, even if the period of the notice to strike were of the right length.

4. For the uninitiated, however, it must be made clear that the law of contract and the law of tort are separate, and a trade union may certainly be sued for a breach of one of its own contracts, either with its own employees or with firms supplying it with goods.

5. Trade union leaders maintain that the individual should abide by the majority decision. On the other hand, the Nuremburg trials did not accept the view that the individual could be relieved of moral responsibility for his own actions. Moreover, the argument of the union leaders would be more convincing if they were equally keen to expel those responsible for leading unofficial strikes.

6. Cmnd. 3888.

7. Self-discipline exercised by unions and the TUC may seem preferable to the threat of legal sanctions. Against this, however, the ultimate threat of expelling a man from a union where a closed shop exists and depriving him of his livelihood is really too serious a sanction to leave to trade unions whose standards of procedure may fall very far short of those of a court of law.

8. The case of leapfrogging on the railways in 1955 was referred to earlier in this chapter.

9. When the NASD eventually sought to comply with the TUC ruling by expelling the former TGWU members it had recruited, some of these challenged the expulsion in the courts and were successful, the union at the time having no rule which allowed it to expel members on the grounds that the TUC considered them to have been 'poached' and had ordered their return to their original union. As a result of this, most unions have now made a rule giving them this power.

10. H. A. Clegg, A. J. Killick, and R. Adams, *Trade Union Officers*, Blackwell, Oxford, 1961.

11. B. C. Roberts, *Trade Union Government and Administration*, Bell, London, 1956, p. 385.

12. The operation of the incomes policy may help to break the regularity of the annual round of wage increases.

13. Apprenticeship

The training necessary to enable workers to play their roles, in industry, in commerce, and in other fields, takes a variety of forms. This training varies from the five or six years spent at university by a doctor followed by a compulsory year in a junior hospital post, to, perhaps, as little as a few days on job instruction for an unskilled worker. It would clearly be an impossible task in a single chapter to consider the variety of forms in which training is provided, and the economic implications of each. The main emphasis will therefore be on the traditional system of apprenticeship for the skilled manual crafts, together with some reference to the problems involved in providing training and, if necessary, retraining for the older worker.

The apprenticeship system

The basis of the system in Britain is an agreement between the apprentice and his master, known as the 'indenture'. The master undertakes to give the apprentice a full training in his craft, while the apprentice agrees, on his part, to remain with the master for the period of the apprenticeship and to be diligent in his work. At the end of the period of apprenticeship, the indenture is endorsed, and this certifies that the apprentice has served his time learning his craft and is entitled to be regarded henceforth as a qualified craftsman.

Detailed figures of the number of apprentices are not readily available, but Liepman, in her study of the subject,[1] quotes the 1951 Census data as showing that there were at the time some 350,000 male apprentices in England and Wales, of whom some 220,000 were in metal manufacture, engineering, shipbuilding, printing, and the 'trowel' trades (bricklaying and plastering).

The maximum age for starting an apprenticeship is 16. This is geared to the five-year duration of the usual apprenticeship and the belief that this should be completed by the time the apprentice reaches the age of 21. This is, perhaps, because the status of the apprentice is felt to be one that is unsuited to someone who has reached the age of legal majority (though this idea does not appear to extend to the professions).

The length of training. There has been great reluctance on the part of British trade unions and employers to depart from the traditional five-year apprenticeship. It would be very curious if it were to prove that it took exactly five years to acquire all the skills of such diverse trades as electrician, plumber, fitter, welder, and so on. Moreover, there is little doubt that in most, or even all, cases the five-year period is unnecessarily long. In Europe, there are comparatively few trades for which the period of training exceeds three years.[2]

There would be a considerable advantage in shortening the period of apprenticeship to three years. At the present time, a man completes his training for a craft at the age of 21. This is quite reasonable, and to shorten the period of apprenticeship to three years would enable the training to be completed by this age, even when the start of the apprenticeship was delayed until 18. On the other hand, there would be no case for making 18 the *normal* starting age. The ideal would be for the apprenticeship to start as soon as a boy leaves school. A school leaving age of 15 and a starting age for apprenticeship of 16 has been shown to have definite disadvantages. The intervening year serves no useful purpose, and a boy going into a job that is relatively well paid, but with few prospects, may be reluctant later to accept the low earnings of an apprentice.

Method and adequacy of training. The usual method of training an apprentice is to let him watch a fully qualified craftsman at work and to pick up the required skill in that way. The craftsman may give the apprentice some hints or instructions, but rarely will there be any systematic teaching. Few of the craftsmen instructing apprentices have been given any training in how best to pass on the skills they themselves possess. Larger firms may make some attempt to provide more systematic instruction: small firms will certainly find it difficult to do so.

The small firm may also find it difficult to provide the apprentice with an adequate all-round training in the craft. The work undertaken by the small firm will often be limited, and it is impossible to teach the apprentice certain aspects of the trade if little or no work of that kind is done. The big firm is, again, in a better position in this respect. Another advantage of the big firm is in respect to day release. Ideally, apprentices should be allowed to spend one day at a technical college learning the more theoretical aspects of their

198

trade. If a firm with only a few apprentices is to release them for one day in five, the disruption of the work of the firm may be considerable. On the other hand, a big firm with many apprentices can more easily arrange schedules for releasing a proportion of its apprentices each day.

Whereas in Britain an apprentice's indenture is automatically endorsed at the end of the five year period, in Europe it is an almost universal rule that some kind of test of competence is imposed, and this is usually conducted by some independent body. The term 'skilled worker' may, in some countries, be applied only to those who have passed a test of this sort, though this need not necessarily prevent a man from working at a particular trade. If such a system were to be introduced into Britain, it would enable an employer to be sure that a man he engaged had reached a certain minimum standard of competence. It need not, if the European model were followed, bar him from engaging a man without such a certificate if he wished to do so.[3]

The imposition of a test of competence by an impartial body also involves a constant review of the nature of the work involved in the craft, and revision of the theoretical and practical training that is appropriate. No doubt a closer supervision of the training given in Britain may be expected to result from the setting up of Industrial Training Boards under an act of 1964.

The cost of training. Although the apprentice may be paid a comparatively low wage, and does some useful work during the period of his apprenticeship, the training of apprentices does involve a firm in some costs. The more conscientiously the firm approaches this task, the greater will be the costs. There is a danger, therefore, that some firms will decide that they would prefer not to train apprentices at all, but to recruit only skilled craftsmen who, at some time, have been trained by other firms. This, of course, is clearly to the disadvantage of firms who do take apprentices: they incur costs in training workers for other employers, and receive no reimbursement for this.

One of the functions of Industrial Training Boards, set up under the Industrial Training Act, 1964, is to equalize the costs of training. The boards are empowered to make levies on firms in an industry, and, among other functions, can make grants to firms undertaking training. In addition, the boards can make recommendations on such matters as the nature, length, and standard of training, and similar matters.

Apprenticeship and demarcation. We have seen already in chapter 12 that serious difficulties may arise from the rigid lines of demarcation between different trades. In Europe, the greater prevelance of industrial unionism has meant that there has not been the same insistence on such lines of demarcation. For each craft, there is a range of skills that have to be learned, but there is inevitably some overlap, and some jobs may be given to members of two or more crafts depending upon circumstances. A man may even be allowed to acquire a qualification in two crafts, which is impossible in Britain.

Training for older workers

A full apprenticeship is unlikely to appeal to the older worker, even if restrictions imposed by trade unions or employers were to be lifted. The low wages normally earned by apprentices would alone ensure that very few older men would be willing to enter upon a normal apprenticeship. Experience abroad has shown, however, that in suitable cases, and with a proper training programme, older men can acquire a skilled trade in a period of about nine months. There will, in a changing economy, be plenty of men whose particular skills become redundant during the course of their working life. Some, at least, of these will be men capable of learning one of the skills normally acquired through apprenticeship, and who should be given the opportunity of doing so through a 'crash' programme of training.

There has been in recent years a shortage of skilled labour. In a very few instances, this has been partly the result of trade union restrictions on the number of apprentices. More commonly, there has been a reluctance on the part of employers to provide training on a scale to meet either the needs of industry or the demand for training from school-leavers. The Industrial Training Act may help to improve matters, but it would be a waste not to provide adequate training (or retraining) facilities for older workers, as well as providing better facilities for the school-leaver.

A start has been made in this direction with the provision of government training centres by the Department of Employment and Productivity. In 1965, 30 such centres were in operation, providing courses in some 40 trades, mostly in the engineering and construction industries. These courses were usually of 6 months' duration, with 12 months as the maximum duration. These centres provided 6000 places in 1965, and a number of additional centres have been established since then. Training is free and a maintenance grant is paid to the trainee by the Department. Selection for training is made by panels on which employers and unions are represented, and, although the courses are shorter than the traditional apprenticeship trainees are recognized as skilled men on completion of the courses. *Training for women.* Very few women enter the trades for which a formal apprenticeship is necessary. It is unlikely that this situation will change. Girls leaving school at 15 or 16, and who typically may expect to marry in their early twenties will hardly think it worth while to undertake a three year apprenticeship. Many women, it is true, may marry, have a family, and be thinking of returning to work in their middle thirties. Nevertheless, few will be so far sighted as to think it worth while to undertake a long apprenticeship, work for only one or two years afterwards, perhaps, and then return to their craft in their thirties. Such women, however, will include many whose true potential will be wasted if they can only secure unskilled or semiskilled work, as at present. The same kind of crash programme that has been suggested for retraining older men might be equally appropriate for women returning to the labour market once their children have ceased to be so completely dependent upon them.

Training for semiskilled jobs

Some measure of training is necessary for jobs below the skilled level which are the subject of formal apprenticeships. The training period may vary, according to the job, from a matter of weeks to a year or two. The rigid distinction between skilled and unskilled work is as artificial and unsatisfactory as the completely rigid lines of demarcation between one skilled craft and another. Just as there is a measure of overlap between different crafts, so there is a continuous gradation in both the degree of skill and in the range of skills required by a job. In all cases, it is important that there should be adequate training without undue prolongation of the training period. Even if the period of training is short, it may well be desirable that the recruit should be given proper instruction, and not just expected to pick up the necessary skill by observation.

There should also be recognition of the changing nature of the jobs being done in a dynamic economy. The degree of skill involved in some jobs may decline, and it may become possible for these to be undertaken by a worker with a limited training rather than a fully trained craftsman, as hitherto. There should be provision, as on the continent of Europe, for recognizing this and for the 'deskilling' of a job. To insist that jobs should continue to be done by a fully trained craftsman, when craftsmen are in very scarce supply, and when the job could be done by somebody less skilled, is a waste of the community's resources. Such restrictions in a period of full employment are completely without justification. Conversely, some jobs may become more difficult. If, however, the job changes so that a skilled man is needed, the employer will, of course, use a craftsman.

NOTES

1. K. Liepman, *Apprenticeship*, Routledge and Kegan Paul, London, 1960, p. 47.

2. This may be the case even with a school leaving age of 14, enabling a man to qualify as a craftsman at 17. See G. Williams *Apprenticeship in Europe*, Chapman and Hall, London, 1963, p. 39.

3. See Williams, op. cit., p. 171.

14. Joint consultation

There is no clear dividing line between joint consultation and collective bargaining. In the present chapter, we shall be considering consultation at the level of the firm. We have seen already in chapter 12 that a JIC may well become a channel for discussion of matters of common interest as well as bargaining in the narrower sense. In this chapter, we shall look briefly at the problem of consultation in British industry, and at a closely related topic, the actual participation of the workers in control. Reference will be made in this latter context to some of the developments in this direction in German industry.

The nature of consultation

Consultation is generally distinguished from both bargaining and control. In consulting the workers on certain issues, the management is not bargaining with them. It may reveal certain intentions, it may ask for the workers' views, it may be ready to modify some of its original intentions if a strong case is made. It is not, however, offering some concession or payment in return for being allowed to introduce certain changes, and to discuss the amount of such concession or payment. In that sense, the management is not bargaining. Neither is it prepared to admit that it will modify its plans because the workers object. It will listen to their views, and may modify its plans if convinced that they are unsound, but, in so far as management retains the right to make the final decision, there is no element of worker-control.

The content of consultation. The subject matter of joint consultation varies a great deal from firm to firm, as does the machinery employed. The works committee (or other body) will certainly be able to discuss such matters as safety precautions, sanitation, and welfare topics generally. During the war, joint production committees were established in many enterprises, and the main function of these was to improve efficiency and increase production in order to help the war effort. After the war, consultation for this kind of objective became far less important. Under normal conditions, workers are unlikely to be keen on measures to improve productivity unless there is some reward for them in doing so. In other words, it is a subject for bargaining rather than consultation.

The Works Committee may, however, discuss more important topics than welfare. The management may, for example, choose to consult the workers on changes that are impending. This may, for example, include changes which will involve redundancies. The discussion may include such matters as compensation (particularly prior to the introduction of the compulsory scheme), procedures to be followed, the order of redundancy, and so on. In such circumstances, the works committee may be an important channel of communication between the management and workers, not merely a place for airing comparatively trivial grievances. On the other hand, it is clearly difficult in such important issues to draw a line between consultation and bargaining. If the workers do not like management's proposals, they will do all they can to bring about a change. If redundancy is inevitable, they may seek greater compensation, or some alternative approach to that of dismissal.

The machinery of consultation. The normal machinery for joint consultation is the works committee or some comparable body including representatives of workers and management. There is no need for the two sides to be represented by equal numbers, since the committee is not an executive body. It may, however, be important that the membership should not be restricted to the representatives of top management and rank and file shopfloor workers. This could create a situation where the views of foremen and others were ignored, and where ordinary shopfloor workers would learn of management's plans before the foremen.

There is, in many firms, a shop stewards' committee. There is no reason why the shop stewards, if necessary with representatives of the foremen and similar grades, should not form the workers' side of a works committee. The inclusion of the shop stewards would be advantageous, in so far as there is the possibility that consultation is going to merge into negotiation, at least on some issues. If the shop stewards are authorized to negotiate (and this depends upon the constitutions of the unions concerned), it is clearly simpler if there is only one body concerned. It is a waste of time for management to negotiate some kind of agreement with a works committee and then have to get it ratified by the shop stewards or some other body that is authorized to negotiate.

Worker participation in control

There have been times when there has been a great deal of interest in the possibility of workers acquiring a measure of control in the enterprises in which they work. A desire for such participation may have had considerable influence, in the early part of the interwar period, on the trade unions and the Labour Party. The abolition of private ownership of the means of production was seen by many as the way to the control of enterprises by those in them. What emerged after the Second World War was something quite different: state ownership replaced private ownership in a number of key industries, the powers of management remained fundamentally unchanged. Former trade unionists were appointed to the boards of nationalized industries and took their place in top management, but they resigned their union posts first. The union attitude was that such appointments were welcomed, but the unions' freedom of action should not be limited in any way by making these appointees union representatives, who might be regarded as committing the unions to decisions taken. While the nationalized industries were placed under a statutory obligation to bargain with the unions and to establish consultative machinery, the worker-management relationship was not basically different from that in private enterprise.

There have been a few examples in British industry or commerce where the majority shareholders in a limited company have converted their controlling equity interest into fixed interest shares and vested the control of the enterprise in the hands of some body representative of the workpeople. In such cases, provision may, however, be made for ensuring that the chief executive retains adequate powers of management, and worker-control does not undermine the effectiveness of routine decision-making. On the other hand, there have been few, if any, British experiments in *shared* control, as there have been, for example, in Germany.

The German experiments. The German company structure is different from the British in important respects, and this facilitates the introduction of a degree of coresponsibility or codetermination in industry. The German enterprise is controlled by two boards, a supervisory board and an executive board. The former is concerned with certain major decisions – whether to undertake some large capital expenditure, or the amount of dividend to declare, and so on. The executive board is responsible for the day-to-day running of the business, and cannot, within its sphere of responsibility, be overruled by the supervisory board. In Britain, the board of directors exercises the supervisory function, but it can also interfere in executive matters. Moreover, the chief executive, the managing director, will also be a member of the board, whereas in Germany the two functions are more sharply divided.

In many German enterprises, there is minority representation of the workers on the supervisory board. In the steel industry, there is stronger worker representation. Here, the supervisory board is made up of equal numbers of representatives of workers and shareholders together with an independent chairman. In addition, there is a labour director among the three members of the executive board.

These arrangements do not interfere with the routine working of the enterprise. At the very least, the machinery provides an additional line of communication in the enterprise and gives the workers access to information that might otherwise not have been available to them. In addition, their views may be heard at the highest levels in the enterprise when new developments are being first considered, as distinct from the trade unions being brought into discussions at a later stage (even if this *is* before a final decision is taken). There is no evidence that the presence of the workers' representatives has reduced enterprise: it may even have had a marginal influence in the opposite direction. On day-to-day matters, works councils are still required to provide a means of contact between workers on the floor and management.

Part 4

The Government and industrial relations

15. The Government and collective bargaining

It is sometimes maintained that the attitude of the Government towards collective bargaining in Britain today is one of neutrality. This is an oversimplification. No doubt, the Government is content enough to leave collective bargaining to the employers and trade unions when all is going smoothly, but the Government cannot remain indifferent to serious disputes between employers and unions which may disrupt the economy. There is, therefore, a long history of measures to try to facilitate the smooth working of collective bargaining. Furthermore, the Government cannot remain indifferent when, in the absence of proper collective bargaining, large numbers of workers receive very low rates of remuneration. There are numerous examples of action taken by the Government to facilitate voluntary collective bargaining, to provide alternative machinery for wage regulation when necessary, to legislate where appropriate provision has not been made through the machinery for collective bargaining, and so on.

The recognition of the right to bargain

For a long time, governments in this country did not recognize the right of the workers to form trade unions and to bargain collectively with employers. It was only in the first quarter of the nineteenth century that trade unions ceased to be illegal organizations. Even after that date, there was a danger that union members could be prosecuted for conspiracy, until an act of 1875 provided that the actions of two or more persons in the course of a trade dispute would not be indictable for conspiracy, unless the acts involved would have been criminal if performed by a single person. It is not criminal for a worker to break his contract of employment by going on strike, nor is it criminal for him to induce a fellow worker to break his contract. These are civil wongs for which the remedy is an action for damages or for an injunction.[1] If, of course, a group of strikers agree to damage their employer's property or to use violence against members of the management or workers who refuse to strike, these are crimes, and the workers concerned would lay themselves open to prosecution on the additional count of criminal conspiracy.

The Government has clearly become much more favourably inclined to the activities of trade unions and to the regulation of wages by collective bargaining. Whereas in 1875 the trade union members were relieved of the threat of criminal prosecution for acts done in furtherance of a trade dispute, legislation in 1906 conferred upon the trade unions themselves virtually complete immunity for torts committed by them, whether in the course of a trade dispute or not. At the same time, a substantial degree of immunity was conferred on officials and members in respect of tortious actions committed in the course of a trade dispute. Thus, both trade unions and members were freed in very large measure from the threat of legal proceedings, both civil and criminal.

By the early years of the present century, some employers were willing enough to negotiate with trade unions; others may have negotiated, albeit somewhat reluctantly; still other employers refused to recognize the right of their workers to organize and bargain collectively. Only a very short time before the outbreak of the First World War, there was a bitter battle between the shipowners and what is now the National Union of Seamen over recognition.

Recognition struggles today. Today most employers recognize the right of workers to form trade unions, and, indeed, see advantages in having strong and effective unions which can represent the views of their members. Nevertheless, difficulties still arise over recognition of unions. In the past, trade union organization has been associated with manual workers. White collar workers have typically been less well organized, certainly in the lower ranks. Today, white collar unionism is increasing, and this increase may produce two kinds of conflict over recognition. First, even employers who have conceded the right of manual workers to organize and bargain collectively may, irrationally, be reluctant to concede a similar right to white collar workers. Second, there is a danger that interunion rivalries may give rise to difficulties. Two or more unions may try to organize the same group of white collar workers, with the result that the employer runs into trouble whichever union he chooses to recognize.[2]

The Government has set up a Commission on Industrial Relations (CIR) which will help to try to solve difficulties of this kind. It will,

210

in the first place, try to achieve a settlement acceptable to the parties concerned. The Government proposes, however, to introduce legislation which will enable effect to be given to the recommendations of the CIR. Where the employer refuses to recognize a union, or unions, and to take part in collective bargaining in good faith, the union, or unions, will be able to go to the Industrial Court and seek a legally enforceable arbitration award. In those cases where the dispute is between unions, the CIR is to be empowered to make recommendations as to which is to be recognized, and the Secretary for Employment and Productivity will then be able to make an order giving effect to these recommendations. When such an order is made, it will be an offence to try to resist the recommendations by coercive action. It is proposed that financial penalties will be imposed by a specially constituted Industrial Board, upon employers, unions, or individual workmen contravening such an order.

Machinery to facilitate collective bargaining

Governments have, as we have seen, long abandoned their earlier hostility to the Trade Union movement. There are still important differences between the attitudes of the political parties to trade unions and to collective bargaining, but the right to form unions and to bargain collectively is recognized by all three major parties. In the preceding section, we have seen something of recent moves to ensure, in practice, the extension of the right of workers to collective bargaining in fields where this has not been possible in the past. Even where collective bargaining is well established, however, it does not always function smoothly. While the Government, in general, prefers to leave bargaining to the parties concerned, it does nevertheless make certain facilities available to them. These are dealt with more fully later in this chapter, but, for the moment, we may note that they include machinery for arbitration and conciliation. If the parties agree, a dispute may, for example, be referred to the Industrial Court for arbitration. The Court will listen to the views of both sides, and then make an award. With conciliation, on the other hand, the emphasis is on helping the two sides to reach an agreement. A great deal of such work is undertaken by the officers of the DEP itself, though there are provisions for appointing other conciliators, if this seems desirable.

There are other situations where it is difficult to organize the workers in an industry effectively, and where there may also be a large number of small employers who might not be willing to join an employers' association. Minimum wage legislation has been introduced covering such industries where remuneration is low. Although the machinery provided in such cases fixes wages by law, the attempt has been made, as far as possible, to reproduce some of the more important elements of collective bargaining. The idea is to bring together representatives of the two sides of industry, assisted by the presence of independent persons, and to try to get the workers and employers to agree on the wage to be fixed. Moreover, this statutory machinery may, in certain instances, be used to give legal force to an agreement already reached in a JIC.

Other government intervention

So far, the emphasis has been on governmental measures to strengthen or facilitate collective bargaining, or to replace it in some measure when it is defective. There are, however, other ways in which the Government intervenes in industrial relations, more so than in, say, the interwar years. This is perhaps natural, for the measure of governmental intervention in the economy as a whole has tended to increase.[3] Two aspects of such intervention may be considered briefly at this stage: manpower planning and incomes policy.

Manpower planning. The formulation of a National Plan by the Government in 1965[4] laid considerable stress on the importance of the supply of labour to the completion of the plan. If a high rate of economic growth is to be achieved, it is important that this should not be hindered by shortages of labour, either in general or in regard to particular types of labour.

Incomes policy. As soon as economists realized that the achievement of full employment by the application of Keynesian policies was a real possibility, they saw the danger that full employment would so strengthen the trade unions that inflationary wage claims would be very difficult to resist. Economists were therefore thinking about a wages policy even before the end of the war. While politicians tried to exhort workers and unions to wage restraint after the war, no serious thought was given to the formulation of a real wages or incomes policy until much later. The pay pause of 1961 was essentially a crisis measure, and was in no sense a long-term policy. Only in 1964, with the return to power of a Labour government in the autumn, was serious attention given to the idea of a long-term policy with the idea of linking wage and salary movements to the rate of growth. The policy formulations since then have all given

212

criteria for departures from the norm of the policy. While these may not be satisfactory, as we shall see in chapter 16, the fact remains that wages increasing more rapidly than productivity may lead to rising prices, with disastrous results for the national economy. Under modern conditions, therefore, the Government cannot be expected to remain indifferent to the outcome of collective bargaining. Here is a way in which the Government is intervening in a very different way from elsewhere. It is not just encouraging collective bargaining, trying to extend it, or trying to alter the rules in favour of one side. It is interfering with the outcome of free bargaining between the parties, imposing, if necessary, its own wishes against those of the two sides of industry, even when they are fully in agreement.

Conciliation

Conciliation may be defined as the attempt to assist the parties to a dispute to adjust their differences and reach agreement. The Conciliation Act, 1896, empowered the President of the Board of Trade to appoint a conciliator or board of conciliation at the request of *either* party to the dispute. The powers of the Board of Trade under this act are now exercised by the Department of Employment and Productivity. The Department also has powers, under the Industrial Courts Act, 1919, to take 'such steps as may seem expedient for promoting a settlement in any dispute reported by or on behalf of one or other of the parties'. At the present time, use is rarely made of these powers to appoint an *ad hoc* conciliator or board of conciliation; an exception was the printing dispute in 1958 when Lord Birkett was appointed as a conciliator. Today, the more usual practice is for the work of conciliation to be undertaken by the Department's own personnel. It has an Industrial Relations Department which is responsible for keeping the Minister in constant touch with the state of industrial relations throughout the country. In each region, there are industrial relations officers who are authorized to take such steps as they think fit to facilitate the settlement of a local dispute. The Department's headquarters staff would act in the event of a national dispute, and, if necessary, the Secretary for Employment and Productivity would step in personally.

Little has been published about the way conciliation works. It is possible, however, to suggest a number of ways in which a conciliator may help to bring about a settlement of a dispute. First, he may be able to lower the temperature of the discussions. This was no doubt particularly important before employers generally had recognized the rightful role of the trade unions in collective bargaining. Even when collective bargaining is the accepted way of fixing wages in an industry, it is still possible for tempers to fray under the stress of negotiation, and the calming influence of a conciliator can still be helpful.

Second, the conciliator may help to clarify the issues involved. If, as may often be the case, the negotiations are complicated, the conciliator may be able to ensure that there are no misunderstandings, and so help to keep attention focused on finding a settlement of the real differences that divide the parties.

Third, although he is not an arbitrator, the conciliator may nevertheless be able to *suggest* a solution. If an *ad hoc* conciliator is appointed, he is likely to be the kind of person who might equally well have been appointed as an arbitrator. He may well suggest the same kind of settlement as he would have put forward had he been arbitrating, and the parties may well be ready to accept his suggestion. This may not always be the case, though. The very fact that the conciliation machinery has been invoked, rather than arbitration, may mean that one or both parties is unwilling to agree, in advance at least, to having a solution laid down from outside.

Fourth, the conciliator may enable both sides to make concessions without loss of face. The reader may be familiar with the accounts of conciliation at the Department of Employment and Productivity. The parties meet in separate rooms with a senior official running from one to the other. The parties may indicate to the official their willingness to make some concession, *if it is known that some concession will be forthcoming from the other side*. If the parties have committed themselves firmly to some 'final ' offer, and this has been widely reported by press, radio, and television, it may be very difficult for one of them to make the first concession. To do so may seem a sign of weakness, and undermine future bargaining strength. Hence the reluctance to make a concession in direct negotiation with the other side, but a readiness to make a concession, if it is known through a third party that this will be matched by a suitable *quid pro quo*.

Arbitration

The role of the arbitrator is to determine a dispute. He is empowered to consider the arguments from the two sides and to make an award which they are then expected to abide by. The Department of Employment and Productivity has powers under the Conciliation

Act to appoint an arbitrator or board of arbitration, but such an *ad hoc* appointment is now unlikely. In a number of industries, machinery for arbitration has been set up, and in other instances a dispute may be referred to the Industrial Court.[5]

The Industrial Court is composed of three members. There is a full-time president, who is a lawyer, and two full-time members, one representing workers and one employers. In addition, there are three panels of part-time members, one of independent persons and the others representative of the two sides of industry. These part-time members may be called upon to serve on the Court if one of the full-time members is not available or if pressure of work should require the Court to sit in more than one division. A dispute will be referred to the Industrial Court only if *both* parties agree and if an attempt has already been made to reach a settlement through the industry's established negotiating machinery. Even if there is no established machinery, some attempt must be made to reach a direct settlement before a dispute is referred to the Industrial Court.

The 'claims' procedure. Most references to the Industrial Court are concerned with disputes over trade union demands for higher wages. There is also a 'claims' procedure which is rather different. This is a relic of the compulsory arbitration that was introduced during the Second World War. The wartime legislation introduced compulsory arbitration in order to prevent the war effort being disrupted by strikes. As well as providing for arbitration by the National Arbitration Tribunal (reformed as the Industrial Disputes Tribunal after the war) in major disputes, this legislation allowed an 'issue' to be raised by the trade unions.

The issue procedure required the National Arbitration Tribunal to consider whether an individual employer was offering wages and conditions of employment that were in line with those generally operating in the particular industry. If not, the employer could be ordered to come into line. In 1958, it was decided to abolish compulsory arbitration: such arbitration was felt to be one-sided in its impact. The awards of the tribunal were legally enforceable. If an employer wanted labour, he had to pay the wage laid down by arbitration. An action could have been brought in the civil courts to recover any wages underpaid. If, however, the workers were not satisfied, there was no obligation on them to work at the prescribed wage.[6] Nevertheless, it was felt by both sides of industry that the issues procedure had some value. Both the unions and the general body of employers were in favour of a measure that forced an employer who was paying wages below the general level to come

215

into line. The procedure was therefore retained in an act of 1959, transferring jurisdiction in issues, now renamed 'claims', to the Industrial Court.

It must be emphasized that this procedure is of limited value. If a claim is adjudicated by the Industrial Court, it will oblige an employer to pay the wages currently normal in the industry *at that time*. If, therefore, most employers negotiate a new agreement with the trade unions, the individual employer who was ordered to come into line remains under an obligation to pay the former wage only: he is under no obligation either to adjust his wages automatically when the general level changes, or to follow the collective agreements made in the industry. When new agreements are negotiated, the claim must be reheard by the Industrial Court if the unions want to keep this employer in line with others.

Enforceability of awards. In defining arbitration, it was said that the arbitrator lays down terms which the parties are expected to accept. There is, however, no legal obligation to do so. With the exception of the claims procedure, arbitration awards, whether of the Industrial Court or of the tribunals which have been set up in particular industries, carry no legal sanction. The obligation to accept the award is a moral one. This must be kept in mind when we consider the nature of the arbitration process as it exists in Britain today.

The basis of arbitration. There are no clear principles which arbitrators are expected to follow. It is quite possible, therefore, that different arbitrators may make awards that are inconsistent. Even if two arbitrators were to take account of the same factors, it would still be possible for them to attach different weights to them. This means that, in a given case, the arbitration award may depend in some measure upon who is chosen to arbitrate. The likelihood of serious inconsistency, however, is very much reduced if arbitration is undertaken by some kind of panel rather than by a single arbitrator.

It is usually supposed that arbitrators exercise some kind of judicial or, at least, quasi-judicial function. Up to a point this is true, but this line of approach can be misleading. In a truly judicial process, it is the task of the judge, sometimes with the help of the jury, to sift the factual evidence put before the court, to decide what actually happened or what probably happened, and what the law states about the particular occurrences. The task of the judge is not an easy one: there may be considerable dispute about the facts, and even if the facts are clear the law may not be. The judge, however, has the guidance of statutes and of precedents established in previous cases. The arbitrator lacks such guidance.[7] He may be presented with

216

evidence about the profitability of an industry, about the level of pay in comparable jobs, and so on. He may be able to say that a 5 per cent rise in pay is needed to bring workers into line with those in comparable fields, or that a 3 per cent rise is the most that firms can pay without putting up prices or accepting a cut in profits. But there are no principles which command general acceptance and which enable an arbitrator to look at data of this sort and say that a certain pay increase is *the* appropriate award. He has to decide whether it is correct to bring these particular workers into line with 'comparable' workers (the selection of those who are comparable itself being open to dispute). He has to decide whether an increase should be limited to what firms can pay without putting up prices, even if this means some cut in profits, or whether an increase should be given which maintains comparability, even at the expense of price increases.

In large measure, then, the arbitrator is not only exercising the functions of a judge, but also those of a legislator. This has not always been understood by those who, at various times, have wrongly accused the Government of interfering with the independence of arbitrators. There would certainly be nothing wrong in Parliament's laying down certain principles that arbitrators should follow. The arbitrators would remain quite free of interference in the interpretation of these criteria and their application to individual cases. Nobody suggests that a judge is not free because he is expected to administer the laws passed by Parliament. Nor is there any valid reason why the Government should not make it known that it believes increases in wages in certain fields, or above a certain level, would be contrary to the public interest. There are plenty of people who are going to comment on such matters, and one cannot expect arbitrators to be unaware of, or uninfluenced by, these discussions, and this is quite proper. It would be quite wrong, even if possible, to expect arbitrators to look at cases in a vacuum. So long as the Government does not try to issue *instructions* to arbitrators, or to secure the removal of arbitrators who make decisions against government policy, there is no improper interference.

Although the arbitrator is not obliged to follow any principles that are formally prescribed, he is not entirely free to make whatever awards he thinks fit. We have seen already that arbitration awards are not legally enforceable, and that, normally, arbitration may only take place when both parties agree. He is, therefore, bound to look for a compromise that will be acceptable to the two parties. He will almost certainly make an award that lies somewhere between what the unions are demanding and what the employers are offering. Even if he thinks the workers are, in some sense, entitled to more than the unions are asking, he will not make an award that exceeds what has been asked. He may well make an award that is well below what the union has asked in such a case, because he knows that, even if the employers accept his award on this occasion, they may be reluctant to accept his or any other arbitrator's intervention on a subsequent occasion. Similarly, he may feel that the unions have not really made a case for *any* increase, but he may well decide that the outright rejection of their case would, in the long run at least, lead to the unions' refusal to accept arbitration.

There are many arguments that unions will use in presenting claims for higher wages, whether in direct negotiation with the employers or before an arbitrator. Pay in comparable industries, the cost of living, the profitability of the industry, whether it is under-manned or threatened with redundancies, changes in the nature of the job, and in the level of productivity, will all be mentioned and must be taken into account by the arbitrator. A careful examination will show, however, that none of these considerations provides an unequivocal guide to the proper level of wages, and one of these criteria may suggest quite a different level from another.

If profits are good, for example, it may be argued that firms could pay higher wages without reducing employment or raising prices. It does not follow that because this is so wages should be raised. If the wages being paid are more or less in line with what is paid in other industries for comparable work, and if the industry has no difficulty in recruiting labour, it would equally well be argued that the present level of wages is correct, and that the firm should consider lowering prices. Again, it is clear that workers may use big profits as a justification for increased pay, but will not accept the corollary, that pay increases should be forgone if losses are being made. Thus, the deficits of British Rail have never deterred the railway unions from making claims for increases in wages. It may well be that, given a high degree of immobility on the part of workers, wages ought to be raised in declining industries, if only to speed contraction and the reallocation of labour: the present point is that profits are used as a one-way argument by the unions. Nevertheless, it may equally be true that employers tend to use poor profits as a reason for rejecting claims for higher pay, but look for other grounds for doing so when profits are good.

The lowest paid workers may need a pay increase when the cost of living rises, although it may be possible to protect them from the

218

effects of rising prices in other ways.[8] An increase in the cost of living is certainly not an indication that *all* workers should receive an increase in pay. The cost of living may rise because imported goods have risen in price, or because of increases in indirect taxation. If imports have become dearer, it may be very undesirable that incomes should rise in order to enable people to go on maintaining the same standard of living. If the country is to avoid running into balance of payments difficulties because imports are costing more, it may be necessary, at the very least, to let rising prices have their natural effect on demand, and not to offset this effect by an adjustment of incomes. Similarly, increased taxation may have been imposed to reduce the purchasing power in the pockets of consumers. To offset this intention by allowing wages to rise would be against the interest of the community as a whole. Up to a point, wages could rise to offset an increase in the cost of living without disastrous results for the whole community, so long as there was some other section of the community to bear the burden. But when wages take something like 75 per cent of the national income, the scope for labour to shift the burden to other sections of the community is limited.

Changes in productivity may, in certain circumstances, provide a valid reason for an increase in pay, but not in all cases. Where increased productivity springs from greater effort, or where a job has become more skilled, there is a fairly clear case for some increase in pay. If, however, productivity is rising simply as a result of increasing mechanization, there may be no good reason why a particular group of workers should expect an increase in pay as a result. This point will be considered more fully in chapter 16 when incomes policy is considered. For the moment, it may be stated that workers in general may reasonably expect to benefit from the general rise in productivity throughout the economy, but a particular group of workers ought not necessarily to expect increases related to a very big increase in their own productivity, unless they have themselves contributed towards this increase in some positive way – that is, beyond accepting the greater degree of mechanization.

Attention must certainly be given to relativities. On the other hand, it must be recognized that the argument for a pay increase based on changed relativities is probably the easiest of all to misuse. It is, for example, quite possible to believe that the pay of any group of workers should bear a reasonable relationship to that of other workers in jobs calling for roughly the same qualifications, skill, and responsibility. This does not mean that one is bound to accept the

219

argument of a trade union to the effect that its members in a particular job have not had a pay increase for a couple of years, that a couple of years ago these members were getting the same as another group of workers who have since had a pay rise of 10 per cent, *therefore these members of ours should now have a 10 per cent rise.* There may be a case for such an increase, but there could equally be reasons for rejecting this line of reasoning. It would need to be demonstrated that the two groups were doing comparable work two years ago, and that the 10 per cent increase received by the one group was not, in fact, a proper recognition of the fact that the work they were doing was more skilled or more responsible. Equally, it would need to be shown before accepting the argument that, even if the jobs were once comparable, they remain so.

Finally, there is the argument that an industry or occupation is undermanned and needs to raise wages in order to increase recruitment. This is most likely to arise in connection with employment in the public sector. In private enterprise, if employers see an opportunity to increase profits by recruiting more labour, they will take the initiative in raising wages. In the public sector, there may be an assumption that a certain level of service to the public must be maintained. A public transport system, for example, may have an establishment based on the need to operate certain routes and maintain a given frequency of service. Should wages be raised to the point where there are no staff shortages? There are, at least, two serious objections to this argument. First, it may not work. The supply of labour to a particular occupation may be inelastic. If the wages of bus drivers are raised, the number of suitable men attracted from other occupations may be very small. Moreover, there is a danger that even if the policy showed signs of succeeding, wages would be raised in other occupations, thus offsetting the incentive for workers to transfer to bus driving. Second, although higher wages might sometimes succeed in recruiting more workers, the impact on costs might undermine the financial structure of the service. Suppose, for example, that municipal bus services are expected to pay their way and not be a charge on the rates. If wages are raised to overcome staff shortages and enable scheduled services to be maintained, an increase in fares might be necessary. If the demand for public transport were inelastic, all would be well. If, however, the demand for public transport is elastic, the result would be such a fall in numbers using public transport that revenue would be reduced and the service make a substantial loss. Genuine undermanning may, in some situations, call for wage increases, but the argument must take

220

full account of the character of the demand for the product and not be based on some purely arbitrary establishment.

To summarize, then, all these arguments are relevant to wage determination, but they cannot provide any automatic rule the arbitrator can apply. He must use his own judgement as to the relative importance of these and, perhaps, other considerations; he must also remember always that he is looking for a compromise that both parties will find acceptable in the long run.

Courts of inquiry

Arbitration is only possible if both sides agree. Conciliation may be undertaken at the request of either party to a dispute, and, indeed, there is nothing to prevent the Department of Employment and Productivity taking the initiative. The parties may be approached and an offer to conciliate made. If it is made clear that such an offer is not welcome or is unlikely to be useful, there remains the power of the Secretary for Employment and Productivity to appoint a court of inquiry. Such courts are

> ... primarily a means of informing Parliament and the public of the facts and underlying causes of a dispute. A court of inquiry is appointed only as a last resort when no agreed settlement of a dispute seems possible, and when an unbiassed examination of the facts is considered to be in the public interest.[9]

The power to appoint such courts of inquiry has been used sparingly. On the average, there were two or three courts of inquiry a year between 1945 and 1961. For earlier years, the average is roughly the same, though there were considerable variations around the average.

A court of inquiry will normally consist of three members, an independent chairman (usually a lawyer or an academic economist) and two other members. These other members are usually an employer and a trade unionist, both of whom have no direct interest in the particular dispute. If the minister thinks fit, the court could be larger, with four representative members, or the inquiry could be entrusted to a single independent person. The appointment of a court of inquiry does not require the consent of the parties, and the court may meet while a strike, or lockout, is in progress.

The court has no power beyond reporting upon the situation as it sees it. Nevertheless, an examination of the history of courts of inquiry show that suggestions in their reports often provide the basis for a settlement. A dispute must sooner or later be settled. The report of an independent court of inquiry, especially if it is the unanimous report of a court of three or five members including one or two prominent trade union leaders, is something that cannot easily be ignored. For this reason, courts of inquiry have often helped pave the way towards a final settlement.

A committee of investigation may be appointed in a similar manner. The composition is similar to that of a court of inquiry, but the process is a less formal one and the report is not laid before Parliament.

Minimum wage legislation

British governments have not favoured a resort to the imposition of a national minimum wage. For the most part, they have been content to allow wages to be fixed largely as a result of collective bargaining, and have only sought to impose a minimum wage in limited areas where collective bargaining is weak or non-existent and where the level of remuneration is such as to call for some special intervention. The chief instrument of minimum wage regulation is the wages council, though there is separate machinery for agriculture. In addition, there are the Fair Wages Resolutions of the House of Commons; the first was passed in 1891, and was aimed at preventing the evils revealed by the Sweating Committee and the abuses resulting from the subcontracting of government work. The resolution aimed at enforcing the payment of the 'current' rates of wages to workers engaged on government contracts. The latest such resolution was passed in 1946; under its terms, a government contractor is required to pay the wages that have been fixed by collective bargaining or arbitration, to observe 'fair' conditions of work as well as 'fair' wages, and to give his workers freedom to join a trade union. (Some local authorities have tried to go further and to require contractors to employ only union labour.) The contractor is required to ensure that these conditions are observed by any subcontractors.

Any question of whether the terms of the resolution are being observed is a matter for the Department of Employment and Productivity. In the absence of agreement between the Department and the contractor, the matter is to be settled by arbitration, usually by the Industrial Court. The purpose of the resolution is to ensure that fair wages and conditions of employment are offered by government contractors, and to encourage the use of the normal machinery of collective bargaining. No rights are conferred on any party other

222

than the Government. The worker on a government contract has no right to sue the employer if he thinks he is being paid less than a 'fair' wage within the meaning of the resolution. Anyone feeling aggrieved may only bring his complaint to the Department of Employment and Productivity and leave the Department to take appropriate action. The ultimate sanction is, of course, the deletion of the contractor's name from the list of those eligible for government contracts.

The wages council machinery. In the past, there have been a number of special procedures for wage regulations. Those that previously existed in catering and road haulage have now been brought within the scope of the ordinary wages council machinery. Only agriculture remains separate, and here the principal difference is that the agricultural wages boards have power to make orders regulating wages, whereas the wages councils make recommendations to the Secretary for Employment and Productivity.

The origins of the wages council system are to be found in the Trade Boards Act, 1909. Initially, four boards were established in trades that paid very low wages. This number has subsequently increased as fresh legislation extended the system to more and more trades. When the latest Wages Council Act was passed in 1959, about three and a half million workers came within the scope of the system.[10]

There are three ways in which a wages council may be set up. First, the Secretary for Employment and Productivity can act on his own initiative if two conditions are satisfied: (a) if there is no adequate machinery for the effective regulation of the wages of some group of workers, and (b) if the existing level of remuneration makes it expedient that a council should be established. The second method is for a Joint Industrial Council or similar body, or organizations representing both workers and employers, to request the Secretary for Employment and Productivity to establish a wages council. This application may be made on the ground that the existing machinery for wage regulation is inadequate, or may cease to be adequate. In this event, the Secretary for Employment and Productivity must, if there is sufficient cause, set up a commission of inquiry. The third method is for the Secretary for Employment and Productivity to take the initiative in setting up a commission of inquiry if he thinks that the machinery for effective regulation of the wages of any group of workers does not exist, or is likely to cease to exist, or is likely to cease to be adequate, and that reasonable remuneration will not be maintained.

The composition of all wages councils is similar. There is an independent chairman and not more than two other independent members, one of whom is usually named as deputy chairman. In addition, there are equal numbers of members representing workers and employers. The number of representative members tends to vary, depending on the different circumstances and interests to be represented. The members must be representative of the different kinds of establishments, different areas, the various trade unions organizing workers, and so on. The more localized and homogeneous the trade, the fewer the representative members will be.

Voting is normally by sides. This means that for a proposal to be carried, it must normally receive the support of a majority of the members present and voting on each side. If the two sides disagree, a majority of the independent members could carry a proposal, but this is not the usual procedure. The role of the independent members, and of the chairman especially, is to try to find a proposal that will command the support of both sides. When agreement is reached, the proposals are submitted to the Secretary for Employment and Productivity, who may then make a wage regulation order.[11]

A wage regulation order may prescribe minimum time or piece rates or both. It may also make regulations about such matters as paid holidays. The Secretary for Employment and Productivity has no power to vary the recommendations of a wages council.[12] He can, however, refer a proposal back to the council. Where this has been done in the past, the council has usually responded by resubmitting the proposals originally made, without modification, and all that is achieved is a measure of delay. This delay may serve two useful purposes, however. First, it makes it clear that the Government considers the proposed increase is against the public interest, perhaps clashing with the incomes policy being pursued. By making its disapproval clear, it is indicating that acceptance of the award is under pressure and should not be taken as a green light for similar increases in other sectors. Second, the delay may serve to reduce the effective rate of increase. If, for example, a 4 per cent increase has been recommended to take effect 12 months from the last increase, this represents a rate of increase of 4 per cent per annum. If the reference back delays the operation of the 4 per cent increase by 4 months, the annual rate of increase is reduced to 3 per cent, which may be acceptable to the Government.

It is an offence to pay a worker less than the wage laid down in a wage regulation order, except in circumstances for which special provision is made. Lower rates of payment may be made to apprentices and learners, and to infirm or incapacitated workers. The employer must, in the latter case, obtain a special permit from the wages council, which may attach such conditions as it deems fit. The act lays down penalties for failing to display prescribed notices, failing to keep proper records, as well as for failing to pay the statutory remuneration. A worker who has been underpaid is entitled to sue for payment of arrears for a period not exceeding two years, or action may be taken on his behalf by the Department's inspectorate.

There has always been provision for the abolition of a wages council if it should prove to be no longer necessary. This provision has rarely been used in the past, although, in general, there has been a great increase in the strength of trade unions. It seems, however, that this growth in union strength has been in limited sectors of industry, and has not altered the traditional weakness of unorganized workers in other sectors.

The impact of minimum wage regulation. It is not easy to assess the impact of minimum wage regulation in Britain. Two separate questions may be asked. First, what has been the impact of wages councils or other machinery on the industries directly concerned? Second, what impact has minimum wage legislation had on wages in general?

It is, in the very nature of things, difficult to prove that the level of wages, either in a particular trade or generally, is higher or lower than it would have been in the absence of minimum wage regulation. In all cases where wages councils are established, the machinery for collective bargaining is weak, and usually the level of remuneration is low. The inadequacy of the arrangements for collective bargaining may spring from weakness on the trade union side. In many of the trades affected, women form a large part of the labour force, and do not organize as readily as men. In other cases, there may be many small employers, and a reluctance on the part of many to join an association. In some cases, both factors may be present. It may be difficult for a trade union to secure a reasonable bargain if a large proportion of workers choose not to join. Again, if many employers remain outside the employers association, associated employers who might otherwise have been willing to concede wage increases may refuse to do so for fear of undercutting. In some instances, wages may be determined by a Joint Industrial Council and this agreement then forms the basis of a wages council recommendation. The effect of this procedure is to ensure that the voluntary agreement is imposed as a statutory obligation on the non-associated employers.

While there can be no conclusive proof, it would appear not unreasonable to suppose that the wages council machinery has kept wages in the trades concerned above the levels that would otherwise have prevailed. The abolition of wages councils, in some cases at least, might be expected to result, if not in a fall in wages, in a slower rate of increase. Where a Joint Industrial Council exists, it might be possible to abolish the wages council, without loss to the workers, if there were some amendment of the Industrial Court claims procedure – for example, to remove the necessity for a case to be brought to the Court each time wages were raised by a fresh agreement.

It may be argued that the minimum rates fixed by wages councils are similar to the basic rates fixed by normal collective bargaining. In both cases, these rates are substantially below actual earnings. Can it be shown that the minima prescribed by wage regulation orders influence the level of actual earnings? Or is it possible that these earnings are determined by market conditions and are not influenced by the wages council minima? This seems unlikely. Although it is true that this gap exists between basic rates and earnings, there is a strong body of belief that there is a super-structure of supplementary payments over and above the basic rates, and that any movement in basic rates therefore tends to influence earnings.[13] It is possible for unorganized workers to obtain very favourable wages if there is a sufficient demand for their services. It seems unlikely that this kind of situation will prevail in the wages council sector. This sector is likely to be oversupplied with labour that is, on the whole, not highly skilled, even when the labour market generally is short of labour.

The existence of monopsony in the labour market, combined with supernormal profits, may permit wages to be forced up without loss of employment. If, however, some firms are not maximizing profits, if management attaches more importance to an easy life than to earning increased money profits, a higher wage rate enforced by trade union or by minimum wage regulation may force the management to increase efficiency. This increased efficiency may enable the same amount of labour to be employed despite the higher wage.[14]

The wages council machinery could have two possible consequences for wage levels generally. One possibility would be that the higher level of wages in the wages council sector would reduce employment in that sector, and so might lead to an increase in the supply of labour to other jobs. This would tend to lower the wage level in other jobs. Alternatively, the enforcement of certain minima

226

by means of the wages councils might have the opposite effect. Trade unions in other parts of the economy might use these minima as some kind of a lever in order to get higher rates under collective agreements. Although there is very little evidence, the probability is that the wages council machinery has made very little difference to the level of wages in the economy as a whole. There is certainly little reason to believe that, where trade unions are strong, the demands they make are in any way related to the awards made by wages councils. The one kind of situation where wages councils awards might have a bigger impact generally is when an incomes policy is being operated. Acceptance of above the norm increases recommended by a wages council might be interpreted as the all-clear for other settlements to go beyond the norm. In such a case, however, the impact is due to the breaching (or apparent breaching) of the incomes policy, rather than the normal impact of the wages council awards. There is equally little reason to suspect that, if the wages council machinery does result in higher wages than would otherwise prevail in the industries covered, the reduction in employment therein would have serious repercussions on other industries. Wages council industries employ a high proportion of women, and the men employed are not the most highly skilled. There is a very real possibility that if any unemployment does result, some of the workers affected are likely to remain unemployed rather than find jobs in other industries and depress wage levels generally. The fact that pay in wages council industries is so low when there is, in general, a shortage of labour, suggests that there is only limited mobility of labour.

A national minimum wage

While there may be doubt about whether the wages council machinery has had any significant impact on wage levels, and, if it has, in what direction, there is no doubt that a good many workers are still earning very low wages. Moreover, the low earners are not confined to any one industry or group of industries. While we might well find a higher proportion of low earners in the wages council sector, nearly every industry has its quota of low earners.

It is, of course, necessary to define what is meant by low earnings. There is no single definition that is satisfactory for all purposes. What many people have in mind, however, is the fact that many men, especially those with children, may be earning less than they would be entitled to under supplementary benefit. The supplementary

227

benefit scales might be regarded as the official 'poverty line', to which everybody will be brought, even if they have no other income at all. In fact, a man in full-time employment cannot receive any supplementary benefit, no matter how low his earnings, and the 'wage-stop' ensures that he cannot, when unemployed, be given the full scale of benefit, if this will make him better off than when in employment.

We can ask what kind of wage a man must earn if he is to be as well off when working as somebody drawing the full supplementary benefit scale. The long-term rate of supplementary benefit, in 1969, gives a married couple £7 19s a week, plus rent (say another 35s). If they have three children aged between 5 and 11 they will get another £4 16s making a total income of £14 10s.[15] If a man is working, he must also pay National Insurance contributions (about £1) and will incur expenses through working (say, at a modest estimate, 13s for meals at work and fares). On the other hand, he will receive 38s in family allowances. If, therefore, he earns £14 5s a week he would be as well off as a man with the same family living on supplementary benefit.

If we are thinking of setting a national minimum wage, however, there are good arguments for making this at least £15 a week. It should be possible for a man with three children in full-time employment to enjoy a standard of living at least a little higher than that possible on supplementary benefit. Some recognition should be given to the fact that a man on supplementary benefit may have some casual earnings disregarded. Finally, it must be remembered that there will be those earning low wages who have more than three children. A minimum wage of £15 a week represents about two-thirds of the average weekly earnings of adult male workers in April 1968. The Ministry of Labour's survey of the spread of earnings in 1960[16] showed that, at that date, about 10 per cent of adult male manual workers were earning less than £10 a week, when average earnings were between £14 10s and £15 a week. We may, therefore, suppose that, today, about 10 per cent of adult males would be earning less than £15 a week. It is clear, therefore, that although the increase in family allowances of 10s per child, made in two stages in October 1967 and April 1968 must have reduced considerably the number of workers likely to fall below the supplementary benefit standard, the remaining problem is still a serious one. The question to be asked is whether a national minimum wage is the best solution or whether some alternative should be sought.

A case can be made for a national minimum wage, but there would be difficulties. In particular, it can be argued that, where employers can obtain cheap labour, there is no real incentive to make the most effective use of labour. The most serious difficulties spring from the present complex wage structure in most industries. It would cost comparatively little to bring all workers up to the £15 a week minimum. Some adjustments would have to be made to the wages of other workers to maintain reasonable differentials, where there was a real difference in the degree of skill or responsibility exercised. Moreover, there would be many instances of workers having to be raised from below £15 to significantly over this figure. It might be difficult, in introducing a national minimum wage to prevent its application to women workers, and this would mean a very big increase in pay for a large number of workers. The cost to industry of a national minimum wage could therefore be very substantial. It would certainly be necessary to ensure that the introduction of a national minimum wage did not lead to a sharp increase in the earnings of all workers who are already earning well over this figure, a very real possibility where scarcely any workers have a basic wage of as much as £15 a week, yet men earn, on average, well over £22 a week.

At the same time, the introduction of a national minimum wage of £15 a week would still leave many workers with more than three children below the poverty line, and a lot more very close to it. It would seem, therefore, that the elimination of poverty can only be brought about through further increases in family allowances or other social policies. If it is felt that the payment of large family allowances by the State is a subsidy to inefficient employers, the remedy might be to adopt the French system, whereby the allowances are met by a payroll tax on employers.

NOTES

1. But see chapter 12 on the legal privileges of trade unions. There may, in fact, now be no effective remedy for the injured employer.

2. It is no solution to recognize all the unions. Even if this did not create difficulties for efficient bargaining, it is quite possible that one union would be set on acquiring exclusive recognition and call a strike or take other action if another union were also recognized.

3. In the 'fifties there was, of course, a gradual abandonment of many of the wartime controls. Nevertheless, there is a long-term trend towards greater intervention.

4. *The National Plan*, Cmnd. 2764, HMSO, London, 1965.

5. For a description of the arbitration machinery that has been established for particular industries, see Ministry of Labour, *Industrial Relations Handbook*, HMSO, London, 1961, or I. Sharpe, *Industrial Conciliation and Arbitration in Great Britain*, Allen and Unwin, London, 1950.

6. In the period to 1951, strikes and lockouts were illegal. Even then, it would not have been possible, in practice, to enforce the penalties provided by imprisoning the large number of workers that might be involved in a major dispute.

7. The argument here refers particularly to arbitration on major wage claims. An arbitrator may, for example, be asked to determine a dispute over the interpretation of some clause in an agreement, or a dispute over the application of agreed disciplinary procedures in a case where there is argument over what actually happened. In these cases, the role of the arbitrator bears a much closer resemblance to that of a judge.

8. In practice, it will be married men with children who are living close to the poverty line as a result of low wages. Very few men earn such low wages that a single man or a childless couple are likely to be near the poverty line, although their standard of living may be quite low. It would therefore be possible to avoid the most serious consequences of rising prices among the low paid by changes in Family Allowances.

9. *Industrial Relations Handbook*, p. 141.

10. The term 'wages council', was first employed in an act of 1945.

11. Before submission to the Secretary for Employment and Productivity, the council publishes its proposals, and must allow at least 14 days for workers or employers to make representations. After this period, the proposals are submitted, with or without modification.

12. There is now, however, provision for referring the recommendations of a wages council, like any collective agreement, to the National Board for Prices and Incomes. The Secretary for Employment and Productivity could, on receiving the Board's report, indicate that no wage regulation order would be made which did not conform to the incomes policy.

13. See, for example, D. J. Robertson, *Factory Wage Structures and National Agreements*, Cambridge U.P., 1960. It is also clear that the PIB believes changes in minimum rates recommended by wages councils may influence the earnings of more highly paid workers in the industry.

14. Increased productivity, however, will enable a given output to be maintained with a reduced labour force. Unless there can be some lowering of price, despite higher wages *and* an elastic demand for the product, some unemployment must result.

15. It must be repeated that the family income will be brought up to this level. Some income may be disregarded, but National Insurance benefit and family allowances will be counted in full.

16. See Table 8.5.

16. Incomes policy

Economists were quick to see the danger that the implementation of Keynesian policies for the maintenance of full employment would increase the bargaining power of trade unions to such an extent that wage inflation would be almost inevitable. There has therefore been much discussion by economists of the possibility of countering this danger by a wages policy, or, in more recent years, by an incomes policy. It is necessary, therefore, to look briefly at the development of ideas on incomes policy, the fundamental relationships involved in such a policy, and finally the attempt by the Government to operate an incomes policy in Britain in the period since 1964.

The development of ideas on incomes policy

Keynesian thinking on the possibility and desirability of maintaining a high and stable level of employment was bound to affect the bargaining power of the trade unions. With the implementation of such policies, the employer would find that labour was scarce: there would be no pool of unemployed men seeking jobs. As a result, men seeking employment might be more particular: they would not rush into the first job offered them unless the wages and conditions of employment were right. There would be much more active competition between employers for labour, and wages would tend to rise. Trade unions would press for higher wages, and would not be inhibited by the fear that a rise in wages would necessarily be accompanied by a fall in the numbers employed. Keynes had demonstrated the fallacy of the argument that a cut in the wage rate is a cure for unemployment. While a fall in wages might, if it affected only one firm, make it possible for more men to be employed, a general fall in wages reduces the aggregate demand for goods and services and might well lead to more unemployment.

In many countries, however, the achievement of full employment came not as a result of the conscious application of Keynesian policies, but as a result of war. During the Second World War in Britain, as in most of the belligerent countries, a large part of the normal labour force was recruited into the armed services. Although output for civilian purposes was drastically curtailed, the demand for equipment for the services meant that the real problem was finding enough workers, rather than finding jobs for the unemployed, which had been the problem in much of the interwar period. There was, of course, in this wartime situation, a danger of wage inflation. In most countries, governments took measures to try to ensure that such inflation did not get out of hand. In Britain, there was legislation which made strikes and lockouts illegal, and any dispute had to be reported to the Ministry of Labour which could refer it to the National Arbitration Tribunal.

Although compulsory arbitration continued in a modified form after the war until 1958, it was largely a dead letter. In practice, the enforcement of the compulsory arbitration against the workers was impossible. The immediate postwar period was one in which there was much 'government by exhortation'. Appeals were made for wage restraint, and with some modest measure of success. For a time, the TUC accepted the policy of wage restraint, although it had no authority to impose this policy on its constituent unions. In this respect, the position of the TUC in Britain is much weaker than that of its counterpart in Sweden, where individual unions are expected to follow closely the key bargain made in central negotiations between the national organizations representing unions and employers. The policy of wage restraint always recognized that there were exceptional cases, and it was all too easy for a union to accept the idea of restraint in principle, but to act on the assumption that most of the cases it was concerned with were among the exceptions. The policy of wage restraint was finally rejected by the TUC in 1950, partly, at least, as a result of the rise in the cost of living which followed devaluation in 1949.

Thereafter, wages or incomes policy continued to be discussed in various economic journals, and appeals for wage restraint were still heard. In the middle 'fifties, there were a number of courts of inquiry which referred to the wider public interest in wage bargaining, and which maintained that this was outside the terms of reference of such courts or ordinary arbitration tribunals, and suggested that some special body should be appointed to study the matter. In 1957, the Council on Prices, Productivity, and Incomes (Cohen Council) was set up and it produced a number of reports. These tended to be theoretical studies in the economics of inflation and

232

had little practical impact. The subject remained an academic one until 1961.

In 1961, Mr Selwyn Lloyd introduced the 'pay pause' as an emergency measure in one of the country's recurrent balance of payments crises. The policy was intended to refer to both wages and dividends. The policy was far from being successful, since it was widely believed that it bore more harshly on wages than profits. There was no control over the level of profits earned: dividends distributed might be held at the previous level for the period of the crisis, but at the end of the period of restraint any profits earned during earlier periods could be distributed. Whereas the wage-earner had to forgo an increase in his wages, the profit-receiver merely had to wait for his.

Furthermore, the pay pause operated unfairly as between wage-earners. The government of the day exercised stringent controls over the pay of workers in the public sector, but it lacked the courage to take powers of controlling the wages of workers in the private sector. A policy of this kind could scarcely be expected to appeal to the workers as a long-run measure, and was, indeed, intensely unpopular, even as a temporary measure.

The pay pause was followed by the period of the 'guiding light' of $2\frac{1}{2}$ per cent. This could be regarded as the forerunner of the norm of the incomes policy that has been operated since 1964. Around this time, the Government also set up the National Incomes Commission. This was given a twofold task: to advise the Government on specific matters relating to the pay of workers in the public sector, and to report on agreements that had been reached in the private sector. It was apparently the belief of the Government that unfavourable reports by the Commission in one case would be enough to dissuade negotiators from behaving in the same irresponsible manner in another case. The Commission's usefulness was limited by the refusal of the trade unions to collaborate.[1]

In the remaining years of life of the Conservative Government, the Commission had no real influence. As the time approached for a general election, the Labour Party laid considerable stress on ending the stop-go policies of the years of Conservative rule, and on the role of an incomes policy in enabling the country to achieve continuous economic growth without inflation. When returned to power in 1964, however, the economic situation was such that the policy of rapid and continuous growth was impossible to implement. The old stop-go policies had to be brought into use once more, except, perhaps, that in the period from 1964 to 1969 there has been precious little of the

233

go. In the circumstances, the incomes policy became, as in 1961, an instrument of restraint rather than the key to expansion. The idea of a policy that would be operated by agreement rapidly gave way to a policy enforced by legal sanctions and, in 1966, to a 'wage freeze' that was much more severe than anything Selwyn Lloyd had contemplated in 1961.

Fundamental relationships

The idea underlying the concept of an incomes policy is that there will be inflation if wages and other incomes rise in money terms more rapidly than the supply of goods and services. The idea that if wages increase at the same rate as productivity all will be well is, however, a very simplified first approximation. A number of important qualifications need to be made.

In practice, we are interested in maintaining both stable prices *and* a healthy balance of payments. In an open economy, there is the possibility that an excessive rise in money incomes will result, in part at least, in increased imports or a diversion of goods from the export market. In this way, the supply of goods is adjusted to the increased level of money incomes. To a limited extent, therefore, a rise in money incomes in excess of the rise in productivity may result in a balance of payments deficit rather than a rise in domestic prices. Some rise in domestic prices is probable, however, because rising wages will mean rising labour costs which are likely to be passed on to the consumer.

The idea that inflation is avoided if money incomes rise at the same rate as productivity also assumes that current incomes are the only source of expenditure. In normal times, this is probably not far from the truth, but in exceptional circumstances it might prove a totally inadequate basis for any kind of economic policy. After the Second World War, for example, consumers in many countries wanted to replace many durable goods which, but for the war, would have been replaced earlier. They were not dependent upon their current earnings when making such purchases, because most people had been induced to save on a substantial scale during the war and were able to draw on these savings for a postwar spending spree. If people are both able and willing to draw on past savings to maintain the standard of consumption they desire, a policy which succeeds in limiting the rate of increase in current incomes to the same level as the rate of increase in productivity may well fail to prevent prices from rising.

234

The most important qualification that has to be considered, however, concerns the relationship between the rate of increase in wages and profits. What matters is that, subject to other qualifications, the level of money incomes should not increase *in aggregate* more rapidly than productivity. There is no reason why any one element in national income should not increase more rapidly than productivity, if others rise less rapidly. Although it may be convenient in much of the discussion of incomes policy to assume that it is desirable that all elements in the national income should rise at the same rate, it is important that we should stop to look a little more closely at the relationship between wages and profits.

A simple model. This problem may be explored by a simple model which concentrates on wages and profits and excludes the other elements of the national income. If productivity increases, it is usually the result of the employment of more capital. Some technical innovations may raise productivity without more capital being employed, but these are exceptional. Increasing output per head is generally accompanied by the employment of more capital per head of worker, certainly when we view the economy as a whole rather than some small sector of it.

If more capital is employed, the increase in output that results may be less than proportionate to the capital employed (the capital to output ratio rises), or it may be proportionate, or it may be more than proportionate (if there is a sufficient rate of technological advance). Suppose that the rate of return on capital needs to be maintained at a constant rate in order to attract funds for investment. This means that the necessary level of profit, as a proportion of total income, will rise, remain the same, or fall, depending upon whether output has risen less than proportionately, proportionately, or more than proportionately to the amount of capital employed. If aggregate profits need to rise more than proportionately to output, wages must rise less than proportionately; if profits need only rise less than proportionately to output, it is possible for wages to rise more than proportionately without any increase in unit costs.

The position may be clarified by a numerical example. Capital employed in year 0 is £1 000 000. Profits, including allowances for depreciation, are £200 000. Two hundred men are employed at an annual wage of £1000. The total wage bill is £200 000 and the national product is £400 000. By year 1, the capital employed in the economy has increased by 5 per cent to £1 050 000. Suppose, however, that output has risen in terms of physical volume by only 4 per cent. If prices are to remain stable, the national product will

235

now be 4 per cent higher than in year 0, in other words, £416 000. If profits must remain at 20 per cent of capital employed, aggregate profits must increase to £210 000 (one-fifth of £1 050 000), leaving wages to increase to £206 000. This is only a 3 per cent increase in wages. If wages had risen by 4 per cent to £208 000, the total national product would have been £418 000, *at year 1 prices*, for an output we know to be worth £416 000 at year 0 prices. In other words, there would, on these figures, have been a rise of about $\frac{1}{2}$ per cent in the level of prices.

The larger the share of wages in the national income, the less important is this consideration. The reader may check this by re-working the example just given with fresh figures.[2]

For completeness, it may be added that it is the gross profit rate that matters, not the net return to the investor. Even if the amount of capital employed rose in the same proportion as output, any tendency for new capital to have a shorter life than old would mean that depreciation allowances would have to be increased and there would be a need for gross profits to increase as a proportion of the national product. Conversely, the share of profits would tend to fall if capital were to become longer-lived.

Incomes policy in Britain

The idea of an incomes policy, as conceived in the months immediately following the election of a Labour Government in 1964, was a policy that would rely largely on voluntary agreement. A norm was to be set, and most wage agreements would have to conform to this, but there would also be criteria for above the norm increases. A National Board for Prices and Incomes (PIB) was established early in 1965. The Government was to have power to refer particular settlements to the PIB, and pay increases could be delayed for a limited period, while the PIB investigation took place.

The policy formulated in 1964 differed in one fundamental way from the pay pause of 1961. The 1961 policy was felt to fall too heavily on wages, and especially wages in the public sector. Not only did the new policy apply equally to all wages, but it also embraced prices. Where the 1961 policy had limited dividends (a temporary impact only, for profits in total were not controlled), the new policy gave the Government power to consider the reasonableness of proposed price increases, and even to consider whether, in certain circumstances, prices ought to be reduced. The new approach to prices was an essential element in securing a measure of trade union support for the incomes policy.

236

The main lines of the policy have remained the same since 1964. Changes that have occurred have been in the direction of requiring advance notice of any major proposal for increasing wages, lengthening the period for which the Government could delay the operation of wage increases, and variations in the norm. Originally, wage increases could be delayed for only a few months, while the PIB made an investigation. With the difficulties experienced by the British economy in 1966 and afterwards, there were such developments as the wage freeze (when all increases were banned), and a period of severe restraint (when there was, in effect, a zero norm, and any increase in wages or salaries had to be justified as a special case). In addition, the delaying powers were increased, so that where the PIB disapproved of a proposed increase it could be withheld for roughly a year. In the Budget Debate in 1969, it was indicated that these powers were due to lapse during the year, and it was not, at the time, the Government's intention to renew them. The position would then be that there could only be a short delay pending a PIB report. Wages council recommendations could also be referred to the PIB, and withheld if the PIB disapproved.

The criteria for above the norm increases. The various White Papers outlining the prices and incomes policy have always given, as criteria for increases in excess of the norm, in brief, the following: (a) a particular group of workers are badly paid, and cannot maintain a reasonable standard of living; (b) a group of workers is seriously underpaid in relation to those doing comparable work, and this is widely recognized; (c) an increase in pay is necessary in order to increase recruitment, or to prevent a loss of manpower, and this is both necessary in the national interest and likely to be effective; and (d) where the workers had made a substantial contribution to greater productivity by accepting new methods of working, and so on.

A great deal depends upon how these criteria are interpreted. There is clearly a danger that almost any claim for higher wages or salaries could be justified under one or other headings. The Government itself has made it clear in various White Papers that it would wish less emphasis to be placed than in the past on changes in the cost of living and in relativities. Nevertheless, workers themselves are unlikely to disregard these matters, and serious difficulties are likely to arise if the Government and the PIB attempt to enforce a policy based on an interpretation of the various criteria that the workers themselves find totally unacceptable. We must therefore look more closely at these criteria, and at some of the difficulties to which they give rise.

237

The idea of above the norm increases for those whose wages are so low that they cannot enjoy a reasonable standard of living will be acceptable to all. In practice, however, the Government has given no guidance on what was meant by 'low pay' in this context. It is undoubtedly true that the basic pay of a very large proportion of the labour force is such that a man with three or four children would be worse off than on supplementary benefit. On the other hand, there are comparatively few men who are getting only the basic minimum, and the PIB has concentrated, therefore, on actual earnings. This is, up to a point, reasonable, although it fails to make adequate provision for those men who are actually on the basic minimum. Given the present structure of wages in Britain, however, it is difficult to see what can be done about this. If adjustments in the minimum basic rate are likely to lead to adjustments in earnings in roughly the same proportion, it is clearly unreasonable to permit an increase in the basic rate if earnings are reasonable, even though it still leaves some men badly off. The real answer may well be a reform of the whole wages structure, but this can hardly be undertaken as part of an incomes policy, particularly a policy that has had to be developed rapidly to cope with severe economic crises.

The 'comparability' criterion is, perhaps, the most difficult of all. Certainly there is no justification for group A to be given an increase because group B has had one, and because in the past there has always been a particular relationship between the pay of groups A and B. This is true, whether it is a case of whether they should continue to receive the same rate of pay or whether there should be some kind of stability in the differential between them. If one merely looks at past relativities, it would always be possible for a trade union to show that a group of its members had lost ground relatively by making an appropriate comparison with some other group at the right date. On the other hand, it is quite reasonable to argue that where the jobs done are reasonably comparable in skill, responsibility, and effort the level of pay should be roughly the same. The criterion is sound provided the right comparisons are made, between groups really doing comparable work at the present time, and not between groups which did so once and were paid the same, but are no longer comparable in any real sense.

It has been argued that acceptance of comparability leads to the perpetuation of the inflationary spiral. The PIB itself used this argument in rejecting the claim of the university teachers at the end of 1968, considering that it was necessary at some point to break the inflationary spiral. The PIB, like many others who have used the
238

same argument, showed a remarkable lack of logic. While it is true that the inflationary spiral must be broken at some point, it does not follow that acceptance of comparability makes the inflationary spiral inevitable. Nor is it true, as the PIB seems to imply, that it was all the same wherever one chose to break the spiral. The correct approach is obvious to anyone who pauses to think a little more deeply. If one group is really paid substantially less than others doing comparable work, they should be allowed an above the norm increase. The point at which the spiral is to be broken is when those who had previously been well paid by comparison with others doing comparable work come to claim an increase on other grounds, or by trying to use the wrong comparisons (i.e., trying to equate themselves with workers on a higher level).

Difficulties and resentment must result if the PIB tries, in one instance, to write off comparability and, at the same time, the Government accepts the comparability argument for other groups. Thus, shortly before the PIB reported on university salaries, the Government had accepted the recommendations of an independent review body on doctors pay which had relied mainly on comparability. And, shortly afterwards, the PIB itself recommended massive increases for the heads of nationalized industries on the same grounds.

The third criterion, the need for higher pay to attract more manpower or to prevent a running down of manpower in a particular sector, also gives rise to difficulties. First, the criterion is subject to a qualification that the maintenance of recruitment is in the national interest. This, however, is not defined. It presumably means some kind of judgement that is independent of purely market considerations. Otherwise, one could argue that any industry that does not have all the labour it wants should raise wages. The *laissez faire* advocate would argue that, if the product is in demand, it is in the national interest to increase its output. While it is obvious that this is not what is meant by the White Paper,[3] no further light is thrown on the matter.

This criterion is also subject to the second qualification, that increased pay would be effective in increasing recruitment. There are, as we have already seen, reasons for doubting whether this will generally be so. If an industry is paying wages substantially less than those offered by most industries, it will have difficulty in recruiting labour. It may well secure some labour—school-leavers who do not know what opportunities are available to them, some older workers who are reluctant to change jobs, and so on. Raising wages to comparability may increase recruitment, but it may not help to go much beyond this level. It will certainly do little good where highly specialized skills are involved, and the supply of labour can only be increased, at the best, slowly. A very modest rise in wages may be all that is required to attract recruits up to the limit set by training facilities. Thereover, the long-run prospects of security in an expanding industry may be more important than remuneration.

The granting of above the norm increases for increased productivity may, at first sight, appear reasonable. This criterion does, admittedly, require that the workers should have made a real contribution towards the increased productivity. There is no question of allowing abnormally large pay increases where productivity has increased from greater mechanization alone. Even so, problems are created by big increases under productivity agreements. There is a better chance of above the norm increases for those workers who have, in the past, adopted restrictive practices and can therefore use these as a counter in productivity bargaining, and also for those workers whose productivity is easily measurable. It is all to the good that any big wage increase should be accompanied by attempts to raise productivity as much as possible. Restrictive practices should be abandoned, but we should not create anomalies in the wage and salary structure by simply buying out these restrictions. In practice, the PIB has maintained that part of the benefit of productivity agreements should go to consumers in the form of lower prices. Nevertheless, it is still unsatisfactory that some workers, who may be equally conscientious, equally skilled, and playing an equally important part in the community's economic life, should be tied to the norm, while others get much bigger increases, perhaps because they have operated more restrictions in the past, or because it happens to be possible to measure their output more easily.

The norm. The norm may be identified with the rate of increase in productivity, subject to the qualifications made above. At this stage, there is one qualification that needs to be considered, a matter of tactics rather than economic substance. Once the norm has been declared, there tends to be an assumption that this is the minimum increase in all wages and salaries, and that where a special case can be established under one of the four criteria more may be given. It is, however, a simple matter of arithmetic, that if productivity goes up by three per cent, and everybody gets a wage increase of *at least* three per cent, and some get a lot more, then the total wage bill is going up by over three per cent and labour costs are rising.

If the norm is actually the rate at which average earnings may
240

increase without inflation, above the norm increases for some groups must be matched by below the norm increases for others. This may be difficult to achieve in practice. The remedy may therefore be to declare a norm which is intended as a minimum increase for all, and to set this below the permissible increase in average earnings so as to allow room for above the norm increases.

The Prices and Incomes Board. The earlier parts of this chapter have touched on some of the inherent difficulties in an incomes policy. A great deal must rest on the PIB itself, and the way in which it interprets its remit. There is good reason for supposing that the PIB is not entirely satisfactory. In the first place, its investigations are comparatively brief. It reports within a matter of months of a reference being made to it. The Monopolies Commission may take as many years to complete one of its investigations. The overall task of the Monopolies Commission may be a greater one, but it is doubtful whether the difference is as great as in the time taken to report. It seems very probable that, by comparison with the Monopolies Commission, the investigations of the PIB are superficial.

There is certainly some evidence that the PIB is prepared to make far-reaching pontifical judgements on the basis of its limited inquiries, and at times even to disregard the limited material at its disposal. In some of its inquiries into the pay of municipal busmen, it made a great deal of the fact that the earnings of these men were not appreciably below the national average, playing down the fact that this was for a very long week and that *hourly* earnings were undoubtedly very low. In its report on university salaries, it made sweeping generalizations about the nature of universities and university teaching, and produced proposals for merit bonuses which would have been castigated as ludicrous if encountered in the course of an investigation of any pay settlement.[4]

It may be that too much blame should not be placed on the PIB. It has a difficult task, and was given little guidance. There are serious dangers in legislation which leaves too much discretionary power in the hands of such bodies. The Monopolies Commission was given little or no guidance as to what constituted the public interest; the PIB has had little guidance; the proposals in the White Paper, *In Place of Strife*,[5] also appear to give wide powers of discretion to the new Commission on Industrial Relations, and to the Minister. It may well be that controls need to be exercised over the economy by such bodies, but in legislation much more thought ought to be given to laying down precise rules for them to follow.

NOTES

1. The Commission made only one report on pay in the public sector, on the pay of university teachers, and recommended substantial increases. This was accepted, and it seems likely, therefore, that the only positive achievement of the Commission, set up primarily to help combat wage inflation, was to bring about large pay increases in one sector.

2. Try an initial assumption of £1 000 000 capital employed, with 200 men employed at a wage of £1000, and the same increases of 5 per cent in capital employed and 4 per cent in output. Wages may rise by $3\frac{1}{2}$ per cent without inflation; and, if they rise by 4 per cent, prices rise by only 0·3 per cent.

3. *Productivity, Prices and Incomes Policy in 1968 and 1969.* H.M.S.O., London, 1968, Cmd. 3590.

4. This proposal was for a £200 bonus to half of the teaching staff for special merit or responsibility. Such bonuses could not be paid without creating anomalies. If paid to half the staff of each department, injustice would occur where everyone was efficient, and equally where the general standard was low. On the other hand, insuperable difficulties would arise in trying to make these awards on a faculty or university basis, and in attempting to compare the assessments made by different departmental heads of the staff under them. In fact, this report was perhaps the most inept of all made by the PIB, and virtually all its recommendations were, in the end, substantially modified. Originally, a four per cent increase in salaries was recommended from October 1968. This was less than the three and a half per cent norm, the last increase having been in April 1966. Even so, the four per cent increase in aggregate was weighted to give substantially bigger increases at the lower end of the salary scale. Another four per cent was to be used for the merit bonuses from October 1969. The Government agreed, however, to use two-thirds of this four per cent to give further straight increases from October 1968, and to use it, moreover, to give increases to those who had received least under the original recommendation. Only the remaining one-third of the four per cent was to be used, from April 1969, to give special awards, and this was to be done by means of special increments within the salary scales.

5. Cmnd. 3888.

Index

244

For selected older vintag

ITALY	06	05	04	03	02	01	00	99	98	97
Barolo, Barbaresco	8	7	9	8	5	9	8	9	8	9
Chianti Classico Ris.	8	6	9	8	5	9	7	9	7	10
Brunello	8	7	9	8	5	9	8	9	8	10
Amarone	8	5	9	8	5	7	9	7	7	10
SPAIN										
Ribera del Duero	6	8	8	8	5	8	7	8	7	6
Rioja (red)	6	8	8	7	6	8	8	7	6	7
PORTUGAL										
South	7	8	8	6	5	8	9	8	6	6
North	5	8	8	8	7	8	9	7	6	8
Port	7	8	8	9	6	7	9	7	6	8
USA										
California Cabernet	8	9	8	8	7	8	7	9	7	7
California Chardonnay	9	8	8	9	8	8	7	8	7	8
Oregon Pinot Noir	8	6	8	8	8	7	9	9	8	5
Wash. State Cabernet	8	9	9	8	7	8	9	9	8	8
AUSTRALIA										
Coonawarra Cabernet	9	10	8	8	9	9	6	8	10	7
Hunter Semillon	8	9	8	8	7	8	9	8	10	9
Barossa Shiraz	8	10	8	7	10	9	8	9	10	8
Marg. River Cabernet	6	9	9	8	8	10	8	10	7	7
NEW ZEALAND										
M'lborough Sauvignon	9	7	8	8	6	9	9	8	5	8
H'kes Bay Cab/Merlot	8	7	8	5	9	7	8	7	10	7
SOUTH AFRICA										
Stellenbosch Cabernet	9	8	8	9	5	9	8	7	8	9
S'bosch Chardonnay	9	8	9	8	6	7	7	8	6	8

Numerals (1–10) represent an overall rating for each year. ◐ Not ready
● Just ready ● At peak ◖ Past best ○ Not generally declared

OZ CLARKE

POCKET WINE
BOOK 2008

PAVILION

This edition first published in 2007 by Pavilion Books

An imprint of
Anova Books Company Ltd
10 Southcombe Street
London W14 0RA

www.anovabooks.com
www.ozclarke.com

Created for Pavilion/Anova by
Websters International Publishers

Editor Maggie Ramsay
Art Director Nigel O'Gorman
Cartographer Andrew Thompson
Indexer Angie Hipkin
Photography Nigel James

16th edition. First published in 1992.
Revised editions published annually.

A CIP catalogue for this book is available from the
British Library.

ISBN-13: 978-1-862-05780-7
ISBN-10: 1-862-05780-X

Printed and bound in China by SNP Leefung

Thanks are due to the following people for their invaluable help with the
2008 edition and the generous spirit in which they have shared their knowl-
edge: Sarah Ahmed, Nicolas Belfrage MW, Dan Berger, Stephen Brook, Bob
Campbell MW, Giles Fallowfield, Peter Forrestal, Roger Harris, James Lawther
MW, John Livingstone-Learmonth, Angela Lloyd, Dan McCarthy, Dave
McIntyre, Charles Metcalfe, Jasper Morris MW, Victor de la Serna, Stephen
Skelton MW, Patricio Tapia, Roger Voss.

CONTENTS

HOW TO USE THIS BOOK

The **World of Wine** section, starting on page 20, gives an overview of all the world's significant wine-producing countries. The most important countries are followed by a full list of the relevant entries in the A–Z section. Remember that regional A–Z entries guide you to further recommended producers in each region or appellation.

The **A–Z section** starts on page 56 and includes over 1600 entries on wines, producers, grapes and wine regions from all over the world. It is followed on page 308 by a **Glossary** of winemaking terms.

Detailed **Vintage Charts**, with information on which of the world's top wines are ready for drinking in 2008, can be found on the inside front and back covers; the front chart features vintages back to 1997; the back chart covers a selection of older vintages for premium wines.

Glass Symbols   These indicate the wines produced.

🍷 Red wine   🍷 Rosé wine   🍷 White wine

The order of the glasses reflects the importance of the wines in terms of volume produced. For example:

🍷 White followed by rosé wine

🍷 Red followed by rosé, then white wine

Grape Symbols   These identify entries on grape varieties.

⣿ Red grape   ⣿ White grape

Star Symbols   These indicate wines and producers that are highly rated by the author.

★   A particularly good wine or producer in its category
★★   An excellent wine or producer in its category – one especially worth seeking out
★★★   An exceptional, world-class wine or producer

Best Years   Recommended vintages are listed for many producer and appellation entries. Those listed in bold, e.g. **2005**, **00**, indicate wines that are ready for drinking now, although they may not necessarily be at their best; those appearing in brackets, e.g. (2006), (04), are preliminary assessments of wines that are not yet ready for drinking.

Cross References   Wine names, producers and regions that have their own entries elsewhere in the A–Z are indicated by SMALL CAPITALS. **Grape varieties** are not cross-referred in this way, but more than 70 varieties, from Albariño to Zinfandel, are included.

Special Features   The A–Z section includes special 2-page features on the world's most important wine styles, regions and grape varieties. These features include recommended vintages and producers, as well as lists of related entries elsewhere in the A–Z.

Index   The Index contains over 4000 recommended producers. Some of the world's most famous brand names are also included.

4

INTRODUCTION

Is this the year that I began to tire of New World flavours? Up to a point. But I must stress that so-called New World flavours are just as likely to happen in Europe as in places like Australia and California. To generalize, what I'm getting tired of is wines that are overripe, overalcoholic, over-oaked and overbearing. Add in a dollop of residual sugar sweetness and a modicum of that thick, soupy fatness that comes from trying to make wine from grapes that have literally shrivelled to death on the vine in the late summer heat – and that stodgy, unrefreshing slab of slobbish flavour – that's what I'm fed up with.

Now I've certainly had my fill of the Californian versions of this, I've had my fill from Australia and South Africa, Chile and Argentina – but also from Spain, from Italy and France. Even in Bordeaux, supposedly the heartland of cool-climate red wine styles, there are wines over 14.5% alcohol that it's hard to manage more than a glass of. I went to Bordeaux three times last year, tasted hundreds of wines – and I only tasted one single wine at a strength as low as 12% alcohol, and the number at 12.5% could be counted on my fingers. Bordeaux used to come to the table at around 11.5%, with its better wines usually fronting up at 12.5%. But suddenly we've got wines from obscure properties muscling in at 14 to 14.5% alcohol, often with a fearsome tannic grip disguised with a wodge of sweet oak, but little in the way of appetizing acidity, freshness or balance. Why should we drink them?

Well, I won't. I don't mean to say I won't drink strong wines. It's all a question of balance. Some grape varieties grown in some warm places seem to need a high alcohol content to achieve balance. A Barossa Shiraz at 12.5% would probably taste of nothing. A Châteauneuf-du-Pape at 12% alcohol might not even be legal. Viognier at 12% alcohol? There'd be no point in growing the grapes because the wine would be devoid of the slightest personality. But a Barossa Shiraz can seem marvellously balanced at 15%. A Châteauneuf can be a most impressive mouthful at 14.5%. A Viognier at 14% should be succulent and scented. These are wines which may need to have high alcohol content to express themselves, and which can exhibit balance as well as power. Fine. So we can make an informed choice as to whether to drink them or not.

No, the trouble lies in all those areas of the world that used to specialize in refreshing wines – red, pink or white – and which are now slavishly following the False High Priest of superripeness. Or overripeness, I'd call it. Some of the world's most influential critics sadly are obsessed with superripe flavours, and many of the world's producers are obsessed with gaining a 'mark' of more than 90 points out of 100, because such marks allow the wine literally to sell itself. Overripeness, sadly, seems to score. And scores sell.

One of the ways this 'dead fruit' flavour is created in wine is by wilfully re-interpreting what might be called 'full physiological ripeness' in the grapes. What was taken as fully ripe a generation ago is now seen as underripe. But it's *not* underripe if you regard wine as a reasonably adult pleasure that sometimes requires a little understanding and patience rather than merely an alcoholic concoction designed for instant gratification and inebriation. Appetizing bitterness is a crucial part of red wine's appeal; acidity is crucial in wines of every colour for the way it refreshes your palate and improves your appreciation of food. And these fundamental components of good wine are lost by the relentless march towards ever riper, ever more baked and shrivelled fruit, as winemaking gurus push 'hang time' – the amount of time that perfectly ripe fruit continues to sit on the vine when it should have been picked – to absurd lengths.

Nowadays, in the Rhône Valley, in Tuscany, in Rioja, in Chile, Australia, South Africa and Argentina, I keep saying to producers – show me your basic wine, not your smarty-pants Icons and Reserve Selections. They look at me as though I'm misguided, or mean, or both. But I don't want to taste the amount of complicated technique and financial investment that has gone into the wine, I just want to taste the essence of the fruit and of its place, nurtured, cherished, but not bullied and bashed, by the men and women who grow the grapes and make the wine. And I want to pay a fair price, neither heavily discounted, nor ridiculously inflated. Above all, I *don't* want too much alcohol, and I *don't* want too much oak. Is that too much to ask?

So what *will* I be drinking this year? Well, quite a lot of European stuff. Most of **France** had a thrilling 2005 and a more problematic 2006. I'll be gulping down irresistible 2005 **Beaujolais** and **Rhône Valley** reds, picking out a few beautifully scented if pricey 2005 **Burgundies**, and I'll continue to stomp around **Languedoc-Roussillon** looking for characterful reds and increasingly good whites. I will drink **Bordeaux**: even at the basic level 2005 is good, though the prices of the top wines are silly, so for smart labels I'll drink the gently classy 2001.

In **Italy** I'll drink the reds from **Sicily** and **Puglia** as well as the bright, juicy **Veneto** reds and **Alto Adige** whites. **Spain** and **Portugal** are really motoring right now – not only famous areas like **Rioja**, **Ribero del Duero** and **Douro**, but also lesser-known places like **Toro**, **Calatayud** and **Campo de Borja** in Spain, **Ribatejo** and **Alentejo** in Portugal. I'll drink those – after I've slaked my thirst on **Austrian Grüner Veltliner** and **Riesling**, and **Mosel Kabinetts** from **Germany**. I will keep searching for decent wines from Eastern Europe, but they're still few and far between. **Slovenia** looks to be doing best.

Chile is setting a fierce pace in South America – new winemaking, new regions for reds *and* whites – and **Argentina** is learning that cooler really is better for growing conditions; the **Uco Valley** may even draw me back to **Chardonnay**. In the **USA**, I'll have more choice than ever before, since there's been an absolute explosion of wineries – Michigan has 103, Virginia 90! If I can find their wines, I'll drink 'em.

And I'll drink pretty much anything I can find from **New Zealand**. It's not just **Sauvignon**: **Riesling** and **Chardonnay** are excellent, **Pinot Noir**'s a thrill and they've discovered how to make a fantastic cool-climate version of **Syrah**. In **Australia** I'll try to avoid the overhyped, over-discounted global brands and focus on wine made by real Australians that can give a glimpse of Australia's brash brilliance. And in **South Africa**, I'll be dodging the big brands and seeking out **Sauvignon** and **Chardonnay**, **Cabernet** and **Shiraz** from the independent producers. And after all that, I'll still find room for a glass of good **English fizz** – if it hasn't sold out. There's now such a demand they've planted hundreds of new acres in southern England, and Pinot Noir and Chardonnay are now England's most widely planted grapes. And some people still say global warming isn't happening.

SOME OF MY FAVOURITES

The following are some of the wines I've enjoyed most this year. They're not definitive lists of 'best wines', but all the wines, regions and producers mentioned here are on an exciting roll in terms of quality. Some are easy to find; others are very rare or expensive, but if you get the chance to try them, grab it! You can find out more about them in the A–Z on pages 56 to 307: the cross-references in SMALL CAPITALS will guide you to the relevant entries.

WORLD-CLASS WINES THAT DON'T COST THE EARTH

- Tim ADAMS Shiraz, Australia
- BOEKENHOUTSKLOOF Syrah, South Africa
- CARMEN Nativa Cabernet Sauvignon, Chile
- Viña Leyda, Cahuil Pinot Noir, SAN ANTONIO, Chile
- Ch. ROC DE CAMBES, Côtes de Bourg, France
- STEENBERG Catharina, South Africa
- TRAPICHE Medalla Cabernet Sauvignon, Argentina
- VILLA MARIA Reserve Merlot, Hawkes Bay, New Zealand

BEST LOOKALIKES TO THE CLASSICS

Bordeaux-style red wines
- CULLEN Cabernet Sauvignon-Merlot, Australia
- OPUS ONE, California
- Miguel TORRES Manso de Velasco, Chile
- VERGELEGEN, South Africa

Burgundy-style white wines
- Ramey, Chardonnay, RUSSIAN RIVER VALLEY, California
- FROMM, Clayvin Vineyard Chardonnay, New Zealand
- HAMILTON RUSSELL Chardonnay, South Africa
- LEEUWIN ESTATE Art Series Chardonnay, Australia

Champagne-style wines
- Jansz (Vintage), YALUMBA, Australia
- NYETIMBER, England
- ROEDERER ESTATE L'Ermitage, California, USA

TOP-VALUE WINES
- CAVA fizz from Spain
- COTES DE GASCOGNE whites, France
- Hungarian whites
- Inycon FIANO, Sicily, Italy
- Old-vines Garnacha reds from Calatayud and Campo de Borja, ARAGON, Spain
- Peter LEHMANN whites, Australia
- Malbec (non-Reserva) from MENDOZA, Argentina
- Marqués de Casa Concha range, CONCHA Y TORO, Chile
- Trincadeira, ALENTEJO, Portugal
- Vin de Pays des Côtes Catalanes, ROUSSILLON, France
- Zonte's Footstep Shiraz-Viognier, Langhorne Creek, SOUTH AUSTRALIA

REGIONS TO WATCH
- BIERZO, Spain
- CAMPANIA, Italy
- CENTRAL OTAGO, New Zealand
- COTEAUX DU LANGUEDOC, France
- COTES DE CASTILLON, France
- Leyda, SAN ANTONIO, Chile
- LIMARI, Chile
- PATAGONIA, Argentina
- Santa Lucia Highlands, MONTEREY COUNTY, California
- Sussex, England
- UCO VALLEY, Mendoza, Argentina

PRODUCERS TO WATCH
- Clos de los Siete, UCO VALLEY, Argentina
- CRAGGY RANGE, Te Muna Road, Martinborough, New Zealand
- The Crossings, Awatere, MARLBOROUGH, New Zealand
- O FOURNIER, Uco Valley, Argentina
- GIRARDIN, Burgundy, France
- Viña Leyda, SAN ANTONIO, Chile
- Noemia, PATAGONIA, Argentina
- PALACIOS family, Spain (in PRIORAT, RIOJA, BIERZO and Valdeorras in GALICIA)
- PONDALOWIE, Victoria, Australia
- Viña Porta, MAIPO, Chile
- Tabalí/SAN PEDRO, Limarí, Chile

AUSTRALIA
- Tim ADAMS Aberfeldy Shiraz
- CAPE MENTELLE Cabernet Sauvignon
- GROSSET Watervale Riesling
- Henschke HILL OF GRACE Shiraz
- HOUGHTON Gladstones Shiraz
- LEEUWIN ESTATE Art Series Chardonnay

- MCWILLIAM'S Lovedale Semillon
- PRIMO ESTATE Moda Amarone Cabernet-Merlot
- ROCKFORD Basket Press Shiraz
- TYRRELL'S Vat 1 Semillon

RED BORDEAUX

- Ch. AUSONE
- Ch. CANON-LA-GAFFELIERE
- Ch. GRAND-PUY-LACOSTE
- Les Forts de LATOUR
- Ch. LEOVILLE-BARTON
- Ch. LEOVILLE-POYFERRE
- Ch. LYNCH-BAGES
- Ch. MARGAUX
- Pich. PICHON-LONGUEVILLE-LALANDE
- Ch. TERTRE-ROTEBOEUF

BURGUNDY

- CARILLON, Bienvenues-Bâtard-Montrachet (white)
- COCHE-DURY, Corton-Charlemagne (white)
- P Damoy, CHAMBERTIN (red)
- B Dugat-Py, Charmes-CHAMBERTIN (red)
- J-N GAGNARD, Bâtard-Montrachet (white)
- Anne GROS, Clos de Vougeot (red)
- LAFON, Volnay Santenots (red)
- Paul Pillot, CHASSAGNE-MONTRACHET (white)
- M Rollin, CORTON-CHARLEMAGNE (white)
- TOLLOT-BEAUT, Corton-Bressandes (red)

CALIFORNIA

- Cline Cellars, Bridgehead ZINFANDEL, Contra Costa County
- DALLA VALLE
- LAUREL GLEN
- Long Meadow Ranch, NAPA VALLEY
- NEWTON Le Puzzle
- Ramey, Hyde Vineyard Chardonnay, CARNEROS
- RIDGE Geyserville Zinfandel
- St Supéry, Dollarhide Cabernet Sauvignon, NAPA VALLEY
- SHAFER Hillside Select Cabernet Sauvignon
- Sean Thackrey, Orion Rossi Vineyard Syrah, NAPA VALLEY
- Viader, NAPA VALLEY

ITALIAN REDS

- ALLEGRINI Amarone
- BOSCARELLI
- D'ALESSANDRO Cortona Syrah

- Giacomo CONTERNO, Barolo, Cascina Francia
- GAJA, Langhe, Sperss
- ISOLE E OLENA Cepparello
- PLANETA Santa Cecilia
- POLIZIANO Le Stanze
- SELVAPIANA Chianti Rufina, Riserva Bucerchiale
- TUA RITA Giusto di Notri

RHÔNE AND SOUTHERN FRANCE

- Ch. de BEAUCASTEL Roussanne Vieilles Vignes (white)
- CUILLERON, Condrieu les Chaillets
- Pierre Gaillard, CONDRIEU
- GRAILLOT, Crozes-Hermitage la Guiraude
- JAMET, Côte-Rôtie
- Dom. de la Janasse, CHATEAUNEUF-DU-PAPE Vieilles Vignes
- Raspail-Ay, GIGONDAS
- Le Vieux Donjon, CHATEAUNEUF-DU-PAPE

CABERNET SAUVIGNON

- SASSICAIA, Tuscany, Italy
- Long Meadow Ranch, NAPA VALLEY, California
- QUEBRADA DE MACUL, Domus Aurea, Chile
- SANTA RITA Floresta, Chile
- RIDGE Monte Bello, California
- STAG'S LEAP WINE CELLARS Fay, California
- TERRAZAS DE LOS ANDES Cheval des Andes, Argentina
- The Willows, BAROSSA VALLEY, Australia

CHARDONNAY

- CARILLON, Bienvenues-Bâtard-Montrachet, France
- COCHE-DURY, Corton-Charlemagne, France
- CONCHA Y TORO Amelia, Chile
- Diamond Valley Vineyards, YARRA VALLEY, Australia
- J-N GAGNARD, Bâtard-Montrachet, France
- GIACONDA, Australia
- GROSSET Piccadilly, Australia
- HAMILTON RUSSELL, South Africa
- KUMEU RIVER, New Zealand
- Morgan, MONTEREY, California
- NEWTON Unfiltered, California
- Ramey, Hudson Vineyard, CARNEROS, California
- RIDGE Monte Bello, California

- SAINTSBURY, Carneros, California
- Tabalí/SAN PEDRO, Reserva Especial, Limarí, Chile

MERLOT

- ANDREW WILL, Washington, USA
- Ch. ANGELUS, St-Émilion, France
- CASA LAPOSTOLLE Cuvée Alexandre, Chile
- CONO SUR 20 Barrels, Chile
- LEONETTI CELLAR, Washington, USA
- ORNELLAIA Masseto, Tuscany, Italy
- Northstar, WALLA WALLA VALLEY, Washington, USA
- Ch. PETRUS, Pomerol, France
- Ch. VALANDRAUD, St-Émilion, France
- WOODWARD CANYON, Washington, USA

PINOT NOIR

- ATA RANGI, New Zealand
- R Chevillon, NUITS-ST-GEORGES les St-Georges, France
- DRY RIVER, New Zealand
- FELTON ROAD, New Zealand
- FLOWERS Camp Meeting Ridge, California
- Freycinet, TASMANIA, Australia
- Anne GROS, Clos de Vougeot, France
- LAFON, Volnay Santenots, France
- Viña Leyda, Lot 21, SAN ANTONIO, Chile
- SAINTSBURY Carneros, California
- E Rouget, ECHEZEAUX, France
- VILLA MARIA, Taylors Pass, Marlborough, New Zealand

RIESLING

- Tim ADAMS, Clare Valley, Australia
- H DONNHOFF Oberhäuser Brücke, Nahe, Germany
- Gobelsburg, KAMPTAL, Austria
- GROSSET Watervale, Clare Valley, Australia
- Fritz HAAG Brauneberger Juffer Sonnenuhr, Mosel, Germany
- Dr LOOSEN Erdener Prälat, Mosel, Germany
- Mount Edward Drumlin, CENTRAL OTAGO, New Zealand
- MOUNT HORROCKS, Australia
- Horst SAUER Escherndorfer Lump, Franken, Germany

SAUVIGNON BLANC

- Cape Campbell, MARLBOROUGH, New Zealand
- Casas del Bosque, CASABLANCA, Chile
- Didier DAGUENEAU, Pouilly-Fumé, France
- Neil ELLIS Groenekloof, South Africa
- Ch. SMITH-HAUT-LAFITTE, Pessac-Léognan, France
- SAINT CLAIR Wairau Reserve, New Zealand
- STEENBERG, South Africa
- VAVASOUR, New Zealand
- VERGELEGEN, South Africa
- VILLA MARIA Reserve Clifford Bay, New Zealand

SYRAH/SHIRAZ

- Tim ADAMS Aberfeldy, Clare Valley, Australia
- BROKENWOOD Graveyard Vineyard, Hunter Valley, Australia
- CAYUSE Cailloux Vineyard, Washington, USA
- Esk Valley Reserve, HAWKES BAY, New Zealand
- JAMET, Côte-Rôtie, France
- Penfolds GRANGE, South Australia
- Trinity Hill Homage, HAWKES BAY, New Zealand
- Tyrrell's Rufus Stone, HEATHCOTE, Australia
- The Willows, BAROSSA Valley, Australia

FORTIFIED WINE

- Cossart Gordon Vintage Bual, MADEIRA WINE COMPANY
- CHAMBERS Rutherglen Muscat
- GONZALEZ BYASS Noé Pedro Ximénez
- GRAHAM'S Vintage Port
- HENRIQUES & HENRIQUES 15-year-old Madeira
- HIDALGO La Gitana Manzanilla
- NIEPOORT Vintage Port

SPARKLING WINE

- BILLECART-SALMON Cuvée N-F Billecart Champagne, France
- CAMEL VALLEY Brut, England
- CLOUDY BAY Pelorus, New Zealand
- DEUTZ Marlborough Cuvée, New Zealand
- Alfred GRATIEN Vintage Champagne, France
- Charles HEIDSIECK Mis en Caves Champagne, France
- Jansz, YALUMBA, Australia
- Charles MELTON Sparkling Red, Australia
- Le Mesnil Blanc de Blancs CHAMPAGNE, France

MODERN WINE STYLES _____

Not so long ago, if I were to have outlined the basic wine styles, the list would have been strongly biased towards the classics – Bordeaux, Burgundy, Sancerre, Mosel Riesling, Champagne. But the classics have, over time, become expensive and unreliable – giving other regions the chance to offer us wines that may or may not owe anything to the originals. *These* are the flavours to which ambitious winemakers the world over now aspire.

WHITE WINES

Ripe, up-front, spicy Chardonnay is the main grape and fruit is the key: apricot, peach, melon, pineapple and tropical fruits, spiced up with the vanilla and butterscotch richness of some new oak – often American oak – to make a delicious, approachable, fruit cocktail of taste. Australia and Chile are best at this style. Oak-aged Chenin and Semillon can have similar characteristics.

Green and tangy New Zealand Sauvignon was the originator of this style – zingy lime zest, nettles and asparagus and passion fruit – and South Africa now has its own tangy, super-fresh examples. Chile's San Antonio and Casablanca regions have started to produce something similar, and there are hopeful signs in southern France and Hungary. Bordeaux and the Loire are the original sources of dry Sauvignon wines, and at last we are seeing an expanding band of modern producers matching clean fruit with zippy green tang. Riesling in Australia is usually lean and limy.

Bone-dry, neutral This doesn't sound very appetizing, but as long as it is well made it will be thirst-quenching and easy to drink. Many Italian whites fit this bill. Southern French wines, where no grape variety is specified, will be like this; so will many wines from Bordeaux, South-West France, Muscadet and Anjou. Modern young Spanish whites and dry Portuguese Vinho Verdes are good examples. I don't like seeing too much neutrality in New World wines, but cheap South African and California whites are 'superneutral'.

White Burgundy By this I mean the nutty, oatmealy-ripe but dry, subtly oaked styles of villages like Meursault at their best. Few people do it well, even in Burgundy itself, and it's a difficult style to emulate. California makes the most effort. Washington, Oregon, New York State and British Columbia each have occasional successes, as do top Australian, South African and New Zealand Chardonnays.

Perfumy, off-dry Gewürztraminer, Muscat and Pinot Gris from Alsace will give you this style and in southern Germany Gewürztraminer, Scheurebe, Kerner, Grauburgunder (Pinot Gris) and occasionally Riesling may also do it. In New Zealand Riesling and Gewürztraminer can be excellent. Irsai Olivér from Hungary and Torrontés from Argentina are both heady and perfumed. Albariño in Spain is leaner but heady with citrus scent. Viognier is apricotty and scented in southern Europe, Australia, Chile and California.

Mouthfuls of luscious gold Good sweet wines are difficult to make. Sauternes is the most famous, but the Loire, and sometimes Alsace, can also come up with rich, intensely sweet wines that can live for decades. Germany's top sweeties are stunning; Austria's are similiar in style to Germany's, but weightier. Hungarian Tokaj has a wonderful sweet-sour smoky flavour. Australia, California and New Zealand also have some exciting examples.

RED WINES

Spicy, warm-hearted Australia is out in front at the moment through the ebullient resurgence of her Shiraz reds – ripe, almost sweet, sinfully easy to enjoy. France's southern Rhône Valley is also motoring, and the traditional appellations in the far south of France are looking good. In Italy Piedmont is producing delicious beefy Barbera and juicy exotic Dolcetto, and Puglia has some excellent, chocolaty Negroamaro. Spain's Ribera del Duero and Toro and Portugal's Alentejo also deliver the goods, as does Malbec in Argentina. California Zinfandel made in its most powerful style is spicy and rich; Lebanese reds have the succulent scent of the kasbah.

Juicy, fruity The excellent 2005 vintage brought Beaujolais' come-hither charms back into the spotlight. Even so, leafy, raspberryish Loire reds and Grenache and Syrah vins de pays are often better bets. Modern Spanish reds from Valdepeñas, Bierzo and La Mancha, and old-vine Garnachas from Campo de Borja and Calatayud, do the trick, as may young Valpolicella and Teroldego in Italy. Argentina has some good examples from Bonarda, Tempranillo, Sangiovese and Barbera.

Deep and blackcurranty Chile has climbed back to the top of the Cabernet tree, though good producers in cooler parts of Australia produce Cabernets of thrilling blackcurrant intensity. New Zealand Merlot and Cabernet Franc are dense and rich yet dry. California too frequently overripens its Cabernet and Merlot, though restrained examples can be terrific. Top Bordeaux is on a rich blackcurranty roll since 2000: it's expensive but exciting – as is top Tuscan Cabernet.

Tough, tannic long-haul boys Bordeaux leads this field, and the best wines are really good after 10 years or so – but, except in years like 2005, minor properties won't age in the same way. It's the same in Tuscany and Piedmont – only the top wines last well – especially Brunello di Montalcino, Vino Nobile di Montepulciano, some IGT and DOCG wines from Chianti Classico, Barolo and Barbaresco. Portugal has some increasingly good Dão and Douro reds.

Soft, strawberryish charmers Good Burgundy definitely tops this group. Rioja in Spain can sometimes get there, as can Navarra and Valdepeñas. Pinot Noir in California, Oregon and New Zealand is frequently delicious, and Chile and Australia increasingly get it right too. Germany can hit the spot with Spätburgunder (Pinot Noir). Italy's Lago di Caldaro often smooches in; and over in Bordeaux, of all places, St-Émilion, Pomerol and Blaye can do the business.

SPARKLING AND FORTIFIED WINES

Fizz This can be white or pink or red, dry or sweet, and I sometimes think it doesn't matter what it tastes like as long as it's cold enough and there's enough of it. Champagne can be best, but frequently isn't – and there are lots of new-wave winemakers making good-value lookalikes. Australia is tops for tasty bargains, followed by California, New Zealand and England. Spain pumps out oceans of good basic stuff.

Fortified wines There's nothing to beat the top ports and sherries in the deep, rich, sticky stakes – though for the glimmerings of a new angle look to Australia, California and South Africa. The Portuguese island of Madeira produces fortifieds with rich, brown smoky flavours and a startling acid bite – and don't forget the luscious Muscats made all round the Mediterranean and in Rutherglen, Australia.

11

MATCHING FOOD AND WINE

Give me a rule, I'll break it – well, bend it anyway. So when I see the proliferation of publications laying down rules as to what wine to drink with what food, I get very uneasy and have to quell a burning desire to slosh back a Grand Cru Burgundy with my chilli con carne.

The pleasures of eating and drinking operate on so many levels that hard and fast rules make no sense. What about mood? If I'm in the mood for Champagne, Champagne it shall be, whatever I'm eating. What about place? If I'm sitting gazing out across the shimmering Mediterranean, hand me anything, just as long as it's local – it'll be perfect.

Even so, there are some things that simply don't go well with wine: artichokes, asparagus, spinach, kippers and mackerel, chilli, salsas and vinegars, chocolate, all flatten the flavours of wines. The general rule here is avoid tannic red wines and go for juicy young reds, or whites with plenty of fruit and fresh acidity. And for chocolate, liqueur Muscats, raisiny Banyuls or Italy's grapy, frothy Asti all work, but some people like powerful Italian reds such as Barolo or Amarone. Don't be afraid to experiment. Who would guess that salty Roquefort cheese and rich, sweet Sauternes would go together? But they do, and it's a match made in heaven. So, with these factors in mind, the following pairings are not rules – just my recommendations.

FISH

Grilled or baked white fish White Burgundy or other fine Chardonnay, white Bordeaux, Viognier, Australian and New Zealand Riesling and Sauvignon.

Grilled or baked oily or 'meaty' fish (e.g. salmon, tuna, swordfish) Alsace or Austrian Riesling, Grüner Veltliner, fruity New World Chardonnay or Semillon; reds such as Chinon or Bourgueil, Grenache/Garnacha, or New World Pinot Noir.

Fried/battered fish Simple, fresh whites, e.g. Soave, Mâcon-Villages, Verdelho, Pinot Gris, white Bordeaux, or a Riesling Spätlese from the Pfalz.

Shellfish Chablis or unoaked Chardonnay, Sauvignon Blanc, Pinot Blanc; *clams and oysters* Albariño, Aligoté, Vinho Verde, Seyval Blanc; *crab* Riesling, Viognier; *lobster, scallops* fine Chardonnay, Champagne, Viognier; *mussels* Muscadet, Pinot Grigio.

Smoked fish Ice-cold basic fizz, manzanilla or fino sherry, Riesling, Sauvignon Blanc, Alsace Gewurztraminer or Pinot Gris.

MEAT

Beef and lamb are perfect with just about any red wine.

Beef/steak *Plain roasted or grilled* tannic reds, Bordeaux, New World Cabernet Sauvignon, Ribera del Duero, Chianti Classico, Pinotage.

Lamb *Plain roasted or grilled* red Burgundy, red Bordeaux, especially Pauillac or St-Julien, Rioja Reserva, New World Pinot Noir, Merlot or Malbec.

Pork *Plain roasted or grilled* full, spicy dry whites, e.g. Alsace Pinot Gris, lightly oaked Chardonnay; smooth reds, e.g. Rioja, Alentejo; *ham, bacon, sausages, salami* young, fruity reds, e.g. Beaujolais, Lambrusco, Teroldego, unoaked Tempranillo or Garnacha, New World Malbec, Merlot, Zinfandel/Primitivo, Pinotage.

Veal *Plain roasted or grilled* full-bodied whites, e.g. Pinot Gris, Grüner Veltliner, white Rioja; soft reds, e.g. mature Rioja or Pinot Noir; *with cream-based sauce* full, ripe whites, e.g. Alsace Pinot Blanc or Pinot Gris, Vouvray, oaked New World Chardonnay; *with rich red-wine sauce* (e.g. *osso* *buco*) young Italian reds, Zinfandel.

Venison *Plain roasted or grilled* Barolo, St-Estèphe, Pomerol, Côte de Nuits, Hermitage, big Zinfandel, Alsace or German Pinot Gris; *with red-wine sauce* Piedmont and Portuguese reds, Pomerol, St-Émilion, New World Syrah/Shiraz or Pinotage, Priorat.

Chicken and turkey Most red and white wines go with these meats – much depends on the sauce or accompaniments. Try red or white Burgundy, red Rioja Reserva, New World Chardonnay.

Duck Pomerol, St-Émilion, Côte de Nuits or Rhône reds, New World Syrah/Shiraz (including sparkling) or Merlot; also full, soft whites from Austria and southern Germany.

Game birds *Plain roasted or grilled* top reds from Burgundy, Rhône, Tuscany, Piedmont, Ribera del Duero, New World Cabernet or Merlot; also full whites such as oaked New World Semillon.

Casseroles and stews Generally uncomplicated, full-flavoured reds. The thicker the sauce, the fuller the wine. If wine is used in the preparation, match the colour. For strong tomato flavours see Pasta.

HIGHLY SPICED FOOD

Chinese Riesling, Sauvignon, Pinot Gris, Gewürztraminer, unoaked New World Chardonnay; fruity rosé; light Pinot Noir.

Indian Aromatic whites, e.g. Riesling, Sauvignon Blanc, Gewürztraminer, Viognier; non-tannic reds, e.g. Valpolicella, Rioja, Grenache.

Mexican Fruity reds, e.g. Merlot, Cabernet Franc, Grenache, Syrah/Shiraz, Zinfandel.

Thai/South-East Asian Spicy or tangy whites, e.g. Riesling, Gewürztraminer, New World Sauvignon Blanc, dry Alsace Muscat. Coconut is tricky: New World Chardonnay may work.

EGG DISHES

Champagne and traditional-method fizz; light, fresh reds such as Beaujolais or Chinon; full, dry unoaked whites; New World rosé.

PASTA, PIZZA

With tomato sauce Barbera, Valpolicella, Soave, Verdicchio, New World Sauvignon Blanc; *with meat-based sauce* north or central Italian reds, French or New World Syrah/Shiraz, Zinfandel; *with cream- or cheese-based sauce* gently oaked Chardonnay, though the Italians would drink unoaked whites from northern Italy; Valpolicella or soft Merlot; *with seafood/fish* dry, tangy whites, e.g. Verdicchio, Vermentino, Grüner Veltliner, Muscadet; *with pesto* New World Sauvignon Blanc, Dolcetto, Languedoc reds. *Basic pizza, with tomato, mozzarella and oregano* juicy young reds, e.g. Grenache/Garnacha, Valpolicella, Austrian reds, Languedoc reds.

SALADS

Sharp-edged whites, e.g. New World Sauvignon Blanc, Chenin Blanc, dry Riesling, Vinho Verde.

CHEESES

Hard Full reds from Italy, France or Spain, New World Merlot or Zinfandel, dry oloroso sherry, tawny port.

Soft LBV port, Zinfandel, Alsace Pinot Gris, Gewürztraminer.

Blue Botrytized sweet whites such as Sauternes, vintage port, old oloroso sherry, Malmsey Madeira.

Goats' Sancerre, Pouilly-Fumé, New World Sauvignon Blanc, Chinon, Saumur-Champigny.

DESSERTS

Chocolate Asti, Australian Liqueur Muscat, Banyuls, Canadian Cabernet Franc icewine.

Fruit-based Sauternes, Eiswein, fortified European Muscats.

MATCHING WINE AND FOOD

With very special bottles, when you have found an irresistible bargain or when you are casting around for culinary inspiration, it can be a good idea to let the wine dictate the choice of food.

Although I said earlier that rules in this area are made to be bent if not broken, there are certain points to remember when matching wine and food. Before you make specific choices, think about some basic characteristics and see how thinking in terms of grape varieties and wine styles can point you in the right direction.

In many cases, the local food and wine combinations that have evolved over the years simply cannot be bettered (think of ripe Burgundy with *coq au vin* or *boeuf bourguignon*; Chianti Riserva with *bistecca alla Fiorentina*; Muscadet and Breton oysters). Yet the world of food and wine is moving so fast that it would be madness to be restricted by the old tenets. Californian cuisine, fusion food, and the infiltration of innumerable ethnic influences coupled with the re-invigoration of traditional wines, continuous experiment with new methods and blends and the opening up of completely new wine areas mean that the search for perfect food and wine partners is, and will remain, very much an on-going process.

Here are some of the characteristics you need to consider, plus a summary of the main grape varieties and their best food matches.

Body/weight As well as considering the taste of the wine you need to match the weight or body of the wine to the intensity of the food's flavour. A heavy alcoholic wine will not suit a delicate dish; and *vice versa*.

Acidity The acidity of a dish should balance the acidity of a wine. High-acid flavours, such as tomato, lemon or vinegar, need matching acidity in their accompanying wines. Use acidity in wine to cut through the richness of a dish but for this to work, make sure the wine is full in flavour.

Sweetness Sweet food makes dry wine taste unpleasantly lean and acidic. With desserts and puddings find a wine that is at least as sweet as the food (sweeter than the food is fine). However, many savoury foods, such as carrots, onions and parsnips, taste slightly sweet and dishes in which they feature prominently will go best with ripe, fruity wines that have a touch of sweetness.

Salt Salty foods and sweet wines match, but salty foods and tannin are definitely best avoided.

Age/Maturity The bouquet of a wine is only acquired over time and should be savoured and appreciated: with age many red wines acquire complex flavours and perfumes and a similar degree of complexity in the flavour of the food is often a good idea.

Tannin Rare red meat can have the effect of softening tannic wine. Avoid eggs and fish.

Oak Oak flavours in wine vary from the satisfyingly subtle to positively strident. This latter end of the scale can conflict with food, although it may be suitable for smoked fish (white wines only) or full-flavoured meat or game.

Wine in the food If you want to use wine in cooking it is best to use the same style of wine as the one you are going to drink with the meal (it can be an inferior version though).

14

RED GRAPES

Barbera Wines made to be drunk young have high acidity that can hold their own with sausages, salami, ham, and tomato sauces. Complex older or oak-aged wines from the top growers need to be matched with rich food such as beef casseroles and game dishes.

Cabernet Franc Best drunk with plain rather than sauced meat dishes, or, slightly chilled, with grilled or baked salmon or trout.

Cabernet Sauvignon All over the world the Cabernet Sauvignon makes full-flavoured reliable red wine: the ideal food wine. Cabernet Sauvignon seems to have a particular affinity for lamb, but it partners all plain roast or grilled meats and game well and would be an excellent choice for many sauced meat dishes such as beef casserole, steak and kidney pie or rabbit stew and substantial dishes made with mushrooms.

Dolcetto Dolcetto produces fruity purple wines that go beautifully with hearty meat dishes such as calves' liver and onions or casseroled game with polenta.

Gamay The grape of red Beaujolais, Gamay makes wine you can drink whenever, wherever, however and with whatever you want – although it's particularly good lightly chilled on hot summer days. It goes well with pâtés, bacon and sausages because its acidity provides a satisfying foil to their richness. It would be a good choice for many vegetarian dishes.

Grenache/Garnacha Generally blended with other grapes, Grenache nonetheless dominates, with its high alcoholic strength and rich, spicy flavours. These are wines readily matched with food: barbecues and casseroles for heavier wines; almost anything for lighter reds and rosés – vegetarian dishes, charcuterie, picnics, grills, and even meaty fish such as tuna and salmon.

Merlot Merlot makes soft, rounded, fruity wines that are some of the easiest red wines to enjoy without food, yet are also a good choice with many kinds of food. Spicier game dishes, herby terrines and pâtés, pheasant, pigeon, duck or goose all team well with Merlot; substantial casseroles made with wine are excellent with top Pomerols; and the soft fruitiness of the wines is perfect for pork, liver, turkey, and savoury foods with a hint of sweetness such as honey-roast or Parma ham.

Nebbiolo Lean but fragrant, early-drinking styles of Nebbiolo wine are best with local salami, pâtés, *bresaola* and lighter meat dishes. Top Barolos and Barbarescos need substantial food: *bollito misto*, rich hare or beef casseroles and *brasato al Barolo* (a large piece of beef marinated then braised slowly in Barolo) are just the job in Piedmont, or anywhere else for that matter.

Pinot Noir The great grape of Burgundy has taken its food-friendly complexity all over the wine world. However, nothing can beat the marriage of great wine with sublime local food that is Burgundy's heritage, and it is Burgundian dishes that spring to mind as perfect partners for the Pinot Noir: *coq au vin, boeuf bourguignon*, rabbit with mustard, braised ham, chicken with tarragon, *entrecôtes* from prized Charolais cattle with a rich red-wine sauce ... the list is endless.

Pinot Noir's subtle flavours make it a natural choice for complex meat dishes, but it is also excellent with plain grills and roasts. New World Pinots are often richer and fruitier – excellent with grills and roasts and a good match for salmon or tuna.

In spite of the prevalence of superb cheese in Burgundy, the best Pinot Noir red wines are wasted on cheese.

Sangiovese Tuscany is where Sangiovese best expresses the qualities that can lead it, in the right circumstances, to be numbered among the great grapes of the world. And Tuscany is very much 'food with wine' territory. Sangiovese wines such as Chianti, Rosso di Montalcino, Vino Nobile di Montepulciano, and the biggest of them all, Brunello, positively demand to be drunk with food. Drink them with *bistecca alla Fiorentina*, roast meats and game, calves' liver, casseroles, hearty pasta sauces, *porcini* mushrooms and Pecorino cheese.

Syrah/Shiraz Whether from France (the Rhône Valley and Languedoc), Australia, California, South America or South Africa, this grape always makes powerful, rich, full-bodied wines that are superb with full-flavoured food. The classic barbecue wine when drunk young, Shiraz/Syrah also goes with roasts, game, hearty casseroles and charcuterie. It can be good with tangy cheeses such as Manchego or Cheshire.

Tempranillo Spain's best native red grape makes juicy wines for drinking young, and matures well in a rich (usually) oaky style. Tempranillo is good with game,

cured hams and sausages, casseroles and meat grilled with herbs; it is particularly good with lamb. It can partner some Indian and Mexican dishes.

Zinfandel California's much-planted, most versatile grape is used for a bewildering variety of wine styles from bland, slightly sweet pinks to rich, succulent, fruity reds. And the good red Zinfandels themselves may vary greatly in style, from relatively soft and light to big and beefy, but they're always ripe and ready for spicy, smoky, unsubtle food: barbecued meat, haunches of lamb, venison or beef, game casseroles, sausages, Tex-Mex or anything rowdy – Zin copes with them all.

WHITE GRAPES

Albariño Light, crisp, aromatic in a grapefruity way, this goes well with crab and prawn dishes as well as Chinese-style chicken dishes.

Aligoté This Burgundian grape can, at its best, make very versatile food wine. It goes well with many fish and seafood dishes, smoked fish, salads and snails in garlic and butter.

Chardonnay More than almost any other grape, Chardonnay responds to different climatic conditions and to the winemaker's art. This, plus the relative ease with which it can be grown, accounts for the marked gradation of flavours and styles: from steely, cool-climate austerity to almost tropical lusciousness. The relatively sharp end of the spectrum is one of the best choices for simple fish dishes; most Chardonnays are superb with roast chicken or other white meat; the really full, rich, New World blockbusters need rich fish and seafood dishes. Oaky Chardonnays are, surprisingly, a good choice for smoked fish.

Chenin Blanc One of the most versatile of grapes, Chenin Blanc makes wines ranging from averagely quaffable dry whites to the great sweet whites of the Loire. The lighter wines can be good as aperitifs or with light fish dishes or salads. The sweet wines are good with fruit puddings and superb with those made with slightly tart fruit.

Gewürztraminer Spicy and perfumed, Gewürztraminer has the weight and flavour to go with such hard-to-match dishes as *choucroute* and smoked fish. It is also a good choice for Chinese or any lightly spiced oriental food and pungent soft cheeses.

Grüner Veltliner In its lightest form, this makes a peppery, refreshing aperitif. Riper, more structured versions keep the pepper but add peach and apple fruit, and are particularly good with grilled or baked fish.

Marsanne These rich, fat wines are a bit short of acidity, so match them with simply prepared chicken, pork, fish or vegetables.

Muscadet The dry, light Muscadet grape (best wines are *sur lie*) is perfect with seafood.

Muscat Fragrant, grapy wines coming in a multitude of styles, from delicate to downright syrupy. The drier ones are more difficult to pair with food, but can be delightful with oriental cuisines; the sweeties really come into their own with most desserts. Sweet Moscato d'Asti, delicious by itself, goes well with rich Christmas pudding or mince pies.

Pinot Blanc Clean, bright and appley, Pinot Blanc is very food-friendly. Classic white wine dishes, modern vegetarian dishes, pasta and pizza all match up well.

Pinot Gris In Alsace, this makes rich, fat wines that need rich, fat food: *choucroute*, *confit de canard*, rich pork and fish dishes. Italian Pinot Grigio wines are light quaffers. New World Pinot Gris is often delightfully fragrant and ideal with grilled fish.

Riesling Good dry Rieslings are excellent with spicy cuisine. Sweet Rieslings are best enjoyed for their own lusciousness but are suitable partners to fruit-based desserts. In between, those with a fresh acid bite and some residual sweetness can counteract the richness of, say, goose or duck, and the fuller examples can be good with oriental food and otherwise hard-to-match salads.

Sauvignon Blanc Tangy green flavours and high acidity are the hallmarks of this grape. Led by New Zealand, New World Sauvignons are some of the snappiest, tastiest whites around. Brilliant with seafood and Oriental cuisine, they also go well with tomato dishes and goats' cheese.

Sémillon/Semillon Dry Bordeaux Blancs are excellent with fish and shellfish; fuller, riper New World Semillons are equal to spicy food and rich sauces, often going even better with meat than with fish; sweet Sémillons can partner many puddings, especially rich, creamy ones. Sémillon also goes well with many cheeses, and Sauternes with Roquefort is a classic combination.

Viognier Viognier is at its best as an aperitif. It can also go well with spicy Indian dishes.

MAKING THE MOST OF WINE

Most wine is pretty hardy stuff and can put up with a fair amount of rough handling. Young red wines can knock about in the back of a car for a day or two and be lugged from garage to kitchen to dinner table without coming to too much harm. Serving young white wines when well chilled can cover up all kinds of ill-treatment – a couple of hours in the fridge should do the trick. Even so, there are some conditions that are better than others for storing your wines, especially if they are on the mature side. And there are certain ways of serving wines which will emphasize any flavours or perfumes they have.

STORING

Most wines are sold ready for drinking, and it will be hard to ruin them if you store them for a few months before you pull the cork. Don't stand them next to the central heating or the cooker, though, or on a sunny windowsill.

Light and extremes of temperature are also the things to worry about if you are storing wine long-term. Some wines, Chardonnay for instance, are particularly sensitive to exposure to light over several months, and the damage will be worse if the bottle is made of pale-coloured glass. The warmer the wine, the quicker it will age, and really high temperatures can spoil wine quite quickly. Beware in the winter of garages and outhouses, too: a very cold snap – say –4°C (25°F) or below – will freeze your wine, push out the corks and crack the bottles. An underground cellar is ideal, with a fairly constant temperature of 10°–12°C (50°–53°F). And bottles really do need to lie on their sides, so that the cork stays damp and swollen, and keeps out the air.

TEMPERATURE

The person who thought up the rule that red wine should be served at room temperature certainly didn't live in a modern, centrally heated flat. It's no great sin to serve a big, beefy red at the temperature of your central heating, but I prefer most reds just a touch cooler. Over-heated wine tastes flabby, and may lose some of its more volatile aromas. In general, the lighter the red, the cooler it can be. Really light, refreshing reds, such as Beaujolais, are nice lightly chilled. Ideally, I'd serve Burgundy and other Pinot Noir wines at larder temperature (about 15°C/59°F), Bordeaux and Rioja a bit warmer (18°C/64°F), Rhône wines and New World Cabernet at a comfortable room temperature, but no more than 20°C/68°F.

Chilling white wines makes them taste fresher, emphasizing their acidity. White wines with low acidity especially benefit from chilling, and it's vital for sparkling wines if you want to avoid exploding corks and a tableful of froth. Drastic chilling also subdues flavours, however – a useful rule if you're serving basic wine, but a shame if the wine is very good. A good guide for whites is to give the cheapest and lightest a spell in the fridge, but serve bigger and better wines – Australian Chardonnays or top white Burgundies – perhaps half-way between fridge and central-heating temperature. If you're undecided, err on the cooler side, for whites or reds. To chill wine quickly, and to keep it cool, an ice bucket is more efficient if filled with a mixture of ice and water, rather than ice alone.

OPENING THE BOTTLE

There's no corkscrew to beat the Screwpull, and the Spinhandle Screwpull is especially easy to use. Don't worry if bits of cork crumble into the wine – just fish them out of your glass. Tight corks that refuse to budge might be loosened if you run hot water over the bottle neck to expand the glass. If the cork is loose and falls in, push it right in and don't worry about it.

Opening sparkling wines is a serious business – point the cork away from people! Once you've started, never take your hand off the cork until it's safely out. Remove the foil, loosen the wire, hold the wire and cork firmly and twist the bottle. If the wine froths, hold the bottle at an angle of 45 degrees, and have a glass at hand.

AIRING AND DECANTING

Scientists have proved that opening young to middle-aged red wines an hour before serving makes no difference whatsoever. The surface area of wine in contact with air in the bottle neck is too tiny to be significant. Decanting is a different matter, because sloshing the wine from bottle to jug or decanter mixes it up quite thoroughly with the air. The only wines that really need to be decanted are those that have a sediment which would cloud the wine if they were poured directly – mature red Bordeaux, Burgundy and vintage port are the commonest examples. Ideally, if you are able to plan that far in advance, you need to stand the bottle upright for a day or two to let the sediment settle in the bottom. Draw the cork extremely gently. As you tip the bottle, shine a bright light through from underneath as you pour in a single steady movement. Stop pouring when you see the sediment approaching the bottle neck.

Contrary to many wine buffs' practice, I would decant a mature wine only just before serving; elderly wines often fade rapidly once they meet with air, and an hour in the decanter could kill off what little fruit they had left. By contrast, a good-quality young white wine can benefit from decanting.

GLASSES

If you want to taste wine at its best, to enjoy all its flavours and aromas, to admire its colours and texture, choose glasses designed for the purpose and show the wine a bit of respect. The ideal wine glass is a fairly large tulip shape, made of fine, clear glass, with a slender stem. When you pour the wine, fill the glass no more than halfway to allow space for aromas. For sparkling wines choose a tall, slender glass, as it helps the bubbles to last longer.

KEEPING LEFTOVERS

Leftover white wine keeps better than red, since the tannin and colouring matter in red wine is easily attacked by the air. Any wine, red or white, keeps better in the fridge than in a warm kitchen. And most wines, if well made in the first place, will be perfectly acceptable, if not pristine, after 2 or 3 days re-corked in the fridge. But for better results it's best to use one of the gadgets sold for this purpose. The ones that work by blanketing the wine with heavier-than-air inert gas are much better than those that create a vacuum in the air space in the bottle.

FRANCE

I've visited most of the wine-producing countries of the world, but the one I come back to again and again, with my enthusiasm undimmed by time, is France. The sheer range of its wine flavours, the number of wine styles produced, and indeed the quality differences, from very best to very nearly worst, continue to enthral me, and as each year's vintage nears, I find myself itching to leap into the car and head for the vineyards of Champagne, of Burgundy, of Bordeaux and the Loire. France is currently going through a difficult period – aware that the New World is making tremendous strides and is the master of innovation and technology, yet unwilling to admit to the quality and character of this new breed of wines. But the best French producers learn from the newcomers while proudly defining their Frenchness.

CLIMATE AND SOIL

France lies between the 40th and 50th parallels north, and the climate runs from the distinctly chilly and almost too cool to ripen grapes in the far north near the English Channel, right through to the swelteringly hot and almost too torrid to avoid grapes overripening in the far south on the Mediterranean shores. In the north, the most refined and delicate sparkling wine is made in Champagne. In the south, rich, luscious dessert Muscats and fortified wines dominate. In between is just about every sort of wine you could wish for.

The factors that influence a wine's flavour are the grape variety, the soil and climate, and the winemaker's techniques. Most of the great wine grapes, like the red Cabernet Sauvignon, Merlot, Pinot Noir and Syrah, and the white Chardonnay, Sauvignon Blanc, Sémillon and Viognier, find conditions in France where they can ripen slowly but reliably – and slow, even ripening always gives the best flavours to a wine. Since grapes have been grown for over 2000 years in France, the most suitable varieties for the different soils and mesoclimates have naturally evolved. And since winemaking was brought to France by the Romans, generation upon generation of winemakers have refined their techniques to produce the best possible results from their different grape types. The great wines of areas like Bordeaux and Burgundy are the results of centuries of experience and of trial and error, which winemakers from other countries of the world now use as role models in their attempts to create good wine.

WINE REGIONS

White grapes generally ripen more easily than red grapes and they dominate the northern regions. Even so, the chilly Champagne region barely manages to ripen its red or white grapes on its chalky soil. But the resultant acid wine is the ideal base for sparkling wine: with good winemaking and a few years' maturing, the young still wine can transform into a golden honeyed sparkling wine of incomparable finesse.

Alsace, on the German border, is warmer and drier than Champagne (the vineyards sit in a rain shadow created by the Vosges mountains that rise above the Rhine Valley) but still produces mainly dry white wines, from grapes such as Riesling, Pinot Gris and Gewurztraminer that are seldom encountered elsewhere in France. With its clear blue skies, Alsace can provide ripeness, and therefore the higher alcoholic strength of the warm south, but also the perfume and fragrance of the cool north.

South-east of Paris, Chablis marks the northernmost tip of the Burgundy region, and the Chardonnay grape here produces very dry wines, usually with a streak of green acidity and minerality, but nowadays with a fuller softer texture to subdue any harshness.

It's a good 2 hours' drive further south to the heart of Burgundy – the Côte d'Or, which runs between Dijon and Chagny. World-famous villages such as Gevrey-Chambertin and Vosne-Romanée (where the red Pinot Noir dominates) and Meursault and Puligny-Montrachet (where Chardonnay reigns) here produce the great Burgundies that have given the region renown over the centuries. Lesser Burgundies – but they're still good – are produced further south in the Côte Chalonnaise, while between Mâcon and Lyon are the white Mâconnais wine villages (Pouilly-Fuissé and St-Véran are particularly tasty) and the villages of Beaujolais, famous for bright, easy-going red wine from the Gamay grape. The 10 Beaujolais Crus or 'growths' are the most important communes and should produce wine with more character and structure.

South of Lyon, in the Rhône Valley, red wines begin to dominate. The Syrah grape makes great wine at Côte-Rôtie and Hermitage in the north, while in the south the Grenache and a host of supporting grapes (most southern Rhône reds will add at least Syrah, Cinsaut or Mourvèdre to their blends) make full, satisfying reds, of which Châteauneuf-du-Pape is the most famous. The white Viognier makes lovely wine at Condrieu and Château-Grillet in the north.

The whole of the south of France has undergone considerable change over the last 20 years. Despite the financial woes of growers who over-extended themselves in the late 1990s, new ownership and a new generation are producing exciting wines from unpromising lands. The traditional Provence, Languedoc and Roussillon vineyards make increasingly impressive reds from Grenache, Syrah, Mourvèdre and Carignan. And, with the new Languedoc appellation (covering the whole of Languedoc and Roussillon), the possibilities and freedom to improve by blending will be extended. Many of the tastiest and most affordable wines are vins de pays. Roussillon also makes fine sweet Muscats and Grenache-based fortifieds.

The south-west of France is dominated by the wines of Bordeaux, but has many other gems benefiting from the cooling influence of the Atlantic. Dry whites from Gascony and Bergerac can be exciting. Jurançon down in the Basque country produces some remarkable dry and sweet wines, while Madiran, Cahors and Bergerac produce good to excellent reds.

But Bordeaux is the king here. The Cabernet Sauvignon and Merlot are the chief grapes, the Cabernet dominating the production of deep reds from the Médoc peninsula and its famous villages of Margaux, St-Julien, Pauillac and St-Estèphe on the left bank of the Gironde river. Round the city of Bordeaux are Pessac-Léognan and Graves, where Cabernet and Merlot blend to produce fragrant refined reds. On the right bank of the Gironde estuary, the Merlot is most important in the plump rich reds of St-Émilion and Pomerol. Sweet whites from Sémillon and Sauvignon Blanc are made in Sauternes, with increasingly good dry whites produced in the Entre-Deux-Mers, and especially in Graves and Pessac-Léognan.

The Loire Valley is the most northerly of France's Atlantic wine regions but, since the river rises in the heart of France not far from the Rhône, styles vary widely. Sancerre and Pouilly in the east produce tangy Sauvignon whites and some surprisingly good Pinot Noir reds. Along the river Cher, which joins the Loire at Tours, the best varieties are Sauvignon and Romorantin for whites, Gamay and Côt/Malbec for reds; watch out for ambitious vins de table. In central Touraine, Saumur and Anjou the focus is squarely on Chenin Blanc in styles which range from bone dry to lusciously sweet, even sparkling and, for the reds, Cabernet Franc with a little Cabernet Sauvignon. Down at the mouth of the river, as it slips past Nantes into the Atlantic swell, the vineyards of Muscadet produce one of the world's most famous and often least memorable dry white wines. Still, in common with the rest of the Loire, better vineyard practices have seen a general uplift in quality.

CLASSIFICATIONS

France has an intricate but eminently logical system for controlling the quality and authenticity of its wines. The system is divided into 4 broad classifications (in ascending order): **Vin de Table**, **Vin de Pays**, **VDQS** (Vin Délimité de Qualité Supérieure) and **AC** (Appellation Contrôlée). Within the laws there are numerous variations, with certain vineyards or producers singled out for special mention. The 1855 Classification in Bordeaux or the Grands Crus of Alsace or Burgundy are good examples. The intention is a system which rewards quality. Vin de Pays and VDQS wines can be promoted to AC, for example, after a few years' good behaviour. However, the AC system is now under increasing attack from critics, both inside and outside France, who feel that it is outmoded and ineffectual and that too many poor wines are passed as of Appellation Contrôlée standard.

2006 VINTAGE REPORT

It was a tricky year in Bordeaux. All looked well at the end of July: the grapes were ripening, the sugar concentration was impressive and producers began to think they might have another 2005 on their hands. Then a cool, wet August set in and to dampen spirits further there were some heavy bouts of rain in September. The accompanying threat of rot meant an accelerated harvest. As usual, those with expertly farmed vineyards fared best, but care was also needed in the cellars to gently extract the fruit and tannins. Expect a mixed bag, with the best reds having good colour and sugar concentration, acidity and a firm tannic edge for aging. 2004 seems the nearest comparative vintage. Dry whites are aromatic and balanced and there's a small volume of decent Sauternes from a careful selection of botrytized grapes in the last week of September.

In Burgundy 2006 looks like a delicious vintage for white wines in a ripe, relatively rich and certainly quite forward style. Chablis picked early and the growers look very happy. The reds will be less regular though, with a few rot problems in the Côte de Beaune. But expect some beautifully fruity if quite forward reds from the Côte de Nuits.

In Beaujolais the vintage was surprisingly good in spite of the weather: good colour, bouquet and flavour with limited tannin and well balanced acidity. A vintage to enjoy.

The Rhône performed well in 2006, better than many French regions. Well-timed rainfall ensured steady ripening. Northern reds are well-fruited and more suitable for aging than in 2004. Southern reds are full of generous fruit, good colour and quite rich foundations. A good year for whites, with loads of freshness.

In Languedoc, it was a similar mixed harvest to other French wine regions. Some areas, such as Minervois, consider they made great wines. In the vast Vin de Pays area, however, the cool August did nothing to help, and a repeat of the superb 2005 was never on the cards. In South-West France, harvesting took place during days of rain and sunshine, hardly a recipe for great wines, although modern equipment and techniques have certainly helped to produce some very drinkable wines.

A vintage of mixed fortunes in the Loire which, save for Muscadet, favoured earlier ripening varieties, particularly Sauvignon Blanc. A hot and dry June/July kept yields down, concentrating flavours; a cool August kept water stress at bay, preserving acidity. Those who picked before September's rains made excellent wines, especially vivaciously fruity Sauvignons. For the later ripening Chenin Blanc and Cabernets, it is a growers' vintage: the best wines reflect meticulous vineyard practices and careful selection. Expect more fruit-driven, fresher, less concentrated wines than 2005 and only a handful of sweet Chenins, predominantly from the Layon. Hit by the tail-end of tropical storms at harvest, Muscadets did not attain such clean, ripe fruit as in 2005.

Heavy late September rain in Alsace put paid to what looked to have been a very promising vintage. The ensuing rot dictated a hasty harvest, and skill in the winery was at a premium. Riesling (thanks to cool conditions in August) and Gewurztraminer seem to have fared the best; Pinot Gris and Pinot Noir were the casualties of the vintage. Yields are considerably down.

After a very hot and dry July in Champagne, it was wet and cool in August and only a miraculous return to warm dry weather at the start of September enabled final ripening and slowed the spread of rot caused by the August rain. Chardonnay generally performed best, though some may be overripe. Pinot Noir did better than Pinot Meunier, with quite high potential alcohol. A season of extremes may produce some high-quality vintage wines in due course.

French entries in the A–Z section (pages 56–307), by region.

ALSACE

ACs
Alsace
Crémant d'Alsace

Producers
Paul Blanck
Marcel Deiss
Hugel
Albert Mann
Réné Muré
Dom. Schoffit
Trimbach
Cave Vinicole de
  Turckheim
Weinbach
Zind-Humbrecht

BORDEAUX

ACs
Barsac
Bordeaux
Bordeaux-Côtes
  de Francs
Bordeaux
  Supérieur
Cadillac
Canon-Fronsac
Cérons
Côtes de Bourg
Côtes de
  Castillon
Entre-Deux-Mers
Fronsac
Graves
Haut-Médoc
Lalande-de-
  Pomerol
Listrac-Médoc
Loupiac
Lussac-St-Émilion
Margaux
Médoc
Montagne-St-
  Émilion
Moulis
Pauillac
Pessac-Léognan
Pomerol
Premières Côtes
  de Blaye
Premières Côtes
  de Bordeaux

Puisseguin-St-
  Émilion
St-Émilion
St-Émilion Grand
  Cru
St-Estèphe
St-Georges-St-
  Émilion
St-Julien
Ste-Croix-du-Mont
Sauternes

Châteaux
Angélus
d'Angludet
l'Arrosée
Ausone
Batailley
Beau-Séjour
  Bécot
Belair
Beychevelle
le Bon Pasteur
Bonnet
Branaire-Ducru
Brane-Cantenac
Calon-Ségur
Canon
Canon-la-
  Gaffeliere
Cantemerle
Chasse-Spleen
Cheval Blanc
Dom. de Chevalier
Clarke

Climens
La Conseillante
Cos d'Estournel
Coutet
Doisy-Daëne
Doisy-Védrines
Ducru-Beaucaillou
l'Eglise-Clinet
l'Évangile
Falfas
de Fargues
Ferrière
de Fieuzal
Figeac
la Fleur-Pétrus
Gazin
Gilette
Gloria
Grand-Puy-
  Ducasse
Grand-Puy-
  Lacoste
Gruaud-Larose
Guiraud
Haut-Bages-
  Libéral
Haut-Bailly
Haut-Bataillley
Haut-Brion
Haut-Marbuzet
d'Issan
Kirwan
Labégorce-Zédé
Lafaurie-
  Peyraguey

Lafite-Rothschild
Lafleur
Lafon-Rochet
Lagrange
la Lagune
Langoa-Barton
Lascombes
Latour
Latour-Martillac
Latour-à-Pomerol
Laville-Haut-Brion
Léoville-Barton
Léoville-Las-
  Cases
Léoville-Poyferré
la Louvière
Lynch-Bages
Magdelaine
Malartic-
  Lagravière
Malescot St-
  Exupéry
Margaux
Maucaillou
Meyney
la Mission-Haut-
  Brion
Monbousquet
Montrose
J P Moueix
Mouton-Cadet
Mouton-
  Rothschild
Nairac
Palmer

Pape-Clément
Pavie
Pavie-Macquin
Petit-Village
Pétrus
de Pez
Pichon-
  Longueville
Pichon-
  Longueville-
  Lalande
le Pin

Pontet-Canet
Potensac
Poujeaux
Prieuré-Lichine
Rauzan-Ségla
Reynon
Rieussec
Roc de Cambes
St-Pierre
Siran
Smith-Haut-Lafitte
Sociando-Mallet

Suduiraut
Talbot
Tertre-Rôteboeuf
la Tour Blanche
Troplong-Mondot
Trotanoy
Valandraud
Vieux-Château-
  Certan
d'Yquem

see also
Bordeaux Red
  Wines
Bordeaux White
  Wines
St-Émilion Premier
  Grand Cru
  Classé

**BURGUNDY and
BEAUJOLAIS
ACs**
Aloxe-Corton
Auxey-Duresses
Bâtard-
  Montrachet
Beaujolais
Beaujolais-
  Villages
Beaune
Blagny
Bonnes-Mares
Bourgogne
Bourgogne-Côte
  Chalonnaise
Bourgogne-
  Hautes-Côtes
  de Beaune
Bourgogne-
  Hautes-Côtes
  de Nuits
Brouilly
Chablis
Chablis Grand
  Cru
Chambertin
Chambolle-
  Musigny
Chassagne-
  Montrachet
Chénas
Chiroubles
Chorey-lès-
  Beaune
Clos des
  Lambrays
Clos de la Roche
Clos St-Denis
Clos de Tart
Clos de Vougeot
Corton
Corton-
  Charlemagne
Côte de Beaune
Côte de Beaune-
  Villages

Côte de Brouilly
Côte de Nuits-
  Villages
Coteaux du
  Lyonnais
Crémant de
  Bourgogne
Échézeaux
Fixin
Fleurie
Gevrey-
  Chambertin
Givry
Irancy
Juliénas
Ladoix
Mâcon
Mâcon-Villages
Maranges
Marsannay
Mercurey
Meursault
Montagny
Monthelie
Montrachet
Morey-St-Denis
Morgon
Moulin-à-Vent
Musigny
Nuits-St-Georges
Pernand-
  Vergelesses
Pommard
Pouilly-Fuissé
Pouilly-Vinzelles
Puligny-
  Montrachet
Régnié
Richebourg
la Romanée
la Romanée-Conti
Romanée-St-
  Vivant
Rully
St-Amour
St-Aubin
St-Bris

St-Romain
St-Véran
Santenay
Savigny-lès-
  Beaune
la Tâche
Viré-Clessé
Volnay
Vosne-Romanée
Vougeot

Producers
Angerville,
  Marquis d'
Boisset
Bouchard Père et
  Fils
Bouzereau
Brocard, Jean-
  Marc
Buxy, Cave des
  Vignerons de
Carillon & Fils,
  Louis
Cathiard, Sylvain
Chablisienne, La
Chandon de
  Briailles
Clair, Bruno
Coche-Dury, J-F
Dauvissat, René &
  Vincent
Drouhin, Joseph
Duboeuf,
  Georges
Dujac
Durup, Jean
Faiveley, Joseph
Gagnard, Jean-
  Noël
Girardin, Vincent
Gouges, Henri
Grivot, Jean
Gros
Hospices de
  Beaune

Jadot, Louis
Lafarge, Michel
Lafon
Laroche, Michel
Latour, Louis
Leflaive, Dom.
Leflaive, Olivier
Leroy, Dom.
Liger-Belair
Méo-Camuzet
Montille,
  Dom. de
Mortet, Denis
Mugnier, J-F
Potel, Nicolas
Ramonet
Raveneau, Jean-
  Marie
Rion
Rodet, Antonin
Romanée-Conti,
  Dom. de la
Roumier, Georges
Rousseau,
  Armand
Sauzet
Tollot-Beaut
Verget
Vogüé, Comte
  Georges de
Vougeraie, Dom.
  de la

see also
Aligoté
Beaujolais
  Nouveau
Burgundy Red
  Wines
Burgundy White
  Wines
Côte de Beaune
Côte de Nuits
Côte d'Or

CHAMPAGNE

Champagne AC
Champagne Rosé
Coteaux
  Champenois AC
Rosé des Riceys
  AC

Producers
Billecart-Salmon
Bollinger
Deutz
Gratien, Alfred
Heidsieck, Charles
Henriot
Jacquesson
Krug

Lanson
Laurent-Perrier
Moët & Chandon
Mumm, G H
Paillard, Bruno
Perrier, Joseph
Perrier-Jouët
Piper-Heidsieck
Pol Roger

Pommery
Roederer, Louis
Ruinart
Taittinger
Veuve Clicquot

JURA and SAVOIE

Arbois AC

Château-Chalon
  AC
Côtes du Jura AC

Crémant du Jura
  AC
l'Étoile AC

Savoie
Seyssel AC

LOIRE VALLEY ACs

Anjou Blanc
Anjou Rouge
Anjou-Villages
Bonnezeaux
Bourgueil
Cabernet d'Anjou
Cheverny
Chinon
Côte Roannaise
Coteaux de
  l'Aubance
Coteaux du
  Layon
Crémant de Loire
Gros Plant du
  Pays Nantais
  VDQS

Jardin de la
  France, Vin de
  Pays du
Jasnières
Menetou-Salon
Montlouis-sur-
  Loire
Muscadet
Pouilly-Fumé
Pouilly-sur-Loire
Quarts de
  Chaume
Quincy
Reuilly
Rosé de Loire
St-Nicolas-de-
  Bourgueil
Sancerre
Saumur

Saumur-
  Champigny
Saumur Mousseux
Savennières
Touraine
Vouvray

Producers
Baumard, Dom.
  des
Blot, Jacky
Bouvet-
  Ladubay
Clos de la Coulée-
  de-Serrant
Clos Naudin,
  Dom. du
Couly-Dutheil
Dagueneau, Didier

Druet, Pierre-
  Jacques
l'Ecu, Dom. de
Huet
Hureau, Ch. du
Mellot, Alphonse
Pithon, Jo
Ragotière, Ch. de
  la
Richou, Dom.
Roches Neuves,
  Dom. des
Vacheron, Dom.
Villeneuve, Ch. de

SOUTHERN FRANCE

CORSICA

Vin de Corse
  AC
Arena, Dom.
  Antoine

LANGUEDOC-ROUSSILLON ACs

Banyuls
Blanquette de
  Limoux
Cabardès
Collioure
Corbières
Coteaux du
  Languedoc
Côtes du
  Roussillon
Côtes du
  Roussillon-
  Villages

Côtes de
  Thongue, Vin de
  Pays des
Faugères
Fitou
Gard, Vin de Pays
  du
Hérault, Vin de
  Pays de l'
Limoux
Maury
Minervois
Muscat de
  Frontignan
Muscat de
  Rivesaltes
Muscat de St-
  Jean-de-
  Minervois
Oc, Vin de Pays d'
Rivesaltes
St-Chinian

Producers
Alquier, Dom.
Bertrand-Bergé,
  Dom.
Borie la Vitarèle
Canet-Valette,
  Dom.
Casenove, Ch. la
Cazes, Dom.
Clos de l'Anhel
Clos Bagatelle
Clos Centeilles
Clos Marie
Clot de l'Oum
Denois, J-L
Estanilles, Ch. des
Gauby, Dom.
Grange des Pères,
  Dom. de la
Hecht & Bannier
l'Hortus, Dom. de
l'Hospitalet, Ch.

Mas Blanc, Dom.
  du
Mas Bruguière
Mas la Chevalière
Mas de Daumas
  Gassac
Mas Jullien
Mont Tauch, les
  Producteurs du
Peyre Rose, Dom.
Prieuré de St-
  Jean de Bébian
Primo Palatum
Sieur d'Arques,
  les Vignerons du
Skalli-Fortant de
  France
Tour Boisée, Ch.
Val d'Orbieu, les
  Vignerons du
Voulte-Gasparets,
  Ch. la

SOUTH-WEST

ACs
Béarn
Bergerac
Buzet
Cahors
Côtes de Duras
Côtes du
  Frontonnais
Côtes de
  Gascogne, Vin
  de Pays des
Côtes du
  Marmandais
Côtes de St-Mont
  VDQS
Crémant de
  Limoux
Gaillac
Irouléguy
Jurançon
Madiran
Marcillac
Monbazillac
Montravel
Pacherenc du Vic-
  Bilh
Pécharmant
Tursan VDQS

Producers
l'Ancienne Cure,
  Dom. de
Buzet, Vignerons
Cauhapé, Dom.
Cèdre, Ch. du
Chapelle Lenclos
Clos Triguedina
Clos Uroulat
Lagrezette, Ch.
Montus, Ch.
Plageoles, Robert
Plaimont,
  Producteurs
Primo Palatum
Tariquet, Dom. du
Tour des Gendres,
  Ch.

PROVENCE

ACs
Bandol
les Baux-de-
  Provence
Bellet
Bouches-du-
  Rhône, Vin de
  Pays des
Cassis
Coteaux d'Aix-en-
  Provence
Coteaux Varois
Côtes de
  Provence
Palette

Producers
d'Eole, Dom.
Pibarnon, Ch. de
Richeaume, Dom.
Trévallon, Dom.
  de
Vannières, Ch.

see also
Clape, La
Languedoc-
  Roussillon
Pic St-Loup
Provence
Roussillon

RHÔNE VALLEY

ACs
Beaumes-de-
  Venise
Château-Grillet
Châteauneuf-du-
  Pape
Clairette de Die
Collines
  Rhodaniennes,
  Vin de Pays des
Condrieu
Cornas
Costières de
  Nîmes
Côte-Rôtie
Coteaux de
  l'Ardèche, Vin
  de Pays des
Coteaux du
  Tricastin
Côtes du
  Lubéron
Côtes du Rhône
Côtes du Rhône-
  Villages
Côtes du
  Ventoux
Côtes du Vivarais
  VDQS
Crémant de Die
Crozes-Hermitage
Gigondas
Hermitage
Lirac
Muscat de
  Beaumes-de-
  Venise
Rasteau
St-Joseph
St-Péray
Tavel
Vacqueyras
Vinsobres

Producers
Allemand, Thierry
Beaucastel, Ch.
  de
Chapoutier, M
Chave, Jean-
  Louis
Clape, A
Clos des Papes
Colombo, Jean-
  Luc
Coursodon, Pierre
Cuilleron, Yves
Delas Frères
Font de Michelle,
  Dom.
Graillot, Alain
Guigal
Jaboulet Aîné,
  Paul
Jamet
l'Oratoire St-
  Martin, Dom. de
Perret, André
Rayas, Ch.
Réméjeanne,
  Dom. la
Rostaing, Réné
St-Désirat, Cave
  de
St-Gayan, Dom.
Sang des
  Cailloux, Dom.
  le
Tain, Cave de
Vieux Télégraphe,
  Dom. du

see also
Cairanne
Rhône Valley

ITALY

The cultivation of the vine was introduced to Italy 2500 to 3000 years ago, by the Greeks (to Sicily and the south) and by the Etruscans (to the north-east and central zones). Despite this great tradition, Italian wines as we know them today are relatively young. New attitudes have resulted, in the last 35 years or so, in a great change in Italian wine. The whole industry has been modernized, and areas like Tuscany are now among the most dynamic of any in the world. With her unique characteristics, challenging wine styles and mass of grape varieties, Italy is now ready again to take on the role of leadership she has avoided for so long.

GRAPE VARIETIES AND WINE REGIONS

Vines are grown all over Italy, from the Austrian border in the north-east to the island of Pantelleria in the far south, nearer to North Africa than to Sicily. The north-west, especially Piedmont, is the home of many of the best Italian red grapes, like Nebbiolo (the grape of Barolo and Barbaresco), Dolcetto and Barbera, while the north-east (Friuli-Venezia Giulia, Alto Adige and the Veneto) is more noted for the success of native white varieties like Garganega and Prosecco, reds like Corvina and Corvinone, and imports like Pinot Grigio, Chardonnay

and Sauvignon. The Po Valley is Lambrusco country west of Bologna, while Sangiovese rules in the hills to the east. Tuscany is best known for its red Chianti and other wines from the native Sangiovese grape as well as its famed Super-Tuscans. On the east coast, Verdicchio and Montepulciano make wines ranging from popular to serious. South of Rome, where the Mediterranean climate holds sway, modern wine-makers are revelling in the chance to make exciting wines from vari-eties of long tradition, such as Negroamaro and Primitivo (in Puglia), Aglianico, Fiano and Greco (in Campania and Basilicata) and Gaglioppo (in Calabria). The islands have their own varieties: red Nero d'Avola and white Inzolia in Sicily, red Cannonau and Carignano and white Vermentino in Sardinia.

CLASSIFICATIONS

Vino da Tavola, 'table wine', is used for wine that is produced either outside the existing laws, or in an area where no delimited zone exists. Both cheap, basic wines and inspired innovative creations like Tig-nanello, Sassicaia and other so-called Super-Tuscans used to fall into this anonymous category. Now the fancy wines have become either DOC (particularly in Piedmont with its Langhe and Piemonte DOCs) or IGT. Remaining Vini da Tavola are labelled simply as *bianco, rosso* or *rosato* without vintages or varietal or geographical indications.

IGT (Indicazione Geografica Tipica) began taking effect with the 1995 vintage to identify wines from certain regions or areas as an equiva-lent of the French Vin de Pays. A great swathe of both ordinary and premium wines traded their Vino da Tavola status for a regional IGT.

DOC (Denominazione di Origine Controllata) is the main classification for wines from designated zones made following traditions that were historically valid but often outdated. Recently the laws have become more flexible, encouraging producers to reduce yields and modernize techniques, while bringing quality wines under new appellations that allow for recognition of communes, estates and single vineyards. If anything, the problem today is a surfeit of DOCs.

DOCG (Denominazione di Origine Controllata e Garantita) was con-ceived as a 'super-league' for DOCs with a guarantee of authenticity that promised high class but didn't always provide it. Wines are made under stricter standards that have favoured improvements, but the best guarantee of quality remains the producer's name.

2006 VINTAGE REPORT

A baking hot and dry late spring and early summer gave way to a cool, rather wet August, but September came to the rescue – despite a few days of torrential downpour in central and northern zones – with sunny days and cool evenings, and in the end most people were pleased with the result qualitatively. In terms of quantity, the centre and north did a bit better than in 2005, the south a bit worse, so the national average was in line with the past 5 years. 2006 is difficult to assess without fairly extensive tasting, but the epithet 'good' or 'very good' (*ottimo*) applied almost everywhere. Puglia, which once again suffered a difficult September, was one of the few zones not to rejoice. There should be some excellent Barolos, Barbarescos, Amarones, Chiantis, Brunellos and super-Tuscans, both for early drinking and for laying down, but careful selection, as always, is essential.

Italian entries in the A–Z section (pages 56–307).

GERMANY

Dull, semi-sweet wines with names like Liebfraumilch, Niersteiner Gutes Domtal and Piesporter Michelsberg used to dominate the export market, but they are rapidly vanishing off all but the most basic radar screens. Instead, and not before time, we are seeing a better range of single-estate wines, with a greatly improved quality. Throughout Germany, both red and white wines are year by year, region by region, grower by grower, becoming fuller, better balanced and drier.

GRAPE VARIETIES
Riesling makes the best wines, in styles ranging from dry to intensely sweet. Other white wines come from Grauburgunder/Ruländer (Pinot Gris), Weissburgunder (Pinot Blanc), Gewürztraminer, Silvaner, Scheurebe and Rieslaner, although Müller-Thurgau produces much of the simpler wine. In the past decade, plantings of red grape varieties have doubled to fully 30% of the nation's vineyard. Good reds can be made in the south of the country from Spätburgunder (Pinot Noir), Dornfelder and Lemberger.

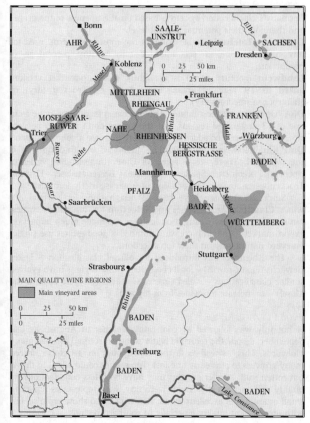

WINE REGIONS

Many of the most delectable Rieslings come from villages such as Bernkastel, Braueberg, Ürzig and Wehlen on the Mosel, and Kiedrich, Johannisberg and Rüdesheim in the Rheingau. The Nahe makes superb Rieslings in Schlossböckelheim and Traisen, and Niederhausen has the best vineyards in the entire region. Rheinhessen is unfortunately better known for its sugary Niersteiner Gutes Domtal than it is for the excellent racy Rieslings produced on steep riverside slopes in the villages of Nackenheim and Nierstein. Franken is the one place the Silvaner grape excels, often made in a powerful, dry, earthy style. The Pfalz is climatically similar to Alsace and has a similar potential for well-rounded, dry whites, plus rapidly improving reds. Baden also produces fully ripe wine styles, which should appeal to an international market accustomed to fuller, drier wines. In Württemberg most of the red wines are thin and dull, but there are a few producers who understand the need for weight and flavour. The other smaller wine regions make little wine and little is exported.

CLASSIFICATIONS

Germany's classification system is based on the ripeness of the grapes and therefore their potential alcohol level.

Deutscher Tafelwein (table wine) is the most basic term, used for any blended wine; it accounts for only a tiny percentage of production.

Landwein (country wine) is a slightly more up-market version, linked to 19 regional areas. These must be Trocken (dry) or Halbtrocken (medium-dry).

QbA (Qualitätswein bestimmter Anbaugebiete) is 'quality' wine from one of 13 designated regions, but the grapes don't have to be very ripe, and sugar can be added to the juice to increase alcoholic content.

QmP (Qualitätswein mit Prädikat) or 'quality wine with distinction' is the top level. There are 6 levels of QmP (in ascending order of ripeness): Kabinett, Spätlese, Auslese, Beerenauslese, Eiswein, Trockenbeerenauslese. The addition of sugar is strictly forbidden.

Since 2000, there have been 2 designations for varietal dry wines: **Classic** for 'good' wines and **Selection** for 'top-quality' wines, but they haven't really caught on: neither has made much impact on export markets. And an increasing number of good estates use single-vineyard names only on their top selections.

The Rheingau has introduced an official classification – Erstes Gewächs (First Growth) – for its best sites. Other regions have evolved similar classifications – called Grosses Gewächs (or Erste Lage in the Mosel) – to indicate top wines from top sites.

2006 VINTAGE REPORT

A hot July was followed by cool rainy weather in August; by late September, despite the return of better weather, rot had invaded many vineyards. This, as well as further downpours on 3 October, forced many growers to pick early and fast. Top estates could afford to throw out rotten fruit; smaller growers may have been less conscientious, so quality will vary greatly. Yields were tiny, with top estates reporting small quantities of excellent wines. Red wines also show promise, but with inconsistent quality especially in southern regions.

German entries in the A–Z section (pages 56–307).

Regions	Iphofen	Emrich-	Rebholz
Ahr	Johannisberg	Schonleber	Richter, Max Ferd
Baden	Kiedrich	Fürst, Rudolf	Sauer, Horst
Franken	Leiwen	Grans-Fassian	Schaefer, Willi
Hessische	Nierstein	Gunderloch	Schäfer-Fröhlich
Bergstrasse	Ockfen	Haag, Fritz	Schloss Lieser
Mittelrhein	Piesport	Haart, Reinhold	Schloss
Mosel-Saar-	Randersacker	Heger, Dr	Reinhartshausen
Ruwer	Rauenthal	Heyl zu	Schloss Saarstein
Nahe	Rüdesheim	Herrnsheim	Schloss Vollrads
Pfalz	Schlossböckelheim	Heymann-	Selbach-Oster
Rheingau	Trittenheim	Löwenstein	Van Volxem
Rheinhessen	Ürzig	Johner, Karl H	Wegeler
Saale-Unstrut	Wachenheim	Jost, Toni	Weil, Robert
Sachsen	Wehlen	Juliusspital	Wittmann
Württemberg	Winkel	Karthäuserhof	Wolf, J L
	Winningen	Keller	Zilliken
Wine towns and	Würzburg	Kesselstatt, Von	
villages		Koehler-Ruprecht	**see also**
Bad Dürkheim	**Producers**	Kühn, Peter Jakob	Kaiserstuhl
Bernkastel	Basserman-	Künstler, Franz	Liebfraumilch
Bingen	Jordan	Leitz, Josef	Ortenau
Brauneberg	Becker, J B	Loosen, Dr	Rieslaner
Eltville	Bercher	Maximin Grünhaus	Riesling
Erbach	Biffar, Josef	Mosbacher,	Scheurebe
Erden	Breuer, Georg	Georg	
Forst	Buhl, von	Müller-Catoir	
Geisenheim	Bürklin-Wolf	Müller-Scharzhof,	
Graach	Darting	Egon	
Hattenheim	Diel, Schlossgut	Prüm, J J	
Hochheim	Dönnhoff	Prüm, S A	

AUSTRIA

I can't think of a European nation where the wine culture has changed so dramatically over a generation as it has in Austria. Austria still makes great sweet wines, but a new order based on world-class medium- and full-bodied dry whites and increasingly fine reds has emerged.

WINE REGIONS AND GRAPE VARIETIES

The Danube runs through Niederösterreich, scene of much of Austria's viticulture. The Wachau produces great Riesling and excellent pepper-dry Grüner Veltliner. The Riesling is powerful and ripe, closer in style to Alsace than Germany. Next along the Danube are Kremstal and Kamptal, rapidly improving as fine dry white regions with a few good reds. The Weinviertel, in the north-east, also produces good reds and Grüner Veltliner whites. Burgenland, south of Vienna, produces the best reds from local varieties Zweigelt, Blaufränkisch and St-Laurent as well as from Cabernet Sauvignon, Merlot and Pinot Noir. Also, around the shores of the Neusiedler See, especially near the town of Rust, Burgenland produces some superb dessert wines. Further south, in Steiermark, Chardonnay and Sauvignon are increasingly oak-aged, though many drinkers still prefer the racy unoaked 'classic' wines from these varieties.

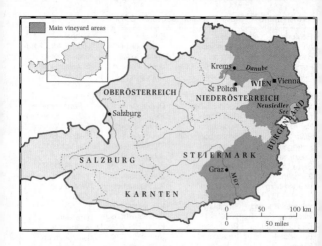

CLASSIFICATIONS

Wine categories are similar to those in Germany, beginning with
Tafelwein (table wine) and **Landwein** (country wine). **Qualitätswein** must come from one of the 16 main wine-producing regions.
Like German wines, quality wines may additionally have a special
category: Kabinett, Spätlese, Auslese, Beerenauslese, Ausbruch,
Trockenbeerenauslese. Since most Austrian wines are dry, these
categories count for less than in Germany. The Wachau has a
ripeness scale for dry whites: Steinfeder wines are made for early
drinking, Federspiel wines can last three years or so and the top wines
are known as Smaragd. The first Austrian appellations, known as
DAC, are starting to appear.

2006 VINTAGE REPORT

After a warm July, August was cool and damp; fine weather returned
in the autumn, with marked differences between day and night
temperatures. Overall, the Wachau and Kremstal produced great white
wines, and quality was high in the Weinviertel and Thermenregion.
Reds, especially Blaufränkisch, fared well in the Burgenland. The crop
was small throughout Austria, but overall quality was exceptional.
There was a good, if reduced, crop of botrytis wine in the Burgenland.

Austrian entries in the A–Z section (pages 56–307).

Regions	Producers		see also
Burgenland	Bründlmayer	Polz	Blaufränkisch
Carnuntum	Feiler-Artinger	Prager	Grüner Veltliner
Donauland	Hirtzberger, Franz	Tement	Schilcher
Kamptal	Knoll, Emmerich	Umathum	
Kremstal	Kracher, Alois	Velich	
Steiermark	Krutzler	Wachau, Freie	
Thermenregion	Nikolaihof	Weingärtner	
Wachau	Opitz, Willi	Wieninger	
Wien	Pichler, Franz X		

SPAIN

The late 1990s provided a dramatic turnaround in the quality of Spain's long-neglected wines. A drastic modernization of winemaking technology has now allowed regions like Priorat, Ribera del Duero, Rueda, Bierzo, Toro and La Mancha to muscle into the limelight, alongside Rioja and Jerez, with potent fruit-driven wines with the impact and style to convert the modern consumer.

WINE REGIONS

Galicia in the green, hilly north-west grows Spain's most aromatic whites. The heartland of the great Spanish reds, Rioja, Navarra and Ribera del Duero, is situated between the central plateau and the northern coast. Further west along the Duero, Rueda produces fresh whites and Toro good ripe reds. Cataluña is principally white wine country (much of it sparkling Cava), though there are some great reds in Priorat and increasingly in Terra Alta and Montsant. Aragón's reds and whites are looking good too, with an impressive relaunch of Aragón's great (but neglected for too long) native grape Garnacha. The central plateau of La Mancha makes mainly cheap reds and whites, though smaller private estates are improving spectacularly. Valencia and La Mancha, known for inexpensive and unmemorable wines, are now producing, with neighbouring Murcia, increasingly ambitious and rich reds. Andalucía's specialities are the fortified wines – sherry, Montilla and Málaga.

CLASSIFICATIONS

Vino de Mesa, the equivalent of France's Vin de Table, is the lowest level, but is also used for a growing number of non-DO 'Super-Spanish'.
Vino de la Tierra is Spain's equivalent of France's Vin de Pays.
DO (Denominación de Origen) is the equivalent of France's AC, regulating grape varieties and region of origin. In Castilla-La Mancha,

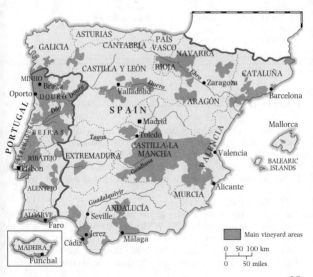

35

this category now encompasses single-estate DOs (Denominación de Origen – Vino de Pago).

DOCa (Denominación de Origen Calificada) is a super-category. Only two regions (Rioja and Priorat) have been promoted.

2006 VINTAGE REPORT
Not as dry as 2005 and 2004, but an early-September heatwave caused generalized problems, with grapes becoming raisined on the vine before they reached full ripeness, and with some rot in the more humid areas in the north-west of Spain. Overall, not as good a vintage as the two previous ones.

Spanish entries in the A–Z section (pages 56–307).

Regions	Rías Baixas	Faustino	Raïmat
Andalucía	Ribera del Duero	Freixenet	Remelluri
Aragón	Rioja	González Byass	Rioja Alta, La
Balearic Islands	Rueda	Guelbenzu	Riojanas
Canary Islands	Somontano	Hidalgo	Rodríguez, Telmo
Castilla-La	Toro	Juvé y Camps	Romeo, Benjamin
Mancha	Utiel-Requena	Leda	Sandeman
Castilla y León	Valdepeñas	López de Heredia	Torres
Cataluña		Lustau, Emilio	Valdespino
Galicia	**Producers**	Marqués de	Vall-Llach
Valencia	Aalto	Cáceres	Vega Sicilia
	Allende	Marqués de	Viñas del Vero
DO/DOCa	Artadi	Griñon	
Bierzo	Barbadilla	Marqués de	**see also**
Cariñena	Berberana	Murrieta	Airén
Cava	Campillo	Marqués de Riscal	Albariño
Costers del Segre	Campo Viejo	Martínez Bujanda	Grenache Noir
Jerez y Manzanilla	Chivite	Mas Doix	Mourvèdre
Jumilla	Clos Erasmus	Mauro	Parellada
Málaga	Clos Mogador	Muga	Tempranillo
La Mancha	Codorniu	Osborne	
Montilla-Moriles	Contino	Palacios, Alvaro	
Navarra	CVNE	Pesquera	
Penedès	Domecq	Pingus, Dominio	
Priorat	Enate	de	

PORTUGAL

Investment and imagination are paying off in this attractive country, with climates that vary from the mild, damp Minho region in the north-west to the subtropical island of Madeira. Innovative use of native grapes and blending with international varieties means that Portugal is now a rich source of inexpensive yet characterful wines.

WINE REGIONS
The lush Vinho Verde country in the north-west gives very different wine from the parched valleys of the neighbouring Douro, with its drier, more continental climate. The Douro, home of port, is also the source of some of Portugal's best unfortified red wines. In Beiras, which includes Bairrada and Dão, soil types are crucial in determining

the character of the wines. Estremadura and Ribatejo use native and international varieties in regions influenced either by the maritime climate or by the river Tagus. South of Lisbon, the Terras do Sado and Alentejo produce some exciting table wines – and the Algarve is waking up. Madeira is unique, a volcanic island 850km (530 miles) out in the Atlantic Ocean.

CLASSIFICATIONS

Vinho de Mesa is the lowest level, but commercially important as so much off-dry to medium-dry rosé is exported under this label.

Vinho Regional (11 in number) is equivalent to French Vin de Pays, with laws and permitted varieties much freer than for IPR and DOC.

IPR (Indicação de Proveniência Regulamentada) is the intermediate step for wine regions hoping to move up to DOC status. Many have been promoted in the past few years, leaving just 4 IPRs, not all of which will definitely become DOCs.

DOC (Denominação de Origem Controlada) Equivalent to France's AC; there are now 25 DOC regions.

2006 VINTAGE REPORT

The winter of 2005–6 brought welcome rain after two years without. It even snowed in Ribatejo and Alentejo. Everything was set for a good vintage after a fine spring. Some vineyards in the Douro were hit by violent hailstorms in mid-June and lost 30% of their grapes, but elsewhere, prospects were good. Summer was hot and mostly dry and gave good white wines, some a little low in acidity. In the baking heat, sugar levels in the Douro shot up, some grapes raisined, but some attractive aromatic ports and red wines have been made. Red wines in the Ribatejo are good, as are some in Dão made from early-ripening grapes. But on 21 September, the rains came to the northern half of Portugal. Later-ripening grapes in Dão never quite made it, so there won't be many Dão reserve wines. In Bairrada, many of the Baga vineyards had shut down in the summer heat and grapes were still unripe. In the rain, they rotted. Down south, alcohol levels are high in Alentejo wines after record August temperatures.

Portuguese entries in the A–Z section (pages 56–307).

USA

The United States has more varied growing conditions for grapes than any other country in the world, which isn't so surprising when you consider that the 50 states of the Union cover an area that is larger than Western Europe; and although Alaska doesn't grow grapes in the icy far north, Washington State does in the north-west, as does Texas in the south and New York State in the north-east, and even Hawaii, lost in the pounding surf of the Pacific Ocean, manages to grow grapes and make wine. Every state, even Alaska (thanks to salmonberry and fireweed), now produces wine of some sort or another; it ranges from some pretty dire offerings, which would have been far better distilled into brandy, to some of the greatest and most original wines to be found in the world today.

GRAPE VARIETIES AND WINE REGIONS

California is far and away the most important state for wine production. In its determination to match the best red Bordeaux and white Burgundy, California proved that it was possible to take the classic European role models and successfully re-interpret them in an area thousands of miles away from their home. However, there is more to California than this. The Central Valley produces the majority of the simple beverage wines that still dominate the American market. Napa and Sonoma Counties north of San Francisco Bay do produce

great Cabernet and Chardonnay, but grapes like Zinfandel and Merlot also make their mark and the Carneros and Russian River Valley areas are highly successful for Pinot Noir, Chardonnay and sparkling wines. In the north, Mendocino and Lake Counties produce good grapes. South of San Francisco, in the cool, foggy valleys between Santa Cruz and Santa Barbara, Chardonnay, Pinot Noir and Syrah are producing exciting cool-climate but ripe-flavoured wines.

Oregon, with a cooler and more capricious climate than most of California, perseveres with Pinot Noir, Chardonnay, Pinot Gris, Pinot Blanc and Riesling with patchy success. Washington, so chilly and misty on the coast, becomes virtual desert east of the Cascade Mountains and it is here, in irrigated vineyards, that superb reds and whites can be made, with thrillingly focused fruit.

In New York, Long Island continues to impress with classically styled Merlot, Cabernet Sauvignon and Cabernet Franc, as well as Chardonnay to pair with the local lobster. Riesling shines in the Hudson Valley and especially the Finger Lakes; Chardonnay and fizz also do well here. Improved vineyard practices have enabled growers to cope with horrible weather through much of the first half of this decade, from vine-killing winter deep freeze to harvest-soaking rains.

Other states have seen dramatic growth in the wine industry this decade. Established industries in Virginia, Maryland, Pennsylvania, Texas and Missouri have led the way, but look also for new growth in North Carolina, Georgia and Michigan.

CLASSIFICATIONS

The AVA (American Viticultural Area) system was introduced in the 1980s. It does not guarantee a quality standard, but merely requires that at least 85% of grapes in a wine come from the specified AVA. There are over 150 AVAs, more than 90 of which are in California.

2006 VINTAGE REPORT

A second successive rainy winter and a cool, wet spring pushed California's north coast harvest schedule back early in the year. High soil moisture encouraged leaf growth in many varieties, necessitating leaf-pulling. Early summer was cool, but a deadly late-July heatwave caused vines to shut down their photosynthesis. However, the heat didn't harm the fruit as much as feared because cool nights in July and August kept acidity high. By mid-September all was back on track for a classic cooler harvest. Unlike the short crop of Pinot Noir suffered by many regions in 2005, Pinot Noir crops rose to normal levels. The harvest was a bit erratic, with some reds coming in before whites, but the large crop was only about two weeks late, with superb quality.

In Washington, a mild winter was followed by a clear and dry spring. Summer was warm, but there were no significant heat spikes and by September, harvest appeared to be coming on schedule. A little Sauvignon Blanc was picked before the weather turned cold. Cooler than average weather in September and October slowed maturation and many vineyards had Cabernet Sauvignon still ripening in November. But the even nature of the weather allowed full ripeness to be achieved and the resulting wines have slightly lower acidity, ripe tannins and are harmonious. It looks to be a vibrant vintage.

In Oregon, the winter was mild and flowering occurred under good to ideal conditions. The crop set was larger than in previous vintages (much needed due to demand for Pinot Noir wines). Brief heat spikes in June and September advanced ripeness. Early September was warm, allowing ripeness to progress, then a change to cool days and intermittent rain prolonged the season. A warm spell compressed the harvest, making for a rapid, stressful vintage. Wines will have plenty of alcohol and acidity and show fragrant aromatics at an early stage.

Growers in the Eastern US were doing cartwheels over the ideal conditions of the 2006 harvest, especially in New York where yields had been hurt by weather in previous years.

USA entries in the A–Z section (pages 56–307) by state.

CALIFORNIA	Calera	Hartford Family	Sanford
AVAs	Caymus	Hartwell	Scharffenberger
Alexander Valley	Chalone	Heitz	Cellars
Anderson Valley	Chateau	Hess Collection	Schramsberg
Carneros	Montelena	Iron Horse	Screaming Eagle
Central Coast	Chateau St Jean	Jordan	Seghesio
Dry Creek Valley	Chimney Rock	Kendall-Jackson	Shafer
Howell Mountain	Clos du Bois	Kenwood	Silver Oak Cellars
Mendocino Ridge	Clos du Val	Kistler	Silverado
Mount Veeder	Coppola, Francis	Kunde Estate	Vineyards
Napa Valley	Ford	Landmark	Simi
Oakville	Cuvaison	Laurel Glen	Sonoma-Cutrer
Paso Robles	Dalla Valle	Marcassin	Spottswoode
Russian River	Dehlinger	Mariah	Stag's Leap Wine
Valley	Diamond Creek	Matanzas Creek	Cellars
Rutherford	Domaine	Merryvale	Steele
Santa Cruz	Carneros	Michael, Peter	Sterling
Mountains	Domaine	Miner Family	Swan, Joseph
Santa Maria Valley	Chandon	Vineyards	Talbott
Santa Rita Hills	Dominus	Mondavi, Robert	Torres, Marimar
Sonoma Coast	Dry Creek	Moon Mountain	Turley
Sonoma Valley	Vineyard	Mumm Napa	Williams Selyem
Stags Leap	Duckhorn	Murray, Andrew	
District	Dunn	Navarro	
	Ferrari-Carano	Newton	**see also**
Producers	Fetzer	Opus One	Central Valley
Acacia	Flora Springs	Phelps, Joseph	Mendocino
Alban	Flowers	Pine Ridge	County
Araujo	Franciscan	Qupé	Monterey County
Arrowood	Gallo	Rasmussen, Kent	Napa Valley
Atlas Peak	Geyser Peak	Ravenswood	San Luis Obispo
Au Bon Climat	Grgich Hills	Ridge	County
Beaulieu Vineyard	Gundlach-	J Rochioli	Santa Barbara
Beringer	Bundschu	Vineyards	County
Bonny Doon	Handley	Roederer Estate	Sonoma County
Bronco Wine Co.	Harlan Estate	Saintsbury	Zinfandel

NEW YORK	**Producers**	Fox Run	Lamoreaux
STATE	Bedell Cellars	Vineyards	Landing
Finger Lakes AVA	Channing	Frank, Dr	Lenz Winery
Long Island	Daughters	Konstantin	

OREGON	**Producers**	Cristom	Wright, Ken
Willamette Valley	Adelsheim	Domaine Drouhin	
AVA	Vineyard	Oregon	
	Argyle	Domaine Serene	
	Beaux Frères	Elk Cove	

WASHINGTON	**Producers**	Columbia Crest	Long Shadows
STATE	Andrew Will	DeLille Cellars	Vintners
AVAs	Winery	Dunham Cellars	Quilceda Creek
Columbia Valley	Cadence	Hedges Cellars	Woodward
Walla Walla Valley	Cayuse Vineyards	Janiuk	Canyon
Yakima Valley AVA	Chateau Ste	L'Ecole No 41	
	Michelle	Leonetti Cellar	

see also	Horton Vineyards	Texas	Virginia

AUSTRALIA

Australian wine today enjoys a reputation still well out of proportion to the quantity of wine produced (total output is about one-fifth that of France), though volumes are mushrooming. The New World wine revolution – emphasizing ripe, rich fruit, seductive use of oak, labelling by grape variety and consumer-friendly marketing – has been led by wine warriors from the southern seas. There's more than enough sunshine and not nearly enough rain to grow the grapes, so most growers are guaranteed ripeness but rely heavily on irrigation for their vines to survive. Dynamic and innovative winemakers ensure a steady supply of new wines, wineries and even regions, but consolidation and internationalization of larger operators seem to be causing an unwarranted and unwelcome dumbing down of flavour.

GRAPE VARIETIES

Varietal wines remain more prized than blends. Shiraz has long been a key varietal and is more fashionable than Cabernet Sauvignon. Renewed respect for old-vine Grenache and Mourvèdre has seen these former workhorse varieties transformed into premium wines. Merlot, and in cooler-climate regions Pinot Noir, lead the pack of alternative red varieties and Australia's endless appetite for experiment has found prospective new stars in Petit Verdot, Tempranillo, Nebbiolo and Sangiovese. Among white grapes the position of Chardonnay remains unchallenged, although Semillon and Riesling both have a longer track record. Rhône varieties Marsanne and Viognier (now fashionably included in blends with Shiraz) are both impressive and Verdelho and Pinot Gris are making a strong case for themselves as alternatives

to Chardonnay. Sweet whites are produced from Semillon and Muscat – both the top-class Brown Muscat (a sub-variety of Muscat Blanc à Petits Grains) and the more workaday Muscat Gordo Blanco.

WINE REGIONS

Western Australia is a vast state, virtually desert except for its south-western coastal strip. The sun-baked region near Perth was best suited to throaty reds and fortified wines, but winery and vineyard expertise has become more sophisticated and good dry whites are now being made. The most exciting wines, both red and white, come from Margaret River and Great Southern down towards the coast.

South Australia dominates the wine scene – it grows the most grapes, makes the most wine and is home to most of the nation's biggest wine companies. There is more to it, however, than attractive, undemanding, gluggable wine. The Clare Valley produces outstanding cool-climate Riesling, as well as excellent Shiraz and Cabernet. The Barossa is home to some of the planet's oldest vines, particularly Shiraz and Grenache. Eden Valley, in the hills to the east of Barossa, excels at crisp, steely Rieslings and scented Shiraz. McLaren Vale, Coonawarra and the Limestone Coast also make many thrilling reds.

Victoria was Australia's major producer for most of the 19th century until her vineyards were devastated by the phylloxera louse. It's only recently that Victoria has regained her position as provider of some of the most startling wine styles in the country: stunning liqueur Muscats; the thrilling dark reds of Central Victoria; and the urbane Yarra Valley and Mornington Peninsula reds and whites.

New South Wales was home to the revolution that propelled Australia to the front of the world wine stage (in the Hunter Valley, an area that remains a dominant force). However, the state is a major bulk producer in Riverina, and a clutch of new regions in the Central Ranges are grabbing headlines.

Tasmania, with its cooler climate, is attracting attention for top-quality Pinot Noirs and Champagne-method sparkling wines. Riesling and Gewürztraminer would almost certainly be excellent, if the producers would give them a chance.

CLASSIFICATIONS

Formal appellation control, restricting certain grapes to certain regions, is virtually unknown; regulations are more of a guarantee of authenticity than a guide to quality. In a country so keen on inter-regional blending for its commercial brands, a system resembling France's AC could be problematic. However, the Label Integrity Program (LIP) guarantees all claims made on labels and the Geographical Indications (GI) committee is busy clarifying zones, regions and sub-regions – albeit with plenty of lively, at times acrimonious, debate about where some regional borders should go.

2007 VINTAGE REPORT

After substantial increases in planting over the past decade and several bumper crops – which have resulted in a prolonged glut – 2007 was the vintage that Australia needed. Yields are down considerably: reds have been harder hit, down almost 40% from the previous vintage, with whites dropping by 17%. The yield in tonnes per hectare is the lowest Australia has experienced in 30 years (since 1976). Most parts of eastern Australia suffered from drought, frost and poor fruit-set; cool-climate regions were hardest hit, with production levels down by an average of 45%. Western Australia was unaffected by the extremes of weather experienced in the East and many winemakers there regard it as potentially their best vintage ever. The warmer regions of the Riverland and the Murray Darling did particularly well, thanks to good rainfall in January which helped vines get through to harvest in better than expected condition. The reds are expected to be especially impressive. The unseasonal weather led to the vintage beginning between 2 and 6 weeks early, with most winemakers enjoying a rare Easter break. Most reports suggest that although quantity is dramatically down, the 2007 vintage will produce wines of very good to excellent quality. The impact of difficult weather conditions during the harvest will affect the development of the vines in 2008. This, together with the likelihood of less water being available for irrigation, means that below average yields are likely once more in 2008.

Australian entries in the A–Z section (pages 56–307).

NEW ZEALAND

New Zealand's wines, though diverse in style, are characterized by
intense fruit flavours, zesty acidity and pungent aromas – the product
of cool growing conditions and high-tech winemaking.

GRAPE VARIETIES

Until recently, New Zealand's fame has rested on one grape variety:
Sauvignon Blanc. The bracing, tangy style of New Zealand's first
Sauvignons redefined the world's expectations of the grape. But this
rapidly maturing wine industry has many more tricks up its sleeve.
The other major white grapes are Chardonnay in a melony, peachy
style and fragrant Riesling, with Gewürztraminer and Pinot Gris on
the rise and Viognier now making an appearance. Among reds,
Cabernet Sauvignon and Merlot are increasingly successful, either
fruity and berryish or in a more serious Bordeaux style blended with
Cabernet Franc; Shiraz is fashionable, dry and scented; and Pinot Noir
is bidding to be taken seriously in the Premier League of world wine.

WINE REGIONS

Nearly 1600km (1000 miles)
separate New Zealand's
northernmost wine region
from the country's (and the
world's) most southerly wine
region, Central Otago. In terms of
wine styles it is useful to divide
the country into two parts. The
warmer climate of Hawkes Bay
and one or two pockets around
Auckland produce the best
Cabernet Sauvignon, Merlot and

44

Cabernet Franc as well as increasingly good Syrah. Waiheke Island and Hawkes Bay's Gimblett Gravels have some of the most exciting red wine vineyards. Martinborough and Wairarapa are noted for Pinot Noir. In the South Island, Nelson is good for Pinot Noir and aromatic whites, while Marlborough is the hub of the industry, famous for Sauvignon Blanc, but also excellent for fizz, Chardonnay, Riesling and Pinot Noir. Waipara is small but produces very characterful reds and whites, while Central Otago produces fabulous Pinot Noir, and a lot else besides.

CLASSIFICATIONS

Labels guarantee geographic origin. The broadest designation is New Zealand, followed by North or South Island. Next come the 10 or so regions. Labels may also name specific localities and individual vineyards.

2007 VINTAGE REPORT

Classic El Niño conditions brought wet, cool weather during flowering, a cyclone with torrential rain in Auckland and Northland, and then a long, dry Indian summer during the critical ripening period. Poor flowering and early frosts reduced the Marlborough Sauvignon Blanc crop by around 20%, although the final tally is expected to be much the same as 2006 thanks to vineyard expansion. On the positive side, every winemaker is crowing about Sauvignon Blanc quality, which may have received a boost through generally lower crop levels.

Cyclone Becky arrived after most of the white grapes had been harvested in Auckland and Northland, although it did promote some rot in mid-season red grapes. Hawkes Bay fared well in both quality and quantity, with reports of 'best-ever' white wines and generally excellent reds. Martinborough and Waipara suffered exceptionally low yields but the quality is mostly very good. As one Martinborough grower said, 'if we got NZ$50 in the hand for every bottle of our Pinot Noir it wouldn't cover the cost of growing the grapes.' Central Otago Pinot Noir will be down in quantity thanks to frosts and poor flowering, but the quality is expected to vary from good to excellent depending on the level of grape selection.

New Zealand entries in the A–Z section (pages 56–307).

Regions	Producers		
Auckland	Ata Rangi	Hunter's	Pegasus Bay
Canterbury	Babich	Isabel Estate	Saint Clair
Central Otago	Cellier Le Brun	Jackson Estate	Seifried
Gisborne	Church Road	Kumeu River	Seresin
Hawkes Bay	Cloudy Bay	Martinborough	Sileni
Kumeu/Huapai	Coopers Creek	Vineyard	Stonyridge
Marlborough	Craggy Range	Matua Valley	Te Mata
Martinborough	Delegat's	Millton	Vavasour
Nelson	Dry River	Montana	Villa Maria
Waiheke Island	Felton Road	Neudorf	Wither Hills
	Fromm	Ngatarawa	
	Giesen	Nobilo	
	Goldwater Estate	Palliser Estate	
		C J Pask	

SOUTH AMERICA

The only countries to have proved their ability to make fine wine are Chile and Argentina, though Uruguay is clearly trying to join them.

ARGENTINA

Affected by several economic crises and political instability during the last decade, the Argentine wine industry now seems to be emerging as one of the brightest stars in the wine world. Better vineyard management and winemaking practices deliver juicy Malbec (Argentina's flagship red grape) not only from the classic Upper Mendoza River region, but also from high-altitude vineyards in Salta's Calchaquí Valley (especially around Cafayate) and down towards Patagonia, in Río Negro and Neuquén. The perfumed and heady white Torrontés grape is also showing its potential, especially when it comes from the high Salta vineyards, while red Bonarda is widely grown and juicily refreshing. Foreign investment is heavily focused on Mendoza, where more than 70% of the country's wine is made. New luxury hotels and spas in the wine country add glamour to this Argentine wine boom.

CHILE

Cabernet Sauvignon is still Chile's best offering to the world of wine, from the complex and sophisticated examples from Maipo, towards the Andes mountains, to soft and fruity versions from the plains in the Central Valley. But Chile's climate is ideal for a wide range of grapes, most of them delivering ripe flavours and intense fruit character. Carménère is better than ever, offering herbal notes and ripe red fruit aromas over a soft texture, especially from the Rapel valleys, while superripe and robust Syrah is emerging everywhere. An ever-

Main vineyard areas

0   250   500 km
0   250 miles

increasing number of coastal-climate reds and whites is appearing from Casablanca and San Antonio valleys, and also from the north in Limarí and Elqui. These areas are the source of crunchy and fresh Sauvignon Blanc and interesting cool-climate Syrah. Diversity – in terms of style, grapes and wine regions – seems to be the keyword for Chilean wine in the future.

URUGUAY

Most of the vines are on clay soils in the Canelones region around Montevideo, which has high rainfall in a relatively cool climate: the thick-skinned, rot-resistant black Tannat grape from South-West France is the leading variety. A clutch of modern wineries are working hard to soften the tannic Tannat; they are also producing snappy Sauvignon Blanc and fresh Cabernet Franc and Merlot. Best producers: Bouza, Carrau, Castillo Viejo, Los Cerros de San Juan, Filgueira, Juanicó, PISANO, Stagnari, Toscanini, Viñedo de los Vientos.

OTHER COUNTRIES

Look at Brazil, how vast it is. Yet in all this expanse, running from 33° South to 5° North, there's nowhere ideal to site a vineyard. The best attempts are made down towards the Uruguayan border, but half of Brazil's wine now comes from the Valle de San Francisco in the torrid north. Peru has seemingly good vineyard sites in the Ica Valley south of Lima, but nothing exciting winewise. Bolivia has few vineyards, but they're incredibly high. Venezuela's chief claim to fame is that some of her subtropical vines give three crops a year!

2007 VINTAGE REPORT

The season is shaping up well, slightly cooler than a normal super-hot year, with little rain to worry about. Many whites were picked early, while reds such as Syrah, Carmenère and Cabernet Sauvignon were picked 2–3 weeks later than usual; winemakers expect fresher fruit with good acidity. On the other side of the Andes, in Mendoza, some intense rain and hail affected Luján de Cuyo and Uco Valley, but well-managed vineyards did not suffer from rot. Optimistic producers expect an even better vintage than in 2006, especially for Malbec.

South American entries in the A–Z section (pages 56–307).

ARGENTINA	Terrazas de Los	San Antonio	Montes
Lujan de Cuyo	Andes	Valley	Quebrada de
Mendoza	Trapiche		Macul
Patagonia	Familia Zuccardi	**Producers**	San Pedro
Salta		Almaviva	Santa Carolina
Uco Valley	**CHILE**	Carmen	Santa Rita
	Casablanca,	Casa Lapostolle	Seña
Producers	Valle de	Casa Marin	Tarapacá
Achaval-Ferrer	Central, Valle	Casablanca, Viña	Torres, Miguel
Altos las	Colchagua, Valle	Concha y Toro	Valdivieso
Hormigas	de	Cono Sur	Villard Estate
Luigi Bosca	Curicó, Valle de	De Martino/Santa	
Catena Zapata	Limarí Valley	Ines	**see also**
Domaine Vistalba	Maipo, Valle de	Errázuriz	Carmenère
O Fournier	Maule, Valle del	La Rosa	Malbec
Norton	Rapel, Valle del	Matetic Vineyards	

SOUTH AFRICA

The worldwide grape glut has not passed by South Africa, and with grape prices falling, some vineyards have been 'mothballed' until they are again economically viable. This comes at a time when all the recent plantings are reaching full production. After many years of growth, both in quantity and price, exports have taken a dive; local consumption also has declined for the sixth year in succession. Amazingly, this scenario has not deterred would-be wine producers from entering the market; new private wineries continue to open at the rate of more than one a week. A brighter side of the picture is that quality, especially among white wines, continues to improve and a new generation of forward-looking winemakers with plenty of foreign experience under their belts looks set to ensure even higher standards.

GRAPE VARIETIES AND WINE REGIONS

The Cape's winelands run roughly 400km (250 miles) north and east of Cape Town, although small pockets of new vineyards are taking the winelands way outside their traditional territory. Wine, albeit in tiny quantities, is now being produced from grapes grown in the mountains above the Eastern Cape town of Plettenberg Bay, better known for its holidaymakers than vines, and the Drakensberg region of KwaZulu-Natal. For the first time in four years, plantings have decreased. White grapes – Chenin Blanc, Chardonnay, Sauvignon Blanc and Colombard – dominate new plantings, and Chenin remains the most planted variety. Red varieties, led by Cabernet Sauvignon and Shiraz, cover just under 46% of the vineyards; Pinotage continues to slide. The emphatic swing towards classic, international varieties continues, with small quantities of Verdelho, Malbec, Nebbiolo, Sangiovese, Tannat and

Tempranillo in the mix. But it is without doubt Rhône varieties that still generate most excitement: as well as Syrah, there's Grenache, Cinsaut and Mourvèdre for reds, and Viognier, Grenache Blanc and Roussanne for whites.

With the major grape varieties being planted over the entire Western Cape winelands, there is little typicity of origin, although some areas are historically associated with specific varieties or styles. Stellenbosch lays claim to some of the best red wines; maritime-influenced Constantia, and Cape Point on the other side of the Peninsula mountain chain, produce exhilarating Sauvignon Blanc, a variety also showing great promise in Durbanville, Darling, upland Elgin and Cape Agulhas. Other cool areas include Walker Bay, where the focus is Pinot Noir. Chardonnay, long associated with inland Robertson, is now making its mark with Cap Classique sparkling wines as well as citrous, nutty still wines. As a warmer area, Robertson is also recognized for fortifieds, both Muscadel (Muscat) and port styles. Inland areas such as Swartland along the west coast appear to have good affinity with Shiraz and other Rhône varieties; white blends including Chenin, Chardonnay, Viognier are also starting to create waves.

CLASSIFICATION
The Wine of Origin (WO) system divides wine-producing areas into regions, districts, wards, estates and single vineyards. Wines can be traced back to their source, but quality is not guaranteed. Varietal, vintaged wines for both export and the local market must be made from at least 85% of the named grape and vintage.

2007 VINTAGE REPORT
After a wet, cold winter and generally cool, dry spring, lasting right through to mid-January, all looked set for a top-quality 2007 harvest. The traditional heatwave hit early and very hard; in some areas temperatures of 40°C or more persisted for over a week. While this adversely affected weaker vineyards and those close to ripening, many well-established vines were nowhere near ripe and came through unscathed. Two subsequent rainy spells and cooler temperatures relieved vineyard stress (but not winemakers' stress!). Sauvignon Blanc, especially from cooler areas, Semillon and Viognier are white stars, though quantities are down. Many reds have good fruit, soft tannins with early accessibility; top wines will be keepers.

South African entries in the A–Z section (pages 56–307).

WINE REGIONS	Boekenhoutskloof	Hamilton Russell	Saxenburg
Constantia WO	Bouchard	Hartenberg Estate	Simonsig
Durbanville WO	Finlayson	Jordan	Spice Route
Elgin WO	Buitenverwachting	Kanonkop	Springfield Estate
Franschhoek WO	Cape Point	Klein Constantia	Steenberg
Paarl WO	Cluver, Paul	KWV	Thelema
Robertson WO	De Trafford	L'Avenir	Veenwouden
Stellenbosch WO	Distell	Meerlust	Vergelegen
Walker Bay WO	Ellis, Neil	Morgenhof	Villiera
	Els, Ernie	Mulderbosch	Warwick
Producers	Fairview	Rust en Vrede	
Beck, Graham	Glen Carlou	Rustenberg	see also
Beyerskloof	Grangehurst	Sadie Family	Pinotage

OTHER WINE COUNTRIES

ALGERIA With many vines over 40 years old, there should be great potential here, but political uncertainty hinders progress despite government support. The western coastal province of Oran produces three-quarters of Algeria's wine, including the soft but muscular Coteaux de Tlemcen wines and dark, beefy reds of the Coteaux de Mascara.

BULGARIA After success in the 1980s and disarray in the 90s, some progress followed the introduction of new wine legislation in 2001, and investment in new vineyards is beginning to gather pace. Entry into the EU in 2007 should encourage a more positive attitude in the vineyards, and there are signs of single-estate wines emerging. New World influences are having some effect, although few wines shine. Cabernet Sauvignon and Merlot dominate, but local grapes – plummy Mavrud, meaty Gamza, deep Melnik, fruity white Dimiat and Misket – can be good. Established wineries such as BOYAR, Khan Krum and Suhindol have been joined by several new operations, Bessa Valley and Stork Nest estates being two of the largest.

CANADA The strict VQA (Vintners Quality Alliance) maintains high standards in British Columbia and Ontario, and there has been enormous progress in the 2 most important regions – OKANAGAN VALLEY in British Columbia and the NIAGARA PENINSULA in Ontario – where the move from hybrid to vinifera varieties has been rapid. Sweet icewine is still Canada's trump card. Pinot Gris, Chardonnay, Riesling and Gewürztraminer lead the way in non-sweet whites; Merlot, Cabernet Franc, Cabernet Sauvignon, even Syrah, show potential in red wines.

CHINA Though China officially promotes wine, its potential remains unfulfilled as the majority of Chinese are reluctant to drink it. However, as the Chinese economy expands, demand for its wines is increasing, particularly in the cities. Home-grown premium wines are emerging and foreign investment proceeds apace with continual improvements in viticulture and winemaking. China now ranks as the sixth biggest wine producer in the world, with massive new plantings every year – mainly international grapes, with some traditional Chinese, German and Russian varieties. Major producers include Changyu, Dynasty, Great Wall, HUADONG and newcomer Xintian. Of course, if the Chinese don't drink this ever-increasing lake of wine, they'll start to export it into an ever-more crowded market.

CROATIA Inland Croatia has an undercurrent of rising potential: bulk whites dominate but small private producers are emerging. Initiatives to sow vines in former minefields are helping to restore Croatia's viticultural heritage. What the country needs now is more investment, more technology in the vineyard and winery and a fair price for the grapes; planned membership of the EU will undoubtedly help. Tourism is flourishing and this should help popularize the wines - so long as foreigners can pronounce them. The best vineyards are on the Dalmatian coast, where international varieties are being planted alongside gutsy indigenous grapes: deep, tannic Plavac Mali – related to Zinfandel – has long produced the top red wines. GRGICH of California has a winery on the Peljesac peninsula. Frano Milos (also on the Peljesac peninsula) and Kozlovic and Matosevic in Istria are other names to look out for.

CYPRUS COMMANDARIA has been famous since the Crusades, but otherwise Cypriot wine has no great reputation. However, Cyprus is modernizing, and regional press houses and wineries are being built in or near the vineyards. Investment by companies like Etko, Keo, Loel and Sodap is at last producing tasty modern reds and whites; Sodap uses Australian consultants. The first efforts with grapes like Cabernet Sauvignon and Sémillon are impressive.

THE CZECH REPUBLIC The vineyards of Bohemia in the north-west and Moravia in the south-east are mainly planted with white varieties – Grüner Veltliner, Müller-Thurgau, Riesling, Pinot Blanc, Pinot Gris – with pockets of red such as St-Laurent and Lemberger (Blaufränkisch).

ENGLAND The UK's winegrowing industry has celebrated more than 50 vintages since the 'revival' of commercial vineyards in the early 1950s. However, with around 800ha (2000 acres) of vines, 330 vineyards (many very small), 115 wineries and an average annual output of around 2 million bottles, it is still minute. Nevertheless, producers have learnt which varieties are successful (Bacchus, Schönburger and Seyval Blanc for whites; Rondo, Regent, Dornfelder and Pinot Noir for reds; and Chardonnay, Pinot Noir and Meunier for quality sparklings), how to train and trellis them to cope with the (usually) cool summers and – most importantly – how to make sound, sometimes excellent, wines. In particular, sparkling wines have shown they can equal Champagne in quality, and even growers from Champagne are taking notice; a producer of very good Champagne has now planted 4ha (10 acres) in Hampshire and more are sure to follow. Regulations now require growers to submit their wines for testing before they can label them 'English'; wines labelled 'UK table wine' should be avoided. The most popular winemaking counties are: Kent (CHAPEL DOWN, Biddenden, Sandhurst), East Sussex (BREAKY BOTTOM, Davenport), West Sussex (NYETIMBER, RIDGEVIEW), Surrey (DENBIES), Berkshire (STANLAKE PARK), Gloucestershire (THREE CHOIRS), Hampshire (Wickham), Devon (SHARPHAM) and Cornwall (CAMEL VALLEY). 2006 was the biggest harvest ever – and the warmest year since records began over 300 years ago.

GEORGIA Georgia faces many challenges – lack of regulation, resistance to change, counterfeiting – but its diverse climates (from subtropical to moderate continental) and soils could produce every style imaginable. The tourist industry is vibrant and helping introduce Georgian wines to a wider audience. International and indigenous varieties abound; the peppery, powerful red Saperavi could be a world-beater. Most wine is still pretty rustic, but investment is beginning to have an effect, with GWS (Georgian Wines & Spirits Company, 75% owned by Pernod Ricard) leading the way.

GREECE Sadly, the Athens Olympics in 2004 made little difference to our minimal enthusiasm for Greek wines. That's a shame, because a new generation of winemakers and grape growers, many of them trained in France, Australia or California, have a clear vision of the flavours they want to achieve and their wines are modern but marvellously original too. Polarization between cheap bulk and expensive boutique wines continues, but large companies such as Boutari, Kourtakis and Tsantalis are upping the quality stakes and flavours improve every vintage. More vineyard and marketing work – many labels are still difficult to understand – is needed. International plantings have led to surprising and successful blends with indigenous varieties such as the red Agiorgitiko, Limnio and Xynomavro, and white Assyrtiko, Moschofilero and Roditis. Quality areas: Naousa and Nemea for reds, SAMOS for sweet Muscats, Patras for dessert Mavrodaphne. Wineries to watch include: Aidarinis, Argyros, ANTONOPOULOS, Gentilini, GEROVASSILIOU, Hatzimichali, Kyr Yanni, Domaine Costa LAZARIDI, Mercouri, Papaïoannou, Strofilia and Tselepos.

HUNGARY Hungary makes remarkably good whites, improving reds and outstanding sweet wines, and has joined the EU, yet few of us have much idea about her as a wine country. Stringent regulations and investment/advice from Australian and western European companies and consultants have put Hungary, with its 22 designated appella-tions, back on the international wine map. There is renewed interest in native varieties such as Furmint and Irsai Olivér for whites, Kékfrankos (Blaufränkisch) and Kadarka for reds, and top Hungarian winemakers – Akos Kamocsay, Vilmos Thummerer and others – are now a solid force. But price and reputation remain low and many vineyards are being abanadoned out of desperation. TOKAJI in particular has yet to develop the world-class reputation its wines deserve.

INDIA India's climate is generally unsuitable for wine production: only a small percentage of the 50,000ha (123,500 acres) of vines is used for wine; both international varieties and ancient Indian ones, such as Arkesham and Arkavati, are planted. Wine consumption is increasing rapidly. CHATEAU INDAGE, with vineyards in the Maharashtra hills east of Mumbai (Bombay), dominates the market and produces still and sparkling wines. Sula is a promising new winery north-east of Mum-bai. Advice from international wine guru Michel Rolland put Grover Vineyards in Bangalore on the map.

ISRAEL More small wineries continue to open and existing ones con-solidate and enlarge. A lack of a decent labelling regime and regulatory authority means that quality is variable and labels not always 100% accurate. Most wine is locally consumed and only a few of the best are exported. Besides GOLAN HEIGHTS, some of Israel's most promising wines now come from Castel in the Judean Hills (particularly good Chardon-nay), Galil Mountain in Galilee and Tishbi in Shomron.

JAPAN As long as there is confusion between which wines are 100% locally grown and which are multi-country blends (which most are), Japanese wines will never really be appreciated by an international audience. One has to assume that the present situation suits most pro-ducers, who sell almost all their wines locally. However, the Japanese are increasingly interested in wine, and their national wine show now attracts entries from around the world. Despite humid conditions, wine is produced in almost every province. SUNTORY is in the best region, Yamanashi, and is expanding its vineyards. Other main players are Mercian, Sapporo, Manns and Domaine Sogga.

LEBANON CHATEAU MUSAR, Kefraya and Ksara survived the 25-year war. Peace has brought a new generation of producers and improved quality from the older companies – new releases from Musar, Kefraya, Ksara, Massaya and Clos St Thomas are vastly superior to those produced just a few years ago and are beginning to find their way into the high streets of the world.

LUXEMBOURG With one of the world's highest levels of wine consumption per capita, very little wine is exported. Co-operatives dominate here and quality is about what you would expect. Elbling and Rivaner (Müller-Thurgau) continue to decline, to be replaced with quality varietals such as Riesling, Pinot Noir, Chardonnay and Gewürztraminer.

MEXICO In the far north-west of Mexico, in Baja California, some good reds are made by L A CETTO as well as by smaller companies such as Monte Xanic and Casa de Piedra. In the rest of the country, only high-altitude areas such as the Parras Valley and Zacatecas have the potential for quality wines. Casa Madero, in the Parras Valley, has some success with Cabernet Sauvignon. Other promising grape varieties include Nebbiolo, Petite Sirah, Tempranillo, Zinfandel and Barbera, with Viognier and Chardonnay also planted.

MOLDOVA Moldovan winegrowers suffered a major setback in 2006 when their main export market, Russia, banned imports of their wines, seemingly in retaliation for Moldova becoming too friendly with the West. Standards of winemaking and equipment leave much to be desired, but fruit quality is good, and international players, including PENFOLDS and winemakers Jacques Lurton, Hugh Ryman and Alain Thiénot, have worked with local wineries. However, chaotic social conditions have led to many attempts being abandoned.

MONTENEGRO This red-wine-dominated part of the former Yugoslavia shows some potential in the beefy Vranac grape with its bitter cherry flavours – but the worst wines are really poor.

MOROCCO Known for big, sweet-fruited reds that once found a ready blending market in France. Since the 1990s massive investment by Castel Frères is instigating a rebirth: the first results are tasty Syrah and Cabernet reds. The important Celliers de Meknes are also on the up.

ROMANIA The huge vineyard area has declined somewhat in recent years as hybrid grape varieties are pulled up, to be replanted with *Vitis vinifera* grapes such as Pinot Noir, Cabernet Sauvignon, Merlot and the native Feteasca Negra for reds, Pinot Gris and Chardonnay for whites. The appellation system is of limited value, although Dealul Mare, Murfatlar and Cotnari all have ancient reputations. Accession to the EU in 2007 may eventually bear fruit, but right now attempts to integrate and conform with EU rules and regulations are proving to be predictably problematic. International-backed ventures such as Cramele Recas, Halewood (Prahova Valley) and Carl Reh are a sign of the mini-revolution, but challenges remain.

SLOVAKIA The eastern part of the old Czechoslovakia, with its cool-climate vineyards, is dominated by white varieties – Pinot Blanc, Riesling, Grüner Veltliner, Irsai Olivér – with the occasional fruity Frankovka (Blaufränkisch) red. Western investment at the state winery at Nitra and smaller wineries such as Gbelce and Hurbanovo near the Hungarian border at Komárno, is rapidly improving the quality. With EU membership we may start to see some examples in the shops.

SLOVENIA Many of the old Yugoslav Federation's best vineyards are here. Potential is considerable, and some interesting wines are emerging, with whites generally better than reds. A simplified appellation system and the increasing popularity of Slovenia as a holiday and second-home region should increase availability. On the Italian border, Brda and Vipava have go-ahead co-operatives, and Kraski Teran is a red wine of repute. The Movia range, from the Kristancic family, looks promising.

SWITZERLAND Fendant (Chasselas) is the main grape for spritzy but neutral whites from the VAUD and VALAIS. Like the fruity DOLE reds, they are best drunk very young. German-speaking cantons produce whites from Müller-Thurgau and mostly light reds and rosés from Pinot Noir (Blauburgunder); top producers, such as Daniel GANTENBEIN, make more powerful versions. Italian-speaking TICINO concentrates on Merlots that have been increasingly impressive since 2000. Serious wines, especially in Valais, use Syrah, Chardonnay, Marsanne and traditional varieties like Amigne and Petite Arvine. See also NEUCHATEL.

THAILAND I first tasted Thai wine a few years ago: it was a light and fruity red and impressive for what I thought of as sub-tropical conditions. Since then, serious Shiraz and Chenin wines have shown that Thailand's high-altitude vineyards are capable of some tasty offerings. Most are sold locally to the tourist industry.

TUNISIA Ancient wine traditions have had an injection of new life from international investment, and results so far are encouraging. Tourism soaks up most of the production and little is exported.

TURKEY The world's sixth-largest grape producer, but 97% ends up as table grapes or raisins. However, with EU membership a possibility in 2012 and with vast vineyards, good growing conditions and cheap labour on hand, Turkey could become a major player if the will-power and the investment are harnessed. Producers such as Diren, Kavaklidere, Turasan and Doluca are using modern technology to produce very drinkable wines. Local variety Buzbag can be good.

UKRAINE The Crimea's vineyards are the most important, producing hearty reds, sweet and sparkling wines; there's a surprisingly good sweet red sparkler, and sweet Muscatels are considered to be a cause for national pride, especially the Massandra brand. The Odessa region is successful with its sparkling wines, the 3 best-known facilities being the Inkerman winery, Novyi Svet and Zolota Balka. Future European investment is said to be in the pipeline, so let's see.

A–Z

OF WINES, PRODUCERS, GRAPES & WINE REGIONS

In the following pages there are over
1600 entries covering the world's top wines, as well as
leading producers, main wine regions and grape
varieties, followed on page 308 by a glossary of wine
terms and classifications.

*On page 4 you will find a full explanation of
How to Use the A–Z. On page 317 there is an index
of all wine producers in the book, to help you find the
world's best wines.*

AALTO *Ribera del Duero DO, Castilla y León, Spain* Former VEGA SICILIA
winemaker Mariano García and former RIBERA DEL DUERO appellation
boss Javier Zaccagnini teamed up to create this new winery in 1999.
From the outset, they have challenged top Spanish producers with
their dense but elegant reds, Aalto★★ and old vines cuvée Aalto
PS★★. Best years: (2005) 04 03 **01 00 99**.

ABRUZZO *Italy* This region stretches from the Adriatic coast to the
mountainous Apennine interior. White Trebbiano d'Abruzzo DOC is
usually dry and neutral; the MONTEPULCIANO D'ABRUZZO DOC is generally a
strapping, peppery red of real character, but increasingly a rosé called
Cerasuolo. Overproduction has been a problem, but quality is on the
increase with new vineyard training techniques and the establishment of
new DOCs, including Controguerra.

ACACIA *Carneros AVA, California, USA* Leading producer of Chardonnay
and Pinot Noir from the CARNEROS region for 2 decades. The regular
Carneros Chardonnay★ is restrained but attractive. Pinot Noirs
include the superb Beckstoffer Vineyard★★ and a Carneros★ – the
wines have moved to a riper, meatier style of late. Best years: (Pinot
Noir) 2005 **03 02 01 00 99** 97 96 95.

ACCADEMIA DEI RACEMI *Manduria, Puglia, Italy* Premium venture from
the Perrucci family, long-established bulk shippers of basic Puglian
wines. Quality, modern-style reds mainly from Primitivo and
Negroamaro under various producers' names: Felline (Vigna del
Feudo★★), Pervini (PRIMITIVO DI MANDURIA Archidamo★★), Masseria Pepe
(Dunico★★). Best years: (reds) (2006) 05 **04 03 01 00**.

ACHAVAL-FERRER *Uco Valley, Mendoza, Argentina* A former garage
winery created by a group of friends in 1998, and now one of
Argentina's most sought-after labels. 80-year-old vines in the La
Consulta area of UCO VALLEY produce Finca Altamira★★★, a Malbec
bursting with personality and a real sense of place. Red blend
Quimera★ is also good. Best years: 2005 **04 03 02 01 99**.

TIM ADAMS *Clare Valley, South Australia* Important
maker of fine, old-fashioned wine from his own
and bought-in local grapes. Classic dry
Riesling★★, oaky Semillon★★, and rich, opulent
Shiraz★★ (sometimes ★★★) and Cabernet★★. The
botrytis Semillon★ can be super, The Fergus★★ is
a glorious Grenache-based blend, and minty,
peppery Aberfeldy Shiraz★★★ is a remarkable, at
times unnerving, mouthful of brilliance from 100-
year-old vines. Best years: (Aberfeldy Shiraz) (2006)
(05) 04 03 02 01 00 **99 98 96 94**.

ADELAIDE HILLS *South Australia* Small and exciting region 30 minutes'
drive from Adelaide. High altitude affords a cool, moist climate ideal
for fine table wines and superb sparkling wine. Consistently good
Sauvignon Blanc and Chardonnay, plus promising Pinot Noir and
steadily improving Shiraz, and even Zinfandel. Best producers: Ashton
Hills★, Bird in Hand★, HENSCHKE★★, Longview, Nepenthe★★,
PETALUMA★★, RIPOSTE, SHAW & SMITH★★, Geoff WEAVER★★.

ADELSHEIM VINEYARD *Willamette Valley AVA, Oregon, USA* Over the
past 3 decades, Adelsheim has established a reputation for excellent,
generally unfiltered, Pinot Noir – especially cherry-scented Elizabeth's

Reserve★ and Bryan Creek Vineyard★ – and for rich Chardonnay Caitlin's Reserve★. Also a bright, minerally Pinot Gris★. Best years: (Elizabeth's Reserve) (2005) 04 03 02 01 **00**.

AGLIANICO DEL VULTURE DOC *Basilicata, Italy*   Red wine from the Aglianico grape grown on the steep slopes of Mt Vulture. Despite the zone's location almost on the same latitude as Naples, the harvest here is sometimes later than in BAROLO, 750km (470 miles) to the north-west, because the Aglianico grape ripens very late at altitude. The best wines are structured, complex and long-lived. Best producers: Basilium★, Consorzio Viticoltori Associati del Vulture (Carpe Diem★), D'Angelo★★, Cantine del Notaio★★, Paternoster★★, Le Querce★. Best years: (2006) (05) 04 **03 01 00 98 97**.

AHR *Germany*   The Ahr Valley is a small (545ha/1345-acre), mainly red wine region south of Bonn. Chief grape varieties are the Spätburgunder (Pinot Noir) and (Blauer) Portugieser. Most Ahr reds used to be made sweet, but this style is on the way out. Meyer-Näkel★, Stodden★ and Deutzerhof★ are the best of a growing band of serious producers.

AIRÉN Spain's – and indeed the world's – most planted white grape can make fresh, modern, but generally neutral-flavoured white wines, with some eye-opening exceptions, such as Ercavio's stunning white from Toledo. Airén is grown all over the centre and south of Spain, especially in La MANCHA, VALDEPENAS and ANDALUCIA (where it's called Lairén).

ALBAN *San Luis Obispo County, California, USA*   Based in the Arroyo Grande district of Edna Valley, RHONE specialist John Alban first produced Viognier in 1991. Today he offers 2 bottlings: Estate★★ and Central Coast★. Roussanne★★ from estate vineyards is laden with honey notes. Syrah is represented by 3 bottlings: Reva★★, Lorraine★★ and Seymour's Vineyard★★. Intense Grenache★★ and Pandora★★, a blend of about 60% Grenache, 40% Syrah, round out the line-up. Local praise has been clamorous despite some reds with extremely high alcohol levels. Best years: (Syrah) 2005 04 03 **02 01 00** 99 98 97 96.

ALBARIÑO Possibly Spain's most characterful white grape. It is a speciality of RIAS BAIXAS in Galicia in Spain's rainy north-west and, as Alvarinho, in Portugal's VINHO VERDE region. When well made, Albariño wines have fascinating flavours of apricot, peach, grapefruit and Muscat grapes, refreshingly high acidity, highish alcohol – and unrefreshingly high prices. The ever-present danger to quality is excessive yields.

ALEATICO Rarely seen, ancient, native Italian grape that produces sweet, scented, high-alcohol dessert wines in central and southern Italy. Best producers: AVIGNONESI, Candido (delicious Aleatico di Puglia★).

ALENQUER DOC *Estremadura, Portugal*   Maritime-influenced hills north of Lisbon, producing wines from (mostly) local grape varieties such as Periquita (Castelão) and Trincadeira, but also from Cabernet, Syrah and Chardonnay. Many wines are simply labelled ESTREMADURA. Best producers: Quinta do Carneiro★, Quinta de Chocapalha★, D F J VINHOS★ (Francos Reserva★★), Quinta do Monte d'Oiro★★, Quinta de Pancas★, Casa SANTOS LIMA★. Best years: (reds) 2005 **04 03 01 00**.

ALENTEJO *Portugal* A large chunk of southern Portugal south and east of Lisbon and, along with the DOURO, one of Portugal's fastest improving red wine regions. Has its own DOC, with 8 sub-regions: Borba, Évora, Granja-Amareleja, Moura, Portalegre, Redondo, Reguengos and Vidigueira. Potential is far from realized, but already some of Portugal's finest reds come from here. Vinho Regional wines are labelled Alentejano. Best producers: (reds) Quinta da Terrugem★★/ALIANÇA, Fundação Eugénio de Almeida (Cartuxa★, Pera Manca★★), BACALHOA VINHOS DE PORTUGAL★ (Tinto da Anfora Grande Escolha★★), Borba co-op★, Quinta do CARMO★, Herdade dos Coelheiros★, CORTES DE CIMA★★, Vinha d'Ervideira★, ESPORAO★★, José Maria da FONSECA★, Mouchão★★, Quinta do Mouro★, João Portugal RAMOS★★, SOGRAPE★. Best years: (reds) 2005 **04 01 00**.

ALEXANDER VALLEY AVA *Sonoma County, California, USA* Important AVA, centred on the northern Russian River, which is fairly warm, with only patchy summer fog. Cabernet Sauvignon is highly successful here, with lovely, juicy fruit not marred by an excess of tannin. Chardonnay may also be good but is often overproduced and lacking in ripe, round flavours. Zinfandel and Merlot can be outstanding from hillside vineyards. Best producers: Alexander Valley Vineyards★, CLOS DU BOIS★, De Lorimier★, GEYSER PEAK★, JORDAN★, Murphy-Goode★★, SEGHESIO★★, SILVER OAK★★, SIMI★, Trentadue★★. See also RUSSIAN RIVER VALLEY AVA, SONOMA COUNTY. Best years: (reds) 2005 04 03 02 **01 00 99 97 95 94 93 91 90**.

ALGARVE *Portugal* Holiday region with feeble, mostly red wines in 4 DOCs: Lagoa, Lagos, Portimão and Tavira. There are exceptions. Look out for reds and rosés from Sir Cliff Richard's Vida Nova label, Quinta do Barranco Longo and Morgado da Torre.

ALIANÇA, CAVES *Beira Litoral, Portugal* Based in BAIRRADA, Aliança makes crisp, fresh whites and soft, approachable red Bairradas★. Also made, either from its own vineyards or bought-in grapes or wines, are reds from the DAO (Quinta da Garrida★) and DOURO; Quinta dos Quatro Ventos★★ from the Douro is a blend of Tinta Roriz, Touriga Franca and Touriga Nacional. The top reds, however, are those from its estate in ALENTEJO, Quinta da Terrugem★★.

ALIGOTÉ French grape, found mainly in Burgundy, whose basic characteristic is a lemony tartness. It can make extremely refreshing wine, especially from old vines, but is generally rather dull and lean. In ripe years it can resemble Chardonnay, especially if a little new oak is used. The best comes from the village of Bouzeron in the COTE CHALONNAISE, where Aligoté has its own appellation. Occasionally also found in Moldova and Bulgaria. Drink young. Best producers: (Burgundy) M BOUZEREAU, COCHE-DURY★, A Ente★, J-H Goisot★, Denis MORTET★, TOLLOT-BEAUT, Villaine★.

ALL SAINTS *Rutherglen, Victoria, Australia* Old winery revived with great flair since 1998 by the late Peter Brown of the BROWN BROTHERS family. Superb fortifieds Rare Tokay★★ and Rare Muscat★★ have rediscovered past glory. Other fortifieds★ are good but still finding their best form. Table wines have shown significant improvement recently.

ALLEGRINI *Valpolicella DOC, Veneto, Italy* High-profile producer in VALPOLICELLA Classico, making single-vineyard La Grola★★ and Palazzo della Torre★★. These are now under the regional Veronese IGT – originally to distance them from the low regard in which much of Valpolicella was held until recently. These, and the barrique-aged La Poja★★★ (made solely with the Corvina grape), show the great potential that exists for Valpolicella as a table wine. Outstanding AMARONE★★★ and RECIOTO Giovanni Allegrini★★. Best years: (Amarone) (2006) 04 **03 01 00 97 95 93 90**.

THIERRY ALLEMAND *Cornas AC, Rhône Valley, France* Thierry Allemand has a smallholding of some 5ha (12 acres) of vines. He is determined to keep yields low, uses little sulphur and seeks to avoid making harsh, tannic wines. With careful vinification he produces 2 intense, unfiltered expressions of CORNAS at its dense and powerful best: Chaillot★★ is marginally the lighter; Reynard★★ is from a parcel of very old Syrah. Also makes a sulphur-free Reynard and St-Péray. Best years: (Reynard) (2006) 05 04 03 01 00 **99 98 96 95 94 91 90**.

ALLENDE *Rioja DOCa, Rioja, Spain* One of the most admired new names in RIOJA. Scented, uncompromisingly concentrated reds include Aurus★★★, Calvario★★ and the affordable Allende★. There is also a delicate white★. Best years: (reds) 2003 **02 01 00 99 98**.

ALMAVIVA★★★ *Valle del Maipo, Chile* State-of-the-art joint venture between CONCHA Y TORO and the Baron Philippe de Rothschild company (see MOUTON-ROTHSCHILD), located in MAIPO Valley's El Tocornal vineyard at the foot of the Andes and – after a slow start – producing a memorably powerful red from old Cabernet Sauvignon vines planted in alluvial, stony soils. It can be drunk at 5 years but should age for 10. Best years: 2003 **02 01 00 99 98 97**.

ALOXE-CORTON AC *Côte de Beaune, Burgundy, France* An important village at the northern end of the CÔTE DE BEAUNE producing mostly red wines from Pinot Noir. Its reputation is based on the 2 Grands Crus, CORTON (mainly red) and CORTON-CHARLEMAGNE (white only). Other vineyards in Aloxe-Corton used to be a source of tasty, good-value Burgundy, but nowadays the reds rarely exhibit their former characteristic blend of ripe fruit and appetizing savoury dryness. Almost all the white wine is classified as Grand Cru. Best producers: d'Ardhuy, CHANDON DE BRIAILLES★★, M Chapuis★, Marius Delarche★, Dubreuil-Fontaine★, Follin-Arvelet★, Camille Giroud★, Antonin Guyon★, JADOT★, Rapet★, Comte Senard★, TOLLOT-BEAUT★★. Best years: (reds) (2006) 05 04 **03 02 01 99 97 96 95**.

DOM. ALQUIER *Faugères, Languedoc, France* The estate which shows best how good FAUGÈRES can be. Barrel aging of all the wines, and low yields for the special cuvées, Les Bastides★★ and La Maison Jaune★. Also a good white blend of Roussanne and Marsanne. Best years: (Bastides) 2005 03 **01 00**.

ALSACE AC *Alsace, France* Tucked away on France's eastern border with Germany, Alsace produces some of the most individual white wines of all, rich in aroma and full of ripe, distinctive flavours. Alsace is almost as far north as CHAMPAGNE, but its climate is considerably warmer and drier. Wines from the 51 best vineyard sites can call themselves Alsace Grand Cru AC and account for 4% of production; quality regulations are more stringent and many individual crus have further tightened the rules. Riesling, Muscat, Gewurztraminer and Pinot Gris are generally considered the finest varieties in Alsace and have been the only ones permitted for Grand Cru wines, although Sylvaner is now legal in Zotzenberg and further changes will follow. Pinot Blanc can produce good wines too. Reds from Pinot Noir are improving fitfully. Alsace labels its wines by grape variety and, apart from Edelzwicker (a blend) and CREMANT D'ALSACE, all Alsace wines are made from a single variety, although blends from Grand Cru sites are emerging (Altenberg de Bergheim). Medium-dry or sweeter wines are now, as of the 2004 vintage, labelled *moelleux*. Vendange Tardive means 'late-harvest'; the grapes (Riesling, Muscat, Pinot Gris or Gewurztraminer) are picked late and almost overripe, giving higher sugar levels and potentially more intense flavours. The resulting wines are usually rich and mouthfilling and often need 5 years or more to show their personality. Sélection de Grains Nobles – late-harvest wines made from superripe grapes of the same varieties – are invariably sweet and usually affected by noble rot; they are among Alsace's finest, but are very expensive to produce (and to buy). Best producers: Jean-Baptiste Adam, L Albrecht★, Barmès-Buecher★, J Becker, Léon Beyer★, P BLANCK★★, Bott-Geyl★★, A Boxler★, E Burn★, DEISS★★★, Dirler-Cadé★★, Pierre Frick★, Rémy Gresser★, HUGEL★, Josmeyer★, Kientzler★, Klur, Kreydenweiss★, S Landmann★, A MANN★★, Meyer-Fonné, Mittnacht Frères, MURE★★, Ostertag★★, Pfaffenheim co-op, Ribeauvillé co-op, Rieflé★, Rolly Gassmann★, M Schaetzel, Charles Schléret, Schlumberger★, SCHOFFIT★★, Louis Sipp, Bruno Sorg★, M Tempé, TRIMBACH★★, TURCKHEIM co-op★, WEINBACH★★, ZIND-HUMBRECHT★★★. Best years: 2005 04 **02 01 00 98 97 96 95.**

ALTARE *Barolo DOCG, Piedmont, Italy* Elio Altare crafts some of the most stunning of Alba's wines: BARBERA D'ALBA★, Dolcetto d'Alba★★ and even finer BAROLO Vigneto Arborina★★★ and Barolo Brunate★★★. Though he is a professed modernist, his wines are intense, full and structured while young, but with clearly discernible fruit flavours, thanks largely to tiny yields. He also makes 3 barrique-aged wines under the LANGHE DOC: Arborina★★★ (Nebbiolo), Larigi★★★ (Barbera) and La Villa★★ (Nebbiolo-Barbera). Altare is one of several producers that make L'Insieme★★ (a Nebbiolo-Cabernet-Barbera blend). Best years: (Barolo) (2006) (04) 03 **01 00 99 98 96 95.**

ALTO ADIGE *Trentino-Alto Adige, Italy* A largely German-speaking province, originally called Südtirol. The region-wide DOC covers 25 types of wine. Reds range from light and perfumed when made from the Schiava grape, to fruity and more structured from the Cabernets or Merlot, to dark and velvety if Lagrein is used. Excess oak can mar their delightful fruit. Whites include Chardonnay, Gewürztraminer, Pinot Bianco, Pinot Grigio, Riesling and Sauvignon, and are usually fresh and fragrant. There is also some good sparkling wine. Much of the wine comes from well-run co-ops. Sub-zones include the previously independent DOCs of Santa Maddalena and Terlano. Best producers: Abbazia di Novacella★, Casòn Hirschprunn★, Peter Dipoli★, Egger-Ramer★, Franz Gojer★, Franz Haas★★, Haderburg★★, Hofstätter★★, Kränzl★, LAGEDER★★, Laimburg★, Loacker★, Josephus Mayr★, Muri-Gries★★, Josef Niedermayr★, Ignaz Niedrist★, Plattner Waldgries★, Peter Pliger-Kuenhof★★, Prima & Nuova/Erste & Neue★, Hans Rottensteiner★, Heinrich Rottensteiner★, TIEFENBRUNNER★★, Elena Walch★, Wilhelm Walch, Baron Widmann★; (co-ops) Caldaro★, Colterenzio★★, Girlan-Cornaiano★, Gries★, Nalles-Magré★, San Michele Appiano★★, Santa Maddalena★, Terlano★, Termeno★. See also TRENTINO.

ALTOS LAS HORMIGAS *Mendoza, Argentina* A rising star in Argentina, founded in 1995 by a group of Italians and Argentines. Altos Las Hormigas Malbec★ is an opulent example of the grape, while Reserva Viña Hormigas★★ is packed with pure, dense blackberry and cherry flavours. Colonia Las Liebres is one of Argentina's best Bonardas. Best years (Viña Hormigas): **2004 03 02 01**.

ALVARINHO See ALBARIÑO.

CASTELLO DI AMA *Chianti Classico DOCG, Tuscany, Italy* Model estate of CHIANTI CLASSICO, with outstanding Chianti Classico★★, plus single-vineyard Riservas★★★ (Bellavista and La Casuccia). L'Apparita★★★ is one of Italy's best Merlots. Also good Chardonnay Al Poggio★. Best years: (Chianti Classico) (2006) 04 **03 01 00 99 98 97 95**.

AMARONE DELLA VALPOLICELLA DOC *Veneto, Italy* A brilliantly individual, bitter-sweet style of VALPOLICELLA made from grapes shrivelled on mats for months after harvest. The wine, which can reach 16% of alcohol and more, differs from the sweet RECIOTO DELLA VALPOLICELLA in that it is fermented to near-dryness, the grapes having been left on the mats a month or two less. Wines from the Classico zone are generally the best, with exceptions from DAL FORNO, Corte Sant'Alda and Roccolo Grassi. Best producers: Accordini★★, ALLEGRINI★★★, Bertani★★, Brigaldara★, Brunelli★, BUSSOLA★★★, Michele Castellani★★, Corte Sant'Alda★★, Valentina Cubi★★, DAL FORNO★★, Guerrieri-Rizzardi★★, MASI★, QUINTARELLI★★★, Le Ragose★★, Roccolo Grassi★, Le Salette★★, Serègo Alighieri★, Speri★★, Tedeschi★★, Tommasi★, Villa Monteleone★★, VIVIANI★★, Zenato★★. Best years: (2006) 04 03 **01 00 97**.

AMIGNE Ancient Swiss grape variety that is virtually limited to the region of Vétroz in the VALAIS. The wine has an earthy, nutty intensity and benefits from a few years' aging. Best producers: Bonvin, Fontannaz, Jean-René Germanier, Caves Imesch.

DOM. DE L'ANCIENNE CURE *Bergerac AC and Monbazillac AC, South-West France* Christian Roche exemplifies the best of BERGERAC, with textured elegant reds, crisp dry whites and balanced, luscious sweet MONBAZILLAC. Both reds and sweet whites have top cuvées called L'Abbaye★ and L'Extase★. Best years: (reds) 2005 03 **01 00**.

ANDALUCÍA *Spain* Fortified wines, or wines naturally so strong in alcohol that they don't need fortifying, are the speciality of this southern stretch of Spain. Apart from sherry (JEREZ Y MANZANILLA DO), there are the lesser, sherry-like wines of Condado de Huelva DO and MONTILLA-MORILES DO, and the rich, sweet wines of MALAGA DO. These regions also make some modern but bland dry whites: the best are from Condado de Huelva. Red wine is now appearing from producers in Málaga, Granada and Almería provinces.

ANDERSON VALLEY AVA *California, USA* Small appellation (less than 245ha/600 acres) in western MENDOCINO COUNTY that produces brilliant wines. Most vineyards are within 15 miles of the Pacific Ocean, making this one of the coldest AVAs in California. Delicate Pinot Noirs and Chardonnays, and one of the few places in the state for first-rate

Gewürztraminer and Riesling. Superb sparkling wines with healthy acidity and creamy yeast are highlights as well. Best producers: Brutocao★, Greenwood Ridge★, HANDLEY★★, Lazy Creek★, NAVARRO★★★, ROEDERER ESTATE★★, SCHARFFENBERGER CELLARS★.

ANDREW WILL WINERY *Washington State, USA* Winemaker Chris Camarda makes delicious blends of BORDEAUX varietals from a range of older WASHINGTON vineyards. At the top are the complex Champoux Vineyard★★★, the opulent Ciel du Cheval★★★ and the tannic yet ageworthy Klipsun Vineyard★★. Wines from 2 newer vineyards, Sheridan Vineyard★ and Two Blondes Vineyard★, still show young vine character. Sorella★★, a blend of the best barrels each vintage, can be outstanding with age. Best years: (reds) (2005) 04 03 **01 00 99**.

CH. ANGÉLUS★★★ *St-Émilion Grand Cru AC, 1er Grand Cru Classé, Bordeaux, France* One of the best-known ST-EMILION Grands Crus (James Bond's choice in *Casino Royale*!), with an energetic owner and talented winemaker. Increasingly gorgeous wines throughout the 1980s and 90s, recognized by promotion to Premier Grand Cru Classé in 1996. Best years: 2005 04 03 02 **01 00 99 98 97 96 95 94 93 92 90 89 88 85**.

MARQUIS D'ANGERVILLE *Volnay, Côte de Beaune, Burgundy, France* The late Jacques d'Angerville for half a century produced an exemplary range of elegant Premiers Crus from VOLNAY, the subtlest of the COTE DE BEAUNE's red wine appellations. Clos des Ducs and Taillepieds are ★★★. All should be kept for at least 5 years. Best years: (top reds) (2006) 05 03 02 99 **98 97 96 95 91 90**.

CH. D'ANGLUDET★ *Margaux AC, Cru Bourgeois, Haut-Médoc, Bordeaux, France* This English-owned château makes a gentle, unobtrusive but generally attractive red that is never overpriced. It ages well for at least a decade. Best years: 2005 04 **03 02 00 98 96 95 94 90 89 88 86 85**.

ANJOU BLANC AC *Loire Valley, France* Ill-defined AC; ranges from bone dry to sweet, from excellent to dreadful; the best are dry. Up to 20% Chardonnay or Sauvignon can be added, but many of the leading producers use 100% Chenin from top sites once dedicated to sweet COTEAUX DU LAYON. Best producers: M Angeli/Sansonnière★★, S Bernaudeau★, des Chesnaies★, P Delesvaux★, Fesles★, L Herbel, Richard Leroy★, Montgilet/V Lebreton★, Mosse★, Ogereau★, Pierre-Bise★, J PITHON★, RICHOU★, Roulerie★, Soucherie/P-Y Tijou★, Yves Soulez★. Best years: (top wines) 2006 05 **04 03** 02 01.

ANJOU ROUGE AC *Loire Valley, France* Anjou reds (from Cabernets Sauvignon and Franc or Pineau d'Aunis) are increasingly successful. Usually fruity, easy-drinking wine, with less tannin than ANJOU-VILLAGES. Wines made from Gamay are sold as Anjou Gamay. Best producers: Brizé★, Chamboureau★, Fesles★, Putille, RICHOU★. Best years: (top wines) 2006 05 04 **03** 02 01 97 96.

ANJOU-VILLAGES AC *Loire Valley, France* Superior Anjou red from 46 villages, and made from Cabernet Franc and Cabernet Sauvignon. Some extremely attractive dry, fruity wines are emerging, with better aging potential than ANJOU ROUGE. Anjou-Villages Brissac is an exciting sub-appellation. Best producers: P Baudouin★, Brizé★, P Delesvaux★, Fesles★, Montgilet/V Lebreton★, de la Motte, Ogereau★, Pierre-Bise★, Putille★, RICHOU (Vieilles Vignes★★), Rochelles/J-Y Lebreton★★, Tigné★, la Varière/Beaujeau. Best years: 2006 05 04 **03** 02 **01 97 96**.

ANSELMI *Veneto, Italy* Roberto Anselmi (and PIEROPAN) has shown that much-maligned SOAVE can have personality when carefully made. Using ultra-modern techniques he has honed the fruit flavours of his San

Vincenzo★★ and Capitel Foscarino★★ and introduced small-barrel-aging for single-vineyard Capitel Croce★★ and luscious, SAUTERNES-like I Capitelli★★ (sometimes ★★★), as well as the Cabernet Sauvignon Realdà. All sold under the regional IGT rather than Soave DOC. Best years: (I Capitelli) (2005) 04 **03 01 00**.

ANTINORI *Tuscany, Italy*   World-famous Florentine family firm that has been involved in wine since 1385, but it is Piero Antinori, the current head, who has made the Antinori name synonymous with quality and innovation. The quality of its CHIANTI CLASSICO wines like Badia a Passignano★ (Riserva★★), Pèppoli★ and Tenute Marchese Antinori Riserva★★ is consistently good, but it was its development of the SUPER-TUSCAN concept of superior wines outside the DOC that launched a quality revolution during the 1970s. Introducing small-barrel-aging to Tuscany, TIGNANELLO★★ and, especially, SOLAIA★★★ can be great wines. Other Tuscan wines include VINO NOBILE La Braccesca★★, Bramasole Syrah from Cortona DOC, BRUNELLO DI MONTALCINO Pian delle Vigne★★ and BOLGHERI's Guado al Tasso★★ (Cabernet-Merlot). Interests further afield include PRUNOTTO in Piedmont, Tormaresca in PUGLIA, FRANCIACORTA's Monte Nisa, Bátaapáti in Hungary and a joint venture with CHATEAU STE MICHELLE in the USA. Best years: (reds) (2006) 04 **03 01 00** 99 98 97. See also CASTELLO DELLA SALA.

ANTONOPOULOS *Patras AO, Peloponnese, Greece*   Boutique winery producing barrel-fermented Chardonnay★★, Cabernet Nea Dris (New Oak)★, a blend of Cabernets Sauvignon and Franc, and Private Collection★, a promising Agiorgitiko-Cabernet blend.

ARAGÓN *Spain*   Aragón stretches south from the Pyrenees to Spain's central plateau. Winemaking has improved markedly, first of all in the cooler, hilly, northern SOMONTANO DO, and now also further south, in Campo de Borja DO, Calatayud DO and CARIÑENA DO; these 3 areas have the potential to be a major budget-price force in a world mad for beefy but fruity reds.

ARAUJO *Napa Valley AVA, California, USA*   Boutique winery whose great coup was to buy the Eisele vineyard, traditionally a source of superb Cabernet under the Joseph PHELPS label. Araujo Cabernet Sauvignon★★★ is now one of California's most sought-after reds, combining great fruit intensity with powerful but digestible tannins. Altagracia is a red BORDEAUX blend; Syrah★★ is impressive. Also Viognier and an attractively zesty Sauvignon Blanc★★.

ARBOIS AC *Jura, France*   The largest of the specific ACs in the Jura region. The majority of wines are red or rosé, but most widely seen outside the region are the whites, made from Chardonnay or the local Savagnin, which can give the wines a sherry-like flavour that is most concentrated in *vin jaune*. There is also a rare, sweet *vin de paille*. Good sparkling CREMANT DU JURA is made mainly from Chardonnay. Best producers: Ch. d'Arlay★, Aviet★, Bourdy★, Désiré★, Dugois★, M Faudot★, F Lornet★, H Maire★, P Overnoy★, La Pinte★, J Puffeney★, Caves de la Reine Jeanne★, Renardière, Rijckaert★, Rolet★, A & M Tissot★, J Tissot★, Tournelle★. Best years: 2005 04 03 02 **01 00** 98.

DOM. ANTOINE ARENA *Patrimonio AC, Corsica, France*   Family-owned vineyard in Patrimonio, which specializes in white wines based on Vermentino, white Bianco Gentile (a local grape which had fallen into disuse) and stunning reds under the Carco, Grotte di Sole★ and Morta Maio labels. Best years: (Grotte di Sole) (2005) 04 03 **01 00**.

ARGIOLAS *Sardinia, Italy* Sardinian star making DOC wines Cannonau (Costera★), Monica (Perdera) and Vermentino (Costamolino★) di Sardegna, but the best wines are the IGT Isola dei Nuraghi blends: Turriga★★ and Korem★ are powerful, spicy reds; Angialis★★ is a golden, sweet white. All the wines are good value.

ARGYLE *Willamette Valley AVA, Oregon, USA* In 1987, Brian Croser and Rollin Soles planned a world-class New World sparkling wine firm; the cool WILLAMETTE VALLEY was ideal for late-ripened Pinot Noir and Chardonnay. Argyle sparkling wine★ was soon followed by barrel-fermented Chardonnay★ and Pinot Noir★. The Reserve★★, Nuthouse★★ and Spirithouse★★ bottlings show just how much potential this large winery possesses. Best years: (Pinot Noir) (2005) 04 03 02 **01 00**.

ARNEIS Italian grape grown in the ROERO hills in PIEDMONT. Arneis is DOC in Roero, producing dry white wines which, at best, have an attractive (appley, herbal) perfume. Good ones can be expensive, but cheaper versions rarely work. Best producers: Brovia★, Cascina Chicco★, Correggia★, Deltetto★, GIACOSA★, Malvirà★, Angelo Negro★, PRUNOTTO★, Sorilaria★, Vietti★, Gianni Voerzio★.

CH. L'ARROSÉE★ *St-Émilion Grand Cru AC, Grand Cru Classé, Bordeaux, France* This small property, just south-west of the historic town of ST-EMILION, makes really exciting wine: rich, chewy and wonderfully luscious, with a comparatively high proportion (40%) of Cabernet. New investment from 2002. Drink after 5 years, but may be cellared for 10 or more. Best years: 2005 04 **03 02 00 98 96 95 90**.

ARROWOOD *Sonoma Valley AVA, California, USA* Richard Arrowood started his own winery in 1986. The wines have mostly been tip-top – beautifully balanced Cabernet★★, superb Merlot★★, deeply fruity Syrah (Saralee's★★, Kuljian★★ and Beau Melange★), lovely, velvety Chardonnay★ (Alary Vineyards★★) and fragrant Viognier★★. In 2006 the winery was acquired by Jackson Family Wines and founder Arrowood left to develop his new brand, Amapola Creek. Best years: (Cabernet Sauvignon) 2003 02 **01 00 99 97 96 95 94 91 90**.

ARTADI *Rioja DOCa, País Vasco, Spain* This former co-op is now producing some of RIOJA's deepest, most ambitious reds. These include Grandes Añadas★★★, Viña El Pisón★★★, Pagos Viejos★★ and Viñas de Gain★. Best years: (2005) 04 03 **01 00 98 96 95 94**.

ASCHERI *Piedmont, Italy* Winemakers in PIEDMONT for at least 5 centuries. The Ascheri style is forward and appealingly drinkable, whether it be BAROLO (Vigna dei Pola★, Sorano★), Dolcetto d'Alba (Vigna Nirane★) or NEBBIOLO D'ALBA. Montalupa Rosso and Bianco are made from Syrah and Viognier. The Cristina Ascheri MOSCATO D'ASTI is delightful.

ASTI DOCG *Piedmont, Italy* Asti Spumante, the world's best-selling sweet sparkling wine, was long derided as light and cheap, though promotion to DOCG signalled an upturn in quality. Made in the province of Asti south-east of Turin, under a denomination which includes the rarer MOSCATO D'ASTI, the wine is now called simply Asti. Its light sweetness and refreshing sparkle make it ideal with fruit and a wide range of sweet dishes. Drink young. Best producers: Araldica, Bera★, Cinzano★, Contero, Giuseppe Contratto★, Cascina Fonda★, FONTANAFREDDA, Gancia★, Martini & Rossi★, Cascina Pian d'Or★, Gianni Voerzio★.

ATA RANGI *Martinborough, North Island, New Zealand* Small, high-quality winery run by 2 families. Stylish, concentrated reds include seductively perfumed cherry/plum Pinot Noir★★★ and an impressive Cabernet-Merlot-Syrah blend called Célèbre★★. Whites include big, rich Craighall Chardonnay★, delicately luscious Lismore Pinot Gris★★ and a concentrated, mouthwatering Sauvignon Blanc★. A succulent Kahu botrytis Riesling is made when vintage conditions allow. Best years: (Pinot Noir) (2006) **03 01 00 99 98 97**.

ATLAS PEAK *Atlas Peak AVA, Napa, California, USA* Established in 1987 by ANTINORI of Italy, this mountaintop winery in the south-east corner of the NAPA VALLEY has been a leader in Californian Sangiovese without ever managing to achieve a consistent style. Consenso★ is a tasty Cabernet-Sangiovese blend; excellent Chardonnay is also grown in these high, cool vineyards. Now owned by Beam Wine Estates, the brand is being re-tooled with more of a focus on Cabernet Sauvignon. Best years: (reds) 2003 **02 01 99 97 95**.

AU BON CLIMAT *Santa Maria Valley AVA, California, USA* Pace-setting winery in this cool region, run by the talented Jim Clendenen, who spends much time in BURGUNDY. The result is a range of lush Chardonnays★★ and intense Pinot Noirs★★ (Isabelle Morgan and Knox Alexander bottlings can be ★★★). He also makes BORDEAUX-style reds and various Italian varietals, both red and white. Cold Heaven Viognier is made by Clendenen's wife, Morgan. QUPE operates from the same winery. Best years: (Pinot Noir) 2005 04 03 02 **01 00 99 98 97 96 95**; (Chardonnay) 2005 04 **03 02 01 00 99 98**.

AUCKLAND *North Island, New Zealand* Vineyards in this region are concentrated in the districts of Henderson, KUMEU/HUAPAI, Matakana and WAIHEKE ISLAND. Clevedon, south of Auckland, is a fledgling area and shows promise. Best years: (Cabernet Sauvignon) 2005 04 **02 00 99 98 96**.

CH. AUSONE★★★ *St-Émilion Grand Cru AC, 1er Grand Cru Classé, Bordeaux, France* This beautiful property is situated on what are perhaps the best slopes in ST-EMILION. Owner Alain Vauthier has taken it to new heights since 1996 and the wines now display stunning texture and depth and the promise of memorable maturity. A high proportion (50%) of Cabernet Franc beefs up the Merlot. Production is 16–20,000 bottles a year (CHEVAL BLANC makes 80,000). Second wine: La Chapelle d'Ausone. Best years: 2005 04 03 02 01 00 **99 98 97 96 95 94 90 89 88 86 85 83 82**.

AUXEY-DURESSES AC *Côte de Beaune, Burgundy, France* Auxey-Duresses is a backwater village up a valley behind MEURSAULT. The reds should be light and fresh but can often lack ripeness. At its best, and at 3–5 years, the white is dry, soft, nutty and hinting at the creaminess of a good Meursault, but at much lower prices. Of the Premiers Crus, Les Duresses is the most consistent. Best producers: (reds) Comte Armand★★, J-P Diconne★, Maison Leroy, Duc de Magenta★, M Prunier★, P Prunier★; (whites) R Ampeau★, d'Auvenay (Dom. LEROY)★★, J-P Diconne★, DROUHIN★, J-P Fichet★, Gras, Olivier LEFLAIVE★, Maison Leroy★, M Prunier★. Best years: (reds) (2006) 05 **03 02 99**; (whites) (2006) 05 **04 02 00**.

AVIGNONESI *Vino Nobile di Montepulciano DOCG, Tuscany, Italy* The Falvo brothers led Montepulciano's revival as one of TUSCANY's best zones. Although international wines like Il Marzocco★ (Chardonnay) and Desiderio★★ (Merlot-Cabernet) at one time received more attention, today the focus is back on the top-quality classics, VINO NOBILE★ and its superior version, made only in top years, Grandi Annate★★. The VIN SANTO★★★ is the most sought-after in Tuscany; there's also a rare red version from Sangiovese, Occhio di Pernice★★★. Best years: (Vino Nobile) (2006) 04 **03 01 00 99**.

BABICH *Henderson, North Island, New Zealand* Family-run winery with some prime vineyard land in MARLBOROUGH and HAWKES BAY. Irongate Chardonnay★ is an intense, steely wine that needs plenty of cellaring, while intense, full-flavoured varietal reds under the Winemakers Reserve label show even greater potential for development. Flagship label The Patriarch features Chardonnay★★ and Cabernet Sauvignon★★, both from Hawkes Bay. Marlborough wines include a stylish Sauvignon Blanc★, a tangy Riesling and a light, fruity Pinot Gris. Best years: (premium Hawkes Bay reds) (2006) 04 **02 00 98**.

BACALHÔA VINHOS DE PORTUGAL *Terras do Sado, Portugal* Forward-looking operation, using Portuguese and foreign grapes with equal ease. Quinta da Bacalhôa★ is an oaky, meaty Cabernet-Merlot blend, Palacio da Bacalhôa★★ even better; Tinto da Ânfora★ a rich and figgy ALENTEJO red (Grande Escolha★★ version is powerful and cedary); and Cova da Ursa★ a toasty, rich Chardonnay. Portugal's finest sparkling wine, vintage-dated Loridos Extra Bruto★, is a pretty decent CHAMPAGNE lookalike, made from Chardonnay. Só Syrah ('só' means 'only' in Portuguese, as in 'only Syrah') is characterful if atypical. Also excellent 20-year-old Moscatel de SETUBAL★★.

BAD DÜRKHEIM *Pfalz, Germany* This spa town has some good vineyards and is the headquarters of the dependable Vier Jahreszeiten co-op. Best producers: DARTING★, Fitz-Ritter, Hensel, Karl Schaefer★, Egon Schmitt. Best years: (2006) 05 04 **03** 02 **01 99 98 97 96**.

BADEN *Germany* Very large wine region stretching from FRANKEN to the Bodensee (Lake Constance). Its dry whites and reds show off the fuller, softer flavours Germany can produce in the warmer climate of its southerly regions. Many of the best non-Riesling German wines come from here, as well as many of the best barrel-fermented and barrel-aged wines. Good co-operative cellars at Achkarren, Bickensohl, Bötzingen, Durbach, Königs-schaffhausen, Pfaffenweiler and Sasbach.

BAGA Important red grape in BAIRRADA, which is one of the few regions in Portugal to rely mainly on one variety. Also planted in much smaller quantities in DÃO and the RIBATEJO. It can give deep, complex, blackberryish wine, but aggressive tannin is a continuing problem.

BAIRRADA DOC *Beira Litoral, Portugal* Bairrada, along with the DOURO, DÃO and ALENTEJO, can be the source of many of Portugal's best red wines. These can brim over with intense raspberry and blackberry fruit, though the tannin levels are severe and may take quite a few years to soften. The whites are coming on fast with modern vinification methods. The region's finest producer, Luis PATO, doesn't use the DOC because of a political disagreement. With an Atlantic climate, vintages can be very variable. Best producers: (reds) Caves ALIANÇA★, Quinta das Bágeiras★, Cantanhede co-op, Quinta do Carvalhinho★, Caves Messias (Garrafeira★), Caves Primavera (Garrafeira★), Quinta da Rigodeira★, Casa de Saima★★, Caves SÃO

JOAO★, SOGRAPE, Sidónio de Sousa★★; (whites) Quinta da Rigodeira★, Casa de Saima★, SOGRAPE (Reserva★, Quinta de Pedralvites★). Best years: (reds) 2005 04 **03 01 00 97**.

BALATONBOGLÁR WINERY *Transdanubia, Hungary* Premium winery in the Lake Balaton region, which has benefited from heavy investment and the expertise of viticulturist Dr Richard Smart, and wine consultant Kym Milne, but still needs to work to improve quality, particularly in the inexpensive but dumbed-down range sold under the Chapel Hill label.

BALEARIC ISLANDS *Spain* Medium-bodied reds and soft rosés were the mainstays of Mallorca's 2 DO areas, Binissalem and Plà i Llevant, until the Anima Negra winery began turning out its impressive, deep reds from the native Callet grape. Best producers: Anima Negra★★, José L Ferrer/Franja Roja, Hereus de Ribas, Miquel Gelabert★, Miquel Oliver, Son Bordils★.

BALNAVES *Coonawarra, South Australia* Long-term residents of COONAWARRA, the grape-growing Balnaves family decided to become involved in making wine in the mid-1990s. With the talented Pete Bissell as winemaker, Balnaves is now among the best producers in the region. Reserve Cabernet The Tally★★ is complex, well structured and deeply flavoured; the regular Cabernet★ is well priced and an excellent example of Coonawarra style.

BANDOL AC *Provence, France* A lovely fishing port with vineyards high above the Mediterranean, producing some of the best reds and rosés in Provence. The Mourvèdre grape gives Bandol its character – dense colour, warm, smoky black fruit and a herby fragrance. The reds happily age for 10 years, sometimes more, but can be very good at 3–4. The rosés, delicious and spicy but often too pricey, should be drunk young. There is a small amount of neutral, overpriced white. Best producers: (reds) la Bastide Blanche★, la Bégude★, Bunan★, Frégate★, le Galantin★, J P Gaussen★★, Gros' Noré★, l'Hermitage★, Lafran-Veyrolles★, la Laidière★, Mas Redorne★, la Noblesse★, PIBARNON★★, Pradeaux★★, Ray-Jane★, Roche Redonne★, Romassan, la Roque, Ste-Anne★, Salettes★, de Souviou★, la Suffrène, Tempier★, Terrebrune★, la Tour du Bon★, VANNIERES★★. Best years: 2004 03 01 **00 99 98 97 96 95**.

BANFI *Brunello di Montalcino DOCG, Tuscany, Italy* High-tech American-owned firm which is now a force in Italy. Chardonnay (Fontanelle★), Cabernet (Tavernelle★★) and Merlot (Mandrielle★) are successful, but even better are BRUNELLO Riserva Poggio all'Oro★★ and Brunello Poggio alle Mura★★. SUPER-TUSCANS Summus★★ (a blend of Sangiovese, Cabernet and Syrah) and Excelsus★★ (Cabernet-Merlot) are also very good. Also has cellars (Vigne Regali) in PIEDMONT for GAVI and fizz. Best years: (top reds) (2006) (04) (03) 01 **99 98 97 95**.

BANNOCKBURN *Geelong, Victoria, Australia* Bannockburn emerged after more than 25 years under Gary Farr as one of Australia's most highly regarded medium-sized wineries. Now that he has moved on to the family By Farr and Farr Rising labels, the challenge is there for Michael Glover to maintain this position. Thus far, the most famous wines have been the powerful, gamy and controversial Pinot Noir★ (Serre★★), MEURSAULT-like Chardonnay★★ and my favourite, the complex and classy Alain GRAILLOT-influenced Shiraz★★. Best years: (Shiraz) (2006) (05) 04 03 02 01 **00 99 98 97 96 94 92 91**.

BANYULS AC *Roussillon, France*   One of the best *vins doux naturels*, made mainly from Grenache, with a strong plum and raisin flavour. *Rimage* – vintaged early bottlings – and tawny (*tuilé*) styles are the best. Generally served as an apéritif in France and deserves a wider audience. Best producers: Cellier des Templiers★, CHAPOUTIER, Clos de Paulilles★, l'Étoile★, MAS BLANC★★, la Rectorie★★, la Tour Vieille★, Vial Magnères★.

BARBADILLO *Jerez y Manzanilla DO, Andalucía, Spain*   The largest sherry company in the coastal town of Sanlúcar de Barrameda makes a wide range of good to excellent wines, in particular salty, dry manzanilla styles (Solear★★) and intense, nutty, but dry amontillados and olorosos, led by Amontillado Principe★★ and Oloroso Cuco★★. Neutral dry white Castillo de San Diego is a bestseller in Spain.

BARBARESCO DOCG *Piedmont, Italy*   This prestigious red wine, grown near Alba in the LANGHE hills south-east of Turin, is often twinned with its neighbour BAROLO to demonstrate the nobility of the Nebbiolo grape. Barbaresco can be a shade softer and less powerful. The wine usually takes less time to mature and is often considered the more approachable of the two, as exemplified by the international style of GAJA. But, as in Barolo, traditionalists also excel, led by Bruno GIACOSA. Even though the area is relatively compact (575ha/1420 acres), wine styles can differ significantly between vineyards and producers. Best vineyards: Asili, Bricco di Neive, Costa Russi, Crichet Pajè, Gallina, Marcorino, Martinenga, Messoirano, Moccagatta, Montestefano, Ovello, Pora, Rabajà, Rio Sordo, San Lorenzo, Santo Stefano, Serraboella, Sorì Paitin, Sorì Tildin. Best producers: Barbaresco co-op★★, Piero Busso★, CERETTO★★, Cigliuti★★, Stefano Farina★★, Fontanabianca★★, GAJA★★★, GIACOSA★★★, Marchesi di Gresy★★, Moccagatta★★, Fiorenzo Nada★★, Castello di Neive★★, Oddero★, Paitin★★, Pelissero★★, Pio Cesare★★, PRUNOTTO★, Albino Rocca★★, Bruno Rocca★★, Sottimano★★, La Spinetta★★, Vietti★★. Best years: (2006) 04 03 **01 00 99 98 97 96 95**.

BARBERA A native of north-west Italy, Barbera vies with Sangiovese as the most widely planted red grape in the country. When grown for high yields its natural acidity shows through, producing vibrant quaffers. Low yields from the top PIEDMONT estates create intensely rich and complex wines. Oaked versions can be stunning. Significant plantings in California, Argentina and Australia.

BARBERA D'ALBA DOC *Piedmont, Italy*   Some outstanding Barbera comes from this appellation. The most modern examples are supple and generous and can be drunk almost at once. More intense, dark-fruited versions require at least 3 years' age, but might improve for as much as 8. Best producers: G Alessandria★★, ALTARE★, Azelia★★, Boglietti★★, Brovia★★, CERETTO★, Cascina Chicco★, Cigliuti★, CLERICO★, Elvio Cogno★★, Aldo CONTERNO★★, Giacomo CONTERNO★★, Conterno-Fantino★, Corino★★, Correggia★★, Elio Grasso★, Giuseppe MASCARELLO★, Moccagatta★, M Molino★★, Monfalletto-Cordero di Montezemolo★★, Oberto★★, Parusso★★, Pelissero★, F Principiano★★, PRUNOTTO★★, RATTI★, Albino Rocca★★, Bruno Rocca★, SANDRONE★★, P Scavino★★, La Spinetta★★, Vajra★★, Mauro Veglio★★, Vietti★★, Gianni Voerzio★, Roberto VOERZIO★★★. Best years: (2006) 04 **03 01 00 99**.

BARBERA D'ASTI DOC *Piedmont, Italy* While Dolcetto d'Asti is usually light and simple, wines made from Barbera show a greater range of quality. Unoaked and barrique-aged examples can compete with the best BARBERA D'ALBA and rival some of the better Nebbiolo-based reds. Best examples can be kept for 5–6 years, occasionally longer. Best producers: Araldica/Alasia★, La Barbatella★★, Pietro Barbero★★, Bava★, Bertelli★★, Braida★★, Cascina Castlèt★, Coppo★★, Hastae (Quorum★), Martinetti★★, Il Mongetto★★, PRUNOTTO★, Cantine Sant'Agata★, La Spinetta★★, Vietti★★, Vinchio-Vaglio Serra co-op★. Best years: (2006) 04 03 01 00 99.

BARDOLINO DOC *Veneto, Italy* Zone centred on Lake Garda, giving, at best, light, scented red and rosé (chiaretto) wines to be drunk young, from the same grape mix as neighbouring VALPOLICELLA. Bardolino Superiore is now DOCG. Best producers: Cavalchina★, Corte Gardoni★, Guerrieri-Rizzardi★, Le Fraghe, MASI, Le Vigne di San Pietro★, Fratelli Zeni.

BAROLO DOCG *Piedmont, Italy* Renowned red wine, named after a village south-west of Alba, from the Nebbiolo grape grown in around 1500ha (3700 acres) of vineyards in the steep LANGHE hills. For a time its austere power, with tough, chewy tannins that took years of cask-aging to soften, was considered too much for modern palates. But for more than 2 decades, many winemakers have applied new methods to make Barolo that is fresher, cleaner, better balanced and ready sooner, with greater colour, richer fruit, softer tannins, and the distinctive 'tar and roses' character so beloved of Barolo fans. Distinct styles of wine are made in the zone's villages. Barolo and La Morra make the most perfumed wines; Monforte and Serralunga the most structured; Castiglione Falletto strikes a balance between the two. Barolo is nowadays frequently labelled by vineyards, though the producer's reputation often carries more weight. Best vineyards: Bricco delle Viole, Brunate, Bussia Soprana, Cannubi Boschis, Cerequio, Conca dell'Annunziata, Fiasco, Francia, Gavarini, Giachini, Ginestra, Monfalletto, Monprivato, Rocche dell'Annunziata, Rocche di Castiglione, Santo Stefano di Perno, La Serra, Vigna Rionda, Villero. Best producers: C Alario★★, G Alessandria★★, ALTARE★★, Azelia★★, Boglietti★★, Bongiovanni★★, Brovia★★, Cappellano★★, CERETTO★★, CHIARLO★, CLERICO★★★, Poderi Colla★★, Aldo CONTERNO★★★, Giacomo CONTERNO★★★, Conterno-Fantino★★, Corino★★, Luigi Einaudi★★, GIACOSA★★★, Elio Grasso★★, M Marengo★★, Bartolo MASCARELLO★★★, Giuseppe MASCARELLO★★★, Monfalletto-Cordero di Montezemolo★★, Oberto★★, Oddero★★, Parusso★★, Pio Cesare★★, Pira★★, E Pira & Figli★★, F Principiano★, PRUNOTTO★★, Renato RATTI★, Revello★★, Giuseppe Rinaldi, Rocche dei Manzoni★★, SANDRONE★★★, P Scavino★★, M Sebaste★★, Vajra★★, Mauro Veglio★★, Vietti★★, Vigna Rionda★★, Gianni Voerzio★★, Roberto VOERZIO★★. Best years: (2006) (04) 03 01 00 99 98 97 96 95 93 90 89 88.

BAROSSA VALLEY See pages 70–1.

BAROSSA VALLEY ESTATE *Barossa, South Australia* Half owned by local growers, with some of the best-sited vineyards in BAROSSA, and half by industry giant HARDY. Flagship reds are huge, gutsy Barossa beauties E&E Black Pepper Shiraz★★, Ebenezer Shiraz★★ and E&E Sparkling Shiraz★★, all of them bursting with ripe plum fruit, spice and plenty of vanilla oak. Other Ebenezer wines include intense, full-flavoured sparkling Pinot Noir. Excellent value Moculta and Spires ranges. Best years: (E&E Black Pepper Shiraz) (2006) (05) (04) 02 01 99 98 96 94.

BAROSSA

South Australia

The Barossa Valley, an hour or so's drive north of Adelaide in South Australia, is the heart of the Australian wine industry. The giants of the industry have their major wineries here – Orlando, Wolf Blass, Penfolds and Yalumba – alongside around 50 or so smaller wineries, producing or processing up to 60% of the nation's wine. However, this percentage is based mostly on grapes trucked in from other regions, because the Barossa's vineyards themselves grow less than 10% of Australia's grapes. Yet Barossa-grown grapes, once rejected as uneconomical for their low yields, are now increasingly prized for those same low yields.

Why? Well, it's highly likely that the world's oldest vines are in the Barossa. The valley was settled in the 1840s by Lutheran immigrants from Silesia, who brought with them vines from Europe, most importantly, as it turned out, cuttings from the Syrah (or Shiraz) variety of France's Rhône Valley. And because Barossa has never been affected by the phylloxera louse, which destroyed many of the world's vineyards in the late 19th century, today you can still see gnarled, twisted old vines sporting just a few tiny bunches of priceless fruit that were planted by refugees from Europe all of a century and a half ago, and are still tended by their descendants. A new wave of winemakers has taken up the cause of the Barossa vines with much zeal and no small amount of national pride, and they now produce from them some of the deepest, most fascinating wines, not just in Australia, but in the world.

GRAPE VARIETIES

Shiraz is prized above all other Barossa grapes, able to conjure headswirling, palate-dousing flavours. Barossa is the main source of Shiraz grapes for Penfolds Grange, the wine that began the revolution in Australian red wine in the 1950s. Cabernet Sauvignon can be very good and similarly potent, as are the Rhône varieties of heady Grenache and deliciously earthy Mourvèdre; some of the most exciting examples are from the original vines planted in the 19th century. All these varieties are largely grown on the hot, dry, valley floor, but just to the east lie the Barossa Ranges, and in these higher, cooler vineyards, especially in those of the neighbouring Eden Valley, some of Australia's best and most fashionable Rieslings are grown, prized for their steely attack and lime fragrance. But even here you can't get away from Shiraz, and some thrilling examples come from the hills, not least Henschke's Hill of Grace and Mount Edelstone.

CLASSIFICATIONS

The Barossa was among the first zones to be ratified within the Australian system of Geographical Indications and comprises the regions of Barossa Valley and Eden Valley. The Barossa lies within South Australia's collective 'super zone' of Adelaide.

See also GRANGE, SOUTH AUSTRALIA; and individual producers.

ROCKFORD

BASKET PRESS

Shiraz

1999

BAROSSA VALLEY

PRODUCED AND BOTTLED AT ROCKFORD WINES, KRONDORF RD., TANUNDA, SOUTH AUSTRALIA 5352   750ml

BEST YEARS

(Barossa Valley Shiraz) (2006)
(05) 04 03 **02 01 99 98 97 96 94
91 90 88**; (Eden Valley Riesling)
2006 05 04 03 02 **01 00 99 98 97
96 95 94 92 91 90 87**

BEST PRODUCERS

Shiraz-based reds

BAROSSA VALLEY ESTATE, Bethany,
Rolf BINDER, Grant BURGE, Burge
Family, Dutschke, Elderton
(Command), GLAETZER, Greenock
Creek (Block Shiraz, Seven
Acres), HENSCHKE, Hewitson,
Jacob's Creek/ORLANDO, Jenke,
Trevor Jones, Kies Family,
Langmeil, Peter LEHMANN,
Charles MELTON, PENFOLDS (RWT,
GRANGE), Chris Ringland,
ROCKFORD, Saltram, ST HALLETT,
Schild Estate, Tim Smith,
Spinifex, Thorn Clarke, TORBRECK,
Torzi Matthews, TURKEY FLAT,
Two Hands, The Willows,
YALUMBA (Octavius).

Riesling

Bethany, Grant BURGE, Leo
Buring (Leonay), HENSCHKE,
Hewitson, Peter LEHMANN,
Jacob's Creek/ORLANDO
(Steingarten, St Helga), Ross
Estate, ST HALLETT, YALUMBA
(Heggies, Mesh/with Jeffrey
GROSSET, Pewsey Vale).

Cabernet Sauvignon-based reds

Rolf BINDER, Grant BURGE,
Greenock Creek, HENSCHKE,
Peter LEHMANN, ST HALLETT, The
Willows.

Other reds (Grenache, Mourvèdre, Shiraz)

Rolf BINDER, Burge Family (Olive
Hill), Grant BURGE, Charles
Cimicky (Grenache), Elderton
(CSM), HENSCHKE, Jenke
(Mourvèdre), Langmeil, Peter
LEHMANN, Charles MELTON,
PENFOLDS (Bin 138 Old Vine),
TORBRECK, TURKEY FLAT (Butcher's
Block, Grenache Noir), Two
Hands.

Semillon

Grant BURGE, HENSCHKE, Heritage,
Jenke, Peter LEHMANN, ROCKFORD,
TURKEY FLAT, The Willows.

JIM BARRY *Clare Valley, South Australia* After buying Australia's most famous Riesling vineyard in 1986, they had to wait until 2005 for the trademark to expire. Now Jim Barry has a flagship white, The Florita★, to head a quartet of classy, perfumed Rieslings. Medium-priced Lodge Hill Shiraz is impressive, but the winery is best known for its rich, fruity McRae Wood Shiraz★★ and heady, palate-busting and expensive Armagh Shiraz★★. Best years: (Armagh Shiraz) (2006) (05) (04) 02 01 99 98 **96 95 92 89**.

BARSAC AC *Bordeaux, France* Barsac, lying close to the river Garonne and with the little river Ciron running along its eastern boundary, is the largest of the 5 communes in the SAUTERNES AC, and also has its own AC, which is used by most, but by no means all, of the top properties. In general, the wines are a little less luscious than other Sauternes, but from good estates they can be marvellous. Best producers: CLIMENS★★★, COUTET★★, DOISY-DAENE★★, Doisy-Dubroca★, DOISY-VEDRINES★★, Myrat★, NAIRAC★★, Piada, Suau★. Best years: 2005 03 **02** 01 **99** 98 97 96 95 90 89 88 86 83.

BASILICATA *Italy* Southern Italian region best known for one wine, the potentially excellent, gutsy red called AGLIANICO DEL VULTURE.

BASSERMANN-JORDAN *Deidesheim, Pfalz, Germany* Since 1996, this famous estate has resumed making rich yet elegant Rieslings of ★★ quality from Deidesheim and FORST. In 2002 the estate was sold to local businessman Achim Niederberger. Best years: (2006) 05 04 **03** 02 **01** 99 98 97 96 90 89 88.

CH. BATAILLEY★ *Pauillac AC, 5ème Cru Classé, Haut-Médoc, Bordeaux, France* A byword for reliability and value for money among the PAUILLAC Classed Growth estates. Marked by a full, obvious blackcurrant fruit, not too much tannin and a luscious overlay of creamy vanilla. Lovely to drink at only 5 years old, the wine continues to age well for at least 15 years. Best years: 2005 04 **03 02** 00 98 96 95 94 90 89 88.

BÂTARD-MONTRACHET AC *Grand Cru, Côte de Beaune, Burgundy, France* This Grand Cru produces some of the world's greatest whites – they are full, rich and balanced, with a powerful mineral intensity of fruit and fresh acidity. There are 2 associated Grands Crus: Bienvenues-Bâtard-Montrachet and the minuscule Criots-Bâtard-Montrachet. All can age for a decade – indeed, they ought to. Best producers: Blain-Gagnard★★, CARILLON★★★, DROUHIN★★★, Fontaine-Gagnard★★, J-N GAGNARD★★★, JADOT★★★, Louis LATOUR★★, Dom. LEFLAIVE★★★, Olivier LEFLAIVE★★, Marc Morey★★★, Pierre Morey★★, Michel Niellon★★★, RAMONET★★★, SAUZET★★★, VERGET★★★. Best years: (2006) 05 04 03 02 01 **00 99 97 95 92 90 89**.

DOM. DES BAUMARD *Coteaux du Layon, Loire Valley, France* Well-sited vineyards produce sensational QUARTS DE CHAUME★★★ which requires aging, as well as rich, honeyed, impeccably balanced COTEAUX DU LAYON Clos de Ste Cathérine★★. Also fine steely, mineral-scented SAVENNIÈRES Clos du Papillon★★ and Clos St-Yves★★, with a late-harvest Trie Spéciale★★ in top years. Idiosyncratic Vert de l'Or Verdelho varies in sweetness according to vintage. CREMANT DE LOIRE and ANJOU reds are OK but unexciting. Baumard made waves in 2006, switching all production to Stelvin screwcap closures. Best years: (Quarts de Chaume) 2003 02 01 99 **97 96 95 90 89**.

LES BAUX-DE-PROVENCE AC *Provence, France* This AC has proved that organic and biodynamic farming can produce spectacular results, mainly due to the warm dry climate. Good fruit and intelligent winemaking produce some of the more easily enjoyable reds in Provence. Best producers: Hauvette★, Lauzières, Mas de la Dame★, Mas de Gourgonnier★, Mas Ste-Berthe★, Romanin★, Terres Blanches★. Best years: 2004 03 **02 01 00 99 98 97**.

BÉARN AC *South-West France* While the rest of South-West France has been busy producing some unusual and original flavours in recent years, Béarn's wines (90% red and rosé) are rarely special, despite some decent grape varieties. Since 2000, however, there seems to have been an improvement in quality. Best producers: Bellocq co-op, Cauhapé, Guilhemas, Lapeyre★, Nigri.

CH. DE BEAUCASTEL *Châteauneuf-du-Pape AC, Rhône Valley, France* François Perrin makes some of the richest, most tannic reds (often ★★★) in CHATEAUNEUF-DU-PAPE, with an unusually high percentage of Mourvèdre and Syrah, which can take at least a decade to show at their best. The white Roussanne Vieilles Vignes★★★ is exquisite and long-lived. Perrin also produces COTES DU RHONE Coudoulet de Beaucastel red★★ and white★ and, under the Domaines Perrin label, a range of increasingly good southern reds, including RASTEAU★ and VINSOBRES★. Best years: (reds) (2006) 05 04 03 **01 00 99 98 97 96 95 94 90 89 88 86 85**; (whites) 2006 05 04 03 **01 00 99 98 97 96 95 94 93 90**.

BEAUJOLAIS AC *Beaujolais, Burgundy, France* Wine region in the beautiful hills that stretch down from Mâcon to Lyon, producing predominantly red wine from the Gamay grape in prolific quantities. Beaujolais is best known for BEAUJOLAIS NOUVEAU, which accounts for 40% of the production. The better-quality reds, each having their own appellation, come from the north of the region and are BEAUJOLAIS-VILLAGES and the 10 single Cru villages; from north to south these are ST-AMOUR, JULIENAS, MOULIN-A-VENT, CHENAS, FLEURIE, CHIROUBLES, MORGON, REGNIE, BROUILLY and COTE DE BROUILLY. Simple Beaujolais comes from the extreme south, and in good vintages is light, fresh, aromatic and delicious to drink, but in poorer vintages the wine can be drab and acidic. A little rosé is also made from Gamay, and a small quantity of Beaujolais Blanc is made from Chardonnay. To combat falling sales, a new Vin de Pays is being considered. Best producers: (reds) J-P Brun/Terres Dorées, L & J-M Charmet/La Ronze★, Chatelus, DUBOEUF, J-F Garlon★, JADOT.

BEAUJOLAIS NOUVEAU *Beaujolais AC, Burgundy, France* Also known as Beaujolais Primeur, this is the first release of bouncy, fruity Beaujolais on the third Thursday of November after the harvest. Once a simple celebration of the new vintage, then over-hyped, and now enjoyed by the true Beaujolais lover. Quality is generally reasonable and the wine is delicious until Christmas and the New Year, but thereafter, while drinkable, is likely to throw a slight sediment.

BEAUJOLAIS-VILLAGES AC *Beaujolais, Burgundy, France* Beaujolais-Villages can come from one of 38 villages in the north of the region, many of the best examples rivalling the quality of the BEAUJOLAIS Crus, having more body, character, complexity and elegance than simple Beaujolais and representing all the pleasure of the Gamay grape at its best. Best villages in addition to the 10 Crus are Lancié, Quincié and Perréon. Best producers: (reds) Ch. de Belleverne★, G Descombes★, DUBOEUF, Manoir du Pavé★.

BEAULIEU VINEYARD *Napa Valley AVA, California, USA* The late André Tchelistcheff, winemaker from the late 1930s to the late 60s, had a major role in creating this icon for Napa Cabernet Sauvignon. After he left, Beaulieu lived on its reputation for too long. However, Private Reserve Cabernet Sauvignon★ seems to have returned to form. Tapestry★ (a meritage red) is good, as are Chardonnay★ and Pinot Noir★ from CARNEROS, and Syrah★. Recent small-lot Cabernets designated Clone 4 and Clone 6 are fascinating. Best years: (Private Reserve) 2004 03 01 00 **99 98 97 96 95 94 92 91 90 87 86 84**.

BEAUMES-DE-VENISE AC *Rhône Valley, France* Area famous for its sweet wine, MUSCAT DE BEAUMES-DE-VENISE. The local red wine is also very good, and received its own appellation from the 2004 vintage. It is full of dark fruit and crisp tannins and can age well for 10 years. Best producers: (reds) Balma Venitia (Beaumes-de-Venise) co-op, Beaumalric, Bernardins, Cassan, Durban, Fenouillet, les Goubert, Redortier.

BEAUNE AC *Côte de Beaune, Burgundy, France* Most of the wines are red, with delicious, soft red-fruits ripeness. There are no Grands Crus but some excellent Premiers Crus, especially Boucherottes, Bressandes, Clos des Mouches, Fèves, Grèves, Marconnets, Teurons, Vignes Franches. White-wine production is increasing – DROUHIN makes outstanding, creamy, nutty Clos des Mouches★★★. Best producers: (growers) Germain/Ch. de Chorey★★, LAFARGE★★, de MONTILLE★★, Albert Morot★, Rateau, TOLLOT-BEAUT★★; (merchants) BOUCHARD PERE ET FILS★★, Champy★, Chanson★, DROUHIN★★, Camille Giroud★★, JADOT★★, Labouré-Roi★. Best years: (reds) (2006) 05 **03 02 99**; (whites) (2006) 05 **04 02**.

CH. BEAU-SÉJOUR BÉCOT★★ *St-Émilion Grand Cru AC, 1er Grand Cru Classé, Bordeaux, France* Demoted from Premier Grand Cru Classé in 1986 and promoted again in 1996, this estate is on top form. Brothers Gérard and Dominique Bécot produce firm, ripe, richly textured wines that need at least 8–10 years to develop. Best years: 2005 04 03 02 **01 00 99 98 96 95 94 90 89 86 85**.

BEAUX FRÈRES *Willamette Valley AVA, Oregon, USA* The goal here is to make ripe, unfiltered Pinot Noir★ that expresses the essence of their 10ha (24-acre) vineyard atop Ribbon Ridge in the Chehalem Valley. A parcel known as the Upper Terrace★★★ yields exceptional fruit from Dijon clones. The Belles Soeurs★ label is used for purchased fruit and selected barrels of estate wine. Best years: (2005) 04 03 **02 01 00**.

GRAHAM BECK WINES *Robertson WO, South Africa* A 2-cellar operation, overseen by Pieter Ferreira. ROBERTSON's potential for Cap Classique sparkling is realized in an elegant, rich NV Brut★, a toastily fragrant, creamy, barrel-fermented and ageworthy Blanc de Blancs★ and an occasional quirky sparkling Pinotage★. Single-vineyard duo The Ridge Syrah★ and flavoursome, succulent Lonehill Chardonnay★ lead the Robertson table wines. Top wines from FRANSCHHOEK include single-vineyard Coffeestone Cabernet Sauvignon★, Old Road Pinotage★ and new Durbanville-sourced Pheasants' Run Sauvignon Blanc★ and The Joshua Shiraz-Viognier★★. The William★, a Cabernet Sauvignon-Pinotage blend, shows much promise and aging potential. Viognier is good, too.

J B BECKER *Walluf, Rheingau, Germany* Becker specializes in long-lived dry Rieslings – usually ★, some Spätlese trocken ★★. He also makes impressive dry Spätburgunder★ (Pinot Noir) reds. Best years: (Riesling Spätlese trocken) (2006) 05 04 **03 02 01 99 98**.

BEDELL CELLARS *Long Island, New York State, USA* Winemaker Kip Bedell helped establish LONG ISLAND's reputation with his high-quality Bordeaux-styled Merlot★ (Reserve★★), Cabernet Sauvignon★ and a red blend called Cupola★★. The wines have continued to improve under new ownership and capital, with Bedell still chief winemaker. Sister winery Corey Creek produces a noteworthy GEWÜRZTRAMINER.

BEECHWORTH *Victoria, Australia* Beechworth was best known as Ned Kelly country before Rick Kinzbrunner planted the hilly slopes of sub-Alpine North-East Victoria and started making wines at GIACONDA. Now boutique wineries produce tiny volumes at high prices and are on a steep learning curve. BROKENWOOD has a major new vineyard here. Best producers: Amulet (Shiraz★★), Castanga★ (Shiraz★★), Cow Hill★, GIACONDA★★★, Savaterre (Chardonnay★★), Sorrenberg★.

BEIRAS *Portugal* This large, central Portuguese province includes the DOCs of DÃO, BAIRRADA, Távora-Varosa and Beira Interior. Vinho Regional wines use Portuguese red and white varieties along with international grapes such as Cabernet Sauvignon and Chardonnay. Best producers: ALIANCA, D F J VINHOS (Bela Fonte), Figueira de Castelo Rodrigo co-op, Quinta de Foz de Arouce★, Filipa PATO★, Luís PATO★★, Rogenda, Caves SÃO JOÃO (Quinta do Poço do Lobo), Quinta dos Termos. Best years: 2005 04 **03 01 00**.

CH. BELAIR★★ *St-Émilion Grand Cru AC, 1er Grand Cru Classé, Bordeaux, France* Belair is next to AUSONE on ST-EMILION's limestone plateau. Under owner-winemaker Pascal Delbeck the estate has been run biodynamically since 1994, and the soft, supremely stylish wines are currently on top form. Drinkable at 5–6 years, but also capable of long aging. Best years: 2005 04 **03 02 01 00 99 98 95 90 89 88 86 85 83 82**.

BELLAVISTA *Franciacorta DOCG, Lombardy, Italy* Specialist in FRANCIACORTA sparkling wines, with a very good Cuvée Brut★★ and 4 distinctive Gran Cuvées★★ (including an excellent rosé). Riserva Vittorio Moretti Extra Brut★★ is made in exceptional years. Also produces lovely still wines, including white blend Convento dell'Annunciata★★★, Chardonnay Uccellanda★★ and red Casotte★ (Pinot Nero) and Solesine★★ (Cabernet-Merlot).

BELLET AC *Provence, France* Tiny AC in the hills behind Nice; the wine, mostly white, is usually overpriced. Ch. de Bellet★, Ch. de Crémat★ and Dom. de Toasc are the most important producers. Best years: (2006) 05 **04 03**.

BENDIGO *Central Victoria, Australia* Warm, dry, former gold-mining region, which is now home to more than 20 small-scale, high-quality wineries. The best wines are rich, ripe, distinctively minty Shiraz and Cabernet. Best producers: Balgownie, Blackjack, Chateau Leamon, Passing Clouds, PONDALOWIE★, Water Wheel. Best years: (Shiraz) (2006) (05) 04 03 02 01 **00 99 98 97 95 94 93 91 90**.

BERBERANA *Rioja DOCa, Rioja, Spain* Now part of Spain's second largest wine company, Arco Bodegas Unidas, incorporating Lagunilla, Marqués de Monistrol and Dominio de Súsar, Berberana makes a pleasant, lightly oaked Crianza and respectable Reservas and Gran Reservas. Best years: (Reserva) 2003 **01 98 96 95 94**.

BERCHER *Burkheim, Baden, Germany* One of the top estates of the KAISERSTUHL. High points are the powerful oak-aged Spätburgunder★★ (Pinot Noir) reds, Grauburgunder★★ (Pinot Gris) dry whites, which marry richness with perfect balance, and dry Muskateller★, which is firm, elegant and tangy. Best years: (whites) (2006) 05 04 **03 02 01 99**; (reds) (2006) 05 04 03 **02 01 99**.

BERGERAC AC *South-West France* Bergerac is the main town of the southern Dordogne and the overall AC for this underrated and improving area on the eastern edge of Bordeaux. The grape varieties are mostly the same as those used in the BORDEAUX ACs. The red is generally like a light, fresh claret, a bit grassy but with a good, raw blackcurrant fruit and hint of earth. Côtes de Bergerac AC wines have a higher minimum alcohol level. In general drink young, although a few estate reds can age for at least 3–5 years. Whites are generally fresh and dry for early drinking. Best producers: l'ANCIENNE CURE★, Bélingard, la Colline★, Court-les-Mûts, Eyssards, Les Miaudoux, Monestier, les Nicots, Panisseau, TOUR DES GENDRES★★, Tourmentine, les Verdots★. Best years: (reds) 2005 **04 03 02 01 00 98 96**.

BERINGER *Napa Valley AVA, California, USA* Beringer, part of the Foster's Wine Group, offers a serious range of top-class Cabernet Sauvignons. The Private Reserve Cabernet can be ★★★ and is one of NAPA VALLEY's finest yet most approachable; the Chabot Vineyard★★ can be equally impressive. The Knight's Valley Cabernet Sauvignon★ is made in a lighter style and is good value. Beringer also makes red★★ and white★ Alluvium (meritage wines) from Knight's Valley. The powerful Private Reserve Chardonnay★★ is ripe and toasty. Bancroft Ranch Merlot★★ from HOWELL MOUNTAIN is also very good. Best years: (Cabernet Sauvignon) 2003 02 **01 00 99 98 97 96 95 94 93 91** 90 87 86 84 81.

BERNKASTEL *Mosel, Germany* Both a historical wine town and in Middle Mosel a large Bereich. Top wines, however, come only from vineyard sites within the town – the most famous of these is the overpriced Doctor vineyard. Many wines from the Graben and Lay sites are often as good and cost a fraction of the price. Best producers: Dr LOOSEN★★, Pauly-Bergweiler★, J J PRUM★★, S A PRUM★, Dr H Thanisch★, WEGELER★★. Best years: (2006) 05 04 02 **01 99 98 97 95 90**.

DOM. BERTRAND-BERGÉ *Fitou AC, Languedoc, France* Old-vine Syrah, Grenache and Carignan produce some impressive FITOU wines: best is Jean Sirven★★, which is aged in wood for 18 months; Ancestrale★ and Mégalithes are good, too. Also some RIVESALTES. Best years: 2004 03 **02 00**.

BEST'S *Grampians, Victoria, Australia* Viv and Chris Thomson run this historical winery, with vineyards dating back to 1868. There have been more recent plantings in the GRAMPIANS and at Lake Boga in the Murray Darling region. There are three ranges: As the Crow Flies quaffers from Lake Boga; medium-priced Kindred Spirits; and the premium Great Western wines. Of these the Bin No. 0 Shiraz★★ is superb, the Cabernet★ is good, and the Riesling★ shows flashes of brilliance. The Thomson Family Shiraz★★ is an outstanding cool-climate Shiraz. Best years: (Thomson Family Shiraz) (2005) 04 01 99 **98 97 95 94 93 91 90**.

CH. BEYCHEVELLE★ *St-Julien AC, 4ème Cru Classé, Haut-Médoc, Bordeaux, France* At its best, this beautiful château can make wine of Second Growth quality. The wine has a charming softness even when young, but takes at least a decade to mature into the cedarwood and blackcurrant flavour for which ST-JULIEN is famous. In the best years it is worth its high price and, after a period of inconsistency, quality has become more regular since the late 1990s. Second wine: Amiral de Beychevelle. Best years: 2005 04 **03 00 99 98 96 95 90 89**.

BEYERSKLOOF *Stellenbosch WO, South Africa* Pinotage (Reserve★★) rules at maestro Beyers Truter's STELLENBOSCH property: it contributes to every style from good fizz to a traditional vintage port style and including a flavoursome dry Pinotage rosé and two versions of a succulent Cabernet-Pinotage-Merlot blend called Synergy (Reserve★). There's also the striking Cabernet Sauvignon-based Beyerskloof★★. Best years: (Beyerskloof) **2002 01 00 99 98 97 96 95**.

BIANCO DI CUSTOZA DOC *Veneto, Italy* Dry white wine from the shores of Lake Garda, made from a blend of grapes including SOAVE's Garganega. Drink young. Best producers: Cavalchina★, Gorgo★, Montresor★, Le Vigne di San Pietro★, Fratelli Zeni★.

BIENVENUES-BÂTARD-MONTRACHET AC See BÂTARD-MONTRACHET.

BIERZO DO *Castilla y León, Spain* Sandwiched between the rainy mountains of GALICIA and the arid plains of CASTILLA Y LEON. The arrival of Alvaro PALACIOS, of PRIORAT fame, and his nephew Ricardo Pérez Palacios, with their inspired Corullón★★ red, shed an entirely new and exciting light on the potential of the Mencía grape. Best producers: Pérez Caramés, Castro Ventosa★, Estefania, Luna Beberide★, Paixar★★, Descendientes de José Palacios★★, Peique★, Pittacum★, Prada a Tope, Dominio de Tares★, Valtuille★★.

JOSEF BIFFAR *Deidesheim, Pfalz, Germany* Frequent changes in winemaker have led to somewhat inconsistent dry and sweet Rieslings (often ★, sometimes ★★) from Deidesheim, Ruppertsberg and WACHENHEIM. Best years: (2006) 05 04 **03** 02 **01** 99 98.

BILLECART-SALMON *Champagne AC, Champagne, France* Top-notch family-controlled CHAMPAGNE house which makes extremely elegant wines that become irresistible with age. Non-vintage Brut★★, non-vintage Brut Rosé★★, Blanc de Blancs★★★, vintage Cuvée N-F

Billecart★★★ and Cuvée Elisabeth Salmon Rosé★★ are all excellent. Clos Saint-Hilaire★★ is a single-vineyard vintage Blanc de Noirs. Best years: 1998 **97** 96 **95 90 89 88 86 85 82**.

ROLF BINDER *Barossa, South Australia* Rolf and Christa Binder's family winery was known as Veritas until 2004, when the name was changed to avoid confusion with a Veritas winery in the US. The motto *In vino veritas* – In wine there is truth – still holds true. There's certainly truth in the bottom of a bottle of Hanisch Shiraz★★★ or Heysen Shiraz★★★. The Shiraz-Mataro Pressings★★ (known locally as Bull's Blood) and 'Heinrich' Shiraz-Grenache-Mataro★★ blends are lovely big reds; Cabernet-Merlot★★ is also good. Under the Christa Rolf label, Shiraz-Grenache★ is good and spicy with attractive, forward black fruit.

BINGEN *Rheinhessen, Germany* A small town and also a Bereich, the vineyards of which fall in both the NAHE and RHEINHESSEN. The best vineyard is the Scharlachberg, which produces some exciting wines, stinging with racy acidity and the whiff of coal smoke. Best producers: Kruger-Rumpf, Villa Sachsen. Best years: (2006) 05 04 02 **01 99 98**.

BIONDI-SANTI *Brunello di Montalcino DOCG, Tuscany, Italy*   Franco
Biondi-Santi's Il Greppo estate has created both a legend and an
international standing for BRUNELLO DI MONTALCINO. However, the
Biondi-Santi style has remained deeply traditional, while that of other
producers has moved on. Yet the very expensive Riserva★★, with
formidable levels of extract, tannin and acidity, deserves a minimum
10 years' further aging after release before serious judgement is passed
on it. Franco's son, Jacopo, has created his own range of wines,
including Sassoalloro★★, a barrique-aged Sangiovese, and
Sangiovese-Cabernet-Merlot blend Schidione★★. Best years: (Riserva)
(2006) (04) (03) 01 99 97 95 90 88 **85 83 82 75 64 55 45**.

BLAGNY AC *Côte de Beaune, Burgundy, France*   The red wine from this
tiny hamlet above MEURSAULT and PULIGNY-MONTRACHET can be fair
value, if you like a rustic Burgundy. Actually much more Chardonnay
than Pinot Noir is grown here, but this is sold as Puligny-Montrachet,
Meursault Premier Cru or Meursault-Blagny. Best producers:
R Ampeau★, Lamy-Pillot★, Matrot★. Best years: (2006) 05 **04 03 02 99**.

DOM. PAUL BLANCK *Alsace AC, Alsace, France*   One of Alsace's most
interesting and reliable domaines, although real character only shows
in the Grand Cru wines. Riesling★★ and Vieilles Vignes
Gewurztraminer★★ from the Furstentum Grand Cru (also the source
of super-rich Pinot Gris SGN★★★) stand out. Riesling Schlossberg★★
and Pinot Gris Altenbourg★★ offer depth and finesse. Best years:
(Grand Cru Riesling) 2005 04 **02 01 00 98 97 96 95**.

BLANQUETTE DE LIMOUX AC *Languedoc-Roussillon, France*   Sharp,
refreshing fizz from the Mauzac grape, which makes up a minimum
90% of the wine and gives it its striking 'green apple skin' flavour –
the balance is made up of Chardonnay and Chenin Blanc. The
traditional (CHAMPAGNE) method is used. The more rustic *méthode
rurale*, finishing off the original fermentation inside the bottle, is used
under a separate appellation, Blanquette Méthode Ancestrale. Best
producers: Collin, Fourn★, Guinot, Martinolles★, SIEUR D'ARQUES★, les
Terres Blanches. See also CRÉMANT DE LIMOUX AC and pages 276–7.

WOLF BLASS *Barossa Valley, South Australia*   Wolf Blass, with its huge
range, remains a cornerstone (with PENFOLDS) of Australia's biggest
wine company, the Foster's Wine Group. The wines do still faintly
reflect the founder's dictum that they must be easy to enjoy, though I
long for them to do better. The reds show overt oak, sometimes
clumsy, and occasionally capture the traditional Blass mint and
blackcurrant charm. Whites are on the oaky side, except for the
Rieslings, which are good, though sweeter and less vibrant than they
used to be, including star Gold Label Riesling★. Black Label★, a red
blend released at 4 years old, is expensive but good. Ultra-expensive
Platinum Label Shiraz★ is quite impressive. Regional varietals under
the Blass label reflect the winemaking style rather than regional taste,
whatever the label says. The Eaglehawk range is reliable quaffing
wine. Best years: (Black Label) (2006) (04) 02 01 **99 98 97 96 95 91 90 88
86**; (Platinum Shiraz) 2003 02 01 **99 98**.

BLAUBURGUNDER See PINOT NOIR.

BLAUER LEMBERGER See BLAUFRÄNKISCH.

BLAUFRÄNKISCH Good, ripe Blaufränkisch has a taste similar to
raspberries and white pepper or even beetroot. Hungarian in origin, it
does well in Austria, where it is the principal red grape of BURGENLAND.

The Hungarian vineyards (where it is called Kékfrankos) are mostly just across the border on the other side of the Neusiedlersee. Called Lemberger in Germany, where almost all of it is grown in WURTTEMBERG. Also successful in New York State and (as Lemberger) in WASHINGTON STATE (getting better with global warming!).

BLAYE See PREMIERES COTES DE BLAYE AC

JACKY BLOT *Loire Valley, France* When he created Domaine de la Taille aux Loups in MONTLOUIS-SUR-LOIRE and VOUVRAY in 1988, Jacky Blot's use of barrel fermentation and new oak caused controversy. However, rigorous selection of pristine, ripe grapes produces sparkling, dry and sweet whites with tremendous fruit purity. Top Montlouis-sur-Loire cuvées Sec Rémus★★ and Liquoreux Romulus★★ are groundbreaking. Since 2002 his methods have produced 4 powerful, well-structured reds at Domaine de la Butte in BOURGUEIL AC: each reflects a distinct parcel from the domaine's south-facing vineyards. Best years: (top whites) 2005 03 02 **97 96 95 90**.

BOEKENHOUTSKLOOF *Franschhoek WO, South Africa* Perched high in the FRANSCHHOEK mountains, this small winery is named after the surrounding Cape beech trees. The flagship trio comprises punchy, savoury Syrah★★; deep, long-lived Cabernet Sauvignon★★; and sophisticated Semillon★★ from 100-year-old vines. Placed between these and the fruit-focused, good-value Porcupine Ridge★ range is the burly, expressive Chocolate Block★★, a Cabernet Sauvignon-Shiraz blend with Grenache and Cinsaut. Best years: (premium reds) **2004 03 02 01 00 99 98 97**.

BOIREANN *Queensland, Australia* Fastidious attention to detail has turned this retirement project 1.5ha (3.5-acre) vineyard – planted to 11 varieties – into QUEENSLAND's most impressive winery. Hatfuls of stunning reds: Merlot★★, Cabernet Sauvignon★, Shiraz★ and Petit Verdot.

BOISSET *Burgundy, France* Jean-Claude Boisset bought his first vineyards in 1964 and began a négociant company whose extraordinary success has enabled him to swallow up many other long-established names such as Jaffelin, Ponelle, Ropiteau and Héritier Guyot in the COTE D'OR, Moreau in CHABLIS, Cellier des Samsons and Mommessin in BEAUJOLAIS and others elsewhere in France. Most of these companies are designed to produce commercially successful rather than fine wine, excepting Domaine de la VOUGERAIE and, perhaps, Boisset itself. Also projects in LANGUEDOC, Canada, Chile and Uruguay.

BOLGHERI DOC *Tuscany, Italy* Zone in the MAREMMA with simple white and rosé wines, plus reds based on Cabernet, Merlot or Sangiovese, with a special sub-zone for SASSICAIA. The DOC Rosso Superiore now covers wines from the prestigious estates of Grattamacco★, Le MACCHIOLE★★, ORNELLAIA★★, Michele Satta★★ and ANTINORI's Guado al Tasso★★. Best years: (reds) (2006) (05) 04 03 **01 00 99 98 97 96 95 94**.

BOLLINGER *Champagne AC, Champagne, France* One of the great CHAMPAGNE houses, with good non-vintage (Special Cuvée★) and vintage wines (Grande Année★★★), made in a full, rich, rather old-fashioned style. (Bollinger is one of the few houses to ferment its base wine in barrels.) It also produces a range of rarer vintages, including a Vintage RD★★★, and a Vieilles Vignes Françaises Blanc de Noirs★★ from ancient, ungrafted Pinot Noir vines. Bollinger bought Champagne Ayala, a near neighbour in Ay, in early 2005. Best years: (Grande Année) 1999 **97** 96 95 **92 90** 89 88 85 82 79.

BORDEAUX RED WINES

Bordeaux, France

This large area of South-West France, centred on the historical city of Bordeaux, produces a larger volume of fine red wine than any other French region. Wonderful Bordeaux-style wines are produced in California, Australia, South Africa and South America, but the home team's top performers still just about keep the upstarts at bay. Around 800 million bottles of red wine a year are produced here. The best wines, known as the Classed Growths, account for a tiny percentage of this figure, but some of their lustre rubs off on the lesser names, making this one of the most popular wine styles.

GRAPE VARIETIES

Bordeaux's reds are commonly divided into 'right' and 'left' bank wines. On the left bank of the Gironde estuary, the red wines are dominated by the Cabernet Sauvignon grape, with varying proportions of Cabernet Franc, Merlot and Petit Verdot. At best they are austere but perfumed with blackcurrant and cedarwood. The most important left bank areas are the Haut-Médoc (especially the communes of Margaux, St-Julien, Pauillac and St-Estèphe) and, south of the city of Bordeaux, the ACs of Pessac-Léognan and Graves. On the right bank, Merlot is the predominant grape, which generally makes the resulting wines more supple and fleshy than those of the left bank. The key areas for Merlot-based wines are St-Émilion and Pomerol, Fronsac and Côtes de Castillon.

CLASSIFICATIONS

Red Bordeaux is made all over the region. At its most basic, the wine is simply labelled Bordeaux or Bordeaux Supérieur. Above this are the more specific ACs covering sub-areas (such as the Haut-Médoc) and individual communes (such as Pomerol, St-Émilion or Margaux). Single-estate Crus Bourgeois are the next rung up on the quality ladder, followed by the Crus Classés (Classed Growths) of the Médoc, Graves and St-Émilion. The famous classification of 1855 ranked the top red wines of the Médoc (plus one from Graves) into 5 tiers, from First to Fifth Growths (Crus); there has been only one change, in 1973, promoting Mouton-Rothschild to First Growth status. Since the 1950s the Graves/Pessac-Léognan region has had its own classification, for red and white wines. St-Émilion's classification (for red wines only) has been revised several times, the last modification being in 2006; the possibility of re-grading can help to maintain quality. Curiously, Pomerol, home of Château Pétrus, arguably the most famous red wine in the world, has no official pecking order. Many top Bordeaux châteaux also make 'second wines', which are cheaper versions of their Grands Vins.

See also BORDEAUX, BORDEAUX-COTES DE FRANCS, BORDEAUX SUPERIEUR, CANON-FRONSAC, COTES DE BOURG, COTES DE CASTILLON, FRONSAC, GRAVES, HAUT-MEDOC, LALANDE-DE-POMEROL, LISTRAC-MEDOC, LUSSAC-ST-EMILION, MARGAUX, MEDOC, MONTAGNE-ST-EMILION, MOULIS, PAUILLAC, PESSAC-LEOGNAN, POMEROL, PREMIERES COTES DE BLAYE, PREMIERES COTES DE BORDEAUX, PUISSEGUIN-ST-EMILION, ST-EMILION, ST-ESTEPHE, ST-GEORGES-ST-EMILION, ST-JULIEN; and individual châteaux.

BEST YEARS

2005 04 03 **01 00 98 96 95 90
89 88 86 85 83 82 78 75 70 66
61**

BEST PRODUCERS

Graves, Pessac-Léognan
Dom. de CHEVALIER, HAUT-
BAILLY, HAUT-BRION, la LOUVIERE,
MALARTIC-LAGRAVIERE, la MISSION-
HAUT-BRION, PAPE-CLEMENT,
SMITH-HAUT-LAFITTE.

Margaux BRANE-CANTENAC,
FERRIERE, MALESCOT ST-EXUPERY,
MARGAUX, PALMER, RAUZAN-
SEGLA, du Tertre.

Pauillac GRAND-PUY-LACOSTE,
HAUT-BAGES-LIBERAL, LAFITE-
ROTHSCHILD, LATOUR, LYNCH-
BAGES, MOUTON-ROTHSCHILD,
PICHON-LONGUEVILLE,
PICHON-LONGUEVILLE-LALANDE,
PONTET-CANET.

Pomerol le BON PASTEUR,
Certan-de-May, Clinet,
la CONSEILLANTE, l'EGLISE-CLINET,
l'EVANGILE, la FLEUR-PETRUS,
GAZIN, LAFLEUR, LATOUR-A-
POMEROL, PETIT-VILLAGE, PETRUS,
le PIN, TROTANOY, VIEUX-CHATEAU-
CERTAN.

St-Émilion ANGELUS, AUSONE,
BEAU-SEJOUR BECOT, BELAIR,
CANON, CANON-LA-GAFFELIERE,
CHEVAL BLANC, Clos Fourtet,
la Dominique, FIGEAC,
Grand Mayne, MAGDELAINE,
MONBOUSQUET, La Mondotte,
PAVIE, PAVIE-MACQUIN, Rol
Valentin, TERTRE-ROTEBOEUF,
TROPLONG-MONDOT, VALANDRAUD.

St-Estèphe CALON-SEGUR, COS
D'ESTOURNEL, HAUT-MARBUZET,
LAFON-ROCHET, les Ormes de
Pez, MONTROSE.

St-Julien BRANAIRE-DUCRU,
DUCRU-BEAUCAILLOU, GRUAUD-
LAROSE, LAGRANGE, LANGOA-
BARTON, LEOVILLE-BARTON,
LEOVILLE-LAS-CASES, LEOVILLE-
POYFERRE, ST-PIERRE, TALBOT.

81

BORDEAUX WHITE WINES

Bordeaux, France

This is France's largest fine wine region but, except for the sweet wines of Sauternes and Barsac, Bordeaux's international reputation is based solely on its reds. From 52% of the vineyard area in 1970, white wines now represent only 12% of the present 120,000ha (296,500 acres) of vines. Given the size of the region, the diversity of Bordeaux's white wines should come as no surprise. There are dry, medium and sweet styles, ranging from dreary to some of the most sublime white wines of all. Bordeaux's temperate southern climate – moderated by the influence of the Atlantic and of 2 rivers, the Dordogne and the Garonne – is ideal for white wine production, particularly south of the city along the banks of the Garonne.

GRAPE VARIETIES

Sauvignon Blanc and Sémillon, the most important white grapes, are both varieties of considerable character and are usually blended together. They are backed up by smaller quantities of other grapes, the most notable of which is Muscadelle (unrelated to Muscat), which lends perfume to sweet wines and spiciness to dry.

DRY WINES

With the introduction of new technology and new ideas, many of them influenced by the New World, Bordeaux has become one of France's most exciting white wine areas. There are both oaked and unoaked styles. The unoaked are leafy, tangy and stony-dry. The barrel-fermented styles are delightfully rich yet dry, custard-cream softness mellowing leafy acidity and peach and nectarine fruit.

SWEET WINES

Bordeaux's most famous whites are its sweet wines made from grapes affected by noble rot, particularly those from Sauternes and Barsac. The noble rot concentrates the flavours, producing rich, honeyed wines replete with pineapple and peach flavours, and which develop a lanolin and beeswax depth and a barley sugar and honey richness with age. On the other side of the Garonne river, Cadillac, Loupiac and Ste-Croix-du-Mont also make sweet wines; these rarely attain the richness or complexity of a top Sauternes, but they are considerably less expensive.

CLASSIFICATIONS

The two largest dry white wine ACs in Bordeaux are Bordeaux Blanc and Entre-Deux-Mers. There are plenty of good dry wines in the Graves and Pessac-Léognan regions; the Pessac-Léognan AC, created in 1987, contains all the dry white Classed Growths. The great sweet wines of Sauternes and Barsac were classified as First or Second Growths in 1855.

See also BARSAC, BORDEAUX, BORDEAUX-COTES DE FRANCS, BORDEAUX SUPERIEUR, CADILLAC, CERONS, COTES DE BOURG, ENTRE-DEUX-MERS, GRAVES, LOUPIAC, PESSAC-LEOGNAN, PREMIERES COTES DE BLAYE, PREMIERES COTES DE BORDEAUX, STE-CROIX-DU-MONT, SAUTERNES; and individual châteaux.

BEST PRODUCERS

Dry wines

Pessac-Léognan Dom. de CHEVALIER, Couhins-Lurton, FIEUZAL, HAUT-BRION, LATOUR-MARTILLAC, LAVILLE-HAUT-BRION, la LOUVIERE, MALARTIC-LAGRAVIERE, SMITH-HAUT-LAFITTE; *Graves* Archambeau, Ardennes, Brondelle, Chantegrive, Clos Floridène, Magneau, Rahoul, Respide-Médeville, St-Robert (Cuvée Poncet-Deville), Vieux-Ch.-Gaubert, Villa Bel Air.

Entre-Deux-Mers BONNET, de Fontenille, Nardique-la-Gravière, Ste-Marie, Toutigeac, Turcaud.

Bordeaux AC l'Abbaye de Ste-Ferme, Bauduc, DOISY-DAENE (Sec), LYNCH-BAGES, Ch. MARGAUX (Pavillon Blanc), REYNON, Roquefort, TALBOT, Thieuley, Tour de Mirambeau.

Premières Côtes de Blaye Charron (Acacia), Haut-Bertinerie, Cave des Hauts de Gironde co-op, Tourtes (Prestige).

Sweet wines

Sauternes and Barsac CLIMENS, Clos Haut-Peyraguey, COUTET, DOISY-DAENE, DOISY-VEDRINES, FARGUES, GILETTE, GUIRAUD, LAFAURIE-PEYRAGUEY, NAIRAC, Raymond-Lafon, RIEUSSEC, Sigalas-Rabaud, SUDUIRAUT, la TOUR BLANCHE, YQUEM.

Cadillac Fayau, Manos, Mémoires.

Cérons Ch. de Cérons, Grand Enclos du Ch. de Cérons.

Loupiac Clos Jean, Cros, Mémoires, Noble.

Ste-Croix-du-Mont Loubens, Pavillon, la Rame.

CH. LE BON PASTEUR★★ *Pomerol AC, Bordeaux, France*   Owned by
Michel Rolland, one of Bordeaux's leading winemakers. The wines are
expensive, but they are always deliciously soft and full of lush fruit.
Best years: 2005 04 **03 01 00 99 98 96 95 94 90 89 88 85 83 82**.

BONNES-MARES AC *Grand Cru, Côte de Nuits, Burgundy, France*   A large
Grand Cru straddling the communes of CHAMBOLLE-MUSIGNY and MOREY-
ST-DENIS, commendably consistent over the last few decades. Bonnes-
Mares generally has a deep, ripe, smoky plum fruit, which starts rich
and chewy and matures over 10–20 years. Best producers: d'Auvenay
(Dom. LEROY)★★★, BOUCHARD PERE ET FILS★★, DROUHIN★★, Drouhin-
Laroze★★, DUJAC★★★, Robert Groffier★★★, JADOT★★★, D Laurent★★,
J-F MUGNIER★★, ROUMIER★★★, de VOGUE★★★, VOUGERAIE★★★. Best years:
(2006) 05 04 03 02 01 **00 99 98 97 96 95 93 90 89**.

CH. BONNET *Entre-Deux-Mers AC, Bordeaux, France*   This region's
pioneering estate for quality and consistency. Large volumes of good,
fruity, affordable Entre-Deux-Mers★, and BORDEAUX AC rosé and red,
particularly the barrel-aged Merlot-Cabernet Réserve★. Drink this at
3–4 years and the others young. A new special cuvée, Divinus★, was
launched with the 2000 vintage. Owner André Lurton is also the
proprietor of La LOUVIERE and other properties in PESSAC-LEOGNAN.

BONNEZEAUX AC *Loire Valley, France*   One of France's great sweet wines,
Bonnezeaux is a zone within the COTEAUX DU LAYON AC. Like SAUTERNES,
the wine is influenced by noble rot, but the flavours are different, as
only Chenin Blanc is used. Quality is variable, but top wines are world
class. It can age very well in good vintages. Best producers:
M Angeli/Sansonnière★★★, Fesles★★★, Godineau★★, des Grandes
Vignes★★, Petit Val★★, Petits Quarts★★, René Renou★★, Terrebrune★,
la Varière★★. Best years: (2006) 05 04 **03** 02 01 **99 97 96 95 90 89**.

BONNY DOON *Santa Cruz Mountains AVA, California, USA*   Randall Grahm
revels in the unexpected. He has a particular love for Rhône, Italian
and Spanish varietals and for fanciful names: Le Cigare Volant★★ is a
blend of Grenache and Syrah is Grahm's homage to CHATEAUNEUF-
DU-PAPE. Old Telegram★★ is 100% Mourvèdre; there's also a lovely
Syrah★★. Particularly delightful are his Ca' del Solo Italianate wines
and various Rieslings, including one entirely from WASHINGTON, and
one a blend of Washington and MOSEL fruit. Grahm has now spread his
net even wider, with the addition of wines from Italy, the LOIRE VALLEY
and elsewhere. The merry-go-round seems never to stop! Best years:
(Old Telegram) 2004 03 02 01 00 **98 97 96 95 94 91**.

BORDEAUX AC *Bordeaux, France*   One of the most important ACs in
France, covering reds, rosés and the dry, medium and sweet white
wines of the entire Gironde region. Most of the best wines are allowed
specific district or commune ACs (such as MARGAUX or SAUTERNES) but a
vast amount of Bordeaux's wine – delicious, atrocious and everything
in between – is sold as Bordeaux AC. At its best, straight red Bordeaux
is marked by bone-dry leafy fruit and an attractive earthy edge, but far
more frequently the wines are tannic and raw – and often overpriced.
Good examples usually benefit from a year or so of aging. Bordeaux
Blanc has joined the modern world with an increasing number of
refreshing, pleasant wines. These may be labelled as Bordeaux
Sauvignon. Drink as young as possible. Bordeaux Clairet is a pale red
wine, virtually rosé but with a little more substance. Best producers:
(reds) BONNET★, d:vin★, Dourthe (Numéro 1), Ducla, Fontenille★, Gadras,
Sirius, Thieuley★, Tour de Mirambeau; (whites) l'Abbaye de Ste-Ferme★,

Bauduc★, DOISY-DAENE★, Dourthe (Numéro 1★), LYNCH-BAGES★, MARGAUX (Pavillon Blanc★★), REYNON★, Roquefort★, TALBOT★, Thieuley★, Tour de Mirambeau★. See also pages 80–3.

BORDEAUX-CÔTES DE FRANCS AC *Bordeaux, France* Tiny area east of ST-EMILION; the top wines are good value. The Thienpont family (Ch. Puygueraud) is the driving force. Best producers: les Charmes-Godard★, Franc-Cardinal, Francs (Les Cerisiers★★), Laclaverie★, Marsau★, Nardou★, Pelan★, la Prade★, Puygueraud★★, Vieux Saule. Best years: 2005 04 **03 01 00 98 97 96 95 94 90**.

BORDEAUX SUPÉRIEUR AC *Bordeaux, France* Covers the same area as the BORDEAUX AC but the wines must have an extra 0.5% of alcohol, a lower yield and a longer period of maturation. Many of the best petits châteaux are labelled Bordeaux Supérieur. Best producers (reds): Barreyre★, Beaulieu Comtes des Tastes★, de Bouillerot★, de Courteillac★, Grand Village★, Parenchère★, Penin★, Pey la Tour★, le Pin Beausoleil★, Reignac★, Tire-Pé★.

BORIE LA VITARÈLE *St-Chinian AC, Languedoc, France* The Izarn family produces two ST-CHINIANS, which express the different soils of their organic vineyard: Les Crès★, dominated by Syrah, is spicy and warm; Les Schistes is cooler, more elegant. Best years: 2004 03 **01 00**.

LUIGI BOSCA *Mendoza, Argentina* Founded by the Arizú family in 1901 and still family-owned, this winery has 400ha (1000 acres) in LUJAN DE CUYO and Maipú, planted mainly with Malbec, Cabernet Sauvignon, Syrah, Chardonnay and Sauvignon Blanc. Try the mineral Finca Los Nobles Chardonnay★, the dense, chocolaty Finca Los Nobles Malbec★ and the more complex and sophisticated Malbec-based blend Gala 1★★ and Cabernet-based Gala 2★. Best years: (reds) 2005 04 03 **02 01 99**.

BOSCARELLI *Vino Nobile di Montepulciano DOCG, Tuscany, Italy* Arguably Montepulciano's best producer, crafting rich and stylish reds with guidance from star enologist Maurizio Castelli. VINO NOBILE★, Riserva del Nocio★★ and the barrique-aged SUPER-TUSCAN Boscarelli★★ are all brilliant. Best years: (2006) 04 **03 01 00 99 97 95**.

BOUCHARD FINLAYSON *Walker Bay WO, South Africa* Pinotphile Peter Finlayson produces classy Pinot Noir (Galpin Peak★ and occasional barrel selection Tête de Cuvée★★). His love of Italian varieties is reflected in Hannibal★★, a multi-cultural mix led by Sangiovese with Pinot Noir, Nebbiolo, Mourvèdre, Barbera and Shiraz. Chardonnays (Kaimansgaat/Crocodile's Lair★ – now fresher, more citrusy and less obviously oaky – and full, nutty home-grown Missionvale★) are plausibly Burgundian. Sauvignon Blanc★ is tangy and fresh. Best years: (Pinot Noir) (2006) 05 **04 03 02 01 00 99 98**.

BOUCHARD PÈRE ET FILS *Beaune, Burgundy, France* Important merchant and vineyard owner, with vines in some of Burgundy's most spectacular sites, including CORTON★★, CORTON-CHARLEMAGNE★★, Chevalier-Montrachet★★ and le MONTRACHET★★★. The firm is owned by Champenois Joseph HENRIOT, who is now realizing the full potential here. Wines from the company's own vineyards are sold under the Domaines du Château de Beaune label. Don't touch anything pre-1996. Best years: (top reds) (2006) 05 04 03 02 **01 00 99 98**.

BOUCHES-DU-RHÔNE, VIN DE PAYS DES *Provence, France* Wines from 3 areas: the coast, a zone around Aix-en-Provence and the Camargue. Mainly full-bodied, spicy reds, but rosé can be good. Best producers: Ch. Bas, l'Île St-Pierre, Mas de Rey, la Michelle, TREVALLON★★, Valdition. Best years: (reds) 2005 **04 03 01 00**.

DOM. HENRI BOURGEOIS *Sancerre AC, Loire Valley, France* Large-scale outfit in SANCERRE with 60ha (150 acres) of domaine vineyards and a substantial négociant business extending into other Loire appellations, plus holdings in New Zealand. Wines are reliable at all levels, from the vin de pays Petit Bourgeois up. The Monts Damnées cuvées, from steep vineyards, have bags of mineral character. Old-vine bottlings Jadis★★, d'Antan★★ and the rare barrel-fermented Étienne Henri★★ are among the finest in Sancerre. Best years: (top wines) 2006 05 04 **02 01 00**.

BOURGOGNE AC *Burgundy, France* Bourgogne is the French name anglicized as 'Burgundy'. This generic AC mops up all the Burgundian wine with no AC of its own, resulting in massive differences in style and quality. The best wines will usually come from a single grower's vineyards just outside the main village ACs of the COTE D'OR; such wines may be the only way we can afford the joys of fine Burgundy. If the wine is from a grower, the flavours should follow a regional style. However, if the address on the label is that of a négociant, the wine could be from anywhere in Burgundy. Pinot Noir is the main red grape, but Gamay from a declassified BEAUJOLAIS cru is, absurdly, allowed. Red Bourgogne is usually light, fruity in an upfront strawberry and cherry way, and should be drunk within 2–3 years. The rosé (from Pinot Noir) can be pleasant, but little is produced. Bourgogne Blanc is a usually bone-dry Chardonnay wine and most should be drunk within 2 years. Bourgogne Passe-tout-Grains is made from Gamay with a minimum 33% of Pinot Noir, while Bourgogne Grand Ordinaire is rarely more than a quaffing wine, drunk in local bars. Best producers: (reds/growers) G Barthod★★, COCHE-DURY★, Dugat-Py★★, Germain/Ch. de Chorey★, LAFARGE★, MEO-CAMUZET★★, P RION★★, ROUMIER★, VOUGERAIE; (reds/merchants) DROUHIN★, GIRARDIN, JADOT★, Labouré-Roi, Maison Leroy★★, N POTEL★★; (reds/co-ops) BUXY★, Caves des Hautes-Côtes★; (whites/growers) M BOUZEREAU★, Boyer-Martenot★, J-M BROCARD★, COCHE-DURY★★, J-P Fichet★, P Javillier★★, Ch. de Meursault★, Pierre Morey★, Guy Roulot★; (whites/merchants) DROUHIN★, FAIVELEY, JADOT★, Olivier LEFLAIVE, RODET★; (whites/co-ops) BUXY, Caves des Hautes-Côtes. Best years: (reds) 2006 **05 03 02**; (whites) **2006 05 04**. See also pages 88–91.

BOURGOGNE ALIGOTÉ AC See ALIGOTÉ.

BOURGOGNE-CÔTE CHALONNAISE AC *Côte Chalonnaise, Burgundy, France* These now sell at a premium over other 'Bourgogne' wines. The AC covers vineyards to the west of Chalon-sur-Saône around the villages of Bouzeron, RULLY, MERCUREY, GIVRY and MONTAGNY. Best producers: X Besson, BUXY CO-OP★, Villaine★. Best years: **2006 05 04**.

BOURGOGNE-HAUTES-CÔTES DE BEAUNE AC *Burgundy, France* The hills behind the great COTE DE BEAUNE are a good source of affordable Burgundy. The red wines are lean but drinkable, as is the slightly sharp Chardonnay. Best producers: Caves des Hautes-Côtes★, J-Y Devevey★, L Jacob★, J-L Joillot★, Ch. de Mercey★/RODET, Naudin-Ferrand★, C Nouveau★. Best years: (reds) (2006) **05 03**; (whites) **2006 05 04**.

BOURGOGNE-HAUTES-CÔTES DE NUITS AC *Burgundy, France* Attractive, lightweight wines from the hills behind the COTE DE NUITS. The reds are best, with an attractive cherry and plum flavour. The whites tend to be rather dry and flinty. Best producers: (reds) Bertagna★, D Duband★, FAIVELEY★, A-F GROS★, M GROS★, A Guyon★, Caves des Hautes-Côtes★, Jayer-Gilles★★, T LIGER-BELAIR★; (whites) Caves des Hautes-Côtes★, Champy★, Jayer-Gilles★★, Thévenot-le-Brun★, A Verdet★. Best years: (reds) (2006) **05 03**; (whites) **2006 05 04**.

BOURGUEIL AC *Loire Valley, France* Fine red wine from between Tours and Angers. Made with Cabernet Franc, sometimes topped up with a little Cabernet Sauvignon; in hot years results can be superb. Given 5–10 years of age, the wines can develop a wonderful raspberry fragrance. Best producers: Y Amirault★★, Audebert (estate wines★), BLOT/la Butte★★, T Boucard★, P Breton★, la Chevalerie, Clos de l'Abbaye★, Max Cognard, DRUET★★, Forges, Lamé-Delisle-Boucard, la Lande/Delaunay, Nau Frères★, Ouches★, Raguenières★. Best years: (2006) 05 04 **03** 02 01 **00 97 96 95**. See also ST-NICOLAS-DE-BOURGUEIL.

BOUVET-LADUBAY *Saumur AC, Loire Valley, France* Sparkling wine producer owned by TAITTINGER. Basic Bouvet Brut and Bouvet Rosé are good. Cuvée Saphir, the top-selling wine, is over-sweet, but Trésor (Blanc★ and Rosé★), fermented in oak casks, is very good. Now also a good Brut Zéro. Weird and wonderful Rubis★ sparkling red is worth trying. The Nonpareils★ range of still wines are pricey for the quality.

BOUZEREAU *Meursault, Côte de Beaune, Burgundy, France* An extended family of vignerons – you'll find a good half dozen domaines with this name in the yellow pages – all making a range of whites from MEURSAULT and neighbouring villages, plus some less interesting COTE DE BEAUNE reds. Best at the moment are Dom. Michel Bouzereau & Fils★ and Vincent Bouzereau★.

BOWEN ESTATE *Coonawarra, South Australia* A COONAWARRA pioneer since the 1970s, Doug Bowen, now joined by his daughter, Emma, continues to make some of the region's best and most peppery Shiraz★★ as well as vibrant blackcurranty Cabernet★. Best years: (Shiraz) (2006) (05) 03 02 01 00 **98 97 96 94 93 92 91**.

BOYAR ESTATES *Bulgaria* The leading distributor of Bulgarian wines, selling more than 65 million bottles worldwide each year. Quality is erratic: many reds are raw and tannic, whites are merely decent.

BRACHETTO An unusual Italian grape native to Piedmont, Brachetto makes every style from dry and still to rich, sweet *passito* and sweet, frothy light red wines with a Muscat-like perfume, as exemplified by Brachetto d'Acqui DOCG. Best producers: (dry) Contero, Correggia★, Scarpa★; (Brachetto d'Acqui) BANFI★, Braida★, G Marenco★.

CH. BRANAIRE-DUCRU★★ *St-Julien AC, 4ème Cru Classé, Haut-Médoc, Bordeaux, France* After a long period of mediocrity, 1994 and subsequent vintages have confirmed a welcome return to full, soft, chocolaty form. Best years: 2005 04 03 02 **01 00 99 98 96 95 94**.

BRAND'S *Coonawarra, South Australia* COONAWARRA firm, owned by MCWILLIAM'S, with 100ha (250 acres) of new vineyards as well as some ancient vines. Ripe Cabernet★ is increasingly attractive; Patron's Reserve★★ (Cabernet with Shiraz and Merlot) is excellent. New life has been breathed into Shiraz★, and the opulent Stentiford's Reserve★★ (from 100-year-old vines) shows how good Coonawarra Shiraz can be. Merlot★★ is among Australia's best examples of the variety. Best years: (reds) (2006) (05) 04 03 02 01 **00 99 98 97 96 94 90**.

CH. BRANE-CANTENAC★★ *Margaux AC, 2ème Cru Classé, Haut-Médoc, Bordeaux, France* After a drab period, Brane-Cantenac returned to form during the late 1990s. Henri Lurton has taken over the family property and is making some superb wines, particularly the 2000, although don't expect flavours to be mainstream – years like 2002 and 2003 are tasty but wild. Best years: 2005 04 **03** 02 **01 00 99 98 96 95 89**.

BURGUNDY RED WINES

Burgundy, France

Rich in history and gastronomic tradition, the region of Burgundy (Bourgogne in French) covers a vast tract of eastern France, running from Auxerre, south-east of Paris, down to the city of Lyon. As with its white wines, Burgundy's red wines are extremely diverse. The explanation for this lies partly in the fickle nature of Pinot Noir, the area's principal red grape, and partly in the historical imbalance of supply and demand between growers – who grow the grapes and make and bottle much of the best wine – and merchants, whose efforts originally established the reputation of the wines internationally.

WINE STYLES

Pinot Noir shows many different flavour profiles according to climate, soil and winemaking. The reds from around Auxerre (Épineuil, Irancy) in the north will be light, chalky and strawberry-flavoured. Also light, though more rustic and earthy, are the reds of the Mâconnais in the south, while the Côte Chalonnaise offers solid reds from Givry and Mercurey.

The top reds come from the Côte d'Or, the heartland of Burgundy. Flavours sweep through strawberry, raspberry, damson and cherry – in young wines – to a wild, magnificent maturity of Oriental spices, chocolate, mushrooms and truffles. The greatest of all – the world-famous Grand Cru vineyards such as Chambertin, Musigny, Richebourg and Clos de Vougeot – are in the Côte de Nuits, the northern part of the Côte d'Or from Nuits-St-Georges up toward Dijon. Other fine reds, especially Volnay, Pommard and Corton, come from the Côte de Beaune. Some villages tend toward a fine and elegant style (Chambolle-Musigny, Volnay), others toward a firmer, more tannic structure (Gevrey-Chambertin, Pommard).

The Beaujolais should really be considered as a separate region, growing Gamay on granitic soils rather than Pinot Noir on limestone, though a small amount of Gamay has also crept north to be included in the lesser wines of Burgundy.

CLASSIFICATIONS

Most of Burgundy has 5 increasingly specific levels of classification: regional ACs (e.g. Bourgogne), specified ACs covering groups of villages (e.g. Côte de Nuits-Villages), village wines taking the village name (Pommard, Vosne-Romanée), Premiers Crus (good village vineyard sites) and Grands Crus (the best individual vineyard sites).

See also ALOXE-CORTON, AUXEY-DURESSES, BEAUJOLAIS, BEAUNE, BLAGNY, BONNES-MARES, BOURGOGNE, BOURGOGNE-COTE CHALONNAISE, BOURGOGNE-HAUTES-COTES DE BEAUNE/NUITS, CHAMBERTIN, CHAMBOLLE-MUSIGNY, CHASSAGNE-MONTRACHET, CHOREY-LES-BEAUNE, CLOS DE LA ROCHE, CLOS ST-DENIS, CLOS DE VOUGEOT, CORTON, COTE DE BEAUNE, COTE DE NUITS, COTE D'OR, CREMANT DE BOURGOGNE, ECHEZEAUX, FIXIN, GEVREY-CHAMBERTIN, GIVRY, IRANCY, LADOIX, MACON, MARANGES, MARSANNAY, MERCUREY, MONTHELIE, MOREY-ST-DENIS, MUSIGNY, NUITS-ST-GEORGES, PERNAND-VERGELESSES, POMMARD, RICHEBOURG, la ROMANEE-CONTI, ROMANEE-ST-VIVANT, RULLY, ST-AUBIN, ST-ROMAIN, SANTENAY, SAVIGNY-LES-BEAUNE, la TACHE, VOLNAY, VOSNE-ROMANEE, VOUGEOT; and individual producers.

BEST PRODUCERS

Côte de Nuits B Ambroise, l'Arlot, Robert Arnoux, Denis Bachelet, G Barthod, Bertagna, A Burguet, Cacheux-Sirugue, S CATHIARD, Charlopin, J Chauvenet, R Chevillon, Chopin-Groffier, B CLAIR, CLOS DES LAMBRAYS, CLOS DE TART, J-J Confuron, P Damoy, Drouhin-Laroze, C Dugat, B Dugat-Py, DUJAC, R Engel, Sylvie Esmonin, Fourrier, Geantet-Pansiot, H GOUGES, GRIVOT, R Groffier, GROS, Hudelot-Noëllat, Jayer-Gilles, F Lamarche, Lechenaut, Philippe Leclerc, Dom. LEROY, LIGER-BELAIR, H Lignier, MEO-CAMUZET, Denis MORTET, Mugneret, Mugneret-Gibourg, J-F MUGNIER, Perrot-Minot, Ponsot, RION, Dom. de la ROMANEE-CONTI, Rossignol-Trapet, Roty, E Rouget, ROUMIER, ROUSSEAU, Sérafin, J & J-L Trapet, de VOGUE, VOUGERAIE.

Côte de Beaune R Ampeau, d'ANGERVILLE, Comte Armand, J Boillot, J-M Boillot, CHANDON DE BRIAILLES, COCHE-DURY, Courcel, Germain/Ch. de Chorey, Michel LAFARGE, LAFON, de MONTILLE, J Prieur, TOLLOT-BEAUT.

Côte Chalonnaise Joblot, M Juillot, Lorenzon, Raquillet, de Suremain, Villaine.

Merchants BOUCHARD PERE ET FILS, Champy, DROUHIN, FAIVELEY, V GIRARDIN, Camille Giroud, JADOT, Labouré-Roi, D Laurent, Maison Leroy, Nicolas POTEL, RODET.

Co-ops BUXY, Caves des Hautes-Côtes.

89

BURGUNDY WHITE WINES

Burgundy, France

White Burgundy has for generations been thought of as the world's leading dry white wine. The top wines have a remarkable succulent richness of honey and hazelnut, melted butter and sprinkled spice, yet are totally dry. Such wines are all from the Chardonnay grape and the finest are generally produced in the Côte de Beaune, the southern part of the Côte d'Or, in the communes of Aloxe-Corton, Meursault, Puligny-Montrachet and Chassagne-Montrachet, where limestone soils and the aspect of the vineyard provide perfect conditions for even ripening of grapes.

WINE STYLES

However, Burgundy encompasses many more wine styles than this, even if no single one quite attains the peaks of quality of those 4 villages on the Côte de Beaune.

Chablis in the north traditionally produces very good steely wines, aggressive and lean when young, but nutty and rounded – though still very dry – after a few years. Modern Chablis is frequently a softer, milder wine, easy to drink young, and sometimes enriched (or denatured) by aging in new oak barrels.

There is no doubt that Meursault and the other Côte de Beaune villages can produce stupendous wine, but it is in such demand that unscrupulous producers are often tempted to maximize yields and cut corners on quality. Consequently white Burgundy from these famous villages must be approached with caution. Lesser-known villages such as Pernand-Vergelesses and St-Aubin often provide good wine at lower prices. There are also good wines from some villages in the Côte de Nuits, such as Morey-St-Denis, Nuits-St-Georges and Vougeot, though amounts are tiny compared with the Côte de Beaune.

South of the Côte d'Or the Côte Chalonnaise is becoming more interesting for quality white wine now that better equipment for temperature control is becoming more widespread and oak barrels are being used more often for aging. Rully and Montagny are the most important villages, though Givry and Mercurey can produce nice white, too. The minor Aligoté grape makes some attractive, if acidic, wine, especially in Bouzeron.

Further south, the Mâconnais is a large region, two-thirds planted with Chardonnay. There is some fair sparkling Crémant de Bourgogne, and some very good vineyard sites, in particular in St-Véran and in Pouilly-Fuissé. Increasingly stunning wines can now be found, though there's still a lot of dross.

See also ALOXE-CORTON, AUXEY-DURESSES, BATARD-MONTRACHET, BEAUJOLAIS, BEAUNE, BOURGOGNE, BOURGOGNE-COTE CHALONNAISE, BOURGOGNE-HAUTES-COTES DE BEAUNE/NUITS, CHABLIS, CHASSAGNE-MONTRACHET, CORTON, CORTON-CHARLEMAGNE, COTE DE BEAUNE, COTE DE NUITS, COTE D'OR, CREMANT DE BOURGOGNE, FIXIN, GIVRY, LADOIX, MACON, MACON-VILLAGES, MARANGES, MARSANNAY, MERCUREY, MEURSAULT, MONTAGNY, MONTHELIE, MONTRACHET, MOREY-ST-DENIS, MUSIGNY, NUITS-ST-GEORGES, PERNAND-VERGELESSES, POUILLY-FUISSE, POUILLY-VINZELLES, PULIGNY-MONTRACHET, RULLY, ST-AUBIN, ST-ROMAIN, ST-VERAN, SANTENAY, SAVIGNY-LES-BEAUNE, VIRE-CLESSE, VOUGEOT; and individual producers.

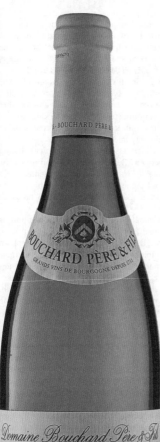

BEST PRODUCERS

Chablis Barat, J-C Bessin, Billaud-Simon, A & F Boudin, J-M BROCARD, D Dampt, R & V DAUVISSAT, D-E Defaix, Droin, DURUP, W Fèvre, J-H Goisot, J-P Grossot, LAROCHE, Long-Depaquit, Malandes, Louis Michel, Picq, Pinson, RAVENEAU, Vocoret.

Côte d'Or (Côte de Beaune) R Ampeau, d'Auvenay (LEROY), Blain-Gagnard, J-M Boillot, Bonneau du Martray, M BOUZEREAU, Boyer-Martenot, CARILLON, CHANDON DE BRIAILLES, Chassorney, Coche-Debord, COCHE-DURY, Marc Colin, Colin-Deléger, Arnaud Ente, J-P Fichet, Fontaine-Gagnard, J-N GAGNARD, A Gras, P Javillier, F Jobard, R Jobard, LAFON, H & O Lamy, Dom. LEFLAIVE, Matrot, Bernard Morey, Marc Morey, Pierre Morey, M Niellon, P Pernot, J & J-M Pillot, RAMONET, M Rollin, G Roulot, SAUZET, VERGET, VOUGERAIE.

Côte Chalonnaise S Aladame, H & P Jacqueson.

Mâconnais D & M Barraud, A Bonhomme, Bret Brothers, Cordier, Corsin, Deux Roches, J-A Ferret, Ch. Fuissé, Guffens-Heynen/VERGET, Guillot-Broux, O Merlin, Robert-Denogent, Ch. des Rontets, Saumaize-Michelin, la Soufrandière, J Thévenet, Valette.

Merchants BOUCHARD PERE ET FILS, Champy, DROUHIN, FAIVELEY, V GIRARDIN, JADOT, Labouré-Roi, Louis LATOUR, Olivier LEFLAIVE, Maison Leroy, Rijckaert, RODET, VERGET.

Co-ops BUXY, la CHABLISIENNE, Lugny, Viré.

91

BRAUNEBERG *Mosel, Germany* Small village with 2 famous vineyard sites, Juffer and Juffer Sonnenuhr, whose wines have a honeyed richness and creamy gentleness rare in the Mosel. Best producers: Bastgen★, Fritz HAAG★★★, Willi Haag★, Paulinshof★, M F RICHTER★★, SCHLOSS LIESER★★. Best years: (2006) 05 04 **03** 02 01 **99 98 97 90**.

BREAKY BOTTOM *Sussex, England* Small vineyard in the South Downs near Lewes. Peter Hall is a quirky, passionate grower, making dry, nutty Seyval Blanc★ that becomes creamy and BURGUNDY-like after 3–4 years. Sparkling wines continue to improve: sparkling Seyval Blanc★ is delicious, but there is a shift to more classic varieties, using early-ripening clones of Chardonnay and Pinot Noir.

GEORG BREUER *Rüdesheim, Rheingau, Germany* Intense dry Riesling from RUDESHEIM Berg Schlossberg★★, Berg Rottland★★ and RAUENTHAL Nonnenberg★★. Also a remarkable Sekt★ from barrel-fermented Pinot Gris, Pinot Blanc and a dash of Riesling – a blend both distinctive and surprisingly successful. Best years: (Berg Schlossberg) (2006) 05 04 03 02 **01 00 99 98 97 96 94**.

BRIGHT BROTHERS *Ribatejo, Portugal* The Fiúza-Bright operation is located in the town of Almeirim; Fiúza-labelled wines are from local vineyards planted to both Portuguese and French varieties. Australian Peter Bright also makes Brightpink, Brightwhite and Brightred table wines, in aluminium bottles, and red and white Fado Alentejo wines.

JEAN-MARC BROCARD *Chablis, Burgundy, France* Dynamic winemaker who has built up this 80ha (200-acre) domaine almost from scratch, and is now one of Chablis' most reliable and satisfying producers. The Premiers Crus (including Montée de la Tonnerre★★, Montmains★★) and slow-evolving Grands Crus (les Clos★★★ stands out) are tremendous, while the basic Chablis, especially Vieilles Vignes★★, are some of the best on the market. Brocard also produces a range of BOURGOGNE Blancs★ from different soil types. Now adopting an increasingly organic – and in some cases biodynamic – approach to his vineyards. Best years: (2006) 05 **04 03 02 00**.

BROKENWOOD *Hunter Valley, New South Wales, Australia* High-profile winery with delicious traditional unoaked HUNTER Semillon★★ (sometimes ★★★). Best wine is classic Hunter Graveyard Vineyard Shiraz★★★; MCLAREN VALE Rayner Vineyard Shiraz★★ is also stunning. Cricket Pitch reds and whites are cheerful, fruity ready-drinkers. New vineyard at BEECHWORTH is making very promising Chardonnay, Viognier and Pinot Noir. Best years: (Graveyard Vineyard Shiraz) (2006) 05 04 03 02 00 99 98 **96 95 94 93 91 90 89 88 86**.

BRONCO WINE CO. *California, USA* Maker of the Charles Shaw range of wines – known as 'Two-Buck Chuck' because of their $2 price tag. There's now a $5 Napa Cabernet Sauvignon. The company is run by maverick Fred Franzia (grand-nephew of the late Ernest GALLO), who owns 14,000ha (35,000 acres) of California vineyard land and markets 10 million cases of wine under more than a dozen brands.

BROUILLY AC *Beaujolais, Burgundy, France* Largest of the 10 BEAUJOLAIS Crus; at its best, the wine is soft, fruity, rich and brightly coloured. Best producers: Ch. de la Chaize★, DUBOEUF (Ch. de Nervers★), A Michaud★, Ch. Thivin★★. Best years: **2006 05**.

BROWN BROTHERS *North-East Victoria, Australia* Highly successful family winery, producing a huge range of varietal wines, which have improved significantly in recent years. Good fizz and fine stickies★★. Top-of-the-range Patricia wines (Cabernet★★, sparkling Pinot-

Chardonnay★★) are Brown's best yet. Premium grapes are from cool King Valley, mountain-top Whitlands and new vineyard at HEATHCOTE.

BRÜNDLMAYER *Kamptal, Niederösterreich, Austria*   Willi Bründlmayer makes wine in a variety of Austrian and international styles, but his outstanding dry Riesling (Alte Reben★★★) from the great Heiligenstein vineyard and Grüner Veltliner (Ried Lamm★★★) are the best; high alcohol is matched by superlative fruit and mineral flavours. Good Sekt★. Best years: (Zöbinger Heiligenstein Riesling) (2006) 05 04 **03** 02 **01 99 98 97**.

BRUNELLO DI MONTALCINO DOCG *Tuscany, Italy*   Powerful red wine produced from Sangiovese (known locally as Brunello). Traditionally needed over 10 years to soften, but modern practices result in more fruit-rich wines, yet still tannic enough to age spectacularly. Best producers: Agostina Pieri★★, Altesino★ (Montosoli★★), BANFI★ (Riserva★★), Barbi★ (Riserva★★), BIONDI-SANTI★, Gianni Brunelli★★, Camigliano★★, La Campana★, Caparzo★ (La Casa★★), Casanova di Neri★★★, Casanuova delle Cerbaie★★, CASE BASSE★★★, Castelgiocondo/FRESCOBALDI (Riserva★), Centolani★ (Pietranera★★), Cerbaiona★★, Ciacci Piccolomini d'Aragona★★, Donatella Cinelli Colombini★, Col d'Orcia★★, COSTANTI★, Fuligni★★, La Gerla★★, Le Gode★★, Gorelli-Due Portine★, Greppone Mazzi★★, Maurizio Lambardi★★, Lisini★★, Mastrojanni★★ (Schiena d'Asino★★★), Siro Pacenti★★★, Pian delle Vigne★★/ANTINORI, Piancornello★★, Pieve Santa Restituta★★, La Poderina★, Poggio Antico★★, Poggio San Polo★★, IL POGGIONE★★, Salvioni★★, Livio Sassetti-Pertimali★★, Talenti★★, La Togata★★, Valdicava★★, Villa Le Prata★★. Best years: (2006) (04) (03) 01 **00** 99 **98 97 95 93 90 88 85**.

BUCELAS DOC *Estremadura, Portugal*   A tiny but historical DOC. The wines are whites based on the Arinto grape (noted for its high acidity). For attractive, modern examples try Quinta da Murta or Quinta da Romeira (Morgado de Santa Catherina★).

VON BUHL *Deidesheim, Pfalz, Germany*   Large estate, sold in 2005 to Achim Niederberger, the new owner of BASSERMANN-JORDAN. Top Rieslings now invariably ★★. Best years: (Grosses Gewächs Rieslings) (2006) 05 04 **03** 02 **01 99 98**.

BUITENVERWACHTING *Constantia WO, South Africa*   Time slows down at this beautiful property, part of the Cape's original CONSTANTIA wine farm. Sauvignon Blanc★ is penetrating and zesty; Husseys Vlei Sauvignon Blanc★ is bigger and more pungent. A ripe, fruit-laden Chardonnay★ has been joined by an elegant, subtle Husseys Vlei★★ version. These and a light racy Riesling can improve with a little aging. The aristocratic Christine★★, with deep flavours and firm, dry structure, remains one of the Cape's most accurate BORDEAUX lookalikes. Best years: (Christine) (2003) 02 **01 00 99 98 97 96 95**.

BULL'S BLOOD *Hungary*   Kékfrankos (Blaufränkisch) grapes sometimes replace robust Kadarka in the blend, thinning the blood; some producers blend with Cabernet Sauvignon, Kékoporto or Merlot. New regulations should improve the quality of Bikavér ('bull's blood') in the 2 permitted regions, Eger and Szekszárd. Winemakers such as Vilmos Thummerer are working hard on this front, and are putting some balls back into the wine.

GRANT BURGE *Barossa Valley, South Australia*   A leading producer in the BAROSSA, with a wide range, including chocolaty Filsell Shiraz★ and rich Meshach Shiraz★★, Cameron Vale Cabernet★ and Shadrach

Cabernet★ (which includes some COONAWARRA fruit), RHONE-style Grenache-Shiraz-Mourvèdre blend Holy Trinity★, fresh Thorn Riesling★, oaky Zerk Semillon, and the excellent-value Barossa Vines range. Recent vintages have shown a welcome reduction in oak. Best years: (Meshach) (2006) (04) 02 01 99 **98 96 95 94 91 90**.

BURGENLAND *Austria* 4 regions: Neusiedlersee, including Seewinkel for sweet wines; Neusiedlersee-Hügelland, famous for sweet wines, now also big reds and fruity dry whites; Mittelburgenland, for robust Blaufränkisch reds; and Südburgenland, for good reds and dry whites. Best producers: FEILER-ARTINGER★★, Gernot Heinrich★★, Juris★, Kollwentz★★, KRACHER★★★, KRUTZLER★★, Helmut Lang★★, M & A Nittnaus★★, OPITZ★, Pöckl★★, Prieler★, Schröck★, Ernst Triebaumer★★, UMATHUM★★, VELICH★★, Robert Wenzel★.

BURGUNDY See BOURGOGNE AC and pages 88–91.

BÜRKLIN-WOLF *Wachenheim, Pfalz, Germany* With nearly 85ha (210 acres) of vineyards, this is one of Germany's largest privately owned estates. Since the mid-1990s it has been securely in the first rank of the PFALZ's producers. Biodynamic since 2005. The powerful, spicy dry Rieslings are now ★★ to ★★★. Best years: (Grosses Gewächs Rieslings) (2006) 05 04 **03** 02 **01** 98 97.

BURMESTER *Port DOC, Douro, Portugal* Shipper established in 1730, and now owned by the Galician firm Sogevinus, which also owns Cálem, Barros and Kopke. Vintage PORT★ is much improved, as is the Vintage released under the Quinta Nova de Nossa Senhora do Carmo★ label. As well as refined 10- and 20-year-old tawnies, there are some outstanding old colheitas★★ which extend back over 100 years. Also decent Late Bottled Vintage and oak-aged DOURO red, Casa Burmester. Gilbert is a range aimed at younger drinkers. Best years: (Vintage) 2003 00 97 **95 94**.

TOMMASO BUSSOLA *Valpolicella DOC, Veneto, Italy* Tommaso Bussola's AMARONE Vigneto Alto★★★ combines elegance with stunning power. Amarone Classico TB★★ is similar with slightly less finesse, and even the basic Amarone BG★ is a challenge to the palate. The Ripasso VALPOLICELLA Classico Superiore TB★★ is one of the best of its genre, and the RECIOTO TB★★★ is consistently excellent. Best years: (2006) (04) 03 **01** 00 99 97 95.

BUXY, CAVE DES VIGNERONS DE *Côte Chalonnaise, Burgundy, France* Now rechristened 'La Buxynoise', this ranks among Burgundy's top co-operatives, producing affordable, well-made Chardonnay and Pinot Noir. The light, oak-aged BOURGOGNE Pinot Noir★ and the red and white Clos de Chenôves★, as well as the nutty white MONTAGNY★, are all good, reasonably priced, and best with 2–3 years' age.

BUZET AC *South-West France* Good BORDEAUX-style red wines from the same mix of grapes, at a lower price. There is very little rosé and the whites are rarely exciting. Best producers: BUZET co-op, Dom. du Pech.

BUZET, VIGNERONS DE *Buzet AC, South-West France* Controlling 90% of the production of BUZET, the local co-op has raised standards in this AC. Some fine single-estate and branded reds, including Château de Padère, Château de Gueyze, Baron d'Ardeuil and the new wood-aged Grande Réserve. Best years: (Grande Réserve) (2005) 04 03 **01** 00.

CA' DEL BOSCO *Franciacorta DOCG, Lombardy, Italy* Model estate, headed by Maurizio Zanella, making some of Italy's finest and most expensive wines: outstanding sparklers in FRANCIACORTA Brut★★, Dosage

Zero★, Satén★★ and the prestige Cuvée Annamaria Clementi★★★. Still wines include good Terre di Franciacorta Rosso★, remarkably good Chardonnay★★★, Pinero★★ (Pinot Noir) and BORDEAUX blend, Maurizio Zanella★★★. Also promising varietal Carmenère, Carmenero★.

CABARDÈS AC *Languedoc, France* Next door to MINERVOIS. Cabernet Sauvignon and Merlot are allowed, as well as the usual French Mediterranean grape varieties. At best, full-bodied – chewy and rustically attractive – and attractively priced. Best producers: Cabrol★, Jouclary, Pennautier★, Salitis, Ventenac. Best years: 2005 04 03 **02 01**.

CABERNET D'ANJOU AC *Loire Valley, France* Rosé made from both Cabernets; generally medium dry or semi-sweet. Drink young. Best producers: Hautes-Ouches, Ogereau, Petites Grouas, Terrebrune.

CABERNET FRANC Often unfairly dismissed as an inferior Cabernet Sauvignon, Cabernet Franc comes into its own in cool zones or areas where the soil is damp and heavy. It can have a leafy freshness linked to raw but tasty blackcurrant-raspberry fruit. In France it thrives in the LOIRE VALLEY and BORDEAUX, especially ST-EMILION and POMEROL. Successful in northern Italy, especially ALTO ADIGE and FRIULI, although some plantings here have turned out to be Carmenère, and increasingly preferred to Cabernet Sauvignon in Tuscany. It is the red of choice for many winemakers in the eastern United States, performing especially well in the FINGER LAKES and VIRGINIA. Experiments with Cabernet Franc on CALIFORNIA's North Coast and in WASHINGTON STATE show promise. There are also some good South African, Chilean and Australian examples.

CABERNET SAUVIGNON See pages 96–7.

CADENCE *Red Mountain AVA, Washington State, USA* Cadence produces vineyard-specific reds. Tapteil Vineyard★★★, a powerful, Cabernet Sauvignon-dominated red, is the flagship until their own vineyard, adjacent to Tapteil, has mature fruit. Ciel du Cheval Vineyard★★★, with a higher percentage of Merlot and Cabernet Franc, is more forward and juicy. Klipsun Vineyard★★ shows the characteristic firm tannins of the site. Best years: (2005) 04 03 02 01 **00 99**.

CADILLAC AC *Bordeaux, France* Sweet wine from the southern half of the PREMIERES COTES DE BORDEAUX. Styles vary from fresh, semi-sweet to richly botrytized. The wines have greatly improved in recent vintages. Drink young. Best producers: Fayau (Cuvée Grains Nobles★), Ch. du Juge, Manos★, Mémoires★, REYNON★. Best years: 2005 **03 02 01 99 98**.

CAHORS AC *South-West France* Important South-West red wine region. This dark, traditionally tannic wine is made from at least 70% Auxerrois (Malbec) and has an unforgettable, rich plummy flavour when ripe and well made – which is less often than I'd wish. Ages well. Best producers: la Caminade★, Cayrou, CEDRE★, Clos la Coutale★, Clos de Gamot★, CLOS TRIGUEDINA★, Gaudou, Gautoul★, Haut-Monplaisir, Haute-Serre, LAGREZETTE★, Lamartine★, les Laquets★, la Reyne, les Rigalets★. Best years: 2003 01 **00 98 96 95 94**.

CAIRANNE *Rhône Valley, France* One of the best of the villages entitled to the COTES DU RHONE-VILLAGES appellation, offering full, herb-scented reds and solid whites. Best producers: D & D Alary★★, Ameillaud★, Brusset★, Cave de Cairanne★, Les Hautes Cances★, ORATOIRE ST-MARTIN★★, Rabasse-Charavin★, M Richaud★★. Best years: (reds) (2006) 05 **04 03 01 00 99 98 95**.

CABERNET SAUVIGNON

Wine made from Cabernet Sauvignon in places like Australia, California, Chile, Bulgaria, even in parts of southern France, has become so popular that many people may not realize where it all started – and how Cabernet became the great, omnipresent red wine grape of the world.

WINE STYLES

Bordeaux Cabernet It all began in Bordeaux. With the exception of a lively bunch of Merlot-based beauties in St-Émilion and Pomerol, the greatest red Bordeaux wines are based on Cabernet Sauvignon, with varying amounts of Merlot, Cabernet Franc and possibly Petit Verdot blended in. The blending is necessary because by itself Cabernet makes such a strong, powerful, aggressive and assertive wine. Dark and tannic when young, the great Bordeaux wines need 10–20 years for the aggression to fade, the fruit becoming sweet and perfumed as fresh blackcurrants, with a fragrance of cedarwood, of cigar boxes, mingling magically among the fruit. It is this character which has made red Bordeaux famous for at least 2 centuries.

Cabernet worldwide When winemakers in other parts of the world sought role models to try to improve their wines, most of them automatically thought of Bordeaux and chose Cabernet Sauvignon. It was lucky that they did, because not only is this variety easy to grow in almost all conditions – cool or warm, dry or damp – but that unstoppable personality always powers through. The cheaper wines are generally made to accentuate the black-currant fruit and the slightly earthy tannins. They are drinkable young, but able to age surprisingly well. The more ambitious wines are aged in oak barrels, often new ones, to enhance the tannin yet also to add spice and richness capable of developing over a decade or more. Sometimes the Cabernet is blended – usually with Merlot, sometimes with Cabernet Franc, and occasionally with other grapes: Shiraz in Australia, Sangiovese in Italy.

Europe Many vineyards in southern France now produce good, affordable Cabernet Sauvignon. Spain has produced some good Cabernet blends, as has Portugal. Italy's red wine quality revolution was sparked off by the success of Cabernet in Tuscany, and all the leading regions now grow it. Eastern Europe grows lots of Cabernet, but of widely varying quality, while the Eastern Mediterranean and North Africa are beginning to produce tasty examples. Germany has tried it but is returning to Pinot Noir. Austria has had more success but is also returning to Blaufränkisch and Zweigelt.

New World There is a general move towards darker, denser, more serious Cabernets, even in countries like Chile and Australia, whose Cabernet triumphs have until now been based on gorgeous blackcurrant fruit, and New Zealand (previously light and green) and South Africa (previously pinched and unfriendly). I hope they don't ditch too much of the fruit, but I have to say a lot of these new contenders are excellent. Argentina is also pitching in with some powerful stuff. California's reputation was created by its strong, weighty Cabernets; she's at a bit of a crossroads right now, with some producers going to superhuman lengths to concentrate and overripen their wines, while others show increasing restraint. I think I'm in the restraint camp for once.

BEST PRODUCERS

France

Bordeaux Dom. de CHEVALIER, COS D'ESTOURNEL, GRAND-PUY-LACOSTE, GRUAUD-LAROSE, LAFITE-ROTHSCHILD, LATOUR, LEOVILLE-BARTON, LEOVILLE-LAS-CASES, LYNCH-BAGES, Ch. MARGAUX, MOUTON-ROTHSCHILD, PICHON-LONGUEVILLE, RAUZAN-SEGLA; *Provence* TREVALLON.

Other European Cabernets

Italy BANFI, CA' DEL BOSCO, Col d'Orcia (Olmaia), GAJA, ISOLE E OLENA, LAGEDER, MACULAN, ORNELLAIA, RAMPOLLA, SAN LEONARDO, SASSICAIA, SOLAIA, TASCA D'ALMERITA, Castello del TERRICCIO (Lupicaia), TUA RITA.

Spain Blecua, MARQUES DE GRINON, TORRES.

New World Cabernets

Australia BALNAVES, CAPE MENTELLE, CULLEN, HOUGHTON (Jack Mann), HOWARD PARK, LEEUWIN (Art Series), MAJELLA, MOSS WOOD, PARKER ESTATE, PENFOLDS (Bin 707), PENLEY ESTATE, PETALUMA, SANDALFORD, WENDOUREE, The Willows, WIRRA WIRRA, Zema.

New Zealand BABICH, Esk Valley, GOLDWATER, Matariki, STONYRIDGE, TE MATA, Vidal, VILLA MARIA.

USA (California) ARAUJO, BERINGER, Bryant Family, CAYMUS, CHIMNEY ROCK, DALLA VALLE, DIAMOND CREEK, DOMINUS, DUNN, Grace Family, HARLAN, HARTWELL, LAUREL GLEN, Long Meadow Ranch, Peter MICHAEL, MINER, MONDAVI, NEWTON, PHELPS, RIDGE, St Supéry, SCREAMING EAGLE, SHAFER, SILVER OAK, SPOTTSWOODE, STAG'S LEAP, Viader; (Washington) ANDREW WILL, DELILLE, LEONETTI, QUILCEDA CREEK, WOODWARD CANYON.

Chile ALMAVIVA, CARMEN, CASABLANCA (Santa Isabel), CONCHA Y TORO, QUEBRADA DE MACUL, SANTA RITA, TORRES.

Argentina CATENA, TERRAZAS DE LOS ANDES.

South Africa BEYERSKLOOF, BOEKENHOUTSKLOOF, BUITEN-VERWACHTING, Neil ELLIS, GLEN CARLOU, KANONKOP, Le Riche, RUSTENBERG, SAXENBURG, THELEMA, VEENWOUDEN, VERGELEGEN.

CALABRIA *Italy* Italy's poorest, most backward and most corrupt region. CIRO, Donnici, Savuto and Scavigna DOC reds from the native Gaglioppo grape, and whites from Greco, are much improved thanks to greater winemaking expertise. In a very restricted field the two leading producers remain Librandi – who have recently added Magno Megonio★★, from the obscure Magliocco variety, to an already fine range – and Odoardi, with their excellent Scavigna Vigna Garrone.

CALERA *San Benito, California, USA* A pace-setter for California Pinot Noir with 5 estate wines: Reed★★, Selleck★★, Jensen★★, Mills★★ and newcomer Ryan★, which shows great potential. They are complex, fascinating wines with power and originality, and capable of aging. Mt Harlan Chardonnay★★ is excitingly original too. CENTRAL COAST Chardonnay★ and Pinot Noir★ are good value. Small amounts of Viognier★★ are succulent with sensuous fruit. Best years: (Pinot Noir) 2004 03 02 **01 00 99 97 96 95**; (Chardonnay) 2005 04 **03 02 01 00 99**.

CALIFORNIA *USA* California's importance is not simply in being the fourth largest wine producer in the world (behind France, Italy and Spain). Most of the revolutions in technology and style that have transformed the expectations and achievements of winemakers in every country of the world – including France – were born in the ambitions of a band of Californian winemakers during the 1960s and 70s. They challenged the old order, with its regulated, self-serving elitism, and democratized the world of fine wine, to the benefit of every wine drinker. This revolutionary fervour is less evident now. And there are times when Californians seem too intent on establishing their own particular New World old order. A few figures: there are around 211,400ha (522,000 acres) of wine grape vineyards, producing around 20 million hectolitres (500 million gallons) of wine annually, about 90% of all wine made in the USA. A large proportion comes from the hot, inland CENTRAL VALLEY. See also CENTRAL COAST, MENDOCINO COUNTY, MONTEREY COUNTY, NAPA VALLEY, SAN LUIS OBISPO COUNTY, SANTA BARBARA COUNTY, SONOMA COUNTY.

CH. CALON-SÉGUR★★ *St-Estèphe AC, 3ème Cru Classé, Haut-Médoc, Bordeaux, France* Long considered one of ST-ESTEPHE's leading châteaux, but in the mid-1980s the wines were not as good as they should have been. Recent vintages have been more impressive, with better fruit and a suppler texture. Second wine: Marquis de Calon. Best years: 2005 04 03 02 **01 00 98 96 95 90 89 86 82**.

CAMEL VALLEY *Cornwall, England* The enterprising Bob Lindo is a sparkling wine specialist who favours Seyval Blanc and Reichensteiner over classic CHAMPAGNE varieties; the result is the quintessentially English Camel Valley Brut★★. Still wines (dry white Bacchus★, Rosé★) are good, too.

CAMPANIA *Italy* Three regions – PUGLIA, SICILY and Campania – lead the revolution in Italy's south. Campania has made excellent progress in the white department, with varietals from Greco di Tufo, Fiano, Falanghina and several other native grapes. On the red side, other producers besides the venerable MASTROBERARDINO have begun to realize the potential of Campania's soil, climate and grapes, especially with the red Aglianico. DOC(G)s of note are FALERNO DEL MASSICO, Fiano di Avellino, Greco di Tufo, Ischia, TAURASI and Vesuvio. The leading red wines are Montevetrano★★★

(Cabernet-Merlot-Aglianico) and Galardi's Terra di Lavoro★★★ (Aglianico-Piedirosso), but also look for top Aglianicos from Antonio Caggiano★★, De Conciliis★, Feudi di San Gregorio★★, Luigi Maffini★, Michele Moio, Salvatore Molettieri, Orazio Rillo★, Cantina del Taburno★, San Paolo and others that fall outside the main DOCs.

CAMPILLO *Rioja DOCa, País Vasco, Spain* An up-market subsidiary of Bodegas FAUSTINO, producing some exciting new red RIOJAS★. The wines are often Tempranillo-Cabernet Sauvignon blends, with masses of ripe, velvety fruit. Best years: (Reserva) 2003 **01 99 98 96 95 94**.

CAMPO DI SASSO *Tuscany, Italy* Brothers Piero and Lodovico ANTINORI's new venture in the commune of Bibbona, near BOLGHERI. Initial plantings include Cabernet Franc as well as Petit Verdot and Merlot. The first wine to emerge was the 2003 Insoglio del Cinghiale; Il Pino di Biserno came on stream in 2006; the top cru, Il Biserno, will follow.

CAMPO VIEJO *Rioja DOCa, Rioja, Spain* The largest producer of RIOJA is owned by Pernod Ricard. Reservas★ and Gran Reservas★ are reliably good, as are the elegant, all-Tempranillo Reserva Viña Alcorta and the barrel-fermented white Viña Alcorta. Albor Tempranillo is a good modern young Rioja, packed with fresh, pastilley fruit. Best years: (Reserva) 2003 **01 98 96 95 94**.

CANARY ISLANDS *Spain* The Canaries have a treasure trove of pre-phylloxera vines, and a total of 9 DOs. The sweet Malvasia from Lanzarote DO and La Palma DO is worth a try, and there are a couple of remarkable fresh dry whites, otherwise stick with the young reds. Best producers: El Grifo, Monje, Viña Norte, Tanajara, Teneguía, Viñátigo.

CANBERRA DISTRICT *New South Wales, Australia* Cool, high altitude (800m/2600ft) may sound good, but excessive cold and frost can be problematic. Lark Hill and Helm make exciting Riesling, Lark Hill and Brindabella Hills some smart Cabernet blends, and Clonakilla increasingly sublime Shiraz. HARDY has poured money in here (Kamberra★). Best producers: Brindabella Hills★, CLONAKILLA★★, Doonkuna★, Helm★, Lake George★, Lark Hill★, Madew★.

DOM. CANET-VALETTE *St-Chinian AC, Languedoc, France* Marc Valette is uncompromising in his quest to make great wine: organic cultivation, low yields, gravity-fed grapes and traditional *pigeage* (foot-stomping) are just some of his methods. The wines offer an enticingly rich expression of ST-CHINIAN's French Mediterranean grape varieties and clay-limestone soils. Cuvées include Une et Mille Nuits (1001 Nights)★ and the powerful, complex Syrah-Grenache Le Vin Maghani★★. Best years: (Le Vin Maghani) (2004) 03 01 **00 99 98**.

CANNONAU Sardinian name of Spain's Garnacha and France's Grenache Noir. In SARDINIA it produces deep, tannic reds, but lighter, modern, dry red wines are gaining in popularity, although traditional sweet and fortified styles can still be found. Best producers: (modern reds) ARGIOLAS, SELLA & MOSCA; Dolianova, Dorgali, Jerzu, Alberto Loi, Ogliastra, Oliena, Santa Maria La Palma and Trexenta co-ops.

CH. CANON★ *St-Émilion Grand Cru AC, 1er Grand Cru Classé, Bordeaux, France* Canon can make some of the richest, most concentrated ST-EMILIONS, but it went into steep decline before being purchased in

1996 by Chanel. Signs are that things have returned to form. Part of the 3.9ha (9.7-acre) vineyard of Grand Cru Classé Ch. Curé-Bon has recently been added to the estate. In good vintages the wine is tannic and rich at first but is worth aging 10–15 years. Second wine: Clos Canon. Best years: 2005 04 **03 02 01 00 98 89 88 85**.

CANON-FRONSAC AC *Bordeaux, France*   This AC is the heart of the ♦ FRONSAC region. The wines are quite sturdy when young but can age for 10 years or more. Best producers: Barrabaque (Prestige★), Canon de Brem★, Cassagne Haut-Canon★, la Fleur Cailleau, Gaby, Grand-Renouil★, Haut-Mazeris, Moulin Pey-Labrie★, Pavillon, Vrai Canon Bouché. Best years: 2005 **03 01 00 98 97 96 95 94 90**.

CH. CANON-LA-GAFFELIÈRE★★ *St-Émilion Grand Cru AC, Grand Cru* ♦ *Classé, Bordeaux, France*   Owner Stephan von Neipperg has placed this property, located at the foot of the town of ST-EMILION, at the top of the list of Grands Crus Classés. The wines are firm, rich and concentrated. Under the same ownership are Clos de l'Oratoire★, Ch. l'Aiguilhe★★ in the COTES DE CASTILLON, and the remarkable *micro-cuvée* La Mondotte★★. Best years: 2005 04 **03 02 01 00 99 98 97 96 95**.

CH. CANTEMERLE★ *Haut-Médoc AC, 5ème Cru Classé, Bordeaux, France* ♦ With La LAGUNE, the most southerly of the Crus Classés. The wines are delicate in style and delightful in ripe vintages. Second wine: Les Allées de Cantemerle. Best years: 2005 04 **03 01 00 98 96 95**.

CANTERBURY *South Island, New Zealand*   The long, cool ripening season of the arid central coast of South Island favours white varieties, particularly Chardonnay, Pinot Gris, Sauvignon Blanc and Riesling, as well as Pinot Noir. The northerly Waipara district produces Canterbury's most exciting wines, especially from Riesling and Pinot Noir. Best producers: Mountford★, PEGASUS BAY★★, Daniel Schuster★, Waipara West★. Best years: (Pinot Noir) (2006) **03 02 01 00 99**; (Riesling) 2006 **04 02 01 00**.

CAPE MENTELLE *Margaret River, Western Australia*   Leading MARGARET ♦ RIVER winery, owned by LVMH. Over the past 2 years, there's been an exodus of key staff, but chief winemaker Rob Mann has good credentials, so there's no reason why Cape Mentelle can't continue to produce superb, cedary Cabernet★★, impressive Shiraz★★ and Chardonnay★★, tangy Semillon-Sauvignon Blanc★★ and wonderfully chewy Zinfandel★★. New Wallcliffe wines are impressive, especially densely concentrated Shiraz★. All wines benefit from cellaring – whites up to 5 years, reds 8–15. Best years: (Cabernet Sauvignon) (2005) (04) 03 02 01 **98 96 95 94 92 91 90**.

CAPE POINT VINEYARDS *Cape Point WO, South Africa*   Pioneering Cape ♦ Peninsula property influenced by bracing Atlantic breezes. Whites respond with vigour and purity. Sauvignon Blanc★★ is astonishing, ocean-fresh, new and original – yet another feather in the cap of new-wave Cape Sauvignon. Partially barrel-fermented Semillon★★ tantalizes with tangerine and lemongrass intensity, while Isliedh★★, a barrel-fermented blend of both varieties, combines power with subtlety. Early reds, from a warmer site, also show promise.

CAPEL VALE *Geographe, Western Australia*   Dr Peter Pratten's winery ♦ sources fruit from its own vineyards in Geographe, Mount Barker, PEMBERTON and MARGARET RIVER. Many of its CV and White Label wines represent good value, especially Sauvignon Blanc-Semillon★ and Riesling★. The top Black Label range has lacked consistency, except for the classy Whispering Hill Riesling★★. Best years: (Whispering Hill Riesling) 2005 04 03 **02 01 00 98 97**.

CARIGNAN The dominant red grape in the south of France is responsible for much boring, cheap, harsh wine. But when made by carbonic maceration, the wine can have delicious spicy fruit. Old vines are capable of dense, rich, impressive reds, as shown by the odd success in France, California, Chile and South Africa. Although initially a Spanish grape (as Cariñena or Mazuelo), it is not that widespread there, but is useful for adding colour and acidity in RIOJA and CATALUNA, and has gained unexpected respect in PRIORAT.

CARIGNANO DEL SULCIS DOC *Sardinia, Italy* Carignano is now producing wines of quite startling quality. Rocca Rubia★, a barrique-aged Riserva from the co-op at Santadi, with rich, fleshy and chocolaty fruit, is one of SARDINIA's best reds. In a similar vein, but a step up, is Baie Rosse★★; even better is the more structured and concentrated Terre Brune★★. Best producer: Santadi co-op. Best years: (reds) (2006) (05) 04 **03 01 00 99 98 97**.

LOUIS CARILLON & FILS *Puligny-Montrachet, Côte de Beaune, Burgundy, France* Excellent family-owned estate in PULIGNY-MONTRACHET. The emphasis is on traditional, finely balanced whites of great concentration, rather than new oak. Look out for Premiers Crus les Referts★★, Champs Canet★★ and les Perrières★★★, and the tiny but exquisite

production of Bienvenues-BATARD-MONTRACHET★★★. Reds from CHASSAGNE-MONTRACHET★, ST-AUBIN★ and MERCUREY★ are good, too. Best years: (whites) (2006) 05 **04 03 02 01 00 99 97**.

CARIÑENA DO *Aragón, Spain* The largest DO of ARAGON, baking under the mercilessly hot sun in inland eastern Spain, Cariñena has traditionally been a land of cheap, deep red, alcoholic wines from the Garnacha grape. (Confusingly the Carignan grape is called Cariñena in Spain.) Since the late 1990s, however, temperature-controlled fermentation has been working wonders with this unfairly despised grape, and Tempranillo and international grape varieties like Cabernet Sauvignon are being planted widely. Best producers: Añadas, San Valero (Monte Ducay, Don Mendo), Solar de Urbezo.

CARLEI *Victoria, Australia* Outstanding biodynamic producer, with Chardonnay★★ and Pinot Noir★ from YARRA VALLEY and Shiraz★★ from HEATHCOTE. Sergio Carlei's signature blends are Tre Rossi★ (Shiraz-Barbera-Nebbiolo), Tre Amici (Sangiovese-Cabernet-Merlot) and Tre Bianchi (Sauvignon with small amounts of Semillon and Chardonnay). The modestly priced Green Vineyards range offers very good regional varietals: Chardonnay and Pinot Noir from the Yarra, Heathcote Shiraz, Central Victorian Cabernet and Cardinia Ranges Pinot Gris.

CARMEN *Maipo, Chile* This winery has some of the best reds in MAIPO, including Gold Reserve★★, a limited release made with Carmen's oldest Cabernet Sauvignon vines, Reserve Carmenère-Cabernet★★, balanced, complex Wine Maker's Reserve★★ and organic Nativa Cabernet Sauvignon★★ (sometimes ★★★) from a project started by Alvaro Espinoza (now at EMILIANA). Best years (reds): (2005) 04 03 **02 01 00 99**.

CARMENÈRE An important but forgotten constituent of BORDEAUX blends in the 19th century, historically known as Grande Vidure. Planted in Chile, it was generally labelled as Merlot until 1996. When ripe and made with care, it has rich blackberry, plum and spice flavours, with an unexpected but delicious bunch of savoury characters – grilled meat, soy sauce, celery, coffee – thrown in. A true original. Also found in northern Italy, Argentina and China. Being replanted in Bordeaux.

CARMIGNANO DOCG *Tuscany, Italy* Red wine from the west of Florence, renowned since the 16th century and revived in the 1970s by Capezzana. The blend (Sangiovese, plus 10–20% Cabernet) is one of Tuscany's more refined wines and can be quite long-lived. Although Carmignano is DOCG for its red wine, DOC applies to a lighter red Barco Reale, a rosé called Vin Ruspo and fine VIN SANTO. Best producers: Ambra★ (Vigne Alte★★), Artimino★, Capezzana★★, Le Farnete/E Pierazzuoli★ (Riserva★★), Piaggia★★, Pratesi★, Villa di Trefiano★. Best years: (2006) 04 **03 02 01 00 99 98 97 95 90 88 85.**

QUINTA DO CARMO *Alentejo, Portugal* Well-established estate. The red★ used to be complex and ageworthy, but in the 1990s quality slumped badly. However, following improvements in both vineyard and winery, wines since the 2000 vintage – especially the Reserva – should restore the Quinta's reputation. Best years: (2004) 03 02 01 **00.**

CARNEROS AVA *California, USA* Hugging the northern edge of San Francisco Bay, Carneros includes parts of both NAPA and SONOMA Counties. Windswept and chilly with morning fog off the Bay, it is a top cool-climate area, suitable for Chardonnay and Pinot Noir as both table wine and a base for sparkling wine. Merlot and even Syrah are also coming on well, but too much vineyard expansion is beginning to worry me. Best producers: ACACIA★★, Buena Vista★, Carneros Creek★, DOMAINE CARNEROS★★, HdV★, Ramey★★, RASMUSSEN★★, SAINTSBURY★★, Truchard★★. Best years: (Pinot Noir) 2004 03 02 **01 99 98.**

CARNUNTUM *Niederösterreich, Austria* 890ha (2200-acre) wine region south of the Danube and east of Vienna, with a strong red wine tradition★. Best producers: Glatzer, G Markowitsch★, Muhr-van der Niepoort★, Pitnauer★.

CASA LAPOSTOLLE *Rapel, Chile* Owned by Marnier-Lapostolle of France, with consultancy from leading BORDEAUX winemaker Michel Rolland. Cuvée Alexandre Merlot★★, from the acclaimed Apalta area in COLCHAGUA, was its first hit back in 1994, now eclipsed by red blend Clos Apalta★★★. Also rich, creamy Cuvée Alexandre Chardonnay★ from the CASABLANCA Valley and Borobo★, a peculiar blend of Pinot Noir, Carmenère, Cabernet Sauvignon, Syrah and Merlot.

CASA MARÍN *San Antonio, Chile* Impressive whites, led by single-vineyard Sauvignon Blancs: Laurel★★ is a powerful wine, full of mineral and intense chilli and fruit flavours, while Cipreses★★★ shows the influence of the Pacific Ocean in its citrus and stony aromas. Casona Vineyard Gewürztraminer★ and Estero Sauvignon Gris★ are good, too – and there's juicy, cool-climate Pinot Noir★.

CASABLANCA, VALLE DE *Aconcagua, Chile* Coastal valley with a cool-climate personality that is powerful proof of Chile's ability to do regional style. Whites dominate, with best results from Chardonnay, Sauvignon Blanc and Gewürztraminer. Even so, the Pinot Noir is some of Chile's best, and Merlot and Carmenère are very good. Best producers: (whites) Casas del Bosque★★, CASA LAPOSTOLLE★,

CASABLANCA★, CONCHA Y TORO★★, EMILIANA★, ERRAZURIZ★, MONTES, Morandé★, Veramonte★. Best years: (whites) 2004 03 02 01.

CASABLANCA, VIÑA *Casablanca, Chile* The cool Santa Isabel Estate in CASABLANCA is the source of top wines such as quince-edged Chardonnay★, minty, exotic Merlot★★ and Cabernet Sauvignon★★. White Label wines use vineyards in Lontué and MAIPO: there is rose- and lychee-filled Gewürztraminer★, excellent tangy, intense Sauvignon Blanc★, inky-black Cabernet Sauvignon★ and low-yield Merlot★. Flagship red blend Neblus★ is made only in the best years.

CASE BASSE *Brunello di Montalcino DOCG, Tuscany, Italy* Gianfranco Soldera unblushingly proclaims his BRUNELLO DI MONTALCINO★★★ and Brunello di Montalcino Riserva★★★ wines (the latter usually under the Intistieti label) to be the best of their genre and, maddeningly, he's right. A fanatical bio-dynamist, Soldera believes perfect grapes are all you need to make great wine. He ages his wines for a minimum of 5 years in large old (and hence neutral) oak barrels; the result is a wine of brilliant colour and an amazing intensity and complexity of perfumes. Best years: (2006) (04) (03) (01) 99 98 97 95 93 90 88 85.

CH. LA CASENOVE *Côtes du Roussillon AC, Roussillon, France* Former photojournalist Étienne Montès, with the help of consultant enologist Jean-Luc COLOMBO, has developed an impressive range, including a perfumed white Vin de Pays Catalan made from Macabeu and Torbat, MUSCAT DE RIVESALTES★, RIVESALTES★ and 2 predominantly Syrah reds: Dom. Saint-Luc Pla del Rei★★ and Commandant François Jaubert★★. Drink this with at least 5 years' bottle age. Best years: (Commandant François Jaubert) 2004 00.

CASSIS AC *Provence, France* A picturesque fishing port near Marseille. The white wine, based on Ugni Blanc and Clairette, is overpriced but can be good if fresh. The red wine is dull, but the rosé can be pleasant (especially from a single estate). Best producers: Bagnol★, Caillol, Clos Ste-Magdelaine★, la Ferme Blanche★, Fontblanche, Mas de Boudard, Ch. de Fontcreuse. Best years: (white) 2005 04 02 01 00 99.

CASTEL DEL MONTE DOC *Puglia, Italy* An arid, hilly zone, and an ideal habitat for the Uva di Troia grape, producing long-lived red wine of astonishing character. There is also varietal Aglianico, some good rosé, and the whites produced from international varieties are improving. Best producers: RIVERA★, Santa Lucia, Tormaresca/ANTINORI, Torrevento★. Best years: (2006) (05) 04 03 01 00 98 97.

CASTELLARE *Chianti Classico DOCG, Tuscany, Italy* Fine estate with excellent CHIANTI CLASSICO★ and deeper, richer Riserva★★. Canonico di Castellare★ (Chardonnay), Coniale di Castellare★★ (Cabernet Sauvignon) and Spartito di Castellare★ (Sauvignon Blanc) are all ripe and fruity. Top wine I Sodi di San Niccolò★★ is an unusual Sangiovese-Malvasia blend, intense but finely perfumed.

CASTILLA-LA MANCHA *Spain* The biggest wine region in the world; hot, dry country with poor clay-chalk soil. The DOs of the central plateau, La MANCHA and VALDEPEÑAS, make white wines from the Airén grape, and some good reds from the Cencibel (Tempranillo). Méntrida DO, Manchuela DO, Ribera del Júcar DO and Almansa DO make fast-improving reds. The most ambitious wines made here are those from MARQUES DE GRIÑON's Dominio de Valdepusa★★ estate and the Dehesa del Carrizal★ estate, both in the Toledo mountains. Uribes Madero's Calzadilla★ in Cuenca province, Finca Sandoval★ from Manchuela and Manuel Manzaneque's Cabernet-based reds★ and Chardonnay from Sierra de Alcaraz in Albacete province are full of promise. Manzaneque now has his own DO, Finca Élez, as do the Dominio de Valdepusa and Dehesa del Carrizal.

CASTILLA Y LEÓN *Spain* This is Spain's harsh, high plateau, with long cold winters and hot summers (but always cool nights). A few rivers, notably the Duero, temper this climate and afford fine conditions for viticulture. After many decades of winemaking ignorance, with a few exceptions like VEGA SICILIA, the situation has changed radically for the better in all of the region's DOs: RIBERA DEL DUERO, RUEDA, BIERZO, Cigales and TORO. Dynamic winemakers such as Telmo RODRIGUEZ and Mariano García of AALTO and MAURO have won huge critical acclaim for the region.

CATALUÑA *Spain* Standards vary among the region's DOs. PENEDES, between Barcelona and Tarragona, has the greatest number of technically equipped wineries in Spain, but doesn't make a commensurate number of superior wines. In the south, mountainous, isolated PRIORAT has become a new icon for its heady, raging reds, and the neighbouring DOs of Montsant and Terra Alta are following in its footsteps. Inland COSTERS DEL SEGRE and Conca de Barberá make potentially excellent reds and whites. Up the coast, Alella makes attractive whites and Ampurdán-Costa Brava (Empordá-Costa Brava), by the French border, is showing signs of life. Cataluña also makes most of Spain's CAVA sparkling wines. The Catalunya DO allows (generally) inexpensive blends from anywhere in the region.

CATENA ZAPATA *Mendoza, Argentina* Argentinian pioneer Nicolás Catena's admiration for California is evident in the ripe, gentle, oaky Alamos and Argento ranges. However, Catena has vines in some of the best terroirs in MENDOZA and the wines in the Alta range – Chardonnay★, Cabernet Sauvignon★★ and Malbec★★ – are developing a recognizable sense of place. Cabernet-based Nicolás Catena Zapata★★ from the Agrelo district is top-flight. Viñas, a collection of single-vineyard Malbecs from the Upper Mendoza River region, is the latest range from this winery. Caro, a joint venture with LAFITE-ROTHSCHILD, successfully combines French restraint with Argentinian panache.

SYLVAIN CATHIARD *Vosne-Romanée, Côte de Nuits, Burgundy, France* Sylvain Cathiard first achieved international recognition in the late 1990s and has made brilliant wines even in difficult vintages since then. The stars are VOSNE-ROMANÉE Les Malconsorts★★★ and ROMANÉE ST-VIVANT★★★ but his village Vosne-Romanée★★ and NUITS-ST-GEORGES Aux Murgers★★ are excellent too. Best years: (2006) 05 04 03 **02 01 00 99**.

DOM. CAUHAPÉ *Jurançon AC, South-West France* Henri Ramonteu has been a major influence in JURANÇON, proving that the area can make complex dry whites as well as more traditional sweet wines. Chant des Vignes★ is a dry, unoaked Jurançon Sec; the oaked version is Sève d'Automne★. Top wines are sweet Noblesse du Temps★★ and barrel-fermented Quintessence★★★. Best years: (sweet wines) (2004) 01 **99**.

CAVA DO *Spain* Cava, the Catalan name for CHAMPAGNE-method fizz, is made in 159 towns and villages throughout Spain, but more than 95% are in CATALUÑA. Grapes used are the local trio of Parellada, Macabeo and

Xarel-lo, although some good Catalan Cavas are made with Chardonnay and Pinot Noir. The best-value, fruitiest Cavas are generally the youngest, with no more than the minimum 9 months' aging. A number of top-quality wines are now produced but are seldom seen abroad, since their prices are too close to those of Champagne to attract international customers. Best producers: Can Feixes, Can Ràfols dels Caus★, Castellblanch, Castell de Vilarnau, CODORNIU★, Colet★, FREIXENET, JUVE Y CAMPS★, Marques de Monistrol, Parxet, RAIMAT, Raventós i Blanc, Rovellats, Agustí Torelló★, Jané Ventura.

CAYMUS VINEYARDS *Napa Valley AVA, California, USA* Caymus Cabernet Sauvignon★ is ripe, intense and generally tannic; it can be outstanding as a Special Selection★★★. Conundrum★ is an exotic, full-flavoured blended white. Also successful MONTEREY Chardonnay under the Mer Soleil★★ label. Best years: (Special Selection) 2004 03 02 **01 00 99 98 97 95 94 91 90 87 86 84**.

CAYUSE VINEYARDS *Walla Walla Valley AVA, Washington State, USA* Winemaker Christophe Baron has created a cult label here. His superb Viognier★★★ is crisp, floral and spicy, yet he is best known for his Syrahs. Using French clones, he farms a vineyard reminiscent of some in CHATEAUNEUF-DU-PAPE for its large stones, called Cobblestone Vineyard. Each parcel of the vineyard has a designation. Syrah Cailloux★★ has a distinctive mineral flavour and chocolate depth. Syrah En Cerise★★ shows more cherry and raspberry flavour but equal richness. The Syrah Bionic Frog★★ sports a cartoon-ish label but is a serious Syrah, reminding me of a northern RHONE version. Cabernet-based Camaspelo is a fascinating redcurrant and jalapeño-scented wine. Best years: (Syrah) (2005) 04 03 02 **01 00**.

DOM. CAZES *Rivesaltes, Roussillon, France* The Cazes brothers make outstanding MUSCAT DE RIVESALTES★★, RIVESALTES Vieux★★ and the superb Aimé Cazes★★, but also produce a range of table wines. Soft red and white Le Canon du Maréchal★ are both good, as are the Syrah-Grenache-Mourvèdre blend Alter★, the Cabernet-based Vin de Pays des Côtes Catalanes Le Credo★, COTES DU ROUSSILLON-VILLAGES Trilogy★ and the small production of barrel-fermented Chardonnay.

CH. DU CÈDRE *Cahors AC, South-West France* Pascal Verhaeghe leads the new generation of CAHORS winemakers. His wines are dark, richly textured, with a generous coating of chocolaty oak. There are 3 cuvées: Le Prestige★; the 100% Auxerrois (Malbec) Le Cèdre★★, which is aged in new oak barrels for 20 months; and Cuvée GC★, which is fermented and aged in oak. All benefit from at least 5–6 years' bottle age. Best years: (Le Cèdre) 2003 01 00 **99 98**.

CELLIER LE BRUN *Marlborough, South Island, New Zealand* CHAMPAGNE-method specialist, with vintage Blanc de Blancs★, and tasty blended vintage and non-vintage bubblies. Quality has languished in recent years but should get a boost from new owner Brian Bicknell, ex-SERESIN. New release 1998 Blanc de Blancs is delicious. Best years: (Blanc de Blancs) **1998 97 96 95 92 91**.

CENCIBEL See TEMPRANILLO.

CENTRAL COAST AVA *California, USA* Huge AVA covering virtually every vineyard between San Francisco and Los Angeles, with a number of sub-AVAs, such as SANTA CRUZ MOUNTAINS, Santa Ynez Valley, SANTA MARIA VALLEY and Monterey. There is superb potential for Pinot Noir and Syrah in Santa Lucia Highlands in the western Monterey area. See also MONTEREY COUNTY, SAN LUIS OBISPO COUNTY, SANTA BARBARA COUNTY.

CENTRAL OTAGO *South Island, New Zealand* The only wine region in New Zealand with a continental rather than maritime climate. Technically the ripening season is long and cool, suiting Pinot Noir, Gewürztraminer, Chardonnay and Pinot Gris, but there are usually periods of considerable heat during the summer to intensify flavour. Long autumns have produced some excellent Rieslings. There are already over 50 wineries and an explosion of plantings, both in good areas like Bannockburn and Lowburn, and in marginal zones. Later expansion is to the Waitaki Valley in northern Otago. Best producers: Akarua★, Black Ridge★, Carrick★★, Chard Farm★, FELTON ROAD★★, Gibbston Valley★, Kawarau Estate★, Mt Difficulty★★, Mount Edward★, Mount Maude, Nevis Bluff★, Peregrine★★, Pisa Range★, Quartz Reef★★, Rippon★★, Two Paddocks★, Wild Earth★. Best years: (Pinot Noir) 2006 05 **03 02 01 99**.

CENTRAL VALLEY/VALLE CENTRAL *Chile* The heart of Chile's wine industry, encompassing the valleys of MAIPO, RAPEL, CURICO and MAULE. Most major producers are located here, and the key factor determining mesoclimate differences is the distance relative to the Coastal Ranges and the Andean Cordillera.

CENTRAL VALLEY *California, USA* This vast area grows 75% of California's wine grapes, used mostly for cheaper styles of wine, along with brandies and grape concentrate. It is a hot area, where irrigated vineyards tend to produce excess tonnages of grapes. It has often been said that it is virtually impossible to produce exciting wine in the Central Valley, but in fact the climatic conditions in the northern half are not unlike those in many parts of Spain and southern France and, viewed overall, the quality has improved over the past few years. Vineyards in the Lodi AVA have expanded to 40,500ha (nearly 100,000 acres), making Lodi the volume and quality leader for Chardonnay, Merlot, Zinfandel and Cabernet. Lodi Zinfandel shows most potential. Other sub-regions with claims to quality are the Sacramento Valley and the Delta area. Best producers: Ironstone★, McManis★, Michael-David★, RAVENSWOOD (Lodi★), Woodbridge/MONDAVI.

CENTRAL VICTORIA *Victoria, Australia* The Central Victoria zone comprises the regions of BENDIGO, HEATHCOTE, Goulburn Valley and the cooler Strathbogie Ranges and Upper Goulburn. Central Victoria, with its mostly warm conditions, produces powerful and individual wines. The few wineries on the banks of the Goulburn River produce fine red Shiraz and white Marsanne, while reds from the high country are rich but scented and dry; whites are delicate and scented. Best producers: Jasper Hill★★, Mitchelton★, Paul Osicka★, PONDALOWIE★, TAHBILK★, Wild Duck Creek★.

CERETTO *Piedmont, Italy* This merchant house was one of the chief modern producers in BAROLO in the 1970s and 80s. Today, Barolo (Bricco Rocche★★, Brunate★★ and Prapò★★), BARBARESCO (Bricco Asili★★), BARBERA D'ALBA Piana★ and white Arneis Blangè, while still good, are being overtaken by smaller, more specialist, growers. Ceretto also produces an oak-aged LANGHE red, Monsordo★★, from Cabernet, Merlot, Pinot Nero and Nebbiolo. An unusual white counterpart, Arbarei, is 100% Riesling. A good sparkler, La Bernardina, is made from Chardonnay and Pinot Noir.

CÉRONS AC *Bordeaux, France* An AC for sweet, soft, mildly honeyed wine in the GRAVES region of Bordeaux. The wine is not quite as sweet as SAUTERNES and not so well known, nor so highly priced. Most producers now make dry wine under the Graves label. Best producers: Ch. de Cérons★, Chantegrive★, Grand Enclos du Château de Cérons★, Haura, Seuil. Best years: 2005 **03 02 01 99 98 97 96 95 90 89**.

L A CETTO *Baja California, Mexico* Mexico's most successful winery relies on mists and cooling Pacific breezes to temper the heat of the Valle de Guadalupe. Italian Camilo Magoni makes ripe, fleshy Petite Sirah★, oak-aged Cabernet Sauvignon, Zinfandel and Nebbiolo. Whites, led by Chardonnay and Chenin, are greatly improved. Also good fizz.

CHABLAIS *Vaud, Switzerland* A sub-region of the VAUD. Most of the vineyards lie on the alluvial plains but 2 villages, Yvorne and Aigle, benefit from much steeper slopes. Most of the thirst-quenchingly dry whites are made from Chasselas. The reds are from Pinot Noir, as is a rosé speciality, Oeil de Perdrix. Drink whites and rosés young. Best producers: Henri Badoux, Conne, J & P Testuz★.

CHABLIS AC *Burgundy, France* Chablis, closer to CHAMPAGNE than to the COTE D'OR, is Burgundy's northernmost outpost. When not destroyed by frost or hail, the Chardonnay grape makes a crisp, dry white wine with a steely mineral fruit which can be delicious. Several producers have taken to barrel-aging for their better wines, resulting in some full, toasty, positively rich dry whites. Others are intentionally producing a soft, creamy, early-drinking style, which is nice but not really Chablis. Outlying areas come under the Petit Chablis AC and should be drunk young. The better straight Chablis AC should be drunk at 2–4 years, while a good vintage of a leading Chablis Premier Cru may take 5 years to show its full potential. About a quarter of Chablis is designated as Premier Cru, the best vineyards on the rolling limestone slopes being Fourchaume, Mont de Milieu, Montmains, Montée de Tonnerre and Vaillons. Best producers: Barat★, J-C Bessin (Fourchaume★★), Billaud-Simon (Mont de Milieu★★), Pascal Bouchard★, A & F Boudin★★, BROCARD★★, la CHABLISIENNE★, Collet★, D Dampt★, R & V DAUVISSAT★★, D-E Defaix★, Droin★, DROUHIN★, Duplessis, DURUP★ (Montée de Tonnerre★★), W Fèvre★★, J-P Grossot (Côte de Troesme★★), LAROCHE★★, Long-Depaquit, Malandes (Côte de Léchêt★★), Louis Michel★★, Picq (Vaucoupin★★), Pinson★, RAVENEAU★★, Vocoret★★. Best years: (Chablis Premier Cru) (2006) 05 **04 02 00 99 98 96**.

CHABLIS GRAND CRU AC *Burgundy, France* The 7 Grands Crus (Bougros, les Preuses, Vaudésir, Grenouilles, Valmur, les Clos and les Blanchots) facing south-west across the town of Chablis are the heart of the AC. Oak barrel-aging takes the edge off taut flavours, adding a rich warmth to these fine wines. Droin and Fèvre are the most enthusiastic users of new oak, but use it less than they used to. Never drink young: 5–10 years are needed before you can see why you spent your money. Best producers: J-C Bessin★★, Billaud-Simon★★, BROCARD★★, la CHABLISIENNE★★, J Dauvissat★, R & V DAUVISSAT★★★, D-E Defaix★★, Droin★★, W Fèvre★★★, LAROCHE★★, Long-Depaquit★★, L Michel★★★, Christian Moreau★, Pinson★★, RAVENEAU★★★, Servin★, Vocoret★★. Best years: (2006) 05 04 03 02 00 **99 98 97 96 95 92 90**.

LA CHABLISIENNE *Chablis AC, Burgundy, France* Substantial co-op producing nearly a third of all CHABLIS. The wines are reliable and can aspire to something much better. The best are the oaky Grands Crus – especially les Preuses★★ and Grenouilles (sold as Ch. Grenouille★★) – but the basic unoaked Chablis★, the Vieilles Vignes★ and the numerous Premiers Crus★ are good, as is the red BOURGOGNE Épineuil. Best years: (whites) (2006) 05 **04 03 02 00 99**.

CHAMPAGNE AC

Champagne, France

The Champagne region produces the most celebrated sparkling wines in the world. It is the most northerly AC in France – a place where grapes struggle to ripen fully, but provide the perfect base wine to make fizz.

Champagne is divided into 5 distinct areas – the best are the Montagne de Reims, where the Pinot Noir grape performs brilliantly, and the Chardonnay-dominated Côte des Blancs south of Épernay. In addition to Chardonnay and Pinot Noir, the other main grape permitted for the production of Champagne is Pinot Meunier.

The wines undergo a second fermentation in the bottle, producing carbon dioxide which dissolves in the wine under pressure. Through this method Champagne acquires its crisp, long-lasting bubbles and a distinctive yeasty, toasty dimension to its flavour. If you buy a bottle of Coteaux Champenois, a still wine from the area, you can see why they decided to make bubbly instead; it usually tastes mean and tart, but is transformed by the Champagne method into one of the most delightfully exhilarating wines of all.

That's the theory anyway, and for 150 years or so the Champenois have persuaded us that their product is second to none. It can be, too, except when it is released too young or sweetened to make up for a lack of richness. When that periodically happens you know that, once again, the powers of marketing have triumphed over the wisdom and skills of the winemaker. But as Champagne expertise begins to turn out exciting sparklers in California, Australia and New Zealand, the Champagne producers must re-focus on quality or lose much of their market for good.

The Champagne trade is dominated by large companies or houses, called négociants-manipulants, recognized by the letters NM on the label. The récoltants-manipulants (RM) are growers who make their own wine, and they are becoming increasingly important for drinkers seeking characterful Champagne.

STYLES OF CHAMPAGNE

Non-vintage Most Champagne is a blend of 2 or more vintages. Quality varies enormously, depending on who has made the wine and how long it has been aged. Most Champagne is sold as Brut, which is a dry, but rarely bone-dry style. Strangely, Extra Dry denotes a style less dry than Brut.

Vintage Denotes Champagne made with grapes from a single vintage. As a rule, it is made only in the best years, but far too many mediocre years were declared in the 1990s.

Blanc de Blancs A lighter, and at best highly elegant, style of Champagne made solely from the Chardonnay grape.

Blanc de Noirs White Champagne made entirely from black grapes, either Pinot Noir, Pinot Meunier, or a combination of the two.

Rosé Pink Champagne, made either from black grapes or (more usually) by mixing a little still red wine into white Champagne.

De luxe cuvée In theory the finest Champagne and certainly always the most expensive, residing in the fanciest bottles.

See also CHAMPAGNE ROSE; and individual producers.

BEST YEARS

1999 98 **96 95 90 89 88 85 82**

BEST PRODUCERS

Houses BILLECART-SALMON, BOLLINGER, Cattier, Delamotte, DEUTZ, Drappier, Duval-Leroy, Gosset, Alfred GRATIEN, Charles HEIDSIECK, HENRIOT, JACQUESSON, KRUG, LANSON, LAURENT-PERRIER, Bruno PAILLARD, Joseph PERRIER, PERRIER-JOUET, Philipponnat, PIPER-HEIDSIECK, POL ROGER, POMMERY, Louis ROEDERER, RUINART, Salon, TAITTINGER, VEUVE CLICQUOT.

Growers Michel Arnould, Paul Bara, Barnaut, Beaufort, Beerens, Chartogne-Taillet, Paul Déthune, Diebolt Vallois, Daniel Dumont, Egly-Ouriet, René Geoffroy, Gimonnet, H Goutorbe, André Jacquart, Lamiable, Larmandier, Larmandier-Bernier, Launois, Margaine, Serge Mathieu, J Michel, Moncuit, Alain Robert, Secondé, Selosse, de Sousa, Tarlant, Vilmart.

Co-ops Beaumont des Crayères, H Blin, Nicolas Feuillatte, Jacquart, Mailly, Le Mesnil, Union Champagne.

De luxe cuvées Belle Époque (PERRIER-JOUET), N-F Billecart (BILLECART-SALMON), Blanc de Millénaires (Charles HEIDSIECK), Clos des Goisses (Philipponnat), Clos de Mesnil (KRUG), Comtes de Champagne (TAITTINGER), Cristal (Louis ROEDERER), Cuvée Josephine (Joseph PERRIER), Cuvée Sir Winston Churchill (POL ROGER), Cuvée William Deutz (DEUTZ), Dom Pérignon (MOET & CHANDON), Dom Ruinart (RUINART), Grand Siècle (LAURENT-PERRIER), Grande Dame (VEUVE CLICQUOT), Noble Cuvée (LANSON), Vintage RD (BOLLINGER).

C **CHALONE**

CHALONE *Monterey County, California, USA* Producers of slow-developing Chardonnay★ and Pinot Noir★ from vineyards on the arid eastern slope of the Coastal Range in mid-MONTEREY COUNTY. Also good Reserve Pinot Noir★ and Chardonnay★, as well as Pinot Blanc★, Chenin Blanc★ and Syrah★. Recent vintages have seemed a bit erratic. Best years: (Chardonnay) 2005 04 **03 02 01 00 99**; (Pinot Noir) 2005 04 03 02 **01 00 99 98 96 95**.

CHAMBERS *Rutherglen, Victoria, Australia* Legendary family winery making sheer nectar in the form of Muscat and Tokay. The secret is Bill Chambers' ability to draw on ancient stocks put down in wood by earlier generations. His 'Special'★★ and 'Rare'★★★ blends are national treasures. The Cabernet and Shiraz table wines are good, the whites pedestrian.

CHAMBERTIN AC *Grand Cru, Côte de Nuits, Burgundy, France* The village of GEVREY-CHAMBERTIN, the largest CÔTE DE NUITS commune, has no fewer than 9 Grands Crus (Chambertin, Chambertin-Clos-de-Bèze, Chapelle-Chambertin, Charmes-Chambertin, Griotte-Chambertin, Latricières-Chambertin, Mazis-Chambertin, Ruchottes-Chambertin and the rarely seen Mazoyères-Chambertin), which can produce some of Burgundy's greatest and most intense red wine. Its rough-hewn fruit, seeming to war with fragrant perfumes for its first few years, creates remarkable flavours as the wine ages. Chambertin and Chambertin-Clos-de-Bèze are neighbours on the slope above the village and the two greatest sites, but overproduction is a recurrent problem with some producers. Best producers: Denis Bachelet★★, BOUCHARD PERE ET FILS★★, Charlopin★, B CLAIR★★, P Damoy★★, DROUHIN★★, Drouhin-Laroze★★, C Dugat★★★, B Dugat-Py★★★, FAIVELEY★★, R Groffier★★, JADOT★★, D Laurent★★, Dom. LEROY★★★, Denis MORTET★★★, H Perrot-Minot★★, Ponsot★★, Rossignol-Trapet★★, J Roty★★, ROUMIER★★, ROUSSEAU★★★, J & J-L Trapet★★, VOUGERAIE★★. Best years: (2006) 05 04 03 02 01 00 99 98 **97 96 95 93 90 88**.

CHAMBERTIN-CLOS-DE-BÈZE AC See CHAMBERTIN AC.

CHAMBOLLE-MUSIGNY AC *Côte de Nuits, Burgundy, France* AC with the potential to produce the most fragrant, perfumed red Burgundy, when not over-cropped. Encouragingly, more young producers are now bottling their own wines. Best producers: Amiot-Servelle★, G Barthod★★, J-J Confuron★, DROUHIN★★, DUJAC★, R Groffier★★, Hudelot-Noëllat★★, JADOT★★, Dom. LEROY★★, F Magnien★★, Marchand-Grillot★★, D MORTET★, J-F MUGNIER★★, RION★★, ROUMIER★★, VOGUE★★. Best years: (2006) 05 04 03 02 01 **00 99 98 97 96 95 93 90**.

CHAMPAGNE See pages 108–9.

CHAMPAGNE ROSÉ *Champagne, France* Good pink CHAMPAGNE – usually a little weightier than white – has a delicious fragrance of cherries and raspberries. The top wines can age well, but most rosé Champagne should be drunk on release, as young as possible. Best producers: (vintage) BILLECART-SALMON★★, BOLLINGER★★, Gosset★★, Charles HEIDSIECK★★, JACQUESSON★★, LAURENT-PERRIER (Grand Siècle Alexandra★★★), MOET & CHANDON★★ (Dom Pérignon★★★), PERRIER-JOUET (Belle Époque★), POL ROGER★★, POMMERY (Louise★★), Louis ROEDERER★★ (Cristal★★★), RUINART (Dom Ruinart★★★), TAITTINGER (Comtes de Champagne★★), VEUVE CLICQUOT★★ (Grande Dame★★★); (non-vintage) Paul Bara★, E Barnaut★★, Beaumont des Crayères★, BILLECART-SALMON★★, Egly-Ouriet★★, Henri Giraud★, Jacquart★, KRUG★★, LANSON★, LAURENT-PERRIER★, MOET & CHANDON, RUINART★,

TAITTINGER, Vilmart★. Best years: 1999 98 96 **95 90 89 88 85 82**. See also pages 108–9.

CHANDON DE BRIAILLES *Savigny-lès-Beaune, Côte de Beaune, Burgundy, France* The de Nicolays – François and his sister Claude – combine modern sophistication with traditional values to produce rich but refined reds from SAVIGNY-LES-BEAUNE★, PERNAND-VERGELESSES★, ALOXE-CORTON★ and CORTON★, and an equally good range of whites from Pernand-Vergelesses★★, Corton★★ and CORTON-CHARLEMAGNE★★★. Best years: (reds) (2006) 05 **03 02 99 98 96**.

CHANNING DAUGHTERS *Long Island, New York State, USA* A boutique winery in LONG ISLAND's Hamptons AVA that produces thrilling but hard-to-find wines, including a racy Sauvignon Blanc★, a Muscat-based blend called Sylvanus★ and a juicy Blaufrankisch★.

CHAPEL DOWN *Kent, England* The UK's largest winery (the result of a merger with Lamberhurst Vineyards), producing around 360,000 bottles from its own vineyards in Tenterden and bought-in grapes from contract growers in the south-east of England. Now embarking on major expansion by persuading growers to plant 400ha (1000 acres) by 2010. A large and excellent range includes sparkling wines, fruity whites (especially Bacchus) and reds from Rondo and Pinot Noir.

CHAPEL HILL *McLaren Vale, South Australia* Chief winemaker Michael Fragos continues to build on the work of Pam Dunsford to produce a range of powerful, classy wines. The Cabernet Sauvignon★★ is a successful blend of mature MCLAREN VALE and COONAWARRA fruit, while the Shiraz★ is all McLaren Vale. Good Unwooded Chardonnay★ and fascinating, bone-dry, honey-scented Verdelho★★. Best years: (Shiraz) (2006) (05) 04 02 01 **98 97 96 95 94 93 91**.

CHAPELLE-CHAMBERTIN AC See CHAMBERTIN AC.

CHAPELLE LENCLOS *Madiran AC, South-West France* One of the leading names in MADIRAN, Patrick Ducournau has tamed the savage Tannat grape with his invention of controlled oxygenation, or *microbullage* – bubbling tiny amounts of oxygen into the wine, either during fermentation or during barrel aging. The technique is now used widely in Bordeaux. The Chapelle Lenclos★★ and Dom Mouréou★ reds are ripe and concentrated, though they need at least 5 years to mature. Also a small amount of sweet white PACHERENC DU VIC-BILH. Best years: (reds) (2005) 03 01 **00 99 98 96**.

M CHAPOUTIER *Rhône Valley, France* Chapoutier is very much in the vanguard of progress, both in viticulture and in winemaking, and is producing a full range of serious, exciting wines. The HERMITAGE la Sizeranne★★ and special Ermitages, les Greffieux★★, l'Ermite★★, le Méal★★★ and le Pavillon★★★; white Hermitage de l'Orée★★ and l'Ermite★★★; CROZES-HERMITAGE les Varonniers★★; ST-JOSEPH les Granits★★ (red and white); and CHATEAUNEUF-DU-PAPE Barbe Rac★ and Croix de Bois★ are all good, but some show a surfeit of new oak. Large-volume Crozes-Hermitage les Meysonniers and COTES DU RHONE Belleruche are good value. Also BANYULS, COTEAUX DU TRICASTIN and Australian joint ventures. Best years: (la Sizeranne) (2006) 05 04 03 01 **00 99 98 95 94 91 90 89 88**.

CHARDONNAY See pages 112–13.

CHARMES-CHAMBERTIN AC See CHAMBERTIN AC.

CHARDONNAY

I never thought I'd see myself write this. Yes, we are getting bored with Chardonnay. Not all Chardonnay: there's probably more top Chardonnay being produced right now than ever before. And for millions of wine drinkers the Chardonnay revolution (easy to pronounce, easy to swallow) has only just begun. But in the heart of the wine world – the middle market, where people care about flavour but also care about price – we're getting fed up. Far too much sugary, over-oaked, unrefreshing junk has been dumped into our laps recently, from countries and producers who should know better. Add to this the increasingly desperate dirt-cheap offerings at the rump end of the market, and you'll see why I think the great golden goose of Chardonnay has the carving knife of cynicism and greed firmly held against its neck. The next few years will show whether it wishes to be the supremely versatile all-rounder or the sloppy jack of all trades and master of none.

WINE STYLES

France Although a relatively neutral variety if left alone (this is what makes it so suitable as a base wine for top-quality Champagne-method sparkling wine), the grape can ripen in a surprising range of conditions, developing a subtle gradation of flavours going from the sharp apple-core greenness of Chardonnay grown in Champagne or the Loire, through the exciting, bone-dry yet succulent flavours of white Burgundy, to a round, tropical flavour in Languedoc-Roussillon.

Other regions Italy produces Chardonnay that can be bone dry and lean or fat, spicy and lush. Spain does much the same. California and Australia virtually created their reputations on great, viscous, almost syrupy, tropical fruits and spice-flavoured Chardonnays; the best producers are now moving away from this style. Some of the best New World Chardonnays, dry but ripe and subtly oaked, are coming from South Africa. Unoaked versions from more mature vines offer increasingly characterful, food-friendly drinking. New Zealand is producing rich, deep, but beautifully balanced Chardonnays, while Chile and Argentina are rapidly learning how to make fine wine from it too. Add Germany, Austria, Canada, New York State, Greece, Portugal, Slovenia, Moldova, Romania, even China, and you'll see it can perform almost anywhere.

Using oak The reason for all these different flavours lies in Chardonnay's wonderful susceptibility to the winemaker's aspirations and skills. The most important manipulation is the use of the oak barrel for fermenting and aging the wine. Chardonnay is the grape of the great white Burgundies and these are fermented and matured in oak (not necessarily new oak); the effect is to give a marvellous round, nutty richness to a wine that is yet savoury and dry. This is enriched still further by aging the wine on its lees.

The New World winemakers sought to emulate the great Burgundies, planting Chardonnay and employing thousands of oak barrels (mostly new), and their success has caused winemakers everywhere else to see Chardonnay as the perfect variety – easy to grow, easy to turn into wine and easy to sell to an adoring public. But as in all things, familiarity can breed contempt.

BEST PRODUCERS

France *Chablis* Billaud-Simon, A & F Boudin, DAUVISSAT, Fèvre, LAROCHE, RAVENEAU; *Côte d'Or* R Ampeau, J-M Boillot, Bonneau du Martray, CARILLON, COCHE-DURY, M Colin, DROUHIN, A Ente, J-P Fichet, J-N GAGNARD, V GIRARDIN, JADOT, F Jobard, R Jobard, LAFON, H Lamy, L LATOUR, Dom. LEFLAIVE, B Morey, M Niellon, RAMONET, G Roulot, SAUZET, VERGET; *Mâconnais* D & M Barraud, Bret Brothers, Guffens-Heynen/VERGET, O Merlin, J Thévenet, Valette.

Other European Chardonnays
Austria TEMENT, VELICH.

Germany JOHNER, REBHOLZ.

Italy Castello di AMA, BELLAVISTA, CA' DEL BOSCO, GAJA, ISOLE E OLENA, LAGEDER, TIEFENBRUNNER (Linticlarus), Vie di Romans, Castello della SALA (Cervaro).

Spain CHIVITE, ENATE, Finca Muñoz, Manzaneque, Señorío de Otazu, TORRES.

New World Chardonnays
Australia BANNOCKBURN, CAPE MENTELLE, CULLEN, GIACONDA, GROSSET, HOWARD PARK, LEEUWIN, PENFOLDS (Yattarna), PETALUMA, PIERRO, SHAW & SMITH, Tapanappa (Tiers Vineyard), TARRAWARRA, TYRRELL'S, VOYAGER.

New Zealand BABICH, CLOUDY BAY, CRAGGY RANGE, DRY RIVER, FELTON ROAD, FROMM, GOLDWATER, ISABEL, KUMEU RIVER, MATUA VALLEY, MILLTON, MONTANA, NEUDORF, PEGASUS BAY, SAINT CLAIR, SERESIN, VAVASOUR, Vidal, VILLA MARIA, WITHER HILLS.

USA ARROWOOD, AU BON CLIMAT, BERINGER, CALERA, CHALONE, CHATEAU ST JEAN, DOMAINE DROUHIN OREGON, FERRARI-CARANO, FLOWERS, HdV, KISTLER, MARCASSIN, MATANZAS CREEK, MERRYVALE, Peter MICHAEL, NEWTON, Ramey, RIDGE, ROCHIOLI, SAINTSBURY, SANFORD, SHAFER, STEELE, TALBOTT.

South Africa BUITENVERWACHTING, Chamonix, Neil ELLIS (Elgin), HAMILTON RUSSELL, JORDAN, MEERLUST, MULDERBOSCH, SPRINGFIELD, THELEMA, VERGELEGEN.

South America CATENA, CONCHA Y TORO (Amelia), CONO SUR (20 Barrels), Tabalí/SAN PEDRO.

113

CHASSAGNE-MONTRACHET AC *Côte de Beaune, Burgundy, France*
Some of Burgundy's greatest white wine vineyards (part of le MONTRACHET and BATARD-MONTRACHET, all of Criots-Bâtard-Montrachet) are within the village boundary. The white Chassagne Premiers Crus are not as well known, but can offer nutty, toasty wines, especially if aged for 4–8 years; Blanchots Dessus, Chaumées, Ruchotte and Morgeots are among the best. Ordinary white Chassagne-Montrachet is usually enjoyable; the red is a little earthy, peppery and plummy and can be an acquired taste. Look out for reds from the following Premiers Crus: Clos de la Boudriotte, Clos St-Jean and Clos de la Chapelle. Best producers: (whites) Blain-Gagnard★★, B Colin, M Colin★★, P Colin★, Colin-Deléger★★, J-N GAGNARD★★, V GIRARDIN★★, V & F Jouard★, H Lamy★, B Morey★★, M Morey★★, M Niellon★★, J & J-M Pillot★★, P Pillot★, RAMONET★, VERGET★★; (reds) CARILLON★, R Clerget★, V GIRARDIN★★, B Morey★★, RAMONET★★. Best years: (whites) (2006) 05 **04 03 02 01 00 99 95**; (reds) (2006) 05 04 03 **02 99 98 96**.

CHASSELAS Chasselas is considered a table grape worldwide. Only in BADEN (where it is called Gutedel) and Switzerland (called FENDANT) is it thought to make decent light, dry wines with a slight prickle. A few Swiss examples, notably from CHABLAIS and DEZALEY, rise above this.

CH. CHASSE-SPLEEN★ *Moulis AC, Cru Bourgeois, Haut-Médoc, Bordeaux, France* Chasse-Spleen is not a Classed Growth – but during the 1980s it built a tremendous reputation for ripe, concentrated and powerful wines under the late proprietor, Bernadette Villars. The château is now run by Villars' daughter Céline, and recent vintages are approaching the form of the old days. Second wine: l'Ermitage de Chasse-Spleen. Best years: 2005 04 **03 02 01 00 99 96 95 94 90 89**.

CHÂTEAU-CHALON AC *Jura, France* The most prized – and pricey – *vin jaune*, it is difficult to find, even in the Jura. But if you do find a bottle, beware – the awesome flavour will shock your tastebuds like no other French wine. Not released until 6 years after the vintage, it can be kept for much longer. Best producers: Baud★, Berthet-Bondet★★, Bourdy★★, Chalandard★★, Crédoz★, Durand-Perron★★, J Macle★, H Maire. Best years: (2000) 99 98 **97 96 95 94 93 92 91 90 89 88 87**.

CHÂTEAU-GRILLET AC★★ *Rhône Valley, France* This rare and *very* expensive RHONE white, made from Viognier and aged in used oak, has a magic reek of orchard fruit and harvest bloom when young but is best drunk after 5 years, and decanted. More reserved in style than CONDRIEU. Best years: 2005 04 **03 01 00 98 95**.

CHATEAU INDAGE *Maharashtra, India* India's first traditional-method sparkling wine appeared in the 1980s, with technical assistance from Champagne's PIPER-HEIDSIECK. Dry sparklers are firm, fresh and chunky – though quality is somewhat erratic. Omar Khayyám is produced from a blend of Chardonnay, Ugni Blanc, Pinot Noir and Pinot Meunier. A demi-sec and a good pink fizz are also produced. Red and white table wines use both international and indigenous Indian grape varieties such as Bangalore Purple and Arkavati.

CHATEAU MONTELENA *Napa Valley AVA, California, USA* NAPA winery producing classic California Chardonnay★★ and an estate Cabernet★★ which are impressive, if slow to develop. The Napa Valley Cabernet★ is an elegant wine for younger consumption. Best years: (Chardonnay) 2005 04 03 **02 01 00 99 98**; (Cabernet) 2003 02 **01 00 99 98 91 90**.

CHATEAU MUSAR *Ghazir, Lebanon* Founded by Gaston Hochar in the 1930s and now run by his Bordeaux-trained son Serge, Musar is famous for having made wine every year bar two (1976 and 84) throughout Lebanon's civil war. From an unlikely blend of primarily Cabernet Sauvignon and Cinsaut comes a wine of real, if wildly exotic, character, with sweet, spicy fruit and good aging potential: Hochar says that red Musar★ 'should be drunk at 15 years'. Some recent vintages have not quite lived up to expectations, but latest harvests are encouraging. There is also a rosé, and a white from local Chardonnay and Sémillon lookalikes Obaideh and Merwah. Hochar Père et Fils is ready to drink upon release, as is Musar Cuvée Reservée, which is not aged in oak. Best years: (red) 2000 99 98 97 **96 95 94 93 91 89 88**; (white) **1999 98 97**.

CHATEAU ST JEAN *Sonoma Valley AVA, California, USA* Once known almost entirely for its range of Chardonnays (Belle Terre★★ and Robert Young★★), St Jean has emerged as a producer of delicious reds, including a BORDEAUX-style blend called Cinq Cépages★★ and a Reserve Merlot★★. Now owned by the Foster's Group. Best years: (Chardonnay) 2005 04 **03 02 01 00 99**; (reds) (2005) 04 03 02 **01 00 99 97 95 94**.

CHATEAU STE MICHELLE *Washington State, USA* Pioneering winery with an enormous range of wines, including several attractive vineyard-designated Chardonnays★ (some ★★), Cabernet Sauvignons★ and Merlots★, especially Cold Creek Vineyard★★ wines. Good Riesling, both dry and sweet, and increasingly interesting pure Meritage★. Partnership with Italy's ANTINORI and Germany's Ernst LOOSEN have produced dark, powerful Tuscan-style red Col Solare★★, a lovely dry Riesling Eroica★★ and a thrilling sweet version, TBA★★★, made in tiny quantities. Quality generally seems to be moving upwards. Best years: (premium reds) (2005) 04 03 02 **01 00 99**.

CHÂTEAUNEUF-DU-PAPE AC *Rhône Valley, France* A large (3350ha/8275-acre) vineyard area between Orange and Avignon. The sweetly fruited red wine is based on Grenache, plus Syrah and Mourvèdre (10 other varieties are also allowed). Always choose Châteauneuf from a single estate, distinguished by the papal coat of arms or mitre embossed on the neck of the bottle. Only 5% of Châteauneuf is white; made mainly from Grenache Blanc, Bourboulenc and Clairette, these wines can be surprisingly good. Top reds, particularly old-vine cuvées, will age for 10 years or more; whites are best young. Best producers: (reds) P Autard★, L Barrot★, BEAUCASTEL★★★, Beaurenard★★, Bois de Boursan★★, H Bonneau★★, Bosquet des Papes★★, du Caillou★, les Cailloux★, Chante-Perdrix★, CHAPOUTIER★, la Charbonnière★★, L Charvin★★, Clos du Mont Olivet★★, CLOS DES PAPES★★, Cristia, Font du Loup★, FONT DE MICHELLE★★, Fortia★★, la Gardine★★, Grand Tinel★, Grand Veneur★, la Janasse★★, Marcoux★★, Millière★★, Monpertuis★★, Mont-Redon★★, la Nerthe★★, Pégaü★★, RAYAS★★★, Roquète★, Roger Sabon★★, Solitude★★, Tardieu-Laurent★★, P Usseglio★★, la Vieille-Julienne★★, Vieux Donjon★, VIEUX TELEGRAPHE★★, Villeneuve★★; (whites) BEAUCASTEL★★★, CLOS DES PAPES★★, FONT DE MICHELLE★★, Grand Veneur★★, Marcoux★★, RAYAS★★, St-Cosme★★, VIEUX TELEGRAPHE★★. Best years: (reds) (2006) 05 **04 03 01 00 99 98 96 95 94 90 89 88**.

JEAN-LOUIS CHAVE *Rhône Valley, France* Jean-Louis Chave's red HERMITAGE★★★ is one of the world's great wines, surpassed only by the Cathelin★★★, produced in exceptional years. His wonderful, richly flavoured white Hermitage★★★ sometimes even outlasts the reds, as it quietly moves toward its honeyed, nutty zenith. Also produces a small amount of excellent red ST-JOSEPH★★ and an occasional stunning traditional sweet Vin de Paille★★. Expensive, but worth the money. Best years: (reds) (2006) 05 04 03 01 **00 99 98 97 96 95 94 92 91 90 89 88 86 85 83 82 79 78**; (whites) (2006) 05 04 03 01 **00 99 98 97 96 95 94 93 92 91 90 89 88 85 83**.

CHÉNAS AC *Beaujolais, Burgundy, France* The smallest of the BEAUJOLAIS Crus, Chénas, while little known, offers a range of styles from light and elegant to austere and needing time to develop Burgundian tones. Best producers: Champagnon★, DUBOEUF, Nathalie Fauvin, H Lapierre★, B Santé★. Best years: **2006 05 03**.

CHENIN BLANC One of the most underrated white wine grapes in the world. In the LOIRE VALLEY, where it is also called Pineau de la Loire, it is responsible for the great sweet wines of COTEAUX DU LAYON, QUARTS DE CHAUME and BONNEZEAUX – some of the longest-lived of all wines – as well as for VOUVRAY, sweet, dry or sparkling, and much other ANJOU white. In South Africa, Chenin Blanc is, ironically, both the most planted and most uprooted variety: vineyard area continues to decrease, but the best sites are being retained and the best wines are being compared favourably with their Loire counterparts. Styles range from sparkling through easy-drinking, dryish wines and modern barrel-fermented versions to botrytized dessert wines. New Zealand and Australia have produced good varietal examples, and it is also grown in California and Argentina.

CH. CHEVAL BLANC★★★ *St-Émilion Grand Cru AC, 1er Grand Cru Classé, Bordeaux, France* Along with AUSONE, the leading ST-EMILION estate. Right on the border with POMEROL, it seems to share some of its sturdy richness, but with an extra spice and purity of fruit that is impressively, recognizably unique. An unusually high percentage

(60%) of Cabernet Franc is often used in the blend. Appealing when young, yet with a remarkable ability to age for many decades. Best years: 2005 04 **03** 02 01 00 **99 98 97 96 95 94 90 89 88 86 85 83 82**.

CHEVALIER-MONTRACHET AC See MONTRACHET AC.

DOM. DE CHEVALIER *Pessac-Léognan AC, Cru Classé de Graves, Bordeaux, France* Some of Bordeaux's finest wines. The red★★ starts out firm and reserved but over 10–20 years gains heavenly cedar, tobacco and blackcurrant flavour. The brilliant white★★★ is both fermented and aged in oak barrels; in the best vintages it will still be improving at 15–20 years. Best years: (reds) 2005 04 03 02 **01** 00 **99 98 96 90 89 88**; (whites) 2005 04 03 02 01 00 99 98 96 95 94 90 89 88.

CHEVERNY AC *Loire Valley, France* A little-known area south of Blois. The local speciality is the white Romorantin grape, which makes a bone-dry wine under the AC Cour-Cheverny, but the best whites are from Chardonnay. Also pleasant Sauvignon, Pinot Noir, Gamay and bracing CHAMPAGNE-method fizz. Drink young. Best producers: Cazin, Cheverny co-op, Courtioux, Gendrier/Huards★, Gueritte, H Marionnet, du Moulin, Salvard, Sauger, C Tessier/la Desoucherie, Tue-Boeuf★.

CHIANTI DOCG *Tuscany, Italy*   The most famous of all Italian wines, but there are many styles, depending on what grapes are used, where they are grown, and by which producer. It can be a light, fresh, easy-drinking red wine with a characteristic hint of bitterness, or it can be an intense, structured yet sleek wine in the same league as the best BORDEAUX. The vineyards are scattered over central Tuscany, either simply as 'Chianti' or Chianti plus the name of one of the 7 sub-zones: Colli Aretini, Colli Fiorentini, Colli Senesi, Colline Pisane, Montalbano, Montespertoli and Rufina. Sangiovese is the main grape; traditionally it was blended with the red Canaiolo and white Malvasia and Trebbiano. Modern winemakers often make Chianti from Sangiovese alone or blended with 20% of Cabernet, Merlot, Syrah or, increasingly, with native grapes like Colorino. See also CHIANTI RUFINA, SUPER-TUSCANS. Best producers: (Chianti Colli Fiorentini) Baggiolino★, Le Calvane, Il Corno, Corzano e Paterno★, Lanciola★, Malenchini★, Pasolini dall'Onda★, Poppiano★, La Querce, Sammontana, San Vito in Fior di Selva; (Chianti Colli Senesi) Campriano, Carpineta Fontalpino★, Casabianca, Casale-Falchini★, Farnetella★, Ficomontanino★, Pacina★, Paradiso★, Pietraserena.

CHIANTI CLASSICO DOCG *Tuscany, Italy*   The original (if slightly enlarged) CHIANTI zone in the hills between Florence and Siena. Classico has led the trend in making richer, more structured and better-balanced wines. Nonetheless, until recently many producers used their best grapes for high-profile SUPER-TUSCANS. Since the 96 vintage, Classico can be made from 100% Sangiovese, though winemakers all too often accept the option of including 20% 'international' grapes (see CHIANTI). Riserva must be aged at least 27 months (usually in barrel) and must use only red grapes. The finest Riserva wines can improve for a decade or more. Many of the estates also offer regular bottlings of red wine, round and fruity, for drinking about 2–5 years after the harvest. Best producers (Riserva or top cru): Castello di AMA★★★, ANTINORI★ (Riserva★★), Badia a Coltibuono★, Brancaia★, Cacchiano★, Capaccia★★, Carpineto★★, Casa Emma★★, Casa Sola★★, Casaloste★★, CASTELLARE★, Castell'in Villa★, Collelungo★★, Colombaio di Cencio★★, Dievole★, FELSINA★★, Le Filigare★, FONTERUTOLI★★, FONTODI★★, ISOLE E OLENA★★, Il Mandorlo★★, La Massa★★, Melini★, Monsanto★★, Il Palazzino★★, Paneretta★★, Panzanello★★, Poggerino★★, Poggiopiano★★, Poggio al Sole (Casasilia★★★), Querceto★, QUERCIABELLA★★★, Castello dei RAMPOLLA★★, RICASOLI (Castello di Brolio★★), RIECINE★★, Rignana★★, Rocca di Castagnoli★★, San Felice★★, San Giusto a Rentennano★★, San Polo in Rosso★, Terrabianca★, Vecchie Terre di Montefili★★, Verrazzano★, Vignamaggio★, Villa Cafaggio★★, VOLPAIA★★. Best years: (2006) 04 **03 01 99 97 95 90**.

CHIANTI RUFINA DOCG *Tuscany, Italy*   Smallest of the CHIANTI sub-zones, situated in an enclave of the Apennine foothills to the east of Florence, where wines were noted for exceptional strength, structure and longevity long before they joined the ranks of Chianti. Today the wines, particularly the long-lived Riserva Bucerchiale from SELVAPIANA and FRESCOBALDI's Montesodi, match the best of CHIANTI CLASSICO. Pomino DOC is a small (100ha/250-acre) high-altitude zone almost entirely surrounded by Chianti Rufina; dominated by Frescobaldi, it makes greater use of French varieties such as Merlot, Cabernet and Chardonnay. Best producers: (Riservas) Basciano★★, Tenuta di Bossi★,

Colognole, FRESCOBALDI★★, Grati/Villa di Vetrice★, Grignano★, Lavacchio★, SELVAPIANA★★★, Castello del Trebbio★. Best years: (2006) 04 03 01 **99 97 95 90 88 85**.

MICHELE CHIARLO *Piedmont, Italy* From his winery base south of Asti, Michele Chiarlo produces stylish wines from several PIEDMONT zones. Single-vineyard BAROLOS★★ and BARBARESCOS★ top the list, but BARBERA D'ASTI★ and GAVI★ are reliable, too. The Monferrato DOC embraces Countacc!★, a Nebbiolo-Barbera-Cabernet Sauvignon blend.

CHIMNEY ROCK *Stags Leap District AVA, California, USA* Powerful yet elegantly sculpted Cabernet Sauvignon★★ (Reserve★★) and a meritage blend called Elevage★★. A tangy Fumé Blanc★ and a Cabernet Franc rosé are also made. Best years: (Elevage) 2003 02 **01 00 99 98 97 96 95 94 91 90**.

CHINON AC *Loire Valley, France* Best red wine of the LOIRE VALLEY, made mainly from Cabernet Franc. Lovely light reds full of raspberry fruit and fresh summer earth to drink young, and heavyweights for keeping; always worth buying a single-estate wine. Best producers: P Alliet★★, B Baudry★★, J & C Baudry, Dom. de Beauséjour, Logis de la Bouchardière, P Breton★, Coulaine★, COULY-DUTHEIL★, J-P Crespin/ Ch. de l'Aulée★, DRUET★★, la Grille★, C Joguet★, la Noblaie, la Perrière★, Roncée★, Rouet, Wilfrid Rousse, P Sourdais★. Best years: (2006) 05 04 **03** 02 **01** 97 96 95.

CHIROUBLES AC *Beaujolais, Burgundy, France* The highest in altitude of the BEAUJOLAIS Crus, producing a light, fragrant, delicious Gamay wine exhibiting all the attractions of a youthful Cru. Best producers: Cheysson★, la Combe au Loup/Méziat★, la Grosse Pierre/A Passot★, J Passot★. Best years: **2006 05**.

CHIVITE *Navarra DO, Navarra, Spain* Longtime leader in exports from NAVARRA. The Gran Feudo★ red and rosé are very good easy drinkers. However, the more up-market reds could be a bit more lively. The top range is called Colección 125 and includes a red Reserva★, classy white Blanco★★ made from Chardonnay, and a characterful sweet Vendimia Tardía★★ from Moscatel (Muscat Blanc à Petits Grains).

CHOREY-LÈS-BEAUNE AC *Côte de Beaune, Burgundy, France* One of those tiny, forgotten villages that make good, if not great, Burgundy at prices most of us can afford, with some committed producers too. Can age for 5–8 years. Best producers: Arnoux★, DROUHIN★, Germain★, Maillard★, TOLLOT-BEAUT★★. Best years: (2006) 05 **03 02 99**.

CHURCH ROAD *Hawkes Bay, North Island, New Zealand* A premium-wine project owned by Pernod Ricard. The reds seem a bit Bordeaux-obsessed, although Reserve wines, made in the best years, can be very good. Reserve Chardonnay★ is rich and smooth with flavours of peach, grapefruit and hazelnut. Best years: (reds) (2006) 04 **02 00 98**.

CHURCHILL *Port DOC, Douro, Portugal* Established in 1981, it was the first new PORT shipper for 50 years. The wines can be good, notably Vintage★, LBV★, Crusted★, single-quinta Gricha and a well-aged, nutty dry white port★, and are much more consistent since Quinta da Gricha was bought in 1999. Since 2003, Churchill Estates, an unfortified DOURO red, has also improved. Best years: (Vintage) 2003 00 97 94 **91 85**; (Quinta da Gricha) 2003 01 99.

CINSAUT Also spelt Cinsault. Found mainly in France's southern RHONE VALLEY, PROVENCE and Languedoc-Roussillon, giving a light wine with fresh, but rather fleeting, neutral fruit. Ideal for rosé wine. In blends,

Cinsaut's low alcohol can help calm high-degree Grenache. Used in the blend for Lebanon's CHATEAU MUSAR. Popular as a bulk blender in South Africa, it is now being rediscovered by enthusiasts of the Rhône style.

CIRÒ DOC *Calabria, Italy* The legend that this was the wine offered to champions in the ancient Olympics has often seemed a more potent reason to buy it than for its quality. Yet Cirò Rosso, a full-bodied red from the Gaglioppo grape, has improved remarkably of late. Non-DOC Gaglioppo-based IGTs, like Librandi's Gravello★★ (an oak-aged blend with Cabernet), are genuinely exciting. The DOC also covers a dry white from Greco and a rare dry rosé. Best producers: Caparra & Siciliani★, Librandi★ (Riserva★★), San Francesco★. Best years: (reds) (2006) (05) 04 **03 01 00 99 97**.

BRUNO CLAIR *Marsannay, Côte de Nuits, Burgundy, France* Excellent wines from vineyards in MARSANNAY, as well as in GEVREY-CHAMBERTIN and VOSNE-ROMANEE, SAVIGNY in the Côte de Beaune and GIVRY in the Côte Chalonnaise. Top wines are CHAMBERTIN Clos de Bèze★★, Gevrey-Chambertin Clos St-Jacques★★ and vineyard-designated Marsannay reds★★. Most of his wine is red, but there is a small amount of white (CORTON-CHARLEMAGNE★★) and a delicious Marsannay rosé★. Best years: (top reds) (2006) 05 03 02 **01 00 99 98 96 90**.

CLAIRETTE DE DIE AC *Rhône Valley, France* Sparkling wine made from a minimum of 75% Muscat, off-dry, with a creamy bubble and an orchard-fresh fragrance. The *méthode Dioise* is used, which preserves the Muscat scent. An ideal light apéritif. Drink young. Best producers: Achard-Vincent★, Clairette de Die co-op, D Cornillon, Jacques Faure, J-C Raspail★. See also CRÉMANT DE DIE.

A CLAPE *Cornas, Rhône Valley, France* The leading estate in CORNAS – dense, tannic, consistently excellent wines, full of rich, roasted fruit and often ★★★. Second wine Renaissance is good lower-key Cornas. Clape also makes fine COTES DU RHONE, both red★ and white★, and decent ST-PERAY★. Best years: (Cornas) (2006) 05 04 03 **02** 01 00 99 **98 97 96 95 94 92 91 90 89 88 86 85 83**.

LA CLAPE *Coteaux du Languedoc AC, Languedoc, France* The mountain of La Clape rises above the flat coastal fields south-east of Narbonne; its vineyards produce some excellent whites from Bourboulenc and Clairette, plus fine, herb-scented reds and rosés, mainly from Grenache, Syrah and Mourvèdre. Whites and reds can age. Best producers: Bouisset, Camplazens★, Capitoul, l'HOSPITALET★, Mire l'Étang, Négly, Pech-Céleyran★, Pech Redon★, Vires. Best years: (reds) 2004 03 **01 00 99**.

CLARE VALLEY *South Australia* Historical upland region north of Adelaide with a deceptively moderate climate, able to grow fine, aromatic Riesling, marvellously textured Semillon, rich, robust Shiraz and Cabernet blends and peppery but voluptuous Grenache. Best producers: (whites) Tim ADAMS★★, Jim BARRY★, Wolf BLASS (Gold Label★), Leo Buring (Leonay★★), Crabtree, GROSSET★★★, KNAPPSTEIN★, LEASINGHAM★, MITCHELL★, MOUNT HORROCKS★★, O'Leary Walker★, PETALUMA★★, Pikes★, Taylors/Wakefield★; (reds) Tim ADAMS★★, Jim BARRY★★, GROSSET★★, Kilikanoon★, LEASINGHAM★, MITCHELL★, Pikes★, Taylors/Wakefield, WENDOUREE★★★. Best years: (Shiraz) (2005) (04) 03 02 **01 99 98 97 96 94 93 92 91 90 88 86**; (Riesling) 2005 **04 03 02 01 99 98 97 96 95 94 93 92 90**.

CLARENDON HILLS *McLaren Vale, South Australia* Winery with a name for high-priced, highly extracted, unfined, unfiltered and unobtainable reds. Single-vineyard Astralis★★ is a hugely concentrated Syrah from old vines, aged in 100% French new oak. Other Syrah ★★ labels offer slightly better value, while Merlot★ and Cabernet Sauvignon★ aim to rub shoulders with great red BORDEAUX – although I'm not sure which ones. Several cuvées of Old Vines Grenache★★ are marked by saturated black cherry fruit and high alcohol. Best years: (Astralis) (2006) (05) 04 03 02 01 00 98 96 **95 94**.

CH. **CLARKE★** *Listrac-Médoc AC, Bordeaux, France* This property had millions spent on it by the late Baron Edmond de Rothschild during the late 1970s, and from the 98 vintage leading Bordeaux winemaker Michel Rolland has been consultant enologist. The wines can have an attractive blackcurrant fruit and now a little more ripeness and polish. With a name like Clarke, how could they possibly fail to seduce? There is also a small production of dry white wine, le Merle Blanc. Best years: 2005 04 **03 01 00 99 98 96**.

DOMENICO CLERICO *Barolo DOCG, Piedmont, Italy* Domenico Clerico produces consistently superlative BAROLO (Ciabot Mentin Ginestra★★★, Pajana★★★, Per Cristina★★★) and excellent BARBERA D'ALBA★ (Trevigne★★), all wonderfully balanced. His range also includes LANGHE Arte★★, a barrique-aged blend of Nebbiolo and Barbera. Best years: (Barolos) (2006) (04) 03 01 **00 99 98 97 96 95 93 90 89 88**.

CH. **CLIMENS★★★** *Barsac AC, 1er Cru Classé, Bordeaux, France* The leading estate in BARSAC, with a deserved reputation for fabulous, sensuous wines, rich and succulent yet streaked with lively lemon acidity. Easy to drink at 5 years, but a good vintage will be richer and more satisfying after 10–15 years. Second wine: les Cyprès (also delicious). Best years: 2005 04 03 **02** 01 00 **99 98 97 96 95 90 89 88**.

CLONAKILLA *Canberra, Australia* Tim Kirk's small family winery, whose stellar Shiraz-Viognier★★★ is regarded as the benchmark for the style in Australia; it is elegant, lavender-scented, fleshily textured and complex, with the structure to age beautifully. Riesling and Viognier★ are good, too. A more modestly priced and increasingly interesting Shiraz is made from grapes purchased from nearby HILLTOPS.

CLOS DE L'ANHEL *Corbières AC, Languedoc, France* In just a few years, Sophie Guiraudon and Philippe Mathias have started to produce remarkable wines with a power unusual even for the CORBIERES. Top wine is smooth, rich Les Dimanches★★; also Les Terrassettes★ and Le Lolo de l'Anhel. Best years: (Les Dimanches) (2004) 03 **01 00**.

CLOS BAGATELLE *St-Chinian AC, Languedoc-Roussillon, France* Siblings Luc and Christine Simon produce various ST-CHINIANS: top wine La Gloire de Mon Père★ is made from Syrah, Mourvèdre and Grenache, and aged in 100% new oak barrels; Sélection in only 25%. Unoaked Marie et Mathieu★ is fruit-driven; Cuvée Camille has spicy, herbal aromas. Also a MUSCAT DE ST-JEAN-DE-MINERVOIS.

CLOS DU BOIS *Alexander Valley AVA, Sonoma County, California, USA* I've always been partial to the house style here: gentle, fruit-dominated SONOMA Chardonnay, Merlot and Cabernet. Top vineyard selections can be exciting, especially the Calcaire★★ and Flintwood★ Chardonnays, as well as the rich, strong Briarcrest Cabernet Sauvignon★★ and Marlstone★★, a red BORDEAUX-style blend. Now part of Beam Wine Estates. Best years: (reds) 2003 02 **01 00 99 97 96 95 94 91 90 88 86**.

CLOS CENTEILLES *Minervois AC, Languedoc-Roussillon, France* Excellent MINERVOIS La Livinière and innovative vins de pays. Impressive Clos Centeilles★★ is the top wine; Capitelle de Centeilles★ and Carignanissime★ are 100% Cinsaut and 100% Carignan respectively. Best years: 2004 03 **01 00 99**.

CLOS DE LA COULÉE-DE-SERRANT *Savennières AC, Loire Valley, France* Fine estate of only 7ha (17 acres) which merits its own AC within the boundaries of SAVENNIÈRES. The Joly family runs the property on fervently biodynamic lines, and the estate wine★★ is a concentrated, long-lived, very pricey Chenin Blanc with a honeyed, floral bouquet. Also produces better-value Savennières Roche aux Moines★★ and Les Vieux Clos★. Best years: 2005 04 03 02 01 00 **97 96 95 93 90 89**.

CLOS ERASMUS★★★ *Priorat DOCa, Cataluña, Spain* Daphne Glorian's tiny estate turns out one of the most profound and personal reds in PRIORAT. Her small winery (formerly Alvaro PALACIOS') also makes a convincing second wine, Laurel★. Best years: (2005) 04 03 02 01 00 99 **98 97 96 94**.

CLOS DES LAMBRAYS AC★★★ *Grand Cru, Côte de Nuits, Burgundy, France* This 8.8ha (22-acre) Grand Cru vineyard in MOREY-ST-DENIS is almost entirely owned by the domaine of the same name, though Taupenot-Merme also has a few rows, not quite enough to make a barrel a year. Thierry Brouin, manager at the Dom. des Lambrays, has raised his game in recent years by a more severe selection of fruit for the Grand Cru, now using only old vines. Best years: (2006) 05 04 03 02 **00 99 96**.

CLOS MARIE *Pic Saint-Loup, Coteaux du Languedoc AC, Languedoc, France* Since 1995, Christophe Peyrus has been making 4 powerful red wines, blends dominated by Syrah, that regularly wow tasters: Glorieuses★, L'Olivette★, Simon★ and Métairies du Clos★. Best years: (2005) 03 **02 00**.

CLOS MOGADOR★★★ *Priorat DOCa, Cataluña, Spain* René Barbier Ferrer was one of the pioneers who relaunched the reputation of PRIORAT in the 1980s. The wine is a ripe, intense, brooding monster built to age. Best years: (2005) 04 03 01 00 99 **98 97 96 95 94 93 92 91 90**.

DOM. DU CLOS NAUDIN *Vouvray AC, Loire Valley, France* Philippe Foreau runs this first-rate VOUVRAY domaine. Depending on the vintage, he produces a range of styles: dry★★, medium-dry★★ and sweet★★ (rare Réserve★★★), as well as Vouvray Mousseux★★ and Pétillant★★. The wines are supremely ageworthy. Best years: (Moelleux Réserve) 2005 03 97 **96 95 90 89**.

CLOS DES PAPES *Châteauneuf-du-Pape AC, Rhône Valley, France* The red CHATEAUNEUF-DU-PAPE★★ has an unusually high amount of Mourvèdre, which gives structure, complexity and potential longevity. Nevertheless, there is enough Grenache to ensure the wine's approachability in its youth and provide an initial blast of fruit. The white★★ takes on the nutty character of aged Burgundy after 5 or 6 years. Best years: (red) (2006) 05 04 03 01 **00 99 98 97 96 95 94 90 89 88 83 81**.

CLOS DE LA ROCHE AC *Grand Cru, Côte de Nuits, Burgundy, France* The best and biggest of the 5 MOREY-ST-DENIS Grands Crus. It has a lovely, bright, red-fruits flavour when young, and should become richly

121

chocolaty or gamy with age. Best producers: DROUHIN★★★, DUJAC★★★, Léchenaut★★, Dom. LEROY★★★, H Lignier★★★, Perrot-Minot★★, Ponsot★★★, ROUSSEAU★★. Best years: (2006) 05 04 **03** 02 **01 00 99 98 97 96 95 93 90**.

CLOS ST-DENIS AC *Grand Cru, Côte de Nuits, Burgundy, France* This small (6.5ha/16-acre) Grand Cru, which gave its name to the village of MOREY-ST-DENIS, produces wines which are sometimes light, but should be wonderfully silky, with the texture that only great Burgundy can regularly achieve. Best after 10 years or more. Best producers: Bertagna★★, Charlopin★★, DUJAC★★★, JADOT★★, Ponsot★★★. Best years: (2006) 05 04 03 02 01 **00** 99 **98 97 96 95 93 90**.

CLOS DE TART AC★★★ *Grand Cru, Côte de Nuits, Burgundy, France* 7.5ha (18-acre) Grand Cru, a monopoly of the Mommessin family, run by Sylvain Pitiot. Intense, concentrated wines made by traditional methods with a modern result. Best years: (2006) 05 04 03 02 01 **00** 99 96 **95 90**.

CLOS TRIGUEDINA★ *Cahors AC, South-West France* Jean-Luc Baldès makes the CAHORS which is for many the reference to this appellation. In Prince Probus★, he unites the strength of Cahors with elegance. His experimental return to the 'black wine' of Cahors (a traditional style in which the must was 'cooked' to enhance colour) is revealed in a limited release, The New Black Wine. Best years: (2005) 03 01 **00 98 95**.

CLOS UROULAT *Jurançon AC, South-West France* Charles Hours makes tiny quantities of stunningly good JURANÇON. Dry Cuvée Marie★★ has ripe fruit yet a deliciously refreshing finish. The rich sweet Jurançon★★ pulls together lemon, lime, honey and apricot: enjoyable young, and ages magnificently. Best years: (sweet) 2003 **01 00 99 98 96 95**.

CLOS DU VAL *Napa Valley AVA, California, USA* Elegant Cabernet Sauvignon★ (STAGS LEAP DISTRICT★★), Chardonnay★, Merlot★, Pinot Noir★ and Zinfandel★. The Reserve Cabernet★ can age well. Ariadne★★, a Semillon-Sauvignon Blanc blend, is a lovely aromatic white. Best years: (Reserve Cabernet) (2003) 02 **01 00 99 97 96 95 94 91 90** 87 86 84.

CLOS DE VOUGEOT AC *Grand Cru, Côte de Nuits, Burgundy, France* Enclosed by Cistercian monks in the 14th century, and today a considerable tourist attraction, this large (50ha/125-acre) vineyard is now divided among 80+ owners. As a result of this division, Clos de Vougeot has become one of the most unreliable Grand Cru Burgundies; the better wine tends to come from the upper and middle parts. When it is good it is wonderfully fleshy, turning deep and exotic after 10 years or more. Best producers: B Ambroise★★, Amiot-Servelle★★, Chopin★★, J-J Confuron★★★, R Engel★★★, FAIVELEY★★, GRIVOT★★★, Anne GROS★★, JADOT★★★, Dom. LEROY★★★, T LIGER-BELAIR★★, MEO-CAMUZET★★★, Denis MORTET★★★, Mugneret-Gibourg★★★, Ch. de la Tour★★, VOUGERAIE★★. Best years: (2006) 05 04 03 02 01 00 99 98 **97 96 95 93 91 90 88**.

CLOT DE L'OUM *Cotes du Roussillon-Villages AC, Roussillon, France* Eric Monné has been making powerful, dense wines since 2001, from 18ha (45 acres) of vines north of Perpignan, which he works organically. Wines include La Compagnie des Papillons★, Saint Bart Vieilles Vignes★ and top wine Numéro Uno★★, a Syrah-Carignan blend.

CLOUDY BAY *Marlborough, South Island, New Zealand* New Zealand's most successful winery, Cloudy Bay achieved cult status with the first release of its zesty, herbaceous Sauvignon Blanc★★ in 1985.

Sauvignon Blanc Te Koko★★ is very different: rich, creamy, oak-matured and bottle-aged. Cloudy Bay also makes Chardonnay★★, a late-harvest Riesling★★, superb ALSACE-style Gewürztraminer★★ and Riesling★★, and good Pinot Noir★. Vintage Pelorus★★ is a high-quality old-style CHAMPAGNE-method fizz and non-vintage Pelorus★★ is excellent too. Best years: (Sauvignon Blanc) **2006 04 03 01**.

PAUL CLUVER *Elgin WO, South Africa* Cool-loving varieties respond well in this high-lying area: Sauvignon Blanc shows mineral refinement, Chardonnay★ is compact and layered. Also an often vibrant, dryish Riesling★ and thrilling Noble Late Harvest botrytis dessert★★ version and a subtle Gewürztraminer★★. A silky Pinot Noir and flavoursome, savoury Cabernet Sauvignon show reds have promise too.

J-F COCHE-DURY *Meursault, Côte de Beaune, Burgundy, France* Jean-François Coche-Dury is a modest superstar, quietly turning out some of the finest wines on the Côte de Beaune. His best wines are his CORTON-CHARLEMAGNE★★★ and MEURSAULT Perrières★★★, but even his BOURGOGNE Blanc★★ is excellent. His red wines, from VOLNAY★★ and MONTHELIE★, tend to be cheaper than the whites and should be drunk younger. But I drank a 15-year-old BOURGOGNE★ last week and it was a delight. Best years: (whites) (2006) 05 04 **03** 02 **01 00 99 97 96 95**.

COCKBURN *Port DOC, Douro, Portugal* Best known for its Special Reserve ruby, Cockburn has more than that to offer. Vintage★ is stylish and Quinta dos Canais★ is a herby single quinta. New Canais DOURO red is aromatic and promising. Best years: (Vintage) 2003 00 97 94 **91 70 63 60 55**; (dos Canais) 2003 01 00 **95 92**.

CODORNÍU *Cava DO, Cataluña, Spain* The biggest CHAMPAGNE-method sparkling wine company in the world. Anna de Codorníu★ and Jaume Codorníu★ are especially good, but all the sparklers are better than the CAVA average. Drink young for freshness. Codorníu also owns RAIMAT in COSTERS DEL SEGRE, Masía Bach in the PENEDES and Bodegas Bilbaínas in RIOJA, and has a stake in Scala Dei in PRIORAT. They also own Artesa in NAPA, California.

COLCHAGUA, VALLE DE *Rapel, Chile* RAPEL sub-region and home to several exciting estates, such as the acclaimed Apalta hillside vineyard, where CASA LAPOSTOLLE, MONTES and others have plantings. Syrah and Carmenère do very well here. Chimbarongo to the east is cool and foggy, while the Nancagua and Santa Cruz are much warmer. New cool vineyards towards the coast in Lolol and Marchígüe are delivering exciting reds and whites. Best producers: Araucano/Lurton★, CASA LAPOSTOLLE★★, Casa Silva★, CONO SUR★★, EMILIANA (Coyam★★), MONTES★★, MontGras, Viu Manent★.

COLDSTREAM HILLS *Yarra Valley, Victoria, Australia* Founded by Australian wine guru James Halliday; owned by Foster's since 2005. Pinot Noir★ is usually good (Reserve★★): sappy and smoky with cherry fruit and clever use of all-French oak. Chardonnay★ (Reserve★★) has subtlety and delicacy but real depth as well. Reserve Cabernet★ can be very good, though not always ripe; Merlot★★ ripens more successfully. Plans to dramatically increase production don't make a lot of sense in a cool region like the YARRA VALLEY. Best years: (Reserve Pinot Noir) (2006) 05 04 02 **00 98 97 96**.

COLLI ORIENTALI DEL FRIULI DOC *Friuli-Venezia Giulia, Italy* This DOC covers 20 different types of wine. Best known are the sweet whites from Verduzzo in the Ramandolo sub-zone and the delicate Picolit, but it is the reds – from the indigenous Refosco and Schioppettino, as well as imports like Cabernet – and dry whites, from Tocai, Ribolla, Pinot Bianco, Pinot Grigio and Malvasia Istriana, that show how exciting the wines can be. Prices are high. Best producers: Ca' Ronesca★, Dario Coos★, Dorigo★, Dri★, Le Due Terre★★, Livio FELLUGA★★, Walter Filiputti★, Adriano Gigante★, Livon★, Meroi★, Miani★★, Davide Moschioni★★, Rocca Bernarda★, Rodaro★, Ronchi di Cialla★, Ronchi di Manzano★★, Ronco del Gnemiz★★, Scubla★, Sirch★, Specogna★, Le Vigne di Zamò★★, Zof★. Best years: (whites) (2006) 04 **02 01 00 99 98 97**.

COLLI PIACENTINI DOC *Emilia-Romagna, Italy*   Home to some of EMILIA-ROMAGNA's best wines, this DOC covers 11 different types, the best of which are Cabernet Sauvignon and the red Gutturnio (a blend of Barbera and Bonarda) as well as the medium-sweet white and bubbly Malvasia. Best producers: Luretta★, Lusenti, Castello di Luzzano/ Fugazza★, Il Poggiarello★, La Stoppa★, Torre Fornello★, La Tosa (Cabernet Sauvignon★). Best years: (reds) (2006) **04 03 01 00 99 98 97 95**.

COLLINES RHODANIENNES, VIN DE PAYS DES *Rhône Valley, France*   Region between Vienne and Valence. The best wines are Gamay and, notably, Syrah, although there are some good juicy Merlots, too. Best producers: P & C Bonnefond★, COLOMBO★, CUILLERON (Viognier★), P Gaillard★, JAMET★, R Jasmin, M Ogier★, ST-DESIRAT co-op, TAIN co-op, G Vernay★, Vins de Vienne (Sotanum★★). Best years: (reds) 2006 **05 04 03 01 99**.

COLLIO DOC *Friuli-Venezia Giulia, Italy*   Some of Italy's best and most expensive dry white wines are from these hills on the Slovenian border. There are 19 types of wine, from local Tocai and Malvasia Istriana to international varieties. The best are ageworthy. Best producers: Borgo Conventi★, Borgo del Tiglio★★, La Castellada★, Damijan★, Livio FELLUGA★★, Marco Felluga★, Fiegl★, GRAVNER★★, JERMANN★★, Edi Keber★, Renato Keber★★, Livon★, Primosic★, Princic★, Puiatti★, Roncùs★, Russiz Superiore★, SCHIOPETTO★, Matijaz Tercic★★, Venica & Venica★★, Villa Russiz★★, Villanova★, Zuani★★. Best years: (whites) (2006) **04 02 01 00 99 98 97 96 95**.

COLLIOURE AC *Roussillon, France*   This tiny fishing port tucked away in the Pyrenean foothills is also an AC, and makes a throat-warming red wine that is capable of aging for a decade but is marvellously rip-roaring when young. Best producers: (reds) Abbé Rous★, Baillaury★, Clos de Paulilles★, MAS BLANC★★, la Rectorie★★, la Tour Vieille★, Vial Magnères★. Best years: 2003 **01 00 99 98 96**.

COLOMBARD   In France, Colombard traditionally has been distilled to make Armagnac and Cognac, but has now emerged as a table wine grape in its own right, notably as a Vin de Pays des COTES DE GASCOGNE. At its best, it has a lovely, crisp acidity and fresh, aromatic fruit. The largest plantings of the grape are in California, where it generally produces rather less distinguished wines. South Africa can produce attractive refreshing wines, though much is used in brandy production. Australia also has some bright-eyed examples.

JEAN-LUC COLOMBO *Cornas AC, Rhône Valley, France*   Colombo has caused controversy with his criticism of traditional methods. His powerful, rich CORNAS has far less tannic grip than some. Top cuvées are les Ruchets★★ and the lush old-vines la Louvée★★, made in tiny quantities. Among négociant wines now produced, CONDRIEU★★,

CHATEAUNEUF-DU-PAPE les Bartavelles★ and red and white HERMITAGE le Rouet★ stand out, although some labels don't always seem fully ripe. Also produces fragrant ST-PERAY la Belle de Mai★, good COTES DU RHONE★ and vins de pays from the RHONE, the Marseille area and ROUSSILLON. Best years: (Cornas) (2006) 05 04 **03 01 00 99 98 97 95 90**.

COLUMBIA CREST *Washington State, USA* Begun as an offshoot of CHATEAU STE MICHELLE, it has grown into the largest winery in Washington State, and continues to produce top-calibre wines at everyday prices. Two Vines budget label is good. Grand Estates Syrah★ and Grand Estates Chardonnay★ are strong suits. For fruit intensity, drink both with 2–3 years' age. Reserve Syrah★ can be heavily oaked but has impressive style. Best years: (reds) (2005) 04 03 **02 01**.

COLUMBIA VALLEY AVA *Washington State, USA* The largest of WASHINGTON's viticultural regions, covering a third of the state's landmass and encompassing both the YAKIMA VALLEY and WALLA WALLA VALLEY. It produces 98% of the state's wine grapes: Merlot, Cabernet Sauvignon and Chardonnay are the most widely planted varieties. Best producers: ANDREW WILL★★, CADENCE★★, CHATEAU STE MICHELLE★, COLUMBIA CREST★, DELILLE CELLARS★★, DUNHAM CELLARS★,

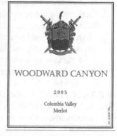

WOODWARD CANYON

2005

Columbia Valley
Merlot

Goose Ridge, HEDGES★, JANUIK WINERY★, L'ECOLE NO 41★★, LONG SHADOWS VINTNERS★★, Matthews Cellars★★, QUILCEDA CREEK★★★, WOODWARD CANYON★★. Best years: (reds) (2006) 04 03 02 01 **00 99**.

COMMANDARIA *Cyprus* Dark brown, treacly wine made from red Mavro and white Xynisteri grapes, sun-dried for 2 weeks before vinification and solera aging. Pretty decent stuff but only potentially one of the world's great rich wines. A lighter, drier style is also produced.

CONCHA Y TORO *Maipo, Chile* Chile's biggest winery, Concha y Toro has around 6000ha (15,000 acres) of vineyards and a talented group of winemakers. Casillero del Diablo★ is the excellent budget label and Marqués de Casa Concha is the next step up (reds★★). Higher up, Trio★ and Terrunyo★★ are good labels for reds and whites. Amelia★★ is the top Chardonnay and small amounts of various excellent reds come out under the Winemaker's Lot label (usually ★★). The classic Cabernet Sauvignon-based Don Melchor★★★ is riper and fleshier in the current (2003) release. Trivento is an exciting Argentinian project. See also ALMAVIVA.

CONDRIEU AC *Rhône Valley, France* Wonderfully fragrant but expensive wine, made entirely from Viognier. Ranging from full and opulent to sweet, late-harvested, Condrieu is a sensation everyone should try, but choose a good producer. Best drunk young. Best producers: G Barge★★, P & C Bonnefond★★, CHAPOUTIER, du Chêne★★, L Chèze★, COLOMBO★★, CUILLERON★★★, DELAS★★, P Dumazet★★, C Facchin★★, P Faury★★, P Gaillard★★, Y Gangloff★★, J-M Gérin, GUIGAL★★ (Doriane★★★), F Merlin★, Monteillet★★, Mouton, R Niéro★★, A Paret★★, A PERRET★★★, C Pichon★★, ROSTAING★★, St-Cosme★★, G Vernay★★★, F Villard★★.

CONO SUR *Rapel, Chile* Dynamic sister winery to CONCHA Y TORO, whose Pinot Noir★ put the grape on the Chilean map. The largely CASABLANCA-sourced 20 Barrels Pinot Noir★★ is rich and perfumed and the wholly Casablanca 20 Barrels Limited Edition★★ and Ocio★★ are positively unctuous. Chardonnay★★, Riesling★★, Merlot★★ and Cabernet Sauvignon★★, under 20 Barrels and Visión labels, are excellent. Also minerally, crunchy 20 Barrels Sauvignon Blanc★★ from one of the coolest sites in Casablanca. Isla Negra offers drier, more 'European' flavours.

CH. LA CONSEILLANTE★★ *Pomerol AC, Bordeaux, France* Elegant, exotic, velvety wine that blossoms beautifully after 5–6 years but can age much longer. Best years: 2005 04 **03** 02 **01** 00 **99 98 96 95 94 90 89**.

CONSTANTIA WO *South Africa* The historical heart of South African wine: three modern wine farms – KLEIN CONSTANTIA, BUITENVERWACHTING and Groot Constantia – were all part of Simon van der Stel's original 1685 land grant. STEENBERG was also one of the earliest wine farms. Today there are nine properties, with many plantings on the steepest slopes. Sauvignon Blanc thrust this cool-climate area into the limelight, but Chardonnays and Semillons are also good. Constantia-Uitsig's elegant, flavoursome Semillon-Sauvignon★ reflects a trend for this blend. Best producers: BUITENVERWACHTING★, Constantia Glen, Constantia-Uitsig★, Groot Constantia, High Constantia, KLEIN CONSTANTIA★, STEENBERG★★. Best years: (whites) **2006 05** 04 03 02 01.

ALDO CONTERNO *Barolo DOCG, Piedmont, Italy* One of BAROLO's finest traditionalist producers. He makes good Dolcetto d'Alba★, excellent BARBERA D'ALBA Conca Tre Pile★★, a barrique-aged LANGHE Nebbiolo Il Favot★★, blended red Quartetto★★ and 2 Langhe Chardonnays: unoaked Printaniè and Bussiador★, fermented and aged in new wood. Pride of the range, though, are his Barolos from the hill of Bussia. In top vintages he produces Barolos Vigna Colonello★★★, Vigna Cicala★★★ and excellent Granbussia★★★, as well as a blended regular Barolo called Bussia Soprana★★. All these Barolos, though accessible when young, need several years to show their true majesty, but retain a remarkable freshness. Best years: (Barolo) (2006) (04) 03 01 **00 99 98 97 96 95 93 90 89 88 85 82**.

GIACOMO CONTERNO *Barolo DOCG, Piedmont, Italy* Aldo's late elder brother Giovanni, now followed by his son Roberto, took an even more traditional approach to winemaking. The flagship wine is BAROLO Monfortino★★★ (only released after some 5 or 6 years in large oak barrels) but Barolo Cascina Francia★★★ is also superb. Also excellent traditional BARBERA D'ALBA★★. Best years: (Monfortino) (2006) (04) (02) (01) (00) 99 **98 97 96 95** 90 89 88 85 82 79 78 74 71.

CONTINO *Rioja DOCa, Rioja, Spain* An estate on some of the finest RIOJA land, half-owned by CVNE. The wines include a Reserva★, a single-vineyard Viña del Olivo★★ and an innovative Graciano★ varietal. Best years: (Reserva) (2005) (04) (03) 02 01 **00 99 98 96 95 94 86 85**.

COONAWARRA *South Australia* On a flat limestone belt thinly veneered with terra rossa soil, Coonawarra can produce sublime Cabernet with blackcurrant leafy flavours and spicy Shiraz that age for years. Merlot can be good, too. An export-led boom fuelled significant new plantings, much of it outside the legendary terra rossa strip, and saw the production of disappointing light reds. An awareness of the risk to the region's reputation has seen substantial changes to viticultural practice over the past 5 years, accompanied by huge investment in revitalizing the vineyards. Best producers: BALNAVES★★, BOWEN★, BRAND'S★★, HOLLICK★, Jacob's Creek/ORLANDO★, KATNOOK★★, Ladbroke Grove, Leconfield★, LINDEMANS, MAJELLA★★★, Murdock, PARKER★★,

PENFOLDS★★, PENLEY★★, PETALUMA★★, WYNNS★★, Zema★★. Best years: (Cabernet Sauvignon) 2005 04 03 02 **01 00 99 98 97 96 94 91 90 86.**

COOPERS CREEK *Auckland, North Island, New Zealand* Successful HAWKES BAY Chardonnay★, especially Swamp Reserve Chardonnay★, and tangy MARLBOROUGH Sauvignon Blanc★★. Dry Riesling★ and Late Harvest Riesling★ styles are also good. A smart range of Reserve reds from Hawkes Bay includes complex Merlot★ and Cabernet Sauvignon blends★. Best years: (Chardonnay) (2006) **04 02 00.**

FRANCIS FORD COPPOLA *Rutherford AVA, California, USA* Movie director Francis Ford Coppola, now a serious wine producer, with volume approaching 1 million cases, has split his winemaking activities between luxury and lifestyle brands. The historical Inglenook Niebaum winery, an elaborate NAPA tourist destination, has been renamed Rubicon Estate. Rubicon★★, a BORDEAUX blend, lacked grace in early vintages but has now taken on a more exciting personality. It still needs 5–6 years of aging. Coppola also offers Cask Cabernet★★, Edizione Pennino★ (Zinfandel), RC Reserve Syrah★ and tiny amounts of Merlot★★ and Cabernet Franc★★, as well as super-premium white blend Blancaneaux★. Big-volume production is now at the former Chateau Souverain winery in SONOMA COUNTY. Brands include Sofia bubblies and good-value Coppola Diamond Collection varietals. Best years: (Rubicon) (2003) 02 **01 00 99 97 96 95 94 91 86.**

CORBIÈRES AC *Languedoc, France* This huge AC now produces some of the best reds in the LANGUEDOC, with juicy fruit and more than a hint of wild hillside herbs. Excellent young, but wines from the best estates can age for years. White Corbières can be tasty – drink as young as possible. Best producers: (reds) Baillat★, Caraguilhes★, Cascadais★, CLOS DE L'ANHEL★, Embres-et-Castelmaure★, Étang des Colombes★, Fontsainte★, Grand Crès★, Grand Moulin★, Haut-Gléon★, Hélène★, l'Ille★, Lastours★, Mansenoble★, Ollieux★, les Palais★, St-Auriol★, VOULTE-GASPARETS★. Best years: (reds) (2005) 04 **03 01 00.**

CORNAS AC *Rhône Valley, France* Pure Syrah wines; attractive alternatives to pricey neighbours HERMITAGE and COTE-ROTIE. When young, the wines are a thick, impenetrable red, almost black in the ripest years. Many need 8 years' aging. Best producers: ALLEMAND★★, F Balthazar★★, CLAPE★★★, COLOMBO★★, Courbis★★, DELAS★, E & J Durand★★, Fauterie★, JABOULET★, J Lemenicier★, Lionnet/ Rochepertuis★★, R Michel★★, V Paris★, TAIN co-op★, Tardieu-Laurent★★, Tunnel★, A Voge★★. Best years: (2006) 05 04 03 **01 00 99 98 97 96 95 94 91 90 89 88 85 83.**

CORSE AC, VIN DE *Corsica, France* Overall AC for CORSICA with 5 superior sub-regions: Calvi, Cap Corse, Figari, Porto Vecchio and Sartène. Ajaccio and Patrimonio are entitled to their own ACs. The most distinctive wines, mainly red, come from local grapes (Nielluccio and Sciacarello for reds, Vermentino for whites). There are some rich sweet Muscats – especially from Muscat du Cap Corse. Best producers: ARENA★, Canarelli★, Clos d'Alzeto★, Clos Capitoro, Clos Culombu★, Clos Landry★, Clos Nicrosi★, Gentile★, Leccia★, Maestracci★, Comte Peraldi★, Renucci★, Saparale, Signadore, Torraccia★.

CORSICA *France* This Mediterranean island has made some pretty dull and undistinguished wines in the past. The last decade has seen a welcome trend toward quality, with co-ops and local growers investing in better equipment and planting noble grape varieties – such as Syrah, Merlot,

Cabernet Sauvignon and Mourvèdre for reds, and Chardonnay and Sauvignon Blanc for whites – to complement the local Nielluccio, Sciacarello and Vermentino. Whites and rosés are pleasant for drinking young; reds are more exciting and can age for 3–4 years. See also CORSE AC.

CORTES DE CIMA *Alentejo, Portugal* Excellent modern Portuguese reds. Local grape varieties – Aragonez (Tempranillo), Trincadeira and Periquita – are used for spicy, fruity Chaminé★, oaked red Cortes de Cima★ and a splendid dark, smoky Reserva★★. Touriga★★ makes an aromatic varietal red and Incógnito★★ is a gutsy, black-fruited blockbuster Syrah. Best years: 2005 04 **03 01 00**.

CORTESE White grape variety planted primarily in south-eastern PIEDMONT in Italy; it can produce good, fairly acidic, dry whites. Sometimes labelled simply as Cortese Piemonte DOC, it is also oaked for GAVI.

CORTON AC *Grand Cru, Côte de Beaune, Burgundy, France* The only red Grand Cru in the COTE DE BEAUNE; ideally the wines should have the burliness and savoury power of the top COTE DE NUITS wines, combined with the seductively perfumed fruit of Côte de Beaune. Red Corton should take 10 years to mature, but many modern examples never get there. Very little white Corton is made. Best producers: B Ambroise★★, d'Ardhuy★★, Bonneau du Martray★★, CHANDON DE BRIAILLES★★, Dubreuil-Fontaine★★, FAIVELEY★★, Camille Giroud★★★, Guyon★★, JADOT★★, Dom. LEROY★★★, MEO-CAMUZET★★★, Prince de Merode★★, Senard★, TOLLOT-BEAUT★★★. Best years: (reds) (2006) 05 04 03 02 01 **00 99 98 96 95 90**.

CORTON-CHARLEMAGNE AC *Grand Cru, Côte de Beaune, Burgundy, France* Corton-Charlemagne, on the west and south-west flanks and at the top of the famous Corton hill, is the largest of Burgundy's white Grands Crus. It can produce some of the most impressive white Burgundies – rich, buttery and nutty with a fine mineral quality. The best show their real worth only at 10 years or more. Best producers: B Ambroise★★, Bonneau du Martray★★★, BOUCHARD PERE ET FILS★★, Champy★★, CHANDON DE BRIAILLES★★★, COCHE-DURY★★★, DROUHIN★★, FAIVELEY★★, V GIRARDIN★★★, JADOT★★★, P Javillier★★, LATOUR★★, Rapet★★, M Rollin★★, TOLLOT-BEAUT★★★, VOUGERAIE★★. Best years: (2006) 05 04 03 02 01 **00 99 97 95 92**.

CH. COS D'ESTOURNEL★★★ *St-Estèphe AC, 2ème Cru Classé, Haut-Médoc, Bordeaux, France* One of the leading châteaux of Bordeaux. Despite a high proportion of Merlot (just under 40%), the wine is classically made for aging and usually needs 10 years to show really well. Recent vintages have been

2003
COS D'ESTOURNEL
SAINT - ESTÈPHE

dark, brooding, powerful and, but for a wobble in 1998 and 99, of the highest order. Second wine: les Pagodes de Cos. Best years: 2005 04 03 02 01 00 **97 96 95 94 90 89 88 86 85**.

COSTANTI *Brunello di Montalcino DOCG, Tuscany, Italy* One of the original, highly respected Montalcino estates making fine BRUNELLO★★ and Rosso★★, as well as Vermiglio★, a tasty partially barrique-aged Sangiovese. Costanti Riserva★★ is archetypal Brunello, austere, elegant and long-lived. Calbello wines, from the hill of Montosoli, include excellent Rosso★★ and Merlot-Cabernet blend Ardingo★★. Best years: (Brunello) (2006) (04) (03) 01 **99 97 95 93 90 88 85 82**.

COSTERS DEL SEGRE DO *Cataluña, Spain*   DO on the 'banks of the Segre' in western CATALUNA. A great array of grape varieties is grown, quality is generally good and prices moderate. Best producers: Castell del Remei★, Celler de Cérvoles★, Tomás Cusiné★, RAIMAT★. Best years: (reds) (2005) (04) 03 **01 00 99 98**.

COSTIÈRES DE NÎMES AC *Rhône Valley, France*   Improving AC between Nîmes and Arles. Reds are generally bright and perfumed, rosés are good young gluggers. Whites are usually tasty versions of Marsanne and Roussanne. Best producers: l'Amarine★, Grande Cassagne★, Lamargue, Mas des Bressades★, Mas Neuf, Mourgues du Grès★, Nages★, d'Or et de Gueules, Tardieu-Laurent, la Tuilerie, Vieux-Relais★. Best years: 2006 **05 04 03 01 00**.

CÔTE DE BEAUNE *Côte d'Or, Burgundy, France*   Southern part of the COTE D'OR; beginning at the hill of CORTON, north of the town of BEAUNE, the Côte de Beaune progresses south as far as LES MARANGES, with white wines gradually taking over from red.

CÔTE DE BEAUNE AC *Côte de Beaune, Burgundy, France*   Small AC, high on the hill above the town of Beaune, named to ensure maximum confusion with the title for the whole region. Best producers: Allexant, VOUGERAIE★. Best years: (2006) 05 04 **03 02**.

CÔTE DE BEAUNE-VILLAGES AC *Côte de Beaune, Burgundy, France*   Red wine AC covering 16 villages, such as AUXEY-DURESSES, LADOIX, MARANGES. If the wine is a blend from several villages it is sold as Côte de Beaune-Villages. It can also cover the red wine production of mainly white wine villages such as MEURSAULT. Best producers: DROUHIN★, JADOT★. Best years: (2006) 05 **03 02 99**.

CÔTE DE BROUILLY AC *Beaujolais, Burgundy, France*   Wine from the higher slopes of Mont Brouilly, a small but abrupt volcanic mountain in the south of the BEAUJOLAIS Crus area. The wine is deeper in colour and fruit and has more intensity than that of BROUILLY. Best producers: O Ravier★, Roches Bleues/Lacondemine★, Ch. Thivin (Zaccharie Geoffray★★), Viornery★. Best years: **2006 05**.

CÔTE CHALONNAISE   See BOURGOGNE-COTE CHALONNAISE.

CÔTE DE NUITS *Côte d'Or, Burgundy, France*   This is the northern part of the great COTE D'OR and is *not* an AC. Almost entirely red wine country, the vineyards start in the southern suburbs of Dijon and continue south in a narrow swathe to below the town of NUITS-ST-GEORGES. The villages are some of the greatest wine names in the world – GEVREY-CHAMBERTIN, VOUGEOT and VOSNE-ROMANEE etc.

CÔTE DE NUITS-VILLAGES AC *Côte de Nuits, Burgundy, France*   Although not much seen, the wines (mostly red) are often good, not very deep in colour but with a nice cherry fruit. Best producers: (reds) D Bachelet★, Chopin-Groffier★, J-J Confuron, JADOT, Jayer-Gilles★, RION★, P Rossignol★. Best years: (reds) (2006) 05 **04 03 02**.

CÔTE D'OR *Burgundy, France*   Europe's most northern great red wine area and also the home of some of the world's best dry white wines. The name, meaning 'golden slope', refers to a 48km (30-mile) stretch between Dijon and Chagny which divides into the COTE DE NUITS in the north and the COTE DE BEAUNE in the south.

CÔTE ROANNAISE AC *Loire Valley, France*   Small, improving AC in the upper LOIRE producing mostly light reds and rosés from Gamay. Non-appellation whites can be good. Best producers: Fontenay★, R Sérol★.

CÔTE-RÔTIE AC *Rhône Valley, France*   The Côte-Rôtie, or 'roasted slope', produces one of France's greatest red wines. On its vertiginous slopes, the Syrah manages to balance super ripeness with freshness, and the small amount of white Viognier sometimes included in the blend gives an unexpected exotic fragrance. Lovely young, it is better aged for 8 years. Best producers: G Barge★★, Bernard★, P & C Bonnefond★★, Bonserine★, B Burgaud★, Clusel-Roch★★, CUILLERON★★, DELAS★, Duclaux★★, Gallet★, Garon★, J-M Gérin★★, GUIGAL★★, JABOULET★, JAMET★★★, Jasmin★★, S Ogier★★, ROSTAING★★, J-M Stéphan★, Tardieu-Laurent★★, Vidal-Fleury★, F Villard★, Vins de Vienne★★. Best years: (2006) 05 04 03 **01 00 99 98 97 95 94 91 90 89 88**.

COTEAUX D'AIX-EN-PROVENCE AC *Provence, France*   The first AC in the south to acknowledge that Cabernet Sauvignon can enormously enhance the traditional local grape varieties such as Grenache, Cinsaut, Mourvèdre, Syrah and Carignan. The reds can age. Some quite good fresh rosé is made, while the whites, mostly still traditionally made, are pleasant but hardly riveting. Best producers: Ch. Bas★, les Bastides★, les Béates★★, Beaupré★, Calissanne★, J-L COLOMBO (Côte Bleue)★, d'EOLE★, Fonscolombe, Revelette★, Vignelaure★. Best years: (reds) 2005 04 **03 01 00 99**.

COTEAUX DE L'ARDÈCHE, VIN DE PAYS DES *Rhône Valley, France*   Increasingly good varietal red wines made from Cabernet Sauvignon, Syrah, Merlot or Gamay and dry, fresh white wines from Chardonnay, Viognier or Sauvignon Blanc. Best producers: Vignerons Ardechois, Colombier, DUBOEUF, G Flacher, Louis LATOUR, Pradel, ST-DESIRAT, Vigier.

COTEAUX DE L'AUBANCE AC *Loire Valley, France*   Smallish AC north of COTEAUX DU LAYON AC for sweet or semi-sweet white wines made from Chenin Blanc. Top sweet wines are now labelled Sélection de Grains Nobles, as in ALSACE. Best producers: Daviau/Bablut★★, Haute Perche★, Montgilet/V Lebreton★, Princé, RICHOU★★, Rochelles★. Best years: (2006) 05 04 **03** 02 **01 99 97 96 90**.

COTEAUX CHAMPENOIS AC *Champagne, France*   Still wines from Champagne. Fairly acid with a few exceptions, notably from Bouzy and Aÿ. The best age for 5 years or more. Best producers: Paul Bara★, BOLLINGER★, Egly-Ouriet★, H Goutorbe, LAURENT-PERRIER, Joseph PERRIER, Ch. de Saran★/MOET & CHANDON. Best years: 2003 02 00 **99 98 96 95**.

COTEAUX DU LANGUEDOC AC *Languedoc, France*   Large and increasingly successful AC situated between Montpellier and Narbonne, producing around 73 million bottles of beefy red and tasty rosé wines. Twelve 'crus', including Montpeyroux, Quatourze and Cabrières, have historically been allowed to append their names to the AC – these are in the process of being delineated by climate and soil type. La CLAPE, Grès de Montpellier and PIC ST-LOUP have already been officially recognized. Best producers: l'Aiguelière★, Aupilhac★, Calage★, Clavel★, CLOS MARIE★, la Coste★, Grès St-Paul★, HECHT & BANNIER★, Lacroix-Vanel★, Mas Cal Demoura★, Mas des Chimères★, MAS JULLIEN★, Mas de Martin, PEYRE ROSE★★, Poujol★, PRIEURE DE ST-JEAN DE BEBIAN★★, Puech-Haut★, St-Martin de la Garrigue★, Terre Megère★. Best years: 2004 03 **01 00 99 98**.

COTEAUX DU LAYON AC *Loire Valley, France*   Sweet wine from the Layon Valley, south of Angers. The wine is made from Chenin Blanc grapes that, ideally, are attacked by noble rot. In great years like 1996, and from a talented grower, this can be one of the world's exceptional sweet wines. Top wines are now labelled Sélection de Grains Nobles, as in ALSACE. Six villages are entitled to use the Coteaux du Layon-Villages AC and put their own name on the label; these wines are definitely underpriced for the quality. Three sub-areas, BONNEZEAUX, Chaume and QUARTS DE CHAUME, have their own ACs. Best producers: P Aquilas★★, P Baudouin★★★, BAUMARD★★, Bergerie★★, Bidet★, Breuil★, Cady★★, P Delesvaux★★★, Forges★★, Ogereau★★, Passavant★, Pierre-Bise★★, J PITHON★★, Quarres★, J Renou★★, Roulerie★★, Sablonnettes★★, Sauveroy★, Soucherie/P-Y Tijou★★, Yves Soulez★★, Touche Noire★. Best years: (2006) 05 04 **03** 02 **01 99 97 96 95 90 89**.

COTEAUX DU LYONNAIS AC *Beaujolais, Burgundy, France* Good, light, BEAUJOLAIS-style reds and a few whites and rosés from scattered vineyards between Villefranche and Lyon. Drink young.

COTEAUX DU TRICASTIN AC *Rhône Valley, France* Bright, fresh, sometimes full, reds and rosés with attractive juicy fruit. Only a little of the nutty white is made but is worth looking out for. Drink it young. Best producers: Décelle, Grangeneuve★, Lônes, St-Luc★, la Tour d'Elyssas, Vieux Micocoulier. Best years: 2006 **05 04 03 01**.

COTEAUX VAROIS AC *Provence, France* North of Toulon, this is an area to watch, with new plantings of classic grapes to improve quality. Best producers: Alysses★, Bremond, Calisse★, Chaberts, Deffends★, Garbelle, Routas★, St-Estève, St-Jean-le-Vieux★, St-Jean-de-Villecroze★, Triennes★. Best years: 2005 04 **03** 01.

CÔTES DE BERGERAC AC See BERGERAC AC.

CÔTES DE BOURG AC *Bordeaux, France* The best red wines are earthy but blackcurranty and can age for 6–10 years. Very little white is made; most of it is dry and dull. Best producers: Brulesécaille★, Bujan★, FALFAS★, Fougas (Maldoror★), Garreau, Guerry, Haut-Guiraud, Haut-Macô★, Haut-Mondésir★, Macay, Mercier★, Nodoz★, ROC DE CAMBES★★, Tayac★, Tour de Guiet★. Best years: 2005 **03 02 01 00 99 98 96 95**.

CÔTES DE CASTILLON AC *Bordeaux, France* Area east of ST-EMILION that has surged in quality recently. There's still good value but prices are beginning to climb. The best wines are full and firm, yet well endowed with the lushness of St-Émilion. Best producers: Dom. de l'A★★, Aiguilhe★★, Belcier, Cap-de-Faugères★, la Clarière Laithwaite, Clos l'Eglise★, Clos Les Lunelles★ (from 2001), Clos Puy Arnaud★★, Côte-Montpezat, Joanin Bécot★, Poupille★, Robin★, Veyry★, Vieux-Ch.-Champs-de-Mars★. Best years: 2005 04 **03 02 01 00 99 98 96 95**.

CÔTES DE DURAS AC *South-West France* AC between ENTRE-DEUX-MERS and BERGERAC, with good, fresh, grassy reds and whites from traditional BORDEAUX grapes. Drink young. Best producers: Clos du Cadaret, Duras co-op, Grand Mayne, Lafon, Landerrouat co-op, Laulan, Mouthes le Bihan★, Petit Malromé. Best years: (reds) 2005 04 03 **01 00**.

CÔTES DE FRANCS See BORDEAUX-COTES DE FRANCS.

CÔTES DU FRONTONNAIS AC *South-West France* From north of Toulouse, some of the most distinctive reds – often juicy and positively silky in texture – of South-West France. Négrette is the chief grape, but certain producers coarsen it with Cabernet, which rather defeats the object. Best producers: Baudare, Bellevue-la-Forêt★, Cahuzac★, la Colombière, Ferran, Flotis, Laurou, Montauriol, la Palme, Plaisance, le Roc★, St-Louis. Best years: 2004 03 **01 00 98**.

CÔTES DE GASCOGNE, VIN DE PAYS DES *South-West France* This is Armagnac country, but the tangy-fresh, fruity white table wines are tremendously good. Best producers: Aurin, Brumont/MONTUS, de Joy, Producteurs PLAIMONT★, St-Lannes, TARIQUET★.

CÔTES DU JURA AC *Jura, France* Jura's regional AC covers a variety of wines, including specialities *vin jaune* and *vin de paille*. Savagnin makes strong-tasting whites, and Chardonnay some good dry whites and CREMANT DU JURA. Distinctive reds and rosés from local Poulsard and Trousseau; wines can be better from Pinot Noir. Drink young. Best producers: Arlay★★, Berthet-Bondet★★, Bourdy★, Chalandard★, Clavelin★, Delay★, Ch. de l'Étoile★, Joly★, A Labet★, J Maclé★★, Reverchon★, Rijckaert★★, Rolet★★, A & M Tissot★.

CÔTES DU LUBÉRON AC *Rhône Valley, France* Production is dominated by the co-ops east of Avignon; their light, easy wines drink young. Domaine wines have more body. Best producers: Bonnieux co-op, Ch. la Canorgue, la Citadelle★, Fontenille★, Ch. de l'Isolette★, la Tour-d'Aigues co-op, Ch. des Tourettes, Val Joanis, la Verrerie★. Best years: 2006 **05 04 03 01**.

CÔTES DU MARMANDAIS AC *South-West France* The red wines are fairly successful BORDEAUX lookalikes; Syrah is also permitted. Best producers: Beaulieu, Cave de Beaupuy, Cocumont co-op, Elian Da Ros★ (Chante Coucou, Clos Baquey★).

CÔTES DE MONTRAVEL AC See MONTRAVEL AC.

CÔTES DE PROVENCE AC *Provence, France* Large AC mainly for fruity reds and rosés to drink young. Whites have improved. Best producers: Barbanau★, la Bernarde★, Clos d'Alari, Commanderie de Peyrassol★, la Courtade★★, Coussin Ste-Victoire★, Cressonnière★, Dupéré-Barrera, Féraud★, Galoupet★, Gavoty★, Jale, Mauvanne★, Minuty★, Ott★, Rabiega★, Réal Martin★, RICHEAUME★, Rimauresq★★, Roquefort★, Maîtres Vignerons de St-Tropez, St-André de Figuière, Sorin★, Élie Sumeire★, Les Valentines.

CÔTES DU RHÔNE AC *Rhône Valley, France* AC for the whole RHONE VALLEY. Over 90% is red and rosé, mainly from Grenache, with some Cinsaut, Syrah, Carignan and Mourvèdre to add warm southern personality. Modern winemaking has revolutionized the style; today's wines are generally juicy, spicy and easy to drink, ideally within 5 years. Most wine is made by co-ops. Best producers: (reds) Amouriers★, d'Andézon★, les Aphillanthes★, A Brunel★, L Charvin★★, CLAPE★, COLOMBO★, Coudoulet de BEAUCASTEL★★, Cros de la Mûre★, Estézargues co-op★, Fonsalette★, FONT DE MICHELLE★, Gramenon★★, Grand Moulas★, Grand Prébois★, GUIGAL★, Haut Musiel, Hugues★, JABOULET, la Janasse★, J-M Lombard★, Mas de Libian★, Mont-Redon, la Mordorée★, REMEJEANNE★, M Richaud★, St-Estève★, ST-GAYAN★, Ste-Anne★, Santa Duc★, Tardieu-Laurent★, Tours★, Vieille Julienne, Vieux-Chêne★; (whites) CLAPE★, Coudoulet de BEAUCASTEL★, P Gaillard★, REMEJEANNE★, Ste-Anne★. Best years: (reds) 2006 **05 04 03 01**.

CÔTES DU RHÔNE-VILLAGES AC *Rhône Valley, France* AC covering 18 villages in the southern COTES DU RHONE that have traditionally made superior wine (especially CAIRANNE, RASTEAU, Laudun, Séguret, Valréas, Sablet, Visan). Best are spicy reds that can age well. Best producers: Achiary★, Amouriers★, Beaurenard★, Bressy-Masson★, de Cabasse★, Cabotte★, Chapoton★, D Charavin★, Charbonnière★, Chaume-Arnaud★, Combe★, Coriançon★, Cros de la Mûre★, Espiguette★, Les Goubert★, Estézargues co-op★, Gourt de Mautens★★, Gramenon★, Grand Moulas★, Grand Veneur★, la Janasse★, Jérôme★, Mourchon★, Pélaquié★, Piaugier★, Rasteau co-op★, REMEJEANNE★, ST-GAYAN★, Ste-Anne★, la Soumade★, Tours★, Trapadis★, Verquière★. Best years: (reds) 2006 **05 04 03 01 00 99 98**.

CÔTES DU ROUSSILLON AC *Roussillon, France* ROUSSILLON's catch-all AC, dominated by co-ops. It's a hot area, and much of the wine is baked and dull. But there's a lively and expanding bunch of estates doing surprisingly good things with white and exciting things with reds. Best producers: (reds) la CASENOVE★★, Vignerons Catalans, CAZES★, Chênes★, J-L COLOMBO★, Ferrer-Ribière★, Força Réal, Joliette, Laporte★, Mas Crémat★, Mossé, Olivier Pithon★, Rivesaltes co-op, Sarda-Malet★. Best years: (reds) 2004 03 **01 00 99 98**.

CÔTES DU ROUSSILLON-VILLAGES AC *Roussillon, France* Wines from the best sites in the northern CÔTES DU ROUSSILLON. Villages Caramany, Latour-de-France, Lesquerde and Tautavel may add their own name. Best producers: Vignerons Catalans, Calvet-Thunevin, CAZES★, Chênes★, Clos des Fées★, CLOT DE L'OUM★★, Fontanel★, Força Réal, Gardiés★, GAUBY★★, Jau, Mas Amiel★, Mas Crémat★, Roc des Anges, Schistes★. Best years: (reds) 2004 03 **01 00 99 98**.

CÔTES DE ST-MONT VDQS *South-West France* A good VDQS for firm but fruity reds and some fair rosés and dry whites. Best producer: Producteurs PLAIMONT★.

CÔTES DE THONGUE, VIN DE PAYS DES *Languedoc, France* Zone north-east of Béziers. Many dull red quaffers, but dynamic estates can produce excellent results. Best producers: l'Arjolle★, Bellevue, les Chemins de Bassac, Condamine l'Évêque, Croix Belle.

CÔTES DU VENTOUX AC *Rhône Valley, France* AC with vineyards on the slopes of Mt Ventoux. When well made, the red wines can have a lovely juicy fruit, or in the case of JABOULET and Pesquié, some real stuffing. Best producers: Anges★, Bedoin co-op, Brusset, Cascavel★, La Croix des Pins★, Font-Sane, Goult/Cave de Lumières★, JABOULET★, la Martinelle, Pesquié★, St-Didier/Cave Courtoise★, Valcombe★, la Verrière, la Vieille Ferme. Best years: (reds) **2006 05 04**.

CÔTES DU VIVARAIS AC *Rhône Valley, France* In the northern Gard and Ardèche, typical southern Rhône grapes (Grenache, Syrah, Cinsaut, Carignan) produce mainly light, fresh reds and rosés for drinking young. Best producers: Vignerons Ardechois, Gallety, Vigier.

QUINTA DO CÔTTO *Douro DOC and Port DOC, Douro, Portugal* Unfortified DOURO wine expert. Quinta do Côtto red and creamy Paço de Teixeró VINHO VERDE are good, and Grande Escolha★★ is one of Portugal's best reds, oaky and powerful when young, rich and ready when mature. Best years: (Grande Escolha) 2001 00 **97 95 94 90 87 85**.

COULY-DUTHEIL *Chinon AC, Loire Valley, France* Large merchant house responsible for 10% of the CHINON AC. Best wines are Clos de l'Écho★, Clos de l'Écho Crescendo★ and Clos de l'Olive★. Top négociant blend is la Baronnie Madeleine★, which combines tasty raspberry fruit with a considerable capacity to age. Also sells a range of other Touraine wines. Best years: (reds) (2006) 05 04 **03** 02 **01 97 96 90 89**.

PIERRE COURSODON *St-Joseph AC, Rhône Valley, France* Family-owned domaine producing rich, oaked ST-JOSEPH★ from very old vines. The red wines need up to 5 years before they show all their magnificent cassis and truffle and violet richness, especially the top wine, La Sensonne★★. Whites, from the Marsanne grape, are good, too. Best years: (reds) 2006 05 **04 03 02 01 00 99 98 95 90**.

CH. COUTET★★ *Barsac AC, 1er Cru Classé, Bordeaux, France* BARSAC'S largest Classed Growth property has been in great form in recent years, and with its finesse and balance is once again a classic Barsac. Extraordinarily intense Cuvée Madame★★★ is made in exceptional years. Best years: 2005 04 03 **02** 01 **00 99** 98 97 96 95 90 89 88.

CRAGGY RANGE *Hawkes Bay and Martinborough, North Island, New Zealand* Premium HAWKES BAY wines include stylish Les Beaux Cailloux Chardonnay★★, a bold Cabernet blend called The Quarry★★, a rich Merlot blend known as Sophia★★ and the flagship Le Sol Syrah★★. Also fine Pinot Noirs★★ and Rieslings★ from MARTINBOROUGH; restrained yet intense Avery Sauvignon Blanc★ and tangy Rapaura Road Riesling★ from MARLBOROUGH; elegant Chardonnay★ and Merlot★, both from the Seven Poplars Vineyard in Hawkes Bay. Best years: (Syrah) (2006) 04 **02** 01.

QUINTA DO CRASTO *Douro DOC and Port DOC, Douro, Portugal* Well-situated property with very good traditional LBV★★ and Vintage★★ port and thoroughly enjoyable red DOURO★, especially Reserva★★ and Touriga Nacional★★. Flagship reds Vinha da Ponte★★ and Maria Teresa★★ can reach ★★★. Best years: (port) 2003 00 99 97 **95** 94; (Reserva) 2004 03 **01 00** 99 98; (Ponte) 2004 00; (Maria Teresa) 2003 01.

CRÉMANT D'ALSACE AC *Alsace, France* Good CHAMPAGNE-method sparkling wine from ALSACE, usually made from Pinot Blanc. Reasonable quality, if not great value for money. Best producers: BLANCK★, Dopff & Irion, Dopff au Moulin★, J Gross★, Kuentz-Bas, MURÉ★, Ostertag★, Pfaffenheim co-op, P Sparr★, A Stoffel★, TURCKHEIM co-op★.

CRÉMANT DE BOURGOGNE AC *Burgundy, France* Most Burgundian Crémant is white and is made either from Chardonnay alone or blended with Pinot Noir. The result, especially in ripe years, can be full, soft, almost honey-flavoured – if you give the wine the 2–3 years' aging needed for mellowness to develop. Best producers: A Delorme, Lucius-Grégoire, Parigot-Richard, Simonnet-Febvre; and the co-ops at Bailly★ (the best for rosé), Lugny★, St-Gengoux-de-Scissé and Viré.

CRÉMANT DE DIE AC *Rhône Valley, France* AC for traditional-method fizz made entirely from the Clairette Blanche grape. Less aromatic than CLAIRETTE DE DIE. Best producers: Jacques Faure, J-C Raspail.

CRÉMANT DU JURA AC *Jura, France* AC for fizz from Jura. Largely Chardonnay-based, with Poulsard for the pinks. Best producers: Ch. de l'Étoile★, la Pinte, Pupillin co-op★.

CRÉMANT DE LIMOUX AC *Languedoc, France* Sparkling wine made from a blend of Chardonnay, Chenin Blanc, Mauzac and Pinot Noir; the wines generally have more complexity than BLANQUETTE DE LIMOUX. Drink young. Best producers: l'Aigle★, Antech, Fourn, Guinot, Laurens★, Martinolles★, SIEUR D'ARQUES★, Valent.

CRÉMANT DE LOIRE AC *Loire Valley, France* CHAMPAGNE-method sparkling wine in Anjou and Touraine, with more fruit and yeast character than those of VOUVRAY and SAUMUR. Good to drink as soon as it is released. Can be excellent value. Best producers: BAUMARD★, Berger Frères★, Brizé★, Fardeau★, Girault★, Gratien & Meyer★, Lambert★, Langlois-Château★, Michaud★, Nerleux/Regis Neau, Passavant★.

CRIOTS-BÂTARD-MONTRACHET AC See BATARD-MONTRACHET AC.

CRISTOM *Willamette Valley AVA, Oregon, USA* Nestled in the Eola Hills, this winery specializes in Pinot Noir (Marjorie Vineyard★, Jessie Vineyard). White wines include barrel-fermented Chardonnay, Pinot Gris and Viognier. Best years: (Pinot Noir) (2005) 04 03 02 **01** 00.

CROFT *Port DOC, Douro, Portugal* Owned by the Fladgate Partnership (along with TAYLOR and FONSECA) since 2001, these wines are showing distinct improvements, especially at basic level. Vintage ports★★ have traditionally been elegant, rather than thunderous. Single-quinta Quinta da Roêda★ is pretty good in recent vintages. Best years: (Vintage) 2003 00 94 **91 77 70 66 63 55 45**; (Roêda) 1997 **95**.

CROZES-HERMITAGE AC *Rhône Valley, France* The largest of the northern Rhône ACs. Ideally, the pure Syrah reds should have a full colour and a strong, clear, black fruit flavour. You can drink them young, but in ripe years from a hillside site the wine improves greatly for 2–5 years. The best whites are fresh and clean. In general drink white Crozes young, before the floral perfume disappears. Best producers: (reds) A Belle★★, CHAPOUTIER★ (Varonniers★★) Y Chave★ (Rouvre★★), Colombier★, Combier★ (Clos des Grives★★), E Darnaud★, DELAS★ (Le Clos, Tour d'Albon★★), O Dumaine★, Entrefaux★, L Fayolle★★, Ferraton★, GRAILLOT★★, Hauts Chassis, JABOULET★, Murinais★, Pavillon-Mercurol★, Pochon★ (Ch. Curson★★), Remizières★★, G Robin★, Rousset (Picaudières★★), M Sorrel★, TAIN co-op (Les hauts du Fief★), Tardieu-Laurent★★, Vins de Vienne★; (whites) Y Chave★, Colombier★, Combier★★, Dard & Ribo★, DELAS★, O Dumaine★, Entrefaux★ (Cuvée des Pends★★) Ferraton★, GRAILLOT★, JABOULET★, Martinelles, Pochon (Ch. Curson★★), Remizières★, M Sorrel★★. Best years: (reds) 2006 **05 04 03 01 00 99 98 95**.

YVES CUILLERON *Condrieu AC, Rhône Valley, France* With wines like Cuilleron's you can understand CONDRIEU's fame and high prices. Les Chaillets Vieilles Vignes★★★ is everything wine made from Viognier should be: opulent and rich, with perfumed honey and apricot aromas. La Petite Côte★★ is also exceptional, and the late-harvest les Ayguets★★★ is an extraordinary sweet whirl of dried apricots, honey and barley sugar. Cuilleron also makes ST-JOSEPH reds★★ and whites★★ and tiny quantities of ripe, dark, spicy CÔTE-RÔTIE★★. A joint venture, les Vins de Vienne, with partners Pierre Gaillard and François Villard, produces Vin de Pays des COLLINES RHODANIENNES Sotanum★★ (100% Syrah) and Taburnum★ (100% Viognier) from ancient terraces just north of Vienne. Best years: (Condrieu) **2006 05 04 03 02 01**.

CULLEN *Margaret River, Western Australia* One of the original and best MARGARET RIVER vineyards, established by Diana and Kevin Cullen and now run by their talented winemaker daughter Vanya. Superb Chardonnay★★★ is complex and satisfying; Sauvignon-Semillon★★ marries nectarines with melon and nuts. The Cabernet Sauvignon-Merlot★★★ is gloriously soft, deep and scented; this wine is now justifiably regarded as one of Australia's greats. Mangan Malbec-Petit Verdot-Merlot★★ is delicious. Best years: (Cabernet Sauvignon-Merlot) (2005) 04 03 02 01 **00 99 98 97 96 95 94 92 91 90 86 84 82**.

CURICÓ, VALLE DE *Valle Central, Chile* Most of the big producers here have planted Cabernet Sauvignon, Merlot, Carmenère, Chardonnay and Sauvignon Blanc. It's a bit warm for whites, but the long growing season provides good fruit concentration for reds. Best producers: Echeverría★★, SAN PEDRO★, Miguel TORRES★★, VALDIVIESO★.

CUVAISON *Napa Valley AVA, California, USA* Red wines include tasty, focused Merlot★, sound Cabernet Sauvignon★ and delicate Pinot Noir★. Decent Chardonnay; silky Reserve Chardonnay★ is worth seeking out. Best years: (Merlot) 2003 **02 01 99 98 97 96 94**.

CVNE *Rioja DOCa, Rioja, Spain* Compañía Vinícola del Norte de España is the full name of this firm, but it's usually known as 'coonay'. Viña Real★ is one of RIOJA's few remaining well-oaked whites. Viña Real Reserva★ and Gran Reserva★ reds can be rich and meaty, and easily surpass the rather commercial Crianzas; Imperial Gran Reserva★ is long-lived and impressive. Real de Asúa★ is a new premium red. Best years: (reds) (2005) (04) (03) **02 01 98 96 95 94 91 90 89 87 86 85**.

DIDIER DAGUENEAU *Pouilly-Fumé AC, Loire Valley, France* A much-needed innovator and quality fanatic in a complacent region. Wines benefit from 4–5 years' aging and, although at times unpredictable, are generally intense and complex. The range starts with En Chailloux★★ and moves up through flinty Buisson Renard★★ to barrel-fermented Silex★★ and Pur Sang★★. Best years: 2006 05 04 **03** 02 01.

ROMANO DAL FORNO *Valpolicella DOC, Veneto, Italy* VALPOLICELLA Superiore★★ from Monte Lodoletta vineyard, outside the Valpolicella Classico area, is a model of power and grace; AMARONE★★★ and RECIOTO DELLA VALPOLICELLA★★★, from the same source, are even more voluptuous. Best years: (Amarone) (2006) (04) (03) 01 00 **97 96 95 93 91 90 88 85**.

TENIMENTI LUIGI D'ALESSANDRO *Cortona DOC, Tuscany, Italy* The vineyards have benefited from massive investment. Il Bosco★★ and the 'second' wine, Cortona Syrah★, are both 100% Syrah. The white Fontarca★ blends Chardonnay with varying amounts of Viognier. Best years: (Il Bosco) (2006) 04 03 01 00 **99 98 97 96 95**.

DALLA VALLE *Napa Valley AVA, California, USA* Stunning hillside winery, producing some of NAPA's most esteemed Cabernets. Maya★★★ is a magnificent blend of Cabernet Sauvignon and Cabernet Franc; the straight Cabernet Sauvignon★★★ is almost as rich. The wines drink well at 10 years, but will keep for 20 or more. Best years: (Maya) (2005) 03 02 01 00 **99 98 97 96 95 94 91 90**.

DÃO DOC *Beira Alta, Portugal* Dão has steep slopes ideal for vineyards, and a great climate for growing local grape varieties, yet it's only just beginning to realize its potential for characterful red and white wines. Best producers: (reds) Caves ALIANCA (Quinta da Garrida★), Boas Quintas (Quinta Fonte do Ouro★), Quinta de Cabriz★ (Virgilio Loureiro★★), Quinta das Maias★, Quinta da Pellada★★, Quinta da Ponte Pedrinha, Quinta dos ROQUES★★, Quinta de Sães★, Caves SAO JOAO★, SOGRAPE★ (Quinta dos Carvalhais★); (whites) Quinta de Cabriz, Quinta das Maias★, Quinta dos ROQUES★★, Quinta de Sães★, SOGRAPE★. Best years: (reds) 2005 04 03 **01 00 99 97 96 95**.

D'ARENBERG *McLaren Vale, South Australia* Chester Osborn makes blockbuster Dead Arm Shiraz★★, Footbolt Old Vine Shiraz★, Custodian Grenache★ and other blends from low-yielding old vines. These are big, brash, character-filled wines, and are continually being joined by more new ideas. Best years: (Dead Arm Shiraz) (2006) (05) 04 03 02 01 00 **97 96 95**.

DARTING *Bad Dürkheim, Pfalz, Germany* Full, rich. fruity wines from sites in BAD DURKHEIM (Spielberg), Ungstein (Herrenberg Riesling Spätlese★★) and WACHENHEIM (Mandelgarten). Best years: (2006) 05 04 **03 02 01 99 98**.

RENÉ & VINCENT DAUVISSAT *Chablis, Burgundy, France* CHABLIS at its most complex – refreshing, seductive and beautifully structured, with the fruit balancing the subtle influence of mostly older oak. Look for la Forest★★, the more aromatic Vaillons★★★ and the powerful les Clos★★★. Best years: (2006) 05 04 **03** 02 **00 99 98 96 95**.

MARCO DE BARTOLI *Sicily, Italy* Marco De Bartoli is most noted for a
dry, unfortified MARSALA-style wine called Vecchio Samperi – his idea of
what Marsala was before the English merchant, John Woodhouse, first
fortified it for export. Particularly fine is the 20-year-old Ventennale –
dry, intense and redolent of candied citrus peel, dates and old, old
raisins. Also excellent MOSCATO PASSITO DI PANTELLERIA Bukkuram★★.

DE BORTOLI *Riverina, New South Wales/Yarra, Victoria, Australia* Large,
family-owned company currently producing some of Australia's most
interesting wines, thanks largely to the restless experimentation of
Steve Webber and his team in the YARRA VALLEY: Sauvignon Blanc★,
Chardonnay★★, Shiraz★★, Cabernet★ and Pinot Noir★★. The RIVERINA
winery first gained prominence by producing a sublime, world-class
botrytized Semillon (Noble One★★★) but in recent times has had
consumers gasping because of the quality of its budget-priced labels –
Sacred Hill, Deen and Montage. VICTORIA-based quaffers such as Sero,
Windy Peak and Gulf Station have their admirers too. Best years:
(Noble One) (2006) (04) 03 02 **00 98 96 95 94 93 90 87 85 84 82**.

DEHLINGER *Russian River Valley AVA, California, USA* Outstanding
Pinot Noir★★★ from vineyards in the cool RUSSIAN RIVER region a few
miles from the Pacific, best at 5–10 years old. Also mouthfilling
Chardonnay★★ and bold, peppery Syrah★★. Recent vintages of
Cabernet★★ and Bordeaux Blend★★ (Cabernet-Merlot) reflect a surge
in quality. Best years: (Pinot Noir) (2005) 04 03 **02 01 00 99 98 97**.

MARCEL DEISS *Alsace AC, Alsace, France* Jean-Michel Deiss is fanatical
about distinctions of *terroir* and,
controversially for ALSACE, his top wines
are now blends, named according to the
vineyard – Grands Crus Altenberg,
Mambourg and Schoenenbourg are all
★★★. These are outstanding wines of
huge character, often with some residual
sugar. Pinot Noir Burlenburg★★ is
vibrant and delicious. Even basic Riesling
St-Hippolyte★ and Pinot Blanc Bergheim
are delightful. Best years: (Grand Cru
blends) 2005 04 03 02 **01 00 99**.

DELAS FRÈRES *Rhône Valley, France* Restored-to-quality merchant
(owned by ROEDERER) selling wines from the entire RHONE VALLEY, but
with its own vineyards in the northern Rhône. Single-vineyard wines
include dense, powerful red HERMITAGE★★ (les Bessards★★★), which
needs a decade or more to reach its peak, perfumed COTE-ROTIE la
Landonne★★ and ST-JOSEPH Ste-Épine★★. The CROZES-HERMITAGE Tour
d'Albon★★ is a good bet, as is the COTES DU RHONE St-Esprit. Look out
for the aromatic CONDRIEU★★. Best years: (premium reds) (2006) 05 04
03 01 **00 99 98 97 96 95 94 91 90 89 88 85 78**.

DELEGAT'S *Henderson, Auckland, North Island, New Zealand* One of New
Zealand's largest family-run wineries, specializing in Chardonnay
(Reserve★), Cabernet and Merlot (Reserve★) from HAWKES BAY. The
Oyster Bay label, based in MARLBOROUGH, is best known for Sauvignon
Blanc★. Best years: (Oyster Bay Sauvignon Blanc) **2006 04 03**.

DELILLE CELLARS *Columbia Valley AVA, Washington State, USA* DeLille
Cellars produces BORDEAUX-style wines from some of the better vineyards
in YAKIMA VALLEY. The flagship is Chaleur Estate Red★★, a powerful,
ageworthy blend of classic Bordeaux varietals. Chaleur Estate Blanc★★

(Semillon and Sauvignon Blanc) has a GRAVES-like character, albeit with a tad more alcohol. The second wine, D2★★, short for Deuxième, is an early-drinking wine. Doyenne Syrah★★ shows outstanding potential. Best years: (Chaleur Estate Red) (2005) 04 03 **02 99**.

DE MARTINO/SANTA INÉS *Maipo, Chile* Old-established winery and now one of MAIPO's rising stars, producing robust, concentrated red wines. Single Vineyard Carmenère★★ is one of Chile's best examples of this grape; De Martino Gran Familia Cabernet Sauvignon★★ is dense and complex. Single Vineyard Chardonnay★ from LIMARI is the best white.

DENBIES *Surrey, England* UK's largest vineyard with 107ha (265 acres) of vines, planted on chalky slopes outside Dorking. First vintage 1989. Wines have been erratic over the years but have now reached a new plateau of quality with remarkably attractive whites, lively, refreshing rosé and decent fizz. Pinot Noir-based Redlands can be good too.

JEAN-LOUIS DENOIS *Vin de Pays d'Oc, Languedoc, France* Producer based in LIMOUX, who can't see a rule without breaking it. First he attempted to plant Riesling and was reprimanded by the French wine authorities (Riesling is permitted only in Alsace). Now he has made a red wine from Merlot and Cabernet, without any of the 'Mediterranean' varieties obligatory in Limoux. This wine is Chloé★, a wine that mixes the flavours of BORDEAUX with just an extra bit of Mediterranean warmth.

DE TRAFFORD *Stellenbosch WO, South Africa* David Trafford is a leading exponent of new-wave Chenin Blanc, in both dry and dessert styles. His rich, ageworthy dry Chenin Blanc★ from venerable Helderberg vines is barrel fermented on its own yeast; the Straw Wine★★ is honey-tinged and succulent. Among the reds, both Cabernet Sauvignon★ and Merlot★ are classically styled and built to age. Shiraz★★, brimming with spicy richness, remains remarkably elegant for its size. Best years: (reds) 2005 04 **03 02 01 00 99 98**.

DEUTZ *Champagne AC, Champagne, France* This small company has been owned by ROEDERER since 1993 and considerable effort and investment have turned a good producer into an excellent one. The non-vintage Brut★★ is now regularly one of the best in Champagne, often boasting a cedary scent, while the top wines are the classic Blanc de Blancs★★, the weightier Cuvée William Deutz★★ and the de luxe vintage blanc de blancs Amour de Deutz★★. Deutz has licensed Pernod Ricard in New Zealand to use its brand on their sparkling wine. Best years: (2002) (00) 99 98 96 **95 90 89 88**.

DÉZALEY *Lavaux, Vaud, Switzerland* The top wine commune in the VAUD, making surprisingly powerful, mineral wines from the Chasselas grape. Best producers: Louis Bovard★, Conne, Les Frères Dubois★, J D Fonjallaz (l'Arbalète★), Pinget★, J & P Testuz★.

D F J VINHOS *Portugal* In the early 1990s, UK wine shippers D & F began working with one of Portugal's most innovative winemakers, José Neiva; in 1999 this relationship evolved into D F J Vinhos. The Bela Fonte brand includes varietal reds Baga, Jaen★ and Touriga Franca★ and a white Bical, all from BEIRAS. Other labels include Segada from the RIBATEJO, Manta Preta★ from ESTREMADURA, Pedras do Monte★ from TERRAS DO SADO, Monte Alentejano from the ALENTEJO and an ALGARVE red, Esplanada. At the top end are the Grand'Arte reds, including an intensely fruity, peppery Trincadeira★★ and beefy Alicante Bouschet★. Three new prestige wines from the DOURO (Escada★), ALENQUER (Francos Reserva★★) and RIBATEJO (Consensus★).

DIAMOND CREEK *Napa Valley AVA, California, USA* Small Diamond
Mountain estate specializing in Cabernet: Volcanic Hill★★★, Red Rock
Terrace★★, Gravelly Meadow★★. Traditionally huge, tannic wines
that, when tasted young, I swear won't ever come round. Yet there's
usually a sweet inner core of fruit that envelops the tannin over
10–15 years; recent releases show wonderful perfume and balance
even in their youth. Best years: (2003) 02 01 00 99 98 **97 96 95 94 92
91 90 87 86 84**.

SCHLOSSGUT DIEL *Burg Layen, Nahe, Germany* Armin Diel has
become one of the leading producers of classic-style Rieslings. Spätlese
and Auslese from Dorsheim's top sites (Burgberg, Goldloch and
Pittermännchen) are regularly ★★. Good Sekt too. Best years: (2006)
05 04 **03** 02 **01 00 99 98 97**.

DISTELL *Stellenbosch, South Africa* South Africa's largest wine company;
some of the allied wineries – such as Neethlingshof★, Stellenzicht★ and
Durbanville Hills★ – are performing well. The Fleur du Cap range is
improving, whites especially. Two wineries in PAARL, Nederburg and
Plaisir de Merle★, are run separately. Nederburg is starting to create a
buzz with some unconventional blends as well as trademark botrytized
dessert Edelkeur★, sold only through an annual auction.

CH. DOISY-DAËNE★★ *Sauternes AC, 2ème Cru Classé, Bordeaux, France*
A consistently good property in BARSAC (although it uses the SAUTERNES
AC for its wines) and unusual in that the sweet wine is made
exclusively from Sémillon. It ages well for 10 years or more. The
extra-rich Extravagant★★★ is produced in exceptional years. Doisy-
Daëne Sec★ is a good, perfumed, dry white. Drink young. Best years:
(sweet) 2005 04 03 **02 01 99 98 97 96 95 90 89**; (dry) 2005 **04 02 01**.

CH. DOISY-VÉDRINES★★ *Sauternes AC, 2ème Cru Classé, Bordeaux,
France* Next door to DOISY-DAENE, Doisy-Védrines is a richly
botrytized wine, fatter and more syrupy than most BARSAC wines. Like
its neighbour, it also sells its wines under the SAUTERNES AC. Best years:
(sweet) 2005 04 03 **02 01 99 98 97 96 95 90 89 88 86 85 83**.

DOLCETTO One of Italy's most charming grapes, producing, for the most
part, purple wines bursting with fruit, though oak-aging is creeping into
the equation a bit too much in the costlier versions. Virtually exclusive
to PIEDMONT and LIGURIA, it boasts 11 DOCs and 1 DOCG (Dogliani) in
Piemonte, with styles ranging from intense and rich in Alba, Ovada and
Diano d'Alba, to lighter and more perfumed in Acqui and Asti. The most
serious, longest-lasting wines are from Dogliani and Alba. Usually best
drunk within 1–2 years, traditionally vinified wines can last 10 years or
more. Best producers: (Alba) Alario★★, ALTARE★★, Boglietti★★, Bon-
giovanni★★, Bricco Maiolica★, Brovia★★, Elvio Cogno★★, Aldo
CONTERNO★, Conterno-Fantino★★, B Marcarini★, Bartolo MASCARELLO★,
Giuseppe MASCARELLO★★, Paitin★, Pelissero★★, PRUNOTTO★, RATTI★,
Albino Rocca★★, SANDRONE★★, Vajra★★, Vietti★, Gianni Voerzio★,
Roberto VOERZIO★; (Dogliani) M & E Abbona★, Chionetti★★, Luigi
Einaudi★★, Pecchenino★★, San Fereolo★★, San Romano★.

DÔLE *Valais, Switzerland* Red wine from the VALAIS that must be made
from at least 51% Pinot Noir, the rest being Gamay. Dôle is generally
a light wine – the deeper, richer (100% Pinot Noir) styles may call
themselves Pinot Noir. Most should be drunk young and lightly
chilled. Best producers: M Clavien, J Germanier, Mathier, Caves Orsat.

DOMAINE CARNEROS *Carneros AVA, California, USA*   Very successful TAITTINGER-owned sparkling wine house. The vintage Brut★ now matches, if not surpasses, Taittinger's fizz from Champagne. Also vintage-dated Le Rêve★★★ and delightful Pinot Noirs★★.

DOMAINE CHANDON *Yarra Valley, Victoria, Australia*   MOËT & CHANDON's Aussie offshoot makes fine Pinot Noir-Chardonnay fizz. Non-vintage Brut, Cuvée Riche and sparkling red Pinot-Shiraz★, and vintage Brut★★, Rosé★★, Blanc de Blancs★, Blanc de Noirs★, YARRA VALLEY Brut★★ and a Tasmanian Cuvée★, plus new vintage ZD★★ (Zero Dosage). Table wines, often of ★★ quality, under the Green Point label. The Green Point name is also used on fizz for export markets.

DOMAINE CHANDON *Napa Valley AVA, California, USA*   California's first French-owned (MOËT & CHANDON) sparkling wine producer majors on reasonable price and acceptable quality, but doesn't match the quality of Moët's subsidiaries in Australia or Argentina. Reserve bottlings can be rich and creamy. Blanc de Blancs is a CARNEROS Chardonnay. Étoile★ is an aged de luxe wine, also made as a flavourful Rosé★.

DOMAINE DROUHIN OREGON *Willamette Valley AVA, Oregon, USA* Burgundy wine merchant Robert DROUHIN bought 40ha (100 acres) in OREGON in 1987, with plans to make fine Pinot Noir on New World land, with an Old World philosophy. The regular Pinot Noir★ is lean but attractive, and the de luxe Pinot Noir Laurène★★ is supple and voluptuous. Pinot Noir Louise★★ is a selection of the finest barrels in the winery. Also very good Chardonnay Arthur★★. Best years: (Pinot Noir) (2006) (05) 04 03 02 01 **00 99 98 97 96 94 93**.

DOMAINE SERENE *Willamette Valley AVA, Oregon, USA*   Ken and Grace Evenstad purchased 17ha (42 acres) of land in the WILLAMETTE VALLEY in 1989, naming the property after their daughter, Serene. Devoted to Pinot Noir and Chardonnay, they have established a fine reputation. The full-bodied Pinot Noir Evenstad Reserve★★ is aged in French oak and has striking black cherry and currant flavours. The Chardonnay Clos du Soleil★★, made from Dijon clones, has a rich apple and hazelnut character. Best years: (Pinot Noir) (2004) (03) 02 01 **00 99 98**.

DOMAINE VISTALBA *Argentina*   French-owned company whose Fabre Montmayou winery in LUJAN DE CUYO produces impressive Malbec★. The almost black, chocolate-and-damsons Grand Vin★★ is a blend of Malbec with Cabernet Sauvignon and Merlot. Latest releases from the Infinitus winery, down in PATAGONIA, are exciting.

DOMECQ *Jerez y Manzanilla DO and Rioja DOCa, Spain*   The largest of the sherry companies, best known for its refreshing fino, La Ina★, is now in a state of flux after the acquisition by Pernod Ricard of Allied Domecq. At the top of the range, dry Amontillado 51-1A★★★, Sibarita Palo Cortado★★★ and Venerable Pedro Ximénez★★ are spectacular. Domecq also makes light, elegant RIOJA, Marqués de Arienzo★.

DOMINUS★★ *Napa Valley AVA, California, USA*   Owned by Christian MOUEIX, director of Bordeaux superstar PETRUS. Wines are based on Cabernet with leavenings of Merlot and Cabernet Franc. Its reputation was marred by excessively tannic early releases, but recent wines are mellow and delicious. Best years: 2003 02 **01 00 99 97 96 95 94 91 90**.

DONAULAND *Niederösterreich, Austria*   Amorphous 2732ha (6750-acre) wine region on both banks of the Danube, stretching from just north of Vienna west to St Pölten. Best are the dry Grüner Veltliners from the Wagram area. Best producers: Josef Bauer★, Karl Fritsch★, Leth★, Bernhard Ott★★, Wimmer-Czerny★.

DÖNNHOFF *Oberhausen, Nahe, Germany* Helmut Dönnhoff is the quiet winemaking genius of the NAHE, conjuring from a string of top sites some of the most mineral dry and naturally sweet Rieslings in the world. The very best are the subtle, long-lived wines from the Niederhäuser Hermannshöhle★★★ and Oberhäuser Brücke vineyards. Eiswein★★★ is equally exciting. Best years: (Hermannshöhle Riesling Spätlese) (2006) 05 04 03 **02 01 00 99 98 97 96 95**.

DOURO DOC *Douro, Portugal* As prices soar for the best wines, deciding whether to use top grapes for unfortified DOURO wine or PORT has become much harder for Douro producers. Quality can be superb when the lush, scented fruit is not smothered by new oak. Reds may improve for 10 years or more. Whites from higher-altitude vineyards have improved, but best drunk young. Best producers: (reds) ALIANCA (Quinta dos Quatro Ventos★), Maria Doroteia Serôdio Borges (Fojo★★), BRIGHT BROTHERS (TFN★), Quinta da Brunheda★, Casal de Loivos★★, Chryseia★★★, Quinta do COTTO (Grande Escolha★★), Quinta do CRASTO★★, FERREIRA★ (Barca Velha★★★, Quinta da Leda★★), Quinta da Gaivosa★, NIEPOORT★★★, Pintas★★, Poeira★★, Quinta do Portal★, RAMOS PINTO★ (Duas Quintas Reserva Especial★★), Quinta de Roriz★, Quinta de la ROSA★, SOGRAPE, Quinta do Vale Dona Maria★★, Quinta do Vale Meao★★, Quinta do Vale da Raposa★, Vallado★ (Sousão★★, Roriz★★), Xisto★★. Best years: (reds) 2005 04 **03 01 00 97 95**.

DOW *Port DOC, Douro, Portugal* The grapes for Dow's Vintage PORT★★★ come mostly from the Quinta do Bomfim, also the name of the excellent single quinta★★★. Dow ports are relatively dry compared with those of GRAHAM'S and WARRE (the 2 other major brands belonging to the Symington family). There are some excellent aged tawnies★★. Quinta Senhora da Ribeira, opposite VESUVIO, has made impressive ports since 1998. Best years: (Vintage) 2003 00 97 94 **91 85 83 80 77 70 66 63 60 55 45**; (Bomfim) 1999 98 95 **92 87 86 84**.

JOSEPH DROUHIN *Beaune, Burgundy, France* Burgundian merchant with substantial vineyard holdings in CHABLIS and the COTE D'OR, and DOMAINE DROUHIN OREGON. Consistently good, if expensive, wines from all over Burgundy. Look for BONNES-MARES★★, ROMANEE-ST-VIVANT★★★, BEAUNE Clos des Mouches (red★★ and white★★★), le MUSIGNY★★★ and le MONTRACHET★★★ from the Marquis de Laguiche. Drouhin offers fine value in Chablis★ and less glamorous Burgundian ACs, such as

RULLY★ and ST-AUBIN★. The BEAUJOLAIS is always good, but overall Drouhin's whites are (just) better than the reds. Top reds and whites should be aged for at least 5 years; often better nearer 10. Best years: (2006) 05 04 03 02 **01 00 99 96 95**.

PIERRE-JACQUES DRUET *Bourgueil AC, Loire Valley, France* A passionate producer of BOURGUEIL and small quantities of CHINON★★. Druet makes 4 Bourgueils – les Cent Boisselées★, Cuvée Beauvais★, Cuvée Grand Mont★★ and Vaumoreau★★ – each a complex expression of the Cabernet Franc grape. Best aged for at least 3–5 years. Best years: (top cuvées) (2006) 05 04 **03 02 01 00 99 97 96 90 89**.

DRY CREEK VALLEY AVA *Sonoma, California, USA* Best known for Sauvignon Blanc, Zinfandel and Cabernet Sauvignon, this valley runs west of ALEXANDER VALLEY AVA, and similarly becomes hotter moving northwards. Best producers: DRY CREEK VINEYARD★, Duxoup★, FERRARI-CARANO★★, GALLO (Zinfandel★, Cabernet Sauvignon★), Lambert Bridge★, Michel-Schlumberger★, Nalle★★, Pezzi King★, Preston★, Quivira★, Rafanelli (Zinfandel★★). Best years: (reds) 2003 02 **01 00 99 98 97 96 95**.

DRY CREEK VINEYARD *Dry Creek Valley AVA, California, USA* An early advocate of Fumé Blanc★, Dry Creek remains faithful to the brisk racy style and also makes a serious Reserve★ which improves with aging. DCV3★ (sometimes ★★) is from original plantings and displays subtle notes of fig and herb. A drink-young Chardonnay (Reserve★) is attractive, but the stars here are red Meritage★, Merlot★, Old Vine Zinfandel★★ and a superb Dry Chenin Blanc★★. Best years: (Old Vine Zin) 2003 02 **01 00 99 97 96 95 94**.

DRY RIVER *Martinborough, North Island, New Zealand* Low yields and an uncompromising attitude to quality at this tiny winery have produced some of the country's top Gewürztraminer★★★ and Pinot Gris★★, an intense, succulent yet minerally Pinot Noir★★★, sleek Chardonnay★★ and powerful, long-lived Craighall Riesling★★★. Excellent Syrah★★ is made in tiny quantities. Best years: (Craighall Riesling) (2006) 03 **01 00 99 98**; (Pinot Noir) (2006) **03 01 00 99**.

GEORGES DUBOEUF *Beaujolais, Burgundy, France* Known as the King of Beaujolais, Duboeuf is responsible for more than 10% of the wine produced in the region. Given the size of his operation, the quality of the wines is good. Duboeuf also makes and blends wine from the Mâconnais (ST-VERAN★), the southern RHONE VALLEY and the LANGUEDOC. His BEAUJOLAIS NOUVEAU is usually reliable, but his top wines are those he bottles for independent growers, particularly Jean Descombes★★ in MORGON, Dom. des Quatre Vents★ and la Madone★ in FLEURIE and Dom. de la Tour du Bief★ in MOULIN-A-VENT.

DUCKHORN *Napa Valley AVA, California, USA* Best known for its very chunky, tannic Merlot★ (Estate Merlot★★) – now, thankfully, softer and riper. The Cabernet Sauvignon★ and Sauvignon Blanc★ provide easier drinking. Paraduxx is a Zinfandel-Cabernet blend; Decoy is the budget line. The company's stellar Pinot Noir★ project is Goldeneye in MENDOCINO. Best years: (Merlot) 2003 02 **01 99 98 97 96 95 94 91 90 86**.

CH. DUCRU-BEAUCAILLOU★★★ *St-Julien AC, 2ème Cru Classé, Haut-Médoc, Bordeaux, France* Traditionally the epitome of ST-JULIEN, mixing charm and austerity, fruit and firm tannins. Vintages from the mid-1980s to 1990 were flawed; back on form since 94. Second wine: la Croix de Beaucaillou. Best years: 2005 04 03 **02 01** 00 **99 98 96 95 94**.

DUJAC *Morey-St-Denis, Côte de Nuits, Burgundy, France* Owner Jacques Seysses' estate is based in MOREY-ST-DENIS, with some choice vineyards also in CHAMBOLLE-MUSIGNY, ECHEZEAUX and GEVREY-CHAMBERTIN. The wines are all perfumed and elegant, including a small quantity of Morey-St-Denis★ white wine, but the outstanding Dujac bottlings are the Grands Crus – Échézeaux★★★, CLOS DE LA ROCHE★★★, BONNES-MARES★★★ and CLOS ST-DENIS★★★ – all of which need to age for a decade or more. From 2005 a host of exciting new vineyards such as VOSNE-ROMANEE Malconsorts will come on stream. He and son Jeremy also make négociant cuvées under the label Dujac Fils et Père. Best years: (Grands Crus) (2006) 05 04 03 02 **01 00 99 98 96 95 93 91 90 89**.

DUNHAM CELLARS *Columbia Valley AVA, Washington, USA* Dunham Cellars is a family-owned winery in a rustic, remodelled World War Two era airplane hangar near the Walla Walla airport. The wines here are powerful and extracted, including Cabernet Sauvignon★★,

Syrah★, a limited-release Lewis Vineyard Syrah Reserve★★, Trutina★ (a BORDEAUX-style blend), Three Legged Red (a table wine named after one of the winery dogs) and a Chardonnay 'Shirley Mays'. Best years: (reds) (2005) 04 03 **02 00**.

DUNN VINEYARDS *Howell Mountain AVA, California, USA* Massive, concentrated, hauntingly perfumed, long-lived Cabernet Sauvignon★★★ is the trademark of Randy Dunn's HOWELL MOUNTAIN wines. His NAPA VALLEY Cabernets★★ are less powerful but still scented. Thankfully he has resisted the move toward high alcohol, and his wines' ability to age beautifully is evidence of this. Best years: 2003 01 **00 99 97 96 95 94 93 92 91 90 88 87 86 85 84 82**.

DURBANVILLE WO *South Africa* Tucked into the folds of the Tygerberg Hills, Durbanville borders Cape Town's northern suburbs. Cool breezes from both the Atlantic Ocean and False Bay suit Sauvignon Blanc: wines are vivid, often with an invigorating minerality. Semillon also does well. Merlot shows promise both as a varietal wine and blended with Cabernet Sauvignon, though the latter sometimes struggles to ripen in cooler years. Best producers: Bloemendal, Durbanville Hills★, Meerendal, Nitida★.

DURIF See PETITE SIRAH.

JEAN DURUP *Chablis, Burgundy, France* The largest vineyard owner in CHABLIS, Jean Durup is a great believer in unoaked Chablis, which tends to be clean without any great complexity. Best are the Premiers Crus Fourchaume★ and Montée de Tonnerre★★. Wines appear under a variety of labels, including l'Eglantière, Ch. de Maligny and Valéry.

ÉCHÉZEAUX AC *Grand Cru, Côte de Nuits, Burgundy, France* The Grands Crus of Échézeaux and the smaller and more prestigious Grands-Échézeaux are sandwiched between the world-famous CLOS DE VOUGEOT and VOSNE-ROMANÉE. Few of the 80 growers here have really made a name for themselves, but there are some fine wines with a smoky, plum richness and a soft texture that age well over 10–15 years to a gamy, chocolaty depth. Best producers: R Arnoux★★, BOUCHARD PERE ET FILS★★, Cacheux-Sirugue★★★, DROUHIN★★, DUJAC★★★, R Engel★★★, GRIVOT★★★, A-F GROS★★★, Jayer-Gilles★★★, Mugneret-Gibourg★★★, Perdrix★, Dom. de la ROMANEE-CONTI★★★, E Rouget★★★. Best years: (2006) 05 04 **03** 02 **01 00 99 98 97 96 95 93 90**.

DOM. DE L'ECU *Muscadet Sèvre-et-Maine, Loire Valley, France* One of the finest producers in MUSCADET, Guy Bossard's biodynamically run estate also produces GROS PLANT DU PAYS NANTAIS white, a velvety red vin de pays Cabernet blend and a refreshing sparkler, Ludwig Hahn. It is his Muscadet, though, that stands out, especially the top cuvées from different soil types: Gneiss, Orthogneiss★ and fuller-bodied, minerally Granite★★. Best years: (Granite) **2005** 04 03 02 01 00.

EDEN VALLEY See BAROSSA, pages 70–1.

CH. L'ÉGLISE-CLINET★★★ *Pomerol AC, Bordeaux, France* A tiny 5.5ha (13-acre) domaine in the heart of POMEROL, with a very old vineyard – one of the reasons for the depth and elegance of the wines. The other is the winemaking ability of owner Denis Durantou. The wine is expensive and in limited supply. It can be enjoyed young, though the best vintages should be cellared for 10 years or more. Second wine: La Petite Église. Best years: 2005 04 **03 02 01 00 99 98 97 96 95 94 93 92 90 89**.

ELGIN WO *South Africa* This high-lying ward within the Overberg District is being targeted by some of the Cape's leading winemakers, and vineyard area is increasing. Summer cloud helps to keep temperatures

143

reasonable, creating the right conditions for pure-fruited Sauvignon Blanc, Chardonnay, Riesling and Pinot Noir. Best producers: Paul CLUVER★, Neil ELLIS★★, Iona, Oak Valley★, THELEMA★.

ELK COVE *Willamette Valley AVA, Oregon, USA* Back in 1974, Elk Cove was one of the pioneers of the WILLAMETTE VALLEY. Today the Campbell family produces Pinot Noir★★, Pinot Gris★, Riesling and a Riesling-based dessert wine called Ultima. The single-vineyard Pinot Noirs – Roosevelt★★, Windhill★ and La Bohème★ – now compete with the elite from the state. Best years: (Pinot Noir) (2005) 04 03 02 **01 00 99**.

NEIL ELLIS *Stellenbosch WO, South Africa* Winemaker and négociant, renowned for powerful, invigorating Groenekloof Sauvignon Blanc★★ and striking STELLENBOSCH reds (blackcurranty Cabernet Sauvignon★★, supple Cabernet-Merlot★). An ageworthy single-vineyard Shiraz★ and Cabernet★ (both from Jonkershoek Valley fruit), and a subtly delicious Chardonnay★★ from cool ELGIN, confirm his versatility. Best years: (Cabernet) **2004** 03 02 01 00 99 98 97; (whites) **2006** 05 04 03 02 01.

ERNIE ELS *Stellenbosch WO, South Africa* Jean Engelbrecht's joint venture with his golfing friend Ernie Els has resulted in a dark, serious BORDEAUX blend under the Ernie Els★ label. Engelbrecht Els★ forges Shiraz with Bordeaux varieties (Cabernets Sauvignon and Franc, Merlot, Malbec and Petit Verdot), in a dense, rich, international style. The Guardian Peak range offers quality blends and good-value varietal wines. Engelbrecht also makes outstanding Cirrus Syrah★★ in partnership with SILVER OAK of California. Best years: (Ernie Els) **2004** 03 02 01 00.

ELTVILLE *Rheingau, Germany* Large wine town, making some of the RHEINGAU's most racy Rieslings. Best producers: Langwerth von Simmern★, Staatsweingut. Best years: (2006) 05 04 **03** 02 **01 00 99 98**.

EMILIA-ROMAGNA *Italy* This region is divided into the western zone of Emilia, best known for LAMBRUSCO, and the eastern zone of ROMAGNA, where Sangiovese is dominant. See also COLLI PIACENTINI.

EMILIANA *Colchagua, Chile* New venture from the Guilisasti family, also main shareholders at CONCHA Y TORO, with leading winemaker Alvaro Espinoza contributing his biodynamic and organic approach to viticulture. Adobe★ is good entry-level range, Novas★★ range is even better, and red five-variety blend Coyam★★ (sometimes ★★★) is one of Chile's most interesting wines. 'Super Coyam', called 'G', is a dense, powerful long-distance runner. Best years: 2005 04 03 **02** 01.

EMRICH-SCHÖNLEBER *Monzingen, Nahe, Germany* Although Monzingen is not the most prestigious of NAHE villages, Werner Schönleber has steadily brought his 14ha (35-acre) property into the front ranks. His vigorous, spicy Rieslings are consistently ★ to ★★ and his Eisweins are ★★★. Best years: (2006) 05 04 03 **02 01 00 99 98**.

ENATE *Somontano DO, Aragón, Spain* Enate and VIÑAS DEL VERO seem to be slugging it out for supremacy in the SOMONTANO DO. Barrel-fermented Chardonnay★ is rich, buttery and toasty, Gewürztraminer★ is exotic and convincing. International grape varieties also feature in the red Crianza, Reserva★ (100% Cabernet Sauvignon), Reserva Especial★★ (Cabernet-Merlot) and blockbuster Merlot-Merlot★. Best years: (reds) (2005) 04 03 **01 00 99 98 96 95 94**.

ENTRE-DEUX-MERS AC *Bordeaux, France* This AC increasingly represents some of the freshest, snappiest dry white wine in France. In general, drink the latest vintage, though better wines will last a year

144

or two. Sweet wines are sold as PREMIERES COTES DE BORDEAUX, St-Macaire, LOUPIAC and STE-CROIX-DU-MONT. Best producers: BONNET★, Castenet Greffier, de Fontenille★, Landereau★, Marjosse★, Nardique la Gravière★, Ste-Marie★, Tour de Mirambeau★, Toutigeac★, Turcaud★.

DOM. D'EOLE *Coteaux d'Aix-en-Provence AC, Provence, France* One of the many organic estates in this corner of Provence. Top wines are Cuvée Caprice★ and Cuvée Léa★★, a 50:50 blend of Syrah and Grenache. Best years: 2005 03 **01 00 98**.

ERBACH *Rheingau, Germany* Erbach's famous Marcobrunn vineyard is one of the top spots for Riesling on the Rhine. The village wines are elegant; those from Marcobrunn more powerful and imposing. Best producers: Jakob Jung★, Knyphausen★, SCHLOSS REINHARTSHAUSEN★★, Schloss Schönborn★, Langwerth von Simmern★. Best years: (2006) 05 04 **03** 02 **01 00 99 98 97**.

ERBALUCE DI CALUSO DOC *Piedmont, Italy* Usually a dry or sparkling white from the Erbaluce grape, but Caluso Passito, where the grapes are semi-dried before fermenting, can be a fine sweet wine. Best producers: (Caluso Passito) Cieck★, Ferrando★, Orsolani★.

ERDEN *Mosel, Germany* Middle MOSEL village with the superb Prälat and Treppchen vineyards. Wines are rich and succulent with a strong mineral character. Best producers: Christoffel★★, Dr LOOSEN★★★, Mönchhof★★, Peter Nicolay★. Best years: (2006) 05 04 **03 02** 01 99 97 95.

ERRÁZURIZ *Aconcagua, Chile* Traditional winery run by dynamic Eduardo Chadwick. Its portfolio includes SEÑA and Arboleda – originally joint ventures with MONDAVI, now 100% Errázuriz. The classic label is Don Maximiano Founder's Reserve★ (sometimes ★★), a red blend from Aconcagua, also the source of La Cumbre Shiraz★ and dense, Cabernet-based The Blend★. Single-vineyard Viñedo Chadwick★★, also a Cabernet-based blend, comes from what some consider the best area of MAIPO. Also very good 'Wild Ferment' Chardonnay★★ and Pinot Noir★ from CASABLANCA. Best years: (reds) 2005 04 **03** 02 01.

ESPORÃO *Reguengos DOC, Alentejo, Portugal* Huge estate in the heart of the ALENTEJO, where Australian David Baverstock makes a broad range of wines. Principal labels are Esporão (red★★ and white★ Reservas), Vinha da Defesa★, Monte Velho and Alandra. Also some delightful varietals: Trincadeira★, Aragonez★, Touriga Nacional★, Syrah★, Alicante Bouschet★ and Verdelho★. Best years: (reds) (2005) 04 **01** 00.

EST! EST!! EST!!! DI MONTEFIASCONE DOC *Lazio, Italy* Trebbiano-based white whose name derives from an old tale of a bishop's servant sent ahead to scout out good wines; he gave this one the thumbs-up code three times. Perhaps it had been a long day. Best producers: Bigi (Graffiti), FALESCO (Poggio dei Gelsi★), Mazziotti (Canuleio★).

CH. DES ESTANILLES *Faugères AC, Languedoc, France* The Louisons know that quality begins in the vineyard. Their best site is the Clos de Fou, with its very steep schistous slope planted with Syrah; the grape 'dominates' the Prestige cuvée★★ (i.e. 100% – but AC regulations do not allow them to say so). Also a wood-fermented and aged rosé, plus fine COTEAUX DU LANGUEDOC white★. Best years: (reds) 2005 **04 02 01**.

ESTREMADURA *Portugal*   Portugal's most productive region, occupying the western coastal strip and with an increasing number of clean, characterful wines. The leading area is ALENQUER, promoted to DOC status along with Arruda, Encostas de Aire, Lourinhã (for brandy only), Óbidos and Torres Vedras. However, much of the wine, including some of the region's best, is simply labelled as Vinho Regional Estremadura. Spicy, perfumed reds are often based on Castelão, but Aragonez, Cabernet Sauvignon, Syrah and Touriga Nacional contribute to top examples, which can benefit from 4 or 5 years' aging. Top producers also make fresh, aromatic whites. Best producers: Agrovitis (Fonte das Mouças★), Quinta de Chocapalha★, Quinta da Cortezia★, D F J VINHOS (Francos Reserva★★), Grand'Arte Touriga Nacional★), Quinta dos Loridos (Merlot★), Quinta do Monte d'Oiro★★, Quinta de Pancas★, Companhia Agricola Sanguinhal, Casa SANTOS LIMA★. See also BUCELAS. Best years: (reds) 2005 04 **03 01 00**.

L'ÉTOILE AC *Jura, France*   A tiny area within the COTES DU JURA which has its own AC for whites, mainly Chardonnay and Savagnin, and for *vin jaune*. Fizz now comes under the CREMANT DU JURA AC. Best producers: Ch. l'Étoile★, Geneletti★, Joly★, Montbourgeau★★.

CH. L'ÉVANGILE★★ *Pomerol AC, Bordeaux, France*   A neighbour to PETRUS and CHEVAL BLANC, this estate has been wholly owned and managed by the Rothschilds of LAFITE-ROTHSCHILD since 1999. The wine is quintessential POMEROL – rich, fat and exotic. Recent vintages have been very good (sometimes ★★★), but expect further improvement as the Rothschild effect intensifies. Second wine: Blason de l'Evangile. Best years: 2005 04 03 02 **01 00 99 98 96 95 94 93 90 89 88 85**.

EVANS & TATE *Margaret River, Western Australia*   A period of over-exuberant expansion led to financially troubled times for Evans & Tate. It has now pared back the operation and focused on MARGARET RIVER where chief winemaker Richard Rowe has quietly produced the company's best-ever wines. Chardonnay★ at all levels is most impressive, but quality and value are evident across the board.

FAIRVIEW *Paarl WO, South Africa*   Owner Charles Back believes South Africa's strength, especially in warmer areas, lies with Rhône varieties. These are expressed in the Goats range: the spicy Goat-Roti★ partners Shiraz with Viognier; Goats do Roam and Goats do Roam in Villages reds and rosé feature Pinotage with Shiraz, Grenache, Cinsaut, Mourvèdre and Viognier, while the whites★ include Grenache Blanc, Clairette and Viognier as part of the mix. Complementing these is Bored Doe, a Merlot-led, classic BORDEAUX-style blend. The French authorities are not amused but fans on both sides of the Atlantic can't get enough. Fine Shiraz★★ (Solitude★★, Beacon Block★★, Jakkalsfontein★★), Carignan★, Merlot★, Cabernet Sauvignon★ and Pinotage★ (Primo★★) and promising all-Italian varietal blend, Agostinelli. Good whites include Oom Pagel Semillon★★, Viognier★ and outstanding sweet wine La Beryl★★★. Back also owns SPICE ROUTE. Best years: (Shiraz) 2006 **05 04 03 02 01 00 99**.

JOSEPH FAIVELEY *Nuits-St-Georges, Côte de Nuits, Burgundy, France*   This Burgundian merchant makes impressive but severely tannic red wines that demand aging (CORTON★★, CHAMBERTIN-Clos-de-Bèze★★, Mazis-Chambertin★★), principally from its own substantial vineyard holdings. In lesser wines, the fruit may not hold out against the tannin, and even aging may not help. The much cheaper MERCUREY reds★ from the Côte Chalonnaise can be attractive, if on the lean side.

Whites from Mercurey★ and RULLY★, and the oak-aged BOURGOGNE Blanc represent reasonably good value. Best years: (top reds) (2006) 05 04 03 99 **98 97 96 95 93 90**; (whites) (2006) 05 **04 03 02 00 99**.

FALERNO DEL MASSICO DOC *Campania, Italy* Falernian was one of the ancient Romans' star wines. The revived DOC, with a white Falanghina and reds from either Aglianico and Piedirosso or from Primitivo, looks promising. Best producers: Michele Moio★, Villa Matilde★ (Vigna Camarato★★). Best years: (reds) (2006) (05) 04 03 **01 00 99 97 95**.

FALESCO *Lazio, Italy* Property of the phenomenal Cotarella brothers: Renzo is ANTINORI's technical director (so responsible for SOLAIA, TIGNANELLO, etc.); Riccardo is a high-profile consultant enologist, working all over Italy from Piedmont to Sicily. Located at Montefiascone, the town of EST! EST!! EST!!!, their Poggio dei Gelsi★ is considered best of the genre, but they are better known for their Merlot Montiano★★, the essence of smooth if somewhat soulless modernity. Best years: (Montiano) (2004) 03 **01 00 99 98 97 96 95 94**.

CH. FALFAS★ *Côtes de Bourg AC, Bordeaux, France* Biodynamic estate making concentrated, structured wine that needs 4–5 years to soften. Le Chevalier★ is an old-vines cuvée. Best years: 2005 **04 03 02 01 00**.

CH. DE FARGUES★★ *Sauternes AC, Bordeaux, France* Property run by the Lur-Saluces family, who until 1999 also owned Ch. d'YQUEM. The quality of this fine, rich wine is more a tribute to their commitment than to the inherent quality of the vineyard. Best years: 2005 04 03 **02 01 99 98 97 96 95 90 89 88 86 83**.

FAUGÈRES AC *Languedoc, France* Vineyards in the schistous hills north of Béziers in the Hérault produce red wines whose ripe, soft, rather plummy flavour marks them out from other LANGUEDOC reds. Best producers: Abbaye Sylva Plana★, ALQUIER★, Léon Barral★, Chenaie★, ESTANILLES★, Faugères co-op, Grézan, Haut-Fabrègues, HECHT & BANNIER★, la Liquière★, Moulin de Ciffre, Ollier-Taillefer (Castel Fossibus★), Saint Antonin. Best years: 2005 04 **03 01 00 99 98**.

FAUSTINO *Rioja DOCa, País Vasco and Rioja, and Cava DO, Spain* Family-owned and technically very well equipped, this RIOJA company makes fair Reserva V and Gran Reserva I red Riojas, as well as a more modern, oak-aged red, Faustino de Autor, and fruit-driven Faustino de Crianza. But they could try harder – and they should. Best years: (reds) (2004) 03 **01 99 98 96 95 94 92 91 90**.

FEILER-ARTINGER *Rust, Neusiedlersee, Burgenland, Austria* Hans Feiler and now his son Kurt make supreme Ausbruch dessert wines★★★. Their dry whites are ★. Solitaire★★ is a suave red blend of Merlot with Blaufränkisch and Zweigelt. Best years: (sweet whites) (2005) 04 02 01 **00 99 98 95 94 91**; (Solitaire) (2006) 05 04 03 **02 01 00 99**.

LIVIO FELLUGA *Colli Orientali del Friuli DOC, Friuli-Venezia Giulia, Italy* A younger generation has continued the great work of Livio Felluga at this large Friuli estate. Merlot-Cabernet blend Vertigo★★, raspberryish straight Merlot Riserva Sossò★★, white Pinot Grigio★, Picolit Riserva★★ and Tocai Friulano★ are all class acts. Shàrjs★ combines Chardonnay with Ribolla and oak, but there's more to stimulate the palate in Terre Alte★★, an aromatic blend of Tocai, Pinot Bianco and Sauvignon. Best years: (whites) (2006) 04 **02 01 00 99 98 97 96**.

FATTORIA DI FELSINA *Chianti Classico DOCG, Tuscany, Italy* Full, chunky CHIANTI CLASSICO★★ wines which improve with several years' bottle age. Quality is generally outstanding; most notable are the single-vineyard Riserva Rancia★★★ and (under the regional IGT Toscana) Sangiovese Fontalloro★★★. Also good are Chardonnay I Sistri★★ and Cabernet Maestro Raro★★. Best years: (Fontalloro) (2006) 04 **03** 01 **00 99 98 97 95 93 90 88 85**.

FELTON ROAD *Central Otago, South Island, New Zealand* Runaway success with vineyards in the old goldfields of Bannockburn. Intensely fruity, seductive Pinot Noir★★ is surpassed by very limited quantities of concentrated, complex Block 3 Pinot Noir★★★ and the equally limited edition Block 5★★★. New Cornish Point Pinot Noir★★ is fleshy and scented. Three classy Rieslings (all ★★) cover the range from dry to sweet. Mineral, citrus unoaked Chardonnay★ can be one of New Zealand's best; barrel-fermented Chardonnay★★ is funky and delicious. Best years: (Pinot Noir) 2006 05 **03 02 01 99**.

FENDANT *Valais, Switzerland* Chasselas wine from the steep slopes of the VALAIS. Good Fendant should be slightly *spritzig*, with a nutty character. However, the average Fendant is overcropped, thin and virtually characterless. Best drunk *very* young. Best producers: Chappaz, Jacques Germanier, Gilliard, Caves Imesch, Maye, Caves Orsat.

FERNGROVE *Great Southern, Western Australia* Ambitious new winery based in Frankland River, where it has 285ha (700 acres) of vines (along with 140ha/345 acres at Mount Barker). The quality potential in Frankland River is unquestioned, being sunny yet cool. Lack of water is a limiting factor, but that also means yields are naturally limited and flavours intensified. So far Majestic Cabernet Sauvignon★★ is stunning, Dragon Shiraz★ and King Malbec★ improve with each vintage, while Cossack Riesling★★ and Diamond Chardonnay★ are very good.

FERNGROVE
FRANKLAND RIVER

WESTERN AUSTRALIA

FERRARI *Trento DOC, Trentino, Italy* Founded in 1902, the firm is a leader for sparkling wine. Consistent, classy wines include Ferrari Brut★, Maximum Brut★, Perlé★, Rosé★ and vintage Giulio Ferrari Riserva del Fondatore★★, aged 8 years on its lees and an Italian classic. Any relation? No, apparently Ferrari is one of the commonest names in Italy.

FERRARI-CARANO *Dry Creek Valley AVA, California, USA* Balanced, elegant Chardonnay; the regular bottling★★ has delicious apple-spice fruit, while the Reserve★★ is deeply flavoured with more than a touch of oak. Fumé Blanc★ is also good. Red wines are equally impressive, including Trésor★★ (a BORDEAUX blend), Siena★★ (Sangiovese-Cabernet Sauvignon), Syrah★, Merlot★ and Zinfandel★. Reds can age for 5–10 years. Best years: (reds) 2003 02 **01 00 99 97 96 95**.

FERREIRA *Port DOC, Douro DOC, Douro, Portugal* Old PORT house owned by SOGRAPE. Ferreira is best known for excellent tawny ports: creamy, nutty Quinta do Porto 10-year-old★ and Duque de Braganza 20-year-old★★. The Vintage Port★★ is increasingly good. Ferreira's unfortified wine operation, known as Casa Ferreirinha, produces Portugal's most sought-after red, Barca Velha★★★; made from DOURO grape varieties (mainly Tinta Roriz), it is produced only in the finest years – just 15 vintages since 1953. Marginally less good years are now sold as Casa Ferreirinha Reserva★ (previously Reserva Especial). Quinta da Leda reds★★ are also fine. Best years: (Vintage) 2003 00 97 95 94 **91 85 83 82 78 77 70 66 63**; (Barca Velha) **1999 95 91 85 83 82 81 78**.

CH. FERRIÈRE★★ *Margaux AC, 3ème Cru Classé, Haut-Médoc, Bordeaux, France* Ferrière was bought by the Merlaut family, owners of Ch. CHASSE-SPLEEN, in 1992. It is now managed by Claire Villars, and the ripe, rich and perfumed wines are among the best in MARGAUX AC. Best years: 2005 04 03 02 **01 00 99 98 96**.

FETZER VINEYARDS *Mendocino County, California, USA* Important winery that I feel could push the quality level a bit higher. Locals swear by the quality of the special cellar door releases, but we never see these in the outside world. Basic wines are good, with tasty Gewürztraminer, Riesling and Syrah★; Barrel Select bottles can be ★. Bargain-priced Valley Oaks line is decent value. Also a leader in organic viticulture with the Bonterra range: Chardonnay, Viognier★, Merlot, Roussanne★, Zinfandel★, Cabernet Sauvignon and Sangiovese. Best years: (Barrel Select reds) 2003 02 01 **99 98 97 96**.

FIANO Exciting, distinctive, low-yielding southern Italian white grape variety. Best producers: (Molise) Di Majo Norante; (Fiano di Avellino DOC in CAMPANIA) Colli di Lapio★, Feudi di San Gregorio★★, MASTROBERARDINO★, Terredora di Paolo★, Vadiaperti★; (others) L Maffini (Kràtos★★), PLANETA (Cometa★★), Settesoli (Inycon★).

CH. DE FIEUZAL *Pessac-Léognan AC, Cru Classé de Graves, Bordeaux, France* Under new ownership since 2001; efforts are being made to recapture the form of the 1980s, with partial success. The red★ is drinkable almost immediately, but can age. The white★★, a gorgeous, perfumed (and ageworthy) wine, is the star performer. Second wine (red and white): l'Abeille de Fieuzal. Best years: (reds) 2005 **00 98 96 95 94 90 89 88 86 85 83 82**; (whites) 2005 **03 02 01 00 99 98 96**.

CH. FIGEAC★★ *St-Émilion Grand Cru AC, 1er Grand Cru Classé, Bordeaux, France* Leading property whose wine traditionally has a delightful fragrance and gentleness of texture. It has an unusually high percentage (70%) of Cabernets Franc and Sauvignon, making it more structured than other ST-EMILIONS. After an unconvincing run of vintages from the mid-1980s, recent vintages have been far more like the lovely Figeac of old. Second wine: la Grange Neuve de Figeac. Best years: 2005 04 **03 02** 01 00 **99 98 95 90 89**.

FINGER LAKES AVA *New York State, USA* Cool region in central NEW YORK STATE, where some winemakers are establishing a regional style for dry Riesling. Chardonnay and sparkling wines also star among the whites, with Pinot Noir and Cabernet Franc the best reds. Best producers: Chateau Lafayette Reneau★, FOX RUN★, Dr Konstantin FRANK★, Heron Hill, LAMOREAUX LANDING★, Red Newt, Swedish Hill, Wagner, Hermann J Wiemer★.

FITOU AC *Languedoc, France* One of the success stories of the 1980s. Quality subsequently slumped, but with the innovative MONT TAUCH co-op taking the lead, Fitou is once again an excellent place to seek out dark, herb-scented reds. Best producers: Abelanet, BERTRAND-BERGE★★, Lerys★, Milles Vignes, MONT TAUCH co-op★, Nouvelles★, Rochelierre, Rolland, Roudène★. Best years: 2004 03 **01 00 99 98**.

FIXIN AC *Côte de Nuits, Burgundy, France* Although it's next door to GEVREY-CHAMBERTIN, Fixin rarely produces anything really magical. The wines are often sold as COTE DE NUITS-VILLAGES. Best producers: Charlopin★, Coillot, Galeyrand, Pierre Gelin★, Alain Guyard★, Dominique Laurent★★. Best years: (reds) (2006) 05 **03 02 01 00 99**.

FLEURIE AC *Beaujolais, Burgundy, France*   The best-known BEAUJOLAIS Cru, Fleurie reveals the happy, carefree flavours of the Gamay grape at its best, plus heady perfumes and a delightful juicy fruit. But demand has meant that too many wines are overpriced and dull. Best producers: J-M Aujoux★, Berrod★, P-M Chermette★★/Vissoux, M Chignard★, Clos de la Roilette★, Depardon★, DUBOEUF (la Madone★, Quatre Vents★), Fleurie co-op★, la Madone/Despres★, Métrat★, A & M Morel★, Verpoix★. Best years: **2006 05 03**.

CH. LA FLEUR-PÉTRUS★★ *Pomerol AC, Bordeaux, France*   Like the better-known PETRUS and TROTANOY, this is owned by the dynamic MOUEIX family. Unlike its stablemates, it is situated entirely on gravel soil and tends to produce tighter wines with less immediate fruit but considerable elegance and cellar potential. Among POMEROL's top dozen properties. Best years: 2005 04 **03** 02 01 **00 99 98 97 96 95 94 90 89**.

FLORA SPRINGS *Napa Valley AVA, California, USA*   Best known for red wines such as Merlot★★, Cabernet Sauvignon★★ and a BORDEAUX blend called Trilogy★★. Barrel-fermented Chardonnay★★ tops the whites, and Soliloquy★, a barrel-fermented Sauvignon Blanc, has attractive melon fruit. The winery also works with Italian varietals; a weighty Pinot Grigio★ and a lightly spiced Sangiovese★ are consistent successes. Best years: (Trilogy) (2005) 04 03 02 **01 00 99 97 96 95 94 91**.

FLOWERS *Sonoma Coast AVA, California, USA*   Small producer whose estate vineyard, Camp Meeting Ridge, a few miles from the Pacific, yields wines of great intensity. Camp Meeting Ridge Pinot Noir★★★ and Chardonnay★★★ are usually made with native yeasts and offer wonderful exotic aromas and flavours. Wines from purchased fruit with a SONOMA COAST designation are ★★. Best years: (Chardonnay) 2005 04 **03 01 00 99**; (Pinot Noir) 2005 04 03 01 **00 99 98 97 96**.

TENUTE AMBROGIO & GIOVANNI FOLONARI *Tuscany, Italy*   A few years ago the Folonari family, owners of the giant RUFFINO, split asunder and these two brothers went their own way. Their properties/brands include Cabreo (Sangiovese-Cabernet Il Borgo★, Chardonnay La Pietra★) and Nozzole (powerful, long-lived Cabernet Il Pareto★★) in CHIANTI CLASSICO, plus VINO NOBILE estate Gracciano-Svetoni, Campo del Mare in BOLGHERI and BRUNELLO producer La Fuga.

FONSECA *Port DOC, Douro, Portugal*   Owned by the same group as TAYLOR (Fladgate Partnership), Fonseca makes ports in a rich, densely plummy style. Fonseca Vintage★★★ is magnificent, the aged tawnies★★ uniformly superb. Fonseca Guimaraens★★ is the 'off-vintage' wine, Fonseca Crusted★ and Late Bottled Vintage★ are among the best examples of their styles, as is Bin No. 27★ of a premium ruby port. Quinta do Panascal is the single quinta vintage. Best years: (Vintage) 2003 00 97 94 92 **85 83 77 75 70 66 63 55**.

JOSÉ MARIA DA FONSECA *Terras do Sado, Portugal*   Go-ahead company making a huge range of wines, from fizzy Lancers Rosé to serious reds. Best include Vinya★ (Syrah-Aragonez), Domingos Soares Franco Private Collection★, and Garrafeiras with codenames like CO★★, RA★★ and TE★★. Optimum★ is top of the range. Periquita is the mainstay, with Clássico★ made only in the best years. Also SETUBAL made mainly from the Moscatel grape: 5-year-old★ and 20-year-old★★. Older vintage-dated Setúbals are rare but superb.

DOM. FONT DE MICHELLE *Châteauneuf-du-Pape AC, Rhône Valley, France*   CHATEAUNEUF-DU-PAPE reds★★, in particular Cuvée Étienne Gonnet★★, and whites★★ that are stylish but still heady, with richness and southern herb fragrance – and not too expensive. Best years: (Étienne Gonnet red) (2006) 05 04 03 01 **00 99 98 97 95 94 90 89**.

FONTANAFREDDA *Barolo DOCG, Piedmont, Italy* One of the largest PIEDMONT estates, based in the old BAROLO hunting lodge of the King of Italy. As well as Barolo Serralunga d'Alba★, it also produces several single-vineyard Barolos★ (La Delizia★★), a range of Piedmont varietals, 4 million bottles of ASTI and a good dry sparkler, Contessa Rosa. Best years: (Barolo) (2006) (04) 03 **01 00 99 97 90 89 88**.

CASTELLO DI FONTERUTOLI *Chianti Classico DOCG, Tuscany, Italy* This estate has belonged to the Mazzei family since the 15th century. The focus is on CHIANTI CLASSICO Riserva★★, along with excellent SUPER-TUSCAN Siepi★★★ (Sangiovese-Merlot). Belguardo★ is a more recent venture in the MAREMMA, with IGT and MORELLINO DI SCANSANO wines.

FONTODI *Chianti Classico DOCG, Tuscany, Italy* The Manetti family has built this superbly sited estate into one of the most admired in the CHIANTI CLASSICO area, with excellent *normale*★★ and fine Riserva Vigna del Sorbo★★. SUPER-TUSCAN Flaccianello della Pieve★★★, produced from a single vineyard of old vines, has served as a shining example to other producers of how excellent Sangiovese can be without the addition of other varieties. Two varietals, Pinot Nero and Syrah★★, are made under the Case Via label. Best years: (Flaccianello) (2006) (04) 03 01 **00 99 97 95 93 90 88 85**.

FORADORI *Teroldego Rotaliano DOC, Trentino, Italy* Producer of dark, spicy, berry-fruited wines, including a regular TEROLDEGO ROTALIANO★ and barrique-aged Granato★★. Foradori's interest in Syrah is producing excellent results, both in the varietal Ailanpa★★ and the smoky, black-cherry lushness of Cabernet-Syrah blend Karanar★. Best years: (Granato) (2006) 04 **03 01 00 99 97**.

FORST *Pfalz, Germany* Village with outstanding vineyard sites, including the Ungeheuer or 'Monster'; wines from the Monster can indeed be quite savage, with a marvellous mineral intensity and richness in the best years. Equally good are the Kirchenstück, Jesuitengarten, Freundstück and Pechstein. Best producers: BASSERMANN-JORDAN★★, VON BUHL★★, BURKLIN-WOLF★★, MOSBACHER★★, WEGELER★, Werlé★, WOLF★★. Best years: (2006) 05 04 **03** 02 **01 99 98 97**.

O FOURNIER *Uco Valley, Argentina* A rising star in the UCO VALLEY, producing exciting Tempranillo and Malbec from old vines in the La Consulta area. Alfa Crux★, a blend of Tempranillo, Merlot and Malbec, is the current top of the line, while Alfa Crux Malbec★★ is an excellent, juicy expression of Argentina's flagship red grape. Also top Syrah★★. B Crux★ is the lighter, but delicious, second label. O Fournier also has a venture in RIBERA DEL DUERO, Spain, producing the top-of-the-line Fournier★★ and Alfa Spiga★ cuvées, and in early 2007 announced a new venture in Chile. Best years: (reds) (2004) 03 **02**.

FOX CREEK *McLaren Vale, South Australia* Impressive, opulent, superripe MCLAREN VALE reds. Reserve Shiraz★★ and Reserve Cabernet Sauvignon★★ have wowed the critics; JSM (Shiraz-Cabernets)★★ is rich and succulent; Merlot★★ is a little lighter but still concentrated and powerful. Vixen sparkling Shiraz★ is also lip-smacking stuff. Whites are comparatively ordinary, albeit fair value for money.

FOX RUN VINEYARDS *Finger Lakes AVA, New York State, USA* A leader in crafting a regional style from Dry Riesling★, as well as a reliable producer of complex, ALSACE-style Gewürztraminer★ and an elegant

Reserve Chardonnay★. There are also spicy, attractive reds from Pinot Noir and Cabernet Franc, and a complex, fruit-forward red Meritage.

FRANCIACORTA DOCG *Lombardy, Italy* CHAMPAGNE-method fizz made from Pinot and Chardonnay grapes. Still whites from Pinot Bianco and Chardonnay and reds from Cabernet, Barbera, Nebbiolo and Merlot are all DOC with the appellation Terre di Franciacorta. Best producers: BELLAVISTA★★, Fratelli Berlucchi★, Guido Berlucchi★, CA' DEL BOSCO★★, Castellino★, Cavalleri★, La Ferghettina★, Enrico Gatti★, Monte Rossa★, Il Mosnel★, Ricci Curbastro★, San Cristoforo★, Uberti★, Villa★.

FRANCISCAN *Napa Valley AVA, California, USA* Consistently good wines at fair prices, from the heart of the NAPA VALLEY. The Cuvée Sauvage Chardonnay★★ is a blockbusting, savoury mouthful, and the Cabernet Sauvignon-based meritage Magnificat★ is very attractive. Part of huge Constellation, which also owns Mount Veeder Winery, where lean but intense Cabernet Sauvignon★★ of great mineral depth and complexity is made, and Estancia, with remarkably good-value Chardonnay★ and Pinot Noir★ from CENTRAL COAST and Cabernet Sauvignon★ from ALEXANDER VALLEY, as well as its own Meritage★. .

DR KONSTANTIN FRANK *Finger Lakes AVA, New York State, USA* The good doctor was a pioneer of vinifera grapes in the FINGER LAKES region of New York State in the 1960s. Now under the direction of his grandson Fred, the winery continues to spotlight the area's talent with Riesling★. There's also some nice Chateau Frank fizz.

FRANKEN *Germany* 6000ha (14,820-acre) wine region specializing in dry wines – recognizable by their squat, green Bocksbeutel bottles (familiar because of the Portuguese wine Mateus Rosé). Silvaner is the traditional variety, although Müller-Thurgau now predominates. The most famous vineyards are on slopes around WURZBURG, RANDERSACKER and IPHOFEN.

FRANSCHHOEK WO *South Africa* Huguenot refugees settled in this picturesque valley, encircled by breathtaking mountain peaks, in the 17th century. Many wineries and other landmarks still bear French names. The valley is recognized for its whites – Semillon is a local speciality (a few vines are 100 years old) – though reds are establishing a reputation. La Motte Shiraz★ and Stony Brook Cabernet Sauvignon Reserve★ are among the most promising. Best producers: Graham BECK★, BOEKENHOUTSKLOOF★★, Cabrière Estate, Chamonix★ (Reserve Chardonnay★★), La Motte★, La Petite Ferme, L'Ormarins, Solms-Delta★, Stony Brook. Best years: (reds) **2004 03 02 01 00 99 98**.

FRASCATI DOC *Lazio, Italy* One of Italy's most famous whites, frequently referred to as Rome's quaffing wine. The wine may be made from Trebbiano or Malvasia or any blend thereof; the better examples have a higher proportion of Malvasia. Good Frascati is worth seeking out, most notably Vigna Adriana★★ (though it's now an IGT) from Castel de Paolis. Other light, dry Frascati-like wines come from neighbouring DOCs in the hills of the Castelli Romani and Colli Albani, including Marino, Montecompatri, Velletri and Zagarolo. Best producers: Casale Marchese★, Castel de Paolis★★, Colli di Catone★, Piero Costantini/Villa Simone★, Fontana Candida★, Zandotti★.

FREIXENET *Cava DO, Cataluña, Spain* The second-biggest Spanish sparkling wine company (after CODORNIU) makes the famous Cordon Negro Brut CAVA in a vast network of cellars in Sant Sadurní d'Anoia. Freixenet also owns the Castellblanch, Segura Viudas, Conde de Caralt and Canals & Nubiola Cava brands as well as PENEDES winery René Barbier and a stake in PRIORAT's Viticultors del Priorat (Morlanda). Its international expansion has gathered pace in recent years with interests in Champagne, California, Australia and Bordeaux.

FRESCOBALDI *Tuscany, Italy* Ancient Florentine company selling large quantities of inexpensive blended wines, but from its own vineyards (some 800ha/1980 acres in total) it produces good to very good wines at Nipozzano (CHIANTI RUFINA Nipozzano Riserva★★ and Montesodi★★), Tenuta di Pomino★, and Castelgiocondo★ in BRUNELLO DI MONTALCINO, where the Sangiovese and Merlot grapes for the SUPER-TUSCAN (and super-expensive) Luce della Vita are grown.

Frescobaldi is now sole owner of the famous Bolgheri estate, ORNELLAIA. Best years: (premium reds) (2006) 04 **03 01 00 99 98 97 95 93 90 88 85**.

FRIULI GRAVE DOC *Friuli-Venezia Giulia, Italy* DOC in western Friuli covering 19 wine types. Good affordable Merlot, Refosco, Chardonnay, Pinot Grigio, Traminer and Tocai. Best producers: Borgo Magredo★, Le Fredis★, Di Lenardo★, Orgnani★, Pighin★, Pittaro★, Plozner★, Pradio★, Russolo★, Vigneti Le Monde★, Villa Chiopris★, Vistorta★. Best years: (whites) (2006) 04 **02 01 00 98**.

FRIULI ISONZO DOC *Friuli-Venezia Giulia, Italy* Classy southern neighbour of COLLIO with wines of outstanding value. The DOC covers 20 styles, including Merlot, Chardonnay, Pinot Grigio and Sauvignon. The best from neighbouring Carso DOC are also good. Best producers: (Isonzo) Borgo San Daniele★, Colmello di Grotta★, Sergio & Mauro Drius★★, Masùt da Rive★ (Silvano Gallo), Lis Neris-Pecorari★★, Pierpaolo Pecorari★, Giovanni Puiatti★, Ronco del Gelso★★, Tenuta Villanova★, Vie di Romans★★; (Carso) Castelvecchio, Edi Kante★★. Best years: (whites) (2006) 04 **03 02 01 00 99 98 97**.

FRIULI-VENEZIA GIULIA *Italy* North-east Italian region bordering Austria and Slovenia. The hilly DOC zones of COLLIO and COLLI ORIENTALI produce some of Italy's finest whites from Chardonnay, Pinot Bianco, Pinot Grigio, Sauvignon and Tocai, and excellent reds mainly from Cabernet, Merlot and Refosco. The DOCs of Friuli Aquileia, FRIULI ISONZO, Friuli Latisana and FRIULI GRAVE, in the rolling hills and plains, produce good-value wines.

FROMM *Marlborough, South Island, New Zealand* Small winery where low-yielding vines and intensively managed vineyards are the secret behind a string of winning white wines, including fine Burgundian-style Clayvin Vineyard Chardonnay★★, German-style Riesling★★ and Riesling Auslese★. Despite its success with whites, Fromm is perhaps best known for intense, long-lived reds, including Clayvin Vineyard Pinot Noir★★★, Fromm Vineyard Pinot Noir★★ and a powerful, peppery Syrah★★. Best years: (Pinot Noir) 2005 04 **03 02 01 00 99**.

FRONSAC AC *Bordeaux, France* Small area west of POMEROL making good-value Merlot-based wines. The top producers have taken note of the feeding frenzy in neighbouring Pomerol and sharpened up their act accordingly, with finely structured wines, occasionally perfumed, and better with at least 5 years' age. Best producers: Dalem★, la

153

Dauphine★, Fontenil★, la Grave★, Haut-Carles★, Magondeau Beau-Site★, Mayne-Vieil (Cuvée Aliénor★), Moulin Haut-Laroque★, Richelieu★, la Rivière★ (Aria★), la Rousselle★, Tour du Moulin, les Trois Croix★, la Vieille Cure★, Villars★. Best years: 2005 **03 01 00 98 96 95 94 90 89 88**.

FUMÉ BLANC See SAUVIGNON BLANC.

RUDOLF FÜRST *Bürgstadt, Franken, Germany* Paul Fürst's dry Rieslings★★ are unusually elegant for a region renowned for its earthy white wines, while his Burgundian-style Spätburgunder (Pinot Noir) reds★★ and barrel-fermented Weissburgunder (Pinot Blanc) whites★★ are some of the best in Germany. Sensual, intellectual wines with excellent aging potential. Best years: (dry Riesling) (2006) 05 04 **03 02 01 99 98**; (reds) (2006) 05 04 03 **02 01 00 99**.

JEAN-NOËL GAGNARD *Chassagne-Montrachet, Côte de Beaune, Burgundy, France* Now run by Gagnard's daughter Caroline Lestimé, who consistently makes some of the best wines of CHASSAGNE-MONTRACHET, particularly Premiers Crus Caillerets★★★ and Morgeot★★. Top wine is rich, toasty BATARD-MONTRACHET★★★. All whites are capable of extended cellaring. Reds★ are good, but not in the same class. Best years: (whites) (2006) 05 04 **03 02 01 00 99 98**.

GAILLAC AC *South-West France* The whites, mainly from Mauzac and Ondenc, with their sharp but attractive green apple bite, are rather stern but, from a decent producer, can be extremely refreshing. Sweet whites are getting better. Some more serious reds are made, which require some aging. The star of Gaillac at the moment is the fizz, ideally not quite dry and packed with fruit. Drink as young as possible. Best producers: Albert, Bosc-Long, Causses-Marines★, Clément-Termes, Escausses, de Gineste, Labarthe★, Labastide-de-Lévis co-op, Mas Pignou, PLAGEOLES★★, Rotier★, Técou co-op★, des Terrisses★.

GAJA *Barbaresco DOCG, Piedmont, Italy* Angelo Gaja brought about the transformation of PIEDMONT from an old-fashioned region that Italians swore made the finest red wine in the world yet the rest of the world disdained, to an area buzzing with excitement. He introduced international standards and charged staggeringly high prices, thus giving other Piedmont growers the chance to get a decent return for their labours. Into this fiercely conservative area, full of fascinating grape varieties but proudest of the native Nebbiolo, he introduced French grapes like Cabernet Sauvignon (Darmagi★★), Sauvignon Blanc (Alteni di Brassica★) and Chardonnay (Gaia & Rey★★). He has also renounced the Barbaresco and Barolo DOCGs for his best wines! Gaja's traditional strength has been in single-vineyard wines from the BARBARESCO region: his Sori San Lorenzo★★★, Sori Tildin★★★ and Costa Russi★★★, now sold under the LANGHE DOC, are often cited as Barbaresco's best of the modern style. Only one premium bottling of Barbaresco DOCG★★★ is now made. Sperss★★★ and Conteisa★★★ – from BAROLO, but sold as Langhe DOC wines – are also outstanding. Barbera Sitorey★ and Nebbiolo-based Langhe Sito Moresco★ are less exciting. Gaja has also invested in BRUNELLO DI MONTALCINO (Pieve Santa Restituta) and BOLGHERI (Cà Marcanda). Best years: (Barbaresco) (2006) (04) 03 01 **00** 99 **98 97 96 95 93 90 89 88 85 82 79 78 71 61**.

GALICIA *Spain* Up in Spain's hilly, verdant north-west, Galicia is renowned for its Albariño whites. There are 5 DOs: RIAS BAIXAS can make excellent, fragrant Albariño, with modern equipment and serious winemaking; Ribeiro DO has also invested heavily in new equipment, and better local white grapes such as Treixadura are now being used; it's a similar story with Godello in the mountainous Valdeorras DO, where new producers such as the young Rafael Palacios, from the ubiquitous Rioja-based family, are reaching new heights for ageworthy, individual whites. Some young reds from the Mencia grape are also made there and in the Ribeira Sacra DO. Monterrei DO is technically backward but shows some potential with its native white grape, Doña Blanca. Most wines are best drunk young.

GALLO *Central Valley, California, USA*   Gallo, the world's second-largest wine company – and for generations a byword for cheap, drab wines – has made a massive effort to change its reputation and our attitudes since the mid-1990s. This began with the release of Sonoma Estate Chardonnay and Cabernet Sauvignon, and their success persuaded the company the future lay in quality rather than vast quantity. The Gallo of Sonoma label has been discontinued and replaced by the umbrella Gallo Family label, with emphasis on Sonoma Chardonnay and Cabernet Sauvignon, Zinfandel and Cabernet Sauvignon from DRY CREEK VALLEY and ALEXANDER VALLEY and other Chardonnay from several vineyards. New vineyards in RUSSIAN RIVER VALLEY and the SONOMA COAST have been planted to Pinot Noir and Pinot Gris. Even so, Gallo continues to produce oceans of ordinary wine. Turning Leaf and Sierra Valley aren't going to turn many heads, but the company has taken Rancho Zabaco upscale and added a parallel brand, Dancing Bull, in which Sauvignon Blanc★ and Zinfandel★★ are budding stars. In 2002, Gallo acquired historical Louis M Martini in NAPA VALLEY, adding the famed Monte Rosso vineyard to its holdings, and then bought Mirassou, Barefoot Cellars and CENTRAL COAST's Bridlewood.

GAMAY   The only grape allowed for red BEAUJOLAIS. In general Gamay wine is rather rough-edged and quite high in raspy acidity, but in Beaujolais, so long as the yield is not too high, it can achieve a wonderful, juicy-fruit gluggability, almost unmatched in the world of wine. Elsewhere in France, it is successful in the Ardèche and the Loire and less so in the Mâconnais. In Switzerland it is blended with Pinot Noir to create DOLE and Goron. There are occasional plantings in Canada, New Zealand, Australia, South Africa, Italy (MONTECARLO DOC) and even England, which could become interesting.

GANTENBEIN *Fläsch, Graubunden, Switzerland*   Since 1982 Daniel Gantenbein has focused on producing intense and powerful versions of the Burgundian varieties, and has won a fine reputation above all for his Pinot Noir★★, as well as Chardonnay and Riesling. Best years: (Pinot Noir) (2005) 04 03 **02 00 99 98**.

GARD, VIN DE PAYS DU *Languedoc, France*   Mainly reds and rosés from the western side of the RHONE delta. Most red is light, spicy and attractive. Rosés can be fresh when young, and with modern winemaking whites can be good. Best producers: des Aveylans★, Baruel★, Cantarelles, Coste Plane, Grande Cassagne★, Guiot★, Mas des Bressades★.

GARNACHA BLANCA See GRENACHE BLANC.

GARNACHA TINTA See GRENACHE NOIR.

155

GATTINARA DOCG *Piedmont, Italy*   One of the most capricious of Italy's top red wine areas. The Nebbiolo wines should be softer and lighter than BAROLO, with a delicious, black plums, tar and roses flavour if you're lucky. Drink within 10 years. Vintages follow those for Barolo. Best producers: Antoniolo★, S Gattinara, Nervi★, Travaglini★.

DOM. GAUBY *Côtes du Roussillon-Villages AC, Roussillon, France*   Gérard Gauby used to make burly but very tannic wines; now his wines are softer but marvellously concentrated and balanced. Highlights include powerful COTES DU ROUSSILLON-VILLAGES Vieilles Vignes★★ and Syrah-dominated La Muntada★★ as well as a gorgeously seductive white vin de pays Calcinaires★★. Best years: (reds) 2004 03 **02 01 00** 99 98.

GAVI DOCG *Piedmont, Italy*   This fashionable and rapidly improving Cortese-based, steely, lemony white can age up to 5 years, providing it starts life with sufficient fruit. La Scolca's Spumante Brut Soldati★ is an admirable sparkling wine. Best producers: Battistina★, Bergaglio★, Broglia★, La Chiara★, CHIARLO★, FONTANAFREDDA, La Giustiniana★★, Pio Cesare, San Pietro★, La Scolca★, Tassarolo★, Villa Sparina★.

CH. GAZIN★★ *Pomerol AC, Bordeaux, France*   One of the largest châteaux in POMEROL, situated next to the legendary PETRUS. The wine, traditionally a succulent, sweet-textured Pomerol, seemed to lose its way in the 1980s but has now got much of its richness and character back under the management of owner Nicolas de Bailliencourt. Best years: 2005 04 **03 02 01 00** 99 98 96 95 94 90 89 88.

GEELONG *Victoria, Australia*   Cool-climate, maritime-influenced region revived in the 1960s after destruction by phylloxera in the 19th century. Can be brilliant; potentially a match for the YARRA VALLEY. Impressive Pinot Noir, Chardonnay, Riesling, Sauvignon and Shiraz. Best producers: Austin's, BANNOCKBURN★, By Farr★, Scotchmans Hill★.

GEISENHEIM *Rheingau, Germany*   Village famous for its wine school, where the Müller-Thurgau grape was bred in 1882. Geisenheim's most famous vineyard is the Rothenberg, which produces strong, earthy wines. Best producers: Johannishof★, WEGELER★. Best years: (2006) 05 04 03 02 **01** 99 98 96.

GEROVASSILIOU *Macedonia AO, Greece*   Bordeaux-trained Evángelos Gerovassiliou has 40ha (100 acres) of vineyards and a modern winery in Epanomi in northern Greece. High-quality fruit results in Syrah-dominated Domaine Gerovassiliou red★ and some fresh, modern whites, including a fine Viognier★ that lacks a little perfume but has fantastic fruit, barrel-fermented Chardonnay and Fumé, and the Domaine Gerovassiliou★ white, a most original Assyrtiko-Malagousia blend.

GEVREY-CHAMBERTIN AC *Côte de Nuits, Burgundy, France*   The wines of Gevrey-Chambertin have at times proved disappointing, but a new generation of growers has restored the reputation of Gevrey as a source of well-coloured, firmly structured, powerful, perfumed wines that become rich and gamy with age. Village wines should be kept for at least 5 years, Premiers Crus and the 8 Grands Crus for 10 years or more, especially CHAMBERTIN and Clos-de-Bèze. The Premier Cru Clos St-Jacques is worthy of promotion to Grand Cru. Best producers: D Bachelet★★, L Boillot★, A Burguet★★, B CLAIR★★, P Damoy★★, DROUHIN★, C Dugat★★★, B Dugat-Py★★, DUJAC★★, S Esmonin★★, FAIVELEY★★, Fourrier★★, Geantet-Pansiot★★, JADOT★★, Denis MORTET★★★, Rossignol-Trapet★, J Roty★★, ROUSSEAU★★★, Sérafin★★, J & J-L Trapet★★. Best years: (2006) 05 04 03 02 **01 00** 99 98 96 95 93 90.

GEWÜRZTRAMINER *Gewürz* means spice, and the wine certainly can be spicy and exotically perfumed, as well as being typically low in acidity. It is thought to have originated in the village of Tramin, in Italy's ALTO ADIGE, and the name Traminer is used by many producers. In parts of Germany and Austria it is known as Clevner and in Switzerland it is called Heida or Paien. It makes an appearance in many wine-producing countries; quality is mixed and styles vary enormously, from the fresh, light, florally perfumed wines produced in Alto Adige to the rich, luscious, late-harvest ALSACE Vendange Tardive. Best in France's Alsace and also good in Austria's Styria (STEIERMARK) and New Zealand.

GEYSER PEAK *Alexander Valley AVA, Sonoma County, California, USA* Australian winemaker Daryl Groom's mainstream wines tend to be accessible and fruit-driven. Typical are the fruity SONOMA COUNTY Cabernet★ and Merlot★ – ripe, juicy and delicious upon release. The Reserve Alexandre Meritage★★, a BORDEAUX-style blend, is made for aging, and the Reserve Shiraz★★ has a cult following. Block Collection features limited production, single-vineyard wines. There's also a highly popular Sauvignon Blanc★. The company is owned by Beam Wine Estates. Best years: (Alexandre) 2002 **01 00 99 98 97 94 91**.

GIACONDA *Beechworth, Victoria, Australia* In spite of (or perhaps because of) Giaconda's tiny production, Rick Kinzbrunner is one of Australia's most influential winemakers. Following on from his

success, BEECHWORTH has become one of the country's most exciting viticultural regions. His tightly structured, minerally, savoury Chardonnay★★★ is one of Australia's best, the Pinot Noir★★★ is both serious and beautiful, the Cabernet★ is ripe, deep and complex, while the Warner Vineyard Shiraz★★

successfully pursues a deep, gamy HERMITAGE style. Because the grapes were affected by bushfires, only the late-ripening Cabernet was released from the 2003 vintage. Best years: (Chardonnay) 2006 05 04 02 01 **00 99 98 96 93 92**.

BRUNO GIACOSA *Barbaresco DOCG, Piedmont, Italy* One of the great winemakers of the LANGHE hills, still basically a traditionalist, though he has reduced maturation time for his BARBARESCOS and BAROLOS to a maximum of 4 years. Superb Barbarescos Asili★★★, Santo Stefano★★★ and Rabaja★★★, and Barolos including Rocche di Falletto★★★ and Falletto★★★. Also excellent Dolcetto d'Alba★, ROERO Arneis★, MOSCATO D'ASTI★★ and sparkling Extra Brut★★.

GIESEN *Canterbury and Marlborough, South Island, New Zealand* A large winery that played a significant part in putting CANTERBURY on the map with a string of fine sweet and dry Rieslings. Has now bought 400ha (1000 acres) of vineyard in MARLBOROUGH and seems intent upon producing vast quantities of budget-priced Sauvignon Blanc rather than stellar Riesling. Best years: (Sauvignon Blanc) **2006 04 03**.

GIGONDAS AC *Rhône Valley, France* Gigondas wines, mostly red and made mainly from Grenache, have fistfuls of chunky personality. Most drink well with 5 years' age; some need a little more. Best producers: P Amadieu★, la Bouissière★★, Brusset★★, Cassan★★, Cayron★★, Clos des Cazaux★★, Clos du Joncuas★★, Cros de la Mûre★★, DELAS★, des Espiers★★, Font-Sane★★, la Fourmone★, les Goubert★, Gour de Chaulé★, Grapillon d'Or★★, GUIGAL★, JABOULET★, Longue-Toque★, Montvac★★, Moulin de la Gardette★★, les Pallières★★, Piaugier★, Raspail-Ay★★, Redortier★, St-Cosme★★, ST-GAYAN★★, Santa Duc★, Tardieu-Laurent★★, la Tourade★★, Trignon★. Best years: 2006 05 **04 03 02 01 00 99 98 97 95 94 90**.

CH. GILETTE★★ *Sauternes AC, Bordeaux, France* These astonishing wines are stored in concrete vats as opposed to the more normal wooden barrels. This virtually precludes any oxygen contact, and it is oxygen that ages a wine. Consequently, when released at up to 30 years old, they are bursting with life and lusciousness. Best years: **1986 85 83 82 81 79 78 76 75 70 67 61 59 55 53 49**.

GIPPSLAND *Victoria, Australia* Diverse wineries along the southern Victoria coast, all tiny but with massive potential. Results are erratic, occasionally brilliant. Nicholson River's BURGUNDY-style Chardonnay can sometimes hit ★★. Bass Phillip Reserve★★ and Premium★★ Pinot Noirs are among the best in Australia, with a cult following. McAlister★, a red BORDEAUX blend, has also produced some tasty flavours. Best producers: Bass Phillip★★, McAlister★, Nicholson River★.

VINCENT GIRARDIN *Santenay, Côte de Beaune, Burgundy, France* The best grower in SANTENAY and now a thriving négociant, with an establishment in MEURSAULT★★. Bright, glossy reds from Santenay★★, MARANGES★ and CHASSAGNE-MONTRACHET★★ are surpassed by excellent VOLNAY★★ and POMMARD Grands Épenots★★★. Chassagne-Montrachet whites (Morgeot★★, Caillerets★★★) are perfectly balanced with good fruit depth. CORTON-CHARLEMAGNE★★★ is exceptional. He has also revived the moribund Henri Clerc estate in PULIGNY-MONTRACHET. Best years: (reds) (2006) 05 04 **03 02 01 99**; (whites) (2006) 05 **04 02 00 99**.

GISBORNE *North Island, New Zealand* Gisborne, with its hot, humid climate and fertile soils, delivers both quality and quantity. Local growers have christened their region 'The Chardonnay Capital of New Zealand' and Gewürztraminer and Chenin Blanc are also a success. Good reds, however, are hard to find. Best producers: MILLTON★★, MONTANA. Best years: (Chardonnay) **2005 04 02**.

GIVRY AC *Côte Chalonnaise, Burgundy, France* Important CÔTE CHALONNAISE village. The reds have an intensity of fruit and ability to age that are unusual in the region. There are some attractive, fairly full, nutty whites, too. Best producers: Bourgeon★, Chofflet-Valdenaire★, B CLAIR★, Clos Salomon★, Joblot★, F Lumpp★★, Ragot★, Sarrazin★. Best years: (reds) (2006) 05 **03 02 99**; (whites) (2006) 05 **04 02**.

GLAETZER *Barossa Valley, South Australia* Colin Glaetzer has been one of the BAROSSA VALLEY's most enthusiastic and successful winemakers for decades. He made his reputation working for other people, and now he and his son Ben are making tip-top Barossa wines under the family label. Fine Semillon★, juicy Grenache-Mourvèdre★ and rich, superripe Bishop Shiraz★★ (from 30–60-year-old vines) and Glaetzer Shiraz★★ (from 80-year-old vines). Ben also makes Amon-Ra Shiraz★★ and Godolphin★★, a deep, dense Shiraz-Cabernet blend, as well as cult MCLAREN VALE Mitolo★★ and exciting reds and whites for the Heartland★★ label. Best years: (Bishop Shiraz) 2006 05 04 02 01 **99 98 96**.

GLEN CARLOU *Paarl WO, South Africa* Started by the Finlaysons in the 1980s and now owned by Donald HESS. David Finlayson remains as winemaker. Three Chardonnays (elegant standard Chardonnay★, richer, toasty Reserve★ and restrained single-vineyard Quartz Stone★★) lead the whites. Reds feature sweet-textured Pinot Noir★; deep, dry Syrah★; Grand Classique★, a red BORDEAUX blend with excellent aging potential; and concentrated Gravel Quarry Cabernet★. Best years: (Chardonnay) 2006 **05 04 03 02 01 00**.

CH. GLORIA★ *St-Julien AC, Haut-Médoc, Bordeaux, France* An interesting property, created out of tiny plots of Classed Growth land scattered all round ST-JULIEN. Generally very soft and sweet-centred, the wine nonetheless ages well. Second wine: Peymartin. Best years: 2005 04 **03** 02 **01 00 99 98 96 95 90 89**.

GOLAN HEIGHTS WINERY *Golan Heights, Israel* Israel's leading quality wine producer. Cool summers, high-altitude vineyards and modern winemaking with kosher standards have resulted in good Sauvignon Blanc and Cabernet Sauvignon★, balanced, oaky Chardonnay★ and good bottle-fermented fizz★. Yarden is the top label.

GOLDMUSKATELLER Moscato Giallo (Muscat Blanc à Petits Grains) is known as Goldmuskateller in the ALTO ADIGE. Here and elsewhere in Italy's north-east, sometimes under the name Fior d'Arancio, it makes scented wines in dry, off-dry and sweet (*passito*) styles. Best producers: Bolognani★, Viticoltori Caldaro★, LAGEDER★, Thurnhof★, Vignalta.

GOLDWATER ESTATE *Waiheke Island, Auckland, New Zealand* The first vineyard on WAIHEKE ISLAND. Top wines are intense, long-lived 'Goldie' Cabernet-Merlot★★ and elegant, cedary Esslin Merlot★★, with considerable depth and structure. Zell Chardonnay★★ from Waiheke looks exciting. Attractive New Dog Sauvignon Blanc★ and Roseland Chardonnay★ from MARLBOROUGH fruit. In 2006 Goldwater merged with Marlborough's VAVASOUR. Best years: (Waiheke reds) **2005 04 02 00 99**.

GONZÁLEZ BYASS *Jerez y Manzanilla DO, Andalucía, Spain* Tio Pepe★ fino is the world's biggest-selling sherry. The old sherries are superb: intense, dry Amontillado del Duque★★★; 2 rich, complex olorosos, sweet Matusalem★★ and medium Apóstoles★★; treacly Noé Pedro Ximénez★★★. One step down is the Alfonso Dry Oloroso★. The firm pioneered the rediscovery of single-vintage (non-solera) dry olorosos★★ and palos cortados★★.

HENRI GOUGES *Nuits-St-Georges, Côte de Nuits, Burgundy, France* The original Henri Gouges was mayor of NUITS-ST-GEORGES in the 1930s and was instrumental in classifying the large number of Premiers Crus in his appellation. Today, the domaine is back on form, producing impressive, meaty, long-lived reds (Les St Georges★★★, Clos des Porrets★★, Les Vaucrains★★) as well as excellent white Nuits-St-Georges Premier Cru La Perrière★★. Best years: (2006) 05 04 02 01 **00 99 98 96 90 78 55 45**.

GRAACH *Mosel, Germany* Important Middle MOSEL wine village with 4 vineyard sites, the most famous being Domprobst (also the best) and Himmelreich. A third, the Josephshöfer, is wholly owned by the von KESSELSTATT estate. The wines have an attractive fullness to balance their steely acidity, and great aging potential. Best producers: von KESSELSTATT★, Dr LOOSEN★★, Markus Molitor★★, J J PRUM★★, S A PRUM★, Max Ferd RICHTER★, Willi SCHAEFER★★★, SELBACH-OSTER★★, Weins-Prüm★. Best years: (2006) 05 04 **03** 02 01 **00 99 98 97 96 94**.

GRACIANO Rare, low-yielding but excellent Spanish grape, traditional in RIOJA, NAVARRA and Extremadura. It makes dense, highly structured, fragrant reds, and its high acidity adds life when blended with low-acid Tempranillo. In Portugal it is called Tinta Miúda. Also grown by BROWN BROTHERS in Australia.

GRAHAM'S *Port DOC, Douro, Portugal* Part of the Symington empire, making rich, florally scented Vintage Port★★★, sweeter than DOW's and WARRE's, but with the backbone to age. In non-declared years makes a fine vintage wine called Malvedos★★. Six Grapes★ is one of the best premium rubies, and 10-year-old★ and 20-year-old★★ tawnies are consistently good. Best years: (Vintage) 2003 00 97 94 91 **85 83 80 77 75 70 66 63 60**; (Malvedos) 2001 99 **95 92 90**.

ALAIN GRAILLOT *Crozes-Hermitage AC, Rhône Valley, France* Excellent estate producing powerfully concentrated, rich, fruity reds. The top wine is CROZES-HERMITAGE la Guiraude★★, but the regular Crozes-Hermitage★★ is wonderful too, and great for early drinking, as are the ST-JOSEPH★★ and a lovely fragrant white Crozes-Hermitage★. Keep top reds for at least 5 years. Son Max has new Dom. des Lises estate. Best years: (la Guiraude) 2006 05 04 **03 01 00 99 96 95 90 89**.

GRAMPIANS AND PYRENEES *Victoria, Australia* Two adjacent cool-climate regions in central western VICTORIA. Both produce some of Australia's most characterful Shiraz, as well as distinguished Riesling, subtle Pinot Gris and savoury Chardonnay. Best producers: BEST'S★, Blue Pyrenees, Dalwhinnie★★, MOUNT LANGI GHIRAN★★, Redbank★, SEPPELT★★, Taltarni. Best years: (Shiraz) 2005 04 03 02 **01 99 98 97 96 94 91 90**.

CH. GRAND-PUY-DUCASSE★ *Pauillac AC, 5ème Cru Classé, Haut-Médoc, Bordeaux, France* After great improvement in the 1980s, form dipped in the early 90s but recovered again in 95. Approachable after 5 years but the best vintages can improve for considerably longer. Second wine: Artigues-Arnaud. Best years: 2005 04 03 **02 00 96 95 90 89**.

CH. GRAND-PUY-LACOSTE★★ *Pauillac AC, 5ème Cru Classé, Haut-Médoc, Bordeaux, France* Classic PAUILLAC, with lots of blackcurrant and cigar-box perfume. It begins fairly dense, but as the wine develops, the flavours mingle with the sweetness of new oak to become one of Pauillac's most memorable taste sensations. Owned by the Borie family of DUCRU-BEAUCAILLOU. Second wine: Lacoste-Borie. Best years: 2005 04 03 02 00 **99 98 96 95 94 90 89 88 86 85 83 82**.

GRANDS-ÉCHÉZEAUX AC See ECHEZEAUX AC.

GRANGE★★★ *Barossa Valley, South Australia* In 1950, Max Schubert, chief winemaker at PENFOLDS, visited Europe and came back determined to make a wine that could match the great BORDEAUX reds. Undeterred by a lack of Cabernet Sauvignon grapes and French oak barrels, he set to work with BAROSSA Shiraz and barrels made from the more pungent American oak. Initially ignored and misunderstood, Schubert eventually achieved global recognition for his wine, a stupendously complex, thrillingly rich red that only begins to reveal its magnificence after 10 years in bottle – but is better after 20. Produced using only the best grapes, primarily from the Barossa with varying amounts from other regions, it is traditionally acknowledged as Australia's greatest red. Best years: (2004) (02) 01 99 98 96 94 92 91 90 **88 86 84 83 80 78 76 71 67 66 63 62 55 53 52**.

DOM. DE LA GRANGE DES PÈRES★★ *Vin de Pays de l'Hérault, Languedoc, France* With only 500 cases produced each year, demand is high for the meticulously crafted unfiltered Cabernet Sauvignon-based red★★. The white★★ is produced in even smaller quantities. Best years: (red) 2003 02 01 00 **99 98**.

GRANGEHURST *Stellenbosch WO, South Africa* Boutique winery known for modern Pinotage★, Cabernet-Merlot★★ with Bordeaux-ish appeal and Nikela★, a blend of all three varieties and owner/winemaker Jeremy Walker's answer to the Cape blend. Recent additions to the range include two Cabernets (Reserve★) and Shiraz-Cabernet Reserve★. Best years: (Cabernet-Merlot) **2002 01 00 99 98 97 95**.

GRANS-FASSIAN *Leiwen, Mosel, Germany* LEIWEN owes its reputation largely to Gerhard Grans. Both sweet and dry Rieslings have gained in sophistication over the years: Spätlese★★ and Auslese★★ from TRITTENHEIMER Apotheke are particularly impressive. Eiswein is ★★★ in good vintages. Best years: (2006) 05 04 **03** 02 **01 99 98** 97 96.

ALFRED GRATIEN *Champagne AC, Champagne, France* This small company makes some of my favourite CHAMPAGNE. Its wines are made in wooden casks, which is very rare nowadays. The non-vintage★★ blend is usually 4 years old when sold, rather than the normal 3 years. The vintage★★★ is deliciously ripe and toasty when released but can age for another 10 years. The prestige cuvée, Cuvée Paradis★★, is non-vintage. Best years: (1999) 97 96 **95 91 90 89 88 85** 83.

GRAVES AC *Bordeaux, France* The Graves region covers the area south of Bordeaux to Langon, but the generally superior villages in the northern half broke away in 1987 to form the PESSAC-LEOGNAN AC. In the southern Graves, a new wave of winemaking has produced plenty of clean, bone-dry whites with lots of snappy freshness, as well as more complex soft, nutty barrel-aged whites, and some juicy, quick-drinking reds. Sweet white wines take the Graves Supérieures AC; the best make a decent substitute for the more expensive SAUTERNES. Best producers: Archambeau★, Ardennes★, Brondelle★, Chantegrive★, Clos Floridène★★, Crabitey★, l'Hospital, Léhoul★, Magence, Magneau★, Rahoul, Respide-Médeville★, St-Robert★, Seuil, Vieux-Ch.-Gaubert★, Villa Bel-Air★; (sweet) Brondelle, Léhoul. Best years: (reds) 2005 **04 01 00 98 96 95** 90; (dry whites) **2005** 04 02 01 00 98 96 95; (sweet whites) 2005 **03 02 01 99 98 97 96 95 90** 89.

GRAVNER *Friuli-Venezia Giulia, Italy* Josko Gravner, FRIULI's most zealous winemaker, sets styles with his wood-aged, oxidative wines. Along with prized and high-priced Chardonnay★★, Sauvignon★★ and Ribolla Gialla★, he combines 6 white varieties in Breg★★. Reds are Rosso Gravner★ (predominantly Merlot) and Rujno★★ (Merlot-Cabernet Sauvignon).

GREAT SOUTHERN *Western Australia* A vast, cool-climate region encompassing the sub-regions of Mount Barker, Frankland River, Denmark, Albany and Porongurup. Mount Barker is particularly successful with Riesling, Shiraz and Cabernet; Frankland River with Riesling, Chardonnay, Shiraz and Cabernet; Denmark with Chardonnay and Pinot Noir; Albany with Pinot Noir; Porongurup with Riesling. Plantings have boomed in recent years, especially in Frankland River. Best producers: Alkoomi★, FERNGROVE★, Forest Hill★, Frankland Estate★,

161

Garlands★, Gilberts★, Goundrey, Harewood★★, HOUGHTON★★, HOWARD PARK★★, Jingalla, PLANTAGENET★★, West Cape Howe★★.

GRECHETTO Italian grape centred on UMBRIA, the main component of ORVIETO DOC, also making tasty, anise-tinged dry white varietals. Occasionally used in VIN SANTO in TUSCANY. Best producers: Antonelli, Barberani-Vallesanta★, Caprai, FALESCO★, Palazzone, Castello della SALA.

GRENACHE BLANC A common white grape in the south of France, but without many admirers. Except me, that is, because I love the pear-scented wine flecked with anise that a good producer can achieve. Low-yield examples take surprisingly well to oak. Generally best within a year of the vintage, although the odd old-vine example can age attractively. Grown as Garnacha Blanca in Spain. A few old vines are contributing to some interesting wines in South Africa.

GRENACHE NOIR Among the world's most widely planted red grapes – the bulk of it in Spain, where it is called Garnacha Tinta. It is a hot-climate grape and in France it reaches its peak in the southern RHÔNE, especially in CHÂTEAUNEUF-DU-PAPE, where it combines great alcoholic strength with rich raspberry fruit and a perfume hot from the herb-strewn hills. It is generally given more tannin, acid and structure by blending with Syrah, Mourvèdre, Cinsaut or other southern French grapes. It can make wonderful rosé in TAVEL, LIRAC and COTES DE PROVENCE, as well as in NAVARRA in Spain. It takes centre stage in ARAGON's Calatayud, Campo de Borja and CARIÑENA, and forms the backbone of the impressive reds of PRIORAT; in RIOJA it adds weight to the Tempranillo. It is also the basis for the *vins doux naturels* of BANYULS and MAURY in southern France. Also grown in CALIFORNIA and SOUTH AUSTRALIA, where it has only recently been accorded much respect as imaginative winemakers realized there was a great resource of century-old vines capable of making wild and massively enjoyable reds. More is being planted in South Africa, where it is a popular component in Rhône-style blends. See also CANNONAU.

GRGICH HILLS CELLAR *Rutherford AVA, California, USA* Mike Grgich was winemaker at CHATEAU MONTELENA when its 1973 Chardonnay shocked Paris judges by finishing ahead of French versions in the famous 1976 tasting. At his own winery he makes classic California Chardonnay★★, which ages for at least a decade, ripe, tannic Cabernet★, plummy Merlot★ and a huge, old-style Zinfandel★. Best years: (Chardonnay) (2005) (04) 03 **02 01 00 99 98 97 95**.

GRIOTTE-CHAMBERTIN AC See CHAMBERTIN AC.

JEAN GRIVOT *Vosne-Romanée, Côte de Nuits, Burgundy, France* Étienne Grivot has settled in to his own interpretation of his father's traditional styles, and has made brilliant wines since 1995, especially RICHEBOURG★★★ and NUITS-ST-GEORGES les Boudots★★. Expensive. Best years: (2006) 05 04 03 02 **01 00 99 98 97 96 95**.

GROS *Côte de Nuits, Burgundy, France* Brilliant COTE DE NUITS wines from various members of the family, especially Anne Gros, Michel Gros, Gros Frère et Soeur and Anne-Françoise Gros. Look out for CLOS DE VOUGEOT★★★, ECHEZEAUX★★★ and RICHEBOURG★★★ as well as good-value HAUTES-COTES DE NUITS★. Best years: (2006) 05 04 03 02 01 **00 99 98 97 96 95 93 90**.

GROS PLANT DU PAYS NANTAIS VDQS *Loire Valley, France* Gros Plant can be searing stuff, but this acidic wine is well suited to the seafood guzzled in the region. Look for a *sur lie* bottling and drink the youngest available. Best producers: Brochet, les Coins, l'ECU, la Grange, Saupin.

GROSSET *Clare Valley, South Australia* Jeffrey Grosset is a perfectionist, crafting tiny quantities of hand-made wines. A Riesling specialist, he bottles Watervale★★★ separately from Polish Hill★★★; both are supremely good and age well. Cabernet blend Gaia★★ is smooth and seamless. Also outstanding Piccadilly (ADELAIDE HILLS) Chardonnay★★★ and very fine Pinot Noir★★ and Semillon-Sauvignon★★. Best years: (Riesling) 2006 05 04 03 **02 01 00 99 98 97 96 94 93 92 90**.

CH. GRUAUD-LAROSE★★ *St-Julien AC, 2ème Cru Classé, Haut-Médoc, Bordeaux, France* One of the largest ST-JULIEN estates, now owned by the same family as CHASSE-SPLEEN and HAUT-BAGES-LIBERAL. Until the 1970s these wines were classic, cedary St-Juliens. Since the early 80s, the wines have been darker, richer and coated with new oak, yet inclined to exhibit an unnerving feral quality. Recent vintages have mostly combined considerable power with finesse, despite disappointments in 02 and 03. Second wine: Sarget de Gruaud-Larose. Best years: 2005 04 **01 00 99 98 96 95 90 89 88**.

GRÜNER VELTLINER Austrian grape, also grown in the Czech Republic, Slovakia and Hungary. It is at its best in Austria's KAMPTAL, KREMSTAL and the WACHAU, where the soil and cool climate bring out all the lentilly, white-peppery aromas. Styles vary from light and tart to savoury, mouthfilling yet appetizing wines equalling the best in Europe.

GUELBENZU *Spain* Family-owned bodega making good Azul★, from Tempranillo, Cabernet and Merlot, and rich concentrated, Cabernet Sauvignon-based Evo★. Lautus★★, from old vines, incorporates Garnacha in the blend. Guelbenzu has estates in both NAVARRA and ARAGON; the wines are non-DO and are labelled as Vinos de la Tierra Ribera del Queiles. Best years: (Evo) (2005) 04 03 **01 00 99 98 97 96**.

GUIGAL *Côte-Rôtie AC, Rhône Valley, France* Marcel Guigal is among the most famous names in the RHONE, producing wines from his own vineyards in COTE-ROTIE under the Château d'Ampuis★★★ label as well as Dom. de Bonserine★ and the Guigal range from purchased grapes (Côte-Rôtie Brune et Blonde is ★★ since 1998). La Mouline, la Turque and la Landonne all rate ★★★ in most critics' opinions. Well, I have definitely had profound wines from La Landonne and La Mouline, and to my surprise and delight the considerable new oak aging had not dimmed the classic Côte-Rôtie beauty and fragrance. However, Guigal is uniquely talented; lesser producers using this amount of new oak rarely manage to save the balance of the wine. CONDRIEU★★ (la Doriane★★★) is wonderfully fragrant. HERMITAGE★★ is also good, ST-JOSEPH★★ improving, as are the COTES DU RHONE★ (red and white) and chunky GIGONDAS★. Best years: (top reds) 2006 05 04 03 01 00 99 **98 97 95 94 91 90 89 88 85 83 82 78**.

CH. GUIRAUD★★ *Sauternes AC, 1er Cru Classé, Bordeaux, France* Since the 1980s this SAUTERNES estate has returned to the top-quality fold. High price reflects the fact that only the best grapes are selected and 50% new oak used each year. Keep best vintages for 10 years or more. Second wine (dry): G de Guiraud. Best years: 2005 04 03 **02 01 99 98 97 96 95 90 89 88 86**.

G | GUNDERLOCH

GUNDERLOCH *Nackenheim, Rheinhessen, Germany*
Fritz and Agnes Hasselbach's estate has become
one of Germany's best. Sensationally
concentrated and luscious Beerenauslese★★
and Trockenbeerenauslese★★★ dessert Rieslings
are expensive for RHEINHESSEN, but worth it. Dry
and off-dry Rieslings, at least ★, however, are
good value. Late-harvest Spätlese and Auslese are
★★ year in, year out. Best years: (2006) 05 04 **03**
02 **01** 00 99 98 97 96 95 93 90.

GUNDERLOCH
2004
Nackenheim
ROTHENBERG
Riesling Auslese

GUNDLACH-BUNDSCHU *Sonoma Valley AVA, California, USA* Family-
owned winery, founded in 1858. From the Rhinefarm Vineyards come
outstanding juicy, fruity Cabernet Sauvignon★★, rich and tightly
structured Merlot★★, Zinfandel★ and Pinot Noir★. Whites include
Chardonnay★, attractive Riesling and lush Gewürztraminer★★. The
Bundschu family also operates the boutique winery Bartholomew
Park, which specializes in Cabernet blends.

FRITZ HAAG *Brauneberg, Mosel, Germany* MOSEL grower with vineyards
in the BRAUNEBERGER Juffer and Juffer Sonnenuhr. Pure, elegant
Rieslings at least ★★ quality, Auslese reaching ★★ or ★★★. Best
years: (2006) 05 04 **03** 02 **01** 99 98 97 96 95 90.

REINHOLD HAART *Piesport, Mosel, Germany* Theo Haart produces
sensational Rieslings – with blackcurrant, peach and citrus aromas –
from the great Piesporter Goldtröpfchen vineyard. Ausleses are often
★★★. Best years: (2006) 05 04 02 **01** 99 98 97 96 95 94.

HAMILTON RUSSELL VINEYARDS *Hemel en Aarde Valley WO, South
Africa* This pioneering WALKER BAY property celebrated 25 years of
winemaking in 2006; the focus remains on Pinot Noir and
Chardonnay. Pinot Noir★★ is broad-shouldered and delicately scented,
while Chardonnay★★ is minerally and exciting – and is pushing
toward ★★★ since recent winemaking changes. Two separate
operations, Southern Right and Ashbourne, focus on Pinotage
(Ashbourne★), while Southern Right Sauvignon Blanc★ is zingy and
easy-drinking. Best years: (Pinot Noir) (2006) **05** 04 03 02 01 00 99 98 97
96; (Chardonnay) 2006 **05** 04 03 02 01 00 99 98 97.

HANDLEY *Mendocino County, California, USA* Outstanding producer of
sparkling wines, including one of California's best Brut Rosés★.
Aromatic Gewürztraminer★★ and Riesling★★ are among the state's
finest. Two bottlings of Chardonnay, from the DRY CREEK VALLEY★ and
ANDERSON VALLEY★, are worth seeking out. The Anderson Valley estate
Pinot Noirs (regular★, Reserve★★) are in a lighter, more subtle style.
A new Syrah★ is excellent. Best years: (Pinot Noir Reserve) (2005) 04 03
01 00 99 98.

HANGING ROCK *Macedon Ranges, Victoria, Australia* Highly individual,
gutsy sparkling wine Macedon Cuvée★★ stands out at John and
Ann (née TYRRELL) Ellis's ultra-cool-climate vineyard high in the
Macedon Ranges. Tangy estate-grown 'The Jim Jim' Sauvignon
Blanc★★ is mouthwatering stuff, while HEATHCOTE Shiraz★★ is the
best red.

HARDY WINE COMPANY *McLaren Vale, South Australia* Despite the
takeover of BRL Hardy by American giant Constellation, wines under
the Hardys flagship label can for still taste reassuringly Australian.
Varietals under the Siegersdorf, Nottage Hill and Tintara (Shiraz★,
Grenache★) labels are among Australia's most reliably good gluggers.

Top of the tree are the commemorative Eileen Hardy Shiraz★★★ and Thomas Hardy Cabernet★★★, both dense reds for hedonists. Eileen Hardy Chardonnay★★ is more elegant and focused than it used to be. Also 'ecologically aware' Banrock Station, inexpensive Insignia wines, good-value Omni sparkling wine and top-quality Arras fizz★. Best years: (Eileen Hardy Shiraz) (2006) (05) (04) 03 02 01 00 98 **97 96 95 93 88 87**.

HARLAN ESTATE *Oakville AVA, California, USA* Estate in the western hills of OAKVILLE, whose BORDEAUX blend has become one of California's most sought-after reds. Full-bodied and rather tannic, Harlan Estate★★★ offers layers of ripe black fruits and heaps of new French oak. Rough upon release, the wine is built to develop for 10 years.

HARTENBERG ESTATE *Stellenbosch WO, South Africa* Bottelary Hills winery quickly returning to the top of the quality ladder. A trio of Shirazes (standard★, The Stork★, single-vineyard Gravel Hill★★) are prime performers in these warm vineyards. Merlot★ and Cabernet also perform well, but The Mackenzie Cabernet-Merlot blend★ tops both. Whites include a pair of Chardonnays (standard and refined, complex The Eleanor★) and an off-dry, limy Riesling★. Best years: (premium reds) **2004 03 02 01 00 98 97**.

HARTFORD FAMILY *Russian River Valley AVA, California, USA* Owned by Jess Jackson (of KENDALL-JACKSON). Very limited production wines from RUSSIAN RIVER, Green Valley and SONOMA COAST fruit bear the Hartford Court label. Pinot Noirs include the massive Arrendell Vineyard★★★. Seascape Vineyard Chardonnay★★ has textbook cool-climate intensity and acidity. Hartford label wines are blended from various sources. Sonoma Coast bottlings of Chardonnay★ and Pinot Noir★ are deeply flavoured and good value. Old-vine Zinfandels include Fanucchi-Wood Road★★, Highwire★, Dina's★ and Russian River Valley★.

HARTWELL *Stags Leap District AVA, Napa Valley, California, USA* Wine collector Bob Hartwell has been producing a gloriously fruity and elegant Cabernet Sauvignon★★★ from his small vineyard in the Stags Leap District since 1993. Recently, an equally supple Merlot★★ and lower-priced Mistique★ Cabernet have been added. Best years: (Cabernet Sauvignon) 2002 **01 00 99 98 97 96 94**.

HATTENHEIM *Rheingau, Germany* Fine RHEINGAU village with 13 vineyard sites, including a share of the famous Marcobrunn vineyard. Best producers: Barth★, Lang, SCHLOSS REINHARTSHAUSEN★★, Schloss Schönborn★. Best years: (2006) 05 04 **03** 02 **01 00 99 98 96 95 94**.

CH. HAUT-BAGES-LIBÉRAL★ *Pauillac AC, 5ème Cru Classé, Haut-Médoc, Bordeaux, France* Little-known PAUILLAC property that has quietly been gathering plaudits for some years now: loads of unbridled delicious fruit, a positively hedonistic style – and its lack of renown keeps the price just about reasonable. The wines will age well, especially the latest vintages. Best years: 2005 04 03 **02 01 00 99 98 96 95 94 90 89**.

CH. HAUT-BAILLY★ *Pessac-Léognan AC, Cru Classé de Graves, Bordeaux, France* Traditionally one of the softest and most charming of the PESSAC-LEOGNAN Classed Growths, and on good form during the 1990s. New ownership from 1998 has produced erratic returns so far, some wines being too tough, some being almost milky soft, some being delicious. Drinkable early, but ages well. Second wine: la Parde-de-Haut-Bailly. Best years: 2005 04 **01** 00 **99 98 96 95 90 89 88 86**.

165

CH. HAUT-BATAILLEY★ *Pauillac AC, 5ème Cru Classé, Haut-Médoc, Bordeaux, France* Despite being owned by the Borie family of DUCRU-BEAUCAILLOU, this estate has produced too many wines that are light, attractively spicy, but rarely memorable. Recent vintages have shown improvement and the wine is becoming a bit more substantial. Best years: 2005 04 **03** 02 01 **00 98 96 95** 90 89 85 83 82.

CH. HAUT-BRION *Pessac-Léognan AC, 1er Cru Classé, Graves, Bordeaux, France* The only Bordeaux property outside the MEDOC and SAUTERNES to be included in the 1855 Classification. The excellent gravel-based vineyard is now part of Bordeaux's suburbs. The red wine★★★ almost always deserves its status. There is also a small amount of white★★★ which, at its best, is magically rich yet marvellously dry, blossoming out over 5–10 years. Second wine: (red) Bahans-Haut-Brion. Best years: (red) 2005 04 03 02 01 00 **99** 98 **96 95 94** 93 90 89 88; (white) 2005 04 **03** 02 01 00 **99** 98 96 95.

CH. HAUT-MARBUZET★★ *St-Estèphe AC, Cru Bourgeois, Haut-Médoc, Bordeaux, France* Impressive ST-ESTEPHE wine with great, rich, mouthfilling blasts of flavour and lots of new oak. Best years: 2005 04 03 02 **01 00 99 98 96 95 94 90 89 88** 86 85 82.

HAUT-MÉDOC AC *Bordeaux, France* The finest gravelly soil is here in the southern half of the MEDOC peninsula; this AC covers all the decent vineyard land not included in the 6 village ACs (MARGAUX, MOULIS, LISTRAC, ST-JULIEN, PAUILLAC and ST-ESTEPHE). Wines vary in quality and style. Best producers: d'Agassac★, Belgrave★, Belle-Vue★, Bernadotte★, Cambon la Pelouse★, Camensac, CANTEMERLE★, Charmail★, Cissac★, Citran★, Coufran, la LAGUNE★, Lanessan★, Malescasse★, Maucamps★, Peyrabon★, Sénéjac★, SOCIANDO-MALLET★★, la Tour-Carnet★, Tour-du-Haut-Moulin★, Villegeorge. Best years: 2005 04 **03 02 01 00 96 95 94** 90 89 88 86 85.

HAUT-MONTRAVEL AC See MONTRAVEL AC.
HAUTES-CÔTES DE BEAUNE AC See BOURGOGNE-HAUTES-CÔTES DE BEAUNE AC.
HAUTES-CÔTES DE NUITS AC See BOURGOGNE-HAUTES-CÔTES DE NUITS AC.

HAWKES BAY *North Island, New Zealand* One of New Zealand's most prestigious wine regions. The high number of sunshine hours, moderately predictable weather during ripening and a complex array of soils make it ideal for a wide range of wine styles. Traditionally known for Cabernet Sauvignon and, particularly, Merlot, it has recently produced some superb Syrahs. Free-draining Gimblett Gravels is the outstanding area, followed by the Triangle. Best producers: Alpha Domus★, CHURCH ROAD★, Clearview★, CRAGGY RANGE★★, Esk Valley★★, Matariki★, MATUA VALLEY★, Newton Forrest★ (Cornerstone★★), NGATARAWA★, C J PASK★, Sacred Hill★, SILENI★, Southbank★, Stonecroft★, Te Awa★, TE MATA★★, Trinity Hill★★, Unison★★, Vidal★★, VILLA MARIA★★. Best years: (premium reds) (2006) **04 02 00 98**.

HEATHCOTE *Central Victoria, Australia* A recent breakaway from the BENDIGO region. Its unique feature is the deep russet Cambrian soil, formed more than 600 million years ago, which is found on the best sites and is proving ideal for Shiraz. Jasper Hill★★★, Heathcote Winery★ and Wild Duck Creek★ are the best of the long-established vineyards, while BROWN BROTHERS and TYRRELL'S (Rufus Stone★★ is outstanding and good value) have extensive new plantings. Heathcote Estate★★ is a brilliant newcomer. Best years: (Shiraz) 2006 05 04 03 02 **01 00 97 96 95 94** 91 90.

HECHT & BANNIER *Languedoc, France* An exciting new partnership of two young Dijon wine marketing graduates, Gregory Hecht and François Bannier. They are selecting and aging some rich, finely crafted wines from MINERVOIS★, COTEAUX DU LANGUEDOC★, FAUGERES★ and ST-CHINIAN★. Coteaux du Languedoc Jonquières★★ is their best wine.

HEDGES *Columbia Valley AVA, Washington State, USA* Top wines here are Cabernet-Merlot blends using fruit from prime Red Mountain AVA vineyards: Three Vineyards★ is powerful and ageworthy, with bold tannins but plenty of cassis fruit; Red Mountain Reserve★ shows more polish and elegance. Red CMS (Cabernets-Merlot-Syrah) and crisp white CMS (Chardonnay-Marsanne-Sauvignon) form the bulk of the production. Best years: (reds) (2005) 04 03 02 01 **00**.

DR HEGER *Ihringen, Baden, Germany* Joachim Heger specializes in powerful, dry Grauburgunder (Pinot Gris)★★, Weissburgunder (Pinot Blanc)★ and red Spätburgunder (Pinot Noir)★, with Riesling a sideline in this warm climate. Winklerberg Grauburgunder★★ is serious stuff, while his ancient Yellow Muscat vines deliver powerful dry wines★ and rare but fabulous TBAs★★. Wines from rented vineyards are sold under the Weinhaus Joachim Heger label. Best years: (white) (2006) 05 04 **03 02 01 00 98 97**.

CHARLES HEIDSIECK *Champagne AC, Champagne, France* Charles Heidsieck, owned by Rémy Cointreau, is the most consistently fine of all the major houses, with vintage★★★ Champagne only declared in the very best years. The non-vintage★★, marked with a bottling date (for example, Mis en Cave en 2003), is regularly of vintage quality; these age well for 5 years. Best years: **1995 90 89 88 85 82**.

HEITZ CELLARS *Napa Valley AVA, California, USA* Star attraction here is the Martha's Vineyard Cabernet Sauvignon★★. Many believe that early bottlings of Martha's Vineyard are among the best wines ever produced in CALIFORNIA. After 1992, phylloxera forced the replanting of Martha's Vineyard and although bottling only resumed in 1996, the 1997 vintage was exceptional and set the tone for the modern era. Heitz also produces a Bella Oaks Vineyard Cabernet Sauvignon★, a Trailside Vineyard Cabernet★ and a straight Cabernet★ that takes time to understand but can be good. Grignolino Rosé is an attractive picnic wine. Best years: (Martha's Vineyard) 2002 97 96 **92** 91 **86 85 75**.

HENRIOT *Champagne AC, Champagne, France* In 1994 Joseph Henriot bought back the name of his old-established family company. Henriot CHAMPAGNES have an austere clarity – no Pinot Meunier is used. The range includes non-vintage Brut Souverain★ and Blanc de Blancs★, vintage Brut★★ and Rosé★ and de luxe Cuvée des Enchanteleurs★★. Best years: 1998 96 **95 90 89 88 85**.

HENRIQUES & HENRIQUES *Madeira DOC, Madeira, Portugal* The wines to look for are the 10-year-old★★ and 15-year-old★★ versions of the classic varieties. Vibrant Sercial and Verdelho, and rich Malmsey and Bual are all fine examples of their styles. Henriques & Henriques also has vintage Madeiras★★★ of extraordinary quality.

HENRY OF PELHAM *Niagara Peninsula VQA, Ontario, Canada* Winery focused on nurturing their vines. Best are Reserve Chardonnay★, Proprietor's Reserve Riesling★, Riesling Icewine★ and a Cabernet-Merlot blend. Best years: (Riesling Icewine) 2004 **03 02 00 99 98**.

HENSCHKE *Eden Valley, South Australia* Fifth-generation winemaker Stephen Henschke and his viticulturist wife Prue make some of Australia's grandest reds from old vines: HILL OF GRACE★★★ is stunning.

167

Mount Edelstone Shiraz★★★, Cyril Henschke Cabernet★★, Johann's Garden Grenache★, Henry's Seven★ Shiraz blend and Keyneton Estate★ are also top wines. The whites are full and intensely flavoured too, led by the seductive, perfumed Julius Riesling★★, toasty yet fruity Louis Semillon★★ and Croft Chardonnay★. Best years: (Mount Edelstone) (2006) (05) 04 02 01 99 **96 94 92 91 90 88 86 84 82**.

HÉRAULT, VIN DE PAYS DE L' *Languedoc, France* A huge region, covering the entire Hérault *département*. Red wines predominate, based on Carignan, Grenache and Cinsaut, and most of the wine is sold in bulk. But things are changing. There are lots of hilly vineyards with great potential, and MAS DE DAUMAS GASSAC followed by GRANGE DES PERES and Gérard Depardieu's Référence are making waves internationally. Whites are improving, too. Best producers: Bosc, Capion★, la Fadèze, GRANGE DES PERES★★, Jany, Limbardié★, Marfée, MAS DE DAUMAS GASSAC★.

HERMITAGE AC *Rhône Valley, France* Great Hermitage, from steep vineyards above the town of Tain l'Hermitage in the northern RHONE, is revered throughout the world as a rare, rich red wine – expensive, memorable and classic. Not all Hermitage achieves such an exciting blend of flavours, but the best growers, with mature red Syrah vines, can create superbly original wine, needing 5–10 years' aging even in a light year and a minimum of 15 years in a ripe vintage. White Hermitage, from Marsanne and Roussanne, is less famous but the best wines, made by traditionalists, can outlive the reds, sometimes lasting as long as 40 years. Best producers: A Belle★, CHAPOUTIER★★ (Pavillon★★★), J-L CHAVE★★★, Y Chave★, Colombier★, COLOMBO★, DELAS★★ (Bessards★★★), B Faurie★★, L Fayolle★, Ferraton★, GUIGAL★★, JABOULET (la Chapelle★), Remizières, J-M Sorrel★, M Sorrel★★, TAIN co-op★★, Tardieu-Laurent★★, les Vins de Vienne★★. Best years: (reds) 2006 05 04 03 01 00 **99 98 97 96 95 94 91 90 89 88 85 83 78**.

THE HESS COLLECTION *Mount Veeder AVA, California, USA* Known for distinctive MOUNT VEEDER Cabernet Sauvignon★ – but after a change in winemaking direction, recent vintages lack both polish and power. Hess Estate Cabernet★ is good value. Chardonnay★ is ripe with tropical fruit and balanced oak. Budget label: Hess Select. Best years: (Cabernet) **2001 00 99 98 97 96 95 94 91 90**.

HESSISCHE BERGSTRASSE *Germany* A small (436ha/1070-acre), warm region near Darmstadt. The co-op, Bergsträsser Winzer, dominates, but better wines, especially lovely Eiswein★★, is made by the Staatsweingut. Riesling is still the most prized grape.

HEYL ZU HERRNSHEIM *Nierstein, Rheinhessen, Germany* Organic estate whose main strength is substantial dry whites from Riesling, Weissburgunder (Pinot Blanc) and Silvaner. However, Auslese and higher Prädikat wines of recent vintages have been of ★★ – and sometimes ★★★ – quality. Only wines from the top sites (Brudersberg, Pettenthal, Oelberg) carry the vineyard designation. Quality slipped recently, but new owner Detler Meyer seems keen to restore its reputation. Best years: (2006) 05 04 **03 02 01 99 98 97 96**.

HEYMANN-LÖWENSTEIN *Winningen, Mosel, Germany* A leading estate of the Lower MOSEL. Its dry Rieslings are unusually full-bodied for the region; those from the Röttgen and Uhlen sites often reach ★★. Also powerful Auslese. Best years: (2006) 05 04 **03 02 01 00 99 98 97**.

HIDALGO *Jerez y Manzanilla DO, Andalucía, Spain*   Hidalgo's Manzanilla La Gitana★★ is deservedly one of the best-selling manzanillas in Spain. Hidalgo is family-owned, and only uses grapes from its own vineyards. Brands include Mariscal★, Fino Especial and Miraflores, Amontillado Napoleon★★, Oloroso Viejo★★ and Jerez Cortado★★.

HILL OF GRACE★★★ *Eden Valley, South Australia*   A stunning wine with dark, exotic flavours made by HENSCHKE from a single plot of Shiraz. The Hill of Grace vineyard was first planted in the 1860s, and the old vines produce a powerful, structured wine with superb ripe fruit, chocolate, coffee, earth, leather and the rest. Can be cellared for 20 years or more. Best years: (2006) (05) (04) (02) 01 99 98 97 96 95 **94 93 92 91 90 88 86 85 82**.

HILLTOP *Neszmély, Hungary*   Under chief winemaker Akos Kamocsay, this winery provides fresh, bright wines, especially white, at friendly prices. Indigenous varieties such as Irsai Oliver and Cserszegi Füszeres line up with Gewürztraminer, Sauvignon Blanc★, Pinot Gris and Chardonnay. Hilltop also produces a good but controversial TOKAJI.

HILLTOPS *New South Wales, Australia*   Promising high-altitude cherry-growing region with a small but fast-growing area of vineyards around the town of Young. Good potential for reds from Cabernet Sauvignon and Shiraz. Best producers: Chalkers Crossing, Grove Estate, MCWILLIAM'S/Barwang★, Woodonga Hill.

FRANZ HIRTZBERGER *Wachau, Niederösterreich, Austria*   One of the WACHAU's top growers. Hirtzberger's finest wines are the concentrated, elegant Smaragd Rieslings from Singerriedel★★★ and Hochrain★★. The best Grüner Veltliner comes from the Honivogl site★★★. Best years: (Riesling Smaragd) (2006) 05 04 **03 02 01** 00 99 98 97 95 94.

HOCHHEIM *Rheingau, Germany*   Village best known for having given the English the word 'Hock' for Rhine wine, but with good individual vineyard sites, especially Domdechaney, Hölle (hell!) and Kirchenstück. Best producers: Joachim Flick, Franz KUNSTLER★★, Werner. Best years: (2006) 05 04 **03 02 01** 99 98 97 96 94.

HOLLICK *Coonawarra, South Australia*   Ian Hollick makes a broader range of good wines than is usually found in COONAWARRA: irresistible sparkling Merlot★ (yes, *Merlot*), subtle Chardonnay★, tobaccoey Cabernet-Merlot★ and richer Ravenswood Cabernet Sauvignon★. Also attractive Sauvignon-Semillon and good limy Riesling★. Best years: (Ravenswood) (2006) (05) (04) (03) 02 01 **99** 98 **96 94 93 91 90 88**.

HORTON VINEYARDS *Virginia, USA*   Horton's Viognier★ established Virginia's potential as a wine region and ignited a rush of wineries wanting to make the next CONDRIEU. Innovations include a sparkling Viognier and varietals such as Tannat and Petit Manseng. The Cabernet Franc★ is consistently among the best wines of the eastern US.

DOM. DE L'HORTUS *Pic St-Loup, Coteaux du Languedoc AC, Languedoc, France*   One of PIC ST-LOUP's leading estates. Bergerie de l'Hortus Cuvée Classique★, a ready-to-drink unoaked Mourvèdre-Syrah-Grenache blend, has delightful flavours of herbs, plums and cherries. Big brother Grande Cuvée★★ needs time for the fruit and oak to come into harmony. The white Grande Cuvée★ is a Chardonnay-Viognier blend. Best years: (Grande Cuvée red) (2005) 04 03 **01 00 99 98**.

HOSPICES DE BEAUNE *Côte de Beaune, Burgundy, France*   Scene of a theatrical auction on the third Sunday in November each year, the Hospices is an historical foundation which sells the wine of the new vintage from its holdings in the COTE D'OR to finance its charitable works.

169

Pricing reflects charitable status rather than common sense, but the auction trend is regarded as an indicator of which way the market is likely to move. Much depends on the skills of the Hospices' wine-making, which has been variable, as well as on the maturation and bottling which are in the hands of the purchaser of each lot.

CH. L'HOSPITALET *La Clape, Côteaux du Languedoc AC, Languedoc, France* With his purchase of this domaine in La CLAPE, Gérard Bertrand has entered the big time in the Languedoc. Best wines are the red Extrême★ and red and white Summum★. He also produces one of the top Vin de Pays d'Oc, Cigalus★★, with 50% Cabernet Sauvignon, as well as CORBIÈRES La Forge, a blend of Syrah and Carignan. Best years (Extrême): (2005) 04 **03 01 00**.

HOUGHTON *Swan District, Western Australia* WESTERN AUSTRALIA's biggest winery, owned by Constellation, sources fruit from its own outstanding vineyards and from growers in premium regions. The budget-priced Line range includes the flavoursome White Classic★ (formerly White Burgundy, or HWB in the EU), good Semillon-Sauvignon Blanc★ and Chenin Blanc; also recently improved Chardonnay and Cabernet. Moondah Brook Cabernet★★ and Shiraz★★ are a leap up in quality and even better value. Houghton has had enormous success with its regional range: a Riesling★★ and Shiraz★★ from Frankland River; a MARGARET RIVER Cabernet★★; and some of the best wines yet seen from the emerging PEMBERTON region. Dense, oaky Gladstones Shiraz★★★ and powerful, lush Jack Mann Cabernet Sauvignon★★★ have also contributed to Houghton's burgeoning profile. Best years: (Jack Mann) (2003) (02) 01 99 98 **96 95 94**.

HOWARD PARK *Margaret River, Western Australia* Howard Park now has wineries at Denmark in GREAT SOUTHERN (for whites) and at MARGARET RIVER (for reds). The classic Cabernet Sauvignon★★★ and occasional Best Barrels Merlot★★ are matched by intense, floral Riesling★★ and supremely classy Chardonnay★★. The Scotsdale Shiraz★★ and Leston Cabernet★ are part of a range of regional reds. The Madfish label is good for Riesling★, Shiraz★, Sauvignon-Semillon★ and unwooded Chardonnay★. Best years: (Cabernet) (2005) (04) 03 02 01 99 **96 94 92 91 90 88 86**; (Riesling) 2006 05 04 03 02 01 **97 95 92 91 89 86**.

HOWELL MOUNTAIN AVA *Napa Valley, California, USA* NAPA's north-eastern corner is noted for powerhouse Cabernet Sauvignon and Zinfandel as well as exotic, full-flavoured Merlot. Best producers: BERINGER (Merlot★★), DUCKHORN★, DUNN★★★, La Jota★★, Ladera★★, Liparita★, PINE RIDGE (Cabernet Sauvignon★), Viader★★★, White Cottage★★. Best years: (reds) 2003 02 **01 00 99 98 97 96 95 94 91 90**.

HUADONG WINERY *Shandong Province, China* The first producer of varietal and vintage wines in China, Huadong has received massive foreign investment as well as state support. Money, however, can't change the climate, and excessive moisture from the summer rainy season causes problems. Even so, Riesling and Chardonnay (under the Tsingtao label) are not at all bad and Cabernet Sauvignon and Chardonnay in special 'feng shui' bottles are pretty tasty.

HUET *Vouvray AC, Loire Valley, France* Complex, traditional VOUVRAY that can age for decades, produced using biodynamic methods. Three excellent sites – le Haut-Lieu, Clos du Bourg and le Mont – yield dry★★, medium-dry★★★ or sweet★★★ wines, depending on the vintage. New investment from American Anthony Hwang is supporting Noël Pinguet's efforts to raise quality even higher. Also very good Vouvray Mousseux★★. Best years: 2006 05 04 **03** 02 **01** 00 99 98 97 96 95 90 89.

HUGEL *Alsace AC, Alsace, France* Best wines are sweet Alsace Vendange Tardive★★ and Sélection de Grains Nobles★★★. Big-volume Tradition wines are rather dull, but Jubilee wines can be ★★. Best years: (Vendange Tardive Riesling) 2005 03 **01** 00 98 97 96 95 90 89 88 83 76.

HUNTER VALLEY *New South Wales, Australia* NEW SOUTH WALES' oldest wine zone overcomes a tricky climate to make fascinating, ageworthy Semillon and rich, buttery Chardonnay. Shiraz is the mainstay for reds, aging well but often developing a leathery overtone; Cabernet is occasionally successful. Premium region is the Lower Hunter Valley; the Upper Hunter has few wineries but extensive vineyards. Best producers: Allandale★, BROKENWOOD★★, Capercaillie, De Iuliis★, Hope★, LAKE'S FOLLY★, Margan Family, MCWILLIAM'S★★, Meerea Park★, ROSEMOUNT, Thomas★, TOWER★, Keith Tulloch★, TYRRELL'S★★. Best years: (Shiraz) 2006 04 03 02 00 99 **98 97 96 94 91**.

HUNTER'S *Marlborough, South Island, New Zealand* One of MARLBOROUGH's stars, with fine, if austere, Sauvignon★, savoury, Burgundian Chardonnay★, vibrant Riesling★ and sophisticated Pinot Noir★. Also attractive Miru Miru fizz★. Best years: (Chardonnay) (2006) **05** 03 01 00.

CH. DU HUREAU *Saumur-Champigny AC, Loire Valley, France* The Vatan family produces exemplary silky SAUMUR-CHAMPIGNY reds. The basic red★ is deliciously bright and fruity. Special cuvées Lisagathe★★ and Fevettes★★ need a bit of time. Jasmine-scented white SAUMUR★ is exceptional in top years. Decent fizz and occasional sweet Coteaux de Saumur, too. Best years: (top reds) 2006 05 04 **03** 02 **01 99 97 96**.

INNISKILLIN *Niagara Peninsula, Ontario, Canada* One of Canada's leading wineries, producing good Pinot Noir★ and Cabernet Franc, beautifully rounded Klose Vineyard Chardonnay★ and rich Vidal Icewine★★, Cabernet Franc Icewine★ and Riesling Icewine★. Another Inniskillin winery is in the OKANAGAN VALLEY in British Columbia. Best years: (Vidal Icewine) 2005 04 **03** 02 00 99 98 97 95 94 92.

IPHOFEN *Franken, Germany* One of the 2 most important wine towns in FRANKEN for dry Riesling and Silvaner. Both are powerful, with a pronounced earthiness. Best producers: JULIUSSPITAL★, Johann Ruck★, Hans Wirsching★. Best years: (2006) 05 04 **03** 02 **01** 00 99 98 97.

IRANCY AC *Burgundy, France* This northern outpost of vineyards, just south-west of CHABLIS, is an unlikely champion of the clear, pure flavours of the Pinot Noir grape. But red Irancy can be delicate and lightly touched by the ripeness of plums and strawberries, and can age well. Best producers: Bienvenu, J-M BROCARD, Cantin, A & J-P Colinot★, Delaloge, Patrice Fort★. Best years: (2006) 05 **03** 02.

IRON HORSE VINEYARDS *Sonoma County, California, USA* Outstanding sparkling wines with vintage Brut★★ and Blanc de Blancs★★ delicious on release but highly suitable for aging. The Brut LD★★★ (Late Disgorged) is a heavenly mouthful of sparkling wine – yeasty and complex. Wedding Cuvée★ blanc de noirs and Brut Rosé★ complete the line-up. Still wines include a lovely Pinot Noir★★, a barrel-fermented Chardonnay★, a seductive Viognier★★ and a sensational Pinot Noir Rosé★.

IROULÉGUY AC *South-West France* A small AC in the Basque Pyrenees. Cabernet Sauvignon, Cabernet Franc and Tannat give fascinating, robust reds that are softer than MADIRAN. Whites are from Petit Courbu and Manseng. Best producers: Arretxea★, Brana★, Etxegaraya, Ilarria★, Irouléguy co-op (Mignaberry★). Best years: (reds) 2004 **03 01 00 98**.

ISABEL ESTATE *Marlborough, South Island, New Zealand* Sauvignon Blanc★ is among New Zealand's best. Aromatic, plum-and-cherry Pinot Noir★★, stylish, concentrated Chardonnay★★ and aromatic Riesling★ and Pinot Gris★ complete the impressive line-up. Best years: (Pinot Noir) **2005 04 03 01 00**.

ISOLE E OLENA *Chianti Classico DOCG, Tuscany, Italy* Paolo De Marchi has long been one of the pacesetters in CHIANTI CLASSICO. His Chianti Classico★★, characterized by clean, elegant and spicily perfumed fruit, excels in every vintage. The powerful SUPER-TUSCAN Cepparello★★★, made from 100% Sangiovese, is the top wine. Excellent Syrah★★, Cabernet Sauvignon★★★, Chardonnay★★ and VIN SANTO★★★. Best years: (Cepparello) (2006) 04 03 01 **00 99 98 97 96 95 93 90 88**.

CH. D'ISSAN★ *Margaux AC, 3ème Cru Classé, Haut-Médoc, Bordeaux, France* This lovely moated property has disappointed me far too often in the past but pulled its socks up in the 1990s. When successful, the wine can be one of the most delicate and scented in the MARGAUX AC. Best years: 2005 04 03 **02 01 00 99 98 96 95 90 89 85**.

PAUL JABOULET AÎNÉ *Rhône Valley, France* During the 1970s, Jaboulet led the way in raising the world's awareness of the great quality of RHONE wines. Although many of the wines are still good, they are no longer the star in any appellation. Best wines are top red HERMITAGE la Chapelle★ (this was a ★★★ wine in its heyday) and white Chevalier de Stérimberg★★. CROZES-HERMITAGE Thalabert★ is famous, but occasional-release Vieilles Vignes★★ is much better nowadays, as are whites Mule Blanche★ and Raymond Roure★. Attractive CORNAS Dom. St-Pierre★, reliable COTES DU RHONE Parallèle 45, good-value COTES DU VENTOUX★ and sweet, perfumed MUSCAT DE BEAUMES-DE-VENISE★★. In January 2006, Jaboulet was bought by Swiss financier Jean-Jacques Frey, owner of Ch. la LAGUNE. Best years: (la Chapelle) (2006) 05 04 03 **01 99 98 97 96 95 94 91 90 89 88 78**.

JACKSON ESTATE *Marlborough, South Island, New Zealand* An established grapegrower with vineyards in MARLBOROUGH's most prestigious district. Tangy, appley Sauvignon Blanc★★ and barrel-fermented Grey Ghost Sauvignon Blanc★★ both improve with a little age; restrained Chardonnay and Pinot Noir and complex, traditional-method fizz. Best years: (Sauvignon Blanc) **2006 04 03 01**.

JACQUESSON *Champagne AC, Champagne, France* Top-class small producer. Its non-vintage is a one-off that will change each year. Cuvée No 729★★ is based on the 2001 harvest. Cuvée 731★★, based on the 2003 harvest, was launched in January 2007. Also makes superb single cru Champagnes from Avize (1996★★), Äy and Dizy. The vintage Blanc de Blancs★★ and vintage Signature Brut★★★ are classic wines. Best years: (1997) 96 **95 93 90 89 88 85**.

LOUIS JADOT *Beaune, Burgundy, France* Leading merchant with a broad range matched only by DROUHIN, and with rights to some estate wines of the Duc de Magenta★★. Jadot has extensive vineyard holdings for red wines, but it is the firm's whites that have earned its reputation. Excellent in Grands Crus like BATARD-MONTRACHET★★★ and CORTON-CHARLEMAGNE★★, but Jadot also shows a more egalitarian side by producing good wines in lesser ACs like ST-AUBIN★ and RULLY★. In recent years has purchased some top BEAUJOLAIS vineyards, such as Ch. des Jacques★ in MOULIN-A-VENT. Best years: (top reds) (2006) 05 04 03 02 01 **00 99 98 97 96 95 90**; (top whites) (2006) 05 04 **03 02 00 99**.

JAMET★★★ *Côte-Rôtie AC, Rhône Valley, France* Jean-Paul and Jean-Luc Jamet are 2 of the most talented growers of COTE-ROTIE. The full-bodied wines, from excellent vineyards, led by the marvellous Côte Brune, age well for a decade or more. Best years: 2006 05 04 03 **01 00 99 98 97 96 95 91 90 89 88**.

JANUIK WINERY *Columbia Valley AVA, Washington State, USA* Before starting his own operation, Mike Januik oversaw all the operations at CHATEAU STE MICHELLE. His experience and knowledge of Washington's vineyards allow him to source fruit from only exceptional sites. His Chardonnays (Elerding★ and Cold Creek★★) are among the top in the state. Lewis Vineyard Syrah★★ is rich, earthy and bold, and Cabernet Sauvignons (Champoux Vineyard★★ and Ciel du Cheval★★) are chocolaty, complex and ageworthy. Best years: (reds) (2005) 04 03 **02**.

JARDIN See JORDAN, South Africa.

JARDIN DE LA FRANCE, VIN DE PAYS DU *Loire Valley, France* This large vin de pays covers most of the LOIRE VALLEY. Annual production averages nearly 80 million bottles of mostly varietal wines. Key whites are Sauvignon Blanc, Chardonnay and Chenin Blanc with some Grolleau Gris, Melon de Bourgogne, Folle Blanche, Pinot Blanc and Arbois. The focus for reds is Gamay, Grolleau, Cabernets Franc and Sauvignon with some Pinot Noir and Abouriou. It is increasingly a refuge for ambitious producers whose wines punch well above the weight of their appellation, especially in TOURAINE. Best producers: Ampelidae, BOUVET-LADUBAY★, Brulée★, l'ECU★, L Herbel, Henry Marionnet★, Alphonse MELLOT★, J-F Merieau★, RAGOTIERE★★, Ricard.

JASNIÈRES AC *Loire Valley, France* Tiny AC north of Tours making long-lived, bone-dry whites from Chenin Blanc. Sweet wine may be made in good years. Best producers: Bellivière★★, J Gigou★★, de Rycke. Best years: 2005 **04 03 02 01 99 97 96 95**.

JEREZ Y MANZANILLA DO/SHERRY See pages 174–5.

JERMANN *Friuli-Venezia Giulia, Italy* Silvio Jermann produces non-DOC Chardonnay★, Sauvignon Blanc★, Pinot Bianco★ and Pinot Grigio★. Deep, long-lived Vintage Tunina★★ is based on Sauvignon-Chardonnay but includes Ribolla, Malvasia and Picolit. Barrel-fermented Chardonnay★★ is labelled 'Were dreams, now it is just wine'. Vinnae★ is based on Ribolla; Capo Martino★ is also a blend of local varieties. The wines are plump but pricey.

JOHANNISBERG *Rheingau, Germany* Probably the best known of all the Rhine wine villages, with 10 vineyard sites, including the famous Schloss Johannisberg. Best producers: Prinz von Hessen★, Johannishof★★, Schloss Johannisberg★. Best years: (2006) 05 04 **03 02 01 99 98 97**.

KARL H JOHNER *Bischoffingen, Baden, Germany* Johner specializes in new oak-aged wines from his native BADEN. The vividly fruity Pinot Noir★ and Pinot Blanc★ are excellent, the Chardonnay SJ★★ is one of Germany's best examples of this varietal, and the rich, silky Pinot Noir SJ★★ can be one of Germany's finest reds. Best years: (Pinot Noir SJ) (2006) 05 04 **03 02 01 00 99**.

JEREZ Y MANZANILLA DO/SHERRY

Andalucía, Spain

The Spanish now own the name outright. At least in the EU, the only wines that can be sold as sherry come from the triangle of vineyard land between the Andalucian towns of Jerez de la Frontera (inland), and Sanlúcar de Barrameda and Puerto de Santa María (by the sea). New agreements signed by the EU have phased out such other appellations as South African Sherry.

The best sherries can be spectacular. Three main factors contribute to the high-quality potential of wines from this region: the chalky-spongy albariza soil where the best vines grow, the Palomino Fino grape – unexciting for table wines but potentially great once transformed by the sherry-making processes – and a natural yeast called flor. All sherry must be a minimum of 3 years old, but fine sherries age in barrel for much longer. Sherries must be blended through a solera system. About a third of the wine from the oldest barrels is bottled, and the barrels topped up with slightly younger wine from another set of barrels and so on, for a minimum of 3 sets of barrels. The idea is that the younger wine takes on the character of older wine, as well as keeping the blend refreshed.

MAIN SHERRY STYLES

Fino and manzanilla Fino sherries derive their extraordinary, tangy, pungent flavours from flor. Young, newly fermented wines destined for these styles of sherry are deliberately fortified very sparingly to just 15–15.5% alcohol before being put in barrels for their minimum of 3 years' maturation. The thin, soft, oatmeal-coloured mush of flor grows on the surface of the wines, protecting them from the air (and thereby keeping them pale) and giving them a characteristic sharp, pungent tang. The addition of younger wine each year feeds the flor, maintaining an even layer. Manzanillas are fino-style wines that have matured in the cooler seaside conditions of Sanlúcar de Barrameda, where the flor grows thickest and the fine, salty tang is most accentuated.

Amontillado True amontillados are fino sherries that have continued to age after the flor has died (after 5 years) and so finish their aging period in contact with air. These should all be bone dry. Medium-sweet amontillados are concoctions in which the dry sherry is sweetened with mistela, a blend of grape juice and alcohol.

Oloroso This type of sherry is strongly fortified after fermentation to deter the growth of flor. Olorosos therefore mature in barrel in contact with the air, which gradually darkens them while they remain dry, but develop rich, intense, nutty and raisiny flavours.

Other styles Manzanilla pasada is aged manzanilla, with greater depth and nuttiness. Palo cortado is an unusual, deliciously nutty, dry style somewhere in between amontillado and oloroso. Sweet oloroso creams and pale creams are almost without exception enriched solely for the export market. Sweet varietal wines are made from sun-dried Pedro Ximénez or Moscatel.

See also individual producers.

BEST PRODUCERS AND WINES

Argüeso (Manzanilla San León, Manzanilla Fina Las Medallas).

BARBADILLO (Manzanilla Eva, Solear Manzanilla Fina Vieja, Amontillado Príncipe, Amontillado de Sanlúcar, Cuco Oloroso Seco, Palo Cortado Obispo Gascon).

Delgado Zuleta (Manzanilla Pasada La Goya).

Díez Mérito (Imperial Fino, Don Zoilo Imperial Amontillado, Victoria Regina Oloroso).

DOMECQ (Fino La Ina, Amontillado 51-1A, Sibarita Palo Cortado, Venerable Pedro Ximénez).

El Maestro Sierra.

Garvey (Palo Cortado, Amontillado Tio Guillermo, Pedro Ximénez Gran Orden).

GONZALEZ BYASS (Tio Pepe Fino, Amontillado del Duque, Matusalem Oloroso Muy Viejo, Apóstoles Oloroso Viejo, Noé Pedro Ximénez, Oloroso Viejo de Añado).

HIDALGO (Manzanilla La Gitana, Manzanilla Pasada, Jerez Cortado, Amontillado Napoleon, Oloroso Viejo).

LUSTAU (Almacenista single-producer wines, Old East India Cream, Puerto Fino).

OSBORNE (Amontillado Coquinero, Fino Quinta, Bailén Oloroso, Solera India Oloroso, Pedro Ximénez).

Rey Fernando de Castilla.

Sánchez Romate (Pedro Ximénez Cardenal Cisneros).

Tradición.

VALDESPINO (Amontillado Coliseo, Amontillado Tio Diego, Amontillado Don Tomás, Cardenal Palo Cortado, Inocente Fino, Oloroso Don Gonzalo, Pedro Ximénez Solera Superior).

Williams & Humbert (Pando Fino, Alegría Manzanilla).

175

JORDAN *Alexander Valley AVA, Sonoma County, California, USA* Ripe, fruity Cabernet Sauvignon★ with a cedar character rare in California. The Chardonnay★ is nicely balanced. J★ fizz is an attractive mouthful, now made independently by Judy Jordan's J Wine Co. J also makes top-notch RUSSIAN RIVER Pinot Noir★. Best years: (Cabernet) 2002 **01 00 99 97 96 95 94 91 86**.

JORDAN *Stellenbosch WO, South Africa* Meticulously groomed hillside vineyards, with a variety of aspects and soils. Chardonnays (regular★★ with creamy complexity; Nine Yards★★, dense, nutty, but balanced) and delicious peppery Chenin★★ head a strong white range. Cabernet Sauvignon★, Merlot★, Syrah★★ and BORDEAUX-blend Cobblers Hill★★ are understated but beautifully balanced for aging. Sophia★ is a rich Bordeaux-blend red. Sold under the Jardin label in the USA. Best years: (Chardonnay) (2006) **05 04 03 02 01 00 99**; (Cobblers Hill) **2004 03 02 01 00 99 98**.

TONI JOST *Bacharach, Mittelrhein, Germany* Peter Jost has put the MITTELRHEIN on the map. From the Bacharacher Hahn site come some delicious, racy Rieslings★; Auslese★★ adds creaminess without losing that pine-needle scent. Best years: (2006) 05 04 **03 02 01 99 98 97 96**.

J P VINHOS See BACALHÔA VINHOS DE PORTUGAL.

JULIÉNAS AC *Beaujolais, Burgundy, France* One of the more northerly BEAUJOLAIS Crus, Juliénas is attractive, 'serious' Beaujolais which can be big and tannic enough to develop in bottle. Best producers: G Descombes★, DUBOEUF★, P Granger★, Ch. de Juliénas★, J-P Margerand★, Pelletier★, B Santé★, M Tête★. Best years: **2006 05 03**.

JULIUSSPITAL *Würzburg, Franken, Germany* A 16th-century charitable foundation known for its dry wines – especially Silvaners from IPHOFEN and WÜRZBURG. Look out for the Würzburger Stein vineyard wines, sappy Müller-Thurgau, grapefruity Silvaners★★ and petrolly Rieslings★★. Best years: (2006) 05 04 **03 02 01 00**.

JUMILLA DO *Murcia and Castilla-La Mancha, Spain* Jumilla's reputation is for big alcoholic reds, but dense, serious reds from Monastrell (Mourvèdre) show the region's potential. Whites are almost non-existent today. Best producers: Casa de la Ermita, Hijos de Juan Gil★, Luzón★, El Nido★, Agapito Rico, Julia Roch (Casa Castillo★★). Best years: **2005 04 03 01 00 99 98 96**.

JURA See ARBOIS, CHATEAU-CHALON, COTES DU JURA, CRÉMANT DU JURA, l'ÉTOILE.

JURANÇON AC *South-West France* The sweet white wine made from late-harvested and occasionally botrytized grapes can be heavenly, with floral, spicy, apricot-quince flavours. The dry wine, Jurançon Sec, can be ageworthy. Best producers: (sweet) Bru-Baché★★, Castera★, CAUHAPE★★, Clos Guirouilh★, Clos Lapeyre★, Clos Thou★, CLOS UROULAT★★, Larrédya★, PRIMO PALATUM★, Souch★★. Best years: (sweet) (2005) 03 **02 01 00 99 98 96**.

JUVÉ Y CAMPS *Cava DO and Penedès DO, Cataluña, Spain* Ultra-traditional and expensive, but unusually for a CAVA outfit most of the grapes come from its own vineyards. Fruitiest Cava is Reserva de la Familia Extra Brut★, but the rosé and the top white Cava Gran Juvé are also good. Ermita d'Espiells is a neutral, dry white wine.

KAISERSTUHL *Baden, Germany* A 4000ha (10,000-acre) volcanic stump rising to 600m (2000ft) and overlooking the Rhine plain and south BADEN. Best producers: BERCHER★★, Dr HEGER★★, Karl H JOHNER★★, Franz Keller★, Königsschaffhausen co-op, Salwey★, Schneider★★. Best years: (dry whites) (2006) 05 04 **02 01 99 98 97**.

KAMPTAL *Niederösterreich, Austria* 3870ha (9560-acre) wine region centred on the town of Langenlois, making some impressive dry Riesling and Grüner Veltliner. Best producers: BRUNDLMAYER★★★, Ehn★★, Hiedler★, Hirsch★, Jurtschitsch★, Fred Loimer★★, Schloss Gobelsburg★★. Best years: (2006) 05 04 **03 02 01 00 99 98**.

KANONKOP *Stellenbosch WO, South Africa* Abrie Beeslaar, only the third winemaker at this estate in four decades, is confidently creating traditional, long-lived red wines – now, thanks to virus-free vine material, often with brighter fruit. Muscular, savoury BORDEAUX-blend Paul Sauer★★ really does mature for 10 years or more. A straight Cabernet Sauvignon★ adds to this enviable red wine reputation: Pinotage★★, from 50-year-old vines, is indelibly associated with the estate. Best years: (Paul Sauer) 2003 02 01 00 99 98 97 96 95 94 91.

KARTHÄUSERHOF *Trier, Ruwer, Germany* Top Ruwer estate which has gone from strength to strength under Christoph Tyrell and winemaker Ludwig Breiling. Rieslings combine aromatic extravagance with racy brilliance. Most wines are now ★★, some Auslese and Eiswein ★★★. Best years: (2006) 05 04 **03** 02 **01 99** 97 95 94 93.

KATNOOK ESTATE *Coonawarra, South Australia* Chardonnay★★ has consistently been the best of the fairly expensive whites, though Riesling★ and Sauvignon★★ are pretty tasty, too. Well-structured Cabernet Sauvignon★ and treacly Shiraz★ lead the reds, with Odyssey Cabernet Sauvignon★★ and Prodigy Shiraz★★ reaching a higher level. Best years: (Odyssey) (2006) (05) (04) 03 02 01 00 99 **98 97 96 94 92 91**.

KÉKFRANKOS See BLAUFRÄNKISCH.

KELLER *Flörsheim-Dalsheim, Rheinhessen, Germany* Klaus Keller and son Klaus-Peter are the leading winemakers in the hill country of RHEINHESSEN, away from the Rhine riverbank. They produce a range of varietal dry wines and naturally sweet Rieslings, as well as extra-special dry Rieslings★★ from the Dalsheimer Hubacker site. Astonishing TBA★★★ from Riesling and Rieslaner. Best years: (2006) 05 04 **03 02 01 00 99**.

KENDALL-JACKSON *Sonoma County, California, USA* Jess Jackson founded KJ in bucolic Lake County in 1982 after buying a vineyard there; the operation has since moved to SONOMA COUNTY as its base, with operations throughout the state, and now produces some 3.5 million cases. With the 2004 vintage, KJ's volume leader, the Vintner's Reserve Chardonnay (2 million cases) was made entirely from estate-grown fruit. Higher levels of quality are found in the Grand Reserve reds and whites, the vineyard-based Highland Estates★ series and the top of the range Stature (red Meritage★★).

KENWOOD *Sonoma Valley AVA, California, USA* Owned by Gary Heck of Korbel sparkling wine fame, this winery has always represented very good quality at reasonable prices. The Sauvignon Blanc★ highlights floral and melon flavours with a slightly earthy finish. Jack London Zinfandel★★ is impressive, while the flagship red remains the long-lived Artist Series Cabernet Sauvignon★★. A RUSSIAN RIVER VALLEY Pinot Noir★ is superb value. Best years: (Zinfandel) (2004) (03) 02 **01 00 99 98 97 96 95 94**.

VON KESSELSTATT *Trier, Mosel, Germany* Good traditional Rieslings (★ to ★★) from some top sites at GRAACH (Josephshöfer) and PIESPORT in the MOSEL, Scharzhofberg in the Saar and Kasel in the Ruwer, but I feel they could do even better. Best years: (2006) 05 04 **03** 02 **01 99 98**.

KIEDRICH *Rheingau, Germany* Small village whose top vineyard is the Gräfenberg, giving long-lived, mineral Rieslings. Wines from Sandgrub and Wasseros are also often good. Best producers: Knyphausen★, WEIL★★★. Best years: (2006) 05 04 **03 02 01 99 98 97 96 95 94**.

CH. KIRWAN★ *Margaux AC, 3ème Cru Classé, Haut-Médoc, Bordeaux, France* This MARGAUX estate has shown considerable improvement since the mid-1990s. Investment in the cellars, more attention to the vineyards and the advice of consultant Michel Rolland have produced wines of greater depth and power but less perfume. Second wine: Les Charmes de Kirwan. Best years: 2005 04 03 **01 00 99 98 96 95**.

KISTLER *Sonoma Valley AVA, California, USA* One of California's hottest Chardonnay producers. Wines are made from many different vineyards (Kistler Vineyard, Durell Vineyard and Dutton Ranch can be ★★★; McCrea Vineyard and the ultra-cool-climate Camp Meeting Ridge Vineyard ★★). All possess great complexity with good aging potential. Kistler also makes a number of single-vineyard Pinot Noirs★★ that go from good to very good. Best years: (Kistler Vineyard Chardonnay) (2005) 04 03 **02 01 00 99 98 97**.

KLEIN CONSTANTIA *Constantia WO, South Africa* Showpiece estate fast regaining deserved stature. The area's aptitude for white wines is reflected in crisp, nicely weighted Sauvignon Blanc★ (expressive, vibrant Perdeblokke★★ from a higher vineyard), good Chardonnay, excellent barrel-fermented white blend Madame Marlbrook★★, attractive off-dry Riesling and Vin de Constance★★ (recent vintages ★★★), a thrilling Muscat dessert wine based on the 18th-century Constantia. In reds, New World-style Shiraz★ looks promising. Best years: (Vin de Constance) **2002** 01 00 99 98 97 96 95 94 93 92 91 90.

KNAPPSTEIN *Clare Valley, South Australia* In 1995 Tim Knappstein quit the company, now owned by Lion Nathan, to make wines in the ADELAIDE HILLS (see RIPOSTE). However, Knappstein is still a market leader, making impressive Riesling: Hand Picked★★ is reliably good and the single-vineyard Ackland★★ (first released in 2005) can be among the best in the country. An intriguing white blend, Three★, combines Gewürztraminer with Riesling and Pinot Gris. There is a subtly-oaked Semillon-Sauvignon★, a Cabernet-Merlot and Chardonnay, plus Shiraz★ and Cabernet Sauvignon★ from the Enterprise vineyard. Best years: (Enterprise Cabernet Sauvignon) (2006) (05) (04) 03 02 01 **00 99 98**.

KNAPPSTEIN LENSWOOD VINEYARDS See RIPOSTE.

EMMERICH KNOLL *Unterloiben, Wachau, Niederösterreich, Austria* Since the late 1970s, some of the greatest Austrian dry white wines. His rich, complex Riesling and Grüner Veltliner are packed with fruit and rarely fail to reach ★★ quality, with versions from both the Loibenberg and Schütt sites ★★★. They repay keeping for 5 years or more. Best years: (Riesling Smaragd) (2006) 05 04 **03 02 01 00 99 98 97 96 95 94 90**.

KOEHLER-RUPRECHT *Kallstadt, Pfalz, Germany* Bernd Philippi makes powerful, very concentrated dry Rieslings★★★ from the Kallstadter Saumagen site, the oak-aged botrytized Elysium★★ and Burgundian-style Spätburgunder (Pinot Noir)★. Philippi is also co-winemaker at Mont du Toit in South Africa. Best years: (Saumagen Riesling) (2006) 05 04 **03 02 01 00 99 98 97 96**.

ALOIS KRACHER *Illmitz, Burgenland, Austria* Unquestionably Austria's greatest sweet winemaker. Nouvelle Vague wines are aged in barriques while Zwischen den Seen wines are spared oak. The Scheurebe Beerenauslesen and TBAs, and the Welschrieslings, Chardonnay-Welschrieslings and Grande Cuvée are all ★★★. Best years: (whites) (2006) 05 04 02 **01 00 99 98 96 95 94**.

KREMSTAL *Niederösterreich, Austria* 2170ha (5365-acre) wine region around Krems, producing some of Austria's best whites, particularly dry Riesling and Grüner Veltliner. Best producers: Malat★★, Mantlerhof★, Sepp Moser★, Nigl★★, NIKOLAIHOF★★, Franz Proidl★, Salomon★★, Stadt Krems★. Best years: (2006) 05 04 **03** 02 **01 00 99 98**.

KRUG *Champagne AC, Champagne, France* Serious CHAMPAGNE house, making seriously expensive wines. The non-vintage Grande Cuvée★★ used to knock spots off most other de luxe brands in its rich, rather over-the-top traditional style. Under new owners LVMH, the style seems to have changed dramatically: it's fresher, leaner, more modern – good, but that's not why I buy Krug. Also an impressive vintage★★, a rosé★★ and ethereal, outrageously expensive, single-vineyard Clos du Mesnil★★★ Blanc de Blancs. Best years: 1995 **90 89 88 85 82 81 79**.

KRUTZLER *Deutsch-Schützen, Südburgenland, Austria* One of Austria's finest red wines, Perwolff★★, is a generously oaked blend of Blaufränkisch and Cabernet Sauvignon. The Blaufränkisch Reserve is almost as fine. Best years: (2006) 05 04 03 **02** 01 **00 99 98 97**.

PETER JAKOB KÜHN *Oestrich, Rheingau, Germany* A brilliant grower and winemaker, Kühn frequently makes headlines with his substantial dry Rieslings and full, juicy Auslese. These wines are usually ★★. Best years: (2006) 05 04 **03 02 01 99 98 97**.

KUMEU/HUAPAI *Auckland, North Island, New Zealand* A small but significant viticultural area north-west of Auckland. The 11 wineries profit from their proximity to New Zealand's largest city. Most producers make little or no wine from grapes grown in their home region. Best producers: COOPERS CREEK★, Harrier Rise, KUMEU RIVER★★, MATUA VALLEY★. Best years: (reds) **2005 04 02 00**.

KUMEU RIVER *Kumeu, Auckland, North Island, New Zealand* This family winery has been transformed by New Zealand's first Master of Wine, Michael Brajkovich, with adventurous, high-quality wines: a big, complex Chardonnay★★★ (Maté's Vineyard★★★), complex oak-aged Pinot Gris★ and a MARLBOROUGH Sauvignon Blanc. Only Pinot Noir disappoints so far. Best years: (Chardonnay) (2006) **05 02 00**.

KUNDE ESTATE *Sonoma Valley, California, USA* The Kunde family have grown wine grapes in SONOMA COUNTY for at least 100 years; in 1990 they started producing wines, with spectacular results. The Chardonnays are all impressive – Kinneybrook★★, Wildwood★★ and the powerful, buttery Reserve★★. The Century Vines Zinfandel★★ gets rave reviews, as does the peppery Syrah★★, the zesty Sauvignon Blanc★★ and the explosively fruity Viognier★★. Best years: (Zinfandel) 2002 **01 00 99 97 96 94**.

FRANZ KÜNSTLER *Hochheim, Rheingau, Germany* Gunter Künstler makes some of the best dry Rieslings in the RHEINGAU – powerful, mineral wines★★, with the Hölle wines often ★★★. Sweet wine quality has been erratic lately, but the best are fantastic. Powerful, earthy and pricey Pinot Noir. Best years: (2006) 05 04 **03** 02 **01 99 98 97 96**.

KWV *Paarl WO, South Africa* This industry giant aims to get back on course with help from Neil ELLIS, Charles BACK (FAIRVIEW) and Ian McKenzie (ex-Southcorp), who are mentoring the winemaking team. The flagship Cathedral Cellar range features bright-fruited, well-oaked Triptych★ (Cabernet-Merlot-Shiraz), rich bold Cabernet Sauvignon★ and modern-style Pinotage. Among whites, barrel-fermented Chardonnay shows pleasing fruit/oak balance, and Sauvignon★ is tangy. Produced in best years only, and in very limited quantities, single-vineyard Perold is an ultra-ripe international-style Shiraz lavishly adorned with new American oak. PORT-style and Muscadel fortifieds remain superb value.

LA ROSA *Cachapoal, Rapel, Chile* Recently rejuvenated old family operation. The La Palma unoaked Chardonnay is pure apricots and figs, and the La Palma Merlot is a delightful easy-drinking style. The La Capitana★ and Don Reca★ labels are a step up in quality and always terrific value.

CH. LABÉGORCE-ZÉDÉ★ *Margaux AC, Cru Bourgeois, Haut-Médoc, Bordeaux, France* Cherished and improved by Luc Thienpont of POMEROL until 2005, this property is now owned by neighbouring Château Labégorce. The wine isn't that perfumed, but is well poised between concentration and finesse. Age for 5 years or more. Second wine: Domaine Zédé. A third wine, Z de Zédé, is a simple BORDEAUX AC. Best years: 2005 04 03 **01 00 99 98 96 95 90 89**.

LADOIX AC *Côte de Beaune, Burgundy, France* Most northerly village in the COTE DE BEAUNE and one of the least known. The village includes some of the Grand Cru CORTON, and the lesser vineyards may be sold as Ladoix-Côte de Beaune or COTE DE BEAUNE-VILLAGES. Reasonably priced reds, quite light in colour and a little lean in style, from several good growers. Best producers: (reds) Cachat-Ocquidant★, Chevalier, E Cornu★, Prince de Merode★, A & J-R Nudant★; (whites) E Cornu, R & R Jacob★, VERGET★. Best years: (reds) (2006) 05 **03 02 99**.

MICHEL LAFARGE *Volnay, Côte de Beaune, Burgundy, France* The doyen of VOLNAY; son Frédéric is now in charge. Some outstanding red wines, notably Volnay Clos des Chênes★★★, Volnay Clos du Château des Ducs★★★ (a monopole) and less fashionable BEAUNE Grèves★★★. BOURGOGNE Rouge★ is good value. Top wines may seem a little lean at first, but will blossom after 10 years' or more aging. Best years: (top reds) (2006) 05 04 03 02 99 **98 97 96 95 93 91 90**.

CH. LAFAURIE-PEYRAGUEY★★ *Sauternes AC, 1er Cru Classé, Bordeaux, France* One of the most improved SAUTERNES properties of the 1980s and now frequently one of the best Sauternes of all, sumptuous and rich when young, and marvellously deep and satisfying with age. Best years: 2005 04 03 **02** 01 **99 98 97 96 95 90 89 88 86 85 83**.

CH. LAFITE-ROTHSCHILD★★★ *Pauillac AC, 1er Cru Classé, Haut-Médoc, Bordeaux, France* This PAUILLAC First Growth is frequently cited as the epitome of elegance, indulgence and expense. Since the late 1990s vintages have been superb, with added depth and body to match the wine's traditional finesse. Second wine: les Carruades de Lafite-Rothschild. Best years: 2005 04 03 02 01 00 **99** 98 **97 96 95 94 90 89 88 86 85 82**.

CH. LAFLEUR★★★ *Pomerol AC, Bordeaux, France* Using some of POMEROL'S most traditional winemaking, this tiny estate can seriously rival the great PETRUS for texture, flavour and aroma. But a high percentage of Cabernet Franc (50%) makes this a more elegant style of wine. Second wine: Pensées de Lafleur. Best years: 2005 04 03 02 01 **00 99 98 96 95 90 89 88**.

LAFON *Meursault, Côte de Beaune, Burgundy, France* One of Burgundy's current superstars, with prices to match. Early exponent of biodynamics for brilliant MEURSAULT including Clos de la Barre★★, Charmes★★★, Perrières★★★, le MONTRACHET★★★ and exciting long-lived reds from VOLNAY (Santenots du Milieu★★★). Since 1999, also MACON★ (Clos du Four★, Clos de la Crochette★). Best years: (whites) (2006) 05 04 **03** 02 **00 99 97 95 93 92**; (reds) (2006) 05 03 02 99 **98 97 96 95 93 91 90**.

CH. LAFON-ROCHET★ *St-Estèphe AC, 4ème Cru Classé, Haut-Médoc, Bordeaux, France* Good-value, affordable Classed Growth claret. Recent vintages have seen an increase of Merlot in the blend, making the wine less austere. Delicious and blackcurranty after 10 years. Best years: 2005 04 **03 02 01 00 99 98 96 95 94 90 89 88 86 85**.

ALOIS LAGEDER *Alto Adige DOC, Trentino-Alto Adige, Italy* Leading producer in ALTO ADIGE, making good, medium-priced varietals and pricey estate and single-vineyard wines such as Löwengang Cabernet★ and Chardonnay★★, Sauvignon Lehenhof★★, Cabernet Cor Römigberg★★, Pinot Noir Krafuss★, Pinot Bianco Haberlehof★ and Pinot Grigio Benefizium Porer★. Also owns the historical Casòn Hirschprunn estate, source of excellent Alto Adige blends. White Contest★★ is based on Pinot Grigio and Chardonnay, with small amounts of Marsanne and Roussanne. The red equivalent, Casòn★★, is Merlot-Cabernet based; a second red, Corolle★, and white Etelle★ show similar style.

LAGO DI CALDARO DOC *Trentino-Alto Adige, Italy* At its best a lovely, barely red, youthful glugger from the Schiava grape, tasting of strawberries and cream and bacon smoke. However, far too much Caldaro is overproduced. Known in German as Kalterersee. Kalterersee Auslese (Lago di Caldaro Scelto) is not sweet, but has 0.5% more alcohol. Best producers: Caldaro co-op★, LAGEDER★, Prima & Nuova/Erste & Neue★, San Michele Appiano co-op, Schloss Sallegg★.

CH. LAGRANGE★★ *St-Julien AC, 3ème Cru Classé, Haut-Médoc, Bordeaux, France* Since the Japanese company SUNTORY purchased this large estate in 1983 it has become a single-minded wine of good fruit, meticulous winemaking and fine quality, an occasional surfeit of tannin being the only cautionary note. Second wine: les Fiefs de Lagrange. Best years: 2005 04 03 02 **01 00 99 98 96 95 94 90 89 88**.

LAGREIN Black grape in Italy's TRENTINO-Alto Adige, producing – when not over-oaked – deep-coloured, brambly, chocolaty reds called Lagrein Dunkel or Scuro, and full-bodied, attractively scented rosé (known as Kretzer). Best producers: Colterenzio co-op (Cornell★), Graziano Fontana★, Franz Gojer★, Gries co-op★, Hofstätter★, LAGEDER★, Laimburg★, Muri-Gries★, J Niedermayr★, I Niedriest★, Plattner-Waldgries★, Hans Rottensteiner★, Santa Maddalena co-op★, Simoncelli★, Terlano co-op★★, Thurnhof★★, TIEFENBRUNNER★★, Zemmer★.

CH. LAGREZETTE *Cahors AC, South-West France* Splendid CAHORS estate owned by Alain-Dominique Perrin, boss of luxury jewellers Cartier. The cellars are overseen by enologist Michel Rolland. There's supple, fruity Moulin Lagrezette, oak-aged Chevaliers and Ch. Lagrezette★. Cuvée Dame Honneur★ and le Pigeonnier★★ are special cuvées, mainly from Malbec. Best years: (2004) 03 02 **01 00 99**.

181

CH. LA LAGUNE ★ *Haut-Médoc AC, 3ème Cru Classé, Haut-Médoc, Bordeaux, France* The closest MEDOC Classed Growth to Bordeaux city. The soils are sandy-gravel and the wines round and elegant in style. Took a dip in the late 1990s but new investment from 2000, and quality has improved. Second wine: Moulin de la Lagune. Best years: 2005 04 **03** 02 **00 98** 96 **95 90 89.**

LAKE'S FOLLY *Hunter Valley, New South Wales, Australia* Charismatic founder Dr Max Lake sold the winery in 2000; the vineyard has been revitalized and the wines, under Rodney Kempe, have reached new levels of excellence and consistency. In best years, austere Chardonnay★★ ages slowly to a masterly antipodean yet Burgundy-like peak. The red, called Cabernets★, is rich, complex and fleshy. Best years: (red) 2005 04 03 02 01 00 99 **98 97 96 93 91** 89 85 83 81; (white) 2005 04 03 02 01 **00 99 98 97 96 94 92 91.**

LALANDE-DE-POMEROL AC *Bordeaux, France* To the north of its more famous neighbour POMEROL, this AC produces ripe, plummy wines with an unmistakable mineral edge that are very attractive to drink at 3–4 years old, but age reasonably well too. Even though they lack the concentration of top Pomerols, the wines are not particularly cheap. Best producers: Annereaux★, Bertineau St-Vincent★, la Croix-St-André★, les Cruzelles★, la Fleur de Boüard★★, Garraud★, Grand Ormeau★, Haut-Chaigneau, les Hauts Conseillants, Jean de Gué★, Laborderie-Mondésir★, Perron (La Fleur★), Sergant, la Sergue★, Siaurac, Tournefeuille, Viaud. Best years: 2005 04 **03 01 00 99 98 96 95.**

LAMBRUSCO *Emilia-Romagna, Italy* 'Lambrusco' refers to a family of black grape varieties, grown in 3 DOC zones on the plains of Emilia and 1 around Mantova in LOMBARDY, but it is the screwcap bottles of non-DOC Lambrusco that made them famous, even though some contain no wine from Lambrusco grapes at all. Proper Lambrusco is a dry or semi-sweet fizzy red with high acidity to partner the rich local foods, such as rich, buttery cheese sauces and salami, and is worth trying (especially Lambrusco di Sorbara and Grasparossa di Castelvetro). Best producers: Barbieri, Barbolini, F Bellei★, Casali, Cavicchioli★, Chiarli, Vittorio Graziano★, Oreste Lini, Stefano Spezia, Venturini Baldini.

LAMOREAUX LANDING *Finger Lakes AVA, New York State, USA* One of the most important wineries in FINGER LAKES. Its Chardonnay Reserve★ is a consistent medal winner, and the Pinot Noir★ is arguably the region's best. Merlot★ and Cabernet Franc★ are also attractive, as are Riesling★ and good, quaffable fizz.

LANDMARK *Sonoma County, California, USA* This producer concentrates on Chardonnay and Pinot Noir. Chardonnays include Overlook★★ and the oakier Damaris Reserve★★ and Lorenzo★★. Tropical-fruited Courtyard Chardonnay★ is lower-priced. Pinot Noir from Kastania Vineyard★★ (SONOMA COAST) is beautifully focused.

LANGHE DOC *Piedmont, Italy* Important DOC covering wines from the Langhe hills around Alba. The range of varietals such as Chardonnay, Barbera and Nebbiolo embrace many former vino da tavola blends of the highest order. Best producers: (reds) ALTARE★★, Boglietti (Buio★★), Bongiovanni (Falletto★★), CERETTO★★, CHIARLO★, Cigliuti★★, CLERICO★★, Aldo CONTERNO★★, Conterno-Fantino (Monprà★★), Luigi Einaudi★,

GAJA★★★, A Ghisolfi★★, Marchesi di Gresy (Virtus★★), F Nada (Seifile★★), Parusso (Bricco Rovella★★), Rocche dei Manzoni (Quatr Nas★), Vajra★, Gianni Voerzio (Serrapiu★★), Roberto VOERZIO★★. Best years: (reds) (2006) 04 03 **01 00 99 98 97 96 95.**

CH. LANGOA-BARTON ★★ *St-Julien AC, 3ème Cru Classé, Haut-Médoc, Bordeaux, France* Owned by the Barton family since 1821, Langoa-Barton is usually, but not always, lighter in style than its ST-JULIEN stablemate LEOVILLE-BARTON, but it is still extremely impressive and excellent value. Drink after 7 or 8 years, although it may keep for 15. Second wine: Réserve de Léoville-Barton (a blend from the young vines of both Barton properties). Best years: 2005 04 **03** 02 **01 00 99 98 96 95 90 89 88 86 85 83 82.**

LANGUEDOC-ROUSSILLON *France* This vast area of southern France, running from Nîmes to the Spanish border and covering the *départements* of the GARD, HERAULT, Aude and Pyrénées-Orientales, is still a source of undistinguished cheap wine, but is also one of France's most exciting wine regions. The transformation is the result of better grape varieties, modern winemaking and ambitious producers, from the heights of GRANGE DES PERES to very good local co-ops. The best wines are the reds, particularly those from CORBIERES, COTEAUX DU LANGUEDOC, MINERVOIS and PIC ST-LOUP, and some new-wave Cabernets, Merlots and Syrahs, as well as the more traditional *vins doux naturels*, such as BANYULS, MAURY and MUSCAT DE RIVESALTES; but we are now seeing exciting whites as well, particularly as new plantings of Chardonnay, Marsanne, Roussanne, Viognier and Sauvignon Blanc mature. From 2008, there is a plan to establish a super-appellation for the whole of Languedoc and Roussillon. Called simply Languedoc AC, it will include all of Coteaux du Languedoc, Corbières, Minervois and the ROUSSILLON appellations. See also BOUCHES-DU-RHONE, COLLIOURE, COSTIERES DE NIMES, COTES DU ROUSSILLON, COTES DE THONGUE, FITOU, MUSCAT DE FRONTIGNAN, MUSCAT DE ST-JEAN-DE-MINERVOIS, OC, RIVESALTES, ST-CHINIAN.

LANSON *Champagne AC, Champagne, France* Non-vintage Lanson Black Label ★ is reliably tasty and, like the rosé ★ and vintage ★★ wines, especially de luxe Noble Cuvée ★★, improves greatly with aging. In March 2006, Lanson (and associated brands Besserat de Bellefon, Gauthier, Massé and Alfred Rothschild) was bought by Boizel Chanoine Champagne, where Bruno PAILLARD is the majority shareholder. Best years: (1999) (98) 97 96 **95 93 90 89 88 85 83 82.**

MICHEL LAROCHE *Chablis, Burgundy, France* Dynamic CHABLIS producer, with good St Martin Vieilles Vignes★ and impressive Grand Cru Les Clos★★★. One of the first Burgundians to use screwtop closures. Also owns MAS LA CHEVALIERE in the Languedoc and L'AVENIR in Stellenbosch, South Africa. Best years: (Chablis) (2006) 05 **04 03 02 00 99.**

CH. LASCOMBES *Margaux AC, 2ème Cru Classé, Haut-Médoc, Bordeaux, France* One of the great underachievers in MARGAUX, with little worth drinking in the 1980s and 90s. New American ownership and investment and the advice of enologist Michel Rolland have begun to make a difference – and the 2004 is the best effort for a generation. Best years: 2005 04 03 **01 00 96 95.**

CH. LATOUR ★★★ *Pauillac AC, 1er Cru Classé, Haut-Médoc, Bordeaux, France* Latour's reputation is based on powerful, long-lasting classic wines. Strangely, in the early 1980s there was an attempt to make lighter, more fashionable wines, with mixed results. The late 80s saw a return to classic Latour, much to my relief. Its reputation for making fine wine in less successful vintages is well deserved. After 30 years in British hands it returned to French ownership in 1993. Spanking new cellars from 2004. Second wine: les Forts de Latour. Best years: 2005 04 03 02 01 00 **99 98 97 96 95 94 93 90 89 88 86**.

LOUIS LATOUR *Beaune, Burgundy, France* Merchant almost as well known for his COTEAUX DE L'ARDECHE Chardonnays as for his Burgundies. Latour's white Burgundies are much better than the reds although the red CORTON-Grancey★★ can be very good. Latour's oaky CORTON-CHARLEMAGNE ★★, from his own vineyard, is his top wine, but there is also good CHEVALIER-MONTRACHET ★★, BATARD-MONTRACHET ★★ and le MONTRACHET ★★. Even so, as these are the greatest white vineyards in Burgundy, there really should be more top performances. Best years: (top whites) (2006) 05 04 03 02 00 **99 97 95**.

CH. LATOUR-MARTILLAC *Pessac-Léognan AC, Cru Classé de Graves, Bordeaux, France* The vineyard here is strictly organic, and has many ancient vines. The deep, dark, well-structured reds★ improved considerably in the 1990s. Whites★ are thoroughly modern and of good quality. Good value as well. Best years: (reds) 2005 04 03 02 01 **00 99 98 96 95 90 88**; (whites) **2005 04 02 01 00 99 98 96 95 94**.

CH. LATOUR-À-POMEROL ★ *Pomerol AC, Bordeaux, France* Directed by Christian MOUEIX of PETRUS fame, this property makes luscious wines with loads of gorgeous fruit and enough tannin to age well. Best years: 2005 04 **03 02 01 00 99 98 95 90 89 88 85 83 82**.

LATRICIÈRES-CHAMBERTIN AC See CHAMBERTIN AC.

LAUREL GLEN *Sonoma Mountain AVA, California, USA* Owner/wine-maker Patrick Campbell makes only Cabernet★★ at his mountaintop winery. This is rich wine with deep fruit flavours, aging after 6–10 years to a perfumed, complex BORDEAUX style. Counterpoint is a label for wine that does not make it into the top-level Cabernet. Terra Rosa is made from bought-in Argentinian wine. A wine called Reds, from Lodi-grown fruit, is great value. Best years: (2005) 02 01 **99 98 97 96 95 94 91 90**.

LAURENT-PERRIER *Champagne AC, Champagne, France* Large, family-owned CHAMPAGNE house, offering flavour and quality at reasonable prices. Non-vintage★ is light and savoury; the vintage★★ is delicious, and the top wine, Cuvée Grand Siècle★★★, is among the finest Champagnes of all. Non-vintage rosé★ is good and vintage Grand Siècle Alexandra★★★ is excellent. Best years: 1997 96 **95 90 88 85 82**.

L'AVENIR *Stellenbosch WO, South Africa* New owner Chablis merchant Michel LAROCHE and winemaker Tinus Els are intent on maintaining the enviable reputation established by the previous partnership of Marc Wiehe and François Naudé. While Pinotage★★ and Cabernet★ are still of their legacy, stylish new vintage Chenin Blanc★ and Chardonnay★ herald a promising new era. Best years: (Pinotage) **2005 04 03 02 01 00 99 98**.

CH. LAVILLE-HAUT-BRION ★★★ *Pessac-Léognan AC, Cru Classé de Graves, Bordeaux, France* One of the finest white PESSAC-LEOGNANS with a price tag to match. Fermented in barrel, it needs 10 years or more to reach its savoury but luscious peak. Best years: 2005 04 **03 02 01 00 99 98 97 96 95 94 93 90 89 85**.

DOMAINE COSTA LAZARIDI *Drama, Greece* This state-of-the-art Bordeaux-inspired winery makes good use of indigenous and international varieties. Fresh gooseberry Amethystos white★

(Sauvignon Blanc, Semillon and Assyrtiko); a fascinatingly intense Viognier★ with a stunning, oily, peach kernel finish; tasty Château Julia Chardonnay★; and the fine Amethystos Cava★, an oak-aged Cabernet from very low yields.

LAZIO *Italy* Region best known for FRASCATI, Rome's white glugger. There are also various bland whites from Trebbiano and Malvasia, such as EST! EST!! EST!!! DI MONTEFIASCONE. The region's most interesting wines are reds based on Cabernet, Merlot and Sangiovese; the local Cesanese can also do well. Some of the best come from Castel de Paolis (Quattro Mori★★), Paolo di Mauro (Vigna del Vassallo★★), Cerveteri co-op (Tertium★) and FALESCO (Montiano★★), with other good wines from Casale del Giglio★, Pietra Pinta★ and Trappolini★.

LEASINGHAM *Clare Valley, South Australia* A wing of HARDY, Leasingham is one of CLARE VALLEY's largest wineries, and is well respected. Riesling★★ can be among Clare's best, and Sparkling Shiraz★★ is excellent. Bin 56 Cabernet-Malbec★ and Bin 61 Shiraz★ are powerful, mid-price reds, while Classic Clare Shiraz★★ and Cabernet★ are high-alcohol, heavily oaked, overpriced blockbusters. Look to the new budget-priced ranges, Magnus and Circa 1893, for value.

L'ECOLE NO 41 *Walla Walla Valley AVA, Washington State, USA* The velvety and deeply flavoured Seven Hills Merlot★ from this winery can be good, as can the Cabernet Sauvignon★ and the lush Syrah★★; a BORDEAUX blend called Apogee★★ from the Pepper Bridge vineyard in WALLA WALLA is dark and challenging. The best wines are the Semillons: a rich, woody, barrel-fermented★★ version and exciting single-vineyard Fries Vineyard Semillon★★ and Seven Hills Vineyard Semillon★★. The Chardonnay★ is pleasant, if simple. Best years: (top reds) (2005) 04 03 02 **01 00**.

LEDA *Castilla y León, Spain* Small winery launched by a bunch of young wine professionals, including the sons of Mariano García (of VEGA SICILIA and MAURO fame). It has taken the country by storm with its profound red Viñas Viejas★★ from very old Tempranillo vines in small plots throughout the Duero region. Best years: 2004 03 **01 00 99**.

LEEUWIN ESTATE *Margaret River, Western Australia* MARGARET RIVER's high flier, with pricey Chardonnay (Art Series★★★) that gets Burgundy lovers drooling. Art Series Cabernet Sauvignon★★ (sometimes ★★★) has improved dramatically since 1998 and exhibits superb blackcurrant and cedar balance. Art Series Riesling★★ is complex and fine, and look out for exceptional Shiraz★★ to come. New labels Prelude and Siblings give Leeuwin pleasure at lower prices. Best years: (Art Series Chardonnay) (2006) (05) 04 02 01 00 **99 98 97 96 95 94 92 90 87**.

DOM. LEFLAIVE *Puligny-Montrachet, Côte de Beaune, Burgundy, France* Famous white Burgundy producer with extensive holdings in some of the greatest vineyards of PULIGNY-MONTRACHET, including les Pucelles★★★, Chevalier-MONTRACHET★★★, BATARD-MONTRACHET★★★ and a tiny slice of le MONTRACHET★★★. After a disappointing patch, Anne-Claude Leflaive has taken the family domaine right back to the top using biodynamic methods. These extraordinarily fine wines can age for 20 years and are understandably expensive. More reasonably priced Mâcon-Verzé was launched in 2004. Best years: (2006) 05 **03** 02 **01 00 99 97 95**.

OLIVIER LEFLAIVE *Puligny-Montrachet, Côte de Beaune, Burgundy, France*
Négociant Olivier Leflaive specializes in crisp, modern white wines from the COTE D'OR and the COTE CHALONNAISE, but standards are far from consistent. Lesser ACs – ST-ROMAIN★, MONTAGNY★, ST-AUBIN★, RULLY★ – offer good value, but the rich, oaky BATARD-MONTRACHET★★★ is the star turn of winemaker Frank Grux. Best years: (top whites) (2006) 05 **04 03 02**.

PETER LEHMANN *Barossa Valley, South Australia* BAROSSA doyen Peter Lehmann buys grapes from many local growers and owns the superb Stonewell vineyard, which contributes its fruit and name to his best Shiraz★★★. Juicy, old-fashioned, fruit-packed reds include Grenache-Shiraz★, Mentor★★ and Eight Songs Shiraz★★. Also lemony Semillon★★ and Chenin★, and dry, long-lived Eden Valley Riesling★★. Bought by California-based Donald HESS in 2003. Best years: (Stonewell Shiraz) (2006) (04) 03 02 01 **99 98 96 94 93 92 91 90 89**.

JOSEF LEITZ *Rüdesheim, Rheingau, Germany* Some of the RHEINGAU's best dry and off-dry Rieslings come from this RÜDESHEIM grower, especially from the Berg Rottland★★ and Berg Schlossberg★★ sites. Best years: (2006) 05 04 **03 02 01 00 99 98**.

LEIWEN *Mosel, Germany* This unspectacular village has become a hotbed of the MOSEL Riesling revolution. Nowhere else in the region is there such a concentration of dynamic estates and new ideas. Best producers: GRANS-FASSIAN★★, Carl Loewen★, Josef Rosch★, St Urbans-Hof★★, Heinz Schmitt★. Best years: (2006) 05 04 **03 02 01 99 98 97**.

LEMBERGER See BLAUFRÄNKISCH.

LENZ WINERY *Long Island AVA, New York State, USA* A leading LONG ISLAND winery going from strength to strength. The Estate Merlot★★ is elegant and powerful with soft, balanced tannins; dry Gewürztraminer★ is spicy and tasty. In good vintages the Pinot Noir★ has deep, ripe fruit. Chardonnay★ is mostly good and Cabernet Franc is appealing.

LEONETTI CELLAR *Walla Walla Valley AVA, Washington State, USA* Rich and velvety Cabernet Sauvignon★★ and Merlot★★ aged in a combination of French and American oak. A dense and powerful Reserve★★★ uses the best barrels. Sangiovese★★ has very fine texture and lots of new wood. The focus is on vineyard management and most of the fruit is now estate grown. Best years: (2005) 04 03 02 **01 00**.

CH. LÉOVILLE-BARTON★★★ *St-Julien AC, 2ème Cru Classé, Haut-Médoc, Bordeaux, France* Made by Anthony Barton, whose family has run this ST-JULIEN property since 1826, this fine claret is a traditionalist's delight. Dark, dry and tannic, and not overly oaked, the wines are often underestimated, but over 10–15 years they achieve a lean yet sensitively proportioned beauty rarely equalled in Bordeaux. Moreover, they are never overpriced. Second wine: Réserve de Léoville-Barton. Best years: 2005 04 03 02 **01 00 99 98 96 95 94 93 90 89 88 86 85 83 82**.

CH. LÉOVILLE-LAS-CASES★★★ *St-Julien AC, 2ème Cru Classé, Haut-Médoc, Bordeaux, France* The largest of the 3 Léoville properties, making wines of startlingly deep, dark concentration. I now find them so dense and thick in texture that it is difficult to identify them as ST-JULIEN. Second wine: Clos du Marquis. Best years: 2005 04 03 02 **01 00 99 98 96 95 94 93 90 89 88 86 85 83 82**.

RÉCOLTE 2002

Grand Vin de Léoville
du Marquis de Las Cases

SAINT-JULIEN-MÉDOC

CH. LÉOVILLE-POYFERRÉ★★ *St-Julien AC, 2ème Cru Classé, Haut-Médoc, Bordeaux, France* Since the 1986 vintage Didier Cuvelier has gradually increased the richness of the wine without wavering from its austere style. A string of excellent wines in the 90s frequently show more classic ST-JULIEN style than those of illustrious neighbour LEOVILLE-LAS-CASES. Second wine: Moulin-Riche. Best years: 2005 04 03 02 **01** 00 **99 98 96 95 94** 90 89 86.

DOM. LEROY *Vosne-Romanée, Côte de Nuits, Burgundy, France* In 1988 Lalou Bize-Leroy bought the former Dom. Noëllat in VOSNE-ROMANEE, renaming it Domaine Leroy, which should not be confused with her négociant house, Maison Leroy, which contains stocks of great mature vintages, or her personal estate, Dom. d'Auvenay. Here she produces fiendishly expensive, though fabulously concentrated, wines with biodynamic methods and almost ludicrously low yields from top vineyards such as CHAMBERTIN★★★, CLOS DE VOUGEOT★★★, MUSIGNY★★★, RICHEBOURG★★★ and ROMANEE-ST-VIVANT★★★. Best years: (top reds) (2006) 05 03 02 01 **00 99 98 97 96 95** 90 89.

LIEBFRAUMILCH *Pfalz, Rheinhessen, Nahe and Rheingau, Germany* Sweetish and low in acidity, Liebfraumilch rightly has a down-market image. It can come from the PFALZ, RHEINHESSEN, NAHE or the RHEINGAU and 70% of the blend must be Müller-Thurgau, Kerner, Riesling and Silvaner.

LIGER-BELAIR *Côte de Nuits, Burgundy, France* Vicomte Louis-Michel Liger-Belair makes stylish, perfumed wines at the family estate in VOSNE-ROMANEE, including the monopoly of la ROMANEE★★★ itself, while his cousin Thibault Liger-Belair makes rich, plump wines from his NUITS-ST-GEORGES base, including Premier Cru les St Georges★★ and Grands Crus RICHEBOURG★★ and CLOS DE VOUGEOT★★. Best years: (Vicomte) (2006) 05 03 02 01 **00 99**; (Thibault) (2006) 05 04 **03 02**.

LIGURIA *Italy* Thin coastal strip of north-west Italy, running from the French border at Ventimiglia to the Tuscan border. Best-known wines are the Cinqueterre, Colli di Luna, Riviera Ligure di Ponente and Rossese di Dolceacqua DOCs.

LIMARÍ VALLEY *Chile* Best known in Chile for pisco (the local brandy), during the past five years this valley – located 400km (250 miles) north of Santiago – has shown that its cold ocean influence and its clay and chalky soil can produce world-class wines. Chardonnay, Syrah and Carmenère are the top performers, all expressing fresh, vibrant flavours and subtle yet clear minerality. Tabalí are the best producers so far (Syrah★★) but expect more in the near future. Best producers: DE MARTINO, Tabalí/SAN PEDRO, Tamaya.

LIMESTONE COAST *South Australia* Zone for south-east of South Australia, including COONAWARRA, PADTHAWAY, Mount Benson and Wrattonbully. Plantings near Mount Gambier, Bordertown and Robe may seek official recognition in the future. New vineyards in this far-flung area have Coonawarra-like terra rossa soil with great potential. The Foster's Wine Group, YALUMBA, HARDY and ORLANDO are all involved.

LIMOUX AC *Languedoc, France* The first AC in the LANGUEDOC to allow Chardonnay and Chenin Blanc, which must be vinified in oak. Production is dominated by the SIEUR D'ARQUES co-op. From 2004 a red Limoux AC has been made from Merlot and Cabernet with local varieties. Best producers: d'Antugnac★, Begude★, SIEUR D'ARQUES★.

LINDEMANS *Murray Darling, Victoria, Australia* Large, historical company that is a key part of the Foster's Wine Group even though it suffered from the corporate chaos of the Southcorp days. Traditionally strong in COONAWARRA, where the best wines are the mineral St George Cabernet★★, spicy Limestone Ridge Shiraz-Cabernet★★ and the red BORDEAUX blend Pyrus★★. Decent mass-market wines such as the Bin range may signal how the company wants to develop. Reserve label reds from the LIMESTONE COAST are good value. Best years: (Coonawarra reds) (2006) (05) (04) 03 02 **01 99 98 96 94 91 90 88 86**.

LIRAC AC *Rhône Valley, France* Underrated AC between TAVEL and CHATEAUNEUF-DU-PAPE. Reds have the dusty, spicy red fruit of Châteauneuf without quite the intensity. They age well but are delicious young. Refreshing rosé has lovely strawberry fruit, and whites can be good – drink them young before the perfume goes. Best producers: Amido★, Aquéria★, Bouchassy★, Duseigneur, la Genestière, Joncier★, Lafond-Roc-Épine★★, Maby, Mont-Redon★, la Mordorée★★, Pélaquié★, Roger Sabon★★, St-Roch★, Ségriès★, Tavel co-op★, Zobel. Best years: 2006 **05 04 03 01 00**.

LISTRAC-MÉDOC AC *Haut-Médoc, Bordeaux, France* Set back from the Gironde and away from the best gravel ridges of the HAUT-MEDOC, Listrac wines can be good without ever being thrilling, and are marked by solid fruit, a slightly coarse tannin and an earthy flavour. More Merlot is now being used to soften the style. Best producers: Cap Léon Veyrin, CLARKE★, Ducluzeau, Fonréaud, Fourcas-Dupré★, Fourcas-Hosten, Fourcas-Loubaney, Grand Listrac co-op, Mayne-Lalande★, Saransot-Dupré. Best years: 2005 **03 01 00 96 95 90**.

LOIRE VALLEY *France* The Loire river cuts right through the heart of France. The middle reaches are the home of world-famous SANCERRE and POUILLY-FUME. The region of TOURAINE makes good Sauvignon Blanc and Gamay, while at VOUVRAY and MONTLOUIS the Chenin Blanc makes some pretty good fizz and still whites, ranging from sweet to very dry. The Loire's best reds are made in SAUMUR-CHAMPIGNY, CHINON and BOURGUEIL, mainly from Cabernet Franc, with ANJOU-VILLAGES improving fast. Anjou is famous for rosé, but the best wines are white, either sweet from the Layon Valley (now also a source of exciting dry white ANJOU), or dry from SAVENNIERES. Near the mouth of the river around Nantes is MUSCADET. See also ANJOU BLANC, ANJOU ROUGE, BONNEZEAUX, CABERNET D'ANJOU, CHEVERNY, COTE ROANNAISE, COTEAUX DE L'AUBANCE, COTEAUX DU LAYON, CRÉMANT DE LOIRE, GROS PLANT DU PAYS NANTAIS, JARDIN DE LA FRANCE, JASNIERES, MENETOU-SALON, MONTLOUIS-SUR-LOIRE, POUILLY-SUR-LOIRE, QUARTS DE CHAUME, QUINCY, REUILLY, ROSÉ DE LOIRE, ST-NICOLAS-DE-BOURGUEIL, SAUMUR, SAUMUR MOUSSEUX.

LOMBARDY *Italy* Lombardy is a larger consumer than producer. Many of the best grapes, especially from OLTREPO PAVESE, go to provide base wine for Italy's *spumante* industry. However, there are some interesting wines in Oltrepò Pavese, VALTELLINA, LUGANA and high-quality sparkling and still wines in FRANCIACORTA.

LONG ISLAND *New York State, USA* Long Island encompasses 3 AVAs: the Hamptons; North Fork; and the broader Long Island AVA. People have likened growing conditions to BORDEAUX, and the long growing season, combined with a maritime influence, does produce similarities. Certainly Merlot and Cabernet Franc are the best reds, with

Chardonnay the best white. Best producers: BEDELL★★, CHANNING DAUGHTERS★, LENZ★★, Macari, Martha Clara, Palmer★, Paumanok★, Pellegrini★, Pindar, Raphael, Shinn Estate, Wölffer★. Best years: (reds) (2006) **02 01 00 98 97**.

LONG SHADOWS VINTNERS *Columbia Valley AVA, Washington State, USA*
Long Shadows Vintners is a series of small partnerships led by Washington wine pioneer Allen Shoup, encompassing a coterie of wineries located in the heart of the COLUMBIA VALLEY appellation. It includes Pedestal★★ with Michel Rolland, Feather★ with Randy DUNN, Poet's Leap★ with Armin Diel of Schlossgut DIEL, Saggi★ with Ambrogio and Giovanni FOLONARI, Sequel★★ with John Duval and Chester-Kidder★ with Allen Shoup and Gilles Nicault, the head winemaker for the group. The arrangement is unique in that each winery is individually owned and managed as a separate partnership. Best years: (reds) (2005) 04.

DR LOOSEN *Bernkastel, Mosel, Germany* Loosen's estate has portions of some of the MOSEL's most famous vineyards: Treppchen and Prälat in ERDEN, Würzgarten in URZIG, Sonnenuhr in WEHLEN, Himmelreich in GRAACH and Lay in BERNKASTEL. Most of the wines achieve ★★, and Spätlese and Auslese from Wehlen, Ürzig and Erden frequently ★★★. His basic Riesling is excellent, year in year out. A joint venture with CHATEAU STE MICHELLE in WASHINGTON is proving exciting. Best years: (2006) 05 04 **03** 02 **01 00 99 98 97 96 95 94**. See also J L WOLF.

LÓPEZ DE HEREDIA *Rioja DOCa, Rioja, Spain* Family-owned RIOJA company, still aging wines in old oak casks. Younger red wines are called Viña Cubillo★, and mature wines Viña Tondonia★ and Viña Bosconia★. Good, oaky whites, especially Viña Gravonia★. Best years: (Viña Tondonia) 1996 **95 94 93 91** 87 86 85 76 54.

LOUPIAC AC *Bordeaux, France* A sweet wine area across the Garonne river from BARSAC. The wines are attractively sweet without being gooey. Drink young in general, though the best can age. Best producers: Clos Jean★, Cros★, Loupiac-Gaudiet, Mémoires★, Noble★, Ricaud, les Roques★. Best years: 2005 **03 02 01 99** 98 97 96 95 90.

CH. LA LOUVIÈRE *Pessac-Léognan AC, Bordeaux, France* The star of PESSAC-LEOGNAN's non-classified estates, its reputation almost entirely due to André Lurton. Well-structured reds★ and fresh, Sauvignon-based whites★★ are excellent value. Best years: (reds) 2005 04 03 **02 01 00** 99 98 96 95 90 89 88; (whites) **2005 04 03** 02 01 00 99 98 96 95 94.

STEFANO LUBIANA *Tasmania, Australia* One of the new stars of the Tasmanian wine scene. Vintage★ and non-vintage★ sparkling wines rank with the best in Australia. Chardonnay★ is restrained and elegant, Sauvignon Blanc shows greengage and passionfruit characters, while the Pinot Noir★ has weight, concentration and a velvety texture.

LUGANA DOC *Lombardy, Italy* Dry white (occasionally sparkling) from the Trebbiano di Lugana grape. Well-structured wines from the better producers can develop excitingly over a few years. Best producers: Ca' dei Frati★★, Ottella★, Provenza★, Visconti★, Zenato★, Fratelli Zeni.

LUJÁN DE CUYO *Mendoza, Argentina* The first DO in Argentina, declared in 1989, with an average altitude of 1000m (3200ft), Luján de Cuyo's reputation lies in its magnificent old Malbec vines. Best producers: Luigi BOSCA★, CATENA★★, Cobos★, Fabre Montmayou/DOMAINE VISTALBA★, Dominio del Plata★, Finca la Anita, TERRAZAS DE LOS ANDES★★, WEINERT★.

LUNGAROTTI *Torgiano DOC, Umbria, Italy* Leading producer of TORGIANO. The Torgiano Riserva (Vigna Monticchio★★) is DOCG. Also makes red San Giorgio★ (Cabernet-Sangiovese) and Chardonnay Palazzi★.

LUSSAC-ST-ÉMILION AC *Bordeaux, France* Much of the wine from this AC, which tastes like a lighter ST-EMILION, is made by the first-rate local co-op and should be drunk within 4 years of the vintage; certain properties are worth seeking out. Best producers: Barbe-Blanche★, Bel-Air, Bellevue, Courlat★, la Grenière, Lussac★, Lyonnat★, Mayne Blanc, des Rochers★. Best years: 2005 **03 01 00 98 96 95 90**.

EMILIO LUSTAU *Jerez y Manzanilla DO, Andalucía, Spain* Specializes in supplying 'own-label' wines to supermarkets. Quality is generally good, and there are some real stars at the top, especially the Almacenista range★★: very individual sherries from small, private producers.

CH. LYNCH-BAGES *Pauillac AC, 5ème Cru Classé, Haut-Médoc, Bordeaux, France* I am a great fan of Lynch-Bages red★★★ – with its almost succulent richness, its gentle texture and its starburst of flavours, all butter, blackcurrants and mint – and it is now one of PAUILLAC's most popular wines. No longer underpriced but it's still worth the money. Impressive at 5 years, beautiful at 10 and irresistible at 20. Second wine: Haut-Bages-Averous. White wine: Blanc de Lynch-Bages★. Best years: (reds) 2005 04 03 02 **01 00 99 98 96 95 94 90 89 88 86 85 83 82**.

LE MACCHIOLE *Bolgheri, Tuscany, Italy* Eugenio Campolmi died prematurely in 2002, having established Le Macchiole as one of the leading quality estates of the new TUSCANY. Mainstay is Paleo Rosso★★, a pure Cabernet (from 2001 100% Cabernet Franc). Best known is the Merlot Messorio★★, while Scrio★★ is one of the best Syrahs in Italy. Best years: (2006) (04) 03 **01 00 99 98 97 96 95.**

MÂCON AC *Mâconnais, Burgundy, France* The basic Mâconnais AC, but most whites in the region are labelled under the superior MACON-VILLAGES AC. The wines are rarely exciting. Chardonnay-based Mâcon Blanc, especially, is a rather expensive basic quaffer. Drink young. Mâcon Supérieur has a slightly higher minimum alcohol level. Best producers: Bertillonnes, Bruyère, DUBOEUF, LAFON★.

MÂCON-VILLAGES AC *Mâconnais, Burgundy, France* Mâcon-Villages should be an enjoyable, fruity, fresh wine for everyday drinking, but because it is made from Chardonnay, the wines are often overpriced. The name can be used by 43 villages, which may also append their own name, as in Mâcon-Lugny. Co-ops dominate production. Best villages: Chaintré, Chardonnay, Charnay, Clessé, Davayé, Igé, Lugny, Prissé, la Roche Vineuse, St-Gengoux-de-Scissé, Uchizy, Viré. Best producers: D & M Barraud★★, A Bonhomme★★, Bret Brothers★★, Deux Roches★, E Gillet★, la Greffière★★, Guillot-Broux★★, LAFON★, J-J Litaud★, Jean Manciat★, O Merlin★★, R Michel★, Rijckaert★, Robert-Denogent★★, Saumaize-Michelin★, J Thévenet★★, Valette★, VERGET★★, J-J Vincent★. Best years: (2006) **05 04 03 02**. See also VIRE-CLESSE.

MACULAN *Breganze DOC, Veneto, Italy* Fausto Maculan makes an impressive range under the Breganze DOC, led by Cabernet-Merlot blend Fratta★★ and Cabernet Palazzotto★, along with excellent reds★★ and whites★★ from the Ferrata vineyards. Even more impressive are sweet Torcolato★★ and outstanding Acininobili★★★, made mainly from botrytized Vespaiolo grapes.

MADEIRA DOC *Madeira, Portugal* The subtropical holiday island of
Madeira seems an unlikely place to find a serious wine. However,
Madeiras are very serious indeed and the best can survive to a great
age. Modern Madeira was shaped by the oïdium epidemic of the
1850s, which wiped out the vineyards, and phylloxera, which struck
in the 1870s. Replantation was with hybrid, non-vinifera vines
greatly inferior to the 'noble' and traditional Malvasia (or Malmsey),
Boal (or Bual), Verdelho and Sercial varieties. There are incentives to
replant the hybrids with European varieties, but progress is slow, and
most of the replantations are of the red Tinta Negra. The typically
burnt, tangy taste of inexpensive Madeira comes from *estufagem*,
heating in huge vats, but modern controls give better flavours than
used to be possible. The best wines are aged naturally in the
subtropical warmth. All except dry wines are fortified early on and
may be sweetened with fortified grape juice before bottling. Basic
3-year-old Madeira is made mainly from Tinta Negra, whereas
higher-quality 10-year-old, 15-year-old and vintage wines (from a
single year, aged in cask for at least 20 years) tend to be made from
1 of the 4 'noble' grapes. Colheita is an early-bottled vintage Madeira,
which can be released after spending 5 years in wood (7 years for
Sercial). Best producers: Barbeito, Barros e Souza, H M Borges,
HENRIQUES & HENRIQUES, Vinhos Justino Henriques, MADEIRA WINE COMPANY,
Pereira d'Oliveira.

MADEIRA WINE COMPANY *Madeira DOC, Madeira, Portugal* This
company ships more than half of all Madeira exported in bottle.
Among the brand names are Blandy's, Cossart Gordon, Leacock and
Miles. Now controlled by the Symington family from the mainland.
Big improvements are taking place in 5-, 10- and 15-year-old wines,
including a tasty 5-year-old (a blend of Malvasia and Bual) called
Alvada★. The vintage wines★★★ are superb. Specially blended 'early
release' colheita wines are surprisingly tasty and complete.

MADIRAN AC *South-West France* The gentle hills of Vic-Bilh, north of
Pau, have seen a steady revival of the Madiran AC. Several of the best
producers use new oak and micro-oxygenation, which helps to soften
the rather aggressive wine, based on the tannic Tannat grape – if
you'll lucky, you'll taste damsons and bitter chocolate. Best
producers: Aydie★★, Barréjat★, Berthoumieu★, Bouscassé★★/MONTUS,
Capmartin★, CHAPELLE LENCLOS★★, du Crampilh★, Cave de Crouseilles,
Laffitte-Teston★, MONTUS★★, Producteurs PLAIMONT, PRIMO PALATUM★,
Viella★. Best years: 2004 03 02 **01 00 98 97 96**.

CH. MAGDELAINE★ *St-Émilion Grand Cru AC, 1er Grand Cru Classé,
Bordeaux, France* Dark, rich, aggressive wines, yet with a load of
luscious fruit and oaky spice. In lighter years the wine has a gushing,
easy, tender fruit and can be enjoyed at 5–10 years. Owned by the
quality-conscious company of MOUEIX. Best years: 2005 04 **03 02 01 00
99 98 96 95 90 89 88 85 82**.

MAIPO, VALLE DEL *Valle Central, Chile* Birthplace of the Chilean wine
industry and increasingly encroached upon by Chile's capital,
Santiago. Cabernet is king and many of Chile's premium-priced reds
come from here. Good Chardonnay is produced from vineyards close
to the Andes. Best producers: ALMAVIVA★★★, Antiyal★★, CARMEN★★,
CONCHA Y TORO★★, Cousiño Macul, DE MARTINO★, El Principal★★,
ERRAZURIZ (Viñedo Chadwick★★★), Haras de Pirque★★, Porta★, QUEBRADA
DE MACUL★★, SANTA RITA★, TARAPACA.

191

MAJELLA *Coonawarra, South Australia* The Lynn family are long-term grapegrowers turned successful winemakers. A trademark lush, sweet vanillin oakiness to the reds is always balanced by dense, opulent fruit. The profound Malleea★★★ (Cabernet-Shiraz) is the flagship, while the Cabernet Sauvignon★★★ (a succulent, fleshy cassis bomb) and Shiraz★★ are almost as good and very reasonably priced; the Musician★★ (Cabernet-Shiraz) is an early-drinking bargain.

MÁLAGA DO *Andalucía, Spain* Málaga is a curious blend of sweet wine, alcohol and juices; production is dwindling. The label generally states colour and sweetness. The best are intensely nutty, raisiny and caramelly. A 'sister' appellation, Sierras de Málaga, was created in 2001 to include wineries outside the city limits of Málaga and non-fortified wines. Best producers: Gomara★, López Hermanos★★, Ordóñez★★, Telmo RODRIGUEZ★, Friedrich Schatz★.

CH. MALARTIC-LAGRAVIÈRE★ *Pessac-Léognan AC, Cru Classé de Graves, Bordeaux, France* A change of ownership in 1997 and massive investment in the vineyard and cellars have seen a steady improvement here since the 98 vintage. The tiny amount of white★★ is made from 100% Sauvignon Blanc and usually softens after 3–4 years into a lovely nutty wine. Best years: (reds) 2005 04 03 **02 01 00 99 98 96 90 89**; (whites) **2005 04 03 02 01 99**.

MALBEC A red grape, rich in tannin and flavour, from South-West France. A major ingredient in CAHORS wines, where it is known as Auxerrois, it is also planted in the LOIRE where it is called Côt. However, it is at its best in Chile and especially in Argentina, where it produces lush-textured, ripe, perfumed, damsony reds. In California, Australia and New Zealand it sometimes appears in BORDEAUX-style blends. In South Africa it is used both in blends and for varietal wines.

CH. MALESCOT ST-EXUPÉRY★ *Margaux AC, 3ème Cru Classé, Haut-Médoc, Bordeaux, France* Once one of the most scented, exotic reds in Bordeaux, a model of perfumed MARGAUX. In the 1980s Malescot lost its reputation as the wine became pale, dilute and uninspired, but since 1995 it has begun to rediscover that cassis and violet perfume and return to its former glory. Can reach ★★, for example in 2004. Best years: 2005 04 03 02 **01 00 99 98 96 95 90**.

MALVASIA This grape, probably of Greek origin, is widely planted in Italy and is found in many guises, both white and red. In Friuli, it is known as the Malvasia Istriana and produces light, fragrant wines of great charm, while in TUSCANY, UMBRIA and the rest of central Italy it is used to improve the blend for wines like ORVIETO and FRASCATI. On the islands, Malvasia is used in the production of rich, dry or sweet wines in Bosa and Cagliari (in SARDINIA) and in Lipari off the coast of SICILY to make really tasty, apricotty sweet wines. As a black grape, Malvasia Nera is blended with Negroamaro in southern PUGLIA and with Sangiovese in CHIANTI. Variants of Malvasia also grow in Spain and mainland Portugal. On the island of MADEIRA it produces sweet, varietal fortified wine, usually known by its English name: Malmsey.

LA MANCHA DO *Castilla-La Mancha, Spain* Spain's vast central plateau is Europe's biggest delimited wine area. Since 1995, DO regulations have allowed for irrigation and the planting of new, higher-quality grape varieties, including Viura, Chardonnay, Cabernet Sauvignon, Merlot and Syrah – and also banned new plantings of the simple white Airén grape. Whites are rarely (see AIRÉN) exciting but nowadays are often fresh and attractive. Reds can be light and fruity, or richer. To the east, the top-notch red wine regions of Ribera del Júcar and Uclés have now seceded from La Mancha, to form their own DOs. Best producers: Ayuso, Vinícola de Castilla (Castillo de Alhambra, Señorío de Guadianeja★), Blas Muñoz★, Rodriguez & Berger (Santa Elena), Torres Filoso (Arboles de Castillejo★), Casa de la Viña.

DOM. ALBERT MANN *Alsace AC, Alsace, France* Powerful, flavoursome and ageworthy wines from a range of Grand Cru vineyards, including intense, mineral Rieslings from Furstentum★★ and Schlossberg★★ and rich Furstentum Gewurztraminer★★. Impressive range of Pinot Gris culminates in some astonishingly concentrated Sélections de Grains Nobles★★★. Basic wines are increasingly stylish. Best years: (Sélection de Grains Nobles Gewurztraminer) 2005 **01 00 98 97 94 89**.

MARANGES AC *Côte de Beaune, Burgundy, France* AC right at the southern tip of the CÔTE DE BEAUNE. Slightly tough red wines of medium depth which are mainly sold as CÔTE DE BEAUNE-VILLAGES. Less than 5% of production is white. Best producers: B Bachelet★, M Charleux★, Contat-Grangé★, DROUHIN, GIRARDIN★. Best years: (reds) (2006) 05 **03 02 99**.

MARCASSIN *Sonoma County, California, USA* Helen Turley focuses on cool-climate Chardonnay and Pinot Noir. Incredible depth and restrained power are the hallmarks here. Tiny quantities of single-vineyard Chardonnays (Alexander Mountain Upper Barn, Three Sisters Vineyard, Marcassin Vineyard) and Pinot Noirs (Marcassin Vineyard, Blue Slide Vineyard) often rank ★★★. Best years: (2004) 03 02 01 **00 99 98 97 96 95**.

MARCHE *Italy* Adriatic region producing increasingly good reds from Montepulciano and Sangiovese, led by ROSSO CONERO and ROSSO PICENO. Good international varietals such as Cabernet, Chardonnay and Merlot under the Marche IGT are becoming more common, as well as blends with the native grapes. Best of the reds are Boccadigabbia's Akronte★★ (Cabernet), Oasi degli Angeli's Kurni★★ (Montepulciano), Monte Schiavo's Adeodato★★ (Montepulciano), Umani Ronchi's Pelago★★ (Montepulciano-Cabernet-Merlot), La Monacesca's Camerte★★ (Sangiovese-Merlot) and Le Terrazze's Chaos★★ (Montepulciano-Merlot-Syrah). However, the truly original wines here are whites based on VERDICCHIO, from Bucci, Colonnara, Coroncino, Garofoli, La Monacesca, Monte Schiavo, Sartarelli, Umani Ronchi.

MARCILLAC AC *South-West France* Strong, dry red wines (and a little rosé), largely made from a local grape, Fer. The reds are rustic but full of fruit and should be drunk at 2–5 years old. Best producers: Cros/Philippe Teulier, Laurens, Marcillac-Vallon co-op, Jean-Luc Matha.

MAREMMA *Tuscany, Italy* The name given to the Tuscan Tyrrhenian coast, notably the southern part, which was only discovered wine-wise in the early 1970s, thanks to SASSICAIA. DOCs include (south to north): Capalbio, Parrina, Bianco di Pitigliano, MORELLINO DI SCANSANO, Montecucco, Monteregio di Massa Marittima, Val de Cornia, BOLGHERI. And of course there's IGT Maremma Toscana. In these climes, compared with inland, Sangiovese comes softer and jammier, the BORDEAUX grapes thrive and vintages count for much less.

MARGARET RIVER *Western Australia* Planted on the advice of agronomist John Gladstones from the late 1960s, this coastal region quickly established its name as a leading area for Cabernet, with marvellously deep, BORDEAUX-like structured reds. Now Chardonnay, concentrated and opulent, vies with Cabernet for top spot, but there is also fine grassy Semillon, often blended with citrus-zest Sauvignon. Increasingly popular Shiraz provides the occasional gem, but there's too much dull stuff. Best producers: Brookland Valley★★, CAPE MENTELLE★★, CULLEN★★★, Devil's Lair★★, EVANS & TATE★, Gralyn★, HOWARD PARK★★, LEEUWIN ESTATE★★★, MOSS WOOD★★★, PIERRO★★, SANDALFORD★★, Suckfizzle★★, VASSE FELIX★, VOYAGER ESTATE★★, Woodlands★. Best years: (Cabernet-based reds) 2005 04 03 02 **01 00 99 98 96 95 94 91 90**.

MARGAUX AC *Haut-Médoc, Bordeaux, France* AC centred on the village of Margaux but including Soussans, Cantenac, Labarde and Arsac. Gravel banks dotted through the vineyards mean the wines are rarely heavy and should have a divine perfume after 7–12 years. Best producers: (Classed Growths) Boyd-Cantenac, BRANE-CANTENAC★★, Dauzac★, FERRIERE★★, Giscours★, ISSAN★, KIRWAN★, LASCOMBES, MALESCOT ST-EXUPERY★, MARGAUX★★★, PALMER★★, PRIEURE-LICHINE★, RAUZAN-SEGLA★★, Tertre★; (others) ANGLUDET★, Bel-Air Marquis d'Aligre★, Eyrins★, la Gurgue★, LABEGORCE-ZEDE★, Monbrison★, SIRAN★. Best years: 2005 04 **03** 02 **01 00 99 96 95**.

CH. MARGAUX★★★ *Margaux AC, 1er Cru Classé, Haut-Médoc, Bordeaux, France* Frequently the greatest wine in the MEDOC. Has produced almost flawless wines since 1978, and inspired winemaker Paul Pontallier continues to produce the best from this great *terroir*. Also some delicious white, Pavillon Blanc★★, from Sauvignon Blanc, but it must be the most expensive BORDEAUX AC wine by a mile. Second wine: Pavillon Rouge★★. Best years: (reds) 2005 04 03 02 01 00 **99 98 96 95 94 93 90 89 88 86 85 83**; (whites) **2005 04 02 01 00 99 98 96 95**.

MARIAH *Mendocino Ridge AVA, Mendocino County, California, USA* Boutique winery producing Zinfandel from a vineyard at 600m (2000ft) overlooking the Pacific Ocean. The wines have cherry fruit and naturally high acidity. Mariah Vineyard Zinfandel★★ is the flagship; Poor Ranch★ is lighter but elegant. A tiny amount of fruit-forward Syrah★ is also made. Best years: (Zinfandel) 2002 **01 00 99**.

MARLBOROUGH *South Island, New Zealand* Marlborough, a wide, flat, pebbly plain around the town of Blenheim, has enjoyed such spectacular success as a quality wine region that it is difficult to imagine that the first commercial vines were planted as recently as 1973. Marlborough is now home to more than half the country's vines. Its long, cool and relatively dry ripening season, cool nights and free-draining stony soils are the major assets. Its snappy, aromatic Sauvignon Blanc first brought the region fame worldwide. Fine-flavoured Chardonnay, steely Riesling, elegant CHAMPAGNE-method fizz and luscious botrytized wines are other successes. Pinot Noir is now establishing a strong regional identity. Best producers: Cape Campbell★, CELLIER LE BRUN, Clifford Bay★, CLOUDY BAY★★, The Crossings★, Dog Point★, Forrest Estate★★, Foxes Island★, FROMM★★, HUNTER'S★, ISABEL★★, JACKSON ESTATE★, Lawson's Dry Hills★, MONTANA, Nautilus★, SAINT CLAIR★★, SERESIN★, Stoneleigh★, VAVASOUR★★, VILLA MARIA★★, WITHER HILLS★★. Best years: (Chardonnay) (2006) **05 03 01**; (Pinot Noir) (2006) **05 04 03 01 00 99 98**; (Sauvignon Blanc) **2006 04 03**.

MARQUÉS DE CÁCERES *Rioja DOCa, Rioja, Spain* Go-ahead RIOJA winery making crisp, aromatic, modern whites★ and rosés★, and fleshy, fruity reds (Reservas★) with the emphasis on aging in bottle, not barrel. There is also a luxury red, Gaudium★. Best years: (reds) 2003 **01 99 98 96 95 94 92 91 90 89 87 85 82**.

MARQUÉS DE GRIÑÓN *Castilla-La Mancha, Spain* From his estate at Malpica, near Toledo, now with its own Dominio de Valdepusa DO, Carlos Falcó (the eponymous Marqués) produces some sensational wines: Dominio de Valdepusa Cabernet Sauvignon★★, Petit Verdot★★, Syrah★★ and the top wine, Eméritus★★, a blend of the 3 varieties. A new Graciano★★ vineyard went into production in 2005, with stunning results. The joint venture with the Arco/BERBERANA group, which developed the Marqués de Griñón wines from RIOJA, is now being phased out. Best years: (Eméritus) 2003 02 **01 00 99 98**.

MARQUÉS DE MURRIETA *Rioja DOCa, Rioja, Spain* The RIOJA bodega that most faithfully preserves the traditional style of long aging. The splendidly ornate Castillo de Ygay★★ label now includes wines other than Gran Reserva. There's a more modern-styled, upmarket cuvée, Dalmau★, and in some vintages a delicious varietal Mazuelo★. Whites are dauntingly oaky, reds packed with savoury mulberry fruit. Best years: (reds) 2004 03 **01 00 99 96 95 94 92 91 89 87 85 68 64**.

MARQUÉS DE RISCAL *Rioja DOCa, País Vasco and Rueda DO, Castilla y León, Spain* A producer which has restored its reputation for classic pungent RIOJA reds (Reserva★). Expensive, Cabernet-based Barón de Chirel★ is made only in selected years. Increasingly aromatic RUEDA whites★. Best years: (Barón de Chirel) 2001 **96 95 94**.

MARSALA DOC *Sicily, Italy* Fortified wines, once as esteemed as sherry or Madeira. A taste of an old Vergine (unsweetened) Marsala, fine and complex, will show why. Today most is sweetened. Purists say this mars its delicate nuances, but DOC regulations allow for sweetening Fine and Superiore versions. Best producers: DE BARTOLI★★, Florio (Baglio Florio★, Terre Arse★), Pellegrino (Soleras★, Riserva 1962★).

MARSANNAY AC *Côte de Nuits, Burgundy, France* Village almost in Dijon, best known for its pleasant but quite austere rosé. Reds are much better, frequently one of Burgundy's most fragrant wines. Best producers: Audoin★, P Charlopin★★, B CLAIR★★, Fougeray de Beauclair★, Geantet-Pansiot★★, JADOT★, MEO-CAMUZET★, D MORTET★★, J & J-L Trapet★. Best years: (reds) (2006) 05 **03 02**.

MARSANNE Undervalued grape yielding rich, nutty, long-lived wines in the northern Rhône (HERMITAGE, CROZES-HERMITAGE, ST-JOSEPH and ST-PERAY), often with the more lively Roussanne. Also used in southern Rhône, PIC ST-LOUP and other Languedoc wines, and performs well in Australia at Mitchelton and TAHBILK. As Ermitage, it produces some good wines in Swiss VALAIS.

MARTINBOROUGH *North Island, New Zealand* A cool, dry climate, free-draining soil and a passion for quality are this region's greatest assets. Mild autumn weather promotes intense flavours balanced by good acidity in all varieties: top Pinot Noir and complex Chardonnay, intense Cabernet, full Sauvignon Blanc and honeyed Riesling. Best producers: ATA RANGI★★, CRAGGY RANGE★, DRY RIVER★★★, Escarpment★, MARTINBOROUGH VINEYARD★★, Murdoch James★, Nga Waka★, PALLISER ESTATE★★, Te Kairanga★. Best years: (Pinot Noir) (2006) **03 01 00**.

MARTINBOROUGH VINEYARD *Martinborough, North Island, New Zealand*
Famous for Pinot Noir★★ but also makes impressive Chardonnay★, spicy Riesling★, creamy Pinot Gris★ and luscious botrytized styles★★ when vintage conditions allow. Winemaker Claire Mulholland has brought added elegance to the often-blockbuster wines of this high-flying producer. Best years: (Pinot Noir) (2006) **03 01 00**.

MARTÍNEZ BUJANDA *Rioja DOCa, País Vasco, Spain* Family-owned firm that makes some of the best modern RIOJA. Whites and rosés are young and crisp, reds★ are full of fruit *and* age well. The single-vineyard Finca Valpiedra★ is a major newcomer. The family has now purchased a large estate in La MANCHA, Finca Antigua. Best years: (reds) 2005 04 03 **01 98 96 95 94 92 91 90 87 86 85**.

MARZEMINO This red grape of northern Italy's TRENTINO province makes deep-coloured, plummy and zesty reds that are best drunk within 3–5 years. Best producers: Battistotti★, La Cadalora★, Cavit★, Concilio Vini★, Isera co-op★, Letrari★, Mezzacorona, Eugenio Rosi★, Simoncelli★, Spagnolli★, De Tarczal★, Vallarom★, Vallis Agri★.

DOM. DU MAS BLANC *Banyuls AC, Roussillon, France* Run by the Parcé family, this estate makes great traditional BANYULS, specializing in the *rimage* (early-bottled vintage) style. La Coume★★ is the top name in this range. Jean-Michel Parcé also makes traditional-style red COLLIOURE★★. Best years: 2003 01 **00 98 96**.

MAS BRUGUIÈRE *Pic St-Loup, Coteaux du Languedoc AC, Languedoc, France* One of the top domaines in PIC ST-LOUP. The basic red★ has rich, spicy Syrah character, while La Grenadière★★ develops buckets of black fruit and spice after 3 years. Super-cuvée Le Septième★★ (seventh generation) is a blend of Mourvèdre with some Grenache. Calcadiz is an easy-drinking red from young vines. Aromatic, fruity and refreshingly crisp Roussanne white Les Mûriers★. Best years: (reds) 2004 03 **01 00 99**.

MAS LA CHEVALIÈRE *Vin de Pays d'Oc, Languedoc, France* State-of-the-art winery created by Chablis producer Michel LAROCHE in the early 1990s. Innovative wines include La Croix Chevalière★, a blend of Syrah, Grenache and Mourvèdre, and Mas la Chevalière Rouge★, from the estate vineyard. Also new range of inexpensive varietals. Best years: 2003 **01 00 99 98**.

MAS DE DAUMAS GASSAC *Vin de Pays de l'Hérault, Languedoc, France* Aimé Guibert proves that the HERAULT, normally associated with cheap table wine, can produce fine, ageworthy reds. The tannic yet rich Cabernet Sauvignon-based red★ and Réserve de Gassac★★ and the lush, scented white★ (Viognier, Chardonnay, Petit Manseng and Chenin)

are impressive, if expensive. Sweet Vin de Laurance★★ is a triumph. Best years: (reds) 2005 **04** 03 02 **01 00 99 98 97 96 95 94**.

MAS DOIX *Priorat DOCa, Cataluña, Spain* The Doix and Llagostera families own some extraordinary old Garnacha and Cariñena vineyards, which provide the grapes for some equally impressive wines. Doix Vinyes Velles★★★ is probably the first of the new generation PRIORATS to reach the heights of the pioneers such as CLOS ERASMUS, CLOS MOGADOR and Alvaro PALACIOS' L'Ermita. Best years: (2005) 04 03 **02 01**.

MAS JULLIEN *Coteaux du Languedoc AC, Languedoc, France* Olivier Jullien makes fine wines in the COTEAUX DU LANGUEDOC. The red Mas Jullien generally rates ★★, while the États d'Ame★ is more forward and fruit driven. White Les Vignes Oubliées★ is also good stuff. Best years: (reds) 2004 03 02 **01 00 99**.

BARTOLO MASCARELLO *Barolo DOCG, Piedmont, Italy* One of the great producers of BAROLO★★★, Bartolo Mascarello died in 2005; his daughter Maria Teresa has run the winery since the early 1990s. Though proudly traditional, the wines have an exquisite perfume and balance. The Dolcetto★ and Barbera★ can need a little time to soften. Best years: (Barolo) (2006) (04) (03) 01 00 **99 98 97** 96 **95 93 90 89 88 86 85 82 78**.

GIUSEPPE MASCARELLO *Barolo DOCG, Piedmont, Italy* The old house of Giuseppe Mascarello (now run by grandson Mauro) is renowned for dense, vibrant Dolcetto d'Alba (Bricco★★) and intense Barbera (Codana★★), but the pride of the house is BAROLO from the Monprivato★★★ vineyard. A little is now produced as a Riserva, Cà d'Morissio★★★, in top years. Small amounts are also made from the Bricco, Santo Stefano di Perno and Villero vineyards. Best years: (Monprivato) (2006) (04) (03) 01 00 **99 98 97** 96 **95 93 91 90 89 88 85 82 78**.

MASI *Veneto, Italy* Family firm, one of the driving forces in VALPOLICELLA. Brolo di Campofiorin★ (effectively if not legally a *ripasso* Valpolicella) is worth looking out for, as is AMARONE (Mazzano★★ and Campolongo di Torbe★★). Valpolicella's Corvina grape is also used in red blends Toar★ and Osar★. The wines of Serègo Alighieri★★ are also produced by Masi. Best years (Amarone): (2006) (04) 03 01 00 **97 95 93 90**.

MASTROBERARDINO *Campania, Italy* This family firm has long flown the flag for CAMPANIA in southern Italy, though it has now been joined by others. Best known for red TAURASI★★ and white Greco di Tufo★ and Fiano di Avellino★. Best years: (Taurasi Radici) (2006) (05) 04 03 **01 99 97** 96 **95 93 90 89 88 85 68**.

MATANZAS CREEK *Bennett Valley AVA, Sonoma County, California, USA* Sauvignon Blanc★★ is taken seriously here, and it shows in a complex, zesty wine; Chardonnay★★ is rich and toasty but not overblown. Merlot★★ has silky, mouthfilling richness. Limited-edition Journey Chardonnay★★ and Merlot★★ are opulent but pricey. Owned by Jess Jackson (of KENDALL-JACKSON). Best years: (Chardonnay) 2005 04 **03 02 01 00 99 98 97**; (Merlot) 2004 03 02 **01 00 99 97 96 95**.

MATETIC VINEYARDS *San Antonio Valley, Chile* Matetic has been producing high-quality wines from the SAN ANTONIO VALLEY – especially under the EQ label – since it burst on to the scene in 2001. Exceptional, concentrated and scented Syrah★★ is the star, but there's also a fleshy Pinot Noir★ and superripe Sauvignon Blanc★.

MATUA VALLEY *Auckland, North Island, New Zealand* In 2001 Matua became part of Beringer-Blass (now Foster's Group), with the consequent introduction of an uninspired budget range. Top wines are still good, with whites more consistent than reds: sensuous, scented Ararimu Chardonnay★★; lush, strongly varietal Gewürztraminer★; tangy MARLBOROUGH Sauvignon Blanc★; fine Merlot★; and Ararimu★, a blend of Cabernet Sauvignon, Merlot and occasionally Syrah. Second label: Shingle Peak. Best years: (Ararimu red) 2004 **02 00 98 96**.

CH. MAUCAILLOU★ *Moulis AC, Cru Bourgeois, Haut-Médoc, Bordeaux, France* Maucaillou shows that you don't have to be a Classed Growth to make high-quality claret. Expertly made by the Dourthe family, it is soft but classically flavoured. It is accessible early on but ages well for 10–12 years. Best years: 2005 **03 02 00 98 96 95 90 89**.

MAULE, VALLE DEL *Valle Central, Chile* The most southerly sub-region of Chile's CENTRAL VALLEY, with wet winters and a large day/night temperature difference. Nearly 30% of Chile's vines are planted here, with nearly 10,000ha (25,000 acres) of Cabernet Sauvignon. Merlot does well on the cool clay soils, and there is some tasty Carmenère and Syrah. Whites are mostly Chardonnay and Sauvignon Blanc. A new and exciting community of producers has recently been redefining Maule's identity, with Calina, Terra Noble, Casa Donoso, Gillmore and Reserva de Caliboro among them, and there's a feeling that Maule's old 'bulk' mentality must give way to a quality focus if the area's great potential is to be realized. Best producers: J Bouchon, Calina★ (KENDALL-JACKSON), Casa Donoso, Terra Noble.

MAURO *Castilla y León, Spain* After making a name for himself as VEGA SICILIA's winemaker for 30 years, Mariano García has propelled his family's estate to the forefront in Spain and abroad. Wines include Crianza★★, Vendimia Seleccionada★★ and Terreus★★★. Best years: (2005) 04 03 **02 01 00 99 98 97 96 95 94**.

MAURY AC *Roussillon, France* A *vin doux naturel* made mainly from Grenache Noir. This strong, sweetish wine can be made in either a young, fresh style (vintage) or the locally revered old *rancio* style. Best producers: la Coume du Roy★, Mas Amiel★★, Maury co-op★, Maurydoré★, la Pleiade★.

MAXIMIN GRÜNHAUS *Grünhaus, Ruwer, Germany* One of Germany's great wine estates. Dr Carl von Schubert vinifies separately the wines of his 2 top vineyards (Abtsberg and Herrenberg), both of monastic origin. He makes chiefly dry and medium-dry wines of great subtlety. In good vintages the wines are certainly ★★★ and are among the most long-lived white wines in the world. Best years: (2006) 05 04 03 **01 00 99 97 95 94 93 92 90 89 88 85 83**.

MAZIS-CHAMBERTIN AC See CHAMBERTIN AC.

MAZOYÈRES-CHAMBERTIN AC See CHAMBERTIN AC.

McLAREN VALE *South Australia* Sunny maritime region south of Adelaide, producing full-bodied wines from Chardonnay, Sauvignon Blanc, Shiraz, Grenache and Cabernet. More than 60 small wineries, plus big boys HARDY and the Foster's Wine Group. Best producers: Cascabel, CHAPEL HILL★★, CLARENDON HILLS★★, Coriole★, D'ARENBERG★★, FOX CREEK★★, HARDY★★, Kangarilla Road★, Maxwell★, Geoff MERRILL★, Mitolo★★, Penny's Hill★, Pirramimma, ROSEMOUNT★, Tatachilla★, WIRRA WIRRA★★★.

McWILLIAM'S *Riverina, New South Wales, Australia* Large family winery, whose Hanwood Estate and JJ McWilliam brands are joint ventures with California's GALLO, delivering good flavours at a fair price. Best are the Mount Pleasant wines from the Lower HUNTER VALLEY: classic bottle-aged Semillons (Elizabeth★★★, Lovedale★★★), buttery Chardonnays★ and special-vineyard Shirazes – Old Paddock & Old Hill, Maurice O'Shea (★★ in the best years) and Rosehill★. Classy liqueur Muscat★★ from RIVERINA, and good table wines from HILLTOPS Barwang★ vineyard. Best years: (Elizabeth Semillon) (2006) (05) (04) (03) 02 01 **00 99 98 97 96 95 94 87 86 84 83 79**.

MÉDOC AC *Bordeaux, France* The Médoc peninsula north of Bordeaux on the left bank of the Gironde river produces a good fistful of the world's most famous reds. These are all situated in the HAUT-MÉDOC, the southern, more gravelly half of the area. The Médoc AC, for reds only, covers the northern part. Merlot dominates in these flat clay vineyards and the wines can be attractive in warm years: dry but juicy. Best at 3–5 years old. Best producers: Bournac★, Escurac★, les Grands Chênes★, Greysac★, Goulée★, L'Inclassable★, Loudenne, Lousteauneuf★, les Ormes-Sorbet★, Patache d'Aux, POTENSAC★, Preuillac, Ramafort★, Rollan-de-By★, la Tour-de-By★, la Tour-Haut-Caussan★, la Tour-St-Bonnet★, Vieux-Robin. Best years: 2005 **04 03 01 00 96 95**.

MEERLUST *Stellenbosch WO, South Africa* New cellarmaster Chris Williams is gradually putting his thoughtful stamp on the classic range from this venerable estate. Chardonnay★ is the earliest beneficiary, showing greater elegance and freshness; Rubicon★, one of the Cape's first BORDEAUX blends, remains complex; Merlot, refined and distinctive. A ripe Pinot Noir completes the range. Best years: (Rubicon) (2004) **03 01 00 99 98 97 96 95 94**; (Chardonnay) (2006) **05 04 03 01 00 99 98**.

ALPHONSE MELLOT *Sancerre AC, Loire Valley, France* Ambitious white and red SANCERRE, made with obsessive attention to detail by Alphonse 'Junior', the 19th generation of the family. The white cuvée La Moussière★ is unoaked, with fresh, intense citrus flavours; the oaked cuvée Edmond★★ needs a few years to mature to a fascinating rich flavour. Red and white Génération XIX★★ are outstanding, with a fine balance of fruit and oak. Since 2005, also makes aromatic, fruity Chardonnay and Pinot Noir, Les Pénitents, in neighbouring Vin de Pays des Coteaux Charitois. Best years: (Edmond) 2006 05 04 **03** 02 01 00 97.

CHARLES MELTON *Barossa Valley, South Australia* One of the leading lights in the renaissance of hand-crafted Shiraz, Grenache and Mourvèdre in the BAROSSA. Fruity Grenache rosé Rose of Virginia★, RHONE blend Nine Popes★★, heady, sumptuous Grenache★★, smoky Shiraz★★ and Sparkling Red★★ have all attained cult status. Cabernet Sauvignon is variable, but ★★ at best. Best years: (Nine Popes) (2006) (05) (04) 03 02 01 99 98 **96 95 94 91 90**.

MENDOCINO COUNTY *California, USA* The northernmost county of the North Coast AVA. It includes cool-climate ANDERSON VALLEY, excellent for sparkling wines and a little Pinot Noir; and the warmer Redwood Valley AVA, with good Zinfandel and Cabernet. Coro is a stylish Zinfandel-based blend made by numerous Mendocino wineries. Best producers: Brutocao★, FETZER, Fife★, Goldeneye★, HANDLEY★★, Husch, Lazy Creek★, McDowell Valley★, NAVARRO★★★, ROEDERER ESTATE★★, SCHARFFENBERGER CELLARS★. Best years: (reds) (2005) 04 03 **01 00 99 97 96 95 94 93 91 90**.

MENDOCINO RIDGE AVA *California, USA* Established in 1997, this is one of the most unusual AVAs in California. Mendocino Ridge starts out at an altitude of 365m (1200ft) on the timber-covered mountaintops of western MENDOCINO COUNTY. Because of the topography, the AVA is non-contiguous: rising above the fog, the vineyards are commonly referred to as 'islands in the sky'. Currently only 30ha (75 acres) are planted, primarily with Zinfandel. Best producers: Edmeades★, MARIAH★, Greenwood Ridge★, STEELE★★.

MERLOT

Red wine without tears. That's the reason Merlot has vaulted from being merely Bordeaux's red wine support act, well behind Cabernet Sauvignon in terms of class, to being the red wine drinker's darling, planted like fury all over the world. It is able to claim some seriousness and pedigree, but – crucially – can make wine of a fat, juicy character mercifully low in tannic bitterness, which can be glugged with gay abandon almost as soon as the juice has squirted from the press. Yet this doesn't mean that Merlot is the jelly baby of red wine grapes. Far from it.

WINE STYLES
Bordeaux Merlot The great wines of Pomerol and St-Émilion, on the Right Bank of the Dordogne, are largely based on Merlot and the best of these – for example, Château Pétrus, which is almost 100% Merlot – can mature for 20–30 years. In fact there is more Merlot than Cabernet Sauvignon planted throughout Bordeaux, and I doubt if there is a single red wine property that does not have some growing, because the variety ripens early, can cope with cool conditions and is able to bear a heavy crop of fruit. In a cool, damp area like Bordeaux, Cabernet Sauvignon cannot always ripen, so the soft, mellow character of Merlot is a fundamental component of the blend even in the best, Cabernet-dominated, Médoc estates, imparting a supple richness and approachability to the wines. Up-and-coming areas like Blaye and Côtes de Castillon depend on it.

Other European regions The south of France has briskly adopted the variety, producing easy-drinking, fruit-driven wines, but in the hot Languedoc the grape often ripens too fast to express its full personality and can seem a little simple, even raw-edged, unless handled well. Italy has long used very high-crop Merlot to produce a simple, light quaffer in the north, particularly in the Veneto, though Friuli and Alto Adige make fuller styles and there are some very impressive examples from Tuscany and as far south as Sicily. The Swiss canton of Ticino is often unjustly overlooked for its intensely fruity, oak-aged versions. Eastern Europe has the potential to provide fertile pastures for Merlot and so far the most convincing, albeit simple, styles have come from Hungary and Bulgaria: the younger examples are almost invariably better than the old. Spain has developed good Merlot credentials since the mid-1990s.

New World Youth is also important in the New World, nowhere more so than in Chile. Chilean Merlot, mostly blended with Carmenère, has leapt to the front of the pack of New World examples with gorgeous garnet-red wines of unbelievable crunchy fruit richness that cry out to be drunk virtually in their infancy. California Merlots often have more serious pretensions, but the nature of the grape is such that its soft, juicy quality still shines through. The cooler conditions in Washington State have produced some impressive wines, and the east coast of the US has produced good examples from places such as Long Island. With some French input, South Africa is starting to get Merlot right, and in New Zealand the warm, dry conditions of Hawkes Bay and Waiheke Island are producing classic styles. Only Australia seems to find Merlot problematic, but there are some fine exceptions from cooler areas, including some surprisingly good fizzes – red fizzes, that is!

BEST PRODUCERS

France
Bordeaux (St-Émilion) ANGELUS, AUSONE, BEAU-SEJOUR BECOT, Clos Fourtet, la Mondotte, TERTRE-ROTEBOEUF, TROPLONG-MONDOT, VALANDRAUD; (Pomerol) le BON PASTEUR, Certan-de-May, Clinet, la CONSEILLANTE, l'EGLISE-CLINET, l'EVANGILE, la FLEUR-PETRUS, GAZIN, LATOUR-A-POMEROL, PETIT-VILLAGE, PETRUS, le PIN, TROTANOY.

Other European Merlots
Italy (Friuli) Livio FELLUGA; (Tuscany) AMA, AVIGNONESI, Castelgiocondo (Lamaione), Ghizzano, Le MACCHIOLE, ORNELLAIA, Petrolo, San Giusto a Rentennano, TUA RITA; (Lazio) FALESCO; (Sicily) PLANETA.

Spain (Navarra) Nekeas; (Penedès) Can Ràfols dels Caus; (Somontano) ENATE.

Switzerland Gialdi (Sassi Grossi), Daniel Huber, La Capellaccia, Christian Zündel.

New World Merlots
USA (California) ARROWOOD, BERINGER, CHATEAU ST JEAN, DUCKHORN, MATANZAS CREEK, MERRYVALE, NEWTON, Pahlmeyer, Paloma, SHAFER, STERLING; (Washington) ANDREW WILL, LEONETTI, QUILCEDA CREEK, WOODWARD CANYON; (New York) BEDELL, LENZ.

Australia BRAND'S, CLARENDON HILLS, COLDSTREAM HILLS, Elderton, Heggies/YALUMBA, James Irvine, PARKER COONAWARRA ESTATE, PETALUMA, Tatachilla.

New Zealand CRAGGY RANGE, Esk Valley, GOLDWATER, Sacred Hill (Broken Stone), SILENI (Triangle), Trinity Hill, VILLA MARIA.

South Africa SAXENBURG, STEENBERG, THELEMA, VEENWOUDEN, VERGELEGEN.

Chile CARMEN, CASA LAPOSTOLLE (Cuvée Alexandre), CASABLANCA (Santa Isabel), CONCHA Y TORO, CONO SUR (20 Barrels).

201

MENDOZA *Argentina* The most important wine province in Argentina, accounting for around 80% of the country's wine. Situated in the eastern foothills of the Andes, Mendoza's bone-dry climate produces powerful, high-alcohol reds. Just south of Mendoza city, Maipú and LUJAN DE CUYO are ideal for Malbec, Syrah and Cabernet Sauvignon. High-altitude regions nearer the Andes, such as UCO VALLEY, produce better whites, particularly Chardonnay, but also thrilling reds. Best producers: ACHAVAL-FERRER★★, ALTOS LAS HORMIGAS★, Luigi BOSCA★, CATENA★★, Cobos★, Finca El Retiro★, O FOURNIER★★, Nieto Senetiner (Cadus★★), NORTON★, Salentein★, TERRAZAS DE LOS ANDES★★, Familia ZUCCARDI★.

MENETOU-SALON AC *Loire Valley, France* Extremely attractive, chalky-clean Sauvignon whites and cherry-fresh Pinot Noir reds and rosés from west of SANCERRE. Best producers: R Champault, Chatenoy★, Chavet★, J-P Gilbert★, P Jacolin, H Pellé★, J-M Roger★, J Teiller★, Tour St-Martin★.

MÉO-CAMUZET *Vosne-Romanée, Côte de Nuits, Burgundy, France* Super-quality estate, run by Jean-Nicolas Méo. New oak barrels and luscious, rich fruit combine in superb wines, which also age well. CLOS DE VOUGEOT★★★, RICHEBOURG★★★ and CORTON★★ are the grandest wines, along with the VOSNE-ROMANEE Premiers Crus, aux Brulées★★, Cros Parantoux★★★ and les Chaumes★★. Fine NUITS-ST-GEORGES aux Boudots★★ and aux Murgers★★, and now also some less expensive négociant wines. Best years: (2006) 05 04 03 02 **01 00 99 97 96 95 93 90**.

MERCUREY AC *Côte Chalonnaise, Burgundy, France* Most important of the 4 main COTE CHALONNAISE villages. The red is usually pleasant and strawberry-flavoured, sometimes rustic, and can take some aging. There is not much white, but I like its buttery, even spicy, taste. Best at 3–4 years old. Best producers: (reds) FAIVELEY★, E Juillot★, M Juillot★, Lorenzon★★, F Raquillet★★, RODET★, de Suremain★, de Villaine★★; (whites) FAIVELEY (Clos Rochette★), Genot-Boulanger★, M Juillot★, O LEFLAIVE★, Ch. de Chamirey★/RODET. Best years: (reds) (2006) 05 **03 02 01 99**.

MERLOT See pages 200–201.

GEOFF MERRILL *McLaren Vale, South Australia* High-profile winemaker with an instinctive feel for wine. There's a nicely bottle-aged Reserve Cabernet★ in a light, early-picked, slightly eccentric style, Reserve Shiraz★ (Henley Shiraz★★) and Chardonnay★ (Reserve★★). Also a moreish unoaked and ageworthy Bush Vine Grenache★★.

MERRYVALE *Napa Valley AVA, California, USA* A Chardonnay powerhouse (Reserve★★, Silhouette★), Starmont★), but reds are not far behind, with BORDEAUX-blend Profile★★ and juicy Reserve Merlot★★. Best years: (Chardonnay) (2005) 04 **03 02 01 00 99**.

MEURSAULT AC *Côte de Beaune, Burgundy, France* The biggest and most popular white wine village in the COTE D'OR. There are no Grands Crus, but a whole cluster of Premiers Crus, of which Perrières, Charmes and Genevrières stand out. The general standard is better than in neighbouring Puligny. The golden wine is lovely to drink young but better aged for 5–8 years. Virtually no Meursault red is now made. Best producers: R Ampeau★★, M BOUZEREAU★★, Boyer-Martenot★★, Coche-Bizouard★★, COCHE-DURY★★★, Deux MONTILLE★, DROUHIN★, A Ente★★★, J-P Fichet★★, V GIRARDIN★★, Grux★★, JADOT★★, P Javillier★★, François Jobard★★, Rémi Jobard★★, LAFON★★★,

Christophe Mary★★, Matrot★★, Pierre Morey★★, G Roulot★★★. Best years: (2006) 05 04 02 **01 00 99 97**.

CH. MEYNEY★ *St-Estèphe AC, Cru Bourgeois, Haut-Médoc, Bordeaux, France* One of the most reliable ST-ESTEPHES, producing broad-flavoured wine with dark, plummy fruit. Second wine: Prieur de Meyney. Best years: 2005 04 03 **02 01 00 99 98 96 95 94 90 89**.

PETER MICHAEL WINERY *Sonoma County, California, USA* British-born Sir Peter Michael has turned a country retreat into an impressive winery known for its small-batch wines. Les Pavots★★ is the estate red BORDEAUX blend, and Mon Plaisir★★ and Cuvée Indigène★ are his top Chardonnays, both noted for their deep, layered flavours. Best years: (Les Pavots) (2005) (04) 03 02 **01 00 99 97 96 95 94 91 90**.

MILLTON *Gisborne, North Island, New Zealand* Organic vineyard using biodynamic methods, whose top wines include the sophisticated Clos St Anne Chardonnay★★, botrytized Opou Vineyard Riesling★★ and complex barrel-fermented Chenin Blanc★. Chardonnays and Rieslings both age well. Best years: (whites) 2005 **04 02 00**.

MINER FAMILY VINEYARDS *Oakville AVA, California, USA* Dave Miner has 32ha (80 acres) planted on a ranch 300m (1000 ft) above the OAKVILLE valley floor. Highlights include yeasty, full-bodied Chardonnay★ (Oakville Ranch★★, Wild Yeast★★) as well as intense Merlot★★ and Cabernet Sauvignon★★ that demand a decade of aging. Also a stylish Viognier★★ and a striking Rosé★ from purchased fruit.

MINERVOIS AC *Languedoc, France* Attractive, mostly red wines from north-east of Carcassonne, made mainly from Syrah, Carignan and Grenache. The local co-ops produce good, juicy, quaffing wine at reasonable prices, but the best wines are made by the estates: full of ripe, red fruit and pine-dust perfume, for drinking young. It can age, especially if a little new oak has been used. A village denomination, La Livinière, covering 6 superior communes whose wines can be particularly scented and fine, can be appended to the Minervois label. Best producers: (reds) Aires Hautes★, Ch. Bonhomme★, Borie de Maurel★, CLOS CENTEILLES★★, Pierre Cros★, Fabas★, la Grave, HECHT & BANNIER★, Maris★, Oustal Blanc★, PRIMO PALATUM★, Pujol, Rieux, Senat★★, Ste-Eulalie★, TOUR BOISÉE★, Villerambert-Julien★. Best years: (2005) 04 **03 01 00 99 98**.

CH. LA MISSION-HAUT-BRION★★★ *Pessac-Léognan AC, Cru Classé de Graves, Bordeaux, France* Traditionally I have found la Mission long on power but short on grace, but in the difficult years of the 1990s it showed impressive consistency allied to challenging intensity and fragrance. Best years: 2005 04 03 02 **01** 00 **98 96 95 94 93 90 89 88 85**.

MISSION HILL *Okanagan Valley VQA, British Columbia, Canada* Recent expansion now allows Kiwi winemaker John Simes to process grapes from extensive holdings in the OKANAGAN VALLEY, which should please new consultant Michel Rolland. He has strengthened the red wines of late: excellent Chardonnay★★, Pinot Blanc★ and Pinot Grigio★ are joined by Merlot★, Cabernet Sauvignon, Pinot Noir and Shiraz★, and a red BORDEAUX-style blend, Oculus★★.

MITCHELL *Clare Valley, South Australia* Jane and Andrew Mitchell turn out some of CLARE VALLEY's most ageworthy Watervale Riesling★★ and a classy barrel-fermented Growers Semillon★. Growers Grenache★ is a huge unwooded and heady fruit bomb, if you're in the mood... Peppertree Shiraz★★ and Sevenhill Cabernet Sauvignon★ are plump, chocolaty and typical of the region.

MITTELRHEIN *Germany* Small (465ha/1150-acre), northerly wine region. Almost 70% of the wine here is Riesling, but the Mittelrhein has been in decline over the last few decades as the vineyard sites are steep and difficult to work. The best growers (like Toni JOST★, Perll★ and Weingart★), clustered around Bacharach and Boppard, make wines of a striking mineral tang and dry, fruity intensity. Best years: (2006) 05 04 **02 01 99 98**.

MOËT & CHANDON *Champagne AC, Champagne, France* Moët & Chandon dominates the CHAMPAGNE market (more than 25 million bottles a year), and has become a major producer of sparkling wine in California, Argentina, Brazil and Australia too. Non-vintage has started to exhibit distressing unreliability, and some recent releases have really not been acceptable. There has been a change of winemaker and hopefully this will put the vintage release at least back on track. Interestingly, the vintage rosé★★ can show a rare Pinot Noir floral fragrance. Dom Pérignon★★★ is the de luxe cuvée. It can be one of the greatest Champagnes of all, but you've got to age it for a number of years after release or you're wasting your money. Best years: (2000) 99 98 **96 95 90 88 86 85 82**.

MONBAZILLAC AC *South-West France* BERGERAC's leading sweet wine. Most is light, pleasant, but forgettable, from the efficient co-op. However, an increasing number of estates are making wines of a richness to approach SAUTERNES, and the ability to age 10 years too. Best producers: l'ANCIENNE CURE★, Bélingard (Blanche de Bosredon★), la Borderie★, Grande Maison★, Haut-Bernasse, Haut-Montlong (Grande Cuvée), Theulet★, Tirecul-la-Gravière★★, Les Verdots★, Treuil-de-Nailhac★. Best years: 2005 03 02 **01 99 98 97 96**.

CH. MONBOUSQUET★ *St-Émilion Grand Cru AC, Grand Cru Classé, Bordeaux, France* Gérard Perse, owner of Ch. PAVIE, has transformed this struggling estate on the Dordogne plain into one of ST-EMILION's 'super-crus'. The reward was promotion to Grand Cru Classé in 2006. Rich, voluptuous and very expensive, the wine is drinkable from 3–4 years but will age longer. Also a plush white Monbousquet★ (BORDEAUX AC). Best years: 2005 04 **03 02 01 00 99 98 97 96 95 94**.

ROBERT MONDAVI *Napa Valley, California, USA* A Californian institution, best known for open and fruity regular Cabernet Sauvignon★ and the Reserve Cabernet★★, possessing enormous depth and power. A regular★ and a Reserve★★ Pinot Noir are velvety smooth and supple wines with style, perfume and balance. For many years the Mondavi signature white was Fumé (Sauvignon Blanc) with ★ Reserve, but in recent years Chardonnay★ (Reserve★★) has overtaken it. The Robert Mondavi Winery is now part of Constellation's Icon Estates portfolio; Mondavi's lower-priced 'lifestyle' lines, Private Selection and Woodbridge (from Lodi in the CENTRAL VALLEY) are promoted separately. Best years: (Cabernet Sauvignon Reserve) (2005) 04 03 02 **01 00 99 98 97 96 95 94 92 91 87**.

MONT TAUCH, LES PRODUCTEURS DU *Fitou, Languedoc-Roussillon, France* A big, quality-conscious co-op producing a large range of wines, from good gutsy FITOU★ and CORBIÈRES to rich MUSCAT DE

RIVESALTES★ and light but gluggable Vin de Pays du Torgan. Top wines: Les Quatre★, Les Douze★. Best years: (Les Douze) (2005) 03 **01** 00.

MONTAGNE-ST-ÉMILION AC *Bordeaux, France* A ST-EMILION satellite which can produce rather good red wines. The wines are normally ready to drink in 4 years but age quite well in their slightly earthy way. Best producers: Calon★, Croix Beauséjour★, Faizeau★, Gachon★, Laurets, Montaiguillon★, Négrit, Roc-de-Calon, Rocher Corbin★, Roudier, Vieux-Ch.-St-André★. Best years: 2005 **03 01** 00 98 96 95 90.

MONTAGNY AC *Côte Chalonnaise, Burgundy, France* Wines from this Côte Chalonnaise village can be rather lean, but are greatly improved now that some producers are aging their wines for a few months in new oak. Generally best with 2–5 years' bottle age. Best producers: S Aladame★★, BOUCHARD PERE ET FILS★, BUXY CO-OP★, Davenay★, FAIVELEY, LATOUR★, O LEFLAIVE★, A Roy★, J Vachet★. Best years: (2006) 05 **04 03** 02.

MONTALCINO See BRUNELLO DI MONTALCINO DOCG.

MONTANA *Auckland, Gisborne, Hawkes Bay and Marlborough, New Zealand* Owned since 2005 by French giant Pernod Ricard, which produces an estimated 40% of New Zealand's wine. Montana's MARLBOROUGH Sauvignon Blanc★ and GISBORNE Chardonnay are in a considerable way to thank for putting New Zealand on the international wine map. Estate bottlings of whites, especially in the Terroir series, are also generally good. Montana is now one of the world's biggest producers of Pinot Noir★, and each vintage the quality improves and the price stays fair. Consistent Lindauer fizz and, with the help of the Champagne house DEUTZ, austere yet full-bodied Deutz Marlborough Cuvée NV Brut★★. CHURCH ROAD, in HAWKES BAY, aims to produce premium reds. As well as Corbans, Pernod Ricard also acquired Stoneleigh, with top-selling Marlborough Sauvignon Blanc★ and Riesling★ and tasty new Rapaura Series★. Extensive plantings in Waipara are now bearing exciting results under the Camshorn label.

MONTECARLO DOC *Tuscany, Italy* Distinctive reds (Sangiovese with Syrah) and whites (Trebbiano with Sémillon and Pinot Grigio). Also non-DOC Cabernet, Merlot, Pinot Bianco, Roussanne and Vermentino. Best producers: (reds) Buonamico★, Carmignani★, Montechiari★, La Torre★, Wandanna★. Best years: (reds) (2006) 04 **03 01** 00 99 97.

MONTEFALCO DOC *Umbria, Italy* Good Sangiovese-based Montefalco Rosso is outclassed by dry Sagrantino di Montefalco DOCG and glorious sweet red Sagrantino Passito from dried grapes. Best producers: (Sagrantino) Adanti★, Antonelli★, Caprai★★ (25 Anni★★★), Colpetrone★★. Best years: (Sagrantino) (2006) 04 03 **01** 00 99 98 97 95.

MONTEPULCIANO Grape grown mostly in eastern Italy (unconnected with TUSCANY's Sangiovese-based wine VINO NOBILE DI MONTEPULCIANO). Can produce deep-coloured, fleshy, spicy wines with moderate tannin and acidity. Besides MONTEPULCIANO D'ABRUZZO, it is used in ROSSO CONERO and ROSSO PICENO in the MARCHE and also in UMBRIA, Molise and PUGLIA.

MONTEPULCIANO D'ABRUZZO DOC *Abruzzo, Italy* The Montepulciano grape's most important manifestation. Quality varies from insipid or rustic to concentrated and characterful. Best producers: Barba, Cataldi Madonna★, Contesa★★, Cornacchia★, Filomusi Guelfi★, Illuminati★, Marramiero★, Masciarelli★★, A & E Monti★, Montori★, Nicodemi★, Roxan★, Cantina Tollo★, Umani Ronchi★, La Valentina★, Valentini★★, L Valori★, Ciccio Zaccagnini★. Best years: (2006) 04 **03 01** 00 98 97 95.

MONTEREY COUNTY *California, USA* Large CENTRAL COAST county south of San Francisco in the Salinas Valley. The most important AVAs are Monterey, Arroyo Seco, Chalone, Carmel Valley and Santa Lucia Highlands. Best grapes are Chardonnay, Riesling and Pinot Blanc, with some good Cabernet Sauvignon, Merlot in Carmel Valley and superb Pinot Noir in the Santa Lucia Highlands in the cool middle of the county. Best producers: Bernardus★★, CHALONE★, Estancia★, Jekel★, Joullian★★, Mer Soleil★★, Morgan★★, TALBOTT★★, Testarossa★★. Best years: (reds) 2005 04 03 **01 00 99 97 96 95 94 91 90**.

MONTES *Colchagua, Chile* One of Chile's pioneering wineries in the modern era, notable for innovative development of top-quality vineyard land on the steep Apalta slopes of COLCHAGUA and the virgin country of Marchígue out toward the Pacific. Sauvignon Blanc★ (Leyda★★) and Chardonnay★ (Alpha★★) are good and fruit-led; all the reds are more austere and need bottle age. From the 2001 vintage, top-of-the-line Montes Alpha M★★ is beginning to shine. The most impressive reds, however, are Montes Alpha★★ and Montes Folly★★, two massive Syrahs from the Apalta slopes, and Purple Angel★★, a vibrant, scented Carmenère from Apalta and Marchígue.

MONTEVERTINE *Tuscany, Italy* Based in the heart of CHIANTI CLASSICO, Montevertine is famous for its non-DOC wines, particularly Le Pergole Torte★★★. This was the first of the SUPER-TUSCANS made solely with Sangiovese, and it remains one of the best. A little Canaiolo is included in the excellent Montevertine Riserva★★. Best years: (Le Pergole Torte) (2006) (04) 03 01 **00 99 98 97 95 93 90 88 85**.

MONTHELIE AC *Côte de Beaune, Burgundy, France* Attractive, mainly red wine village lying halfway along the CÔTE DE BEAUNE behind MEURSAULT and VOLNAY. The wines generally have a lovely cherry fruit and make pleasant drinking at a good price. Best producers: Boussey, COCHE-DURY★, Darviot-Perrin★, P Garaudet★, R Jobard★, LAFON★, G Roulot★★, de Suremain★. Best years: (reds) (2006) 05 04 **03 02 99**.

MONTILLA-MORILES DO *Andalucía, Spain* Sherry-style wines that used to be sold almost entirely as lower-priced sherry substitutes. However, the wines *can* be superb, particularly the top dry amontillado, oloroso and rich Pedro Ximénez styles. Best producers: Alvear (top labels★★), Aragón, Gracia Hermanos, Pérez Barquero★, Toro Albalá★.

DOM. DE MONTILLE *Côte de Beaune, Burgundy, France* Brought to fame by *Mondovino* star, Hubert de Montille, and now run by son Étienne. Consistent producer of stylish reds that demand aging, from VOLNAY (especially Mitans★★, Champans★★, Taillepieds★★★) and POMMARD (Pezerolles★★, Rugiens★★). Also top PULIGNY Les Caillerets★★★. Very expensive. From 2005 some exciting Côte de Nuits vineyards have been added. Étienne and his sister have also started a négociant business, Deux Montille★. Best years: (2006) 05 04 **03** 02 99 96 **93 88 85 83**.

MONTLOUIS-SUR-LOIRE AC *Loire Valley, France* On the opposite bank of the Loire to VOUVRAY, Montlouis makes similar styles (dry, medium, sweet and CHAMPAGNE-style fizz), if a touch less fine. Mousseux, the green, appley fizz, is best drunk young. Still wines need 5–10 years, particularly the sweet Moelleux. Best producers: L Chatenay★, Chidaine★, Delétang★★, Levasseur-Alex Mathur★, des Liards/Berger★, Taille aux Loups★★/BLOT. Best years: (2006) 05 04 **03 02 01 99 97 96 95**.

MONTRACHET AC *Côte de Beaune, Burgundy, France* This world-famous Grand Cru straddles the boundary between the villages of CHASSAGNE-MONTRACHET and PULIGNY-MONTRACHET. Wines have a unique combination of concentration, finesse and perfume; white Burgundy at its most sublime. Chevalier-Montrachet, immediately above it on the slope, yields slightly leaner wine that is less explosive in its youth, but good examples become ever more fascinating with age. Best producers: BOUCHARD★★, M Colin★★★, DROUHIN (Laguiche)★★★, LAFON★★★, LATOUR★★, Dom. LEFLAIVE★★★, LEROY★★★, RAMONET★★★, Dom. de la ROMANEE-CONTI★★★, SAUZET★★, Thénard★★. Best years: (2006) 05 04 03 02 01 00 99 **97 95 92 90 89 85**.

MONTRAVEL AC *South-West France* Dry, medium-dry and sweet white wines from the western end of the red BERGERAC region. Sweet ones from Côtes de Montravel AC and Haut-Montravel AC. Red Montravel, from 2001, is made from a minimum 50% Merlot. Best producers: le Bondieu, Masburel★, Moulin Caresse★, Perreau, Pique-Sègue, Puy-Servain★, le Raz. Best years: (sweet) 2002 **01 98 96 95**; (red) 2005 03 **01**.

CH. MONTROSE★★ *St-Estèphe AC, 2ème Cru Classé, Haut-Médoc, Bordeaux, France* A leading ST-ESTEPHE property, once famous for its dark, brooding wine that would take around 30 years to reach its prime. In the late 1970s and early 80s the wines became lighter, but Montrose has now returned to a powerful style, though softer than before. Recent vintages have been extremely good. Sold in 2006, so let's see what happens to the style. Second wine: la Dame de Montrose. Best years: 2005 04 03 01 00 **99 98 96 95**.

CH. MONTUS *Madiran AC, South-West France* Alain Brumont has led MADIRAN's revival, using 100% Tannat and deft public relations. The top wine is aged in new oak. He has 3 properties: Montus (Prestige★★), Bouscassé (Vieilles Vignes★★) and Meinjarre. Montus and Bouscassé also make enjoyable dry PACHERENC DU VIC-BILH★ and COTES DE GASCOGNE, while Bouscassé has fine Moelleux★★. Best years: (Prestige) 2005 03 01 **00 99 98 97 96 95**.

MOON MOUNTAIN *Sonoma Valley AVA, California, USA* Formerly known as Carmenet (which is now a brand of the Foster's Group – the wines are not related), Moon Mountain specializes in intensely flavoured reds from mountain vineyards. Full-throttle Cabernet Franc★★ and Reserve Cabernet Sauvignon★★ can age for a decade. Reserve Sauvignon Blanc★★ from Edna Valley grapes features plenty of creamy oak. Best years: (reds) (2005) (04) (03) 02 **01 00 99 98 97 96 95 94**.

MORELLINO DI SCANSANO DOC *Tuscany, Italy* Morellino is the local name for the Sangiovese grape in the south-west of TUSCANY. The wines can be broad and robust, but the best are delightfully perfumed. Best producers: E Banti★, Belguardo★/FONTERUTOLI, Carletti/POLIZIANO (Lohsa★), Cecchi★, Il Macereto★, Mantellassi★, Morellino di Scansano co-op★, Moris Farms★★, Poggio Argentaria★★, Le Pupille★★. Best years: (2006) **04 03 01 00 99 98 97**.

MOREY-ST-DENIS AC *Côte de Nuits, Burgundy, France* Morey has 5 Grands Crus (CLOS DES LAMBRAYS, CLOS DE LA ROCHE, CLOS ST-DENIS, CLOS DE TART and a share of BONNES-MARES) as well as some very good Premiers Crus. Basic village wine is sometimes unexciting, but from a quality grower the wine has good fruit and acquires an attractive depth as it ages. A tiny amount of startling nutty white wine is also made. Best producers: Pierre Amiot★, Arlaud★★, Dom. des Beaumonts, CLAIR★★, DUJAC★★★, Dom. des Lambrays★★, H Lignier★★★, H Perrot-Minot★★, Ponsot★★, ROUMIER★★, ROUSSEAU★★, Sérafin★★. Best years: (2006) 05 04 03 02 **01 00 99 98 97 96 95 93 90**.

MORGENHOF *Stellenbosch WO, South Africa*   A 300-year-old Cape farm grandly restored and run with French flair by owner Anne Cointreau-Huchon. The range spans Cap Classique sparkling to PORT styles. Best are a well-oaked, muscular Chenin Blanc, structured Merlot★ and the dark-berried, supple Première Sélection★, a BORDEAUX-style blend.

MORGON AC *Beaujolais, Burgundy, France*   The longest-lasting of BEAUJOLAIS Crus, wines that should have the structure to age and delightful cherry fruit. There are, however, many more Morgons, made in a commercial style for early drinking, which are nothing more than a pleasant, fruity – and pricey – drink. Best producers: N Aucoeur★, DUBOEUF (Jean Descombes★), J Foillard, M Jonchet★, M Lapierre★. Best years: **2006** 05 03.

MORNINGTON PENINSULA *Victoria, Australia*   Exciting cool-climate maritime region dotted with small vineyards. Chardonnay runs the gamut from honeyed to harsh; Pinot Noir can be very stylish in warm years. Best producers: Kooyong★★, Main Ridge★, Moorooduc★, Paringa Estate★★, Port Phillip Estate★, STONIER★★, T'Gallant★, Tuck's Ridge, Yabby Lake★★. Best years: (Pinot Noir) 2006 05 04 03 02 **01 00 99 98 97 95 94**.

MORRIS *Rutherglen, Victoria, Australia*   Historical winery, ORLANDO-owned, with David Morris making old favourites like Liqueur Muscat★★ and Tokay★★ (Old Premium★★★), 'ports', 'sherries' and robust table wines.

DENIS MORTET *Gevrey-Chambertin, Côte de Nuits, Burgundy, France*   Before his untimely death in January 2006, Denis Mortet had built a brilliant reputation for his GEVREY-CHAMBERTIN (various cuvées, all ★★★) and tiny amounts of CHAMBERTIN★★★. Early vintages are deep coloured and powerful; recent years show increased finesse. Best years: (2006) 05 04 03 02 **01 00** 96 **95 93**.

GEORG MOSBACHER *Forst, Pfalz, Germany*   This small estate makes dry white and dessert wines in the village of FORST. Best of all are the dry Rieslings★★ from the Forster Ungeheuer site, which are among the lushest in Germany. Delicious young, but worth cellaring for more than 3 years. Best years: (2006) 05 04 **02 01 99 98 97 96**.

MOSCATO D'ASTI DOCG *Piedmont, Italy*   Utterly beguiling, delicately scented, gently bubbling wine, made from Moscato Bianco grapes grown in the hills between Acqui Terme, Asti and Alba in north-west Italy. The DOCG is the same as for ASTI, but only select grapes go into this wine, which is frizzante (semi-sparkling) rather than fully sparkling. Drink while they're bubbling with youthful fragrance. Best producers: Araldica/Alasia★, ASCHERI★, Bava★, Bera★★, Braida★, Cascina Castlèt★, Caudrina★★, Michele CHIARLO, Giuseppe Contratto★, Coppo★, Cascina  Fonda★, Forteto della Luja★, Icardi★, Marenco★, Beppe Marino★, La Morandina★, Marco Negri★, Perrone★, Cascina Pian d'Or★, Saracco★★, Scagliola★, La Spinetta★★, I Vignaioli di Santo Stefano★.

MOSCATO PASSITO DI PANTELLERIA DOC *Sicily, Italy*   Powerful dessert wine made from the Muscat of Alexandria, or Zibibbo, grape. Pantelleria is a small island south-west of SICILY, closer to Africa than it is to Italy. The grapes are picked in mid-August and laid out in the hot sun to shrivel for a couple of weeks. They are then crushed and fermented to give an amber-coloured, intensely flavoured sweet

Muscat. The wines are best drunk within 5–7 years of the vintage. Best producers: Benanti★, D'Ancona★, DE BARTOLI★★, Donnafugata (Ben Ryé★), Murana★, Nuova Agricoltura co-op★, Pellegrino.

MOSEL-SAAR-RUWER *Germany*   A collection of vineyard areas on the Mosel and its tributaries, the Saar and the Ruwer, amounting to 9080ha (22,435 acres). The Mosel river rises in the French Vosges before forming the border between Germany and Luxembourg. In its first German incarnation in the Upper Mosel the light, tart Elbling grape holds sway, but with the Middle Mosel begins a series of villages responsible for some of the world's very best Riesling wines: PIESPORT, BRAUNEBERG, BERNKASTEL, GRAACH, WEHLEN, URZIG and ERDEN. The wines have tremendous slatiness and an ability to blend the greenness of citrus leaves and fruits with the golden warmth of honey. Great wines are rarer in the lower part of the valley as the Mosel approaches Koblenz, although WINNINGEN is an island of excellence. The Saar can produce wonderful, piercing wines in villages such as Serrig, Ayl, OCKFEN and Wiltingen. Ruwer wines are slightly softer; the estates of MAXIMIN GRUNHAUS and KARTHAUSERHOF are on every list of the best in Germany. From late 2007 only the name 'Mosel' will appear on labels.

MOSS WOOD *Margaret River, Western Australia*   Seminal MARGARET RIVER winery at the top of its form. Supremely good, scented Cabernet★★★ needing 5 years to blossom, classy Chardonnay★★, pale, fragrant Pinot Noir★ or crisp, fruity but ageworthy Semillon★★. Range is expanding with excellent Ribbon Vale★★ wines. Best years: (Cabernet) (2005) (04) 03 02 01 **00 99 98 96 95 94 91 90 85**.

J P MOUEIX *Bordeaux, France*   As well as owning PETRUS, la FLEUR-PETRUS, MAGDELAINE, TROTANOY and other properties, the Moueix family runs a thriving merchant business specializing in the wines of the right bank, particularly POMEROL and ST-EMILION. Quality is generally high.

MOULIN-À-VENT AC *Beaujolais, Burgundy, France*   Potentially the greatest of the BEAUJOLAIS Crus, taking its name from an ancient (now renovated) windmill that stands above Romanèche-Thorins. The granitic soil yields a majestic wine that with time transforms into a rich Burgundian style more characteristic of the Pinot Noir than the Gamay. Best producers: Champagnon★, DUBOEUF (Tour du Bief★), Ch. des Jacques★/JADOT, Ch. du Moulin-à-Vent★, Dom. Romanesca★, P Sapin (Le Vieux Domaine). Best years: **2006 05 03**.

MOULIS AC *Haut-Médoc, Bordeaux, France*   Small AC within the HAUT-MEDOC. Much of the wine is excellent – delicious at 5–6 years old, though good examples can age 10–20 years – and not overpriced. Best producers: Anthonic, Biston-Brillette★, Branas-Grand-Poujeaux, Brillette, CHASSE-SPLEEN★, Duplessis, Gressier-Grand-Poujeaux★, MAUCAILLOU★, Moulin-à-Vent, POUJEAUX★. Best years: 2005 03 **02 01 00 96 95 90 89 88**.

MOUNT HORROCKS *Clare Valley, South Australia*   Stephanie Toole has transformed this label into one of the CLARE VALLEY's best, with taut, minerally, limy Riesling★★★ from a single vineyard in Watervale; classy, cedary Semillon★; complex, savoury Shiraz★; and a delicious sticky (dessert wine), the Cordon Cut Riesling★★, which shows varietal character with a satisfying lush texture.

MOUNT LANGI GHIRAN *Grampians, Victoria, Australia*   This winery made its reputation with remarkable dark plum, chocolate and pepper Shiraz★★. Delightful Riesling★, honeyed Pinot Gris★ and melony unwooded Chardonnay★. Joanna★★ Cabernet is dark and intriguing. Best years: (Shiraz) 2004 03 99 **98 97 96 95 94 93 92 90 89**.

MOUNT MARY *Yarra Valley, Victoria, Australia* This classic property continues in spite of the death of its founder, John Middleton. It uses only estate-grown grapes along BORDEAUX lines, with dry white Triolet★★ blended from Sauvignon Blanc, Semillon and Muscadelle, and Quintet (★★★ for committed Francophiles), from Cabernets Sauvignon and Franc, Merlot, Malbec and Petit Verdot, that ages beautifully. The Pinot Noir★★ is almost as good. Best years: (Quintet) (2004) 03 02 01 00 99 98 97 96 **95 94 93 92 91 90 88 86 84**.

MOUNT VEEDER AVA *Napa Valley, California, USA* Small AVA in south-west NAPA, with Cabernet Sauvignon and Zinfandel in an impressive, rough-hewn style. Best producers: Chateau Potelle★, Robert Craig★★, HESS COLLECTION, Lokoya★★, Mayacamas★, Mount Veeder Winery★.

MOURVÈDRE The variety originated in Spain, where it is called Monastrell. It dominates the JUMILLA DO and also Alicante, Bullas and Yecla. It needs lots of sunshine to ripen, which is why it performs well on the Mediterranean coast at BANDOL. It is increasingly important as a source of body and tarry, pine-needle flavour in the wines of CHATEAUNEUF-DU-PAPE and parts of Languedoc-Roussillon. It is beginning to make a reputation in Australia and California, where it is sometimes known as Mataro, and is also starting to make its presence felt in South Africa.

MOUTON-CADET *Bordeaux AC, Bordeaux, France* The most widely sold red BORDEAUX in the world was created by Baron Philippe de Rothschild in the 1930s. Blended from the entire Bordeaux region, the wine is undistinguished – and never cheap. A new label and somewhat fruitier style were introduced in 2004. Also a white, rosé, MEDOC and GRAVES.

CH. MOUTON-ROTHSCHILD★★★ *Pauillac AC, 1er Cru Classé, Haut-Médoc, Bordeaux, France* Baron Philippe de Rothschild died in 1988, having raised Mouton from a run-down Second Growth to its promotion to First Growth in 1973, and a reputation as one of the greatest wines in the world. It can still be the most magnificently opulent of the great MEDOC reds, but inexcusable inconsistency frequently makes me want to downgrade it. Recent vintages seem back on top form. When young, it is rich and indulgent on the palate, aging after 15–20 years to a complex bouquet of blackcurrant and cigar box. There is also a white wine, Aile d'Argent. Second wine: Petit-Mouton. Best years: (red) 2005 04 03 02 01 00 **99 98 96 95 90 89 88 86 85 83 82**.

MUDGEE *New South Wales, Australia* Small, long-overlooked region neighbouring HUNTER VALLEY, with a higher altitude and marginally cooler temperatures. Major new plantings are giving it a fresh lease of life and producers are beginning to make the best use of very good fruit. Best producers: Abercorn, Farmer's Daughter, Huntington Estate★, Miramar★, ORLANDO (Poet's Corner★), ROSEMOUNT.

MUGA *Rioja DOCa, Rioja, Spain* A traditional family winery making high-quality, rich red RIOJA★, especially the Gran Reserva, Prado Enea★★. It is the only bodega in Rioja where every step of red winemaking is still carried out in oak containers. The modern Torre Muga Reserva★ marks a major stylistic change. The new top cuvée is Aro★★. Whites and rosés are good too. Best years: (Torre Muga Reserva) 2001 **99 98 96 95**.

J-F MUGNIER *Chambolle-Musigny, Côte de Nuits, Burgundy, France*
Since giving up his other career as an airline pilot in 1998, Frédéric Mugnier has produced a series of beautifully crafted, lightly extracted wines at the Château de Chambolle-Musigny, especially from les Amoureuses★★ and Grand Cru le MUSIGNY★★★. In 2004 the 9ha (23-acre) NUITS-ST-GEORGES Clos de la Maréchale★★ vineyard came back under his control; first vintages are very stylish and a small section has been grafted over to white wine production. Best years: (2006) 05 04 02 01 **00 99 98 96 93 90 89.**

MULDERBOSCH *Stellenbosch WO, South Africa* Consistency is one of the hallmarks of this white-dominated range. Sleek, gooseberry-infused Sauvignon Blanc★★ is deservedly a cult wine; drink young and fresh. Purity and intensity mark out the Chardonnays (regular★ and barrel-fermented★★) and oak-brushed Chenin Blanc★ (previously labelled Steen op Hout)★. The handful of reds includes Faithful Hound, a Cabernet-Merlot blend, BORDEAUX-like but easy-drinking. Best years: (barrel-fermented Chardonnay) **2005 04 03 02 01 00 99 98**.

MÜLLER-CATOIR *Neustadt-Haardt, Pfalz, Germany* This PFALZ producer makes wine of a piercing fruit flavour and powerful structure unsurpassed in Germany, including Riesling, Scheurebe, Rieslaner, Gewürztraminer, Muskateller and Pinot Noir – all ★★. BA and TBA are invariably ★★★. In 2002 veteran winemaker Hans-Günther Schwarz retired and was replaced by Martin Tranzen. Best years: (2006) 05 04 **03** 02 **01 99 98 97 96 94.**

EGON MÜLLER-SCHARZHOF *Scharzhofberg, Saar, Germany* Some of the world's greatest – and most expensive – sweet Rieslings are this estate's Auslese, Beerenauslese, Trockenbeerenauslese and Eiswein, all usually rate ★★★. Regular Kabinett and Spätlese wines are pricey but classic. Best years: (2006) 05 04 03 02 01 **99 97 95 93 90 89 88 83 76**.

MÜLLER-THURGAU The workhorse grape of Germany, largely responsible for LIEBFRAUMILCH, with 14% of the country's vineyards, but steadily diminishing. When yields are low it produces pleasant floral wines, but this is rare since modern clones are all super-productive. It is occasionally better in England – and a few good examples, with a slightly green edge to the grapy flavour, come from Switzerland, Luxembourg and Italy's ALTO ADIGE and TRENTINO. In New Zealand, Müller-Thurgau acreage is in terminal decline.

G H MUMM *Champagne AC, Champagne, France* Mumm's top-selling non-vintage brand, Cordon Rouge, disappointing in the 1990s, improved when Dominique Demarville took over as winemaker in 1998, but he left in 2006 to join VEUVE CLICQUOT. It remains to be seen whether his efforts at improving quality, confirmed by the 2005 release of Mumm Grand Cru★, will be continued under Pernod Ricard's ownership. Best years: 1998 96 **95 90 89 88 85 82.**

MUMM NAPA *Napa Valley AVA, California, USA* The California offshoot of Champagne house MUMM has always made good bubbly, but the style is now leaner and meaner, which is a pity. Cuvée Napa Brut Prestige is a fair drink; Blanc de Noirs★ is better than most pink Champagnes. Also elegant vintage-dated Blanc de Blancs★ and the flagship DVX★. Now part of Pernod Ricard.

MUSCAT

It's strange, but there's hardly a wine grape in the world which makes wine that actually tastes of the grape itself. Yet there's one variety which is so joyously, exultantly grapy that it more than makes up for all the others – the Muscat, generally thought to be the original wine vine. In fact there seem to be about 200 different branches of the Muscat family worldwide, but the noblest of these and the one that always makes the most exciting wine is called Muscat Blanc à Petits Grains (the Muscat with the small berries). These berries can be crunchily green, golden yellow, pink or even brown – as a result Muscat has a large number of synonyms. The wines they make may be pale and dry, rich and golden, subtly aromatic or as dark and sweet as treacle.

WINE STYLES

France Muscat is grown from the far north-east right down to the Spanish border, yet is rarely accorded great respect in France. This is a pity, because the dry, light, hauntingly grapy Muscats of Alsace are some of France's most delicately beautiful wines. It pops up sporadically in the Rhône Valley, especially in the sparkling wine enclave of Die. Mixed with Clairette, the Clairette de Die Tradition is a fragrant grapy fizz that deserves to be better known. Muscat de Beaumes-de-Venise is a delicious manifestation of the grape, this time fortified, fragrant and sweet. Its success has encouraged the traditional fortified winemakers of Languedoc-Roussillon, especially in Frontignan and Rivesaltes, to make fresher, more perfumed wines than the flat and syrupy ones they've produced for generations.

Italy Muscat, mainly Moscato Bianco, is grown in Italy for fragrantly sweet or (rarely) dry table wines in the north and for *passito*-style wines in the south (though Muscat of Alexandria is sometimes preferred below Rome). The most delicate Muscats in Italy are those of Asti, where the grape is called Moscato di Canelli. As either Asti or Moscato d'Asti, this brilliantly fresh fizz can be a blissful drink. Italy also has red varieties: the Moscato Nero for rare sweet wines in Lazio, Lombardy and Piedmont; and Moscato Rosa/ Rosenmuskateller for delicately sweet wines in Trentino-Alto Adige and Friuli-Venezia Giulia. Moscato Giallo/Goldmuskateller (Orange Muscat) is often preferred to Moscato Bianco in the north-east.

Other regions Elsewhere in Europe, Muscat is a component of some Tokajis in Hungary, Crimea has shown how good it can be in the Massandra fortified wines, and the rich golden Muscats of Samos and Patras are among Greece's finest wines. As Muskateller in Austria and Germany it makes primarily dry, subtly aromatic wines. In Spain, Moscatel de Valencia is sweet, light and sensational value, Moscatel de Grano Menudo is on the resurgence in Navarra and it has also been introduced in Mallorca. Portugal's Moscatel de Setúbal is also wonderfully rich and complex. California grows Muscat, often calling it Muscat Canelli, but South Africa and Australia make better use of it. With darker berries, and called Brown Muscat in Australia and Muscadel in South Africa, it makes some of the world's sweetest and most luscious fortified wines, especially in the north-east Victoria regions of Rutherglen and Glenrowan in Australia.

BEST PRODUCERS

Sparkling Muscat
France (CLAIRETTE DE DIE)
Achard-Vincent, Clairette de
Die co-op, Jean-Claude
Raspail.

Italy (Asti) G Contratto, Gancia;
(Moscato d'Asti) Bera, Braida,
Caudrina, Saracco,
La Spinetta.

Dry Muscat
Austria (Muskateller) Gross,
Lackner-Tinnacher, POLZ,
TEMENT.

France (Alsace) J Becker,
Dirler-Cadé, Kientzler,
Kuentz-Bas, Rolly Gassmann,
Ostertag, SCHOFFIT, WEINBACH,
ZIND-HUMBRECHT.

Germany (Muskateller)
BERCHER, Dr HEGER,
MULLER-CATOIR, REBHOLZ.

Spain (Alicante) Bocopa co-
op; (Málaga) Ordóñez, Telmo
RODRIGUEZ; (Penedès) TORRES
(Viña Esmeralda).

Italy (Goldmuskateller) LAGEDER.

Sweet Muscat
Australia (Liqueur Muscat)
ALL SAINTS, Baileys of
Glenrowan, BROWN BROTHERS,
Buller, Campbells, CHAMBERS,
MCWILLIAM'S, MORRIS, SEPPELT,
Stanton & Killeen, YALUMBA.

France (Alsace) E Burn,
Fernand Engel, Rolly
Gassmann, René MURE,
SCHOFFIT; (Beaumes-de-Venise)
Bernardins, Durban, Paul
JABOULET, Pigeade; (Frontignan)
la Peyrade; (Lunel) Lacoste;
(Rivesaltes) CAZES, Jau.

Greece SAMOS co-op.

Italy (Goldmuskateller)
Viticoltori Caldaro, Thurnhof;
(Pantelleria) DE BARTOLI, Murana.

Portugal (Moscatel de Setúbal)
BACALHOA VINHOS DE PORTUGAL,
J M da FONSECA.

South Africa KLEIN CONSTANTIA.

Spain (Navarra) Camilo
Castilla, CHIVITE; (Terra Alta)
Vinos Piñol; (Valencia) Gandía;
(Alicante) Gutiérrez de la Vega,
Enrique Mendoza, Primitivo
Quiles; (Sierras de Málaga)
Ordóñez, Telmo RODRIGUEZ.

M **RENÉ MURÉ**

RENÉ MURÉ *Alsace AC, Alsace, France* The pride and joy of this
🍷 domaine's fine vineyards is the Clos St-Landelin, a parcel within the
Grand Cru Vorbourg and the label for all the top wines. The Clos is
the source of lush, concentrated wines, with particularly fine Riesling★★
and Pinot Gris★★. The Muscat Vendange Tardive★★ is rare and
remarkable, as is the opulent old-vine Sylvaner Cuvée Oscar★. The
Vendange Tardive★★ and Sélection de Grains Nobles★★★ wines are
among the best in Alsace. Best years: (Clos St-Landelin Riesling) 2005
04 **02 01 00 97 96 95**.

ANDREW MURRAY VINEYARDS *Santa Barbara County, California, USA*
🍷 Working with RHONE varieties, winemaker Andrew Murray has created
an impressive array of wines. Rich, aromatic Viognier★ and
Roussanne★★ as well as several Syrahs, including Roasted Slope★★
and Hillside Reserve★★. Espérance★ is a spicy blend patterned after a
serious COTES DU RHONE. Best years: (Syrah) 2004 03 02 **01 00 99 98 97 96**.

MUSCADET AC *Loire Valley, France* Muscadet is the general AC for the
♀ region around Nantes in north-west France, best drunk young and
fresh as an apéritif or with the local seafood. Wines from three better
quality zones (Muscadet Coteaux de la Loire, Muscadet Côtes de
Grand-Lieu and Muscadet Sèvre-et-Maine) are typically labelled *sur lie*.
They must be matured on the lees for a maximum of 12 months and
show greater depth of flavour. Ironically, top cuvées from specific
vineyards or soils (granite, gneiss, schist) are usually aged *sur lie* for
well over 12 months so cannot use this term on the label. Best
producers: Serge Bâtard★, Bidière, Bonhomme, Bonnet-Huteau,
Chéreau-Carré, Choblet/Herbauges★, Bruno Cormerais★, Michel David★,
Dorices★, Douillard, l'ECU★, Gadais★, Jacques Guindon★, Hautes-
Noëlles★, l'Hyvernière, Landrons★, Luneau-Papin★, Metaireau★,
RAGOTIERE★, Sauvion★, la Touché★. Best years: (sur lie) 2005 **03 02**.

MUSCAT See pages 212–13.

MUSCAT OF ALEXANDRIA Muscat of Alexandria rarely shines in its own
🌾 right but performs a useful job worldwide, adding perfume and fruit to
what would otherwise be dull, neutral white wines. It is common for
sweet and fortified wines throughout the Mediterranean basin (in
Sicily it is called Zibibbo) and in South Africa (where it is also known
as Hanepoot), as well as being a fruity, perfumed bulk producer there
and in Australia, where it is known as Gordo Blanco or Lexia.

MUSCAT DE BEAUMES-DE-VENISE AC *Rhône Valley, France* Delicious
♀ Muscat *vin doux naturel* from the southern Rhône. It has a fruity
acidity and a bright fresh feel, and is best drunk young to get all that
lovely grapy perfume at its peak. Best producers: Beaumalric★,
Beaumes-de-Venise co-op, Bernardins★★, DELAS★, Durban★★,
Fenouillet★, JABOULET★★, Pigeade★★, Vidal-Fleury★.

MUSCAT BLANC À PETITS GRAINS See MUSCAT, pages 212–13.

MUSCAT DE FRONTIGNAN AC *Languedoc, France* Muscat *vin doux*
♀ *naturel* on the Mediterranean coast. Quite impressive but can be a bit
cloying. Muscat de Mireval AC, a little further inland, can have a
touch more acid freshness, and quite an alcoholic kick. Best
producers: (Frontignan) Cave de Frontignan, la Peyrade★, Robiscau;
(Lunel) Lacoste★; (Mireval) la Capelle★, Mas des Pigeonniers, Moulinas.

MUSCAT DE LUNEL AC, MUSCAT DE MIREVAL AC See MUSCAT DE
FRONTIGNAN.

MUSCAT DE RIVESALTES AC *Roussillon, France* Made from Muscat
♀ Blanc à Petits Grains and Muscat of Alexandria, the wine can be very
good from go-ahead producers who keep the aromatic skins in the
juice for longer periods to gain extra perfume and fruit. Most
delicious when young. Best producers: Baixas co-op (Dom. Brial★, Ch.
les Pins★), la CASENOVE★, CAZES★★, Chênes★, Corneilla, Fontanel★,
Força Réal★, l'Heritier, Jau★, Laporte★, MONT TAUCH★, de Nouvelles★,
Piquemal★.

MUSCAT DE ST-JEAN-DE-MINERVOIS AC *Languedoc, France* Up in
♀ the remote Minervois hills, a small AC for fortified Muscat made from
Muscat Blanc à Petits Grains. Less cloying than some Muscats from
the plains of LANGUEDOC-ROUSSILLON, more tangerine and floral. Best
producers: CLOS BAGATELLE, Combebelle, Vignerons de Septimanie.

MUSIGNY AC *Grand Cru, Côte de Nuits, Burgundy, France* One of a
♏ handful of truly great Grands Crus, combining power with an
exceptional depth of fruit and lacy elegance – an iron fist in a velvet
glove. Understandably expensive. A tiny amount of BOURGOGNE Blanc
is currently made from the Musigny vineyard by de VOGUE★★. Best
producers: DROUHIN★★★, JADOT★★★, D Laurent★★★, Dom. LEROY★★★,
J-F MUGNIER★★★, J Prieur★★, ROUMIER★★★, VOGUE★★★, VOUGERAIE★★★.
Best years: (2006) 05 04 03 02 01 **00** 99 98 **97** 96 95 **93 90 89 88**.

NAHE *Germany* 4120ha (10,180-acre) wine region named after the
River Nahe, which rises below Birkenfeld and joins the Rhine by BINGEN,
opposite RUDESHEIM in the RHEINGAU. Riesling, Müller-Thurgau and
Silvaner are the main grapes, but the Rieslings from this geologically
complex region are considered some of Germany's best. The finest
vineyards are those of Niederhausen and SCHLOSSBOCKELHEIM, situated in
the dramatic, rocky Upper Nahe Valley, and at Dorsheim and Münster in
the lower Nahe.

CH. NAIRAC★★ *Barsac AC, 2ème Cru Classé, Bordeaux, France* An
♀ established star in BARSAC which, by dint of enormous effort and considerable investment, produces a wine sometimes on a par with the
First Growths. The influence of aging in new oak casks, adding spice
and even a little tannin, makes this sweet wine a good candidate for
aging 10–15 years. Best years: 2005 04 03 **02** 01 **99 98 97 96 95**.

NAPA VALLEY See pages 218–19.

NAPA VALLEY AVA *California, USA* An AVA designed to be so inclusive
♏ that it is almost completely irrelevant. It includes vineyards that are
outside the Napa River drainage system – such as Pope Valley and
Chiles Valley. Because of this a number of sub-AVAs have been and
are in the process of being created; a few such as CARNEROS and STAGS
LEAP DISTRICT are discernibly different from their neighbours, but the
majority are similar in nature, and many fear that these sub-AVAs
will simply dilute the magic of Napa's name. See also HOWELL MOUNTAIN,
MOUNT VEEDER, NAPA VALLEY, OAKVILLE, RUTHERFORD.

NAVARRA DO *Navarra, Spain* This buzzing region has increasing
♏ numbers of vineyards planted to Cabernet Sauvignon, Merlot and
Chardonnay in addition to Tempranillo, Garnacha and Moscatel
(Muscat). This translates into a wealth of juicy reds, barrel-fermented
whites and modern sweet Muscats, but quality is still more
haphazard than it should be. Best producers: Camilo Castilla
(Capricho de Goya Muscat★★), CHIVITE★, Magaña★, Alvaro Marino★,

215

Castillo de Monjardin★, Nekeas co-op★, Ochoa, Palacio de la Vega★, Príncipe de Viana★, Señorío de Otazu★. Best years: (reds) 2005 **04 03 01 99 98**.

NAVARRO VINEYARDS *Anderson Valley AVA, California, USA* Small but extremely high-calibre family-owned producer of sensational Gewürztraminer★★★, Pinot Gris★★, Riesling★★, Dry Muscat★★ and late-harvest Riesling★★★, perfectly balanced Pinot Noir★★ and a dozen other stellar wines.

NEBBIOLO The grape variety responsible for the majestic wines of BAROLO and BARBARESCO, found almost nowhere outside north-west Italy. Its name may derive from the Italian for fog, *nebbia*, because it ripens late when the hills are shrouded in autumn mists. It needs a thick skin to withstand this fog, so often gives very tannic wines that need years to soften. When grown in the limestone soils of the Langhe hills around Alba, Nebbiolo produces wines that are only moderately deep in colour but have a wonderful array of perfumes and an ability to develop great complexity with age. Barolo is usually considered the best and longest-lived of the Nebbiolo wines; the myth that it needs a decade or more to be drinkable has been dispelled by new-style Barolo, and the best Barolos now reach a plateau within 10 years and then subtly mature for decades. Barbaresco also varies widely in style between the traditional and the new. NEBBIOLO D'ALBA and ROERO produce lighter styles. The variety is also used for special barrique-aged blends, often with Barbera and/or Cabernet and sold under the LANGHE DOC. Nebbiolo is also the principal grape for reds of northern PIEDMONT – Carema, GATTINARA and Ghemme. In LOMBARDY it is known as Chiavennasca and is the main variety of the Valtellina DOC and VALTELLINA SUPERIORE DOCG wines. Outside Italy, rare good examples have been made in Australia, California and South Africa.

NEBBIOLO D'ALBA DOC *Piedmont, Italy* Red wine from Nebbiolo grown around Alba, but excluding the BAROLO and BARBARESCO zones. Vineyards in the LANGHE and ROERO hills are noted for sandy soils that produce a fragrant, fruity style for early drinking, though some growers make wines that improve for 5 years or more. Best producers: Alario★, ASCHERI, Bricco Maiolica★★, CERETTO, Cascina Chicco★, Correggia★★, GIACOSA★, Giuseppe MASCARELLO★, Pio Cesare★, PRUNOTTO★, RATTI★, SANDRONE★, Vietti★. Best years: (2006) **04 03 01 00 99 98**.

NELSON *South Island, New Zealand* A range of mountains separates Nelson from MARLBOROUGH at the northern end of South Island. Nelson is made up of a series of small hills and valleys with a wide range of mesoclimates. Pinot Noir, Chardonnay, Riesling and Sauvignon Blanc do well. Best producers: Greenhough★, Kina Beach, NEUDORF★★, Rimu Grove★, SEIFRIED★, Spencer Hill. Best years: (whites) (2006) **05 04 03 02 01**.

NERO D'AVOLA The name of SICILY's great red grape derives from the town of Avola near Siracusa, although it is now planted all over the island. Its deep colour, high sugars and acidity make it useful for blending, especially with the lower-acid Nerello Mascalese, but also with Cabernet, Merlot and Syrah. On its own, and from the right soils, it can be brilliant, with a soft, ripe, spicy black fruit character. Examples range from simple quaffers to many of Sicily's top reds.

NEUCHÂTEL *Switzerland* Swiss canton with high-altitude vineyards, mainly Chasselas whites and Pinot Noir reds and rosé. Best producers: Ch. d'Auvernier, Châteney, Montmollin, Porret.

NEUDORF *Nelson, South Island, New Zealand* Owners Tim and Judy Finn produce some of New Zealand's most stylish and sought-after wines, including gorgeous, honeyed Chardonnay★★★, rich but scented Pinot Noir★★, Sauvignon Blanc★★ and Riesling★★. Best years: (Chardonnay) (2006) 05 04 03 02 01; (Pinot Noir) 2005 03 02 01 00.

NEW SOUTH WALES *Australia* Australia's most populous state is responsible for about 25% of the country's grape production. The largest centres of production are the irrigated areas of RIVERINA, and Murray Darling, Swan Hill and Perricoota on the Murray River, where better viticultural and winemaking practices and lower yields have led to significant quality improvements. Smaller premium-quality regions include the old-established HUNTER VALLEY, Cowra and higher-altitude MUDGEE, Orange and HILLTOPS. CANBERRA is an area of tiny vineyards at chilly altitudes, as is Tumbarumba at the base of the Snowy Mountains.

NEW YORK STATE *USA* Wine grapes were first planted on Manhattan Island in the mid-17th century, but it wasn't until the early 1950s that a serious wine industry began to develop in the state as vinifera grapes were planted to replace natives such as *Vitis labrusca*. Weather conditions, particularly in the north, can be challenging, but improved vineyard practices have made a good vintage possible in most recent years. The most important region is the FINGER LAKES in the north of the state, but LONG ISLAND is the most exciting; the Hudson River Region has a couple of good producers and a few upstarts are producing noteworthy wines amid the ocean of plonk along the shores of Lake Erie. Best producers: (Hudson River) Clinton, Millbrook★. See also FINGER LAKES and LONG ISLAND.

NEWTON *Napa Valley AVA, California, USA* Spectacular winery and steep vineyards high above St Helena, owned by French luxury giant LVMH. Cabernet Sauvignon★★, Merlot★★ and Claret★ are some of California's most pleasurable examples. Even better is the single-vineyard Cabernet Sauvignon-based Le Puzzle★★★. Newton pioneered the unfiltered Chardonnay★★★ style and this lush mouthful is one of California's best. Age Chardonnays for up to 5 years, reds for 10–15. Best years: (Cabernet Sauvignon) 2003 02 01 00 99 97 96 95 94 91 90.

NGATARAWA *Hawkes Bay, North Island, New Zealand* Viticulture here is organic, with Chardonnay, botrytized Riesling and Cabernet-Merlot under the premium Alwyn Reserve label. The Glazebrook range includes attractive Chardonnay★ and Cabernet-Merlot★, both of which are best drunk within 5 years. Best years: (reds) (2006) 04 02 00 98.

NIAGARA PENINSULA *Ontario, Canada* Sandwiched between lakes Erie and Ontario, the Niagara Peninsula benefits from regular through-breezes created by the Niagara escarpment, the cool climate bringing out distinctive characteristics in the wine. Icewine, from Riesling and Vidal, is the showstopper, with growing international acclaim. Chardonnay leads the dry whites, with Pinot Noir, Merlot and Cabernet Franc showing most promise among the reds. Best producers: Cave Spring★, Chateau des Charmes★, HENRY OF PELHAM★, INNISKILLIN★★, Konzelmann★, Reif Estate★, Southbrook★, Stoney Ridge, THIRTY BENCH★. Best years: (icewines) 2004 03 02 00 99 98.

NAPA VALLEY

California, USA

From the earliest days of California wine, and through all its ups and downs, the Napa Valley has been the standard-bearer for the whole industry and the driving force behind quality and progress. The magical Napa name – derived from an Indian word for plenty – applies to the fertile valley itself, the county in which it is found and the AVA for the overall area, but the region is so viticulturally diverse that the appellation is virtually meaningless.

The valley was first settled by immigrants in the 1830s, and by the late 19th century Napa, and in particular the area around the communities of Rutherford and Oakville, had gained a reputation for exciting Cabernet Sauvignon. Despite the long, dark years of Prohibition, this reputation survived and when the US interest in wine revived during the 1970s, Napa was ready to lead the charge.

GRAPE VARIETIES

Most of the classic French grapes are grown and recent replantings have done much to match varieties to the most suitable locations. Cabernet Sauvignon is planted in profusion and Napa's strongest reputation is for varietal Cabernet and Bordeaux-style (or meritage) blends, mostly Cabernet-Merlot. Pinot Noir and Chardonnay, for both still and sparkling wines, do best in the south, from Yountville down to Carneros. Zinfandel is grown mostly at the north end of the valley. Syrah and Sangiovese are relatively new here.

SUB-REGIONS

The most significant vine-growing area is the valley floor running from Calistoga in the north down to Carneros, below which the Napa River flows out into San Pablo Bay. It has been said that there are more soil types in Napa than in the whole of France, but much of the soil in the valley is heavy, clayish, over-fertile, difficult to drain and really not fit to make great wine. Some of the best vineyards are tucked into the mountain slopes at the valley sides or in selected spots at higher altitudes.

There is as much as a 10° temperature difference between torrid Calistoga and Carneros at the mouth of the valley, cooled by Pacific fog and a benchmark for US Pinot Noir and cool-climate Chardonnay. About 20 major sub-areas have been identified along the valley floor and in the mountains, although there is much debate over how many have a real claim to individuality. Rutherford, Oakville and Yountville in the mid-valley produce Cabernet redolent of dust, dried sage and ultra-ripe blackcurrants. Softer flavours come from Stags Leap to the east. The higher-altitude vineyards of Diamond Mountain, Spring Mountain and Mount Veeder along the Mayacamas mountain range to the west produce deep Cabernets, while Howell Mountain in the north-east has stunning Zinfandel and Merlot.

See also CARNEROS AVA, HOWELL MOUNTAIN AVA, MOUNT VEEDER AVA, NAPA VALLEY AVA, OAKVILLE AVA, RUTHERFORD AVA, STAGS LEAP DISTRICT AVA; and individual producers.

VIADER

NAPA VALLEY

(2005) (04) 03 **02 01 00 99 97 95 94 91 90 87 86**

BEST PRODUCERS

Cabernet Sauvignon and meritage blends

Abreu, Altamura, Anderson's Conn Valley, ARAUJO, Barnett (Rattlesnake Hill), BEAULIEU, BERINGER, Bryant Family, Burgess Cellars, Cafaro, Cakebread, CAYMUS, CHATEAU MONTELENA, Chateau Potelle (VGS), CHIMNEY ROCK, Cliff Lede, Clos Pegase, CLOS DU VAL, Colgin, Conn Creek (Anthology), Corison, Cosentino, Robert Craig, DALLA VALLE, Darioush, Del Dotto, DIAMOND CREEK, DOMINUS, DUCKHORN, DUNN, Elyse, Etude, Far Niente, FLORA SPRINGS, Forman, Freemark Abbey, Frog's Leap, Grace Family, Groth, HARLAN ESTATE, HARTWELL, HEITZ, Jarvis, La Jota, Ladera, Lewis Cellars, Livingston, Lokoya, Long Meadow Ranch, Long Vineyards, Markham, Mayacamas, MERRYVALE, Peter MICHAEL, MINER, MONDAVI, Monticello, Mount Veeder Winery/FRANCISCAN, NEWTON, Oakford, OPUS ONE, Pahlmeyer, Paradigm, Robert Pecota, Peju Province (HB Vineyard), PHELPS, PINE RIDGE, Plumpjack, Pride Mountain, Quintessa, Raymond, Rombauer (Meilleur du Chai), Rubicon/COPPOLA, Rudd Estate, Saddleback, St Clement, SCREAMING EAGLE, Seavey, SHAFER, SILVER OAK, SILVERADO, SPOTTSWOODE, Staglin Family, STAG'S LEAP WINE CELLARS, STERLING, Swanson, The Terraces, Philip Togni, Turnbull, Viader, Villa Mt Eden (Signature Series), Vine Cliff, Vineyard 29, Von Strasser, Whitehall Lane, ZD.

NIEPOORT *Port DOC, Douro, Portugal* Remarkable small PORT shipper of Dutch origin. Outstanding Vintage ports★★★, old tawnies★★★ and Colheitas★★★. Unfiltered LBVs★★ are among the best in their class – intense and complex. The Vintage Port second label is called Secundum★★. Niepoort also produces fine red and white DOURO Redoma★★ and red Vertente★★; Batuta★★★ and Charme★★ are already established as two of Portugal's leading reds. Best years: (Vintage) 2005 03 00 97 94 92 91 **87 85 82 80 77 70 66 63**.

NIERSTEIN *Rheinhessen, Germany* Both a small town and a large Bereich which includes the infamous Grosslage Gutes Domtal. The town boasts 23 vineyard sites and the top ones (Pettenthal, Brudersberg, Hipping, Oelberg and Orbel) are some of the best in the Rhine Valley. Best producers: GUNDERLOCH★★, HEYL ZU HERRNSHEIM★★, Kühling-Gillot★, St Antony★, Schneider★. Best years: (2006) 05 04 **03 02 01 99 98**.

NIKOLAIHOF *Wachau, Niederösterreich, Austria* The Saahs family makes some of the best wines in the WACHAU as well as in nearby Krems-Stein in KREMSTAL, including steely, intense Rieslings from the famous Steiner Hund vineyard, always ★★. A biodynamic estate. Best years: (2006) 05 04 02 01 **99 98 97**.

NOBILO *Kumeu/Huapai, Auckland, North Island, New Zealand* Wines range from medium-dry White Cloud to premium varietals. Tangy though restrained Sauvignon Blanc and a vibrant Chardonnay★ are the top wines from MARLBOROUGH. In 1998 Nobilo bought Selaks, with wineries in AUCKLAND and Marlborough (Drylands); since then they have added the intense Drylands Marlborough Sauvignon Blanc★, Chardonnay★ and Riesling★ to their list. The Selaks label has the most character. Nobilo is now part of Constellation Brands.

NORTON *Luján de Cuyo, Mendoza, Argentina* Austrian-owned winery where reds impress more than whites, with good, chocolaty Sangiovese, soft, rich Merlot★ and good Barbera. Higher up the scale, quality has enormously improved in the past few vintages, especially in single vineyard★★ and Reserva★ releases, while top-of-the-line Privada★★ is enjoyable young but ages beautifully. Perfumed Torrontés★ and snappy Sauvignon Blanc★ are good whites.

NOVAL, QUINTA DO *Port DOC, Douro, Portugal* Owned by AXA-Millésimes, this immaculate property is the source of extraordinary Quinta do Noval Nacional★★★, made from ungrafted vines – some say the best vintage PORT made, but virtually unobtainable except at auction. Other Noval ports (including Quinta do Noval Vintage★★★ and Silval★★) are excellent too. Also fine Colheitas★★ and some stunning 40-year-old tawnies★★★. Best years: (Nacional) 2003 00 97 94 87 85 70 **66 63 62 60 31**; (Vintage) 2004 03 00 97 95 94 91 **87 85 70 66 63 60 31**.

NUITS-ST-GEORGES AC *Côte de Nuits, Burgundy, France* This large AC is one of the few reliable 'village' names in Burgundy. Although it has no Grands Crus, many of its Premiers Crus (it has 38!) are extremely good. The red can be rather slow to open out, often needing at least 5 years, but it ages to a delicious, chocolaty, deep figs-and-prune fruit. Minuscule amounts of white are made by GOUGES★, l'Arlot, Chevillon and RION. Best producers: l'Arlot★★, R Arnoux★★, S CATHIARD★, J Chauvenet★★, R Chevillon★★, J-J Confuron★★, FAIVELEY★★, H GOUGES★★, GRIVOT★★, Jayer-Gilles★★, Lechenaut★★, T LIGER-BELAIR★★, MEO-CAMUZET★★, A Michelot★, Mugneret★★, J-F MUGNIER★★, POTEL★★, RION★★. Best years: (reds) (2006) 05 04 03 02 **01 00 99 98 97 96 95 93 90**.

NYETIMBER *West Sussex, England* England's flagship sparkling wine producer, using classic CHAMPAGNE varieties. Two wines are made – Classic Cuvée★★ (Chardonnay, Pinot Noir and Pinot Meunier) and Chardonnay-based Blanc de Blancs★★ – though they have also released a 2003 Pinot Meunier Blanc de Noirs. Winemaker changes are worrying, though the same Champagne-based enologist has been there from the start, and the wines continue to exhibit exceptional depth, with delicious toasty flavours and great length. The estate has now been sold to Dutch investor Eric Heerema, and I pray all the good work won't be undone. Best years: **1999 98 96 95 94**.

OAKVILLE AVA *Napa Valley, California, USA* This region is cooler than RUTHERFORD, which lies immediately to the north. Planted primarily to Cabernet Sauvignon, the area contains some of NAPA's best vineyards, both on the valley floor (MONDAVI, OPUS ONE, SCREAMING EAGLE) and hillsides (HARLAN ESTATE, DALLA VALLE), producing wines that display lush, ripe black fruits and firm tannins. Best years: (Cabernet Sauvignon) (2005) (04) 03 02 **01 00 99 97 96 95 94 91 90**.

OC, VIN DE PAYS D' *Languedoc-Roussillon, France* Important Vin de Pays covering LANGUEDOC-ROUSSILLON. Overproduction and consequent underripeness have not helped its reputation, but an increasing number of fine reds and whites show what can be done. Best producers: l'Aigle★, Condamine Bertrand, J-L DENOIS★, l'HOSPITALET, J & F Lurton★, MAS LA CHEVALIERE, Ormesson★, Pech-Céleyran (Viognier★), Quatre Sous★, St-Saturnin★, SKALLI-FORTANT, VAL D'ORBIEU (top reds★), Virginie.

OCKFEN *Saar, Germany* Village with one famous individual vineyard site, the Bockstein. The wines can be superb in a sunny year, never losing their cold steely streak but packing in delightful full-flavoured fruit as well. Best producers: St Urbans-Hof★★, Dr Heinz Wagner★★, ZILLIKEN★★. Best years: (2006) 05 04 **03** 02 **01 99 97 95 93**.

OKANAGAN VALLEY *British Columbia, Canada* The oldest and most important wine-producing region of British Columbia and first home of Canada's rich, honeyed icewine. The Okanagan Lake helps temper the bitterly cold nights but October frosts can be a problem. Chardonnay, Pinot Blanc, Pinot Gris and Pinot Noir are the top performers. South of the lake, Cabernet, Merlot and even Shiraz are now being grown successfully. Best producers: Blue Mountain★, Burrowing Owl★, Gehringer★, INNISKILLIN, MISSION HILL★★, Quails' Gate, SUMAC RIDGE★, Tinhorn Creek. Best years: (reds) 2005 04 03 **02 01 00**.

OLTREPÒ PAVESE DOC *Lombardy, Italy* Italy's main source of Pinot Nero, used mainly for sparkling wines that may be called Classese when made here by the CHAMPAGNE method, though base wines supply *spumante* industries elsewhere. Still reds from Barbera, Bonarda and Pinot Nero and whites from the Pinots, Riesling and Chardonnay can be impressive. Best producers: Cà di Frara★, Le Fracce★, Frecciarossa★, Fugazza, Castello di Luzzano, Mazzolino★, Monsupello★, Montelio★, Vercesi del Castellazzo★, Bruno Verdi★. Best years: (reds) (2006) **04 03 01 00 99**.

WILLI OPITZ *Neusiedlersee, Burgenland, Austria* The eccentric and publicity-conscious Willi Opitz produces a remarkable, unusual range of dessert wines from his 12ha (30-acre) vineyard, including red Eiswein. The best are ★★, but dry wines are simpler and less consistent.

OPUS ONE★★ *Oakville AVA, California, USA* BORDEAUX-blend wine, a joint venture initially between Robert MONDAVI and the late Baron Philippe de Rothschild of MOUTON-ROTHSCHILD, now between Constellation and

Baroness Philippine de Rothschild. Various Opus bottlings have been in the ★★ range, one or two nudging ★★★, in a beautifully cedary, minty manner. Best years: 2003 02 **01 99 98 97 96 95 94 93 92 91 90 86 85 84**.

DOM. DE L'ORATOIRE ST-MARTIN *Côtes du Rhône AC, Rhône Valley, France* Careful fruit selection in the vineyard is the secret of Frédéric and François Alary's concentrated Côtes du Rhône-Villages CAIRANNE reds and whites. Haut-Coustias white★ is ripe with peach and exotic fruit aromas, while the red★★ is a luscious mouthful of raspberries, herbs and spice.

Top red Cuvée Prestige★★ is deep and intense with darkly spicy fruit. Best years: (Cuvée Prestige) 2006 **05 04 03 01 00 99 98 95**.

OREGON *USA* Oregon shot to international stardom in the early 1980s following some perhaps overly generous praise of its Pinot Noir, but it is only with the release of a succession of fine recent vintages and some soul-searching by the winemakers about what style they should be pursuing that we can now begin to accept that some of the hype was deserved. Consistency is still a problem, however, with surprisingly warm weather now offering challenges along with the traditional ones of overcast skies and unwelcome rain. Chardonnay can be quite good in an austere, understated style. The rising star is Pinot Gris which can be delicious, with surprising complexity. Pinot Blanc is also gaining momentum. The WILLAMETTE VALLEY is considered the best growing region, although the more BORDEAUX-like climate of the Umpqua and Rogue Valleys can produce good Cabernet Sauvignon and Merlot. Best producers: (Rogue, Umpqua) Abacela★, Bridgeview★, Calahan Ridge, Foris★, Henry Estate, Valley View Winery. Best years: (reds) (2005) 04 03 02 **01 00 99**.

ORLANDO *Barossa Valley, South Australia* Australia's third-biggest wine company, and the force behind export colossus Jacob's Creek, is owned by Pernod Ricard. It encompasses MORRIS, Russet Ridge, Wickham Hill, Gramp's, Richmond Grove and Wyndham Estate, and MUDGEE winery Poet's Corner, home to the Henry Lawson and Montrose brands. The company is taking advantage of the strength of the Jacob's Creek name to rebrand Orlando wines, hence Jacob's Creek Steingarten Riesling★★ from Eden Valley, Jacob's Creek St Hugo Cabernet Sauvignon★ from COONAWARRA and rich Jacob's Creek Centenary Hill Shiraz★★ from the BAROSSA. Flagship reds remain Jacaranda Ridge Cabernet★ from Coonawarra and Lawson's Shiraz★★ from PADTHAWAY. Jacob's Creek Reserve and Limited Release★★ wines are excellent. Basic Jacob's Creek Cabernet and Semillon-Chardonnay seem stretched, but Riesling★ and Grenache-Shiraz are fine. Best years: (St Hugo) (2006) (05) (04) 03 02 01 **00 99 98 96 94 91 90 88 86**.

ORNELLAIA, TENUTA DELL' *Bolgheri, Tuscany, Italy* This beautiful property in the heart of BOLGHERI was developed by Lodovico ANTINORI, brother of Piero. Ornellaia★★, a Cabernet-Merlot blend, doesn't quite have the style of neighbouring SASSICAIA. Also small amounts of outstanding Merlot, Masseto★★★. Now owned by FRESCOBALDI. Best years: (Ornellaia) (2006) (05) 04 03 **01 00 99 98 97 96 95**.

ORTENAU *Baden, Germany* A chain of steep granitic hills between Baden-Baden and Offenburg, which produce the most elegant (generally dry) Rieslings in BADEN, along with fragrant, medium-bodied Spätburgunder (Pinot Noir) reds. Best producers: Laible★★, Männle, Nägelsförst★, Schloss Neuweier★, Wolff Metternich★.

ORVIETO DOC *Umbria, Italy* Traditionally a lightly sweet (*abboccato*) white wine, Orvieto is now usually dry and characterless. In the superior Classico zone, however, the potential for richer, more biscuity wines exists. Not generally a wine for aging. There are also some very good botrytis-affected examples. Best producers: (dry) Barberani-Vallesanta★, La Carraia★, Decugnano dei Barbi★, Palazzone★, Castello della SALA★, Salviano★, Conte Vaselli★, Le Velette★; (sweet) Barberani-Vallesanta★, Decugnano dei Barbi★, Palazzone★★, Castello della SALA★.

OSBORNE *Jerez y Manzanilla DO, Andalucía, Spain* The biggest drinks company in Spain, Osborne does most of its business in brandy and other spirits. Its sherry arm in Puerto de Santa María specializes in the light Fino Quinta★. Amontillado Coquinero★, rich, intense Bailén Oloroso★★ and Solera India Oloroso★★ are very good indeed.

PAARL WO *South Africa* Paarl is South Africa's second most densely planted district after Worcester, accounting for 18% of all vineyards. A great diversity of soil and climate favour everything from Cap Classique sparkling wines to sherry styles, but reds are setting the quality pace, especially Shiraz. Its white RHONE counterpart, Viognier, solo and in some expressive white blends, is also performing well. FRANSCHHOEK, Simonsberg-Paarl, Voor Paardeberg and Wellington are smaller designated areas (wards) within the Paarl district. Best producers: (Paarl) Boschendal, DISTELL (Nederburg, Plaisir de Merle★), FAIRVIEW★★, GLEN CARLOU★, Rupert & Rothschild★ VEENWOUDEN★★, Vilafonté★, Welgemeend★; (Wellington) Diemersfontein★, Mont du Toit★. Best years: (premium reds) 2005 **04 03 02 01 00 99 98**.

PACHERENC DU VIC-BILH AC *South-West France* Individual whites from an area overlapping the MADIRAN AC in north-east Béarn. The wines are mainly dry, but there are some medium-sweet/sweet late-harvest wines. Most Pacherenc is best drunk young. Best producers: Aydie★, Berthoumieu★, Brumont (Bouscassé★, MONTUS★), du Crampilh★, Damiens, Laffitte-Teston★, Producteurs PLAIMONT★, Sergent★, Viella. Best years: (2006) 05 **04 03 02 01 00**.

PADTHAWAY *South Australia* This wine region has always been the alter ego of nearby COONAWARRA, growing whites to complement Coonawarra's reds; Chardonnay has been particularly successful. Nowadays there are some excellent reds, especially from Henry's Drive; even GRANGE has included Padthaway grapes. ORLANDO's premium Lawson's Shiraz★★ is 100% Padthaway, HARDY's Eileen Hardy Shiraz★★★ sometimes includes Padthaway fruit. Best producers: Browns of Padthaway, Henry's Drive★★, LINDEMANS★, ORLANDO★, Padthaway Estate, SEPPELT, Stonehaven★.

BRUNO PAILLARD *Champagne AC, Champagne, France* Bruno Paillard is one of the very few individuals to have created a new CHAMPAGNE house over the past century. Paillard still does the blending himself. Non-vintage Première Cuvée★ is lemony and crisp; Réserve Privée★ is a blanc de blancs; vintage Brut★★ is a serious wine. De luxe cuvée Nec Plus Ultra★★ is a barrel-fermented blend of Grands Crus made in top vintages. Also owns Philipponnat and the great single-vineyard site, Clos des Goisses★★★. Best years: 1996 **95 90 89 88**.

ALVARO PALACIOS *Priorat DOCa, Cataluña, Spain* The young Alvaro
Palacios was already a veteran with Bordeaux and Napa experience
when he launched his boutique winery in the rough hills of southern
CATALUÑA in the late 1980s. He is now one of the driving forces of the
area's rebirth. His expensive, highly concentrated reds (L'Ermita★★★,
Finca Dofí★★, Les Terrasses★) from old Garnacha vines and a dollop
of Cabernet Sauvignon, Merlot, Cariñena and Syrah have won a cult
following. Best years: (2005) (04) 03 01 **00 99 98 97 96 95 94**.

PALETTE AC *Provence, France* Tiny AC just east of Aix-en-Provence.
Even though the local market pays high prices, I find the reds and
rosés rather tough and charmless. However, Ch. Simone manages to
achieve a white wine of some flavour from basic southern French
grapes. Best producers: Crémade, Ch. Simone★.

PALLISER ESTATE *Martinborough, North Island, New Zealand* State-of-
the-art winery producing some of New Zealand's best Sauvignon
Blanc★★ (certainly the best outside MARLBOROUGH) and Riesling★,
delightful Chardonnay★★ and Pinot Gris★, with some impressive,
rich-textured Pinot Noir★★. Exciting botrytized dessert wines appear
in favourable vintages. Méthode★ fizz is also impressive. Best years:
(Pinot Noir) (2006) **03 01 00 99 98**.

CH. PALMER★★ *Margaux AC, 3ème Cru Classé, Haut-Médoc, Bordeaux,*
France This estate was named after a British major-general who
fought in the Napoleonic Wars, and is one of the leading properties in
MARGAUX AC. The wine is wonderfully perfumed, with irresistible plump
fruit. The very best vintages can age for 30 years or more. Second
wine: Alter Ego (frequently an excellent, scented red). Best years: 2005
04 03 02 **01 00 99** 98 96 95 90 89 88 86 85 83 82.

CH. PAPE-CLÉMENT *Pessac-Léognan AC, Cru Classé de Graves,*
Bordeaux, France The expensive red wine★★ from this GRAVES
Classed Growth has not always been as consistent as it should be – but
things settled down into a high-quality groove during the 1990s. In
style it is mid-way between the refinement of HAUT-BRION and the
firmness of la MISSION-HAUT-BRION. More elegance and seduction since
2001. Also produces a small amount of fine, aromatic white wine★★.
Second wine: (red) Clémentin. Best years: (reds) 2005 04 03 02 01 00 **99**
98 96 95 90 89 88 86; (white) 2005 **04 03 02 01 00** 99 98 96.

PARELLADA This Catalan exclusivity is the lightest of the trio of white
grapes that go to make CAVA wines in north-eastern Spain. It also
makes still wines, light, fresh and gently floral, with good acidity. Drink
it as young as possible, while it still has the benefit of freshness.

PARKER COONAWARRA ESTATE *Coonawarra, South Australia* Things
have finally settled down following the death of founder John Parker;
the estate has been bought by the Rathbone family who own Yering
Station in the YARRA VALLEY and MOUNT LANGI GHIRAN. The top label,
cheekily named First Growth★★ in imitation of illustrious BORDEAUX
reds, has enjoyed much critical acclaim. It is released only in better
years. Second-label Terra Rossa Cabernet Sauvignon★ is lighter and
leafier. The Merlot★★ is among the best produced in Australia. Best
years: (First Growth) (2006) (05) (04) 01 99 **98 96 93 91 90**.

C J PASK *Hawkes Bay, North Island, New Zealand* Chris Pask made the
first wine in the now-famous Gimblett Gravels area of HAWKES BAY. The
winery is best known for Reserve reds, including a rich and powerful

Reserve Merlot, an elegant, long-lived Reserve Syrah★ and, in the best vintages, a classy red blend called Reserve Declaration★. Best years: (reds) (2006) **04 02 00 98**.

PASO ROBLES AVA *California, USA* A large AVA at the northern end of SAN LUIS OBISPO COUNTY. Cabernet Sauvignon and Zinfandel perform well in this warm region, and Syrah is gaining an important foothold, but too many producers are chasing OTT alcohol levels. The Perrin family from Ch. de BEAUCASTEL selected this AVA to plant RHONE varieties for their California project, Tablas Creek, whose whites so far outshine the reds. Best producers: Adelaida★, Eberle★, Justin★, J Lohr★, Peachy Canyon★, Tablas Creek★, Wild Horse★.

PATAGONIA *Argentina* Located 750 km (465 miles) south of MENDOZA, Patagonia used to be called 'the vineyards of the winds'. Those constant winds, along with relentless sunshine and cool nights, allow a super-healthy viticulture where Malbec flavours are fresh and scented and plump, Cabernet and Merlot are juicy and, perhaps, Pinot Noir may flourish. There are two main areas: Río Negro, to the east, is where the first vines were planted in the 19th century. The newly planted Neuquén area to the north-west has seen dramatic development during the past 5 years. Best producers: (Río Negro) Humberto Canale★, Chacra★★, Infinitus★★/DOMAINE VISTALBA, Noemía★★; (Neuquén) Fin del Mundo★, NQN★, Familia Schroeder★.

LUÍS PATO *Bairrada, Beira Litoral, Portugal* Leading 'modernist' in BAIRRADA, passionately convinced of the Baga grape's ability to make great reds on clay soil. He now labels his wines as BEIRAS after arguing with Bairrada's bosses. Wines such as the Vinhas Velhas★, Vinha Barrosa★★, Vinha Pan★★ and the flagship Quinta do Ribeirinho Pé Franco★★ (from ungrafted vines) rank among Portugal's finest modern reds, and some can reach ★★★ with age. Homenagem★★ combines Baga with Touriga Nacional from Quinta de Cabriz (DÃO). Good white, Vinha Formal★, is 100% Bical. Daughter Filipa makes delightful reds and whites under Lokal★★ and Ensaios FP★★ labels. Best years: (reds) 2005 04 **03 01 00 97 96 95 92**.

PAUILLAC AC *Haut-Médoc, Bordeaux, France* The deep gravel banks around the town of Pauillac in the HAUT-MEDOC are the heartland of Cabernet Sauvignon. For many wine lovers, the king of red wine grapes finds its ultimate expression in the 3 Pauillac First Growths (LATOUR, LAFITE-ROTHSCHILD and MOUTON-ROTHSCHILD). The large AC also contains 15 other Classed Growths. The uniting characteristic of Pauillac wines is their intense blackcurrant fruit flavour and heady cedar and pencil-shavings perfume. These are the longest-lived of BORDEAUX's great red wines. Best producers: Armailhac★, BATAILLEY★, Clerc-Milon★, Duhart-Milon★, Fonbadet, GRAND-PUY-DUCASSE★, GRAND-PUY-LACOSTE★★, HAUT-BAGES-LIBERAL★, HAUT-BATAILLEY★, LAFITE-ROTHSCHILD★★★, LATOUR★★★, LYNCH-BAGES★★★, MOUTON-ROTHSCHILD★★★, Pibran★, PICHON-LONGUEVILLE★★★, PICHON-LONGUEVILLE-LALANDE★★★, PONTET-CANET★★. Best years: 2005 04 03 02 **01** 00 **96 95 90 89 88 86**.

CH. PAVIE★★ *St-Émilion Grand Cru AC, 1er Grand Cru Classé, Bordeaux, France* The style of the wine may be controversial – dense, rich, succulent – and it has as many enemies as friends, but there's no doubting the progress made at Pavie since Gérard Perse acquired the property in 1998. The price has also soared. Pavie-Decesse★ and MONBOUSQUET★ are part of the same stable. Best years: 2005 04 03 **02** 01 00 **99 98 90 89 88 86**.

225

CH. PAVIE-MACQUIN★★ *St-Émilion Grand Cru AC, 1er Grand Cru Classé,*
Bordeaux, France This has become one of the stars of the ST-EMILION
GRAND CRU since the 1990s, with promotion to Premier Grand Cru
Classé in 2006. Management and winemaking are in the hands of
Nicolas Thienpont (of BORDEAUX-COTES DE FRANCS) and Stéphane
Derenoncourt, who consults to CANON-LA-GAFFELIERE and PRIEURE-LICHINE,
among others. Rich, firm and reserved, the wines need 7–8 years and
will age longer. Best years: 2005 04 03 02 **01 00 99 98 97 96 95 94 90**.

PÉCHARMANT AC *South-West France* Improving red wines from small
AC north-east of BERGERAC. The wines are quite light in body but have
a delicious, full, piercing flavour of blackcurrants and attractive grassy
acidity. Good vintages easily last 10 years and match a good HAUT-
MEDOC. Best producers: Beauportail, Bertranoux, Costes★, Grand Jaure,
Haut-Pécharmant★, Métairie-Haute★, Tiregand★. Best years: 2005 04
03 01 **00 98 96**.

PEGASUS BAY *Canterbury, South Island, New*
Zealand Matthew Donaldson and Lynette
Hudson make lush, mouthfilling
Chardonnay★★, an almost chewy Pinot
Noir★★ and its even richer big sister Prima
Donna Pinot Noir★★, powerful Sauvignon
Blanc-Semillon★★ and very stylish
Riesling★★. These are some of the most
original wines in New Zealand, and all will
age well. Best years: (Pinot Noir) (2006) 05 04
03 02 01 00 99.

PEMBERTON *Western Australia* Exciting emergent region, deep in the
karri forests of the south-west, full of promise for cool-climate Pinot
Noir, Shiraz, Chardonnay, Merlot and Sauvignon Blanc. HOUGHTON
leads the way – thanks to the outstanding fruit coming from the
vineyard they purchased a decade ago – with its Pemberton range:
sparkling Chardonnay-Pinot Noir★, Sauvignon Blanc★★,
Chardonnay★★, but dull Merlot. Best producers: Bellarmine,
HOUGHTON★★, Lillian, Merum, Picardy★, Salitage, Smithbrook.

PENEDÈS DO *Cataluña, Spain* The booming CAVA industry is based in
Penedès, and the majority of the still wines are white, made from the
Cava trio of Parellada, Macabeo and Xarel-lo, clean and fresh when
young, but never exciting. Better whites are made from Chardonnay.
The reds are variable, the best made from Cabernet Sauvignon and/or
Tempranillo and Merlot. Best producers: Albet i Noya★, Can Feixes★,
Can Ràfols dels Caus★★, Cavas Hill, JUVE Y CAMPS, Jean León★, Marques
de Monistrol, Masía Bach★, Albert Milá i Mallofré, Puig y Roca★, Sot
Lefriec★, TORRES★, Vallformosa, Jané Ventura★.

PENFOLDS *Barossa Valley, South Australia* While it was part of the giant
Southcorp group, Penfolds proved that quality *can* go hand in hand
with quantity, but so far its performance as part of the giant Foster's
Wine Group hasn't been inspiring. It still makes the country's most
famous red wine, GRANGE★★★, and a welter of other reds such as RWT
Shiraz, Magill Estate★★, St Henri, Bin 707 Cabernet★★, Bin 389
Cabernet-Shiraz★, Bin 28 Kalimna★ and Bin 128 Coonawarra Shiraz,
but as you go further down the range to previously reliable wines like
Koonunga Hill and Rawson's Retreat a dispiriting blandness enters in.
Whites are led by overpriced Yattarna Chardonnay★★; there's also a
tasty wooded Semillon★★, citrus Eden Valley Riesling★ and Rawson's

Retreat Riesling. Thomas Hyland Cabernet, Shiraz and Chardonnay are pretty good. Best years: (top reds) 2004 02 **98 96 94 91 90**.

PENLEY ESTATE *Coonawarra, South Australia* Kym Tolley, a member of the PENFOLD family, combined the names when he left Southcorp and launched Penley Estate in 1991. From 1997 Cabernet Sauvignon★★★ has been outstanding. Chardonnay and Hyland Shiraz can reach ★★; Gryphon Merlot★ and fizz★ are also worth a try. Best years: (Cabernet Reserve) (2006) (05) 04 02 00 99 98 **96 94 93 92 91**.

PERNAND-VERGELESSES AC *Côte de Beaune, Burgundy, France* The little-known village of Pernand-Vergelesses contains a decent chunk of the great Corton hill, including much of the best white CORTON-CHARLEMAGNE Grand Cru vineyard. The red wines sold under the village name are very attractive when young, with a nice raspberry pastille fruit and a slight earthiness, and will age for 6–10 years. As no one ever links poor old Pernand with the heady heights of Corton-Charlemagne, the whites sold under the village name can be a bargain. The wines can be a bit lean and dry to start with but fatten up beautifully after 2–4 years in bottle. Best producers: (reds) CHANDON DE BRIAILLES★★, C Cornu★, Denis Père et Fils★, Dubreuil-Fontaine★, Laleure-Piot★; (whites) CHANDON DE BRIAILLES★★, Dubreuil-Fontaine★, Germain/ Ch. de Chorey, A Guyon, JADOT, Laleure-Piot★, J-M Pavelot★, Rapet★, Rollin★. Best years: (reds) (2006) 05 **03 02 99**; (whites) (2006) 05 **04 02**.

ANDRÉ PERRET *Condrieu AC, Rhône Valley, France* A top CONDRIEU grower, with 2 standout cuvées: Clos Chanson★★ is direct and full, Chéry★★★, made with some later-picked grapes, is musky, floral and rich. Impressive white and red ST-JOSEPH, notably Les Grisières★★ from old Syrah vines. Best years: (Condrieu) 2006 05 **04 03 01**.

JOSEPH PERRIER *Champagne AC, Champagne, France* The NV Cuvée★ is biscuity and creamy, Prestige Cuvée Josephine★★ has length and complexity, but the much cheaper Cuvée Royale Vintage★★ is the best deal. Best years: (1999) 98 96 **95 90 89 88 85 82**.

PERRIER-JOUËT *Champagne AC, Champagne, France* Perrier-Jouët has had three owners in the past 8 years (it's now owned by Pernod Ricard). This doesn't help consistency, but Perrier-Jouët had fallen so low during the 1990s that any change would be beneficial. Certainly the NV is now a decent drink once more, the Blason Rosé★ is charming and the de luxe vintage cuvée Belle Époque★ reasonably classy. So keep up the improvement for this great label which, for me, always oozes self-indulgence – and I want this reflected in the flavour. Best years: (2002) 99 96 **95 90 89 85 82**.

PESQUERA *Ribera del Duero DO, Castilla y León, Spain* Tinto Pesquera reds, richly coloured, firm, fragrant and plummy-tobaccoey, have long been among Spain's best. Made by the small firm of Alejandro Fernández, they are 100% Tempranillo and sold as Crianza and Reserva★. Gran Reserva★★ and Janus★★★ are made in the best years. Condado de Haza (Alenza★) is a separate estate. New ventures in Zamora (Dehesa La Granja★) and La MANCHA (Vínculo). Best years: (Pesquera Crianza) 2004 **01 99 98 96 95 94 93 92 91 90 89**.

PESSAC-LÉOGNAN AC *Bordeaux, France* AC created in 1987 for the northern (and best) part of the GRAVES region and including all the Graves Classed Growths. The supremely gravelly soil tends to favour red wines over the rest of the Graves. Now, thanks to cool fermentation and the use of new oak barrels, this is also one of the most exciting areas of France for top-class white wines. Best producers: (reds) les Carmes Haut-Brion★, Dom. de CHEVALIER★★, FIEUZAL★, HAUT-BAILLY★, HAUT-BRION★★★, Larrivet-Haut-Brion★, LATOUR-MARTILLAC★, la LOUVIERE★, MALARTIC-LAGRAVIERE★, la MISSION-HAUT-BRION★★★, PAPE-CLEMENT★★, SMITH-HAUT-LAFITTE★★, la Tour Haut-Brion★; (whites) Brown★, Carbonnieux★, Dom. de CHEVALIER★★★, Couhins-Lurton★★, FIEUZAL★★, HAUT-BRION★★★, LATOUR-MARTILLAC★, LAVILLE-HAUT-BRION★★★, la LOUVIERE★★, MALARTIC-LAGRAVIERE★★, PAPE-CLEMENT★★, Rochemorin★, SMITH-HAUT-LAFITTE★★. Best years: (reds) 2005 04 02 01 00 99 98 96 95; (whites) 2005 04 02 01 00 99 98 96 95.

PETALUMA *Adelaide Hills, South Australia* This public company, which includes KNAPPSTEIN, STONIER, Mitchelton in Victoria and Smithbrook in Western Australia, was founded by Brian Croser, probably Australia's most influential winemaker. It was taken over by brewer Lion Nathan in 2001. CHAMPAGNE-style Croser★ is stylish but lean. Chardonnay★★ and COONAWARRA (Cabernet-Merlot)★★ are consistently fine and Hanlin Hill Riesling★★ from the CLARE VALLEY is at the fuller end of the spectrum and matures superbly. Best years: (Coonawarra) (2006) (05) (04) (03) 02 01 00 **99 97 94 91 90 88**.

PETIT VERDOT A rich, tannic variety, grown mainly in Bordeaux's HAUT-MEDOC to add depth, colour and violet fragrance to top wines. Late ripening and erratic yield limit its popularity, but warmer-climate plantings in Australia, California, Chile, Argentina, Spain and Italy are giving exciting results. There are a few promising varietal wines in South Africa but generally it is blended with other BORDEAUX varieties.

CH. PETIT-VILLAGE★ *Pomerol AC, Bordeaux, France* This top POMEROL wine used to be rather dry and dense, but has considerably softened up in the last few vintages. In general it is worth aging the wine for 8–10 years. Best years: 2005 04 03 01 **00 99 98 96 95 94 90 89 88 85 82**.

PETITE ARVINE A Swiss grape variety from the VALAIS, Petite Arvine has a bouquet of peach and apricot, and develops a spicy, honeyed character. Dry, medium or sweet, the wines have good aging potential – thank goodness: I've got one from 1969. Best producers: Chanton★, Chappaz★, Caves Imesch★, Maye, Dom. du Mont d'Or★, Varone.

PETITE SIRAH Once used primarily as a blending grape in California, this variety (identical to the Rhône blender Durif) now has its own cheering society, a trade group called P.S. I Love You, founded in 2002. Some 275 California wineries now make a varietal Petite Sirah. At its best, it is deep, tannic and long-lived, but can be monstrously huge and unfriendly. Australian and Mexican examples are softer though still hefty, and can occasionally develop a floral scent and blackberry fruit. Best producers: L A CETTO★ (Mexico), De Loach★, FETZER, Fife, Foppiano, RAVENSWOOD★, Stags' Leap Winery★★, TURLEY★★.

CH. PÉTRUS★★★ *Pomerol AC, Bordeaux, France* One of the most expensive red wines in the world (alongside other superstars from POMEROL, such as le PIN). The powerful, concentrated wine produced here is the result of the caring genius of Pétrus' owners, the MOUEIX family, who have maximized the potential of the vineyard of almost solid clay, although the impressive average age of the vines has been much reduced by recent replantings. Drinkable for its astonishingly rich, dizzying blend of fruit and spice flavours after a decade, but top years will age for much longer, developing exotic scents of tobacco and chocolate and truffles as they mature. Best years: 2005 04 03 02 01 00 **99 98 96 95 90 89 88 86 85**.

DOM. PEYRE ROSE *Coteaux du Languedoc AC, Languedoc, France* Organic viticulture, ultra-low yields and total absence of oak are all marks of the **97** individuality of Marlène Soria's wines. Syrah is the dominant grape in both the raisin- and plum-scented Clos des Cistes★★ and the dense, velvety Clos Syrah Léone★★. Best years: (reds) 2003 01 **00 99 98 97 96**.

CH. DE PEZ★ *St-Estèphe AC, Cru Bourgeois, Haut-Médoc, Bordeaux, France* One of ST-ESTEPHE's leading non-Classed Growths, de Pez makes mouthfilling, satisfying claret with sturdy fruit. Slow to evolve, good vintages often need 10 years or more. Owned by Champagne house ROEDERER. Best years: 2005 04 03 02 **01 00 99 98 96 95 90 89 88**.

PFALZ *Germany* This immense wine region, with 23,360ha (57,720 acres), makes a lot of mediocre wine, but the quality estates are capable of matching the best that Germany has to offer. The Mittelhaardt has a reputation for Riesling, especially round the villages of BAD DÜRKHEIM, WACHENHEIM, FORST and Deidesheim, though Freinsheim, Kallstadt, Ungstein, Gimmeldingen and Haardt also produce fine Riesling as well as Scheurebe, Rieslaner and Pinot Gris. In the Südliche Weinstrasse the warm climate makes the area an ideal testing ground for Spät-, Weiss- and Grauburgunder (aka Pinots Noir, Blanc and Gris), as well as Gewürztraminer, Scheurebe, Muscat and red Dornfelder, the last often dark and tannic, sometimes produced with oak influence.

JOSEPH PHELPS *Napa Valley AVA, California, USA* Joseph Phelps' BORDEAUX-blend Insignia★★★ is consistently one of California's top reds, strongly fruit-driven with a lively spicy background. Phelps' pure Cabernets include Napa Valley★ and huge Backus Vineyard★★, beautifully balanced with solid ripe fruit. The Napa Merlot★ is ripe and elegant, with layers of fruit. Phelps was the first California winery to major on Rhône varietals, and makes an  intense Viognier★ and complex Syrah★. A separate wine, Le Mistral★, is a splendid Rhône red blend from Phelps' vineyards in MONTEREY COUNTY. Soon to release Chardonnay and Pinot Noir from a project at cold Freestone near the Sonoma coast. Best years: (Insignia) (2005) (04) 2003 02 **01 00 99 96 95 94 93 91 85**.

CH. DE PIBARNON *Bandol AC, Provence, France* Blessed with excellently located vineyards, Pibarnon is one of BANDOL's leading properties. The reds★★, extremely attractive when young, develop a truffly, wild herb character with age. Average white and a ripe, strawberryish rosé. Best years: (red) 2005 03 01 **00 99 98 97 96 95**.

PIC ST-LOUP *Coteaux du Languedoc AC, Languedoc, France* This COTEAUX DU LANGUEDOC Cru, north of Montpellier, is one of the coolest growing zones in the Midi and, along with la CLAPE, produces some of the best reds in the Languedoc. Syrah is the dominant variety, along with Grenache and Mourvèdre. Whites from Marsanne, Roussanne,

Rolle and Viognier are showing promise. Best producers: Cazeneuve★, CLOS MARIE★, Ermitage du Pic St-Loup, l'Euzière★, l'HORTUS★, Lancyre★, Lascaux★, Lavabre★, MAS BRUGUIERE★, Mas de Mortiès★. Best years: (reds) 2005 04 **03 01 00 99 98**.

FRANZ X PICHLER *Wachau, Niederösterreich, Austria* Austria's most famous producer of dry wines. Top wines Grüner Veltliner and Riesling 'M'★★★ (for monumental) and Riesling Unendlich★★★ (endless) – alcoholically potent but balanced – are amazing. Since 1997 he has teamed up with Szemes and TEMENT in BURGENLAND to make red Arachon★★. Best years: (Riesling/Grüner Veltliner Smaragd) (2006) 05 04 **03** 02 **01 00 99 98 97 95**.

CH. PICHON-LONGUEVILLE★★★ *Pauillac AC, 2ème Cru Classé, Haut-Médoc, Bordeaux, France* Despite its superb vineyards, Pichon-Longueville (called Pichon-Baron until 1988) wines were 'also-rans' for a long time. In 1987 the property was bought by AXA and Jean-Michel Cazes of LYNCH-BAGES took over the management. The improvement was immediate and thrilling. Cazes has now left, but most recent vintages have been of First Growth standard, with firm tannic structure and rich dark fruit. Cellar for at least 10 years, although it is likely to keep for 30. Second wine: les Tourelles de Pichon. Best years: 2005 04 03 02 01 00 **99 98 97** 96 **95 90 89 88 86 82**.

CH. PICHON-LONGUEVILLE-LALANDE★★★
Pauillac AC, 2ème Cru Classé, Haut-Médoc, Bordeaux, France The inspirational figure of May de Lencquesaing forged the modern reputation of this property. It's now (2007) controlled by Champagne house ROEDERER but with the same winemaking and management team. Divinely scented and

lush at 6–7 years, the wines usually last for 20 at least. Recent years have been excellent. Second wine: Réserve de la Comtesse. Best years: 2005 04 03 02 **01** 00 **99 98 97 96 95 91 90 89 88 86 85 83 82**.

PIEDMONT *Italy* The most important Italian region for the tradition of quality wines. In the north, there is Carema, Ghemme and GATTINARA. To the south, in the LANGHE hills, there's BAROLO and BARBARESCO, both masterful examples of the Nebbiolo grape, and other wines from Dolcetto and Barbera grapes. In the Monferrato hills, in the provinces of Asti and Alessandria, the Barbera, Moscato and Cortese grapes hold sway. Recent changes in the system have created the broad DOCs of Langhe and Monferrato and the regionwide Piemonte appellation, designed to classify all wines of quality from a great range of grape varieties. See also ASTI, ERBALUCE DI CALUSO, GAVI, MOSCATO D'ASTI, NEBBIOLO D'ALBA, ROERO.

PIEROPAN *Veneto, Italy* Leonildo Pieropan produces exceptionally good SOAVE Classico★ and, from 2 single vineyards, Calvarino★★ and La Rocca★★. Excellent RECIOTO DI SOAVE Le Colombare★★ and opulent Passito della Rocca★★, a barrique-aged blend of Sauvignon, Riesling Italico and Trebbiano di Soave. Single-vineyard Soaves can improve for 5 years or more, as can the Recioto and other sweet styles.

PIERRO *Margaret River, Western Australia* Mike Peterkin doesn't make that much Pierro Chardonnay★★★, yet still it is a masterpiece of elegance and complexity. The Semillon-Sauvignon LTC★ is full with just a hint of leafiness, while the Pinot Noir★ approaches ★★ as the vines age. Dark, dense Cabernet Sauvignon-Merlot★ is the serious, BORDEAUX-like member of the family. The Fire Gully range is sourced from a nearby vineyard. Best years: (Chardonnay) (2006) (05) 04 03 02 **01 00 99**.

PIESPORT *Mosel, Germany* The generic Piesporter Michelsberg wines, soft, sweet and forgettable, have nothing to do with the excellent Rieslings from the top Goldtröpfchen site. With their intense peach and blackcurrant aromas they are unique among MOSEL wines. Best producers: GRANS-FASSIAN★★, Reinhold HAART★★, Kurt Hain★, von KESSELSTATT★, Lehnert-Veit, St Urbans-Hof★★. Best years: (2006) 05 04 02 **01 00 99 98 97 96 95**.

CH. LE PIN★★★ *Pomerol AC, Bordeaux, France* Now one of the most expensive wines in the world, with prices at auction sometimes overtaking those for PETRUS. The first vintage was 1979 and the wines, which are concentrated but elegant, are produced from 100% Merlot. The tiny 2ha (5-acre) vineyard lies close to those of TROTANOY and VIEUX-CH.-CERTAN. Best years: 2005 04 02 **01 00 99 98 96 95 94 90 89 88 86 85**.

PINE RIDGE *Stags Leap District AVA, California, USA* Wines come from several NAPA AVAs, but its flagship Cabernet remains the supple, plummy STAGS LEAP DISTRICT★★. Andrus Reserve★★, a BORDEAUX blend, has more richness and power, while the HOWELL MOUNTAIN Cabernet★ offers intense fruit and structure for long aging. CARNEROS Merlot★ is spicy and cherry fruited, and Carneros Chardonnay★ looks good. Best years: (Stags Leap Cabernet) 2003 02 **01 00 99 97 96 95 94 91**.

PINGUS, DOMINIO DE *Ribera del Duero DO, Castilla y León, Spain* Peter Sisseck's tiny vineyards and winery have attracted worldwide attention since 1995 due to the extraordinary depth and character of the cult wine they produce, Pingus★★★. Second wine Flor de Pingus★ is also super. Best years: (Pingus) (2005) 04 03 **01 00 99 96 95**.

PINOT BIANCO See PINOT BLANC.

PINOT BLANC Wines have a clear, yeasty, appley taste, and good examples can age to a delicious honeyed fullness. In ALSACE it is taking over the 'workhorse' role from Sylvaner and Chasselas and is the mainstay of most CREMANT D'ALSACE. Important in northern Italy as Pinot Bianco and taken seriously in southern Germany and Austria (as Weissburgunder), producing imposing wines with ripe pear and peach fruit and a distinct nutty character. Also successful in Hungary, Slovakia, Slovenia and the Czech Republic and promising in California, Oregon and Canada.

PINOT GRIGIO See PINOT GRIS.

PINOT GRIS At its finest in ALSACE; with reasonable acidity and a deep colour the grape produces fat, rich wines that mature wonderfully. It is very occasionally used in BURGUNDY (as Pinot Beurot) to add fatness to a wine. Italian Pinot Grigio, often boring, occasionally delicious, is currently so popular worldwide that New World producers are tending to use the Italian name in preference to the French version. Also successful in Austria and Germany as Ruländer or Grauburgunder, and as Malvoisie in the Swiss VALAIS. There are good Romanian and Czech examples, as well as spirited ones in Hungary (as Szürkebarát). In a crisp style, it is successful in Oregon and showing promise in California, Virginia and Okanagan Valley in Canada. Becoming fashionable in New Zealand and cooler regions of Australia.

PINOT NOIR

There's this myth about Pinot Noir that I think I'd better lay to rest. It goes something like this. Pinot Noir is an incredibly tricky grape to grow and an even more difficult grape to vinify; in fact Pinot Noir is such a difficult customer that the only place that regularly achieves magical results is the thin stretch of land known as the Côte d'Or, between Dijon and Chagny in France, where mesoclimate, soil conditions and 2000 years of experience weave an inimitable web of pleasure.

This just isn't so. The thin-skinned, early-ripening Pinot Noir is undoubtedly more difficult to grow than other great varieties like Cabernet or Chardonnay, but that doesn't mean that it's impossible to grow elsewhere – you just have to work at it with more sensitivity and seek out the right growing conditions. And although great red Burgundy is a hauntingly beautiful wine, many Burgundians completely fail to deliver the magic, and the glorious thing about places like New Zealand, California, Oregon, Chile, Australia and Germany is that we are seeing an ever-increasing number of wines that are thrillingly different from anything produced in Burgundy, yet with flavours that are unique to Pinot Noir.

WINE STYLES

France All France's great Pinot Noir wines come from Burgundy's Côte d'Or. Rarely deep in colour, they should nonetheless possess a wonderful fruit quality when young – raspberry, strawberry, cherry or plum – that becomes more scented and exotic with age, the plums turning to figs and pine, and the richness of chocolate mingling perilously with truffles and well-hung game. Strange, challenging, hedonistic. France's other Pinots – in north and south Burgundy, the Loire, Jura, Savoie, Alsace and now occasionally in the south of France – are lighter and milder, and in Champagne its pale, thin wine is used to make sparkling wine.

Other European regions Since the 1990s, helped by good vintages, German winemakers have made considerable efforts to produce serious Pinot Noir (generally called Spätburgunder). Italy, where it is called Pinot Nero, and Switzerland (as Blauburgunder) both have fair success with the variety. Austria and Spain have produced a couple of good examples, and Romania, the Czech Republic and Hungary produce significant amounts of Pinot Noir, though of generally low quality.

New World Light, fragrant wines have bestowed upon Oregon the reputation for being 'another Burgundy'; but I get more excited about the sensual wines of the cool, fog-affected areas of California: the ripe, stylish Russian River Valley examples; the exotically scented wines of Carneros, Anderson Valley and Sonoma Coast; the startlingly original offerings from Santa Barbara County and Santa Lucia Highlands on east-facing slopes of western Monterey County.

New Zealand produces wines of thrilling fruit and individuality, most notably from Martinborough, Canterbury's Waipara district and Central Otago. In the cooler regions of Australia – including Yarra Valley, Adelaide Hills, north-east Victoria and Tasmania – producers are beginning to find their way with the variety. New Burgundian clones bode well for South African Pinot Noir. Chile's Leyda and Bio-Bio areas are beginning to shine.

BEST PRODUCERS

France *Burgundy* d'ANGERVILLE,
l'Arlot, Comte Armand,
D Bachelet, G Barthod,
J-M Boillot, CATHIARD, CHANDON
DE BRIAILLES, R Chevillon, CLAIR,
J-J Confuron, DROUHIN,
C Dugat, B Dugat-Py, DUJAC,
R Engel, FAIVELEY, GIRARDIN,
GOUGES, GRIVOT, Anne GROS,
JADOT, Labouré-Roi, LAFARGE,
LAFON, Dom. LEROY, H Lignier,
MEO-CAMUZET, de MONTILLE,
MORTET, J-F MUGNIER, Ponsot,
POTEL, RION, Dom. de la
ROMANEE-CONTI, E Rouget,
ROUMIER, ROUSSEAU, Sérafin,
TOLLOT-BEAUT, de VOGUE.

Germany BECKER, BERCHER,
FURST, Huber, JOHNER, Meyer-
Näkel, REBHOLZ.

Switzerland GANTENBEIN.

Italy CA' DEL BOSCO, Franz Haas,
Haderburg, Hofstätter, Castello
della SALA.

New World Pinot Noirs
USA (California) ACACIA, AU BON
CLIMAT, Byron, CALERA, CHALONE,
Clos Pepe, Davis Bynum,
DEHLINGER, Dutton-Goldfield,
Merry Edwards, Etude, Gary
Farrell, FLOWERS, HARTFORD
FAMILY, KISTLER, La Crema,
LANDMARK, Littorai, MARCASSIN,
Morgan, Patz & Hall, RASMUSSEN,
ROCHIOLI, SAINTSBURY, SANFORD,
Siduri, SWAN, Talley, WILLIAMS
SELYEM; (Oregon) ARGYLE, BEAUX
FRERES, DOMAINE DROUHIN, Torii
Mor, Ken WRIGHT.

Australia Ashton Hills,
BANNOCKBURN, Bass Phillip, Bindi,
COLDSTREAM HILLS, Curly Flat,
Diamond Valley, Freycinet,
GIACONDA, Kooyong, Paringa,
STONIER, TARRAWARRA, Yabby Lake.

New Zealand ATA RANGI, Carrick,
CRAGGY RANGE (Te Muna Road),
DRY RIVER, FELTON ROAD, FROMM,
Greenhough (Hope Vineyard),
ISABEL, MARTINBOROUGH VINEYARD,
NEUDORF, PALLISER ESTATE, PEGASUS
BAY, Peregrine, Quartz Reef,
SERESIN, VAVASOUR, WITHER HILLS.

South Africa BOUCHARD
FINLAYSON, HAMILTON RUSSELL.

Chile CONO SUR (20 Barrels,
Ocio), Viña Leyda, Porta, Villard.

PINOT MEUNIER An important ingredient in CHAMPAGNE, along with Pinot Noir and Chardonnay – though it is the least well known of the three. Occasionally found in the LOIRE, and also grown in Germany under the names Müllerrebe, Müller-Traube or Schwarzriesling.

PINOT NERO See PINOT NOIR.
PINOT NOIR See pages 232–3.

PINOTAGE A Pinot Noir x Cinsaut cross, conceived in South Africa in 1925 and covering 6% of the country's vineyards. Highly versatile; classic versions are full-bodied and well-oaked with ripe plum, spice and maybe some mineral, banana or marshmallow flavours. New Zealand and California have interesting examples. A little is also grown in Brazil and Zimbabwe. Best producers: (South Africa) Ashbourne★, Graham BECK★, Bellingham (Premium★), BEYERSKLOOF★★, Clos Malverne★, DeWaal★ (Top of the Hill★★), Diemersfontein★, FAIRVIEW★, GRANGEHURST★, Kaapzicht★, KANONKOP★★, L'AVENIR★★, Newton Johnson★, SIMONSIG★, Stony Brook★, Tukulu; (New Zealand) Te Awa★.

PIPER-HEIDSIECK *Champagne AC, Champagne, France* They've put a big effort into restoring Piper's reputation and the work has paid off. Non-vintage★ is now gentle and biscuity, and the vintage★★ is showing real class. They've also launched a plethora of new cuvées: Sublime (demi-sec), Divin (blanc de blancs), Rosé Sauvage and Rare★★, a de luxe non-vintage blend. Best years: (2000) 96 **95 90 89 85 82**.

PIPERS BROOK VINEYARD *Northern Tasmania, Australia* Keenly sought, well-made wines: steely Riesling★★, classically reserved Chardonnay★★, fragrant Gewürztraminer★, refreshing Pinot Gris★ and increasingly good Pinot Noir (Reserve★, Blackwood★, Lyre★★). Its traditional-method sparkling wine, Kreglinger★★ (formerly Pirie) is one of Australia's best. Ninth Island★, the second label, is good. Best years: (Riesling) 2005 04 03 02 **01 00 99 98 97 95 94 93 92 86 82**.

PISANO *Canelones, Uruguay* This family-owned winery can make some of Uruguay's truest expressions of the Tannat grape: RPF is a good example and pure, dense Axis Mundi is from old vines. The more sophisticated Arretxea★ is a blend of Tannat, Cabernet Sauvignon and Merlot. Best years: (reds) 2005 04 **02 00**.

DOM. JO PITHON *Coteaux du Layon AC, Loire Valley, France* Pithon is renowned among the Layon-based producers for his powerful sweet and dry wines with an increasingly subtle use of new oak. Fine sweet COTEAUX DU LAYON★★ and QUARTS DE CHAUME★★ made entirely from botrytized fruit see plenty of oak and drink well fairly young. Les Bonnes Blanches★★ is the most striking of 4 trailblazing dry ANJOU BLANCS, and a young-vines SAVENNIERES shows promise, as does new red ANJOU Les Cabernets. Best years: (dry whites) (2006) 05 04 **03 02 01**.

DOM. ROBERT PLAGEOLES *Gaillac AC, South-West France* Both traditionalist and modernizer, Robert Plageoles has revived 14 ancient grape varieties, which he blends in his sweet Vin d'Autan★★. His dry wines include Mauzac, Ondenc and a bone-dry Mauzac Nature★ fizz.

PLAIMONT, PRODUCTEURS *Madiran AC, Côtes de St-Mont VDQS and Vin de Pays des Côtes de Gascogne, South-West France* This grouping of 3 Gascon co-ops is the largest, most reliable and most go-ahead producer of COTES DE GASCOGNE and COTES DE ST-MONT. The whites, full of crisp fruit, are reasonably priced and are best drunk young. The reds, especially Ch. de la Roque★ and Ch. de Sabazan★, are very good too. Also good MADIRAN (Arte Benedicte) and PACHERENC DU VIC-BILH.

PLANETA *Sicily, Italy* Rapidly expanding, dynamic estate. Chardonnay★★ is already one of the best in southern Italy; Cabernet Sauvignon Burdese★★ and Merlot★★ are becoming some of Italy's most impressive; and rich, peppery Santa Cecilia★★ (Nero d'Avola) has star quality. The white Cometa★★ is a fascinating Sicilian version of FIANO. Gluggable Cerasuolo di Vittoria★ and La Segreta red★ and white★ blends are marvellously fruity.

PLANTAGENET *Great Southern, Western Australia* Influential winery in the GREAT SOUTHERN region, with spicy Shiraz★★, limy Riesling★★, melony/nutty Chardonnay★ and classy Cabernet Sauvignon★. Omrah is the second label, made from bought-in grapes – Sauvignon Blanc★, Chardonnay★, Shiraz★ and Pinot Noir★ stand out. Best years: (Shiraz) 2005 04 03 02 01 **99 98** 97 95 93 90 86 85.

TENUTA IL POGGIONE *Brunello di Montalcino DOCG, Tuscany, Italy* Extensive property (more than 100ha/250 acres of vineyard) which set the standard for traditional-style BRUNELLO DI MONTALCINO★★ (Riserva★★) at a reasonable price. Also fine ROSSO DI MONTALCINO★ and SUPER-TUSCAN Cabernet-Sangiovese blend San Leopoldo★. Best years: (2006) (04) (03) 01 **99 98** 97 95 93 90 88 85.

POL ROGER *Champagne AC, Champagne, France* Non-vintage Brut Réserve★ (formerly known as White Foil) is biscuity and dependable rather than thrilling. Pol Roger also produces a vintage★★, a vintage rosé★★ and a vintage Chardonnay★★. Its top Champagne, the Pinot-dominated Cuvée Sir Winston Churchill★★, is a deliciously refined drink. All vintage wines will improve with at least 5 years' keeping. Best years: (1999) **98** 96 **95** 90 89 88 85 82.

POLIZIANO *Vino Nobile di Montepulciano DOCG, Tuscany, Italy* A leading light in Montepulciano. VINO NOBILE★★ is far better than average, especially the Riserva Vigna Asinone★★. SUPER-TUSCAN Le Stanze★★★ (Cabernet Sauvignon-Merlot) has been outstanding in recent vintages – the fruit in part coming from owner Federico Carletti's other estate, Lohsa, in MORELLINO DI SCANSANO. Best years: (Vino Nobile) (2006) 04 **03** 01 **99 98** 97 95.

POLZ *Steiermark, Austria* Polz is probably the most consistent producer of aromatic dry white wines in Styria. Few wines here fail to reach ★, and with Weissburgunder (Pinot Blanc), Morillon (Chardonnay), Muskateller and Sauvignon Blanc the combination of intensity and elegance frequently deserves ★★. Steierische Klassik indicates wines vinified without any new oak. Best years: (2006) 05 04 **03 02** 01 00.

POMEROL AC *Bordeaux, France* The Pomerol AC includes some of the world's most sought-after red wines. Pomerol's unique quality lies in its deep clay (though gravel also plays a part in some vineyards) in which the Merlot grape flourishes. The result is seductively rich, almost creamy wine with wonderful mouthfilling fruit flavours: often plummy, but with blackcurrants, raisins and chocolate, too, and mint to freshen it up. Best producers: Beauregard★, Bonalgue, le BON PASTEUR★★, Certan-de-May★, Clinet★★, Clos l'Église★★, Clos René, la CONSEILLANTE★★, l'EGLISE-CLINET★★★, l'EVANGILE★★, la FLEUR-PETRUS★★, GAZIN★★, Hosanna★★ (previously Certan-Guiraud), LAFLEUR★★★, LATOUR-A-POMEROL★, Montviel, Nénin★, PETIT-VILLAGE★, PETRUS★★★, Le PIN★★★, TROTANOY★★, VIEUX-CHATEAU-CERTAN★★. Best years: 2005 04 **01 00** 98 96 95 94 90 89 88 86 85 83 82.

POMINO DOC See CHIANTI RUFINA.

POMMARD AC *Côte de Beaune, Burgundy, France* The first village
south of Beaune. At their best, the wines should have full, round,
beefy flavours. Can age well, often for 10 years or more. There are no
Grands Crus but les Rugiens Bas and les Épenots (both Premiers Crus)
occupy the best sites. Best producers: Aleth-Girardin★, Comte
Armand★★★, J-M Boillot★★, Courcel★★, Dancer★, M Gaunoux★,
V GIRARDIN★★, LAFARGE★★, Lejeune★, de MONTILLE★★, J & A Parent★,
Ch. de Pommard★, Pothier-Rieusset★. Best years: (2006) 05 03 02 99 **98
97 96 95 90**.

POMMERY *Champagne AC, Champagne, France* High-quality CHAMPAGNE
house now owned by Vranken, who have maintained the traditional
Pommery style but in recent years have launched 9 – yes 9 – non-
vintage cuvées! I can't keep up. Along with Brut Royal and
Apanage★, the range now includes Summertime blanc de blancs,
Wintertime blanc de noirs and Springtime, a Pinot Noir-dominated
rosé. Austere vintage Brut★ is delicious with maturity, and the
prestige cuvée Louise, both white★★ and rosé★★, is the epitome of
discreet, perfumed elegance. Best years: (1998) 96 **95 92 90 89 88 85 82**.

PONDALOWIE *Bendigo, Victoria, Australia* Dominic and Krystina Morris
are dynamic producers making a name for their red wines, including
some absolutely ripper Shiraz★, Shiraz-Viognier★ and Tempranillo★.

CH. PONTET-CANET★★ *Pauillac AC, 5ème Cru Classé, Haut-Médoc,
Bordeaux, France* This property's vineyards are located close to
those of MOUTON-ROTHSCHILD. Since 1975, when the Tesserons of LAFON-
ROCHET bought the property, there has been a gradual return to the
typical PAUILLAC style of big, chewy, intense claret that develops a
beautiful blackcurrant fruit, and since 2000 the property has been on
fine form. It's one of the wines of the vintage in 2005 – and that's
saying something. One of the best value of the Classed Growths. Best
years: 2005 04 03 02 **01** 00 **99 98 96 95 94 90 89 86 85**.

PORT See pages 238–9.

NICOLAS POTEL *Burgundy, France* Energetic young négociant producing
consistently fine wines at attractive prices. Particularly strong in his
native VOLNAY★★ and in NUITS-ST-GEORGES★★. Now increasing white
wine production. Owned by large négociant Labouré-Roi. Best years:
(2006) 05 **04** 03 **02 01 00** 99.

CH. POTENSAC★★ *Médoc AC, Cru Bourgeois, Bordeaux, France* Owned
and run by the Delon family, of LEOVILLE-LAS-CASES, Potensac's fabulous
success is based on quality, consistency and value for money. The
wine can be drunk at 4–5 years, but fine vintages will improve for at
least 10 years. Best years: 2005 04 03 02 **01 00 99 98 96 95 90 89 88**.

POUILLY-FUISSÉ AC *Mâconnais, Burgundy, France* Chardonnay from 5
villages, including Pouilly and Fuissé. After a period of poor value,
there are now some committed growers producing buttery, creamy
wines that can be delicious at 2 years but will often develop
beautifully for up to 10. Best producers: D & M Barraud★★, Bret
Brothers★★, Cordier★★, Corsin★★, C & T Drouin★, J-A Ferret★★, Ch.
Fuissé★★, Guffens-Heynen (VERGET)★★, R Lassarat★★, R Luquet★, O
Merlin★★, Robert-Denogent★★, Ch. des Rontets★★, Saumaize-
Michelin★★, Valette★★. Best years: (2006) 05 **04** 03 **02 01 00** 99.

POUILLY-FUMÉ AC *Loire Valley, France* Fumé means 'smoked' in
French and a good Pouilly-Fumé has a pungent smell often likened to
gunflint. The grape is Sauvignon Blanc, and the extra smokiness

comes from a flinty soil called silex. Despite the efforts of a few producers, this is a disappointingly underperforming and overpriced AC. Best producers: F Blanchet★, Henri BOURGEOIS★, A Cailbourdin★, J-C Chatelain★, Didier DAGUENEAU★★, Serge Dagueneau★, André Dezat, A & E Figeat, Ladoucette★, Landrat-Guyollot★, Masson-Blondelet★, M Redde★, Seguin, Sellier, Tinel-Blondelet★, Ch. de Tracy★. Best years: 2006 05 **04 02 00**.

POUILLY-LOCHÉ AC See POUILLY-VINZELLES AC.

POUILLY-SUR-LOIRE AC *Loire Valley, France* Light appley wines from the Chasselas grape from vineyards around Pouilly-sur-Loire, the town which gave its name to POUILLY-FUMÉ. Drink as young as possible.

POUILLY-VINZELLES AC *Mâconnais, Burgundy, France* Small AC which, with its neighbour Pouilly-Loché, lies somewhat in the shadow of POUILLY-FUISSÉ. Most wines come through the co-operative, but there are some good domaines. Best producers: Cave des Grands Crus Blancs, la Soufrandière★★, Tripoz★, Valette★. Best years: (2006) **05 04 03 02**.

CH. POUJEAUX★ *Moulis AC, Cru Bourgeois, Haut-Médoc, Bordeaux, France* Frequently Poujeaux is the epitome of MOULIS – beautifully balanced, gentle ripe fruit jostled by stony dryness – but just lacking that something extra to propel it to a higher plane. Attractive at 5–6 years old, good vintages can easily last for 10–20 years. Best years: 2005 04 03 02 **01 00 99 98 96 95 90 86 85**.

PRAGER *Wachau, Niederösterreich, Austria* Toni Bodenstein is one of the pioneers of the WACHAU, producing top dry Rieslings from the Achleiten and Klaus vineyards★★★ and excellent Grüner Veltliners from the Achleiten vineyard★★. Best years: (Riesling/Grüner Veltliner Smaragd) (2006) 05 04 **03** 02 **01 00 99 98 97 96 95**.

PREMIÈRES CÔTES DE BLAYE AC *Bordeaux, France* A much improved AC on the right bank of the Gironde. The fresh, Merlot-based reds are ready at 2–3 years but will age for more. Top red wines can be labelled under the new, quality-driven Blaye AC from 2000. Best producers: (reds) Bel-Air la Royère★, Confiance★, Gigault (Cuvée Viva★), Les Grands Maréchaux, Haut-Bertinerie★, Haut-Colombier★, Haut-Grelot, Haut-Sociando, les Jonqueyres★, Mondésir-Gazin★, Montfollet★, Roland la Garde★, Segonzac★, Tourtes★; (whites) Haut-Bertinerie★, Charron (Acacia★), Cave des Hauts de Gironde, Tourtes (Prestige★). Best years: 2005 **04 03 01 00 98 96 95**.

PREMIÈRES CÔTES DE BORDEAUX AC *Bordeaux, France* Hilly region overlooking GRAVES and SAUTERNES across the Garonne. For a long time the AC was best known for its Sauternes-style sweet wines, particularly from the communes of CADILLAC, LOUPIAC and STE-CROIX-DU-MONT, but the juicy reds and rosés have now forged ahead. These are usually delicious at 2–3 years old but should last for 5–6 years. Dry whites are designated BORDEAUX AC. Best producers: (reds) Bauduc★, Carignan★, Chelivette, Clos Ste-Anne, Grand-Mouëys★, Lamothe-de-Haux, Lezongars★, Mont-Pérat★, Plaisance★, Puy-Bardens★, REYNON★, Ste-Marie (Alios★), Suau★. Best years: (reds) **2005 00 98 96 95**.

CH. PRIEURÉ-LICHINE★ *Margaux AC, 4ème Cru Classé, Haut-Médoc, Bordeaux, France* Seriously underachieving property that saw several false dawns before being sold in 1999. Right Bank specialist Stéphane Derenoncourt of PAVIE-MACQUIN and CANON-LA-GAFFELIÈRE fame is now the consultant winemaker, and the wines now have more fruit, finesse and perfume, especially the 2004. Best years: 2005 04 **03** 02 **01 00 99 98 96 95 90 89 86**.

PORT DOC
Douro, Portugal

The Douro region in northern Portugal, where the grapes for port are grown, is wild and beautiful, and now classified as a World Heritage Site. Steep hills covered in vineyard terraces plunge dramatically down to the Douro river. Grapes are one of the few crops that will grow in the inhospitable climate, which gets progressively drier the further inland you travel. But not all the Douro's grapes qualify to be made into port. A quota is established every year, and the rest are made into increasingly good unfortified Douro wines.

Red port grapes include Touriga Franca, Tinta Roriz, Touriga Nacional, Tinta Barroca, Tinta Cão and Tinta Amarela. Grapes for white port include Codega, Malvasia Fina, Rabigato and Gouveio. Grapes for both are partially fermented, and then *aguardente* (grape spirit) is added – fortifying the wine, stopping the fermentation and leaving sweet, unfermented grape sugar in the finished port.

PORT STYLES

Vintage Finest of the ports matured in bottle, made from grapes from the best vineyards. Vintage port is not 'declared' every year (usually there are 3 or 4 declarations per decade), and only during the second calendar year in cask if the shipper thinks the standard is high enough. It is bottled after 2 years, and may be consumed soon afterwards, as is not uncommon in the USA; at this stage it packs quite a punch. The British custom of aging for 20 years or more can yield exceptional mellowness. Vintage port throws a thick sediment, so requires decanting.

Single quinta (Vintage) A true single-quinta wine comes from an individual estate; however, many shippers sell their vintage port under a quinta name in years which are not declared as a vintage, even though it may be sourced from 2 or 3 different vineyards. It is quite possible for these 'off vintage' ports to equal or even surpass the vintage wines from the same house.

Aged tawny Matured in cask for 10, 20, 30 or even 40 years before bottling, older tawnies have delicious nut and fig flavours.

Colheita Tawny from a single vintage, matured in cask for at least 7 years – potentially the finest of the aged tawnies.

Late Bottled (Vintage) (LBV) Port matured for 4–6 years in vat, then usually filtered to avoid sediment forming in the bottle. Traditional unfiltered LBV has much more flavour and requires decanting; it can generally be aged for another 5 years or more.

Crusted Making a comeback, this is a blend of good ports from 2–3 vintages, bottled without filtration after 3–4 years in cask. A deposit (crust) forms in the bottle and the wine should be decanted.

Reserve (most can be categorized as Premium Ruby) has an average of 3–5 years' age. A handful represent good value.

Ruby The youngest red port with only 1–3 years' age. Ruby port should be bursting with young, almost peppery fruit, and there has been an improvement in quality of late, except at the cheapest level.

Tawny Cheap tawny is either an emaciated ruby, or a blend of ruby and white port, and is both dilute and raw.

White Only the best taste dry and nutty from wood-aging; most are coarse and alcoholic, best with tonic water and a slice of lemon.

BEST PRODUCERS

Vintage BURMESTER, CHURCHILL,
COCKBURN, CROFT, Delaforce,
DOW, FERREIRA, FONSECA,
GRAHAM'S, NIEPOORT, Quinta do
NOVAL, Portal, RAMOS PINTO,
SMITH WOODHOUSE, TAYLOR,
WARRE.

Single quinta (Vintage)
CHURCHILL (Quinta da Gricha),
COCKBURN (Quinta dos Canais),
Quinta do CRASTO,
CROFT (Quinta da Roêda),
DOW (Quinta do Bomfim),
FONSECA (Guimaraens),
GRAHAM'S (Malvedos), Martinez
(Quinta da Eira Velha),
NIEPOORT (Quinta do
Passadouro), NOVAL (Silval),
Quinta de la ROSA, SMITH
WOODHOUSE (Madalena), TAYLOR
(Quinta de Terra Feita, Quinta
de Vargellas), Quinta Vale
Dona Maria, Quinta do Vale
Meão, Quinta do Vallado,
Quinta do VESUVIO, WARRE
(Quinta da Cavadinha).

Aged tawny Barros,
BURMESTER, COCKBURN, DOW,
FERREIRA, FONSECA, GRAHAM'S,
Krohn, NIEPOORT, NOVAL, RAMOS
PINTO, SANDEMAN, TAYLOR, WARRE.

Colheita Andresen, Barros,
BURMESTER, Feist, Kopke,
Krohn, NIEPOORT, NOVAL.

**Traditional Late Bottled
Vintage** Andresen, CHURCHILL,
CRASTO, FONSECA, Infantado,
NIEPOORT, NOVAL, Poças,
RAMOS PINTO, la ROSA,
SMITH WOODHOUSE, WARRE.

Crusted CHURCHILL, DOW.

Ruby COCKBURN, FERREIRA,
FONSECA, GRAHAM'S, la ROSA,
SANDEMAN, SMITH WOODHOUSE,
TAYLOR, WARRE.

White CHURCHILL, NIEPOORT.

239

PRIEURÉ DE ST-JEAN DE BÉBIAN *Coteaux du Languedoc AC, Languedoc, France* One of the pioneering estates in the Midi. It took a dip in the early 1990s but is once more back on form, producing an intense, spicy, generous red★★, second after La Chapelle de Bébian and a barrel-fermented white. Best years: (red) 2002 **01 00 99 98**.

PRIMITIVO DI MANDURIA DOC *Puglia, Italy* The most important appellation for PUGLIA's Primitivo grape, which has been enjoying a renaissance of interest since it was found to be almost identical to California's Zinfandel. The best wines combine outstanding ripeness and concentration with a knockout alcohol level. Good Primitivo is also sold as IGT Primitivo del Tarantino. Best producers: Felline★★, Pervini★★, Giovanni Soloperto. Best years: (2006) (05) **04 03 01 00**.

PRIMO ESTATE *Adelaide Plains/McLaren Vale, South Australia* Innovative Joe Grilli has worked miracles over the years, making a virtue out of the heat of the Adelaide Plains. While the Colombard vineyards remain on the Adelaide Plains, much of the focus has shifted to MCLAREN VALE. The premium label is Joseph: Grilli adapts the Italian *amarone* method for Moda Amarone Cabernet-Merlot★★ (★★★ with 10 years' age!) and makes a dense, eye-popping Joseph Red fizz★. He also does a sensuous Botrytis Riesling La Magia★★, fabulous honeyed fortified Fronti★★★, surprising dry white La Biondina Colombard★, and cherry-ripe Il Briccone★, a Shiraz-Sangiovese blend, fine Nebbiolo★ – and superb olive oils★★★. Best years: (Cabernet-Merlot Joseph) 2006 05 04 02 01 **00 99 98 97 96 95 94 93 91 90**.

PRIMO PALATUM *Languedoc and South-West France* One of the new breed of négociants working between many appellations. Xavier Copel selects the best wines from CAHORS★, JURANÇON★, MADIRAN★, MINERVOIS★ and COTES DU ROUSSILLON as well as buying wine from Bordeaux. Cahors cuvées Classica and Mythologia are dark and concentrated.

PRIORAT DOCa *Cataluña, Spain* A hilly, isolated district with very low-yielding vineyards planted on precipitous slopes of deep slate soil. Old-style fortified *rancio* wines used to attract little attention. Then in the 1980s a group of young winemakers revolutionized the area, bringing in state-of-the-art winemaking methods and grape varieties such as Cabernet Sauvignon to back up the native Garnacha and Cariñena. Their rare, expensive wines have taken the world by storm. Ready at 5 years old, the best will last much longer. The region was elevated to DOCa status in 2001. Best producers: Bodegas B G (Gueta-Lupiá★), Capafons-Ossó★, Cims de Porrera★★, CLOS ERASMUS★★★, CLOS MOGADOR★★★, Combier-Fischer-Gerin★★ (Trio Infernal 2/3★★★), La Conreria d'Scala Dei★, Costers del Siurana (Clos de l'Obac★), J M Fuentes (Gran Clos★★), Ithaca★, MAS DOIX★★★, Mas d'en Gil (Clos Fontà★), Mas Martinet (Clos Martinet★), Mas Romaní★★, Alvaro PALACIOS★★★, Pasanau Germans (Finca la Planeta★), Rotllan Torra★, Scala Dei★, VALL-LLACH★★. Best years: (reds) (2005) (04) 03 01 **00 99 98 96 95 94 93**.

PROSECCO DI CONEGLIANO-VALDOBBIADENE DOC *Veneto, Italy* The Prosecco grape gives soft, scented wine made sparkling by a second fermentation in tank, though Prosecco can also be still, or *tranquillo*. Generally, however, it is a spumante or frizzante for drinking young. The Cartizze sub-zone near Valdobbiadene produces the most refined wines. Best producers: Adami★, Bernardi★, Bisol★, Carpenè Malvolti★, Le Colture, Col Vetoraz★, Nino Franco★, La Riva dei Frati★, Ruggeri & C★, Tanorè★, Zardetto★.

PROVENCE *France* Provence is home to France's oldest vineyards but the region has been better known for its beaches and arts festivals than for its wines. However, it seems even Provence is caught up in the revolution sweeping through the vineyards of southern France. The area has 5 small ACs (BANDOL, les BAUX-DE-PROVENCE, BELLET, CASSIS and PALETTE), but most of the wine comes from the much larger areas of the COTES DE PROVENCE, COTEAUX VAROIS, Coteaux de Pierrevert and COTEAUX D'AIX-EN-PROVENCE. Vin de Pays des BOUCHES-DU-RHONE is also becoming increasingly important. Provençal reds are generally better than whites and rosés.

J J PRÜM *Bernkastel, Mosel, Germany* Estate making some of Germany's best Riesling in sites like the Sonnenuhr★★★ in WEHLEN, Himmelreich★★ in GRAACH and Lay★★ and Badstube★★ in BERNKASTEL. All have great aging potential. Best years: (2006) 05 04 03 02 01 **99 98 97 96 95 94 93 90 88 85 83**.

S A PRÜM *Wehlen, Mosel, Germany* There are a confusing number of Prüms in the MOSEL – the best known is J J PRUM, but S A Prüm comes a decent second. The estate's most interesting wines are Riesling from WEHLENer Sonnenuhr, especially Auslese★★, but it also makes good wine from sites in BERNKASTEL★ and GRAACH★. Best years: (2006) 05 04 03 02 01 **99 97 95 93**.

PRUNOTTO *Barolo DOCG, Piedmont, Italy* One of the great BAROLO producers, now ably run by Albiera, the eldest of Piero ANTINORI's 3 daughters. Highlights include Barolo Bussia★★★ and Cannubi★★, BARBERA D'ALBA Pian Romualdo★★, BARBERA D'ASTI Costamiòle★★, BARBARESCO Bric Turot★★ and NEBBIOLO D'ALBA Occhetti★. Also good MOSCATO D'ASTI★, Barbera d'Asti Fiulot★ and ROERO Arneis★. Best years: (Barolo) (2006) (04) 03 01 **00 99 98 97 95 93 90 89 88 85**.

PUGLIA *Italy* This southern region is a prolific source of blending wines, but exciting progress has been made with native varieties: red Uva di Troia in CASTEL DEL MONTE; white Greco for characterful Gravina, revived by Botromagno; and Verdeca and Bianco d'Alessano for Locorotondo. The red Primitivo, led by examples from producers under the ACCADEMIA DEI RACEMI umbrella, make a big impact (whether under the PRIMITIVO DI MANDURIA DOC or more general IGTs). But it is the Negroamaro grape grown on traditional bush-trained or *alberello* vines in the Salento peninsula that provides the best wines, whether red or rosé. Outstanding examples include Vallone's Graticciaia★★, Candido's Duca d'Aragona★★ and Taurino's Patriglione★★. Brindisi and SALICE SALENTINO are two good-value, reliable DOCs.

PUISSEGUIN-ST-ÉMILION AC *Bordeaux, France* Small ST-EMILION satellite AC. The wines are generally fairly solid but with an attractive chunky fruit and usually make good drinking at 3–5 years. Best producers: Bel-Air, Branda, Durand-Laplagne★, Fongaban, Guibeau-la-Fourvieille, Laurets, la Mauriane★, Producteurs Réunis, Soleil★. Best years: 2005 **03 01 00 98 96 95**.

PULIGNY-MONTRACHET AC *Côte de Beaune, Burgundy, France* Puligny is one of the finest white wine villages in the world and adds the name of its greatest Grand Cru, le MONTRACHET, to its own. There are 3 other Grands Crus (BATARD-MONTRACHET, Bienvenues-BATARD-MONTRACHET and Chevalier-MONTRACHET) and 11 Premiers Crus. The flatter vineyards use the Puligny-Montrachet AC. Good vintages really need 5 years' aging, while Premiers Crus and Grands Crus may need 10 years and can last for 20 or more. A few barrels of red wine are made. Best producers: J-M Boillot★★, CARILLON★★★, Chavy★, Deux MONTILLE★, DROUHIN★★, A Ente★★, B Ente★, JADOT★★, Larue★★, LATOUR★, Dom. LEFLAIVE★★★, O LEFLAIVE★, P Pernot★★, Ch. de Puligny-Montrachet★★, RAMONET★★, SAUZET★★. Best years: (2006) 05 **04 02 01 00 99**.

PYRENEES See GRAMPIANS AND PYRENEES.

QUARTS DE CHAUME AC *Loire Valley, France*   The Chenin Blanc grape finds one of its most rewarding mesoclimates here. Quarts de Chaume is a 40ha (100-acre) AC within the larger COTEAUX DU LAYON AC and, as autumn mists begin to curl off the river Layon, noble rot attacks the grapes. The result is intense, sweet wines which can last for longer than almost any in the world – although many can be drunk after 5 years. Best producers: BAUMARD★★★, Bellerive★★, Laffourcade★, Pierre-Bise★★, J PITHON★★, Plaisance★, Joseph Renou★★, Suronde★★, la Varière★. Best years: (2006) 05 04 **03** 02 01 **99 97 96 95 90 89**.

QUEBRADA DE MACUL *Maipo, Chile*   Located toward the east of Santiago, at the foot of the Andes, this garage winery was created by winemaker Ignacio Recabarren to produce superbly idiosyncratic Cabernet Sauvignon-based Domus Aurea★★, a red packed with MAIPO character. Recabarren left in 2002 and Bordelais Patrick Valette is now in charge as a consultant winemaker; the wines have become a little more mainstream. Best years: (Domus Aurea) 2003 02 **01 99 97**.

QUEENSLAND *Australia*   The Queensland wine industry is expanding fast and now produces more than TASMANIA. Here wine is closely linked to tourism. About 60 wineries perch on rocky hills in the main region, the Granite Belt, near the NEW SOUTH WALES border. New areas South Burnett (north-west of Brisbane), Darling Downs (around the town of Toowoomba) and Mount Tamborine in the Gold Coast hinterland are showing promise. Best producers: Albert River, Barambah Ridge, BOIREANN★, Robert Channon★, Clovely Estate, Heritage, Jimbour Station, Preston Peak★, Robinsons Family, Sirromet, Summit Estate.

QUERCIABELLA *Chianti Classico DOCG, Tuscany, Italy*   This model of a modern Chianti producer serves up a gorgeously scented, rich-fruited CHIANTI CLASSICO★★. But it has made an even greater splash with its three SUPER-TUSCANS: BURGUNDY-like white Batàr★★ from Pinot Bianco and Chardonnay; tobaccoey, spicy Sangiovese-Cabernet blend Camartina★★★; and Palafreno★, a blend of Sangiovese and Merlot. Best years: (Camartina) (2006) (04) 03 **01 99 97 95 93 90 88**.

QUILCEDA CREEK *Washington State, USA*   One of America's top Cabernet Sauvignons★★★, a wine with intense concentration and exceptional character. It benefits from cellaring for 7–10 years. Supple, rich Merlot★★★ is produced in small quantities. A less expensive Columbia Valley Red★★ offers a tantalizing glimpse of the winemaking style. Best years: (2005) (04) 03 **02 01 99 97**.

QUINCY AC *Loire Valley, France*   Appealingly aggressive gooseberry-flavoured, dry white wine from Sauvignon Blanc vineyards west of Bourges. Can age for a year or two. Best producers: Ballandors★, H BOURGEOIS★, Mardon★, J Rouzé, Silices de Quincy★, Trotereau★.

QUINTARELLI *Valpolicella DOC, Veneto, Italy*   Giuseppe Quintarelli is the great traditional winemaker of VALPOLICELLA. His philosophy is one of growing only the very best grapes and leaving nature to do the rest. His Classico Superiore★★ is left in cask for about 4 years and his famed

AMARONE★★★ and RECIOTO★★ for up to 7 years before release. Alzero★★ is a spectacular Amarone-style wine made from Cabernets Franc and Sauvignon. Best years: (Amarone) (2004) (03) 01 99 **97 95 93 90 88 85 83**.

QUPÉ *Santa Maria Valley AVA, California, USA* Owner/winemaker Bob Lindquist makes a savoury, tasty Bien Nacido Syrah★. His Reserve Chardonnay★★ and Bien Nacido Cuvée★★ (a Chardonnay-Viognier blend) have sublime appley fruit and perfume. A leading exponent of red and white RHONE-style wines, including Viognier★ and Marsanne★. Best years: (Syrah) (2005) 04 03 **02 01 00 99 98 97 96 95 94 91 90**.

CH. DE LA RAGOTIÈRE *Muscadet Sèvre-et-Maine, Loire Valley, France* The inventive Couillaud brothers claim to have salvaged the reputation of Muscadet in US restaurants with M★★, an old-vines wine matured *sur lie* for over 2 years. The standard Muscadet★ is elegant and built to last, too; lighter ones come from the Couillauds' other property, Ch. la Morinière. Vin de pays Chardonnay is a speciality (Auguste Couillaud★) and a host of experimental varieties appear under the Collection Privée label (Sauvignon Gris★). Les Zunics is an exciting, fragrant vin de table blend. Best years: (M) **2001 99 97**.

RAÏMAT *Costers del Segre DO, Cataluña, Spain* Owned by CODORNIU, this large, irrigated estate makes pleasant and refreshingly balanced wines from Tempranillo, Cabernet Sauvignon (Mas Castell vineyard★) and Chardonnay. Lively 100% Chardonnay CAVA and upscale red blend 4 Varietales. Best years: (reds) 2004 **03 01 00 99 98**.

RAMONET *Chassagne-Montrachet, Côte de Beaune, Burgundy, France* The Ramonets (Noël and Claude) produce some of the most complex of all white Burgundies from 3 Grands Crus (BATARD-MONTRACHET★★★, Bienvenues-BATARD-MONTRACHET★★★ and le MONTRACHET★★★) and Premiers Crus including Ruchottes★★★, Caillerets★★★, Boudriotte★★, Vergers★★, Morgeot★★ and Chaumées★★★. If you want to spare your wallet try the ST-AUBIN★★ or the CHASSAGNE-MONTRACHET white★★ or red★★. Best years: (whites) (2006) 05 04 03 02 **01 00 99 98 97 92 90 89**.

JOÃO PORTUGAL RAMOS *Alentejo, Portugal* João Portugal Ramos is one of Portugal's foremost winemakers. Smoky, peppery Trincadeira★★, spicy Aragonês (Tempranillo)★, powerful Syrah★ and intensely dark-fruited red blend Vila Santa★★ are all superb. Marquês de Borba★ is the label for everyday reds and whites, and a brilliant red Reserva★★ is also made. New World-style Tagus Creek is setting new standards in juicy, affordable styles. Best years: **2005 04 01 00 99 97**.

RAMOS PINTO *Douro DOC and Port DOC, Douro, Portugal* Innovative PORT company owned by ROEDERER, making complex, full-bodied Late Bottled Vintage★ and aged tawnies (10-year-old Quinta da Ervamoira★★ and 20-year-old Quinta do Bom Retiro★★★). Vintage Ports★★ are rich and early maturing. DOURO reds Duas Quintas (Reserva★, Reserva Especial★★) and Bons Ares★ are reliable. Best years: (Vintage) 2004 03 00 97 **95 94 83**.

CASTELLO DEI RAMPOLLA *Chianti Classico DOCG, Tuscany, Italy* Outstanding CHIANTI CLASSICO★★. SUPER-TUSCAN Sammarco, sometimes ★★★, is mostly Cabernet with some Sangiovese; Vigna d'Alceo★★★ adds Petit Verdot to Cabernet Sauvignon. Best years: (Sammarco) (2006) 04 03 **01 00 99 98 97 95**; (Vigna d'Alceo) (2006) (04) 03 01 **00 99 98 97**.

243

RANDERSACKER *Franken, Germany* Important wine village just outside the city of Würzburg in FRANKEN, producing excellent, medium-bodied dry Rieslings, dry Silvaners, spicy Traminer and piercingly intense Rieslaner. Best producers: JULIUSSPITAL★, Schmitt's Kinder★, Störrlein★. Best years: (2006) 05 04 **03 02 01 00 99 98**.

RAPEL, VALLE DEL *Valle Central, Chile* One of Chile's most exciting red wine regions, Rapel covers both the Valle del Cachapoal in the north and the Valle de COLCHAGUA in the south. Both are the cradle of Chilean Carmenère. Best producers: Altaïr★/SAN PEDRO, Anakena, CASA LAPOSTOLLE★★, CONCHA Y TORO★★, CONO SUR★, EMILIANA★★, Gracia★, LA ROSA★, MONTES★★, MontGras, Torreón de Paredes, Viu Manent★.

KENT RASMUSSEN *Carneros AVA, California, USA* Burgundian-style Chardonnay★★ capable of considerable aging and a fascinating juicy Pinot Noir★★ are made by ultra-traditional methods. Also occasional delightful oddities like Alicante and Dolcetto under the Ramsay label. Best years: (Pinot Noir) (2005) 02 **01 00 99 98 95 94 91 90**.

RASTEAU *Rhône Valley, France* The single-village AC is for fortified Grenache red or white wine and a *rancio* version which is left in barrel for 2 or more years. However, much of the best wine from Rasteau is full-bodied dry red, which comes under the COTES DU RHONE-VILLAGES AC. Best producers: Beaurenard★, Cave des Vignerons, Mourt de Gautens★★, Perrin★, Rabasse-Charavin, Santa Duc, la Soumade★, du Trapadis★.

RENATO RATTI *Barolo DOCG, Piedmont, Italy* The late Renato Ratti led the revolution in winemaking in the Alba area with BAROLO and BARBARESCO of better balance, colour and richness and softer in tannins than the traditional models. Today his son Pietro and nephew Massimo Martinelli produce sound Barolo★ from the Marcenasco vineyards at La Morra, as well as good BARBERA D'ALBA Torriglione★, Dolcetto d'Alba Colombè★, NEBBIOLO D'ALBA Ochetti★ and Monferrato DOC Villa Pattono★, a blend of Barbera with Cabernet and Merlot.

RAUENTHAL *Rheingau, Germany* Sadly, only a few producers live up to the reputation earned by this RHEINGAU village's great Baiken and Gehrn sites for intense, spicy Rieslings. Best producers: Georg BREUER★★, Staatsweingut. Best years: (2006) 05 04 03 02 **01 00 99 98 97**.

CH. RAUZAN-SÉGLA★★ *Margaux AC, 2ème Cru Classé, Haut-Médoc, Bordeaux, France* A dynamic change of winemaking regime in 1982 and the purchase of the property by Chanel in 1994 have propelled Rauzan-Ségla up the quality ladder. Now the wines have a rich blackcurrant fruit, almost tarry, thick tannins and weight, powerful woody spice and good concentration. Second wine: Ségla. Best years: 2005 04 03 02 **01 00 99 98 96 95 94 90 89 88 86 85 83**.

JEAN-MARIE RAVENEAU *Chablis, Burgundy, France* Beautifully nuanced CHABLIS from 3 Grands Crus (Blanchot★★★, les Clos★★★, Valmur★★★) and 4 Premiers Crus (Montée de Tonnerre★★★, Vaillons★★, Butteaux★★★, Chapelot★★), using a combination of old oak and stainless-steel fermentation. The wines can age for a decade or more. Best years: (top crus) (2006) 05 04 **03 02 00 99 97 95 92 90 89**.

RAVENSWOOD *Sonoma Valley AVA, California, USA* Joel Peterson, one of California's best-known Zin experts, established Ravenswood in 1976. During the lean years, when most Zinfandel was pink and sweet, he added an intense Chardonnay, a sometimes very good Cabernet Sauvignon★ and several tasty Merlots (Sangiacomo★★). But Zinfandel remains the trump card. Early 21st-century offerings were disappointing – especially large-volume Vintners Blend – but this has now picked up, and Amador★ and Lodi★ wines are tasty and characterful, and sometimes outperform the Sonoma products (some single-vineyard wines can be ★★). The Constellation group purchased the winery in 2001. Best years: (Zins) 2002 **01 00 99 97 96 95 94 91 90**.

CH. RAYAS *Châteauneuf-du-Pape, Rhône Valley, France* Emmanuel Reynaud, nephew of the eccentric Jacques Reynaud, runs this estate in his uncle's inimitable rule-breaking style, producing usually exotically rich reds★★★ and whites★★ which also age well. Prices are not cheap and the wines are not consistent, but at its best Rayas is thrilling. The red is made entirely from low-yielding Grenache vines – the only such wine in the AC – while the white is a blend of Clairette, Grenache Blanc and (so rumour has it) Chardonnay. Second-label Pignan can also be impressive. COTES DU RHONE Ch. de Fonsalette★★ is usually wonderful. Best years: (Châteauneuf-du-Pape) (2005) 04 03 01 **99 98 96 95 94 91 90 89 88 86**; (whites) 2005 04 03 01 **00 99 98 97 96 95 94 91 90 89**.

REBHOLZ *Siebeldingen, Pfalz, Germany* This estate in the southern PFALZ produces crystalline Riesling★★, Weissburgunder★★ and Grauburgunder★, with vibrant fruit aromas. Top of the range are intensely mineral dry Riesling★★★ from the Kastanienbusch and Sonnenschein vineyards, powerful dry Gewürztraminer★★ and extravagantly aromatic dry Muskateller★★. The sparkling wine★★, from barrel-fermented Pinot varieties, is among Germany's most elegant. Also Germany's finest Chardonnay★★ and serious Spätburgunder★★ (Pinot Noir) reds. Best years: (whites) (2006) 05 04 **03** 02 01 **00 99 98**; (reds) (2006) 05 04 **03 02 01 00 99 98**.

RECIOTO DELLA VALPOLICELLA DOC *Veneto, Italy* The great sweet wine of VALPOLICELLA, made from grapes picked earlier than usual and left to dry on straw mats until February or even March. The wines are deep in colour, with a rich, bitter-sweet cherryish fruit. Top wines age well for 10 years, but most are best drunk young. As with Valpolicella, the Classico tag is important, if not essential. Best producers: Accordini★, ALLEGRINI★★, Bolla (Spumante★★), Brigaldara★, BUSSOLA★★★, Michele Castellani★★, DAL FORNO★★★, MASI★, QUINTARELLI★★, Le Ragose★, Le Salette★, Serègo Alighieri★★, Speri★, Tedeschi★, Tommasi★, Villa Monteleone★★, Viviani★. Best years: (2005) 04 **03 01 00 98 97**.

RECIOTO DI SOAVE DOCG *Veneto, Italy* Sweet white wine made in the SOAVE zone from dried grapes, like RECIOTO DELLA VALPOLICELLA. Garganega grapes give wonderfully delicate yet intense wines that age well for up to a decade. One of the best, ANSELMI's I Capitelli, is now sold as IGT Veneto. Best producers: ANSELMI★★, La Cappuccina★★, Cà Rugate★, Coffele★★, Gini★★, PIEROPAN★★, Bruno Sartori★, Tamellini★★. Best years: (2006) 04 **03 01 00 98 97**.

RÉGNIÉ AC *Beaujolais, Burgundy, France* In good years this BEAUJOLAIS Cru is light, aromatic and enjoyable along the style of CHIROUBLES, but can be thin in lesser years. Best producers: DUBOEUF (des Buyats★), Rampon, Gilles Roux/de la Plaigne★, Tracot/ Dubost★. Best years: **2006 05**.

DOM. LA RÉMÉJEANNE *Côtes du Rhône AC, Rhône Valley, France* First-class property making a range of strikingly individual, sometimes heady wines. COTES DU RHONE-VILLAGES les Genèvriers★★ has the weight and texture of good CHATEAUNEUF-DU-PAPE, while COTES DU RHONE Syrah les Eglantiers★★ is superb. Both need at least 3–5 years' aging. Also good Côtes du Rhône les Chèvrefeuilles★ and les Arbousiers (red and white). Best years: (les Eglantiers) 2006 **05 04 03 01 00**.

REMELLURI *Rioja DOCa, País Vasco, Spain* Organic RIOJA estate producing red wines with far more fruit than usual and good concentration for aging – the best are ★★. There is also a delicate, barrel-fermented white blend★★. Best years: (Reserva) 2002 01 **99 98 96 95 94 91 89**.

RETSINA *Greece* Resinated white (and rosé) wine common all over Greece – although both production and sales are falling. Poor Retsina is diabolical but the best are deliciously oily and piny. Drink young – and cold.

REUILLY AC *Loire Valley, France* Extremely dry but attractive Sauvignon from west of SANCERRE. Also some pale Pinot Noir red and Pinot Gris rosé. Best producers: Henri Beurdin★, Gérard Bigonneau, Denis Jamain, Denis Jaumier.

CH. REYNON *Premières Côtes de Bordeaux AC, Bordeaux, France* Property of enology professor Denis Dubourdieu. The dry whites, particularly the fruity, minerally Sauvignon Blanc★, are delightful and the red★ has come on tremendously since 1997. In the same stable is the lovely GRAVES Clos Floridène★★, which is vinified at Reynon. Best years: (reds) 2005 **04 03 01 00 99 98**; (whites) 2005 **04 02 01 00 99**.

RHEINGAU *Germany* 3106ha (7675-acre) wine region on a south-facing stretch of the Rhine flanking the city of Wiesbaden, planted with 78% Riesling and 13% Spätburgunder (Pinot Noir). Traditionally considered Germany's most aristocratic wine region, both in terms of the racy, slow-maturing wines and because of the number of noble estate owners. But famous names are no longer a guarantee of top quality, as a new generation of winemakers is producing many of the best wines. See also ELTVILLE, ERBACH, GEISENHEIM, HATTENHEIM, HOCHHEIM, JOHANNISBERG, KIEDRICH, RAUENTHAL, RUDESHEIM, WINKEL. Best years: (2006) 05 04 **03** 02 **01 99 98 97 96**.

RHEINHESSEN *Germany* 26,228ha (64,810-acre) wine region to the south and west of Mainz. On the Rheinfront between Mainz and Worms are a number of very famous top-quality estates, especially at Bodenheim, Nackenheim, NIERSTEIN and Oppenheim. BINGEN, to the north-west, also has a fine vineyard area along the left bank of the Rhine. Further away from the river a handful of growers, such as KELLER and WITTMANN, are making a name for themselves. Riesling accounts for barely 10% of the vineyard area; Weissburgunder (Pinot Blanc) is the rising star. Best years: (2006) 05 04 **03** 02 **01 00 99 98**.

RHÔNE VALLEY *France* The Rhône starts out as a river in Switzerland, ambling through Lake Geneva before hurtling southwards into France. In the area south of Lyon, between Vienne and Avignon, the valley becomes one of France's great wine regions. In the northern part vertigo-inducing slopes overhang the river and the small amount of wine produced is of remarkable individuality. The Syrah grape reigns here in COTE-ROTIE and on the great hill of HERMITAGE. ST-JOSEPH, CROZES-HERMITAGE and CORNAS also make excellent reds, while the white Viognier grape yields perfumed, musky wine at CONDRIEU and the tiny CHATEAU-GRILLET. In the southern part the steep slopes give way to hot, wide plains, with hills both in the west and east. Most of these vineyards are either COTES DU RHONE or COTES DU RHONE-VILLAGES, reds, whites and rosés, but there are also specific ACs, the best known being CHATEAUNEUF-DU-PAPE, GIGONDAS and the luscious, golden dessert wine, MUSCAT DE BEAUMES-DE-VENISE. See also BEAUMES-DE-VENISE, CAIRANNE, CLAIRETTE DE DIE, COSTIERES DE NIMES, COTEAUX DE L'ARDECHE, COTEAUX DU TRICASTIN, COTES DU LUBÉRON, COTES DU VENTOUX, LIRAC, RASTEAU, ST-PÉRAY, TAVEL, VACQUEYRAS, VINSOBRES.

RÍAS BAIXAS DO *Galicia, Spain*   The best of GALICIA's DOs, Rías Baixas is making some of Spain's best whites (apart from a few Chardonnays in the north-east). The magic ingredient is the Albariño grape, making dry, fruity whites with a glorious fragrance and citrus tang. Drink young or with short aging. Best producers: Agro de Bazán★★, Castro Martín, Martín Códax★, Condes de Albarei★, Quinta de Couselo, Fillaboa★★, Adegas Galegas★, Lagar de Fornelos★, Lusco do Miño★★, Gerardo Méndez (Do Ferreiro Cepas Vellas★★), Viña Nora★, Pazo de Barrantes★, Pazo de Señorans★★, Santiago Ruiz★, Terras Gauda★★.

RIBATEJO *Portugal*   Portugal's second-largest wine region straddles the river Tagus (Tejo). Hotter and drier than ESTREMADURA to the west, vineyards in the fertile flood plain are being uprooted in favour of less vigorous soils away from the river, though D F J VINHOS still believes in the quality of the original alluvial sites. The Ribatejo DOC includes 6 sub-regions. Vinho Regional wines are labelled Ribatejano. Best producers: (reds) Quinta da Alorna, Quinta do Alqueve, Casa Cadaval★, Quinta do Casal Branco (Falcoaria★), D F J VINHOS★, Caves Dom Teodosio, Quinta do Falcão, Falua (Reserva★), Fiúza-BRIGHT, Quinta da Lagoalva da Cima★, Companhia das Lezírias, Quinta da Ribeirinha (Vale de Lobos).

RIBERA DEL DUERO DO *Castilla y León, Spain*   The dark, mouthfilling reds in this DO, from Tinto Fino (Tempranillo), sometimes with Cabernet Sauvignon and Merlot, are nowadays generally more exciting than those of RIOJA. But excessive expansion of vineyards, increase in yields and excessive use of oak may threaten its supremacy. Best producers: AALTO★★, Alión★★, Arroyo, Arzuaga★, Astrales★, Dominio de Atauta★★, Balbás★, Hijos de Antonio Barceló★, Briego★, Felix Callejo, Cillar de Silos★, Convento San Francisco★, O FOURNIER★, Hermanos Cuadrado García, Hacienda Monasterio★★, Montecastro★★, Emilio Moro★★, Pago de los Capellanes★★, Pago de Carraovejas★, Parxet, Pedrosa, PESQUERA★★, PINGUS★★★, Protos★, Rodero★, Telmo RODRIGUEZ★, Hermanos Sastre★★, Tarsus★, Valduero★, Valtravieso, VEGA SICILIA★★★, Viñedos y Bodegas Matarromera★, Alonso del Yerro★★. Best years: 2004 03 01 **00 99 96 95 94 91 90 89 86 85**.

BARONE RICASOLI *Chianti Classico DOCG, Tuscany, Italy*   The estate where modern CHIANTI was perfected by Baron Bettino Ricasoli in the mid-19th century. The flagship wine is Castello di Brolio Chianti Classico★★; wine labelled Brolio is effectively a second selection. Riserva Guicciarda★ is good value. SUPER-TUSCAN Casalferro★★ is a Sangiovese-Merlot blend. Best years: (Casalferro) (2006) 04 **03 01 00 99 97**.

DOM. RICHEAUME *Côtes de Provence AC, Provence, France*   German-owned property, run on organic principles and producing impressively deep-coloured reds★ (Columelle★★) full of smoky spice and power. Best years: (Columelle) 2004 **02 01 00 99**.

RICHEBOURG AC *Grand Cru, Côte de Nuits, Burgundy, France* Rich, fleshy wine from the northern end of VOSNE-ROMANEE. Most domaine-bottlings are exceptional. Best producers: GRIVOT★★★, Anne GROS★★★, A-F GROS★★★, Hudelot-Noëllat★★, Dom. LEROY★★★, T LIGER-BELAIR★★, MEO-CAMUZET★★★, Dom. de la ROMANEE-CONTI★★★. Best years: (2006) 05 04 03 02 01 **00** 99 98 **97** 96 **95 93 91 90**.

DOM. RICHOU *Loire Valley, France* One of the most consistent and good-value domaines in the LOIRE. Best are the ANJOU-VILLAGES Brissac Vieilles Vignes★★ and sweet COTEAUX DE L'AUBANCE les Trois Demoiselles★★. Rogeries★ is a good example of modern dry ANJOU BLANC. Best years: (les Trois Demoiselles) (2006) 05 04 **03** 02 **01** 99 97 96 95 90 89.

MAX FERD RICHTER *Mülheim, Mosel-Saar-Ruwer, Germany* Racy Rieslings from some of the best sites in the MOSEL, including WEHLENer Sonnenuhr★★, BRAUNEBERGer Juffer★★ and GRAACHer Domprobst★. Richter's Mülheimer Helenenkloster vineyard produces a magical Eiswein★★★ virtually every year (although not in 1999). Best years: (2006) 05 04 **03 02 01** 99 98 98 97 96 95 94.

RIDGE VINEYARDS *Santa Cruz Mountains AVA, California, USA* Paul Draper's Zinfandels★★★, made with grapes from various sources, have great intensity and long life. Other reds, led by Monte Bello Cabernet★★★, show impressive personality. Three Valleys★★ is a fascinating blend of Zinfandel with Carignan, Syrah and Petite Sirah. There's fine Chardonnay★★, too. Best years: (Monte Bello) 2003 02 01 **00** 99 98 97 95 94 93 92 91 90 87 85 84.

RIDGEVIEW *West Sussex, England* Specialist sparkling wine producer using classic CHAMPAGNE varieties to make an excellent – and improving – range of wines. Cavendish★★ and Bloomsbury★★ are traditional 3-variety blends; Knightsbridge★ is a blanc de noirs; Fitzrovia★ is a Chardonnay-Pinot Noir rosé. Best years **2003 02 99 98**.

RIECINE *Chianti Classico DOCG, Tuscany, Italy* Small estate in Gaiole making exquisite wines. Yields are low, so there is a great intensity of fruit and a superb definition of spiced cherry flavours. English winemaker Sean O'Callaghan continues to fashion ever better CHIANTI CLASSICO★★, Riserva★★★ and barrique-aged La Gioia★★★. Best years: (La Gioia) (2006) 04 03 **01** 99 98 97 95 90.

RIESLANER One of the few German grape crossings of real merit, Rieslaner resembles Riesling, but with greater breadth and even higher acidity. This makes it an ideal sweet wine grape, as MULLER-CATOIR (Pfalz), KELLER (Rheinhessen) and some Franken growers have demonstrated, with wines frequently ★★.

RIESLING See pages 250–1.

RIESLING ITALICO Unrelated to the great Riesling of the Rhine, this grape is decreasingly planted in northern Italy, where it produces decent dry whites. As Olasz Rizling, it is highly esteemed in Hungary. Elsewhere in Europe it is known as Welschriesling; in Austria it makes some of the best sweet wines, but tends to be rather dull as a dry wine.

CH. RIEUSSEC★★★ *Sauternes AC, 1er Cru Classé, Bordeaux, France* Apart from the peerless Ch. D'YQUEM, Rieussec is often the richest, most succulent wine of SAUTERNES. Cellar for at least 10 years. Dry white 'R' is nothing special. Second wine: Carmes de Rieussec.

Owned by LAFITE-ROTHSCHILD. Best years: 2005 04 03 02 01 **99 98 97 96 95 90 89 88**.

RIOJA DOCa *Rioja, Navarra, País Vasco and Castilla y León, Spain* Rioja, in northern Spain, is not all oaky, creamy white wines and elegant, barrel-aged reds, combining oak flavours with wild strawberry and prune fruit. Over half Rioja's red wine is sold young, never having seen the inside of a barrel, and most of the white is fairly anonymous. Wine quality, as could be expected from such a large region with more than 300 producers, is inconsistent but a bevy of ambitious new producers is taking quality seriously. Best producers: (reds) ALLENDE★★, Altos de Lanzaga★/Telmo RODRIGUEZ, Amézola de la Mora, ARTADI★★, Baron de Ley★, BERBERANA★, Bodegas Bilbaínas, CAMPILLO★, CAMPO VIEJO★, Luis Cañas, CONTINO★★, El Coto★, CVNE, DOMECQ★, FAUSTINO★, Lan (Culmen★), LOPEZ DE HEREDIA★, MARQUES DE CACERES★, MARQUES DE MURRIETA★★, MARQUES DE RISCAL★★, Marqués de Vargas★★, MARTINEZ BUJANDA★★, Abel Mendoza★★, Montecillo★, MUGA★, Palacios Remondo★, REMELLURI★★, Fernando Remírez de Ganuza★★, La RIOJA ALTA★★, RIOJANAS★, Roda★★, Benjamin ROMEO★★, Sierra Cantabria★★, Señorío de San Vicente★★, Viña Ijalba; (whites) CAMPO VIEJO, CVNE★, LOPEZ DE HEREDIA★, MARQUES DE CACERES★, MARQUES DE MURRIETA, MARTINEZ BUJANDA★, Montecillo★, La RIOJA ALTA★, RIOJANAS★. Best years: (reds) 2005 04 01 **00 96 95 94 91 89 87 85 82 81 78**.

LA RIOJA ALTA *Rioja DOCa, Rioja, Spain* One of the best of the older RIOJA producers, making mainly Reservas and Gran Reservas. Its only Crianza, Viña Alberdi, fulfils the minimum age requirements for a Reserva anyway. There is a little good, lemony-oaky Viña Ardanza Reserva★ white. Red Reservas, Viña Arana★ and Viña Ardanza★★, age splendidly, and Gran Reservas, Reserva 904★★ and Reserva 890★★★ (made only in exceptional years), are among the very best of Rioja wines. Best years: (Gran Reserva 890) **1989 87 85 82 81 78**.

BODEGAS RIOJANAS *Rioja DOCa, Rioja, Spain* Quality winery producing Reservas and Gran Reservas in 2 styles – elegant Viña Albina★ and richer Monte Real★ – plus refined Gran Albina★★. White Monte Real Blanco Crianza★ is one of RIOJA's best. The whites and Reservas can be kept for 5 years after release, Gran Reservas for 10 or more. Best years: (Monte Real Gran Reserva) 1998 **96 95 94 91 89 87 85 83 82 81**.

RION *Nuits-St-Georges, Côte de Nuits, Burgundy, France* Patrice Rion was the winemaker at Dom. Daniel Rion from 1979 to 2000, making consistently fine but often austere reds such as VOSNE-ROMANEE les Beauxmonts★★ and les Chaumes★★, ECHEZEAUX and CLOS DE VOUGEOT. His own label brings rich, concentrated BOURGOGNE Rouge★★, CHAMBOLLE-MUSIGNY les Cras★★, and NUITS-ST-GEORGES Clos des Argillières★★ from his own vines plus, since 2000, a small négociant range. Best years: (top reds) (2006) 05 **04 03** 02 **01 00 99**.

RIPOSTE *Adelaide Hills, South Australia* Since leaving KNAPPSTEIN to move to the cool ADELAIDE HILLS, Tim Knappstein has run Lenswood Vineyard and TK Wines. In 2003, the Knappsteins sold the Lenswood Vineyard, although Tim is still able to access its fruit. He now acts as contract winemaker for half a dozen Adelaide Hills labels and has started his own brand, Riposte. His current focus is on Pinot Noir, Sauvignon Blanc and Gewürztraminer, and the first batch of wines is very good.

RIVERA *Puglia, Italy* One of southern Italy's better-known producers. The CASTEL DEL MONTE Riserva Il Falcone★ is a good, full-blooded southern red. Also a series of varietals under the Terre al Monte label, best of which are Aglianico★, Pinot Bianco and Sauvignon Blanc.

RIESLING

If you have tasted wines with names like Laski Riesling, Olasz Riesling, Welschriesling, Gray Riesling, Riesling Italico and the like and found them bland or unappetizing – do not blame the Riesling grape. These wines have filched Riesling's name, but have nothing whatsoever to do with the great grape itself.

Riesling is Germany's finest contribution to the world of wine – and herein lies the second problem. German wines fell to such a low level of general esteem through the proliferation of wines like Liebfraumilch during the 1980s that Riesling, even true German Riesling, has been dragged down with it.

So what *is* true Riesling? It is a very ancient German grape, probably the descendant of wild vines growing in the Rhine Valley. It certainly performs best in the cool vineyard regions of Germany's Rhine and Mosel Valleys, and in Alsace and Austria. It also does well in Canada, New Zealand and both warm and cool parts of Australia. It is widely planted in California, less so in northern Italy, and there's a tiny amount in South Africa.

Young Rieslings often show a delightful floral perfume, sometimes blended with the crispness of green apples, often lime, peach, nectarine or apricot, sometimes even raisin, honey or spice depending upon the ripeness of the grapes. As the wines age, the lime often intensifies, and a flavour perhaps of slate, perhaps of petrol/kerosene intrudes. In general Rieslings may be drunk young, but top dry wines can improve for many years, and the truly sweet German styles can age for generations.

WINE STYLES

Germany These wines have a marvellous perfume and an ability to hold on to a piercing acidity, even at high ripeness levels, so long as the ripening period has been warm and gradual rather than broiling and rushed. German Rieslings can be bone dry, through to medium and even lusciously sweet. Styles range from crisp elegant Mosels to riper, fuller wines from the Rheingau and Nahe, with rounder, fatter examples from the Pfalz and Baden regions in the south. The very sweet Trockenbeerenauslese (TBA) Rieslings are made from grapes affected by noble rot; for Eiswein (icewine), also intensely sweet, the grapes are picked and pressed while frozen.

Other regions In the valleys of the Danube in Austria, Riesling gives stunning dry wines that combine richness with elegance, but the most fragrant wines, apart from German examples, come from France's Alsace. The mountain vineyards of northern Italy and the cool vineyards of the Czech Republic, Slovakia and Switzerland can show a floral sharp style. Australia is the southern hemisphere's world-class producer, with cool areas of South Australia, Victoria and Western Australia all offering superb – and different – examples typified by a citrus, mineral scent, and often challenging austerity. New Zealand's style is floral, fresh and frequently attractively off-dry, but with enough acidity to age. South Africa's best examples so far are usually sweetly botrytized, although cool-climate producers are dedicating more energy to the variety, especially drier styles. The USA has fragrant dry examples from New York and the Pacific Northwest and sweet styles from California, and Canada has its icewines.

SELBACH-OSTER

2002

ZELTINGER SONNENUHR
RIESLING SPÄTLESE *

QUALITÄTSWEIN MIT PRÄDIKAT · PRODUCE OF GERMANY
C/ABFÜLLUNG WEINGUT SELBACH-OSTER · D-54492 ZELTINGEN
L - A.P.NR. 2 608 119 023 03

J · Saar · R.
al.85% vol · 750 ml e

BEST PRODUCERS

Germany
Dry BASSERMANN-JORDAN,
Georg BREUER, BURKLIN-WOLF,
Christmann, HEYMANN-
LOWENSTEIN, KELLER, KOEHLER-
RUPRECHT, KUNSTLER, J LEITZ,
REBHOLZ, SAUER, J L WOLF.

Non-dry DIEL, DONNHOFF,
GUNDERLOCH, HAAG, HAART,
HEYMANN-LOWENSTEIN,
KARTHAUSERHOF, von KESSELSTATT,
KUHN, KUNSTLER, Carl Loewen,
Dr LOOSEN, MAXIMIN GRUNHAUS,
MULLER-CATOIR, Egon MULLER-
SCHARZHOF, J J PRUM, St
Urbans-Hof, Willi SCHAEFER,
SELBACH-OSTER, WEIL.

Austria
Dry Alzinger, BRUNDLMAYER,
Gobelsburg, Hiedler,
HIRTZBERGER, J Högl, KNOLL,
Loimer, Nigl, NIKOLAIHOF,
F X PICHLER, Rudi Pichler,
PRAGER, Schmelz.

France
(Alsace) *Dry* P BLANCK,
A Boxler, DEISS, Dirler-Cadé,
HUGEL, Josmeyer, Kientzler,
Kreydenweiss, A MANN, MURE,
Ostertag, SCHOFFIT, TRIMBACH,
WEINBACH, ZIND-HUMBRECHT.

Non-dry Léon Beyer, DEISS,
HUGEL, Ostertag, TRIMBACH,
WEINBACH, ZIND-HUMBRECHT.

Australia
Tim ADAMS, Bay of Fires,
Leo Buring (Leonay), FERNGROVE,
Freycinet, GROSSET, HENSCHKE,
HOUGHTON, HOWARD PARK,
Jacob's Creek (Steingarten),
KNAPPSTEIN, Mesh, MOUNT
HORROCKS, Peter LEHMANN
(Reserve), O'Leary Walker,
Pewsey Vale (Contours),
PETALUMA (Hanlin Hill),
PIPERS BROOK, Skillogallee.

New Zealand
DRY RIVER, FELTON ROAD, Foxes
Island, FROMM, MILLTON, Mt
Difficulty, Mount Edward,
PEGASUS BAY, Stoneleigh,
VILLA MARIA, Waipara West.

South Africa
Sweet CLUVER, Neethlingshof.

USA
(Washington) CHATEAU STE
MICHELLE (Eroica), LONG SHADOWS
(Poet's Leap); (New York)
Dr Konstantin FRANK.

RIVERINA *New South Wales, Australia* Centred on the town of Griffith and irrigated by the waters of the Murrumbidgee River, the Riverina is an important source of reliable cheap quaffing wines. Many of Australia's best-known brands, though not mentioning the Riverina on the label, are based on wines from here. The potential for quality is definitely there, and locally based companies such as DE BORTOLI (with Sacred Hill, Deen and Montage), MCWILLIAM'S (Hanwood, Inheritance), Nugan Estate★ (Cookoothama, Talinga Park), Westend★ (Richland) and Casella (YELLOWTAIL, Yendah) have lifted quality at budget prices. The range of sweet wines is remarkable, generally ★ level, led by Noble One Botrytis Semillon★★★ from De Bortoli.

RIVERLAND *Australia* This important irrigated region, responsible for about 12% of the national grape crush, lies along the Murray River in SOUTH AUSTRALIA near the border with VICTORIA. A great deal goes to cask wine and cheap quaffers but an increased awareness of quality has seen inferior varieties replaced and yields lowered. Here and there, wines of real character are emerging, including some remarkable reds from the Petit Verdot grape. Best producers: Angove's, HARDY (Banrock Station, Renmano), Kingston Estate, YALUMBA (Oxford Landing).

RIVESALTES AC *Roussillon, France* *Vin doux naturel* from a large area around the town of Rivesaltes. These fortified wines are some of southern France's best and can be made from an assortment of grapes, mainly white Muscat (when it is called MUSCAT DE RIVESALTES) and Grenache Noir, Gris and Blanc. A *rancio* style ages well. Best producers: Baixas co-op, la CASENOVE★, CAZES★★, Chênes★, Fontanel★, Força Réal★, GAUBY★, Joliette★, Laporte, Nouvelles★, Rivesaltes co-op, Sarda-Malet★, Trouillas co-op.

ROBERTSON WO *South Africa* Hot, dry inland area with lime-rich soils, uncommon in the Cape, that are ideal for vines. Chenin Blanc and Colombard remain the major white wine varieties, though a quarter of all South Africa's Chardonnay also grows here, for both still and sparkling styles. Sauvignon can also be good. Muscadel (Muscat Blanc à Petits Grains) yields a benchmark fortified wine, usually unoaked and released young. A red revolution is under way: Shiraz, Merlot and Cabernet have made an excellent start. Best producers: Graham BECK★, Bon Courage, De Wetshof, Quando, Robertson Winery, SPRINGFIELD ESTATE★, Van Loveren, Weltevrede, Zandvliet.

CH. ROC DE CAMBES★★ *Côtes de Bourg AC, Bordeaux, France* François Mitjavile of TERTRE-ROTEBOEUF has applied diligence and genius to this property since he acquired it in 1988. Full and succulent, with ripe dark fruit, this wine takes the COTES DE BOURG appellation to new heights. Best years: 2005 04 **03 02 01 00** 99 98 97 96 95.

DOM. DES ROCHES NEUVES *Saumur-Champigny AC, Loire Valley, France* A shift to biodynamic methods and more hands-off winemaking (including less extraction and new oak) has elevated already very good wines to a higher level. Fresh, pure and mineral, top cuvées Insolite★★ (Chenin Blanc) and Marginale★★ (Cabernet Franc) are excellent expressions of fruit and terroir. Best years: (red) (2006) 05 **04** 03 **02** 01 **00** 99 97.

J ROCHIOLI *Russian River Valley AVA, California, USA* Well-known grape growers, the Rochioli family are equally good at winemaking, offering silky, black cherry Pinot Noir★★ and a richer, dramatic West Block Reserve Pinot★★. Also a fine Sauvignon Blanc★ and a range of cult Chardonnays★★. Best years: (Pinot Noir) (2005) 04 03 02 **01 00** 99 98 97.

ROCKFORD *Barossa Valley, South Australia* Wonderfully nostalgic wines from Robert O'Callaghan, a great respecter of the old vines so plentiful in the BAROSSA, who delights in using antique machinery to create wines of irresistible drinkability. Masterful Basket Press Shiraz★★, Riesling★★, Moppa Springs★ (Grenache-Shiraz-Mourvèdre), Rifle Range Cabernet★★ and cult sparkling Black Shiraz★★★. Best years: (Basket Press Shiraz) (2006) (05) 04 03 02 01 **99 98 96 95 92 91 90 86.**

ANTONIN RODET *Mercurey, Côte Chalonnaise, Burgundy, France* Merchant specializing in COTE CHALONNAISE, but with an excellent range throughout Burgundy. Rodet owns or co-owns 5 domaines – Ch. de Rully★, Ch. de Chamirey★, Ch. de Mercey★, Dom. des Perdrix★ and Jacques Prieur★★ – which are the source of the best wines. BOURGOGNE Vieilles Vignes★ is one of the best inexpensive Chardonnays available. Also owns Dom. de l'Aigle in LIMOUX. Best years: (reds) (2006) 05 **04 03 02 99**; (whites) (2006) 05 **04 02 00 99.**

TELMO RODRÍGUEZ *Spain* The former winemaker for REMELLURI has formed a 'wine company' that is active throughout Spain. With a team of enologists and viticulturists, it forms joint ventures with local growers and manages the winemaking process. The results are often spectacular. Top wines: Molino Real★ (Sierras de MALAGA), Alto Matallana★★ (RIBERA DEL DUERO), Altos de Lanzaga★ (RIOJA), Dehesa Gago Pago La Jara★★ (TORO), Viña 105 (Cigales), Basa★ (RUEDA).

LOUIS ROEDERER *Champagne AC, Champagne, France* Renowned firm making some of the best, full-flavoured CHAMPAGNES around. As well as the excellent non-vintage★★ and pale vintage rosé★★, it also makes a big, exciting vintage★★, delicious vintage Blanc de Blancs★★ and the famous Roederer Cristal★★★ and Cristal Rosé★★★, de luxe cuvées which are nearly always magnificent. Both the vintage and Cristal can usually be aged for 10 years or more; the non-vintage benefits from a bit of aging, too. Best years: 1999 97 96 **95 90 89 88 85.**

ROEDERER ESTATE *Anderson Valley AVA, California, USA* Californian offshoot of Louis ROEDERER. The Brut★★ (sold in the UK as Quartet) is austere but impressive, a step back from the upfront fruit of many California sparklers, but it will age beautifully if you can wait. Lovely rosé★★, and the top bottling, L'Ermitage★★★, is stunning. Best years: (L'Ermitage) 1999 97 96 **94 92 91.**

ROERO DOCG *Piedmont, Italy* The Roero hills lie across the Tanaro river from the LANGHE hills, home of BAROLO and BARBARESCO. Long noted as a source of supple, fruity Nebbiolo-based red wines to drink in 2–5 years, Roero has recently been turning out Nebbiolos of Barolo-like intensity from producers such as Correggia and Malvirà. Roero is also the home of the white Arneis grape. Best producers: (reds) G Almondo★, Ca' Rossa★, Cascina Chicco★, Correggia★★, Deltetto★★, Funtanin★, F Gallino★, Malvirà★★, Monchiero Carbone★, Angelo Negro★, Porello★. Best years: (reds) (2006) 04 **03 01 00 99.** See also ARNEIS.

ROMAGNA *Emilia-Romagna, Italy* Romagna's wine production is centred on 4 DOCs and 1 DOCG. The whites are from Trebbiano (ineffably dull), Pagadebit (showing promise as both dry and sweet wine) and Albana (Albana di Romagna DOCG can be dry or sweet). The best of the Sangiovese-based reds can rival good CHIANTI CLASSICO. Best producers: (Sangiovese) La Berta★, Castelluccio★★, L Conti★, Drei Donà-La Palazza★★, G Madonia★, San Patrignano co-op/Terre del Cedro★ (Avi★★), Tre Monti★, Zerbina★★.

LA ROMANÉE AC *Grand Cru, Côte de Nuits, Burgundy, France* Tiny Grand Cru★★★ of the very highest quality, owned and now made by Vicomte LIGER-BELAIR; up to 2002 it was distributed by BOUCHARD PERE ET FILS. Best years: (2006) 05 03 02 99 **98 97 96**.

LA ROMANÉE-CONTI AC *Grand Cru, Côte de Nuits, Burgundy, France* For many extremely wealthy wine lovers this is the pinnacle of red Burgundy★★★. It is an incredibly complex wine with great structure and pure, clearly defined fruit flavour, but you've got to age it 15 years to see what all the fuss is about. The vineyard, wholly owned by Dom. de la ROMANEE-CONTI, covers only 1.8ha (4½ acres). Best years: (2006) 05 04 03 02 01 **00** 99 98 **97** 96 95 93 **90 89 88 85 78**.

DOM. DE LA ROMANÉE-CONTI *Vosne-Romanée, Côte de Nuits, Burgundy, France* This famous red wine domaine owns a string of Grands Crus in VOSNE-ROMANEE (la TACHE★★★, RICHEBOURG★★★, ROMANEE-CONTI★★★, ROMANEE-ST-VIVANT★★★, ECHEZEAUX★★★ and Grands-Échézeaux★★★) as well as a small parcel of le MONTRACHET★★★. The wines are ludicrously expensive but can be sublime – full of fruit when young, but capable of aging for 15 years or more to an astonishing marriage made in the heaven and hell of richness and decay. Best years: (reds) (2006) 05 04 03 02 01 **00** 99 98 **97** 96 95 93 **90 89 85 78**.

ROMANÉE-ST-VIVANT AC *Grand Cru, Côte de Nuits, Burgundy, France* The largest of VOSNE-ROMANEE's 6 Grands Crus. At 10–15 years old the wines should reveal the keenly balanced brilliance of which the vineyard is capable, but a surly, rough edge sometimes gets in the way. Best producers: l'Arlot★★, R Arnoux★★★, S CATHIARD★★★, J-J Confuron★★★, DROUHIN★★★, Hudelot-Noëllat★★, JADOT★★★, Dom. LEROY★★★, Dom. de la ROMANEE-CONTI★★★. Best years: (2006) 05 04 03 02 01 **00** 99 98 **97** 96 95 **93 90**.

BENJAMIN ROMEO *Rioja DOCa, La Rioja, Spain* ARTADI's former wine-maker launched his own estate with a collection of tiny old vineyards, and immediately caused a sensation with his velvety, Burgundian and yet powerful wines, Contador★★★, La Viña de Andrés Romeo★★ and La Cueva de Contador★★. Best years: (2005) (04) 03 02 01 **00**.

QUINTA DOS ROQUES *Dão DOC, Beira Alta, Portugal* One of DÃO's finest producers, the wines of 2 estates with quite different characters are made here. Quinta dos Roques red★ is ripe and supple, while Quinta das Maias★ is a smoky, peppery red. The top wines are the dos Roques Reserva★★, made from old vines and aged in 100% new oak, and Touriga Nacional★★. Both estates also have a decent dry white, especially Roques Encruzado★. Best years: (2005) (04) 03 01 **00 97 96**.

QUINTA DE LA ROSA *Douro DOC and Port DOC, Douro, Portugal* The Bergqvist family have transformed this property into a small but serious producer of both PORT and unfortified DOURO★ (Reserve★★) wines. The Vintage Port★★ is excellent, as is unfiltered LBV★★; Finest Reserve and 10-year-old tawny★ are also good. A special selection vintage port, Vale do Inferno★★, was made in 1999 and shows a lovely old vine intensity. Best years: (Vintage) 2004 03 00 97 96 95 94 **92 91**.

ROSÉ DE LOIRE AC *Loire Valley, France* Dry rosé from ANJOU, SAUMUR and TOURAINE. It can be a lovely drink, full of red berry fruits, but drink as young as possible, chilled. It's far superior to Rosé d'Anjou AC, which is usually sweetish without much flavour – though Rosé d'Un Jour is very good rosé from 8 rebellious growers led by Mark Angeli. Best producers: Hautes Ouches, Passavant, St-Arnoud, Trottières.

ROSÉ DES RICEYS AC *Champagne, France* Still, dark pink wine made from Pinot Noir grapes in the southern part of the CHAMPAGNE region. Best producers: Alexandre Bonnet★, Devaux★, Guy de Forez, Morel.

ROSEMOUNT ESTATE *Hunter Valley, New South Wales, Australia* Winery buying and growing grapes in several regions to produce some of Australia's most popular wines, but many seem sweeter and flatter than before and any sense of 'estate' has virtually disappeared. Even top-level Show Reserves are far less focused. The flagship Roxburgh Chardonnay★ is undergoing a dramatic and not entirely successful style change. Best of the other whites is Orange Vineyard Chardonnay★. Show Reserve reds are a bit stodgy, as is dense Balmoral Syrah, but GSM★ (Grenache-Syrah-Mourvèdre) can be good. After an inspiring start in MUDGEE, the Hill of Gold range has dipped, though Mountain Blue Shiraz-Cabernet★ can be excellent. Best years: (Balmoral Syrah) (2005) 04 03 02 01 00 **98 97 96 94 92 91 90**.

ROSSO CÒNERO DOC *Marche, Italy* The best wines in this zone, on the Adriatic coast, are made solely from Montepulciano, and have a wonderfully spicy richness. Best producers: Fazi Battaglia★, Garofoli★ (Grosso Agontano★★), Lanari★ (Fibbio★★), Leopardi Dittajuti★, Malacari★, Mecella (Rubelliano★), Monte Schiavo (Adeodato★★), Moroder★ (Dorico★★), Le Terrazze★ (Sassi Neri★★, Visions of J★★), Umani Ronchi★ (Cúmaro★★). Best years: (2006) 04 **03 01 00**.

ROSSO DI MONTALCINO DOC *Tuscany, Italy* The little brother of BRUNELLO DI MONTALCINO spends less time aging in wood, enabling the wines to retain a wonderful exuberance of flavour. In lesser years the best Brunello grapes may cascade here, so off-years (like 2002) can be surprisingly good. Best producers: Agostina Pieri★★, Altesino★, Argiano★, Brunelli★, Camigliano★, Caparzo★, Casanova di Neri★★, Ciacci Piccolomini d'Aragona★★, Col d'Orcia★, Collemattoni★, COSTANTI★, Fuligni★, Gorelli-Due Portine★, M Lambardi★★, Lisini★, Siro Pacenti★★, Poggio Antico★, il POGGIONE★, Poggio Salvi★, Salicutti★★, San Filippo-Fanti★, Talenti★, Valdicava★. Best years: (2006) 05 **04 03 02 01 00**.

ROSSO DI MONTEPULCIANO DOC *Tuscany, Italy* Some VINO NOBILE producers use this DOC in order to improve selection for the main wine; the best deliver delightfully plummy, chocolaty flavours. Best producers: La Braccesca★/ANTINORI, La Ciarliana★, Contucci★, Dei★, Del Cerro★, Il Faggeto★, Fassati★, Nottola★, POLIZIANO★, Salcheto★★, Valdipiatta★, Villa Sant'Anna★. Best years: (2006) **04 03 01**.

ROSSO PICENO DOC *Marche, Italy* Often considered a poor relative of ROSSO CONERO, but it can be rich and seductive when the full complement (40%) of Montepulciano is used. Best producers: Boccadigabbia★ (Villamagna★★), Le Caniette★, Laurentina★, Monte Schiavo★, Saladini Pilastri★, Velenosi★. Best years: (2006) **04 03 01 00**.

RENÉ ROSTAING *Côte-Rôtie AC, Rhône Valley, France* Modern, oaked, rich, ripe wines with deep colour and soft fruit flavours, from some of the best sites in COTE-ROTIE: classic Côte-Rôtie★, Côte Blonde★★ and la Landonne★★. There's a very good CONDRIEU★★ too. Best years: (top crus) 2006 05 04 03 **01 00 99 98 95 94 91 90 88**.

GEORGES ROUMIER *Chambolle-Musigny, Côte de Nuits, Burgundy, France* Christophe Roumier is one of Burgundy's top winemakers, devoting as much attention to his vineyards as to cellar technique, believing in severe pruning, low yields and stringent grape selection. Roumier rarely uses more than one-third new oak. His best wine is often BONNES-MARES★★★, but his other Grands Crus include MUSIGNY★★★, Ruchottes-Chambertin★★ and CORTON-CHARLEMAGNE★★. The best value are usually the village CHAMBOLLE★★ and an exclusively owned Premier Cru in MOREY-ST-DENIS, Clos de la Bussière★★. Best years: (reds) (2006) 05 04 03 02 **01 00** 99 **98 97 96 95 90**.

ROUSSANNE The RHONE VALLEY's best white grape, frequently blended with Marsanne. Roussanne is the more aromatic and elegant of the two, less prone to oxidation and with better acidity, but growers usually prefer Marsanne due to its higher yields. Now being planted in the Midi. There are some examples in Savoie and Australia. While much of the Roussanne planted in California has been identified as Viognier, there are a few true plantings that produce fascinating, complex wines.

ARMAND ROUSSEAU *Gevrey-Chambertin, Côte de Nuits, Burgundy, France* One of the most highly respected CHAMBERTIN estates, with vineyards in Chambertin★★★, Clos-de-Bèze★★★, Mazis-Chambertin★★ and Charmes-Chambertin★★ as well as GEVREY-CHAMBERTIN Clos St-Jacques★★★ and CLOS DE LA ROCHE★★★ in MOREY-ST-DENIS. The long-lived traditional wines are outstandingly harmonious, elegant, yet rich. Charles Rousseau has been making these great wines since 1959, though recent vintages have been slightly inconsistent. Best years: (2006) 05 04 03 **02** 99 **96 93** 91 **90** 89 88 85.

ROUSSILLON *France* The snow-covered peaks of the Pyrenees form a spectacular backdrop to the ancient region of Roussillon, now the Pyrénées-Orientales *département*. The vineyards produce a wide range of fairly priced wines, mainly red, ranging from the ripe, raisin-rich *vins doux naturels* to light, fruity-fresh vins de pays, and there are now some really exciting table wines, both white and red, being made in Roussillon, especially by individual estates. See also BANYULS, COLLIOURE, COTES DU ROUSSILLON, COTES DU ROUSSILLON-VILLAGES, MAURY, MUSCAT DE RIVESALTES, RIVESALTES.

RUCHOTTES-CHAMBERTIN AC See CHAMBERTIN AC.

RÜDESHEIM *Rheingau, Germany* Village producing silky, aromatic wines from some steep terraced vineyards high above the Rhein (Berg Schlossberg, Berg Rottland, Berg Roseneck and Bischofsberg). Not to be confused with the NAHE village of the same name. Best producers: Georg BREUER★★, Johannishof★, Kesseler★★, Josef LEITZ★★, Ress. Best years: (2006) 05 04 03 02 **01 00 99 98 97 96**.

RUEDA DO *Castilla y León, Spain* The RIOJA firm of MARQUES DE RISCAL launched the reputation of this white wine region in the 1970s, first by rescuing the almost extinct Verdejo grape, then by introducing Sauvignon Blanc. Fresh young whites have been joined by barrel-fermented wines aiming for a longer life, particularly at Castilla La Vieja, Ossian and Belondrade y Lurton. Best producers: Alvarez y Diez★, Antaño (Viña Mocén★), Belondrade y Lurton★, Bodegas de Crianza Castilla La Vieja★, Cerrosol (Doña Beatriz), Hermanos Lurton, MARQUES DE RISCAL★, Viñedos de Nieva★, Ossian★, José Pariente★, Javier Sanz★, Vinos Sanz, Viña Sila★ (Naia, Naiades), Angel Rodríguez Vidal (Martinsancho★).

RUFFINO *Tuscany, Italy*   Huge operation now partly owned by American giant Constellation Brands; production is still controlled by brothers Marco and Paolo Folonari, and is increasingly orientated toward quality. SUPER-TUSCANS include La Solatia★ (Chardonnay); Modus★ (Sangiovese-Cabernet-Merlot); Nero del Tondo★ (Pinot Noir); and the unique blend of Colorino and Merlot, Romitorio di Santedame★★. Ruffino also owns VINO NOBILE estate Lodola Nuova, BRUNELLO Il Greppone Mazzi and Borgo Conventi in COLLIO. See also FOLONARI.

RUINART *Champagne AC, Champagne, France*   Ruinart has a surprisingly low profile given the quality of its wines. Non-vintage★ is very good, as is Blanc de Blancs★★, but the top wines here are the supremely classy Dom Ruinart Blanc de Blancs★★★ and the Dom Ruinart Rosé★★★. Best years: (1998) 96 **95 90 88 85 83 82**.

RULLY AC *Côte Chalonnaise, Burgundy, France*   Best known for white wines, often oak-aged. Reds are light, with a fleeting strawberry and cherry perfume. Most wines are reasonably priced. Best producers: (whites) d'Allaines★, J-C Brelière★, M Briday★, DROUHIN★, Dureuil-Janthial★, Duvernay, FAIVELEY★, V GIRARDIN★, H & P Jacqueson★★, JADOT★, O LEFLAIVE★, RODET★, Villaine★; (reds) Dureuil-Janthial★, la Folie, H & P Jacqueson★. Best years: (whites) (2006) **05 04 02**; (reds) **05 03 02**.

RUSSIAN RIVER VALLEY AVA *Sonoma County, California, USA*   Beginning south of Healdsburg this valley cools as it meanders toward the Pacific. Green Valley, a sub-AVA, is home to IRON HORSE and Marimar TORRES. It is now challenging CARNEROS as the top spot in North Coast California for Pinot Noir and Chardonnay. Best producers: Davis Bynum★, DEHLINGER★★, De Loach★, Dutton-Goldfield★★, Merry Edwards★, Gary Farrell★★, IRON HORSE★★, Ramey★★, ROCHIOLI★★, SONOMA-CUTRER★, Rodney Strong★, Joseph SWAN★, Marimar TORRES★★, WILLIAMS SELYEM★★. Best years: (Pinot Noir) (2005) 04 03 02 **01 00 99 97 95**.

RUST EN VREDE *Stellenbosch WO, South Africa*   Jean Engelbrecht, son of original owner/winemaker Jannie Engelbrecht, is once again running this red-only property. Cellar renovations and a new winemaker, Coenie Snyman, should bring stability and a return to form for this farm's excellent reds. Rust en Vrede★, a Cabernet-Shiraz-Merlot blend, reflects the farm's terroir, Shiraz★, Merlot and Cabernet all benefit from young, virus-free vines, showing fine, soft tannins and fresh fruit. Best years: (Rust en Vrede estate wine) **2003 02 01 00 99 98 97**.

RUSTENBERG *Stellenbosch WO, South Africa*   Top-notch wines led by single-vineyard Peter Barlow★★, a big but classically structured Cabernet, and bold Five Soldiers★★ (Chardonnay). There's also a complex, layered BORDEAUX-style blend John X Merriman★★ and lean but scented Roussanne, a first in South Africa. The Last Straw★★ is a heavenly sticky. A delightful, heady Viognier★★ and increasingly complex savoury Shiraz★ are the pick of the value

Brampton range. Best years: (Peter Barlow) (2005) **04 03 02 01 99 98 97**; (Five Soldiers) **2005 04 03 02 01 00 99 98**.

RUTHERFORD AVA *Napa Valley, California, USA*   This viticultural area in mid-NAPA VALLEY has inspired hours of argument over whether it has a distinct identity. The heart of the area, the Rutherford Bench, does seem to be a prime Cabernet Sauvignon zone, and many traditional Napa Cabernets come from here and exhibit the 'Rutherford dust' flavour. Best producers: BEAULIEU★★, Cakebread, FLORA SPRINGS★, Freemark Abbey★, Rubicon/COPPOLA★★, Quintessa★, Staglin★★. Best years: (Cabernet) (2005) (04) 03 02 01 00 **99 96 95 94 93 91 90 86**.

RUTHERGLEN *Victoria, Australia*   This region in north-east VICTORIA is the home of heroic reds from Shiraz, Cabernet and Durif, and luscious, world-beating fortifieds from Muscat and Tokay (Muscadelle). Good sherry- and PORT-style wines. Best producers: (fortifieds) ALL SAINTS★, Buller★★, Campbells★★, CHAMBERS★★, MORRIS★★, Stanton & Killeen★★.

SAALE-UNSTRUT *Germany*   Located in the former East Germany, Saale-Unstrut's 658ha (1625 acres) of vineyards have been extensively replanted since 1989, but these vineyards must mature before first-class wines can be produced. Weissburgunder (Pinot Blanc) is the most important quality grape. Best producers: Gussek, Lützkendorf★, Pawis.

SACHSEN *Germany*   Until recently one of Europe's forgotten wine regions (411ha/1015 acres) on the river Elbe in former East Germany. Now beginning to produce some good wines, the best being dry Riesling, Gewürztraminer, Weissburgunder (Pinot Blanc) and Grauburgunder (Pinot Gris) with snappy acidity and surprisingly high alcohol. Best producers: Schloss Proschwitz★, Schloss Wackerbarth, Klaus Zimmerling★.

THE SADIE FAMILY *Swartland WO, South Africa*   Eben Sadie takes a non-interventionist approach in his warm Swartland vineyards, with biodynamics playing an increasing role. He crafts a red and a white wine, both of which benefit from aging. Columella★★, Shiraz with a little Mourvèdre, combines richness and power and is clearly influenced by Eben's project in Spain, a PRIORAT called Dits del Terra. Palladius★★ blends Viognier, Chenin Blanc, Chardonnay and Grenache Blanc into a generously textured dry white wine whose flavours evolve endlessly in the glass. Second-label Sequillo★★ is a bright, mineral-fresh, delicious red. Best years: (Columella) **2004 03 02 01 00**.

ST-AMOUR AC *Beaujolais, Burgundy, France*   The most northerly of the BEAUJOLAIS crus, much in demand through the romantic connotation of its name. The granitic vineyards produce wines with great intensity of colour that may be initially harsh, needing a few months to soften. Best producers: des Billards/Loron★, DUBOEUF★ (des Sablons★), des Duc★. Best years: **2006 05 03**.

ST-AUBIN AC *Côte de Beaune, Burgundy, France*   Some of Burgundy's best-value wines. Good reds, especially from Premiers Crus like les Frionnes and les Murgers des Dents de Chien. Also reasonably priced, oak-aged whites. Best producers: d'Allaines★, Bernard Bachelet, F & D Clair★★, M Colin★★, Deux MONTILLE★, DROUHIN★, JADOT★, H & O Lamy★★, Lamy-Pillot★, Larue★★, O LEFLAIVE★, B Morey★, RAMONET★★. Best years: (reds) (2006) 05 **03** 02; (whites) (2006) 05 **04** 03 02.

ST-BRIS AC *Burgundy, France*   Recently promoted appellation for Sauvignon Blanc; paradoxically, producing less interesting wines than a decade ago. Drink young. Best producer: J-H Goisot.

ST-CHINIAN AC *Languedoc, France*   Large AC of hill villages set back from the coast, covering strong, spicy red wines with more personality and fruit than run-of-the-mill HERAULT. Best producers: Berloup co-op, BORIE LA VITARELE★, CANET-VALETTE★★, Cazal-Viel★, CLOS BAGATELLE★,

HECHT & BANNIER★, Jougla★, Mas Champart★, Maurel Fonsalade★, Moulin de Ciffre, Moulinier, Rimbert★, Roquebrun co-op, Tabatau (Lo Tabataire★) . Best years: 2005 04 **03 01 00 99**.

SAINT CLAIR *Marlborough, South Island, New Zealand* A top performer thanks to some great vineyard sites. Several Sauvignons are led by the intensely fruity Wairau Reserve Sauvignon Blanc★★. Excellent Reserve Chardonnay★★, tasty Riesling★ and Gewürztraminer★. Vicar's Choice is impressive entry-level label. Various Pinot Noirs★ (Doctor's Creek★★) and serious, chocolaty Rapaura Reserve Merlot★ lead the reds. Best years: (Sauvignon Blanc) **2006 04** 03.

ST-DÉSIRAT, CAVE DE *St-Joseph AC, Rhône Valley, France* One of the best co-ops in the RHONE VALLEY. The intense, smoky red ST-JOSEPH★ is a bargain, as are local vins de pays. In 2005 it took over the nearby co-op of Sarras, and now accounts for over 50% of all St-Joseph.

ST-ÉMILION AC *Bordeaux, France* The scenic Roman hill town of St-Émilion is the centre of Bordeaux's most historic wine region. The finest vineyards are on the plateau and *côtes*, or steep slopes, around the town, although an area to the west, called the *graves*, contains 2 famous properties, CHEVAL BLANC and FIGEAC. It is a region of smallholdings, with over 1000 properties, and consequently the co-operative plays an important part. The dominant early-ripening Merlot grape gives wines with a 'come hither' softness and sweetness rare in red BORDEAUX. St-Émilion AC is the basic generic AC, with 4 'satellites' (LUSSAC, MONTAGNE, PUISSEGUIN, ST-GEORGES) allowed to annex their name to it. The best producers, including the Classed Growths, are found in the more tightly controlled ST-EMILION GRAND CRU AC category. Best years: 2005 **03 01 00 98 96 95** 90.

ST-ÉMILION GRAND CRU AC *Bordeaux, France* ST-EMILION's top-quality AC, which includes the estates classified as Grand Cru Classé and Premier Grand Cru Classé (below). The 2006 Classification lists 46 Grands Crus Classés. It also includes many of the new wave of limited edition *vins de garage*. Best producers: (Grands Crus Classés) l'ARROSEE★, Balestard-la-Tonnelle★, CANON-LA-GAFFELIERE★★, Clos de l'Oratoire★, la Dominique★, Fleur Cardinale★, Grand Mayne★★, Grand Pontet★, Larcis Ducasse★, Larmande★, MONBOUSQUET★, Pavie-Decesse★, la Tour Figeac★; (others) Bellevue★, Faugères★, Fombrauge★, la Gomerie★, Gracia★, La Mondotte★, Moulin St-Georges★, Quinault l'Enclos★, Rol Valentin★, TERTRE-ROTEBOEUF★, Teyssier★, VALANDRAUD★★. Best years: 2005 **03 01 00 98 96 95 90 89 88**.

ST-ÉMILION PREMIER GRAND CRU CLASSÉ *Bordeaux, France* The St-Émilion élite level, divided into 2 categories – 'A' and 'B' – with only the much more expensive CHEVAL BLANC and AUSONE in category 'A'. There are 13 'B' châteaux, with PAVIE-MACQUIN and TROPLONG MONDOT added in the 2006 Classification. Best producers: ANGELUS★★★, AUSONE★★★, BEAU-SEJOUR BECOT★★, Beauséjour★, BELAIR★, CANON★, CHEVAL BLANC★★★, Clos Fourtet★, FIGEAC★★, la Gaffelière★, MAGDELAINE★, PAVIE★★, PAVIE-MACQUIN★★, TROPLONG MONDOT★★, Trottevieille★. Best years: 2005 04 03 02 **01 00 99 98 96 95 90 89 88 86 85**.

ST-ESTÈPHE AC *Haut-Médoc, Bordeaux, France* Large AC north of PAUILLAC with 5 Classed Growths. St-Estèphe wines have high tannin levels, but given time (10–20 years) those sought-after flavours of blackcurrant and cedarwood do peek out. More Merlot has been planted to soften the wines and make them more accessible at an earlier age. As summers get drier and hotter, these wines are coming into their own. Best producers: CALON-SEGUR★★, COS D'ESTOURNEL★★★, Cos Labory, HAUT-MARBUZET★★, LAFON-ROCHET★, Lilian-Ladouys★, Marbuzet★, MEYNEY★, MONTROSE★★, les Ormes-de-Pez★, PEZ★, Phélan Ségur★. Best years: 2005 04 **03** 02 **01 00 96 95 94 90 89 88 86 85**.

DOM. ST-GAYAN *Gigondas AC, Rhône Valley, France* The Meffre family's holdings include some very old vines, which lend power to the chunky GIGONDAS★ (★★ in top years). Other reds, such as Rasteau, are good value. Best years: (Gigondas) 2006 05 04 **03 01 00 99 98 97 96 95 90**.

ST-GEORGES-ST-ÉMILION AC *Bordeaux, France* The smallest satellite of ST-EMILION, with lovely, soft wines that can nevertheless age for 6–10 years. Best producers: Calon, Macquin St-Georges★, St-André Corbin★, Ch. St-Georges★, Tour-du-Pas-St-Georges★, Vieux-Montaiguillon. Best years: 2005 **03 01 00 98 96 95 90**.

ST HALLETT *Barossa Valley, South Australia* Change is afoot at the home of the venerable Old Block Shiraz★ and its Shiraz siblings Blackwell★ and Faith★. Following a merger with MCLAREN VALE's Tatachilla, then a joint takeover of ADELAIDE HILLS' Hillstowe, all 3 wineries were snapped up by brewer Lion Nathan. So far, the bargain Gamekeeper's Reserve★ red, Poacher's Blend★ white, EDEN VALLEY Riesling★ and The Reward Cabernet★★ all seem to be performing pretty well, but production is now centred on St Hallett, which may strain resources. Best years: (Old Block) (2006) (04) 03 02 **98 96 94 93 91 90**.

ST-JOSEPH AC *Rhône Valley, France* Large, mainly red AC, on the opposite bank of the Rhône to HERMITAGE. Made from Syrah, the reds have mouthfilling fruit with irresistible blackcurrant richness. Brilliant at 1–2 years, they can last for up to 10. The white wines are usually pleasant and flowery to drink young, although an increasing number can age. Best producers: (reds) CHAPOUTIER★, J-L CHAVE★★, Chêne★, L Chèze★, COLOMBO★, Courbis★, COURSODON★★, CUILLERON★★, DELAS★★, E & J Durand★, P Faury★, Florentin★, P Gaillard★★, Gonon★★, GRAILLOT★★, B Gripa★★, GUIGAL★★, JABOULET★, Monier★, Monteillet★★, Paret★, A PERRET★★, C Pichon★, ST-DESIRAT co-op★, TAIN co-op★, Tardieu-Laurent★, G Vernay★, F Villard★★; (whites) CHAPOUTIER (Granits★★), Chêne★★, L Chèze★, Courbis★ (Royes★★), CUILLERON★★, DELAS★, Ferraton★, P Finon, G Flacher, Florentin★, P Gaillard★★, Gonon★★, B Gripa★, GUIGAL, Monteillet★, A PERRET★, Villard★★. Best years: (reds) 2006 **05 03 01 00 99 98 95**; (whites) 2006 **05 04 03 00 99 98**.

ST-JULIEN AC *Haut-Médoc, Bordeaux, France* For many, St-Julien produces perfect claret, with an ideal balance between opulence and austerity and between the brashness of youth and the genius of maturity. It is the smallest of the HAUT-MEDOC ACs but almost all is first-rate vineyard land and quality is high. Best producers: BEYCHEVELLE★, BRANAIRE-DUCRU★★, DUCRU-BEAUCAILLOU★★★, GLORIA★, GRUAUD-LAROSE★★, LAGRANGE★★, LANGOA-BARTON★★, LEOVILLE-BARTON★★★, LEOVILLE-LAS-CASES★★★, LEOVILLE-POYFERRE★★, ST-PIERRE★★, TALBOT★. Best years: 2005 04 03 02 **01 00 99 98 97 96 95 94 90 89 88 86 85**.

CHÂTEAU BEYCHEVELLE
GRAND VIN 2003
— SAINT-JULIEN —

ST-NICOLAS-DE-BOURGUEIL AC *Loire Valley, France* An enclave within the larger BOURGUEIL AC, and similarly producing light wines from vineyards toward the river, sturdier bottles from up the hill. Almost all the wine is red and with the same piercing red fruit flavours of Bourgueil, and much better after 7–10 years, especially in warm vintages. Best producers: Y Amirault★★, Clos des Quarterons★, Dom. de la Cotelleraie/Vallée★, L & M Cognard-Taluau★, Vignoble de la Jarnoterie, F Mabileau★★, J-C Mabileau★, Dom. Pavillon du Grand Clos★, J Taluau★. Best years: (2006) 05 04 **03** 02 **01 00** 97 96 95.

ST-PÉRAY AC *Rhône Valley, France*   Rather hefty, CHAMPAGNE-method fizz from Marsanne and Roussanne grapes. Still white is usually dry, fragrant and mineral on the finish. Best producers: S Chaboud★, CLAPE★, COLOMBO★, DELAS, Fauterie★, B Gripa★★, J Lemenicier★, TAIN co-op★, Tardieu-Laurent★, J-L Thiers★, Tunnel★, Vins de Vienne, A Voge★. Best years: **2006 05 04 03 01 00** 99.

CH. ST-PIERRE★★ *St-Julien AC, 4ème Cru Classé, Haut-Médoc, Bordeaux, France*   Small ST-JULIEN property making wines that have become a byword for ripe, lush fruit wrapped round with the spice of new oak. Drinkable early, but top vintages can improve for 20 years. Best years: 2005 04 03 02 **01 00 99** 98 96 95 94 90 89 85.

ST-ROMAIN AC *Côte de Beaune, Burgundy, France*   Red wines with a firm, bitter-sweet cherrystone fruit and flinty-dry whites. Both are usually good value by Burgundian standards, but take a few years to open out. Best producers: (whites) Bazenet★, H & G Buisson, Chassorney★★, A Gras★★, O LEFLAIVE★, VERGET★★; (reds) A Gras★. Best years: (whites) (2006) 05 **04 03** 02; (reds) (2006) 05 **03** 02.

ST-VÉRAN AC *Mâconnais, Burgundy, France*   Often thought of as a POUILLY-FUISSE understudy, this is gentle, fairly fruity, normally unoaked Mâconnais Chardonnay. Overall quality is good. Drink young. Best producers: D & M Barraud★, Cordier★, Corsin★★, Deux Roches★, DUBOEUF★, Gerbeaux★, R Lassarat★, O Merlin★, Saumaize-Michelin★, J C Thévenet★, J-L Tissier★, VERGET★, J-J Vincent★.

STE-CROIX-DU-MONT AC *Bordeaux, France*   Best of the 3 sweet wine ACs that gaze jealously at SAUTERNES and BARSAC across the Garonne river (the others are CADILLAC and LOUPIAC). The wine is mildly sweet rather than splendidly rich. Top wines can age for at least a decade. Best producers: Crabitan-Bellevue★, Loubens★, Lousteau-Vieil, Mailles, Mont, Pavillon★, la Rame★. Best years: 2005 **03 02 01** 99 98 97 96 95.

SAINTSBURY *Carneros AVA, California, USA*   Deeply committed CARNEROS winery. Its Pinot Noirs★★ are brilliant examples of the perfume and fruit quality of Carneros; the new line of vineyard-designated Pinots, led by the exquisite Brown Ranch★★★, are deeper and oakier, while Garnet★ is a delicious lighter style. The Chardonnays★★ are also impressive, best after 2–3 years. Best years: (Pinot Noir) 2005 04 03 02 01 **00 99** 98 97 96 95.

CASTELLO DELLA SALA *Orvieto DOC, Umbria, Italy*   Belongs to the ANTINORI family, making good ORVIETO★ and outstanding oak-aged Cervaro★★★ (Chardonnay and a little Grechetto). Also impressive Pinot Nero★ and sweet Muffato della Sala★★.

DUCA DI SALAPARUTA *Sicily, Italy*   Corvo is the brand name for Sicilian wines made by this firm. Red and white Corvo are pretty basic, but there are superior whites, Colomba Platino★ and Bianca di Valguarnera★, and 2 fine reds, Terre d'Agala★ and Duca Enrico★★.

SALICE SALENTINO DOC *Puglia, Italy*   One of the better DOCs in the Salento peninsula, using Negroamaro tempered with a dash of perfumed Malvasia Nera for ripe, chocolaty wines that acquire hints of roast chestnuts and prunes with age. Drink after 3–4 years, although they may last as long again. The DOCs of Alezio, Brindisi, Copertino,

Leverano and Squinzano are similar. Best producers: Candido★, Casale Bevagna★, Leone De Castris★, Due Palme★, Taurino★, Vallone★★, Conti Zecca. Best years: (reds) (2006) 04 **03 01 00.**

SALTA *Argentina*   The vineyards of Salta province, 700km (435 miles) north of Mendoza, are concentrated along the Calchaquí Valley. The most important location is Cafayate, at about 1750m (5750 ft), where all the traditional producers are located, but Colomé (2200m/7200 ft) is also showing tremendous potential and there are new vineyards going as high as 3100m (over 10,000 ft) – truly the highest in the world. High altitude, sandy soils and almost no rain produce wines of intense colour and high alcohol content, with scented white Torrontés and lush red Malbec. Best producers: (Cafayate) Etchart, Finca Las Nubes, San Pedro de Yacochuya; (Colomé) Colomé.

SAMOS *Greece*   The island of Samos has a centuries-old reputation for rich, sweet, Muscat-based wines. The Samos co-op's wines include deep gold, honeyed Samos Nectar★★, made from sun-dried grapes; apricotty Palaio★, aged for up to 20 years; and seductively complex Samos Anthemis★, fortified and cask-aged for up to 5 years.

SAN ANTONIO VALLEY *Chile*   This region is really in two parts – the more northerly, actually called San Antonio, and the more southerly Leyda. Closeness to the Pacific Ocean and the icy Humboldt Current decides whether you are best at snappy Sauvignon Blanc and fragrant Pinot Noir (Leyda), or scented, juice-laden Syrah (San Antonio). There are half a dozen estates, but big companies like CONCHA Y TORO and MONTES are also making exciting wine from the region's fruit. Water shortage is a problem, but expect Leyda in particular to become a new mini-CASABLANCA. Best producers: CASA MARIN★★, Garcés Silva/Amayna★, Viña Leyda★★, MATETIC★.

SAN LEONARDO *Trentino, Italy*   Marchese Carlo Guerrieri Gonzaga, a former winemaker at SASSICAIA, has established his Cabernet-Merlot blend San Leonardo★★ as the northern equivalent of the famous Tuscan. Recently launched is an almost equally impressive Merlot called Villa Gresti★★. Best years: (2006) 04 03 **01 00 99 97 96 95**.

SAN LUIS OBISPO COUNTY *California, USA*   CENTRAL COAST county best known for Chardonnay, Pinot Noir, a bit of old-vine Zinfandel, Syrah and Cabernet Sauvignon. There are 5 AVAs – Edna Valley, PASO ROBLES, SANTA MARIA VALLEY (shared with SANTA BARBARA COUNTY), Arroyo Grande Valley and York Mountain. Best producers: Claiborne & Churchill★, Eberle★, Edna Valley★★, Justin★, Laetitia, J Lohr (Hilltop Cabernet Sauvignon★★), Meridian★, Norman★, Saucelito Canyon★, Savannah-Chanelle★, Talley★★, Wild Horse★. Best years: (reds) 2005 04 03 02 **01 00 99 98 97 95 94**.

SAN PEDRO *Curicó, Chile*   This giant operation produced little of note before Jacques Lurton arrived as a consultant in 1994. He's gone now, but the French influence lingers in a venture with ST-EMILION Ch. Dassault called Altaïr★, a fine, sophisticated Cabernet Sauvignon-based red; the second wine, Sideral, is chewy and ripe. San Pedro's 35 South range is pretty good, Castillo de Molina Reservas★ are ripe and full-bodied, and 1865 Malbec★★ and Cabernet★★ are excellent, powerful, dark-fruited reds. The Tabalí winery, in LIMARI VALLEY, is producing memorable Chardonnay★★ and Syrah★★.

SANCERRE AC *Loire Valley, France*   White Sancerre can provide the perfect expression of the bright green tang of the Sauvignon grape, and from a good grower can be deliciously refreshing – as can the rare Pinot Noir rosé – but the very best also age well. Some growers produce a richer style using new oak. Pinot Noir reds from top producers are now a serious proposition. The wines are more consistent than those of neighbouring POUILLY. Prices reflect the appellation's popularity. Best producers: F & J Bailly★, Balland-Chapuis★, H BOURGEOIS★★, H Brochard★, R Champault★, F Cotat★★, L Crochet★, Delaporte★, Gitton★, P Jolivet★, Serge Laloue★, Dom. Martin★, A MELLOT★★, J Mellot★, P Millérioux★, Mollet-Maudry★, H Natter★, A & F Neveu★, R Neveu★, V Pinard★★, J Reverdy★, P & N Reverdy★, J-M Roger★, VACHERON★★, André Vatan★. Best years: 2006 **05 04 02**.

SANDALFORD *Swan Valley, Western Australia* One of Western Australia's original wineries (founded in 1840) and a pioneer of the MARGARET RIVER, where Sandalford planted a large vineyard in 1972. However, it generally underperformed until the arrival of winemaker Paul Boulden in 2001. With the premium wines, Bouldon has focused on the Margaret River, and quality has leaped ahead. Whites – Sauvignon Blanc-Semillon, Verdelho★ and Chardonnay★ – are impressive, while the reds are perhaps even better: dark and classically ripe, fleshy Shiraz★★ and Cabernet Sauvignon★★★. Lush Cabernet Prendiville Reserve★★★ raises the bar even further. Budget ranges – Element and Protégé – offer quality at fair prices. Best years: (Cabernet Sauvignon) (2005) 04 03 02 01 00 **99**.

SANDEMAN *Port DOC, Douro, Portugal and Jerez y Manzanilla DO, Spain* The port operation is now owned by SOGRAPE, but run by George Sandeman (7th-generation descendant of the founder). Excellent aged tawnies: 20-year-old★ and 30-year-old★★. Vintage ports are more patchy. Vau Vintage★★ is the second label, for early drinking. In 2004 Sogrape sold its Jerez assets to Nueva Rumasa (Garvey), which now makes the Sandeman brands as a sub-contractor. Best years: (Vintage) 2003 00 97 94 **66 63 55**.

LUCIANO SANDRONE *Barolo DOCG, Piedmont, Italy* Luciano Sandrone has become one of PIEDMONT's leading wine stylists, renowned for his BAROLO Cannubi Boschis★★★ and Le Vigne★★★, as well as BARBERA D'ALBA★★ and Dolcetto d'Alba★★, which rank with the best.

SANFORD *Santa Rita Hills AVA, California, USA* Richard Sanford planted the great Benedict vineyard in the Santa Ynez Valley in 1971, thus establishing SANTA BARBARA as a potentially top-quality vineyard region. An estate vineyard planted west of Highway 101 is in the SANTA RITA HILLS, an area that subsequently burst on to the Pinot Noir scene with some spectacular wines. Sanford now makes sharply focused, dark-fruited Pinot Noir★★, Chardonnay★★ and Sauvignon Blanc★. Richard Sanford left the project in 2005 to found high-quality Alma Rosa label. Best years: (Pinot Noir) 2005 04 03 02 01 00 **99 98 97 96 95**.

DOM. LE SANG DES CAILLOUX *Vacqueyras AC, Rhône Valley, France* Top VACQUEYRAS estate with big, authentic red wines led by the old-vines Grenache-Syrah Cuvée de Lopy★★ that bursts with fruit and vigour over 10 or more years. Doucinelle★ and Azalaïs★ reds are more restrained. Best years: 2006 05 **04 03 01 00 99 98**.

SANGIOVESE Sangiovese, the most widely planted grape variety in Italy, reaches its greatest heights in central TUSCANY, especially in Montalcino, whose BRUNELLO must be 100% varietal. This grape has produced a wide range of sub-varieties that make generalization difficult. Much care is being taken in the current wave of replanting, whether in CHIANTI CLASSICO, Brunello di Montalcino or VINO NOBILE DI MONTEPULCIANO. Styles range from pale, lively and cherryish through vivacious, mid-range Chiantis to excellent top Riservas and SUPER-TUSCANS. Some fine examples are also produced in ROMAGNA. California producers like ATLAS PEAK, SHAFER, Robert Pepi and SEGHESIO are having a go at taming the grape, without much success. Australia has good examples from King Valley in VICTORIA (Gary Crittenden, Pizzini) and MCLAREN VALE (Coriole), but poor-quality clones have thus far hampered progress. Also grown in Argentina and Chile, and both South Africa and NEW YORK are trying it.

SANTA BARBARA COUNTY *California, USA* CENTRAL COAST county, north-west of Los Angeles, known for Chardonnay, Riesling, Pinot Noir and Syrah. The main AVAs are SANTA RITA HILLS, Santa Ynez Valley and most of SANTA MARIA VALLEY (the remainder is in SAN LUIS OBISPO COUNTY), all top areas for Pinot Noir. Best producers: AU BON CLIMAT★★, Babcock, Beckmen★★, Brewer-Clifton★★, Byron★★, Cambria, Foxen★★, Hitching Post★★, Lane Tanner★★, Longoria★, Melville★, Andrew MURRAY★★, Ojai★★, Fess Parker★, QUPE★★, SANFORD★★, Whitcraft★★, Zaca Mesa★. Best years: (Pinot Noir) 2005 04 03 02 **01 00 99 98 97 95 94**.

SANTA CAROLINA *Maipo, Chile* Long-established winery that is at last catching up with the modern world. You'll find fresh Reserva whites★ with good fruit definition, and substantial, ripe, if oaky, Barrica Selection reds★. Top of the range is the Cabernet-based VSC★.

SANTA CRUZ MOUNTAINS AVA *California, USA* A sub-region of the CENTRAL COAST AVA. Notable for long-lived Chardonnays and Cabernet Sauvignons, including the stunning Monte Bello from RIDGE. Also small amounts of robust Pinot Noir. Best producers: BONNY DOON★★, David Bruce★★, Clos La Chance★, Kathryn Kennedy★★, Mount Eden Vineyards★★, RIDGE★★★, Santa Cruz Mountain Vineyard★.

SANTA MARIA VALLEY AVA *Santa Barbara County and San Luis Obispo County, California, USA* Cool Santa Maria Valley is coming on strong as a producer of Chardonnay, Pinot Noir and Syrah. Look for wines made from grapes grown in Bien Nacido vineyards by several small wineries. Best producers: AU BON CLIMAT★★, Byron★★, Cambria, Foxen★★, Lane Tanner (Pinot Noir★★), Longoria★, QUPE★★.

SANTA RITA *Maipo, Chile* Long-established MAIPO giant. Red blends such as superb Triple C★★ (Cabernet Franc, Cabernet Sauvignon, Carmenère) and Syrah-Cabernet Sauvignon-Carmenère★★ show real flair. Floresta whites (Leyda Sauvignon Blanc★★) and reds★★ – both single varietal and blends (expect ★★★ here soon) – are tremendous. Casa Real★ is expensive and old fashioned, but some people love it.

SANTA RITA HILLS AVA *Santa Barbara County, California, USA* Established in 2002, this small AVA lies at the western edge of the Santa Ynez Hills in SANTA BARBARA COUNTY. Fog from the Pacific keeps temperatures cool. Pinot Noir is the primary grape (along with small amounts of Syrah and Chardonnay) and the wines have deeper colour, greater varietal intensity and higher acidity than others in the region. Best producers: Babcock, Brewer-Clifton★★, Clos Pepe★★, Fiddlehead★★, Foley★★, Lafond★, Melville★, SANFORD★★, Sea Smoke★★.

SANTENAY AC *Côte de Beaune, Burgundy, France* Red Santenay wines often promise good ripe flavour, though they don't always deliver it, but are worth aging for 4–6 years in the hope that the wine will open out. Many of the best wines, both red and white, come from les

Gravières Premier Cru on the border with CHASSAGNE-MONTRACHET. Best producers: (reds) R Belland★★, F & D Clair★, M Colin★, J Girardin★, V GIRARDIN★★, Monnot★, B Morey★★, L Muzard★★, N POTEL★, Prieur-Brunet; (whites) V GIRARDIN★, Jaffelin, René Lequin-Colin★. Best years: (reds) (2006) 05 **04 03 02 99**.

CASA SANTOS LIMA *Alenquer DOC, Estremadura, Portugal* A beautiful estate with an expanding range. Light, fruity and tasty Espiga reds and whites, spicy red★ and creamy, perfumed white Palha Canas, and red and white Quinta das Setencostas★. Also Touriz★ (from DOURO varieties), varietal Touriga Nacional★, Touriga Franca★, Trincadeira★ and Tinta Roriz★ and peachy, herby Chardonnay★.

CAVES SÃO JOÃO *Beira Litoral, Portugal* A pioneer of cool-fermented, white BAIRRADA, and has made some very good Cabernet Sauvignons from its own vines. Rich, complex traditional reds include outstanding Reserva★★ and Frei João★ from Bairrada and Porta dos Cavaleiros★★ from DAO – they demand at least 10 years' age to show their quality.

SARDINIA *Italy* Grapes of Spanish origin, like the white Vermentino and Torbato and the red Monica, Cannonau and Carignano, dominate production on this huge, hilly Mediterranean island, but they vie with a Malvasia of Greek origin and natives like Nuragus and Vernaccia. The cooler northern part favours whites, especially Vermentino, while the southern and eastern parts are best suited to reds from Cannonau and Monica, with Carignano dominating in the south-west. The wines used to be powerful, alcoholic monsters, but the current trend is for a lighter, modern, more international style. Foremost among those in pursuit of quality are ARGIOLAS, SELLA & MOSCA and the Santadi co-op. See also CARIGNANO DEL SULCIS.

SASSICAIA DOC★★★ *Tuscany, Italy* Legendary Cabernet Sauvignon-Cabernet Franc blend. Vines were planted in 1944 to satisfy the Marchese Incisa della Rocchetta's thirst for fine red Bordeaux, which was in short supply during the war. The wine remained purely for

family consumption until nephew Piero ANTINORI and winemaker Giacomo Tachis persuaded the Marchese to refine production practices and to release several thousand bottles from the 1968 vintage. Since then, Sassicaia's fame has increased as it proved itself to be one of the world's great Cabernets, combining a blackcurrant power of blistering intensity with a heavenly scent of cigars. It is the first Italian single-owner estate wine to have its own DOC, within the BOLGHERI appellation, from the 1995 vintage. Best years: (2006) 04 **03 01 99 98 97 95 90 88 85 68**.

HORST SAUER *Escherndorf, Franken, Germany* Horst Sauer shot to stardom in the late 1990s. His dry Rieslings★★ and Silvaners★ are unusually juicy and fresh for a region renowned for blunt, earthy wines. His late-harvest wines are unchallenged in the region and frequently ★★★; they will easily live a decade, sometimes much more. Best years: (dry Riesling, Silvaner) (2006) 05 04 **03 02 01 00 99**.

SAUMUR AC *Loire Valley, France* Dry white wines, mainly from Chenin Blanc, with up to 20% Chardonnay; the best combine bright fruit with a mineral seam. The reds are lighter than those of SAUMUR-

CHAMPIGNY. Also dry to off-dry Cabernet rosé, and sweet Coteaux de Saumur in good years. Best producers: Château-Gaillard★, Clos Rougeard★★, Collier★, Filliatreau★, Fosse-Seche, HUREAU★, Langlois-Château★, R-N Legrand★, la Paleine★, ROCHES NEUVES★★, St-Just★, Saumur co-op, Tour Grise, VILLENEUVE★★, Yvonne★★. Best years: (whites) 2006 05 04 **03 02 01**.

SAUMUR-CHAMPIGNY AC *Loire Valley, France* Saumur's best red wine. Cabernet Franc is the main grape, and in hot years the wine can be superb, with a piercing scent of blackcurrants and raspberries easily overpowering the earthy finish. Delicious young, it can age for 6–10 years. Best producers: Clos Rougeard★★, de la Cune, Filliatreau★, HUREAU★★, Lavigne, R-N Legrand★, Nerleux★, la Perruche★, Retiveau-Rétif★, ROCHES NEUVES★★, St-Vincent★, Patrick Vadé★, Varinelles★, VILLENEUVE★★, Yvonne★. Best years: 2006 05 04 **03 02 01 97 96**.

SAUMUR MOUSSEUX AC *Loire Valley, France* Reasonable CHAMPAGNE-method sparkling wines, mainly from Chenin Blanc. Adding Chardonnay and Cabernet Franc makes the wine softer and more interesting. Usually non-vintage. Small quantities of rosé are also made. Best producers: BOUVET-LADUBAY★, Gratien & Meyer★, Grenelle★, la Paleine★, la Perruche★, St-Cyr-en-Bourg co-op★, Veuve Amiot.

SAUTERNES AC *Bordeaux, France* The name Sauternes is synonymous with the best sweet wines in the world. Sauternes and BARSAC both lie on the banks of the little river Ciron and are 2 of the very few areas in France where noble rot occurs naturally. Production of these intense, sweet, luscious wines from botrytized grapes is a risk-laden and extremely expensive affair, and the wines are never going to be cheap. From good producers the wines are worth their high price – as well as 14% alcohol they have a richness full of flavours of pineapples, peaches, syrup and spice. Good vintages should be aged for 5–10 years and often last twice as long. Best producers: Bastor-Lamontagne★, Clos Haut-Peyraguey★★, Cru Barréjats★, DOISY-DAENE★★, DOISY-VEDRINES★★, FARGUES★, GILETTE★, GUIRAUD★★, Haut-Bergeron★, les Justices★, LAFAURIE-PEYRAGUEY★★, Lamothe-Guignard★, Malle★, Rabaud-Promis★, Raymond-Lafon★★, Rayne-Vigneau★, RIEUSSEC★★★, Sigalas Rabaud★★, SUDUIRAUT★★, la TOUR BLANCHE★★, YQUEM★★★. Best years: 2005 03 **02** 01 **99** 98 97 96 95 90 89 88 86 83.

SAUVIGNON BLANC See pages 268–9.

SAUZET *Puligny-Montrachet, Côte de Beaune, Burgundy, France* A producer with a reputation for classic, rich, full-flavoured white Burgundies, made in an opulent, fat style, but recently showing more classical restraint. Sauzet owns prime sites in PULIGNY-MONTRACHET★ and CHASSAGNE-MONTRACHET★ (Premiers Crus usually ★★), as well as small parcels of BATARD-MONTRACHET★★★ and Bienvenues-BATARD-MONTRACHET★★★. Best years: (2006) 05 **04 03 02**.

SAVENNIÈRES AC *Loire Valley, France* Wines from Chenin Blanc, produced on steep vineyards south of Anjou. Usually steely and dry, although some softer wines are being produced by a new generation using new oak and malolactic fermentation. The top wines usually need at least 8 years to mature, and can age for longer. There are 2 extremely good vineyards with their own ACs: la Coulée-de-Serrant and la Roche-aux-Moines. Best producers: BAUMARD★★, Bergerie, Clos de Coulaine★, CLOS DE LA COULEE-DE-SERRANT★★, Closel★★, Épiré★★, Forges★, aux Moines★, Eric Morgat★, Pierre-Bise★★, Jo PITHON,

P Soulez/Chamboureau★, P-Y Tijou★★. Best years: (2006) 05 04 03 02 **01 99 97 96 95 90 89**.

SAVIGNY-LÈS-BEAUNE AC *Côte de Beaune, Burgundy, France* Large village with reds dominating; usually dry and lean, they need 4–6 years to open out. The top Premiers Crus, such as Lavières, Peuillets and La Dominode, are more substantial. The white wines show a bit of dry, nutty class after 2–3 years. The wines are generally reasonably priced. Best producers: S Bize★, Camus-Bruchon★★, Champy★, CHANDON DE BRIAILLES★, B CLAIR★★, M Écard★★, J J Girard★, P Girard★, V GIRARDIN★, L Jacob★★, Dom. LEROY★★, C Maréchal★, J-M Pavelot★★, TOLLOT-BEAUT★★. Best years: (reds) (2006) 05 **03 02 99 96**.

SAVOIE *France* Savoie's high Alpine vineyards produce fresh, snappy white wines with loads of flavour, when made from the Altesse (or Roussette) grape. Drink them young. There are some attractive light reds and rosés, too, and, in hot years, some positively Rhône-like reds from the Mondeuse grape. Most of the better wines use the Vin de Savoie AC and should be drunk young or with 3–4 years' age. The 15 best villages, including Abymes, Apremont, Chignin and Montmélian, can add their own name to the label. Between Lyon and Savoie are the vineyards of the Vin du Bugey VDQS, with light, easy-drinking reds and whites. Best producers: Bouvet★, Charlin, Dupasquier★, Jacquin★, Magnin★, C Marandon★, Monin, Neyroud, Perret★, A & M Quénard★, R Quénard★, Ripaille★, Rocailles★, Saint-Germain, C Trosset★; (Bugey) Charlin. See also SEYSSEL.

SAXENBURG *Stellenbosch WO, South Africa* In-demand red wines, led by dense, burly Private Collection Shiraz★★ and an even richer, bigger Shiraz Select★★, plus excellent Cabernet★★ and Merlot★. Private Collection Sauvignon Blanc★★ and Chardonnay★ head the white range. Drink whites young; reds will improve for 5–8 years. Best years: (premium reds) (2004) **03 02 01 00 99 98 97**.

WILLI SCHAEFER *Graach, Mosel, Germany* Classic MOSEL wines: Riesling Spätlese and Auslese from the GRAACHER Domprobst vineyard have a balance of piercing acidity and lavish fruit that is every bit as dramatic as Domprobst's precipitous slope. Extremely long-lived, they're frequently ★★★, as is the sensational Beerenauslese Schaefer produces in good vintages. Even his QbA wines are ★. Best years: (Riesling Spätlese, Auslese) (2006) 05 04 **03 02 01 99 98 97 96 95 94 90**.

SCHÄFER-FRÖHLICH *Bockenau, Nahe, Germany* From vineyards in SCHLOSSBOCKELHEIM and the more obscure Bockenau, Tim Fröhlich has since 2003 been producing racy dry Rieslings★★ and sumptuous nobly sweet wines★★★. Best years (2006) 05 04 03 02 **01 99**.

SCHARFFENBERGER CELLARS *Anderson Valley AVA, California, USA* Owned by ROEDERER. Non-vintage Brut★★, with lovely toasty depth, exuberant Rosé★★, and vintage Blanc de Blancs★★ are all excellent.

SCHEUREBE Silvaner x Riesling crossing found in Germany's PFALZ and RHEINHESSEN. In Austria it is sometimes labelled Sämling 88. At its best in Trockenbeerenauslese and Eiswein. When ripe, it has a marvellous flavour of honey, exotic fruits and the pinkest of pink grapefruit.

SCHILCHER Rosé wine from the Blauer Wildbacher grape, a speciality of the West STEIERMARK in Austria. Its very high acidity means you either love it or detest it. For me, it's a mood thing. Best producer: Strohmeier.

SAUVIGNON BLANC

 Of all the world's grapes, the Sauvignon Blanc is leader of the 'love it or loathe it' pack. It veers from being wildly fashionable to totally out of favour depending upon where it is grown and which country's wine writers are talking, but you, the consumers, love it – and so do I. Sauvignon is always at its best when full rein is allowed to its very particular talents, because this grape does give intense, sometimes shocking flavours, and doesn't take kindly to being put into a straitjacket. Periodically, producers lose confidence in its fantastic, brash, tangy personality and try to calm it down. Don't do it. Let it run free – it's that lip-smacking, in-yer-face nettles and lime zest and passionfruit attack that drinkers love. There's no more thirst-quenching wine than a snappy, crunchy young Sauvignon Blanc. Let's celebrate it.

WINE STYLES

Sancerre-style Sauvignon Although it had long been used as a blending grape in Bordeaux, where its characteristic green tang injected a bit of life into the blander, waxier Sémillon, Sauvignon first became trendy as the grape used for Sancerre, a bone-dry Loire white whose green gooseberry fruit and slightly smoky perfume inspired the winemakers of other countries to try to emulate, then often surpass, the original model.

The range of styles Sauvignon produces is as wide as, if less subtly nuanced than, those of Chardonnay. It is highly successful when picked not too ripe, fermented cool in stainless steel, and bottled early. This is the Sancerre model followed by growers elsewhere. New Zealand is now regarded as the top Sauvignon country, and many new producers in places like Australia, South Africa, southern France, Hungary and Chile are emulating this powerful mix of passionfruit, gooseberry and lime. South African Sauvignons are starting to move away from the mono-dimensional, fruit-driven style, showing more structure and character reflecting their origin.

Using oak Sauvignon also lends itself to fermentation in barrel and aging in new oak, though less happily than does Chardonnay. This is the model of the Graves region of Bordeaux, although generally here Sémillon would be blended in with Sauvignon to good effect.

New Zealand again excels at this style, and there are good examples from California, Australia, northern Italy and South Africa. In Austria, producers in southern Styria (Steiermark) make powerful, aromatic versions, sometimes with a touch of oak. In all these regions, the acidity that is Sauvignon's great strength should remain, with a dried apricots fruit and a spicy, biscuity softness from the oak. These oaky styles are best drunk either within about a year, or after aging for 5 years or so, and can produce remarkable, strongly individual flavours that you'll either love or loathe.

Sweet wines Sauvignon is also a crucial ingredient in the great sweet wines of Sauternes and Barsac from Bordeaux, though it is less susceptible than its partner Sémillon to the sweetness-enhancing 'noble rot' fungus, botrytis.

Sweet wines from the USA, South Africa, Australia and, inevitably, New Zealand range from the interesting to the outstanding – but the characteristic green tang of the Sauvignon should stay in the wine even at ultra-sweet levels.

BEST PRODUCERS

France
Pouilly-Fumé J-C Chatelain, Didier DAGUENEAU, Ladoucette, Masson-Blondelet, de Tracy; *Sancerre* H BOURGEOIS, F Cotat, L Crochet, A MELLOT, Pinard, J-M Roger, VACHERON; *Pessac-Léognan* Dom. de CHEVALIER, Couhins-Lurton, FIEUZAL, HAUT-BRION, LAVILLE-HAUT-BRION, SMITH-HAUT-LAFITTE.

Other European Sauvignons
Austria Gross, Lackner-Tinnacher, POLZ, TEMENT.

Italy Colterenzio co-op, Peter Dipoli, GRAVNER, Edi Kante, LAGEDER, SCHIOPETTO, Vie di Romans, Villa Russiz.

Spain (Rueda) Alvarez y Diez (Mantel Blanco), MARQUES DE RISCAL, Javier Sanz; (Penedès) TORRES (Fransola).

New Zealand
Astrolabe, Cape Campbell, Clifford Bay, CLOUDY BAY, Crossings, Forrest Estate, ISABEL, JACKSON ESTATE, Lawson's Dry Hills, NEUDORF, PALLISER, SAINT CLAIR, SERESIN, VAVASOUR, VILLA MARIA, WITHER HILLS.

Australia
Bird in Hand, Bridgewater Mill, Brookland Valley, Edwards, HANGING ROCK, HOUGHTON (PEMBERTON), KATNOOK ESTATE, Lenton Brae, SHAW & SMITH, Stella Bella, Tamar Ridge, Geoff WEAVER.

USA
California Abreu, ARAUJO, FLORA SPRINGS (Soliloquy), KENWOOD, KUNDE, Mason, MATANZAS CREEK, MONDAVI (Reserve Fumé), Murphy-Goode, Navarro, Quivira, ROCHIOLI, SPOTTSWOODE, St. Supery, Voss.

Chile
CASA MARIN, Casas del Bosque, CONCHA Y TORO (Terrunyo), Viña Leyda, MONTES (Leyda), SANTA RITA (Floresta), Tabalí/SAN PEDRO.

South Africa
CAPE POINT VINEYARDS, Neil ELLIS, Flagstone, Havana Hills, MULDERBOSCH, SAXENBURG, SPRINGFIELD ESTATE, STEENBERG, THELEMA, VERGELEGEN.

269

SCHIOPETTO *Friuli-Venezia Giulia, Italy* The late Mario Schiopetto pioneered the development of scented varietals and high-quality, intensely concentrated white wines from COLLIO. Outstanding are Tocai Friulano★★, Pinot Bianco★★ and Sauvignon★★, which open out with age to display fascinating flavours. New COLLI ORIENTALI vineyards Poderi dei Blumeri can only add further prestige.

SCHLOSS LIESER *Lieser, Mosel, Germany* Since Thomas Haag (son of Wilhelm, of the Fritz HAAG estate) took over the winemaking in 1992 (and then bought the property in 97), this small estate has shot to the top. MOSEL Rieslings★★ marry richness with great elegance. Best years: (2006) 05 04 **03 02 01 99 98 96**.

SCHLOSS REINHARTSHAUSEN *Erbach, Rheingau, Germany* Estate formerly owned by the Hohenzollern family, rulers of Prussia. Top sites include the great ERBACHER Marcobrunn. Interesting organic Weissburgunder-Chardonnay blend from Erbacher Rheinhell, an island in the Rhine. Good Rieslings (Auslese, Beerenauslese, TBA ★★) and Sekt★. Best years: (2006) 05 04 **03 02 01 99 98 97 96 95**.

SCHLOSS SAARSTEIN *Serrig, Mosel-Saar-Ruwer, Germany* Fine Saar estate with somewhat austere Riesling Trocken; Riesling Kabinett★, Spätlese★ and Auslese★★ are better balanced, keeping the startling acidity but coating it with fruit, often with the aromas of slightly unripe white peaches. Saarstein makes the occasional spectacular Eiswein★★★. Best years: (2006) 05 04 **03** 02 **01 99 97 95 90**.

SCHLOSS VOLLRADS *Oestrich-Winkel, Rheingau, Germany* Quality at this historical estate has improved greatly this century, with some brilliant Eiswein★★ and TBA★★. Best years: (2006) 05 04 **03 02 01 99**.

SCHLOSSBÖCKELHEIM *Nahe, Germany* This village's top sites are the Felsenberg and Kupfergrube, but good wines also come from Mühlberg and Königsfels. Best producers: Dr Crusius★, DONNHOFF★★★, Gutsverwaltung Niederhausen-Schlossböckelheim★, SCHAFER-FROHLICH★★. Best years: (2006) 05 04 **03 02 01 00 99 98**.

DOM. SCHOFFIT *Alsace AC, Alsace, France* One of the two main owners of the outstanding Rangen Grand Cru vineyard, also making a range of deliciously fruity non-cru wines. Top-of-the-tree Clos St-Théobald wines from Rangen are often ★★★ and will improve for at least 5–6 years after release, Rieslings for even longer. The Cuvée Alexandre range is essentially declassified Alsace Vendange Tardive. Best years: (Clos St-Théobald Riesling) 2005 04 **02 01 00 99 98 97 96 95**.

SCHRAMSBERG *Napa Valley AVA, California, USA* The first CALIFORNIA winery to make really excellent CHAMPAGNE-style sparklers from the classic grapes. Though all releases do not achieve the same heights, these wines can be among California's best, and as good as most Champagne. The Crémant★ is an attractive sweetish sparkler, the Blanc de Noirs★★ and the Blanc de Blancs★ are more classic. Bold, powerful J Schram★★ is rich and flavoursome and increasingly good. Top of the line is the Reserve Brut★★. Vintage-dated wines can be drunk with up to 10 years' age. In 2005, the winery debuted its first red wine, a 2002 J Davies Cabernet Sauvignon★★ from Diamond Mountain, in honour of the late founder, Jack Davies.

SCREAMING EAGLE *Oakville AVA, California, USA* Real estate agent Jean Phillips first produced a Cabernet Sauvignon from her OAKVILLE valley floor vineyard in 1992. Made in very limited quantities, Screaming Eagle★★★ is one of California's most sought-after Cabernets each vintage, a huge, brooding wine that displays all the lush fruit of

Oakville. Sold in March 2006; the new owners propose to change as little as possible – except the price. That's gone up to $500 a bottle!

SEGHESIO *Sonoma County, California, USA* Having grown grapes in SONOMA COUNTY for a century, the Seghesio family is today known for its own Zinfandel. All bottlings, from Sonoma County★★ to the single-vineyard San Lorenzo★★ and Cortina★★, display textbook black fruit and peppery spice. Sangiovese from 1910 vines, known as Chianti Station★, is one of the best in the state. Also look for fascinating Aglianico★ and crisp Italian whites such as Pinot Grigio★ and Arneis★.

SEIFRIED *Nelson, South Island, New Zealand* Estate founded in 1974 by Austrian Hermann Seifried and his New Zealand wife Agnes. The best wines include Sauvignon Blanc★, Gewürztraminer★ and botrytized Riesling★★. Best years: (whites) (2006) **05 04 03 02 01**.

SELBACH-OSTER *Zeltingen, Mosel, Germany* Johannes Selbach is one of the MOSEL's new generation of star winemakers, producing very pure, elegant Riesling★★ from the Zeltinger Sonnenuhr site. Also fine wine from WEHLEN, GRAACH and BERNKASTEL. Best years: (2006) 05 04 **03** 02 **01 00 99 98 97 96 95 94**.

SELLA & MOSCA *Sardinia, Italy* As well as the rich, port-like Anghelu Ruju★ made from semi-dried Cannonau grapes, this much-modernized old firm, today part of the Campari group, produces good dry whites, Terre Bianche★ (Torbato) and La Cala★ (Vermentino), and oak-aged reds, Marchese di Villamarina★ (Cabernet) and Tanca Farrà★ (Cannonau-Cabernet). Best years: (Marchese di Villamarina) (2006) (05) 04 **01 00 97 95**.

SELVAPIANA *Chianti DOCG, Tuscany, Italy* This estate has always produced excellent CHIANTI RUFINA. But since 1990 it has vaulted into the top rank of Tuscan estates, particularly with the single-vineyard crus Fornace★★ and Vigneto Bucerchiale Riserva★★★. VIN SANTO★★ is very good. Best years: (Bucerchiale) (2006) (04) 01 **99 98 95 93 91 90 88 85**.

SÉMILLON Found mainly in South-West France, especially in the sweet wines of SAUTERNES and BARSAC, because it is prone to noble rot (*Botrytis cinerea*). Also blended for its waxy texture with Sauvignon Blanc to make dry wine – almost all the great GRAVES Classed Growths are based on this blend. Performs well in Australia (aged Semillon from the HUNTER, BAROSSA and CLARE VALLEY can be wonderful) on its own or as a blender with Chardonnay (the accent over the é is dropped on New World labels). Sémillon is also blended with Sauvignon in Australia, New Zealand, California and WASHINGTON STATE. In cooler regions of South Africa it is producing some outstanding results, often barrel-fermented, and, increasingly, in flagship blends with Sauvignon.

SEÑA★ *Aconcagua, Chile* Seña is one of those trailblazing wines – initially a joint venture with MONDAVI – that was supposed to change the face of Chilean wine, but didn't, because it was too Californian. Now 100% Chilean-owned (by the Chadwick family of ERRAZURIZ), this Cabernet-based super-blend may indeed blaze a trail with its impressively ripe and dense *Chilean*-styled fruit. Best years: 2003 02 01 **00 99**.

SEPPELT *Grampians, Victoria, Australia* In one of the year's most controversial moves, Foster's has put Seppeltsfield (the BAROSSA base of Seppelt and its entire fortified resources) up for sale so that it can more vigorously chase the almighty dollar. The perceived threat to the most significant fortified stocks in the country has aroused the ire of the wine media and the Barossa community. The DP fortifieds★★ remain excellent value and the 100-year-old Para Liqueur Tawny★★★ a world-class wine of incomparable quality. From its GRAMPIANS base, Seppelt continues to excel with its flagship St Peters Shiraz★★, the definitive Show Sparkling Shiraz★★★ and the Original Sparkling Shiraz★. The sparkling whites are disappointing and appear to be suffering from a lack of focus. Drumborg Riesling★ from the super-cool Henty region of southern Victoria stands out, and there are some excellent budget-priced table wines in the Victorian range.

SERESIN *Marlborough, South Island, New Zealand*
Film producer Michael Seresin's winery has made a big impact on the MARLBOROUGH scene with his range of stylish organic wines. Intense Sauvignon Blanc★ is best within a year or two of the vintage, but creamy Chardonnay★★, succulent Pinot Gris★ and rich, oaky Pinot Noir★ will age for up to 3 years. Best years: (Sauvignon Blanc) 2006 04 03.

SETÚBAL DOC *Portugal* Fortified wine from the Setúbal Peninsula south of Lisbon, which is called 'Moscatel de Setúbal' when made from at least 85% Moscatel, and 'Setúbal' when it's not. Best producers: BACALHOA VINHOS DE PORTUGAL★★, José Maria da FONSECA★★.

SEYSSEL AC *Savoie, France* Known for its feather-light, sparkling wine, Seyssel Mousseux. With the lovely sharp, peppery bite of the Molette and Altesse grapes smoothed out with a creamy yeast, it is an ideal summer gulper. The still white is light and floral, and made only from Altesse. Best producers: Mollex★, Varichon & Clerc.

SEYVAL BLANC Hybrid grape whose disease resistance and ability to continue ripening in a damp autumn make it a useful variety in England, Canada, NEW YORK STATE and other areas in the eastern US. Gives clean, sappy, grapefruit-edged wines that are sometimes a very passable imitation of bone-dry CHABLIS.

SHAFER *Stags Leap District AVA, California, USA* One of the best NAPA wineries, making unusually fruity One Point Five Cabernet★★ and Reserve-style Hillside Select★★★. Merlot★★ is also exciting. Relentless★ is made from estate-grown Syrah. Red Shoulder Ranch Chardonnay★★★ is classic CARNEROS style. Best years: (Hillside Select) (2005) (04) (03) 02 **01 00 99 98 97 96 95 94 93 91 90 84**.

SHARPHAM *Devon, England* Beautiful vineyard with consistent winemaking and a stylish range of still and sparkling wines, including Bacchus★ white and Beenleigh red (Cabernet Sauvignon-Merlot).

SHAW & SMITH *Adelaide Hills, South Australia* Tangy Sauvignon Blanc★★ was a runaway success from the first vintage in 1989. The range now includes Unwooded Chardonnay★, an increasingly brilliant single-vineyard M3 Chardonnay★★★ and impressive, fleshy, cool-climate Shiraz★. Best years: (M3 Chardonnay) (2005) 04 **03 02 01 00**.

SHERRY See JEREZ Y MANZANILLA DO, pages 174–5.

SHIRAZ See SYRAH, pages 284–5.

SICILY *Italy* Sicily is emerging with a renewed spirit and attitude to wine production. Those who lead the way, such as PLANETA, Duca di SALAPARUTA and TASCA D'ALMERITA, have been joined by others, including Donnafugata, the revitalized Spadafora and transformed Settesoli (headed by Diego Planeta; Inycon is its tasty budget label). Other exciting estates include Abbazia Santa Anastasia, especially noted for its Cabernet Sauvignon-Nero d'Avola blend, Litra★★; Cottanera, for excellent varietal Merlot (Grammonte★★), Mondeuse (L'Ardenza★★) and Syrah (Sole di Sesta★★); Cusumano, for 100% Nero d'Avola (Sàgana★) and a Nero d'Avola-Cabernet-Merlot blend (Noà★); Morgante, for another pure Nero d'Avola (Don Antonio★★); Palari, for its Nerello Mascalese-Cappuccio blend (Faro Palari★★); and Ceuso, for a Nero d'Avola-Merlot-Cabernet blend (Ceuso Custera★). Firriato, aided by consultant Kym Milne, also makes excellent reds★ and whites★. See also MARSALA, MOSCATO PASSITO DI PANTELLERIA.

SIEUR D'ARQUES, LES VIGNERONS DU Limoux AC and Blanquette de Limoux AC, Languedoc, France This modern co-op makes around 80% of the still and sparkling wines of LIMOUX. The BLANQUETTE DE LIMOUX★ and CREMANT DE LIMOUX★ are reliable, but the real excitement comes with the Toques et Clochers Chardonnays★ (occasionally ★★). The co-op also makes a range of white and red varietal vins de pays and has a joint venture with Philippine de Rothschild (MOUTON-CADET), Baron'arques, and with GALLO in California (Red Bicyclette).

SILENI Hawkes Bay, North Island, New Zealand Established by millionaire Graeme Avery, with a view to making nothing but the best, this modern winery brings a touch of the NAPA VALLEY to HAWKES BAY. Refreshing unoaked Chardonnay★, tangy MARLBOROUGH Sauvignon★ and ripe, mouthfilling Semillon★ are all tasty. Pinot Noir★ is good (from Hawkes Bay and Marlborough), as is Merlot (The Triangle★), and new Syrah★★ is delicate and scented. Best years: (reds) (2006) 04 02 00 98.

SILVER OAK CELLARS Napa Valley, California, USA Only Cabernet Sauvignon is made here, with bottlings from ALEXANDER VALLEY★★ and NAPA VALLEY★★ grapes. Forward, generous, fruity wines, impossible not to enjoy young, yet with great staying power. Best years: (Napa Valley) (04) (03) 02 01 00 99 97 96 95 94 93 92 91 90 86 85 84.

SILVERADO VINEYARDS Stags Leap District AVA, California, USA The regular Cabernet Sauvignon★ has intense fruit and is drinkable fairly young; Solo★★ and Limited Reserve★★ have more depth and are capable of aging; a STAGS LEAP DISTRICT Cabernet Sauvignon★★ displays the cherry fruit and supple tannins of this AVA. Also a fruity Merlot★, refreshing Sauvignon Blanc★ and Chardonnay★ with soft, inviting fruit and a silky finish. Best years: (Limited Reserve Cabernet) (2005) (04) (03) 02 01 99 95 94 91 90.

SIMI Alexander Valley AVA, California, USA Historical winery purchased by Constellation in 1999. Currently the ALEXANDER VALLEY Cabernet Sauvignon★, Chardonnay★ (Reserve★★) and Sauvignon Blanc★ attain fair standards. Best years: (reds) 2001 99 97 95 94 91 90.

SIMONSIG Stellenbosch WO, South Africa Family-run property with broad range of styles. Most consistent are the reds: regular Shiraz and lavishly oaked Merindol Syrah; a delicious unwooded Pinotage★ and well-oaked old-vine Redhill Pinotage★; the svelte BORDEAUX-blend Tiara★; and dense, powerful Frans Malan Reserve★, a Cape blend of Pinotage, Cabernet Sauvignon and Merlot. Whites are sound, if less exciting. Cap Classique sparklers, Kaapse Vonkel and occasional Cuvée Royale, are biscuity and creamy. Best years: (premium reds) (2005) 04 03 02 01 00 99 98 97.

CH. SIRAN★ *Margaux AC, Cru Bourgeois, Haut-Médoc, Bordeaux, France*
Owned by the same family since 1848, this estate produces consistently good claret – increasingly characterful, approachable young, but with enough structure to last for as long as 20 years. Second wine: S de Siran. Best years: 2005 04 03 02 **01 00 99 98 96 95 90 89 86**.

SKALLI-FORTANT DE FRANCE *Languedoc-Roussillon, France* Now one of the most important producers in the south of France, Robert Skalli was a pioneer of varietal wines in the Midi. Modern winemaking and the planting of international grape varieties were the keys to success. The Fortant de France brand includes a range of single-variety Vins de Pays d'oc. Grenache and Chardonnay are among the best, along with Reserve F Merlot and Cabernet Sauvignon.

CH. SMITH-HAUT-LAFITTE *Pessac-Léognan AC, Cru Classé de Graves, Bordeaux, France* This property was floundering until a change of ownership in 1990 heralded a decade of hard graft, resulting in massively improved quality. The reds, traditionally lean, now have much more fruit and perfume and can approach ★★. The 100% Sauvignon white is a shining example of modern white Bordeaux and at best is ★★★. Best years: (reds) 2005 04 **03** 02 **01 00 99 98 96 95 94**; (whites) **2005 04 03 02 01 00 99 98 96 95 94 93**.

SMITH WOODHOUSE *Port DOC, Portugal* Underrated but consistently satisfying PORT from this shipper in the Symington group. The Vintage★★ is always worth looking out for, as is single-quinta Madalena★ (made since 1995), and its Late Bottled Vintage Port★★ is the rich and characterful, figgy, unfiltered type. Best years: (Vintage) 2003 00 97 94 92 **91 85 83 80 77 70 63**; (Madalena) 2001 99 98 **95**.

SOAVE DOC *Veneto, Italy* In the hilly Soave Classico zone near Verona, the Garganega and Trebbiano di Soave grapes can produce ripe, nutty, scented wines. Since 1992, the blend may include 30% Chardonnay, and good examples are definitely on the increase. Soave Superiore has been DOCG for 3 years, but the top private producers continue to ignore it in protest at the anomalous rules governing the denomination. Best producers: Bertani★, Ca' Rugate★, La Cappuccina★, Coffele★★, Gini★★, Inama★, MASI★, Pasqua/Cecilia Beretta★, PIEROPAN★★, Portinari★, Prà★★, Suavia★★, Tamellini★. See also ANSELMI, RECIOTO DI SOAVE DOCG.

CH. SOCIANDO-MALLET★★ *Haut-Médoc AC, Haut-Médoc, Bordeaux, France* It wasn't classified in 1855, but every single vintage nowadays outshines many properties that were. The wines massively repay 10–20 years' aging, but exhibit classic Bordeaux flavours from as early as 5 years old. Best years: 2005 04 03 02 **01 00 99 98 97 96 95 94 90 89 88 86 85 83 82**.

SOGRAPE *Portugal* This Portuguese giant revolutionized quality in some of Portugal's most reactionary wine regions. Mateus Rosé is still the company's golden egg, but Sogrape makes good to very good wines, including VINHO VERDE (Quinta de Azevedo★★), DOURO (Reserva Tinto★), DÃO and ALENTEJO (Vinha do Monte and Herdade do Peso★★). A high-tech winery in Dão produces Duque de Viseu★ and premium Quinta dos Carvalhais. Varietal Encruzado★ (white) and Touriga Nacional (red) are promising. A (red) Reserva★★ is a further step up. Callabriga★ is Sogrape's new baby, Aragonez-based reds from Douro, Alentejo and Dão, blended with local varieties. Subsidiaries FERREIRA, SANDEMAN and Offley provide top-flight PORTS. Also owns Finca Flichman in Argentina.

SOLAIA★★★ *Tuscany, Italy* One of ANTINORI'S SUPER-TUSCANS, sourced, like TIGNANELLO, from the Santa Cristina vineyard. Solaia is a blend of Cabernet Sauvignon, Sangiovese and Cabernet Franc. Intense, with rich fruit and a classic structure, it is not produced in every vintage. Best years: (2006) 04 03 **01 99 98 97 95 94 93 91 90 88 86 85**.

SOMONTANO DO *Aragón, Spain* Up-and-coming region in the foothills of the Pyrenees. Reds and rosés from the local grapes (Moristel and Tempranillo) can be light, fresh and flavourful, and international varieties such as Chardonnay and Gewürztraminer are already yielding promising wines. An interesting development is the rediscovery of the powerful native red grape, Parraleta, and of old-vines Grenache. Best producers: Otto Bestué, Blecua★★, ENATE★★, Fábregas, Irius★, Lalanne★, Pirineos★, VIÑAS DEL VERO★. Best years: (reds) 2005 04 **03 01 99 98 96**.

SONOMA COAST AVA *California, USA* A huge appellation, defined on its western boundary by the Pacific Ocean, that attempts to bring together the coolest regions of SONOMA COUNTY. It encompasses the Sonoma part of CARNEROS and overlaps parts of SONOMA VALLEY and RUSSIAN RIVER. The heart of the appellation are vineyards on the high coastal ridge only a few miles from the Pacific. Intense Chardonnays and Pinot Noirs are the focus. Best producers: FLOWERS★★, HARTFORD FAMILY★★, KISTLER★★, Littorai (Hirsch Pinot Noir★★★), MARCASSIN★★, W H Smith★★, Sonoma Coast Vineyards★★, Wild Hog★.

SONOMA COUNTY *California, USA* Sonoma's vine-growing area is big and sprawling – some 25,500ha (63,000 acres), with dozens of soil types and mesoclimates, from the fairly warm SONOMA VALLEY and ALEXANDER VALLEY regions to the cool Green Valley and lower RUSSIAN RIVER VALLEY. The best wines are from Chardonnay, Sauvignon Blanc, Cabernet Sauvignon, Pinot Noir and Zinfandel. Often the equal of rival NAPA in quality and originality of flavours. See also CARNEROS, DRY CREEK VALLEY, SONOMA COAST.

SONOMA-CUTRER *Russian River Valley AVA, Sonoma County, California, USA* Rich, oaky, popular, but often overhyped Chardonnays. Single-vineyard Les Pierres★★ is the most complex and richest; Cutrer★★ can also have a complexity worth waiting for; Founders Reserve★★ is made in very limited quantities. Russian River Ranches★ is much improved in recent releases. Best years: (2005) 04 03 02 **01 00 99 98 97 95**.

SONOMA VALLEY AVA *California, USA* The oldest wine region north of San Francisco, Sonoma Valley is situated on the western side of the Mayacamas Mountains, which separate it from NAPA VALLEY. Best varieties are Chardonnay and Zinfandel, with Cabernet and Merlot from hillside sites also good. Best producers: ARROWOOD★★, CHATEAU ST JEAN★, B R Cohn, Fisher★, GUNDLACH-BUNDSCHU★★, KENWOOD★, KUNDE★★, LANDMARK★★, LAUREL GLEN★★, MATANZAS CREEK★★, MOON MOUNTAIN★★, RAVENSWOOD★, St Francis★, Sebastiani★. Best years: (Zinfandel) (2003) **01 00 99 98 97 96 95 94**.

SOUTH AUSTRALIA Australia's biggest grape-growing state, with some 70,000ha (173,000 acres) of vineyards and almost half the country's total production. Covers many climates and most wine styles, from bulk wines to the very best. Established regions are ADELAIDE HILLS, Adelaide Plains, CLARE, BAROSSA and Eden Valleys, MCLAREN VALE, Langhorne Creek, COONAWARRA, PADTHAWAY and RIVERLAND. Newer regions creating excitement include Mount Benson and Wrattonbully, both in the LIMESTONE COAST zone.

SPARKLING WINES OF THE WORLD ___

Made by the Traditional (Champagne) Method

Although Champagne is still the benchmark for top-class sparkling wines all over the world, the Champagne houses themselves have taken the message to California, Australia and New Zealand via wineries they've established in these regions. However, Champagne-method fizz doesn't necessarily have to feature the traditional Champagne grape varieties (Chardonnay, Pinot Noir and Pinot Meunier), and this allows a host of other places to join the party. Describing a wine as Champagne method is strictly speaking no longer allowed (only original Champagne from France is officially sanctioned to do this), but the use of a phrase like Traditional Method should not distract from the fact that these wines are still painstakingly produced using the complex system of secondary fermentation in the bottle itself.

STYLES OF SPARKLING WINE

France French fizz ranges from the sublime to the near-ridiculous. The best examples have great finesse and include appley Crémant d'Alsace, produced from Pinot Blanc and Riesling; often inexpensive yet eminently drinkable Crémant de Bourgogne, based mainly on Chardonnay; and some stylish examples from the Loire, notably in Saumur and Vouvray. Clairette de Die and Cremant de Limoux in the south confuse the issue by sometimes following their own idiosyncratic method of production, but the result is delicious.

Rest of Europe Franciacorta DOCG is a success story for Italy. Most metodo classico sparkling wine is confined to the north, where ripening conditions are closer to those of Champagne, but a few good examples do pop up in unexpected places – Sicily, for instance. Asti, Lambrusco and Prosecco are not Champagne-method wines. In Spain, the Cava wines of Cataluña offer an affordable style for everyday drinking. German Sekt comes in two basic styles: one made from Riesling grapes, the other using Champagne varieties. England is proving naturally suited to growing grapes for sparkling wine.

Australia and New Zealand Australia has a wide range of styles, though there is still little overt varietal definition. Blends are still being produced using fruit from many areas, but regional characters are starting to emerge. Cool Tasmania is the star performer, making some top fizz from local grapes. Red sparklers, notably those made from Shiraz, are an irresistible Australian curiosity with an alcoholic kick. Cool-climate New Zealand is coming up fast for fizz with some premium and pricy examples; as in Australia, some have Champagne connections.

USA In California, some magnificent examples are produced – the best ones using grapes from Carneros or the Anderson Valley. Quality has been transformed by the efforts of French Champagne houses. Oregon is also a contender in the sparkling stakes.

South Africa Cap Classique is the local name for the Champagne method. The best are very good and those from the limy soils of Robertson are starting to show particularly well, but generally there are problems with consistency.

See also individual producers.

BEST PRODUCERS

Australia BROWN BROTHERS, Cope-Williams, DOMAINE CHANDON (Green Point), Freycinet (Radenti), HANGING ROCK, HARDY, Stefano LUBIANA, Charles MELTON, PETALUMA (Croser), PIPERS BROOK (Kreglinger), ROCKFORD (Black Shiraz), SEPPELT (Sparkling Shiraz), Taltarni (Clover Hill), Tamar Ridge, YALUMBA (Jansz), Yarrabank, Yellowglen.

Austria BRUNDLMAYER, Schlumberger.

France *Alsace* Ostertag; *Burgundy* Bailly co-op, Lugny co-op; *Die* J-C Raspail; *Limoux* SIEUR D'ARQUES; *St-Péray* Chaboud, J-L Thiers; *Saumur* BOUVET-LADUBAY, Gratien & Meyer; *Vouvray* CLOS NAUDIN, HUET.

Germany *Franken* Schloss Sommerhausen; *Pfalz* Bergdolt, REBHOLZ; *Rheingau* BREUER, WEGELER.

Italy *Franciacorta* BELLAVISTA, CA' DEL BOSCO; *Trento* FERRARI; *Sicily* TASCA D'ALMERITA.

New Zealand CELLIER LE BRUN, CLOUDY BAY (Pelorus), DEUTZ, HUNTER'S, Nautilus, No 1 Family Estate, PALLISER.

Portugal Caves ALIANCA, Quinta dos Loridos/BACALHOA, Vertice (Super-Reserva).

South Africa Graham BECK, STEENBERG, Twee Jonge Gezellen, VILLIERA.

Spain *Cava* Can Ràfols dels Caus, CODORNIU, FREIXENET, JUVE Y CAMPS, Agustí Torelló.

UK BREAKY BOTTOM, CAMEL VALLEY, CHAPEL DOWN, NYETIMBER, RIDGEVIEW.

USA *California* DOMAINE CARNEROS, DOMAINE CHANDON, Gloria Ferrer, HANDLEY, IRON HORSE, J Wine, Laetitia, MUMM NAPA, ROEDERER ESTATE, SCHARFFENBERGER CELLARS, SCHRAMSBERG; *Oregon* ARGYLE.

277

SOUTH-WEST FRANCE As well as the world-famous wines of BORDEAUX, South-West France has many lesser-known, less expensive ACs, VDQS and Vins de Pays, over 10 *départements* from the Atlantic coast to LANGUEDOC-ROUSSILLON. Bordeaux grapes (Cabernet Sauvignon, Merlot and Cabernet Franc for reds; Sauvignon Blanc, Sémillon and Muscadelle for whites) are common, but there are lots of interesting local varieties as well, such as Tannat (in MADIRAN), Petit Manseng (in JURANÇON) and Mauzac (in GAILLAC). See also BERGERAC, BUZET, CAHORS, COTES DE DURAS, COTES DU FRONTONNAIS, IROULÉGUY, MONBAZILLAC, MONTRAVEL, PACHERENC DU VIC-BILH, PÉCHARMANT.

SPÄTBURGUNDER See PINOT NOIR.

SPICE ROUTE WINE COMPANY *Swartland WO, South Africa* Owned by Charles Back of FAIRVIEW. Ripe, well-oaked Flagship Syrah★★ and polished Malabar★ – Shiraz-based and featuring any or all of Mourvèdre, Merlot, Grenache, Viognier and Pinotage, reflecting its Malmesbury *terroir* – now head the pack. Whites showing promise include rich, barrel-fermented Chenin Blanc★ and elegant Viognier. Best years: (premium reds) 2004 03 02 01 00 99 98.

SPOTTSWOODE *Napa Valley AVA, California, USA* Replanted in the mid-1990s, this beautifully situated 16ha (40-acre) vineyard west of St Helena has not missed a beat since the winery opened in 1982. Deep, blackberry- and cherry-fruited Cabernet Sauvignon★★★ is wonderful to drink early, but is best at 5–10 years. Sauvignon Blanc★★ (blended with a little Semillon and barrel fermented) is a sophisticated treat. Best years: (Cabernet) (2005) (04) 03 02 **01 00 99 98 97 96 95 94** 91.

SPRINGFIELD ESTATE *Robertson WO, South Africa* Abrie Bruwer's approach is strictly hands-off in his efforts to capture his vineyard's *terroir*. Méthode Ancienne Chardonnay★ is barrel fermented with vineyard yeasts and bottled without any fining or filtration. Not every vintage makes it! Cabernet Sauvignon is also made as Méthode Ancienne★. The unwooded Wild Yeast Chardonnay★ and flinty, lively Life from Stone Sauvignon Blanc★★ are also notably expressive. The Cabernet Franc-Merlot-based Work of Time★ is the farm's first blend.

STAGS LEAP DISTRICT AVA *Napa County, California, USA* One of California's best-defined appellations. Located in south-eastern NAPA VALLEY, it is cooler than OAKVILLE or RUTHERFORD to the north, so the red wines here are more elegant in nature. A little Sauvignon Blanc and Chardonnay are grown, but the true stars are Cabernet Sauvignon and Merlot. Best producers: CHIMNEY ROCK★★, Cliff Lede★, CLOS DU VAL★★, HARTWELL★★, PINE RIDGE★★, SHAFER★★★, SILVERADO★★, Robert Sinskey★★, STAG'S LEAP WINE CELLARS★★, Stags' Leap Winery★★.

STAG'S LEAP WINE CELLARS *Stags Leap District AVA, California, USA* The winery rose to fame when its Cabernet Sauvignon came first at the famous Paris tasting of 1976. Cabernet Sauvignon★★ can be stunning, particularly the SLV★★★ from estate vineyards and the Fay★★; the Cask 23 Cabernet Sauvignon★★ can be very good, but is overhyped. After a dip in quality, late 90s vintages were back on form. A lot of work has gone into the Chardonnay★ (Arcadia Vineyard★★) and the style is one of NAPA's more successful. Sauvignon Blanc★ (Rancho Chimiles★★) is intensely flavoured, with brisk acidity. Best years: (Cabernet) (2003) 02 **01 00 99 98 97 96 95 94** **91 90 86**.

STANLAKE PARK *Berkshire, England* Formerly known as Valley Vineyards, this 10ha (25-acre) vineyard has, over the past 20 years, produced many stunning wines. The range includes toasty oaky Fumé and fragrant Regatta and Hinton Grove★ whites; barrel-aged Pinot Noir and Ruscombe red; sparkling Heritage Brut (from Seyval Blanc and other grapes) and Stanlake Park★ (Pinot Noir and Chardonnay).

STEELE *Lake County, California, USA* Owner/winemaker Jed Steele is a master blender. He sources grapes from all over California and blends them into exciting wines, usually featuring vivid fruit with supple mouthfeel. He also offers single-vineyard wines and has, in current release, 4–6 Chardonnays, most ★★. His Zinfandels★★ and Pinot Noirs★★ (CARNEROS, SANTA MARIA VALLEY) are usually very good. Shooting Star label provides remarkable value in a ready-to-drink style.

STEENBERG *Constantia WO, South Africa* The oldest farm in the CONSTANTIA valley produces some of South Africa's best and most consistent Sauvignon Blanc: Reserve★★ is smoky and flinty with underlying fruit richness; straight Sauvignon★★ is pure upfront fruit. Barrel-fermented Semillon★★ (occasionally pushing ★★★) matches them in quality. Reds include an irresistible minty Merlot★★, gaining more nuance each year; Catharina★★, a blend featuring the Bordeaux varieties with Shiraz and a dab of Nebbiolo; and exciting, smoky Shiraz★★. Fast-improving Steenberg 1682 Brut★ Cap Classique fizz is elegant and biscuity. Best years: (whites) **2006 05 04 03 02 01 00**.

STEIERMARK *Austria* This 3291ha (8130-acre) region (Styria in English) in south-east Austria is divided into 3 areas: Süd-Oststeiermark, Südsteiermark and Weststeiermark. Technically it is the warmest of the Austrian wine regions, but the best vineyards are in cool, high-altitude sites. The tastiest wines are Morillon (unoaked Chardonnay, though oak is catching on), Sauvignon Blanc and Gelber Muskateller (Muscat). Best producers: Gross★★, Lackner-Tinnacher★, POLZ★★, E Sabathi★, Sattlerhof★, TEMENT★★, Winkler-Hermaden★, Wohlmuth★.

STELLENBOSCH WO *South Africa* This district boasts the greatest concentration of wineries in the Cape, though only third in vineyard area; the vineyards straddle valley floors and stretch up the many mountain slopes. Climates and soils are as diverse as wine styles; smaller units of origin – wards – are now being demarcated to more accurately reflect this diversity. The renowned reds are matched by some excellent Sauvignon Blanc and Chardonnay, as well as modern Chenin Blanc and Semillon. Best producers: BEYERSKLOOF★, Cordoba★, Delaire★, De Toren★, DE TRAFFORD★★, DeWaal★, Dornier★, Eikendal, Neil ELLIS★★, ERNIE ELS★, Ken Forrester★, The Foundry★, GRANGEHURST★★, HARTENBERG★, JORDAN★★, KANONKOP★★, L'AVENIR★, Le Riche★★, MEERLUST★, Meinert★, MORGENHOF★, Morgenster★, MULDERBOSCH★★, Neethlingshof★, Overgaauw★, RUST EN VREDE★, RUSTENBERG★★, SAXENBURG★★, SIMONSIG★, Stellenzicht★, THELEMA★★, Tokara★, VERGELEGEN★★, VILLIERA★, WARWICK★, Waterford★.

STERLING VINEYARDS *Napa Valley AVA, California, USA* Merlot is the focus here, led by Three Palms★★ and Reserve★★, both impressively packed with ripe, dense fruit. Reserve Cabernet is now ★★, and the regular bottling is improving, as is Winery Lake Pinot Noir★. The Winery Lake Chardonnay★ delivers honey and apple fruit in an elegant package. Best years: (Merlot) 2002 **01 00 99 97 96 94**.

SUPER-TUSCANS

Tuscany, Italy

The term 'Super-Tuscans', first used by English and American writers, has now been adopted by Italians themselves to describe the new-style red wines of Tuscany. The 1970s and 80s were a time when enormous strides were being made in Bordeaux, Australia and California, yet these changes threatened to bypass Italy completely because of its restrictive wine laws. A group of winemakers, led by Piero Antinori – who created the inspirational Tignanello and Solaia from vineyards within the Chianti Classico DOCG – abandoned tradition to put their best efforts and best grapes into creative wines styled for modern tastes.

Old large oak casks were replaced with French barriques, while Cabernet Sauvignon and other trendy varieties, such as Cabernet Franc, Merlot and Syrah, were planted alongside Sangiovese in vineyards that emerged with sudden grandeur as crus. Since the DOC specifically forbade such innovations, producers were forced to label their wines as plain Vino da Tavola. The 'Super-Tuscan' Vino da Tavolas, as they were quickly dubbed, were a phenomenal success: brilliant in flavour with an approachable, upfront style. Some found it hard to believe that table wines with no official credentials could outrank DOCG Chianti. A single mouthful was usually enough to convince them.

Today, however, the market has turned against these wines (with few exceptions) as overpriced and over-internationalized. Sales have declined alarmingly and producers are having trouble clearing their warehouses of wines which until recently were on allocation.

WINE STYLES

Sangiovese, the Cabernets and Merlot are the basis for most Super-Tuscans, usually in a blend. All also appear varietally, with Sangiovese forming the largest group of top-quality varietal Super-Tuscans. To some Sangiovese-based wines, a small percentage of other native varieties such as Colorino, Canaiolo or Malvasia Nera is added. Syrah is of growing importance, mostly varietally, but also in innovative new blends such as Argiano's Solengo. Super-Tuscan wines also show considerable differences in vinification and aging. Top wines are invariably based on ripe, concentrated grapes from a site with special attributes.

CLASSIFICATIONS

A law passed in 1992 has finally brought the Super-Tuscans into line with official classifications. Sassicaia now has its own DOC under Bolgheri. Chianti Classico's now independent DOCG could cover many a Sangiovese-based Super-Tuscan, but the majority are currently sold under the region-wide IGT Toscana alongside wines made from international varieties. There are also 3 sub-regional IGTs, but only a few producers use these.

See also BOLGHERI, CHIANTI CLASSICO, SASSICAIA, SOLAIA, TIGNANELLO; and individual producers.

BEST YEARS

(2006) 04 03 **01 00 99 98 97 95**

BEST PRODUCERS

Sangiovese and other Tuscan varieties Badia a Coltibuono (Sangioveto), BOSCARELLI, CASTELLARE (I Sodi di San Niccolò), FELSINA (Fontalloro), FONTODI (Flaccianello della Pieve), ISOLE E OLENA (Cepparello), Lilliano (Anagallis), MONTEVERTINE (Le Pergole Torte), Paneretta (Quattrocentenario, Terrine), Poggio Scalette (Il Carbonaione), Poggiopiano (Rosso di Sera), Querceto (La Corte), RIECINE (La Gioia), San Giusto a Rentennano (Percarlo), VOLPAIA (Coltassala).

Sangiovese-Cabernet and Sangiovese-Merlot blends Argiano (Solengo), BANFI (Summus), Colombaio di Cencio (Il Futuro), FONTERUTOLI (Siepi), Gagliole, Montepeloso (Nardo), QUERCIABELLA (Camartina), RICASOLI (Casalferro), Sette Ponti (Oreno), TIGNANELLO.

Cabernet Col d'Orcia (Olmaia), Fossi (Sassoforte), ISOLE E OLENA (Collezione), Le MACCHIOLE (Paléo Rosso), Nozzole (Il Pareto), RAMPOLLA (Sammarco, Vigna d'Alceo), SOLAIA.

Merlot AMA (L'Apparita), Le MACCHIOLE (Messorio), ORNELLAIA (Masseto), Petrolo (Galatrona), TUA RITA (Redigaffi).

Cabernet-Merlot blends ANTINORI (Guado al Tasso), BANFI (Excelsus), Capezzana (Ghiaie della Furba), ORNELLAIA (Ornellaia), Poggio al Sole (Seraselva), POLIZIANO (Le Stanze), Le Pupille (Saffredi), Trinoro, TUA RITA (Giusto di Notri).

281

STONIER *Mornington Peninsula, Victoria, Australia* The peninsula's biggest winery and one of its best, though Lion Nathan, via PETALUMA, now has a controlling interest. Single Vineyard and Reserve Chardonnay★★ and Single Vineyard and Reserve Pinot★★ are usually outstanding, and there are fine standard bottlings in warm vintages.

STONYRIDGE *Waiheke Island, Auckland, North Island, New Zealand* The leading winery on WAIHEKE ISLAND, Stonyridge specializes in reds made from Cabernet Sauvignon, Merlot, Petit Verdot, Malbec and Cabernet Franc. The top label, Larose★★★, is a remarkably BORDEAUX-like red of real intensity; it is one of New Zealand's most expensive wines. Best years: (Larose) **2005 04 02 00 99 98**.

CH. SUDUIRAUT★★ *Sauternes AC, 1er Cru Classé, Bordeaux, France* Together with RIEUSSEC, Suduiraut is regarded as a close runner-up to d'YQUEM. Although the wines are delicious at only a few years old, the richness and excitement increase enormously after a decade or so. Seemed to be under-performing in the 1980s and mid-90s but now owned by AXA (see PICHON-LONGUEVILLE) and back on irresistible song. Best years: 2005 04 03 **02** 01 **99 98 97 96 95 90 89 86 82**.

SUMAC RIDGE *Okanagan Valley VQA, British Columbia, Canada* Excellent Sauvignon Blanc★ and Gewürztraminer Reserve★, fine Pinot Blanc and one of Canada's best CHAMPAGNE-method fizzes, Steller's Jay Brut★. Top reds include Cabernet Sauvignon, Cabernet Franc, Merlot, Pinot Noir and Meritage★.

SUNTORY *Japan* Red Tomi and sweet white Noble d'Or (made from botrytized grapes) are top brands for wine made exclusively from grapes grown in Japan. Classic varieties – Cabernets Sauvignon and Franc, Chardonnay, Semillon and Sauvignon – are also having success.

SUPER-TUSCANS See pages 280–1.

SWAN DISTRICT *Western Australia* The original WESTERN AUSTRALIA wine region and the hottest stretch of vineyards in Australia, spread along the fertile silty flats of Perth's Swan River. It used to specialize in fortified wines, but SOUTH AUSTRALIA and north-east VICTORIA do them better. New-wave whites and reds are fresh and generous. Best producers: Paul Conti, Faber, HOUGHTON★★, John Kosovich, Lamont★, Oakover, SANDALFORD★★, Upper Reach.

JOSEPH SWAN VINEYARDS *Russian River Valley AVA, California, USA* The late Joseph Swan made legendary Zinfandel in the 1970s and was one of the first to age Zinfandel★★ in French oak. In the 80s he turned to Pinot Noir★★ which is now probably the winery's best offering. Best years: (Zinfandel) **2002 01 99 98 97 96 95**.

SYRAH See pages 284–5.

LA TÂCHE AC★★★ *Grand Cru, Côte de Nuits, Burgundy, France* Along with la ROMANÉE and la ROMANÉE-CONTI, the greatest of the great VOSNE-ROMANÉE Grands Crus, owned by Dom. de la ROMANÉE-CONTI. The wine provides layer on layer of flavours; keep it for 10 years or you'll only experience a fraction of the pleasure you paid big money for. Best years: (2006) 05 04 03 02 01 00 99 98 **97** 96 95 93 **90 89** 88 **85 78**.

TAHBILK *Goulburn Valley, Central Victoria, Australia* Wonderfully old-fashioned family company making traditionally big, gumleafy/minty reds, matured largely in old wood. Reserve Shiraz, 1860 Vines Shiraz★ and Cabernet are full of character, even if they need years of cellaring. White Marsanne★★ is perfumed and attractive, as is a floral-scented Viognier★. Other whites tend to lack finesse. Best years: (Reserve Shiraz) 2005 04 03 02 01 00 99 **98 97 96 94 93**.

TAIN, CAVE DE *Hermitage, Rhône Valley, France* Progressive co-op offering good-value wines from the northern Rhône. Reasonably high quality, despite annual production of 500,000 cases and rather dull basic 'supermarket' cuvées. Impressive CROZES-HERMITAGE les Hauts du Fief★, fine CORNAS★ and both red and white ST-JOSEPH★ and HERMITAGE★★. Topping the range are an old-vine red Hermitage Gambert de Loche★★ and a Vin de Paille★★. Also still and sparkling ST-PERAY★. Best years: (top reds) 2006 05 04 03 **01 00 99 98 97 95**.

TAITTINGER *Champagne AC, Champagne, France* The top wine, Comtes de Champagne Blanc de Blancs★★★, can be memorable for its creamy, foaming pleasures and the Comtes de Champagne rosé★★ is elegant and oozing class. Prélude is an attractive, fuller-bodied non-vintage style (50% Chardonnay, 50% Pinot Noir) made from 4 Grands Crus and aged for 4 years before release. Les Folies de la Marquetterie is a new non-vintage style from a steeply sloping single vineyard planted in alternate rows of Chardonnay and Pinot Noir. Best years: (2002) 00 99 98 96 **95 90 89 88 85 82**.

CH. TALBOT★ *St-Julien AC, 4ème Cru Classé, Haut-Médoc, Bordeaux, France* Chunky, soft-centred but sturdy, capable of aging well for 10–20 years and increasingly good this century. Also a tasty white wine, Caillou Blanc de Talbot★. Second wine: Connétable de Talbot. Best years: 2005 04 03 02 **01 00 99 98 96 95 90 89 88 86 85 83 82**.

TALBOTT *Monterey County, California, USA* This estate is known for its Chardonnays from vineyards in the Santa Lucia Highlands in MONTEREY COUNTY. Sleepy Hollow Vineyard★★, Cuvée Cynthia★★ and Diamond T Estate★★ are all packed with ripe tropical fruit and ample oak. Kali Hart Chardonnay★ gives a taste of the style on a budget. Also Chardonnay and Pinot Noir under the Logan label.

TARAPACÁ *Maipo, Chile* Flagship winery for the Fósforos group, which also owns Misiones de Rengo, Viña Mar and Casa Rivas. American Ed Flaherty arrived in 2006 after a successful stint with ERRAZURIZ, and should provide the talent to kickstart an operation that is full of potential but short on achievement. So far Reserve Syrah★ and Carmenère★ are good, as is basic Sauvignon Blanc. New single-vineyard MAIPO bottlings are uneven but promising.

DOM. DU TARIQUET *Vin de Pays des Côtes de Gascogne, South-West France* On his huge 853-ha (2,100-acre) property, Yves Grassa, innovative COTES DE GASCOGNE producer, transformed Gascony's thin raw whites into some of the snappiest, fruitiest, almost-dry wines in France. Grassa also makes oak-aged★ and late-harvest★ styles. Also wines under the brand name Domaine la Hitaire.

TARRAWARRA *Yarra Valley, Victoria, Australia* Founder Marc Besen wanted to make a MONTRACHET, and hang the expense. It's a long haul, but the winemakers are doing well: Chardonnay★★ is deep and multi-faceted. Pinot Noir★★ has almost COTE DE NUITS flavour and concentration. Tin Cows is a less pricey brand for both these grapes, plus Shiraz and Merlot. Best years: (Pinot Noir) 2003 02 **01 99 98 97 96 94 92**.

TASCA D'ALMERITA *Sicily, Italy* This estate in the highlands of central SICILY makes some of southern Italy's best wines. Native grape varieties give excellent Rosso del Conte★★ (based on Nero d'Avola) and white Nozze d'Oro★ (based on Inzolia), but there are also Chardonnay★★ and Cabernet Sauvignon★★ of extraordinary intensity and elegance. Almerita Brut★ (Chardonnay) is a fine CHAMPAGNE-method sparkler. Relatively simple Regaleali Bianco and Rosato are good value.

SYRAH/SHIRAZ

Syrah's popularity is rising fast and it now produces world-class wines in France; in Australia, where as Shiraz it produces some of the New World's most remarkable reds; and in California and possibly South Africa and Chile, too. And wherever it appears it trumpets a proud and wilful personality based on loads of flavour and unmistakable originality.

When the late-ripening Syrah grape is grown in the coolest, most marginal areas for full ripening, such as Côte-Rôtie, it is capable of producing wines of immense class and elegance. However, producers must ensure low yields if they are to produce high-quality wines. Syrah's heartland – Hermitage and Côte-Rôtie in the Rhône Valley – comprises a mere 365ha (900 acres) of steeply terraced vineyards, producing hardly enough wine to make more than a very rarefied reputation for themselves. This may be one reason for its relatively slow uptake by growers in other countries, who simply had no idea as to what kind of flavour the Syrah grape produced, so didn't copy it. But the situation is rapidly changing and Syrah's spread round the warmer wine regions of the world is at last accelerating.

WINE STYLES
French Syrah The flavours of Syrah are most individual, but with modern vineyard practices and winemaking techniques they are far less daunting than they used to be. Traditional Syrah had a savage, almost coarse, throaty roar of a flavour. And from the very low-yielding Hermitage vineyards, the small grapes often showed a bitter tannic quality. But better selections of clones in the vineyard and improved winemaking have revealed that Syrah in fact gives a wine with a majestic depth of fruit – all blackberry and damson, loganberry and plum – some quite strong tannin, occasionally bacon smoke, but also a warm creamy aftertaste, and a promise of chocolate and occasionally a scent of violets. It is these characteristics that have made Syrah popular throughout the south of France as an 'improving' variety for its rather traditional red wines.
Australian Shiraz Australia's most widely planted red variety has become, in many respects, its premium varietal. Shiraz gives spectacularly good results when taken seriously – especially in the Barossa, Clare, Eden Valley and McLaren Vale regions of South Australia. An increasingly diverse range of high-quality examples are also coming from Victoria's high country vineyards, more traditional examples from New South Wales' Hunter Valley and Mudgee, and exciting, more restrained styles from the Great Southern, Grampians, Pyrenees and Adelaide Hills regions, as well as patches of Canberra and Queensland. Just about everywhere, really. Flavours are rich, intense, thick sweet fruit coated with chocolate, and seasoned with leather, herbs and spice, or fragrant, floral and flowing with damson and blackberry fruit.
Other regions In California and Washington State producers are turning out superb Rhône-style blends as well as varietal Syrahs modelled closely on Côte-Rôtie or Hermitage. In South Africa and Chile, more exciting varietal wines and blends appear every vintage. Italy, Spain, Portugal, Argentina and New Zealand are beginning to shine, and even Switzerland and North Africa are having a go.

BEST PRODUCERS

France

Rhône ALLEMAND, F Balthazar, G Barge, A Belle, B Burgaud, CHAPOUTIER, CHAVE, Y Chave, Chêne, CLAPE, Clusel-Roch, COLOMBO, Combier, Courbis, COURSODON, CUILLERON, DELAS, E & J Durand, B Faurie, L Fayolle, Gaillard, J-M Gérin, Gonon, GRAILLOT, Gripa, GUIGAL, JAMET, Jasmin, R Michel, ROSTAING, S Ogier, M Sorrel, Tardieu-Laurent, F Villard, Vins de Vienne; *Languedoc* ALQUIER, GAUBY, Mas Champart, PEYRE ROSE, PRIEURE DE ST-JEAN DE BEBIAN.

Other European Syrah

Italy Bertelli, D'ALESSANDRO, FONTODI, Fossi, ISOLE E OLENA, Le MACCHIOLE, Poggio al Sole.

Spain Albet i Noya, Dehesa del Carrizal, MARQUES DE GRINON, Enrique Mendoza.

New World Syrah/Shiraz

Australia Tim ADAMS, BAROSSA VALLEY ESTATE, Jim BARRY, BEST'S, Rolf BINDER, BRAND'S, BROKENWOOD, CLARENDON HILLS, CLONAKILLA, Craiglee, Dalwhinnie, D'ARENBERG, Dutschke, FOX CREEK, GLAETZER, HARDY, Heartland, Henry's Drive, HENSCHKE, Hewitson, HOUGHTON, HOWARD PARK, Jasper Hill, Peter LEHMANN, Charles MELTON, MOUNT LANGI GHIRAN, PENFOLDS, PLANTAGENET, Pondalowie, ROCKFORD, SEPPELT, SHAW & SMITH, TORBRECK, TURKEY FLAT, TYRRELL'S, WENDOUREE, The Willows, WIRRA WIRRA, YALUMBA, Yering Station, Zema.

New Zealand CRAGGY RANGE, DRY RIVER, Esk Valley, FROMM, Passage Rock, SILENI, Stonecroft, Te Awa, TE MATA, Trinity Hill, Vidal, VILLA MARIA.

South Africa BOEKENHOUTSKLOOF, FAIRVIEW, The Foundry, SADIE FAMILY, SAXENBURG, SPICE ROUTE, STEENBERG, Stellenzicht.

USA (California) ALBAN, ARAUJO, Cline, DEHLINGER, Dutton-Goldfield, Edmunds St John, Havens, Jade Mountain, Lewis, Andrew MURRAY, QUPE, Swanson, Thackrey, Truchard.

Chile ERRAZURIZ, Falernia, MATETIC, MONTES, Tabalí/SAN PEDRO.

TASMANIA *Australia* Tasmania may be a minor state viticulturally, with only 1200ha (2965 acres) of vines, but the island has a diverse range of mesoclimates and sub-regions. The generally cool climate has always attracted seekers of greatness in Pinot Noir and Chardonnay, and good results are becoming more consistent. Riesling, Gewürztraminer and Pinot Gris perform well, but the real star is fabulous premium fizz. Best producers: Apsley Gorge, Freycinet★★, HARDY (Bay of Fires★★), Stefano LUBIANA★, Moorilla★, PIPERS BROOK★★, Providence, Tamar Ridge★, Wellington★. Best years: (Pinot Noir) 2005 03 **02 01 00 99 98 97 95 94 93 92 91**.

TAURASI DOCG *Campania, Italy* MASTROBERARDINO created Taurasi's reputation; now the great potential of the Aglianico grape is being exploited by others, both within this DOCG and elsewhere in CAMPANIA. Drink at 5–10 years. Best producers: A Caggiano★★, Feudi di San Gregorio★, MASTROBERARDINO★★, S Molettieri★, Struzziero, Terredora★. Best years: (2006) 04 03 **01 00 98 97 96 94 93 92 90**.

TAVEL AC *Rhône Valley, France* Big, alcoholic rosé from north-west of Avignon. Grenache and Cinsaut are the main grapes. Drink Tavel at one year old if you want it cheerful, heady, yet refreshing, with food. Best producers: Aquéria★, la Forcadière★, Genestière★, GUIGAL, Lafond Roc-Épine, Montézargues★, la Mordorée★★, Vignerons de Tavel, Trinquevedel★.

TAYLOR *Port DOC, Douro, Portugal* The aristocrat of the PORT industry, over 300 years old and still going strong. Now part of the Fladgate Partnership, along with FONSECA, CROFT and Delaforce. Its Vintage★★★ (sold as Taylor Fladgate in the USA) is superb; Quinta de Vargellas★★ is an elegant, cedary, single-quinta vintage port made in the best of the 'off-vintages'. Quinta de Terra Feita★★, the other main component of Taylor's Vintage, is also often released as a single-quinta in non-declared years. Taylor's 20-year-old★★ is a very fine aged tawny. First Estate is a successful premium ruby. Best years: (Vintage) 2003 00 97 94 92 **85 83 80 77 75 70 66 63 60 55 48 45 27**; (Vargellas) 2001 99 98 **96 95 91 88 87 86 82 78 67 64 61**.

TE MATA *Hawkes Bay, North Island, New Zealand* HAWKES BAY's glamour winery, best known for its reds, Coleraine★★ and Awatea★★, both based on Cabernet Sauvignon with varying proportions of Merlot and Cabernet Franc. Also delicious toasty Elston Chardonnay★. Exceptional vintages of all 3 wines might be aged for 5–10 years. Bullnose Syrah★★ is a scented, elegant, peppery red. Woodthorpe Viognier★ is a New Zealand trailblazer for the variety. Best years: (Coleraine) **2004 02 00 98 96**.

TEMENT *Südsteiermark, Austria* Austria's best Sauvignon Blanc★★ (single-site Zieregg★★★) and Morillon (Chardonnay)★★. Both varieties are fermented and aged in oak, giving power, depth and subtle oak character. The Gelber Muskateller are unusually racy – perfect apéritif wines. Red Arachon★★ is a joint venture with PICHLER and Szemes in BURGENLAND. Best years: (Morillon Zieregg) (2006) 05 04 **03 02 01 00**.

TEMPRANILLO Spain's best native red grape can make wonderful wine with wild strawberry and spicy, tobaccoey flavours. It is important in RIOJA, PENEDES (as Ull de Llebre), RIBERA DEL DUERO (as Tinto Fino or Tinta del País), La MANCHA and VALDEPENAS (as Cencibel), NAVARRA, SOMONTANO, UTIEL-REQUENA and TORO (as Tinta de Toro). In Portugal it is found in the ALENTEJO (as Aragonez) and in the DOURO, DAO and ESTREMADURA (as

Tinta Roriz). Wines can be deliciously fruity for drinking young, but Tempranillo also matures well, and its flavours blend happily with oak. It is now being taken more seriously in Argentina, and new plantings have been made in California, Oregon, Washington (CAYUSE), Australia and South Africa.

TEROLDEGO ROTALIANO DOC *Trentino-Alto Adige, Italy* Teroldego is a TRENTINO grape variety, producing mainly deep-coloured, grassy, blackberry-flavoured wine from gravel soils of the Rotaliano plain. Best producers: Barone de Cles★, M Donati★, Dorigati★, Endrizzi★, FORADORI★★, Conti Martini★, Mezzacorona (Riserva★), Cantina Rotaliana★, A & R Zeni★. Best years: (2006) 04 03 **01 00 99 97 96 95 93**.

TERRAS DO SADO *Setúbal Peninsula, Portugal* Warm, maritime area south of Lisbon. SETUBAL produces sweet fortified wine. The better reds (based on Castelão) come from the Palmela DOC. A few good whites. Best producers: (reds) Caves ALIANCA (Palmela Particular★), BACALHOA VINHOS DE PORTUGAL★★, D F J VINHOS★, Ermelinda Freitas★, José Maria da FONSECA★★, Hero do Castanheiro, Pegões co-op★, Pegos Claros★. Best years: 2005 04 03 **01 00 99 97 96 95**.

TERRAZAS DE LOS ANDES *Mendoza, Argentina* Offshoot of the Chandon empire, and a terrific source of reds from high-altitude vineyards around LUJAN DE CUYO. Top reds used to be known as Gran Malbec★★ and Gran Cabernet Sauvignon★★, but are now labelled Afincado and heading for ★★★. A joint venture with CHEVAL BLANC of ST-EMILION has yielded Cheval des Andes★★★, a stunning Cabernet Sauvignon-Malbec blend.

CASTELLO DEL TERRICCIO *Tuscany, Italy* Estate in the Pisan hills south of Livorno. Changes in philosophy seem to have deprived top red Lupicaia★★ (Cabernet-Merlot) and less pricey Tassinaia★ (Sangiovese-Cabernet-Merlot) of much of their exciting, scented, potentially ★★★ personality. Rondinaia (Chardonnay)★★ and Con Vento (Sauvignon Blanc)★ are the most interesting whites. Capannino is an inexpensive red. Best years: (Lupicaia) (2006) (04) (03) 01 **00 98 97 96 95 94 93**.

CH. TERTRE-RÔTEBOEUF★★ *St-Émilion Grand Cru AC, Bordeaux, France* ST-EMILION's most exceptional unclassified estate. The richly seductive, Merlot-based wines sell at the same price as the Premiers Grands Crus Classés – and so they should. Under the same ownership as the outstanding ROC DE CAMBES. Best years: 2005 04 **03** 02 **01 00 99 98 97 96 95 94 90 89 88**.

TEXAS *USA* Texas has enjoyed the tremendous wine industry growth that has hit the USA this decade, with the number of wineries tripling to 129. The state has 8 AVAs, with the Texas High Plains the most significant. Plantings are tending away from BORDEAUX varieties in favour of natives, hybrids and Rhône and Italian grapes. Thunderstorms are capable of destroying entire crops in minutes. Best producers: Becker, Fall Creek, Flat Creek, Llano Estacado, McPherson, Messina Hof.

THELEMA *Stellenbosch WO, South Africa* Meticulous attention to detail, both in vineyards and cellar, has helped this mountainside farm maintain a top ranking among Cape wineries for nearly 20 years. Consistently good, leafy yet blackcurranty Cabernet Sauvignon★★, ripe fleshy Merlot★ (Reserve★★), spicy, accessible Shiraz★, barrel-fermented Chardonnay★★, vibrant Sauvignon Blanc★★ and citrus Riesling★. New ELGIN venture is already showing exciting Sauvignon★ and Shiraz★. Best years: (Cabernet Sauvignon) (2005) **03 02 01 00 99 98 97 96 95**; (Chardonnay) 2006 **05 04 03 02 01 00 99 98**.

THERMENREGION *Niederösterreich, Austria* This warm, 2330ha (5760-acre) region, south of Vienna, takes its name from the spa towns of Baden and Bad Vöslau. Near Vienna is the village of Gumpoldskirchen with its rich and sometimes sweet white wines. The red wine area around Baden produces large amounts of Blauer Portugieser together with improving examples of Pinot Noir and Cabernet. Best producers: Alphart, Biegler, Fischer★, Johanneshof★, Schellmann, Stadlmann★. Best years: (sweet whites) (2006) 05 04 **03 02 01 00**.

THIRTY BENCH *Niagara Peninsula VQA, Ontario, Canada* A collaboration of 3 winemakers, Thirty Bench is known for its excellent Rieslings, including Late Harvest and Icewine★, very good BORDEAUX-style red Reserve Blend★ and a fine barrel-fermented Chardonnay★.

THREE CHOIRS *Gloucestershire, England* Martin Fowke makes a large range of wines from 30ha (74 acres) of vines, plus bought-in grapes. New Release is a fresh, fruity white, released in November of vintage year (as with BEAUJOLAIS NOUVEAU). Other successful wines are Bacchus, Schönburger and Sieggerebe varietals, plus Late Harvest dessert wine. Sparkling wines and Seyval-based wines are not always so tasty.

TICINO *Switzerland* Italian-speaking, southerly canton of Switzerland. The most important wine here is Merlot, usually soft and gluggable, but sometimes more serious with some oak barrel-aging. Best producers: Brivio, La Capellaccia★, Delea★, Gialdi, Huber★, Werner Stucky★, Christian Zündel★. Best years: (2006) 05 04 **03 02 01 00** 97.

TIEFENBRUNNER *Alto Adige DOC, Trentino-Alto Adige, Italy* Herbert Tiefenbrunner began his career at this castle (Schloss Turmhof) as a teenager in 1943. He still helps son Christof in the winery, producing 20-plus wine styles, mostly under the ALTO ADIGE DOC. The focus is on purity of fruit and varietal character, mainly among whites, the star being Müller-Thurgau 'Feldmarschall'★★ which, at 1,000m (3280 ft), is too high to qualify as DOC under Italy's relentlessly silly laws. Best years: (Feldmarschall) (2006) 04 03 **01 00 99 98 97**.

TIGNANELLO★★ *Tuscany, Italy* In the early 1970s, Piero ANTINORI employed the previously unheard-of practice of aging in small French oak barrels and used Cabernet Sauvignon (20%) in the blend with Sangiovese. The quality was superb, and Tignanello's success sparked off the SUPER-TUSCAN movement. Top vintages are truly great; lesser years are of decent CHIANTI CLASSICO quality. Best years: (2006) 04 **03 01 00 99 98 97 95 93 90 88 85**.

TINTA RORIZ See TEMPRANILLO.

TOCAI FRIULANO Tocai Friulano is a north-east Italian grape producing dry, nutty, oily whites of great character in COLLIO and COLLI ORIENTALI. At the time of writing, Friuli producers are awaiting a final ruling on the name, but it looks like they, under pressure from the Hungarians, will have to change it. Perhaps to just plain Friulano? But that, too, is under challenge. Best producers: Borgo del Tiglio★, Livio FELLUGA★, JERMANN★, Edi Keber★★, Miani★★, Princic★, Ronco del Gelso★★, Russiz Superiore★★, SCHIOPETTO★★, Le Vigne di Zamò★★, Villa Russiz★.

TOKAJI *Hungary* Hungary's classic, liquorous wine of historical reputation, with its unique, sweet-and-sour, sherry-like tang, comes from 28 villages on the Hungarian–Slovak border. Mists from the Bodrog river ensure that noble rot on the Furmint, Hárslevelü and Muscotaly (Muscat Ottonel) grapes is a fairly common occurrence. Degrees of sweetness are measured in *puttonyos*. Discussions continue about traditional oxidized styles versus fresher modern versions. Best producers: Disznókö★★, Château Megyer★★, Oremus★, Château Pajzos★★, Royal Tokaji Wine Co★★, Istvan Szepsy (6 Puttonyos 95★★★, Essencia★★★), Tokaji Kereskedöház★. Best years: 2000 **99 97 93**.

TOLLOT-BEAUT *Chorey-lès-Beaune, Burgundy, France* High-quality COTE DE BEAUNE reds with lots of fruit and a pronounced new oak character. The village-level CHOREY-LES-BEAUNE★★, ALOXE-CORTON★★ and SAVIGNY-LES-BEAUNE★★ wines are all excellent, as is the top BEAUNE Premier Cru Clos du Roi★★. Whites are more variable, but at best delicious. Best years: (reds) (2006) 05 **04** 03 02 **01** 99 96.

TORBRECK *Barossa Valley, South Australia* Dave Powell specializes in opulent, well-structured reds from 60–120-year-old Shiraz, Grenache and Mataro (Mourvèdre) vines. Made in minute quantities, the flagship RunRig★★★, single-vineyard Descendant★★ and Factor★★ are all  richly concentrated, powerful and complex Shiraz. The Steading★ and Juveniles★ are Grenache-Mataro-Shiraz blends (the latter unoaked) while the Woodcutters White (Semillon) and Red (Shiraz) are lightly oaked, mouth-filling quaffers.

TORGIANO DOC & DOCG *Umbria, Italy* A zone near Perugia dominated by one producer, LUNGAROTTI. Lungarotti's basic Rubesco Torgiano★ is ripely fruity; the Torgiano Riserva DOCG Vigna Monticchio★★ is a fine black cherry-flavoured wine, aged for up to 8 years before release.

TORO DO *Castilla y León, Spain* Mainly red wines, which are robust, full of colour and tannin, and pretty high in alcohol. The main grape, Tinta de Toro, is a variant of Tempranillo, and there is some Garnacha. In the late 1990s, the arrival of some of the top wineries in Spain gave the sleepy area a major boost. Best producers: Viña Bajoz, Fariña★, Frutos Villar (Muruve★), Garanza, Matarredonda, Maurodos★★, Numanthia-Termes (Numanthia★★, Termanthia★★★), Pintia★★/VEGA SICILIA, Quinta de la Quietud★, Sobreño, Telmo RODRIGUEZ★★, Toresanas/Bodegas de Crianza Castilla la Vieja★, Vega Saúco, Villaester.

TORRES *Penedès DO, Cataluña, Spain* Large family winery led by visionary Miguel Torres, making good wines with local grapes, (Parellada, Tempranillo) and international varieties. Viña Sol★ is a good, citrony quaffer, Viña Esmeralda★ (Muscat Blanc à Petits Grains and Gewürztraminer) is grapy and spicy, Fransola★★ (Sauvignon Blanc with some Parellada) is rich yet leafy, and Milmanda★ is a delicate, expensive Chardonnay. Successful reds are soft, oaky and blackcurranty Gran Coronas★ (Tempranillo and Cabernet), fine, relatively rich Mas la Plana★ (Cabernet Sauvignon), floral, perfumed Mas Borrás (Pinot Noir) and raisiny Atrium★ (Merlot). The top reds – Grans Muralles★★, a blend of Catalan grapes, and Reserva Real★★, a BORDEAUX-style red blend – are interesting but very expensive. Best years: (Mas la Plana) 2001 **00 99 98 96 95 94 91** 90 88 87 83 81 79 76.

MARIMAR TORRES ESTATE *Sonoma County, California, USA* The sister
of Spanish winemaker Miguel TORRES has established her own winery
in the cool Green Valley region of SONOMA COUNTY, only a few miles from
the Pacific Ocean. She specializes in Chardonnay and Pinot Noir, the
best of which are from the Don Miguel Vineyard. The Chardonnay★★
is big and intense, initially quite oaky, but able to age gracefully to
fascinating maturity at 10 years old. Recent vintages of full-flavoured
Pinot Noir★★ are the best yet. Best years: 2003 02 **01 00 99 98 97 95 94**.

MIGUEL TORRES *Curicó, Chile* Now producing its best ever wines:
snappy Sauvignon Blanc★★, grassy, fruity Santa Digna rosé★,
weighty, blackcurrant Manso de Velasco Cabernet★★, exciting,
sonorous old-Carignan-based Cordillera★★ and the new Conde de
Superunda★★, a tremendous, dense blend based on Cabernet and
Tempranillo. Best years: (Manso) 2003 02 **01 00 99**.

CH. LA TOUR BLANCHE★★ *Sauternes AC, 1er Cru Classé, Bordeaux,
France* This estate regained top form in the 1980s with the
introduction of new oak barrels for fermentation, lower yields and
greater selection. Full-bodied, rich and aromatic, it now ranks with the
best of the Classed Growths. Second wine: Les Charmilles de la Tour
Blanche. Best years: 2005 04 03 **02** 01 **99 98 97 96 95 90 89 88 86**.

CH. TOUR BOISÉE *Minervois AC, Languedoc, France* Top wines here
are the red Jardin Secret★, Cuvée Marie-Claude★, aged for 12 months
in barrel, the fruity Cuvée Marielle et Frédérique★, and the white Cuvée
Marie-Claude★, with a hint of Muscat Blanc à Petits Grains for added
aroma. Best years: (red) 2004 **03 01 00**.

CH. TOUR DES GENDRES *Bergerac AC, South-West France* Luc de
Conti's BERGERACS are made with as much sophistication as the better
Crus Classés of BORDEAUX. Generously fruity Moulin des Dames★ and
the more serious la Gloire de Mon Père★★ reds are mostly Cabernet
Sauvignon. Full, fruity and elegant Moulin des Dames★★ white is a
Bordeaux blend of Sémillon, Sauvignon Blanc and Muscadelle. Best
years: (la Gloire de Mon Père) 2005 03 **01 00 99 98 96**.

TOURAINE AC *Loire Valley, France* General AC in the central LOIRE;
largely everyday wines to drink young, though its tradition for wines
that could do with some aging is being restored by an ambitious
minority, many of whose wines are confusingly labelled Vin de Table.
Most reds are from Gamay and, in hot years, can be juicy, rustic-fruited
wines. There is a fair amount of red from Cabernets Sauvignon and
Franc too, and some good Côt (Malbec). Best whites are Sauvignon
Blanc, which can be a good substitute for SANCERRE at half the price, and
the rare Romorantin; decent Chenin and Chardonnay. White and
rosé sparkling wines are made by the traditional method but rarely
have the distinction of the best VOUVRAY and CREMANT DE LOIRE. Best
producers: Acacias★, Brulée★, Clos de la Briderie★, Corbillières, J
Delaunay★, Robert Denis★, David Levin, Marcadet★, H Marionnet/la
Charmoise★, J-C Mandard, J-F Merieux★, Michaud★, Octavie★, Pavy★,
Pré Baron★, J Preys★, Ricard★, Roche Blanc★, Sauvète. Best years:
(reds) (2006) 05 **04 03 02**.

TOURIGA NACIONAL High-quality red Portuguese grape, rich in aroma
and fruit. It contributes deep colour and tannin to PORT, and is rapidly
increasing in importance for table wines throughout the country.
Small but important plantings in South Africa enhance some of the
impressive port-styles emerging across the country.

TOWER ESTATE *Hunter Valley, New South Wales, Australia* Len Evans' last venture continues without the chairman's guiding hand. The syndicate focuses on sourcing top-notch grapes from their ideal regions. So, there is powerful, stylish COONAWARRA Cabernet★★, top-flight BAROSSA Shiraz★★, fine floral CLARE Riesling★★, fruity ADELAIDE HILLS Sauvignon Blanc★ and classic Semillon★★, Shiraz★ and Chardonnay★ from the HUNTER VALLEY.

TRAPICHE *Mendoza, Argentina* The fine wine arm of Peñaflor, Argentina's biggest wine producer, where chief winemaker Daniel Pi has triumphantly turned quality around since taking over in 2002. Medalla Cabernet Sauvignon★★ is now dense and satisfying, Iscay★ solid and rich, while single-vineyard Malbecs★★ are sumptuous and individual. Also punchy Sauvignon and melony Chardonnay.

TRÁS-OS-MONTES *Portugal* Impoverished north-eastern province, producing pretty rustic stuff. However, the Vinho Regional regions Transmontano and Duriense cover a handful of good reds, most from around the DOURO. Best producers: Quinta de Cidrô (Chardonnay★), RAMOS PINTO (Quinta de Bons Ares★), Valle Pradinhos.

TREBBIANO The most widely planted white Italian grape variety. As Trebbiano Toscano, it is the base for EST! EST!! EST!!! and any number of other neutral, dry whites, as well as much VIN SANTO. But there are other grapes masquerading under the Trebbiano name that aren't anything like as neutral. The most notable are the Trebbianos from SOAVE, LUGANA and ABRUZZO – grapes capable of full-bodied, fragrant wines. Called Ugni Blanc in France, where it is primarily used for distilling, as it should be.

TRENTINO *Italy* Region of northern Italy. The wines rarely have the verve or perfume of ALTO ADIGE examples, but can make up for this with riper, softer flavours, where vineyard yields have been kept in check. The Trentino DOC covers 20 different styles of wine, including whites Pinot Bianco and Grigio, Chardonnay, Moscato Giallo, Müller-Thurgau and Nosiola, and reds Lagrein, Marzemino and Cabernet. Trento Classico is a DOC for CHAMPAGNE-method fizz. Best producers: N Balter★, N Bolognani★, La Cadalora★, Castel Noarna★, Cavit co-op, Cesconi★★, De Tarczal★, Dorigati, FERRARI★★, Graziano Fontana★, FORADORI★★, Letrari★, Longariva★, Conti Martini★, Maso Cantanghel★★, Maso Furli★, Maso Roveri★, Mezzacorona, Pojer & Sandri★, Pravis★, SAN LEONARDO★★, Simoncelli★, E Spagnolli★, Vallarom★, La Vis co-op. See also TEROLDEGO ROTALIANO.

DOM. DE TRÉVALLON *Provence, France* Iconoclastic Eloi Dürrbach makes brilliant reds★★ (at best ★★★) – a tradition-busting blend of Cabernet Sauvignon and Syrah, mixing herbal wildness with a sweetness of blackberry, blackcurrant and black, black plums – and a tiny quantity of white★★★. Both are labelled Vin de Pays des BOUCHES-DU-RHONE. The reds age well, but are intriguingly drinkable in their youth. Best years: (reds) (2005) 04 03 **01 00 99 98 97**.

TRIMBACH *Alsace AC, Alsace, France* An excellent grower/merchant whose trademark is beautifully structured, emphatically dry, subtly perfumed elegance. Top wines are Gewurztraminer Cuvée des Seigneurs de Ribeaupierre★★, Riesling Cuvée Frédéric Émile★★ and Riesling Clos Ste-Hune★★★. Also very good Vendange Tardive★★ and

Sélection de Grains Nobles★★. Trimbach basics are a bit pricey, but enjoyable in their austere manner. Best years: (Clos Ste-Hune) (2005) (04) 03 02 01 **00 99 98 97 96 95 93 92 90**.

TRITTENHEIM *Mosel, Germany* Important village with some excellent vineyard sites, notably the Apotheke (pharmacy) and Leiterchen (little ladder). The wines are sleek, with crisp acidity and plenty of fruit. Best producers: Ernst Clüsserath★, Clüsserath-Weiler★, GRANS-FASSIAN★★, Milz-Laurentiushof★. Best years: (2006) 05 04 **03** 02 01 **99 98 97**.

CH. TROPLONG-MONDOT★★ *St-Émilion Grand Cru AC, 1er Grand Cru Classé, Bordeaux, France* Owner Christine Valette has been producing quality wines at this property since the mid-1980s. Her compensation – elevation to Premier Grand Cru Classé in 2006. The wines are powerfully structured and mouthfillingly textured for long aging. Best years: 2005 04 03 02 01 **00 99 98 97 96 95 94 90 89**.

CH. TROTANOY★★ *Pomerol AC, Bordeaux, France* Another POMEROL estate (like PETRUS and LATOUR-A-POMEROL) which has benefited from the brilliant touch of the MOUEIX family. Back on form after a dip in the mid-80s. Best years: 2005 04 03 **02** 01 **00 99 98 97 96 95 94 90 89 88 82**.

TUA RITA *Tuscany, Italy* Since the early 1990s, this estate in the MAREMMA has established itself at the top of the Italian Merlot tree with Redigaffi★★; Cabernet-Merlot blend Giusto di Notri★★ is almost as renowned. Best years: (2006) (05) 04 03 **01 00 99 98 97 96 95**.

CAVE VINICOLE DE TURCKHEIM *Alsace AC, Alsace, France* Important co-op with good basics in all varieties. The Reserve tier of all wines merits ★, while Brand★, Hengst★★ and Ollwiller★ bottlings are rich and concentrated. Reds, rosés and CREMANT D'ALSACE★ are consistent. Best years: (Grand Cru Gewurztraminer) 2005 04 **02 01 00 99 98 97 95**.

TURKEY FLAT *Barossa, South Australia* The Schultz family, Barossa growers with substantial holdings of old-vine Shiraz (planted 1847) and Grenache, turned to winemaking in 1990. Deeply flavoured, lush Shiraz★★, delicious Grenache★ and one of Australia's top Rosés★.

TURLEY *Napa Valley AVA, California, USA* Larry Turley's ultra-ripe Zinfandels★★, from a number of old vineyards, are either praised for their profound power and depth or damned for their tannic, high-alcohol, PORT-like nature. Petite Sirah★★ is similarly built. Best years: (Zins) (2005) 04 **03 02 01 00 99 98 97 96 95**.

TURSAN VDQS *South-West France* These wines are made on the edge of les Landes, the sandy coastal area south of Bordeaux. The white is the most interesting: made from the Baroque grape, it is clean, crisp and refreshing. Best producers: Baron de Bachen, Dulucq, Tursan co-op.

TUSCANY *Italy* Tuscany's rolling hills, clad with vines, olive trees and cypresses, have produced wine since at least Etruscan times. Today, its many DOC/DOCGs are based on the red Sangiovese grape and are led by CHIANTI CLASSICO, BRUNELLO DI MONTALCINO and VINO NOBILE DI MONTEPULCIANO, as well as famous SUPER-TUSCANS like ORNELLAIA and TIGNANELLO. White wines, despite sweet VIN SANTO, and the occasional excellent Chardonnay and Sauvignon, do not figure highly. See also BOLGHERI, CARMIGNANO, MAREMMA, MONTECARLO, MORELLINO DI SCANSANO, ROSSO DI MONTALCINO, ROSSO DI MONTEPULCIANO, SASSICAIA, SOLAIA, VERNACCIA DI SAN GIMIGNANO.

TYRRELL'S *Hunter Valley, New South Wales, Australia* Top-notch family-owned company with prime Lower HUNTER vineyards, now expanding into COONAWARRA, MCLAREN VALE and HEATHCOTE, with impressive results.

Comprehensive range, from good-value quaffers (Old Winery★, Lost Block★) to excellent Vat 47 Chardonnay★★★ and Vat 9 Shiraz★. Semillon is the speciality, with 4 single-vineyard wines (all ★★) – Lost Block, Stevens, Belford and the rare HVD – and, best of all, the superb Vat 1★★★. Best years: (Vat 1 Semillon) (2003) (02) 01 00 99 **98 97 96 95 94 93 92 91 90 89 87 86 77 76 75**; (Vat 47 Chardonnay) 2003 02 01 **00 99** 98 97 96 95 94 91 89.

UCO VALLEY *Mendoza, Argentina* This valley, in the foothills of the Andes, is an old secret of Argentine viticulture, newly rediscovered. Most vineyards are new but there are precious old plantings too. With vineyards at 1000–1500m (3200–4900 ft) above sea level, it's Argentina's best spot for Chardonnays, especially from the Tupungato area. Reds are also showing fascinating flavours – especially Merlot, Malbec, Syrah, Tempranillo and Pinot Noir. Best producers: ACHAVAL-FERRER★★, CATENA★★, Clos de los Siete★★, O FOURNIER★★, Salentein★, TERRAZAS DE LOS ANDES★★.

UGNI BLANC See TREBBIANO.

UMATHUM *Frauenkirchen, Neusiedlersee, Burgenland, Austria* Resisting the trend in Austria to produce heavily oaked blockbuster reds, Josef Umathum emphasizes finesse and sheer drinkability. The single-vineyard Ried Hallebühl★★ is usually his top wine, but the St Laurent Vom Stein★ and the Zweigelt-dominated Haideboden★ sometimes match it in quality. Best years: (reds) 2005 04 **03 01 00** **99 97**.

UMBRIA *Italy* Wine production in this Italian region is dominated by ORVIETO, accounting for almost 70% of DOC wines. However, some of the most characterful wines are reds from TORGIANO and MONTEFALCO. Latest interest centres on international-style reds made by the ubiquitous Riccardo Cotarella at estates such as Pieve del Vescovo (Lucciaio★★), La Carraia (Fobiano★★), Lamborghini (Campoleone★★) and La Palazzola (Rubino★★).

ÜRZIG *Mosel, Germany* Middle MOSEL village with the famous red slate Würzgarten (spice garden) vineyard tumbling spectacularly down to the river and producing marvellously spicy Riesling. Drink young or with at least 5 years' age. Best producers: J J Christoffel★★, Dr LOOSEN★★★, Merkelbach, Mönchhof★★, Peter Nicolay★. Best years: (2006) 05 04 **03** 02 **01 00 99 98 97 96**.

UTIEL-REQUENA DO *Valencia, Spain* Renowned for its rosés, mostly from the Bobal grape. Reds, with Tempranillo often complementing Bobal, are on the up. The groundbreaking Mustiguillo★★ winery now has its own appellation, Vinos de la Tierra Terrerazo. Best producers: Coviñas, Gandía, Palmera (L'Angelet★), Schenk, Torre Oria, Dominio de la Vega.

DOM. VACHERON *Sancerre AC, Loire Valley, France* Unusually for a SANCERRE domaine, Vacheron, now biodynamic, is more reputed for its Pinot Noir reds than for its whites, but the whole range is currently on top form. Intense and expensive Belle Dame★★ red and Les Romains★★ red and white lead the way. The basic Sancerres – a cherryish red★ and a grapefruity white★ – have reserves of complexity that set them above the crowd. Best years: (Belle Dame) 2006 05 04 **03** **02 01 00 99**.

VACQUEYRAS AC *Rhône Valley, France* Red wines, mainly Grenache, account for 95% of production; dark in colour, they have a warm, spicy bouquet and a rich deep flavour that seems infused with the herbs and pine dust of the south. Lovely to drink at 2–3 years, though good wines will age for 10 years. Best producers: Amouriers★, la Charbonnière★, Clos des Cazaux★★, Couroulu★, DELAS★, Font de Papier★, la Fourmone★, la Garrigue★, JABOULET★, Monardière★★, Montirius★★, Montmirail★, Montvac★, SANG DES CAILLOUX★★, Tardieu-Laurent★★, la Tourade★, Ch. des Tours★, Vacqueyras co-op, Verquière★. Best years: 2006 05 **04 03 01 00 99 98**.

VAL D'ORBIEU, LES VIGNERONS DU *Languedoc-Roussillon, France* This growers' association is one of France's largest wine-exporting companies, selling in excess of 20 million cases a year. Membership includes several top co-ops (Cucugnan, Cuxac, Montredon, Ribauté) and individual producers (Dom. de Fontsainte, Ch. la VOULTE-GASPARETS). It also owns Cordier (BORDEAUX), and markets the wines of Ch. de Jau and the excellent BANYULS and COLLIOURE estate, Les Clos de Paulilles. Its upmarket blended wines (Cuvée Chouette★, Chorus★, Elysices★, Réserve St-Martin, la Cuvée Mythique★) are a mix of traditional Mediterranean varieties with Cabernet or Merlot.

VALAIS *Switzerland* Swiss canton flanking the Rhône. Between Martigny and Sierre the valley turns north-east, creating an Alpine suntrap, and this short stretch of terraced vineyard land provides many of Switzerland's most individual wines from Fendant, Johannisberger (Silvaner), Pinot Noir and Gamay, and several stunning examples from Syrah, Chardonnay, Ermitage (Marsanne) and Petite Arvine. Best producers: Bonvin★, M Clavien★, J Germanier★, Didier Joris★, Mathier, Dom. du Mont d'Or★, Caves Orsat, Provins Valais, Zufferey.

CH. VALANDRAUD★★ *St-Émilion Grand Cru AC, Bordeaux, France* The precursor of the 'garage wine' sensation in ST-EMILION, a big, rich, extracted wine from low yields, from grapes mainly grown in different parcels around St-Émilion. Recently the core of the wine has been a top-quality limestone-based property and we can now see a real, impressive, consistent Valandraud style developing. Best years: 2005 04 03 02 **01 00 99 98 97**.

VALDEPEÑAS DO *Castilla-La Mancha, Spain* Valdepeñas offers some of Spain's best inexpensive oak-aged reds, but there is an increasing number of unoaked, fruit-forward reds as well. In fact, there are more whites than reds, at least some of them modern, fresh and fruity. Best producers: Miguel Calatayud, Los Llanos, Luís Megía, Real, Félix Solís, Casa de la Viña.

VALDESPINO *Jerez y Manzanilla DO, Andalucía, Spain* New owner Grupo Estévez (Marqués del Real Tesoro, Tio Mateo) is probably the quality leader in Jerez today and, thank goodness, the pristine quality of Valdespino's sherries has not been affected. Fino Inocente★★, Palo Cortado Cardenal★★ and dry Amontillado Coliseo★★★ are stunning examples of sherry's different styles.

VALDIVIESO *Curicó, Chile* Important winery, struggling to get back on track after a few lean years. Varietals are attractive and direct, Reserves from cooler regions a definite step up, and some of the Single Vineyards are quite impressive (Chardonnay★, Malbec★). Multi-varietal, multi-vintage blend Caballo Loco★★ (mad horse) is always fascinating and unpredictable, and Eclat★★, based on old Carignan, is chewy and rich.

VALENCIA *Spain*   The best wines from Valencia DO are the inexpensive, sweet, grapy Moscatels. Simple, fruity whites, reds and rosés are also good. Alicante DO to the south produces a little-known treasure, the Fondillón dry or semi-dry fortified wine, as well as a cluster of wines made by a few quality-conscious modern wineries. Monastrell (Mourvèdre) is the main red grape variety. Best producers: (Valencia) Gandía, Los Pinos★, Celler del Roure★, Schenk, Cherubino Valsangiacomo (Marqués de Caro); (Alicante) Bocopa★, Gutiérrez de la Vega (Casta Diva Muscat★★), Enrique Mendoza★★, Salvador Poveda★, Primitivo Quiles★. See also UTIEL-REQUENA.

VALL-LLACH *Priorat DOCa, Spain*   This tiny winery, owned by Catalan folk singer Lluís Llach, has joined the ranks of the best PRIORAT producers with its powerful reds★★ dominated by old-vine Cariñena. Best years: 2001 00 **99 98**.

VALLE D'AOSTA *Italy*   Tiny Alpine valley sandwiched between PIEDMONT and the French Alps in northern Italy. The regional DOC covers 17 wine styles, referring either to a specific grape variety (like Gamay or Pinot Nero) or to a delimited region like Donnaz, a northern extension of Piedmont's Carema, producing a light red from the Nebbiolo grape. Perhaps the finest wine from these steep slopes is the sweet Chambave Moscato. Best producers: R Anselmet★, C Charrère/Les Crêtes★, La Crotta di Vegneron★, Grosjean, Institut Agricole Regional★, Onze Communes co-op, Ezio Voyat★.

VALPOLICELLA DOC *Veneto, Italy*   Styles range from a light, cherryish red to rich, PORT-like RECIOTO and AMARONE. Most of the better examples are Valpolicella Classico Superiore from the hills north-west of Verona and are made predominantly from Corvina and Corvinone grapes. The most concentrated, ageworthy examples are made either from a particular vineyard, or by refermenting the wine on the skins and lees of the Amarone, a style called *ripasso*, or by using a portion of dried grapes. Best producers: Accordini★, ALLEGRINI★, Bertani★, Brigaldara★, Brunelli★, BUSSOLA★, Michele Castellani★, DAL FORNO★★, Guerrieri-Rizzardi★, MASI★, Mazzi★, Pasqua/Cecilia Beretta★, QUINTARELLI★★, Le Ragose★, Le Salette★, Serègo Alighieri★, Speri★, Tedeschi★, Villa Monteleone★, VIVIANI★★, Zenato★, Fratelli Zeni★. Best years: (Valpolicella Superiore): 2004 **03 01 00 97 95 93 90**.

VALTELLINA SUPERIORE DOCG *Lombardy, Italy*   Red wine produced on the precipitous slopes of northern LOMBARDY. There is a basic, light Valtellina DOC red, made from at least 70% Nebbiolo (here called Chiavennasca), but the best wines are made under the Valtellina Superiore DOCG as Grumello, Inferno, Sassella and Valgella. From top vintages the wines are attractively perfumed and approachable. Sfursat or Sforzato is a dense, high-alcohol red (up to 14.5%) made from semi-dried grapes. Best producers: La Castellina★, Enologica Valtellinese★, Fay★, Nino Negri★, Nera★, Rainoldi★, Conti Sertoli Salis★, Triacca★. Best years: (2006) 04 03 **01 99 98 97 95 93 90 88 85**.

CH. VANNIÈRES *Bandol AC, Provence, France*   Leading BANDOL estate, owned by the Boisseaux family since the 1950s. Under a new winemaker, it has leapt into the top ranks. Wood has replaced cement tanks, wines are bottled unfiltered, and the percentage of Mourvèdre has gone from 50 to 95. Besides red Bandol★★, Vannières produces COTES DE PROVENCE and Vin de Pays. Best years: 2005 03 01 00 98 **97 96**.

VAN VOLXEM *Wiltingen, Saar, Germany* Roman Niewodniczanski bought
this estate, with its great old vineyards in Scharzhofberg and Wiltinger
Gottesfuss, in 2000. His style, off-dry and opulent, is atypical and
controversial, but often ★★. Best years (2006) 05 **04 03 01 00**.

VASSE FELIX *Margaret River, Western Australia* Under a new
winemaking team this winery has become more focused on the
region. The flagship Heytesbury Chardonnay★★ is tighter, leaner and
finer than before, while the powerful Heytesbury Cabernet★ shows
greater elegance. There's a decadently rich, profound Cabernet
Sauvignon★ and oak-led Shiraz★, and the Chardonnay★ is
pleasurable drinking for a modest price. Best years: (Heytesbury
Cabernet Sauvignon) (2005) (04) 02 01 **99 97 96 95**.

VAUD *Switzerland* The Vaud's main vineyards border Lake Geneva (Lac
Léman), with 5 sub-regions: la Côte, Lavaux, CHABLAIS, Côtes de
l'Orbe-Bonvillars, Vully. Fresh light white wines are made from
Chasselas; at DEZALEY it gains depth. Reds from Gamay and Pinot Noir.
Best producers: Henri Badoux, Louis Bovard★, Dubois, Massy, Obrist,
J & P Testuz★.

VAVASOUR *Marlborough, South Island, New Zealand* First winery in
MARLBOROUGH's Awatere Valley, now enjoying spectacular success. One
of New Zealand's best Chardonnays★★, a fine, lush Pinot Noir★★ and
palate-tingling, oak-tinged Sauvignon Blanc★★. Second-label
Dashwood is also top stuff, particularly the tangy Sauvignon Blanc★★.
Vavasour recently merged with high-flying Waiheke winery
GOLDWATER. Best years: (Sauvignon Blanc) **2006 04 03**.

VEENWOUDEN *Paarl WO, South Africa* The focus here is on reds based
on BORDEAUX varieties: sumptuous, well-oaked Merlot★★; firm and
silky-fruited Veenwouden Classic★★; and Vivat Bacchus★, with a
distinctive Malbec component. A tiny quantity of fine Chardonnay★ is
made. Best years: (Merlot, Classic) **2003 02 00 99 98 97 96 95**.

VEGA SICILIA *Ribera del Duero DO, Castilla y León, Spain* Among
Spain's most expensive wines, rich, fragrant, complex and very slow
to mature, and by no means always easy to appreciate. This estate
was the first in Spain to introduce French varieties, and almost a
quarter of the vines are now Cabernet Sauvignon, two-thirds are
Tempranillo and the rest Malbec and Merlot. Vega Sicilia Unico★★★ –
the top wine – was traditionally given about 10 years' wood aging,
but since 1982 this has been reduced to 5 or 6. Second wine:
Valbuena★★. A subsidiary winery produces the more modern
Alión★★, and the new Pintia★★ winery makes some of the most
distinctive wines in TORO. Best years: (Unico) 1996 94 91 **90 89 87 86 85
83 82 81 80 79 76 75 74 70 68**.

VELICH *Neusiedlersee, Burgenland, Austria* Roland and Heinz Velich
make Austria's most mineral and sophisticated Chardonnay★★ from
old vines in the Tiglat vineyard. Also spectacular dessert wines of ★★
and ★★★ quality. Best years: (Tiglat Chardonnay) (2006) 05 04 **03 02 01
00**; (sweet whites) (2006) 05 04 02 **01 00 99 98 96 95**.

VENETO *Italy* This region takes in the wine zones of SOAVE, VALPOLICELLA,
BARDOLINO and Piave in north-east Italy. It is the source of a great deal of
inexpensive wine, but the Soave and Valpolicella hills are also capable of
producing high-quality wine. Other hilly areas like Colli Berici and Colli
Euganei produce large quantities of dull varietal wines, but can offer the
odd flash of brilliance. The great dry red of this zone is AMARONE. See also

BIANCO DI CUSTOZA, PROSECCO DI CONEGLIANO-VALDOBBIADENE, RECIOTO DELLA VALPOLICELLA, RECIOTO DI SOAVE.

VERDICCHIO DEI CASTELLI DI JESI DOC *Marche, Italy* Verdicchio, grown in the hills near the Adriatic around Jesi and in the Apennine foothills enclave of Matelica, has blossomed into central Italy's most promising white variety. When fresh and fruity it is the ideal wine with fish, but some Verdicchio can age into a white of surprising depth of flavours. A few producers, notably Garofoli with Serra Fiorese★★, age it in oak, but even without wood it can develop an almost Burgundy-like complexity. A little is made sparkling. Best producers: (Jesi) Brunori★, Bucci★★, Colonnara★, Coroncino★★, Fazi Battaglia★, Garofoli★★, Mancinelli★, Terre Cortesi Moncaro★, Monte Schiavo★★, Santa Barbara★, Sartarelli★★, Tavignano★, Umani Ronchi★, Fratelli Zaccagnini★; (Matelica) Belisario★, Bisci★, Mecella★, La Monacesca★★.

VERGELEGEN *Stellenbosch WO, South Africa* This historical farm's reputation is built on quality and consistency. Sauvignon Blancs are considered benchmarks: the regular bottling★★ is aggressive and racy, streaked with sleek tropical fruit: the single-vineyard Reserve★★ is flinty, dry and fascinating. Topping both is the barrel-fermented white Vergelegen★★ – a Semillon-Sauvignon blend that ages superbly for 3–6 years. There is also a ripe-textured, stylish Chardonnay Reserve★★. The reds are even more attention grabbing: Vergelegen★★★, a BORDEAUX blend, shows classic mineral intensity, Merlot★★ and Cabernet Sauvignon★★ are some of the best in South Africa. Single-vineyard Cabernet Sauvignon-based 'V'★★★ is brilliantly individual. Best years: (premium reds) 2004 **03 02 01 00 99 98**.

VERGET *Mâconnais, Burgundy, France* Négociant house run by Jean-Marie Guffens-Heynen, an exuberant character with his own domaine. The Guffens-Heynen wines include excellent MACON-VILLAGES★★ and POUILLY-FUISSE★★. The Verget range has outstanding Premiers Crus and Grands Crus from the COTE D'OR, notably CHASSAGNE-MONTRACHET★★ and BATARD-MONTRACHET★★★. But beware, the wines are made in a *very* individualistic style. Best years: (2006) 05 04 **03 02 01 00 99**.

VERITAS See Rolf BINDER.

VERMENTINO The best dry white wines of SARDINIA generally come from the Vermentino grape. Light, dry, perfumed and nutty, the best examples tend to be from the north-east of the island, where the Vermentino di Gallura zone is located. Occasionally it is made sweet or sparkling. Vermentino is also grown in LIGURIA and TUSCANY, though its character is quite different. It is believed to be the same as Rolle, found in many blends in LANGUEDOC-ROUSSILLON. Best producers: (Sardinia) ARGIOLAS★, Capichera★★, Cherchi★, Gallura co-op★, Piero Mancini★, Pedra Majore★, Santadi co-op★, SELLA & MOSCA★, Vermentino co-op★.

VERNACCIA DI SAN GIMIGNANO DOCG *Tuscany, Italy* Dry white wines – generally light quaffers – made from the Vernaccia grape grown in the hills around San Gimignano. It is debatable whether the allowance of up to 10% Chardonnay in the blend is a forward step. There is a

San Gimignano DOC for the zone's up-and-coming reds, though the best super-tuscans are sold as IGT wines. Best producers: Cà del Vispo★, Le Calcinaie★, Casa alle Vacche★, Casale-Falchini★, V Cesani★, La Lastra (Riserva★), Melini (Le Grillaie★), Montenidoli★, G Panizzi★, Il Paradiso★, Pietrafitta★, La Rampa di Fugnano★, Guicciardini Strozzi★, Teruzzi & Puthod (Terre di Tufi★★), Vagnoni★.

QUINTA DO VESÚVIO★★ *Port DOC, Douro, Portugal* A consistently top vintage PORT from the Symington stable that appears only when the high quality can be maintained. Best with at least 10 years' age, but I still think its greatest strength is as the backbone of top vintage blends. Best years: 2004 03 01 00 99 97 **96 95 94 92 91 90**.

VEUVE CLICQUOT *Champagne AC, Champagne, France* Produced by the LVMH luxury goods group, these CHAMPAGNES can still live up to the high standards set by the original Widow Clicquot at the beginning of the 19th century, although many are released too young. The non-vintage is full, toasty and satisfyingly weighty, or lean and raw, depending on your luck; the vintage★ used to be reliably impressive, but recent releases have shown none of the traditional Clicquot class. The de luxe Grande Dame★★★, however, is both powerful and elegant. Grande Dame Rosé★★★ is exquisite. Best years: 2000 99 **98** 96 **95 90** 89 88 85 82.

VICTORIA *Australia* Despite its relatively small area, Victoria has arguably more land suited to quality grape-growing than any other state in Australia, with climates ranging from hot Murray Darling and Swan Hill on the Murray River to cool MORNINGTON PENINSULA and GIPPSLAND in the south. The range of flavours is similarly wide and exciting. With more than 500 wineries, Victoria leads the boutique winery boom, particularly in Mornington Peninsula. See also BEECHWORTH, BENDIGO, CENTRAL VICTORIA, GEELONG, GRAMPIANS AND PYRENEES, HEATHCOTE, RUTHERGLEN, YARRA VALLEY.

VIEUX-CHÂTEAU-CERTAN★★ *Pomerol AC, Bordeaux, France* Slow-developing, tannic red with up to 30% Cabernet Franc and 10% Cabernet Sauvignon in the blend, which after 15–20 years finally resembles more a fragrant refined MEDOC than a hedonistic POMEROL. Best years: 2005 04 02 01 **00 99 98 96 95 90 89 88 86 85 83 82**.

DOM. DU VIEUX TÉLÉGRAPHE *Châteauneuf-du-Pape AC, Rhône Valley, France* The vines are some of the oldest in CHATEAUNEUF and the Grenache-based red★★★ is among the best modern-style wines produced in the RHONE VALLEY. There is also a small amount of white★★, which is rich and heavenly when very young. Good second wine, Vieux Mas des Papes. Also owns la Roquète★ in Châteauneuf and les Pallières★★ in GIGONDAS. Best years: (reds) 2006 05 04 03 **01 00** 99 98 97 96 95 90 89 88.

VILLA MARIA *Auckland and Marlborough, New Zealand* Founder George Fistonich also owns Esk Valley and Vidal (both in HAWKES BAY). Villa Maria Reserve Merlot-Cabernet★★★, Reserve Merlot★★, Esk Valley The Terraces★★★ and Vidal Merlot-Cabernet★★ are superb. New Syrahs are among New Zealand's best: Esk Valley and Villa Maria Reserve both ★★★. Reserve Chardonnay from Vidal★★ and Villa Maria★★ are power-packed wines. The Villa Maria Reserve range includes at least 9 MARLBOROUGH Sauvignon Blancs, with Clifford Bay★★, Ballochdale★★ and Richmond Brook★★ single estates outstanding. Also from Marlborough, impressive Riesling★ and Pinot

Gris★ and stunning botrytized Noble Riesling★★★. Best years: (Hawkes Bay reds) (2006) **04 02 00 98**.

CH. DE VILLENEUVE *Saumur-Champigny AC, Loire Valley, France* The secret of this property's success lies in low yields, picked when properly ripe. First-class SAUMUR-CHAMPIGNY★, with concentrated, mineral Vieilles Vignes★★ and le Grand Clos★★. Also good white, stainless steel-fermented SAUMUR★ and barrel-fermented Saumur Les Cormiers★★. Best years: 2006 05 04 **03** 02 **01 97 96**.

VILLIERA *Stellenbosch WO, South Africa* The speciality is Cap Classique sparklers; stand-outs are Monro Brut★ and the additive-free Brut Natural Chardonnay★. Still whites include Sauvignon Blanc (Bush Vine★), a consistent Riesling and 2 delicious Chenin Blancs★ with different degrees of oaking. Monro, a structured Merlot-led BORDEAUX blend, is best among the reds. Fired Earth★ is a tasty Late Bottled PORT style. Also 'mentor' to neighbouring M'hudi project (Pinotage★).

VIN SANTO *Tuscany, Italy* The 'holy wine' of TUSCANY can be one of the world's great sweet wines – but it has also been one of the most wantonly abused wine terms in Italy (happily the *liquoroso* version, made by adding alcohol to partially fermented must, is no longer recognized as a legitimate style of vin santo). Made from grapes either hung from rafters or laid on mats to dry, the resulting wines, fermented and aged in small barrels (*caratelli*) for up to 7–8 years, should be nutty, oxidized, full of the flavours of dried apricots and crystallized orange peel, concentrated and long. Also produced in UMBRIA, and in TRENTINO as Vino Santo using the Nosiola grape. Best producers: Castello di AMA★, AVIGNONESI★★★, Fattoria di Basciano★★, Bindella★★, Cacchiano★, Capezzana★★, Fattoria del Cerro★★, Corzano & Paterno★★, FONTODI★★, ISOLE E OLENA★★★, Romeo★★, San Felice★★, San Gervasio★★, San Giusto a Rentennano★★★, SELVAPIANA★★, Villa Sant'Anna★★, Villa di Vetrice★, VOLPAIA★.

VIÑAS DEL VERO *Somontano DO, Aragón, Spain* Buttery but mineral unoaked Chardonnay and its toasty barrel-fermented counterpart★ are joined by more original whites such as Clarión★, a blend of Chardonnay, Gewürztraminer and Macabeo; flavours are back on track after a few years of lightening up. Top reds – Gran Vos★ (Merlot-Cabernet-Pinot Noir) and the red blend made by its subsidiary Blecua★★ – still deliver the goods.

VINHO VERDE DOC *Minho and Douro Litoral, Portugal* 'Vinho Verde' can be red *or* white – 'green' only in the sense of being young. The whites are the most widely seen outside Portugal and range from sulphured and acidic to aromatic, flowery and fruity. One or two that fall outside the DOC regulations are sold as Vinho Regional Minho. Best producers: Quinta de Alderiz, Quinta do Ameal★, Quinta da Aveleda, Quinta da Baguinha★, Encostas dos Castelos, Quinta da Franqueira★, Moncão co-op (Deu la Deu Alvarinho★, Muralhas de Moncão), Muros de Melgaço (Alvarinho★), Quintas de Melgaço, Palácio de Brejoeira, Dom Salvador, Casa de Sezim★, Quinta de Soalheiro★, SOGRAPE (Gazela, Quinta do Azevedo★), Quinta do Tamariz (Loureiro★).

VINO NOBILE DI MONTEPULCIANO DOCG *Tuscany, Italy* The 'noble wine' from the hills around the town of Montepulciano is made from the Sangiovese grape, known locally as Prugnolo, with the help of a little Canaiolo and Mammolo (and increasingly, today, Merlot and Cabernet). At its best, it combines the power and structure of BRUNELLO DI MONTALCINO with the finesse and complexity found in top CHIANTI.

Unfortunately, the best was a rare beast until relatively recently; improvement in the 1990s has been impressive. The introduction of what is essentially a second wine, ROSSO DI MONTEPULCIANO, has certainly helped. Best producers: AVIGNONESI★★, Bindella★, BOSCARELLI★★, La Braccesca★★/ANTINORI, Le Casalte★, La Ciarliana★, Contucci★, Dei★★, Del Cerro★★, Fassati★★, Gracciano★, Il Macchione★, Nottola★★, Palazzo Vecchio★, POLIZIANO★★, Redi★, Romeo★, Salcheto★★, Trerose★ (Simposio★★), Valdipiatta★. Best years: (2006) 04 **03 01 00 99 97 95**.

VINSOBRES AC *Rhône Valley, France*   Southern RHONE village whose red moved up to full AC in 2005. A good area for Syrah, which goes into the blend with Grenache. Best producers: Chaume-Arnaud★, Coriançon★, Deurre★, Jaume★, Moulin★, Perrin★, Peysson, Rouanne, la Vinsobraise co-op.

VIOGNIER Traditionally grown only in the northern RHONE, and a poor yielder, prone to disease and difficult to vinify. The wine can be delicious: peachy, apricotty with a soft, almost waxy texture, usually a fragrance of spring flowers and sometimes a taste like crème fraîche. New, high-yielding clones are now found in LANGUEDOC-ROUSSILLON, Ardèche and the southern Rhône as well as in Spain, Switzerland, Italy, Austria, California, Argentina, Chile, Australia and South Africa.

VIRÉ-CLESSÉ AC *Mâconnais, Burgundy, France*   Appellation created in 1998 out of 2 of the best MACON-VILLAGES. Controversially, the rules have outlawed wines with residual sugar, thus excluding Jean Thévenet's extraordinary cuvées. Best producers: A Bonhomme★★, Bret Brothers★, O Merlin★, R Michel★★, Rijckaert★, Cave de Viré★, Ch. de Viré★. Best years: (2006) **05 04 02**.

VIRGINIA *USA*   Thomas Jefferson failed miserably at growing grapes at his Monticello estate, but his modern-day successors have created a rapidly growing and improving wine industry. Virginia now has more than 110 wineries and 6 AVAs. Aromatic Viognier and earthy Cabernet Franc show most promise. Best producers: Barboursville★, Chrysalis, HORTON★, Kluge, Linden★, Rockbridge, Valhalla★, Veritas, White Hall★.

VIVIANI *Valpolicella DOC, Veneto, Italy*   Claudio Viviani's 9ha (22-acre) site is turning out some beautifully balanced VALPOLICELLA. The top AMARONE, Casa dei Bepi★★★, is a model of enlightened modernity, and the Valpolicella Classico Superiore Campo Morar★★ and RECIOTO★★ are of a similar quality. Best years: (2006) 04 **03 01 00 97**.

ROBERTO VOERZIO *Barolo DOCG, Piedmont, Italy*   One of the best of the new wave of BAROLO producers. Dolcetto (Priavino★) is successful, as is Vignaserra★★ – barrique-aged Nebbiolo with a little Cabernet – and the outstanding BARBERA D'ALBA Riserva Vigneto Pozzo dell'Annunziata★★★. Barriques are also used for fashioning his Barolo, but such is the quality and concentration of fruit coming from densely planted vineyards that the oak does not overwhelm. Single-vineyard examples made in the best years are Brunate★★, Cerequio★★★, La Serra★★ and Riserva Capalot★★★. Best years: (Barolo) (2006) (04) 03 01 **00 99 98 97 96 95 93 91 90 89 88 85**.

COMTE GEORGES DE VOGÜÉ *Chambolle-Musigny AC, Côte de Nuits, Burgundy, France*   De Vogüé owns substantial holdings in 2 Grands Crus, BONNES-MARES★★★ and MUSIGNY★★★, as well as in Chambolle's top Premier Cru, les Amoureuses★★★. Since 1990 the domaine has been on magnificent form. It is the sole producer of minute quantities of Musigny Blanc★★, but because of recent replanting the wine is currently being sold as (very expensive) BOURGOGNE Blanc. Best years: (Musigny) (2006) 05 04 03 00 99 98 **97** 96 93 **92 91 90**.

VOLNAY AC *Côte de Beaune, Burgundy, France* Some of the most elegant red wines of the COTE DE BEAUNE; attractive when young, good examples can age well. The top Premiers Crus are Caillerets, Champans, Clos des Chênes, Santenots and Taillepieds. Best producers: R Ampeau★, d'ANGERVILLE★★, H Boillot★, J Boillot★★, J-M Boillot★★, J-M Bouley★, COCHE-DURY★★, V GIRARDIN★★, LAFARGE★★★, LAFON★★★, Matrot★★, MONTILLE★★★, N POTEL★★, J Prieur★★, Roblet-Monnot★, N Rossignol★, J Voillot★★. Best years: (2006) 05 04 03 02 99 **98 97 96 95** 93 91 90.

CASTELLO DI VOLPAIA *Chianti Classico DOCG, Tuscany, Italy* Light, perfumed but refined CHIANTI CLASSICO★ (Riserva★★). Two stylish SUPER-TUSCANS, Balifico★★ and Coltassala★★, are both predominantly Sangiovese. Sometimes good but not great VIN SANTO★. Riccardo Cotarella is consultant enologist.

VOSNE-ROMANÉE AC *Côte de Nuits, Burgundy, France* The greatest village in the COTE DE NUITS, with 6 Grands Crus and 13 Premiers Crus (notably les Malconsorts, aux Brûlées and les Suchots) which are often as good as other villages' Grands Crus. The quality of Vosne's village wine is also high. In good years the wines need at least 6 years' aging, but 10–15 would be better. Best producers: R Arnoux★★★, Cacheux Sirugue★★, S CATHIARD★★★, B CLAIR★★, B Clavelier★★, R Engel★★, GRIVOT★★★, Anne GROS★★★, A-F GROS★★, M GROS★★★, F Lamarche★★, Dom. LEROY★★★, Vicomte LIGER-BELAIR★★★, MEO-CAMUZET★★★, Mugneret-Gibourg★★, RION★★, Dom. de la ROMANEE-CONTI★★★, E Rouget★★★. Best years: (2006) 05 04 03 02 01 **00** 99 **98 97** 96 **95 93 91 90**.

VOUGEOT AC *Côte de Nuits, Burgundy, France* Outside the walls of CLOS DE VOUGEOT there are 11ha (27 acres) of Premier Cru and 5ha (12 acres) of other vines. Look out for Premier Cru Les Cras (red) and the Clos Blanc de Vougeot, first planted with white grapes in 1110. Best producers: Bertagna★★, Chopin★★, C Clerget★, VOUGERAIE★★. Best years: (reds) (2006) 05 04 03 02 01 **00 99 98 97 96**.

DOM. DE LA VOUGERAIE *Côte de Nuits, Burgundy, France* An estate created by Jean-Claude BOISSET in 1999 out of the numerous vineyards – often excellent but under-achieving – which came with Burgundy merchant houses acquired during his rise to prominence since 1964. Wines have been generally outstanding, notably Clos Blanc de VOUGEOT★★★, GEVREY-CHAMBERTIN les Évocelles★★, le MUSIGNY★★★ and Vougeot les Cras★★ reds. Best years: (reds) (2006) 05 04 03 02 **01 00 99**.

CH. LA VOULTE-GASPARETS *Corbières AC, Languedoc, France* CORBIERES with flavours of thyme and baked earth from old hillside vines. Good basic Voulte-Gasparets and more expensive Cuvée Réservée★ and Romain Pauc★★. Can be drunk young, but ages well. Best years: (Romain Pauc) 2004 03 **01 00 99 98**.

VOUVRAY AC *Loire Valley, France* Dry, medium-dry, sweet and sparkling wines from Chenin grapes east of Tours. The dry wines acquire beautifully rounded flavours after 6–8 years. Medium-dry wines, when well made from a single domaine, are worth aging for 20 years or more. Spectacular noble-rot-affected sweet wines can be produced when conditions are right. The fizz is some of the LOIRE's best. Best producers: Aubuisières★★, Bourillon-Dorléans★★,

Champalou★, CLOS NAUDIN★★, la Fontainerie★★, Gaudrelle★, Gautier★★, Haute Borne★, HUET★★★, Pichot★★, F Pinon★★, Taille aux Loups★★/BLOT, Vigneau Chevreau★. Best years: 2006 05 04 **03 02 01 99 97 96 95 93 90 89**.

VOYAGER ESTATE *Margaret River, Western Australia* Originally planted in 1978 and owned since 92 by mining magnate and teetotaller Michael Wright, who has built one of the most impressive cellar door complexes in MARGARET RIVER. Stellar Chardonnay★★★, vibrant Sauvignon Blanc-Semillon and grassy Sauvignon Blanc. The Cabernet Sauvignon★ and Shiraz have leapt up a notch in recent vintages.

WACHAU *Niederösterreich, Austria* This stunning 1390ha (3400-acre) stretch of the Danube is Austria's top region for dry whites, from Riesling and Grüner Veltliner. Best producers: F HIRTZBERGER★★★, Högl★★, KNOLL★★★, NIKOLAIHOF★★, F X PICHLER★★★, PRAGER★★★, Schmelz★★, Freie Weingärtner WACHAU★. Best years: (2006) 05 04 **03 02 01 00 99 98 97 95 94 93 90**.

WACHAU, FREIE WEINGÄRTNER *Wachau, Niederösterreich, Austria* Co-op producing fine WACHAU white wines, especially vineyard-designated Grüner Veltliners★★ and Rieslings★★. Now sells its top wines under the name Domäne Wachau. Its brilliant winemaker left in 2003, and quality dipped until 2005. Best years: (2006) 05 04 03 02 01 **99 98 97**.

WACHENHEIM *Pfalz, Germany* Wine village made famous by the BURKLIN-WOLF estate, its best vineyards can produce rich yet beautifully balanced Rieslings. Best producers: Josef BIFFAR★, BURKLIN-WOLF★★, Karl Schaefer★, J L WOLF★★. Best years: (2006) 05 04 **03 02 01 99 98 97 96**.

WAIHEKE ISLAND *North Island, New Zealand* GOLDWATER pioneered wine-making on this island in Auckland harbour in the early 1980s, and this tiny region is now home to over 30 wineries. Hot, dry ripening conditions have made high-quality Cabernet-based reds that sell for high prices. Chardonnay is now appearing, together with experimental plots of Syrah and Viognier. Best producers: Fenton★, GOLDWATER★★, Obsidian, Passage Rock, STONYRIDGE★★★, Te Whau★. Best years: (reds) **2005 04 02 00 99 98**.

WALKER BAY WO *South Africa* This maritime district on the south coast is home to a mix of grape varieties, but the holy grail of the majority is Pinot Noir, with the hub of activity in the Hemel en Aarde (heaven and earth) Valley. Also steely Sauvignon Blanc, minerally Chardonnay and refined Pinotage. Best producers: Ashbourne★, BOUCHARD FINLAYSON★, HAMILTON RUSSELL★★, Hermanuspietersfontein, Newton Johnson★. Best years: (Pinot Noir) (2006) **05 04 03 02 01 00 99 98**.

WALLA WALLA VALLEY AVA *Washington State, USA* Walla Walla has over 80 of WASHINGTON's wineries, but 35 have only been producing wine since 1999. Similarly, vineyard acreage, although only 4% of the state total, has trebled since 99 – and is still growing. If you think there's a gold-rush feel about this clearly exciting area you wouldn't be far wrong. Best producers: CAYUSE VINEYARDS★★, DUNHAM CELLARS★, K Vintners★, L'ECOLE NO 41★★, LEONETTI CELLAR★★★, LONG SHADOWS VINTNERS★★, Northstar★, Pepper Bridge Winery★, Reininger★, WOODWARD CANYON★★.

WARRE *Port DOC, Douro, Portugal* Part of the Symington group, with top-quality Vintage PORT★★★ and a good 'off-vintage' port from Quinta da Cavadinha★★. LBV★★ is in the traditional, unfiltered style. Warrior★ is a reliable ruby and Otima a solid 10-year-old tawny; Otima★ 20-year-old is much better. Best years: (Vintage) 2003 00 97 94 **91 85 83 80 77 70 66 63**; (Cavadinha) 2001 99 98 96 **95 92 90 88 87 86 82 78**.

WARWICK *Stellenbosch WO, South Africa* Situated in the heart of prime red wine country, Warwick produces the complex Trilogy★ BORDEAUX-style blend and a refined, fragrant Cabernet Franc★. The Three Cape Ladies★ red blend includes Pinotage along with Cabernet Sauvignon and Merlot. Whites are represented by an unwooded Sauvignon Blanc and full-bodied, lightly oaked Chardonnay★. Best years: (Trilogy) 2005 **04 03 02 01 00 99 98**.

WASHINGTON STATE *USA* Second-largest premium wine-producing state in the US with more than 460 wineries. The chief growing areas are in irrigated high desert, east of the Cascade Mountains, where the COLUMBIA VALLEY AVA encompasses the smaller AVAs of YAKIMA VALLEY, WALLA WALLA VALLEY, Wahluke Slope, Horse Heaven Hills, Columbia Gorge, Rattlesnake Hills and Red Mountain. Although the heat is not as intense as in California, long summer days with extra hours of sunshine due to the northern latitude seem to increase the intensity of fruit flavours and result in both red and white wines of great depth. Cabernet, Merlot, Syrah, Chardonnay and Semillon can produce very good wines here.

GEOFF WEAVER *Adelaide Hills, South Australia* Low-yielding vines at Geoff Weaver's Lenswood vineyard produce top-quality fruit, from which he crafts limy Riesling★★, crisply gooseberryish Sauvignon★★ and stylish cool-climate Chardonnay★★. Pinot Noir is promising.

WEGELER *Bernkastel, Mosel; Oestrich-Winkel, Rheingau; Deidesheim, Pfalz, Germany* The Wegeler family's 3 estates are dedicated primarily to Riesling, and dry wines make up the bulk of production. Whether dry or naturally sweet Auslese, the best merit ★★ and will develop well with 5 or more years of aging. Consistently good 'Geheimrat J' Sekt★★, too. Best years: (Mosel-Saar-Ruwer) (2006) 05 04 **03 02 01 99 98 97 96 95**.

WEHLEN *Mosel, Germany* Village whose steep Sonnenuhr vineyard produces some of the most intense Rieslings in Germany. Best producers: Kerpen, Dr LOOSEN★★★, J J PRÜM★★★, S A PRÜM★, Max Ferd RICHTER★★, SELBACH-OSTER★★, WEGELER★, Dr Weins-Prüm★. Best years: (2006) 05 04 **03 02 01 99 98 97 95 94 93**.

ROBERT WEIL *Kiedrich, Rheingau, Germany* This estate has enjoyed huge investment from Japanese drinks giant SUNTORY which, coupled with Wilhelm Weil's devotion to quality, has returned it to the RHEINGAU's premier division. Majestic sweet Auslese, Beerenauslese and Trockenbeerenauslese Rieslings★★★, and dry Rieslings★ are crisp and elegant, although the regular wines have been a little disappointing in recent vintages. Best years: (2006) 05 04 **03 02 01 99 98 96 95 94**.

WEINBACH *Alsace AC, Alsace, France* This Kaysersberg estate is run by Colette Faller and her two daughters, Laurence (the winemaker) and Catherine. The range is quite complicated. The lightest wines are named in honour of Mme Faller's late husband Théo★★. Ste-

Cathérine★★ bottlings come from the Schlossberg and are late picked, though not technically Vendange Tardive; Laurence wines are from the non-cru Altenbourg. Superior bottlings in both ranges include the vineyard name, and the top dry wine is the special selection Ste-Cathérine Riesling Grand Cru Schlossberg L'Inédit★★★. Quintessence – a super-concentrated Sélection de Grains Nobles from Pinot Gris★★★ or Gewurztraminer★★★ – is not produced every year. All the wines are exceptionally balanced and, while delightful on release, can age for many years. Best years: (Grand Cru Riesling) 2005 04 **02 01 00 99 98 97 96 95 94 93 92 90**.

WEINERT *Mendoza, Argentina* Buying grapes from some of the oldest vineyards in LUJAN DE CUYO, Weinert has built a reputation for Malbec. Its oxidative approach to winemaking creates complex, long-lived reds such as mocha and black cherry Gran Vino★★. Estrella (Star) Malbec★★ is an eccentric red released decades after the vintage.

WEISSBURGUNDER See PINOT BLANC.

WELSCHRIESLING See RIESLING ITALICO.

WENDOUREE *Clare Valley, South Australia* Small winery using old-fashioned methods to make enormous, ageworthy reds★★★ from paltry yields off their own very old Shiraz, Cabernet, Malbec and Mataro (Mourvèdre) vines, plus tiny amounts of sweet Muscat★. Reds can, and do, age beautifully for 30 years or more. Best years: (reds) (2006) (05) (04) 03 02 01 99 98 96 **95 94 92 91 90 86 83 82 81 80 78 76 75**.

WESTERN AUSTRALIA Only the south-west corner of this vast state is suited to vines, the SWAN DISTRICT and Perth environs being the oldest and hottest area, with present attention (and more than 230 producers) focused on GREAT SOUTHERN, MARGARET RIVER, Geographe and PEMBERTON. The state produces just over 4% of Australia's grape crush but about 20% of its premium wines.

WIEN *Austria* Region within the city limits of Wien (Vienna). The best wines come from south-facing sites in Grinzing, Nussdorf and Weiden; and the Bisamberg hill east of the Danube. Best producers: Christ, Edlmoser, Mayer, Schilling, WIENINGER★★, Zahel. Best years: (2006) 05 04 **03 01 00**.

WIENINGER *Stammersdorf, Wien, Austria* Fritz Wieninger has risen above the parochial standards of many Viennese growers to offer a range of elegant, well-crafted wines from Chardonnay and Pinot Noir. The best range is often the Select★★, the pricier Grand Select★ being often over-oaked. Recent additions are brilliant white wines from the renowned Nussberg★★ vineyard. Best years: (2006) 05 04 **03 01 00**.

WILLAMETTE VALLEY AVA *Oregon, USA* Wet winters, generally dry summers, and a so-so chance of long, cool autumn days provide sound growing conditions for cool-climate varieties such as Pinot Noir, Pinot Gris and Chardonnay. Dundee Hills, with its volcanic hillsides, is considered the best sub-region. Best producers: ADELSHEIM★, ARGYLE★, BEAUX FRERES★★, CRISTOM★, DOMAINE DROUHIN★★, DOMAINE SERENE★★, ELK COVE★★, Evesham Wood★, Sineann★, Torii Mor★, WillaKenzie★, Ken WRIGHT★. Best years: (reds) (2006) (05) 04 03 **02 01 00**.

WILLIAMS SELYEM *Russian River Valley AVA, California, USA* Purchased in 1998 by John Dyson, a vineyard owner from New York. The cult following for the Pinot Noirs★★, especially the J Rochioli Vineyard★★, has diminished somewhat in recent years. The wine has become relatively lighter in weight, sometimes very fruity and sometimes just a bit off the wall. Best years: (Pinot Noir) (2005) 04 **03 02 01 00 99 98 97 96 95 94**.

WINKEL *Rheingau, Germany* RHEINGAU village whose best vineyard is the large Hasensprung but the most famous one is Schloss Vollrads – an ancient estate that does not use the village name on its label. Best producers: Eser, von Hessen, Johannishof★★, SCHLOSS VOLLRADS★ (since 1999), WEGELER★. Best years: (2006) 05 04 03 02 **01 99 98 96**.

WINNINGEN *Mosel, Germany* A small group of dedicated growers have shown that the steep slopes of this little-known village, particularly the Ühlen and Röttgen sites, can produce excellent Rieslings, especially in a rich dry style, plus occasional TBAs. Best producers: HEYMANN-LOWENSTEIN★★, Reinhard Knebel★★, Richard Richter★. Best years: (2006) 05 04 **03 02 01 99 97**.

WIRRA WIRRA *McLaren Vale, South Australia* Consistent maker of whites with more finesse than is customary in the region; now reds are as good, too. Well-balanced Sauvignon Blanc★, ageworthy Semillon blend★, buttery Chardonnay★★ and soft reds led by delicious The Angelus Cabernet★★, chocolaty RSW Shiraz★★, decadent Original Blend Grenache-Shiraz★, and seductive Allawah BAROSSA Grenache★★. Best years: (RSW Shiraz) (2006) (05) 04 03 02 01 98 **96 94 91 90**.

WITHER HILLS *Marlborough, South Island, New Zealand* Quality-focused winery, bought in 2002 by New Zealand brewing group Lion Nathan; talented founder/winemaker Brent Marris resigned as manager after the 2007 vintage to focus on his label 'The Ned'. A trio of stylish MARLBOROUGH wines – concentrated, pungent Sauvignon Blanc★★, fruit-focused Chardonnay★★ and vibrant Pinot Noir★★ – get the best out of grapes that perform with distinction in this region. Will the style change post-Marris? We'll have to wait and see. Best years: (Sauvignon Blanc) **2006 04 03**.

WITTMANN *Westhofen, Rheinhessen, Germany* Philipp Wittmann has worked wonders at his family's organic estate, succeeding equally with bold dry Rieslings★★ and voluptuous Trockenbeerenauslese ★★★. Best years: (2006) 05 04 **03 02 01 99**.

J L WOLF *Wachenheim, Pfalz, Germany* Ernst Loosen, of Dr LOOSEN, took over this underperforming estate in 1996. A string of concentrated, mostly dry Rieslings★★ have won it a place among the region's top producers. Best years: (2006) 05 04 **03 02 01 99 98**.

WOODWARD CANYON *Walla Walla Valley AVA, Washington State, USA* Big, barrel-fermented Chardonnays (Celilo Vineyard★) were the trademark wines for many years, but today the focus is on reds, with a fine Artist Series★★ Cabernet Sauvignon and Old Vines★★ Cabernet Sauvignon leading the line-up. Merlot★★ is rich, velvety and deeply perfumed. White and red★ BORDEAUX-style blends are labelled Charbonneau, the name of the vineyard where the fruit is grown. Best years: (Cabernet Sauvignon) (2005) 04 03 02 01 **00 99**.

KEN WRIGHT CELLARS *Willamette Valley AVA, Oregon, USA* Ken Wright produces more than a dozen succulent, single-vineyard Pinot Noirs. Bold and rich with new oak flavour, they range from good to ethereal, led by the Carter★★, Savoya★★, Guadalupe★★, McCrone★★ and Shea★★. Fine WASHINGTON Chardonnay from the Celilo Vineyard★★, expressive French clone OREGON Chardonnays from Carabella★ and McCrone★ and a zesty Freedom Hill Vineyard Pinot Blanc★ make up the portfolio of whites. Best years: (Pinot Noir) (2005) 04 03 **02 01 00 99**.

WÜRTTEMBERG *Germany*   11,500ha (28,415-acre) region centred on the river Neckar. Two-thirds of the wine made is red, and the best comes from Lemberger (Blaufränkisch) or Spätburgunder (Pinot Noir) grapes. Massive yields are often responsible for pallid wines, especially from the locally popular Trollinger grape. However, a few of the many marvellously steep sites are now producing perfumed reds and racy Riesling. Best years: (reds) (2005) 04 **03** 02 01 **99** 97.

WÜRZBURG *Franken, Germany*   The centre of FRANKEN wines. Some Rieslings can be great, but the real star is Silvaner. Best producers: Bürgerspital, JULIUSSPITAL★★, Staatlicher Hofkeller, Weingut am Stein★. Best years: (2006) 05 04 03 **02 01 00 99 97 94**.

WYNNS *Coonawarra, South Australia*   Wynns' name is synonymous with COONAWARRA. It is now part of the giant Foster's Wine Group, but its personality seems to have suffered less than most of the group's other brands and, except at the top end, prices remain fair. Investment in vineyard rejuvenation is paying off. Attractive Chardonnay★ and delightful Riesling★. However, Wynns is best known for reds. The Shiraz★ and Black Label Cabernet Sauvignon★★ are both good. Top-end John Riddoch Cabernet Sauvignon★★ and Michael Shiraz★★ were deep, ripe, oaky styles, but latest releases show much more restraint and elegance. Look for new Johnson's Block Shiraz-Cabernet★. Best years: (John Riddoch) (2005) (04) 03 **99 96 94 91 90 88 86**.

YAKIMA VALLEY AVA *Washington State, USA*   This important valley lies within the much larger COLUMBIA VALLEY AVA. Yakima is planted mostly to Chardonnay, Merlot and Cabernet Sauvignon and has more than 40 wineries. Best producers: Chinook★, DELILLE CELLARS★★, Hogue Cellars, Wineglass Cellars★.

YALUMBA *Barossa Valley, South Australia*   Distinguished old firm, owned by the Hill-Smith family, making a wide range of wines under its own name, as well as Heggies Vineyard (restrained Riesling★, plump Merlot★★, opulent Viognier★ and botrytis Riesling★★), Hill-Smith Estate (Sauvignon Blanc★) and Pewsey Vale (fine Riesling★★ and Cabernet Sauvignon★). Flagship reds are The Signature Cabernet-Shiraz★★, Octavius Shiraz★★ and The Menzies Cabernet★★ and all cellar well. New premiums include Old Vine Grenache★★, Contour Riesling★★, Virgilius Viognier★★ and Shiraz-Viognier★. High quality quaffers like Y Series varietals★ (sometimes ★★) and Oxford Landing Chardonnay, Sauvignon★ and Cabernet-Shiraz are consistently impressive. Angas Brut is big-volume enjoyable fizz, while TASMANIA's Jansz★ (Vintage★★) has added a class act to the flight. Museum Release fortifieds (Muscat★★) are excellent, but rare. Best years: (The Signature red) (2006) (05) (04) 03 02 01 00 99 98 **97 96 95 93 92 91 90 88**.

YARRA VALLEY *Victoria, Australia*   With its cool climate, the Yarra is asking to be judged as Australia's best Pinot Noir region. Exciting also for Chardonnay and Cabernet-Merlot blends and as a supplier of base wine for fizz. Best producers: Arthur's Creek★, COLDSTREAM HILLS★★, DE BORTOLI★★, CARLEI★★, Diamond Valley★★, DOMAINE CHANDON/Green Point★, Métier, MOUNT MARY★★, St Huberts, TARRAWARRA★★, Yarra Burn★, Yarra Ridge, Yarra Yering★★, Yeringberg★, Yering Station★★.

YELLOWTAIL *Riverina, New South Wales, Australia*   Yellowtail, Australia's fastest-growing export brand ever, has made the modestly-sized RIVERINA family winery, Casella, a major world player. Artfully crafted but overly sweet wines.

CH. D'YQUEM★★★ *Sauternes AC, 1er Cru Supérieur, Bordeaux, France*
♀ Often rated the most sublime sweet wine in the world, Yquem's total commitment to quality is unquestionable. Despite a large vineyard (100ha/250 acres), production is tiny. Only fully noble-rotted grapes are picked, often berry by berry, and low yield means each vine produces only a glass of wine! This precious liquid is then fermented in new oak barrels and left to mature for 3–4 years before bottling. It is one of the world's most expensive wines, in constant demand because of its richness and exotic flavours. The wines took a step forward in quality during the 1990s and seem to have gone even further during the 2000s. A dry white, Ygrec, is made in some years. In 1999 LVMH won a 3-year takeover battle with the Lur-Saluces family, owners for 406 years. Best years: 2005 04 03 02 01 **00 99 98 97 96 95 94 93 91 90 89 88 86 83 82 81 80 79 76 75 71 70 67 62**.

ZILLIKEN *Saarburg, Mosel-Saar-Ruwer, Germany* Estate specializing in
♀ Rieslings★★ (Auslese, Eiswein often ★★★) from the Saarburger Rausch vineyard. Best years: (2006) 05 04 03 02 **01 99 97 95 94 93**.

ZIND-HUMBRECHT *Alsace AC, Alsace, France* Olivier Humbrecht is one
♀ of France's outstanding winemakers, with an approach that emphasizes the individuality of each site and each vintage. Wines from 4 Grand Cru sites – Rangen, Goldert, Hengst and Brand – are superlative (Riesling★★★, Gewurztraminer★★★, Pinot Gris★★★ and Muscat★★), the Rangen in particular producing wines unlike any others in Alsace. Wines from specific non-Grand Cru vineyards such as Clos Windsbuhl and Clos Jebsal are also exceptional. Vendange Tardive and Sélection de Grains Nobles wines are almost invariably of ★★★ quality. Even basic Sylvaners★ and Pinot Blancs★★ are fine. Wines often have some residual sugar, but it's all natural. Best years: (Grand Cru Riesling) 2005 04 03 02 01 **00 99 98 97 96 95**.

ZINFANDEL CALIFORNIA's versatile red grape can make big, juicy, fruit-
packed wine – or insipid, sweetish 'blush' or even late-harvest dessert wine. Some Zinfandel is now made in other countries, with notable examples in Australia and South Africa. Best producers: (California) Brown★★, Cline Cellars★★, Dashe★★, DRY CREEK VINEYARD★★, Dutton Goldfield★★, Gary Farrell★★, FETZER★, HARTFORD★, MARIAH★, Martinelli★★, Nalle★★, Preston★, Rafanelli★★, RAVENSWOOD★, RIDGE★★★, Rosenblum★★, Saddleback★, St Francis★, SEGHESIO★★, Trinitas★★, TURLEY★★; (Australia) CAPE MENTELLE★★, Kangarilla Road, Nepenthe★★. See also PRIMITIVO DI MANDURIA.

FAMILIA ZUCCARDI *Mendoza, Argentina* One of Argentina's great
success stories. Dynamic owner José Zuccardi saw the potential for export before his compatriots and set about creating a range of utterly enjoyable easy-drinking wines. Basic Santa Julia reds★ are very successful. Santa Julia Reservas and Zuccardi 'Q'★ (Tempranillo★★) wines have improved dramatically with the introduction of up-to-date equipment and storage facilities. Top-of-the-line Zeta★★, a blend of Tempranillo and Malbec, is a serious yet sensual red. Zuccardi also experiments with more grape varieties than anyone else in Argentina; future triumphs will include such varieties as Marselan, Caladoc, Tannat and Touriga Nacional. Son Sebastian is a whizz-kid with sparklers (red Bonarda★ is ace) and sweeties. He's even made a sweet botrytized Cabernet! My kind of guy.

GLOSSARY OF WINE TERMS

AC/AOC (APPELLATION D'ORIGINE CONTRÔLÉE)
The top category of French wines, defined by regulations covering vineyard yields, grape varieties, geographical boundaries, alcohol content and production method. Guarantees origin and style of a wine, but not its quality.

ACID/ACIDITY
Naturally present in grapes and essential to wine, providing balance and stability and giving the refreshing tang in white wines and the appetizing grip in reds.

ADEGA
Portuguese for winery.

AGING
An alternative term for maturation.

ALCOHOLIC CONTENT
The alcoholic strength of wine, expressed as a percentage of the total volume of the wine. Typically in the range of 7–15%.

ALCOHOLIC FERMENTATION
The process whereby yeasts, natural or added, convert the grape sugars into alcohol (Ethyl alcohol, or Ethanol) and carbon dioxide.

AMONTILLADO
Traditionally dry style of sherry. *See* Jerez y Manzanilla in main A–Z.

ANBAUGEBIET
German for growing region; these names will appear on labels of all QbA and QmP wines. There are 13 *Anbaugebiete*: Ahr, Baden, Franken, Hessische Bergstrasse, Mittelrhein, Mosel-Saar-Ruwer, Nahe, Pfalz, Rheingau, Rheinhessen, Saale-Unstrut, Sachsen and Württemberg.

AUSBRUCH
Austrian Prädikat category used for sweet wines from the town of Rust.

AUSLESE
German and Austrian Prädikat category meaning that the grapes were 'selected' for their higher ripeness.

AVA (AMERICAN VITICULTURAL AREA)
System of appellations of origin for US wines.

AZIENDA AGRICOLA
Italian for estate or farm. It also indicates wine made from grapes grown by the proprietor.

BARREL AGING
Time spent maturing in wood, usually oak, during which wine takes on flavours from the wood.

BARREL FERMENTATION
Oak barrels may be used for fermentation instead of stainless steel to give a rich, oaky flavour to the wine.

BARRIQUE
The *barrique bordelaise* is the traditional Bordeaux oak barrel of 225 litres (50 gallons) capacity.

BAUMÉ
A scale measuring must weight (the amount of sugar in grape juice) to estimate potential alcohol content.

BEERENAUSLESE
German and Austrian Prädikat category applied to wines made from 'individually selected' berries (i.e. grapes) affected by noble rot (*Edelfäule* in German). The wines are rich and sweet. Beerenauslese wines are only produced in the best years in Germany, but in Austria they are a regular occurrence.

BEREICH
German for region or district within a wine region or *Anbaugebiet*. Bereichs tend to be large, and the use of a Bereich name, such as Bereich Bingen, without qualification is seldom an indication of quality – in most cases, quite the reverse.

BIODYNAMIC VITICULTURE
This approach works with the movement of the planets and cosmic forces to achieve health and balance in the soil and in the vine. Vines are treated with infusions of mineral, animal and plant materials, applied in homeopathic quantities, with some astonishing results.

BOTTLE SIZES

CHAMPAGNE

Magnum	1.5 litres	2 bottles
Jeroboam	3 litres	4 bottles
Rehoboam	4.5 litres	6 bottles
Methuselah	6 litres	8 bottles
Salmanazar	9 litres	12 bottles
Balthazar	12 litres	16 bottles
Nebuchadnezzar	15 litres	20 bottles

BORDEAUX

Magnum	1.5 litres	2 bottles
Marie-Jeanne	2.25 litres	3 bottles
Double-magnum	3 litres	4 bottles
Jeroboam	4.5 litres	6 bottles
Imperial	6 litres	8 bottles

BLANC DE BLANCS
White wine made from one or more white grape varieties. Used especially for sparkling wines; in Champagne, denotes wine made entirely from the Chardonnay grape.

BLANC DE NOIRS
White wine made from black grapes only – the juice is separated from the skins to avoid extracting any colour. Most often seen in Champagne, where it describes wine made from Pinot Noir and/or Pinot Meunier.

BLENDING
(assemblage) The art of mixing together wines of different origin, styles or age, often to balance out acidity, weight etc.

BODEGA
Spanish for winery.

BOTRYTIS
See noble rot.

BRUT
French term for dry sparkling wines, especially Champagne.

CARBONIC MACERATION
Winemaking method used to produce fresh fruity reds for drinking young. Whole (uncrushed) bunches of grapes are fermented in closed containers – a process that extracts lots of fruit and colour, but little tannin.

CHAMPAGNE METHOD
Traditional method used for all of the world's finest sparkling wines. A second fermentation takes place in the bottle, producing carbon dioxide which, kept in solution under pressure, gives the wine its fizz.

CHAPTALIZATION
Legal addition of sugar during fermentation to raise a wine's alcoholic strength. More necessary in cool climates where lack of sun produces insufficient natural sugar in the grape.

CHARMAT
See cuve close.

CHÂTEAU
French for castle, used to describe a variety of wine estates.

CHIARETTO
Italian for a rosé wine of very light pink colour from around Lake Garda.

CLARET
English for red Bordeaux wines, from the French clairet, which was traditionally used to describe a lighter style of red Bordeaux.

CLARIFICATION
Term covering any winemaking process (such as filtering or fining) that involves the removal of solid matter either from the must or the wine.

CLONE
Strain of grape species. The term is usually taken to mean laboratory-produced, virus-free clones, selected to produce higher or lower quantity, or selected for resistance to frost or disease.

CLOS
French for a walled vineyard – as in Burgundy's Clos de Vougeot – also commonly incorporated into the names of estates (e.g. Clos des Papes), regardless of whether they are walled or not.

COLD FERMENTATION
Long, slow fermentation at low temperature to extract maximum freshness from the grapes.

COLHEITA
Aged tawny port from a single vintage. See Port in main A–Z.

COMMUNE
A French village and its surrounding area or parish.

CO-OPERATIVE
In a co-operative cellar, growers who are members bring their grapes for vinification and bottling under a collective label. In terms of quantity, the French wine industry is dominated by co-ops. They often use less workaday titles, such as Caves des Vignerons, Producteurs Réunis, Union des Producteurs or Cellier des Vignerons.

CORKED/CORKY
Wine fault derived from a cork which has become contaminated, usually with Trichloroanisole or TCA. The mouldy, stale smell is unmistakable. Nothing to do with pieces of cork in the wine.

COSECHA
Spanish for vintage.

CÔTE
French word for a slope or hillside, which is where many, but not all, of the country's best vineyards are found.

CRÉMANT
French term for traditional-method sparkling wine from Alsace, Bordeaux, Burgundy, Die, Jura, Limoux, Loire and Luxembourg.

CRIANZA
Spanish term for the youngest official category of oak-matured wine. A red Crianza wine must have had at least 2 years' aging (1 in oak, 1 in bottle) before sale; a white or rosé, 1 year.

CRU
French for growth, meaning a specific plot of land or particular estate. In Burgundy, growths are divided into Grands (great) and

309

Premiers (first) Crus, and apply solely to the actual land. In Champagne the same terms are used for whole villages. In Bordeaux there are various hierarchical levels of Cru referring to estates rather than their vineyards. In Italy the term is used frequently, in an unofficial way, to indicate a single-vineyard or special-selection wine.

CRU BOURGEOIS
French term for wines from the Médoc that are ranked immediately below the Crus Classés (last revised in 2003). Many are excellent value for money.

CRU CLASSÉ
The Classed Growths are the aristocracy of Bordeaux, ennobled by the Classifications of 1855 (for the Médoc, Barsac and Sauternes), 1955, 1969, 1986, 1996 and 2006 (for St-Émilion) and 1953 and 1959 (for Graves). Curiously, Pomerol has never been classified. The modern classifications are more reliable than the 1855 version, which was based solely on the price of the wines at the time of the Great Exhibition in Paris, but in terms of prestige the 1855 Classification remains the most important. With the exception of a single alteration in 1973, when Ch. Mouton-Rothschild was elevated to First Growth status, the list has not changed since 1855. It certainly needs revising.

CUVE CLOSE
A bulk process used to produce inexpensive sparkling wines. The second fermentation, which produces the bubbles, takes place in tank rather than in the bottle. Also called Charmat.

CUVÉE
French for the contents of a single vat or tank, but usually indicates a wine blended from either different grape varieties or the best barrels of wine.

DÉGORGEMENT
Stage in the production of Champagne-method wines when the sediment, collected in the neck of the bottle during *remuage*, is removed.

DEMI-SEC
French for medium-dry.

DO (DENOMINACIÓN DE ORIGEN)
Spain's equivalent of the French AC quality category, regulating origin and production methods.

DOC (DENOMINAÇÃO DE ORIGEM CONTROLADA)
Portugal's top regional classification for wines.

DOCa (DENOMINACIÓN DE ORIGEN CALIFICADA)
Spanish quality wine category, intended to be one step up from DO. So far only Rioja and Priorat qualify.

DOC (DENOMINAZIONE DI ORIGINE CONTROLLATA)
Italian quality wine category, regulating origin, grape varieties, yield and production methods.

DOCG (DENOMINAZIONE DI ORIGINE CONTROLLATA E GARANTITA)
The top tier of the Italian classification system.

DOSAGE
A sugar and wine mixture added to sparkling wine after *dégorgement* which affects how sweet or dry it will be.

EDELZWICKER
Blended wine from Alsace, usually bland.

EINZELLAGE
German for an individual vineyard site which is generally farmed by several growers. The name is preceded on the label by that of the village; for example, the Wehlener Sonnenuhr is the Sonnenuhr vineyard in Wehlen. The mention of a particular site should signify a superior wine. Sadly, this is not necessarily so.

EISWEIN
Rare, chiefly German and Austrian, late-harvested wine made by picking the grapes and pressing them while frozen. This concentrates the sweetness of the grape as most of the liquid is removed as ice. *See also* Icewine.

ESCOLHA
Portuguese for selection.

FEINHERB
Disliking the unsatisfactory term Halbtrocken, some producers prefer the term Feinherb. It lacks legal definition but usually applies to wines with 9–25g per litre of residual sugar.

FILTERING
Removal of yeasts, solids and any impurities from a wine before bottling.

FINING
Method of clarifying wine by adding a coagulant (e.g. egg whites, isinglass, bentonite) to remove soluble particles such as proteins and excessive tannins.

FINO
The lightest, freshest style of sherry. *See* Jerez y Manzanilla in main A–Z.

FLOR
A film of yeast which forms on the surface of fino sherries (and some other wines) in the barrel, preventing oxidation and imparting a tangy, dry flavour.

FLYING WINEMAKER
Term coined in the late 1980s to describe enologists, many Australian-trained, brought in to improve the quality of wines in many underperforming wine regions.

FORTIFIED WINE
Wine which has high-alcohol grape spirit added, usually before the initial fermentation is completed, thereby preserving sweetness.

FRIZZANTE
Italian for semi-sparkling wine, usually made dry, but sometimes sweet.

GARAGE WINE
See vin de garage.

GARRAFEIRA
Portuguese term for wine from an outstanding vintage, with 0.5% more alcohol than the minimum required, and 2 years' aging in vat or barrel followed by 1 year in bottle for reds, and 6 months of each for whites. Also used by merchants for their best blended and aged wines. Use of the term is in decline as producers opt for the more readily recognized Reserva as an alternative on the label.

GRAN RESERVA
Top category of Spanish wines from a top vintage, with at least 5 years' aging (2 of them in cask) for reds and 4 for whites.

GRAND CRU
French for great growth. Supposedly the best vineyard sites in Alsace, Burgundy, Champagne and parts of Bordeaux and should produce the most exciting wines.

GRANDES MARQUES
Great brands – the Syndicat des Grandes Marques was once Champagne's self-appointed élite. It disbanded in 1997.

GROSSLAGE
German term for a grouping of vineyards. Some are not too big, and have the advantage of allowing small amounts of higher QmP wines to be made from the grapes from several vineyards. But sometimes the use of vast Grosslage names (e.g. Niersteiner Gutes Domtal) deceives consumers into believing they are buying something special. Top estates have agreed not to use Grosslage names on their labels.

HALBTROCKEN
German for medium dry. In Germany and Austria medium-dry wine has 9–18g per litre of residual sugar, though sparkling wine is allowed up to 50g per litre. See Feinherb.

ICEWINE
A speciality of Canada, produced from juice squeezed from ripe grapes that have frozen on the vine. See also Eiswein.

IGT (INDICAZIONE GEOGRAFICA TIPICA)
The Italian equivalent of the French vin de pays. As in the Midi, both premium and everyday wines may share the same appellation. Many of the Super-Tuscan vini da tavola are now sold under a regional IGT.

IPR (INDICAÇÃO DE PROVENIÊNCIA REGULAMENTADA)
The second tier in the Portuguese wine classifications, for regions awaiting approval for DOC. Or not (see page 37).

KABINETT
Term used for the lowest level of QmP wines in Germany.

LANDWEIN
German or Austrian 'country' wine; the

equivalent of French vin de pays. The wine must have a territorial definition and may be chaptalized to give it more alcohol.

LATE HARVEST
See Vendange Tardive.

LAYING DOWN
The storing of wine which will improve with age.

LEES
Sediment – dead yeast cells, grape pips (seeds), pulp and tartrates – thrown by wine during fermentation and left behind after racking. Some wines are left on the fine lees for as long as possible to take on extra flavour.

MALOLACTIC FERMENTATION
Secondary fermentation whereby harsh malic acid is converted into mild lactic acid and carbon dioxide. Normal in red wines but often prevented in whites to preserve a fresh, fruity taste.

MANZANILLA
The tangiest style of sherry, similar to fino. See Jerez y Manzanilla in main A–Z.

MATURATION
Term for the beneficial aging of wine.

MERITAGE
American term for red or white wines made from a blend of Bordeaux grape varieties.

MESOCLIMATE
The climate of a specific geographical area, be it a vineyard or simply a hillside or valley.

MIDI
A loose geographical term, virtually synonymous with Languedoc-Roussillon, covering the vast, sunbaked area of southern France

311

between the Pyrenees and the Rhône Valley.

MOELLEUX
French for soft or mellow, used to describe sweet or medium-sweet wines.

MOUSSEUX
French for sparkling wine.

MUST
The mixture of grape juice, skins, pips and pulp produced after crushing (but prior to completion of fermentation), which will eventually become wine.

MUST WEIGHT
An indicator of the sugar content of juice – and therefore the ripeness of grapes.

NÉGOCIANT
French term for a merchant who buys and sells wine. A négociant-éléveur is a merchant who buys, makes, ages and sells wine.

NEW WORLD
When used as a geographical term, New World includes the Americas, South Africa, Australia and New Zealand. By extension, it is also a term used to describe the clean, fruity, upfront style now in evidence all over the world, but pioneered in the USA and Australia.

NOBLE ROT
(*Botrytis cinerea*) Fungus which, when it attacks ripe white grapes, shrivels the fruit and intensifies their sugar while adding a distinctive flavour. A vital factor in creating many of the world's finest sweet wines, such as Sauternes and Trockenbeerenauslese.

OAK
The wood used almost exclusively to make barrels for fermenting and aging fine wines.

OECHSLE
German scale measuring must weight (sugar content).

OLOROSO
The darkest, most heavily fortified style of sherry. *See* Jerez y Manzanilla in main A–Z.

OXIDATION
Over-exposure of wine to air, causing loss of fruit and flavour. Slight oxidation, such as occurs through the wood of a barrel or during racking, is part of the aging process and, in wines of sufficient structure, enhances flavour and complexity.

PASSITO
Italian term for wine made from dried grapes. The result is usually a sweet wine with a raisiny intensity of fruit. The drying process is called *appassimento*. *See also* Moscato Passito di Pantelleria, Recioto della Valpolicella, Recioto di Soave and Vin Santo in main A–Z.

PERLWEIN
German for a lightly sparkling wine.

PÉTILLANT
French for a lightly sparkling wine.

PHYLLOXERA
The vine aphid *Phylloxera vastatrix* attacks vine roots. It devastated European and consequently other vineyards around the world in the late 1800s soon after it arrived from America. Since then, the vulnerable *Vitis vinifera* has generally been grafted on to vinously inferior, but phylloxera-resistant, American rootstocks.

PRÄDIKAT
Grades defining quality wines in Germany and Austria. These are (in ascending order) Kabinett (not considered

as Prädikat in Austria), Spätlese, Auslese, Beerenauslese, the Austrian-only category Ausbruch, and Trockenbeerenauslese. Strohwein and Eiswein are also Prädikat wines. Some Spätleses and even a few Ausleses are now made as dry wines.

PREMIER CRU
First Growth; the top quality classification in parts of Bordeaux, but second to Grand Cru in Burgundy. Used in Champagne to designate vineyards just below Grand Cru.

PRIMEUR
French term for a young wine, often released for sale within a few weeks of the harvest. Beaujolais Nouveau is the best-known example.

QbA (QUALITÄTSWEIN BESTIMMTER ANBAUGEBIETE)
German for quality wine from designated regions. Sugar can be added to increase the alcohol content. Usually pretty ordinary, but from top estates this category offers excellent value for money. In Austria *Qualitätswein* is equivalent to the German QbA.

QmP (QUALITÄTSWEIN MIT PRÄDIKAT)
German for quality wine with distinction. A higher category than QbA, with controlled yields and no sugar addition. QmP covers 6 levels based on the ripeness of the grapes: *see* Prädikat.

QUINTA
Portuguese for farm or estate.

RACKING
Gradual clarification of wine; the wine is transferred from one barrel or container to another, leaving the lees behind.

RANCIO
A fortified wine deliberately exposed to the effects of oxidation, found mainly in Languedoc-Roussillon, Cataluña and southern Spain.

REMUAGE
Process in Champagne-making whereby the bottles, stored on their sides and at a progressively steeper angle in *pupitres*, are twisted, or riddled, each day so that the sediment moves down the sides and collects in the neck of the bottle on the cap, ready for *dégorgement*.

RESERVA
Spanish wines that have fulfilled certain aging requirements: reds must have at least 3 years' aging before sale, of which one must be in oak barrels; whites and rosés must have at least 2 years' age, of which 6 months must be in oak.

RÉSERVE
French for what is, in theory at least, a winemaker's finest wine. The word has no legal definition in France.

RIPASSO
A method used in Valpolicella to make wines with extra depth. Wine is passed over the lees of Recioto or Amarone della Valpolicella, adding extra alcohol and flavour, though also extra tannin and a risk of higher acidity and oxidation.

RISERVA
An Italian term, recognized in many DOCs and DOCGs, for a special selection of wine that has been aged longer before release. It is only a promise of a more pleasurable drink if the wine had enough fruit and structure in the first place.

SEC
French for dry. When applied to Champagne, it actually means medium-dry.

'SECOND' WINES
A second selection from a designated vineyard, usually lighter and quicker-maturing than the main wine.

SEDIMENT
Usually refers to residue thrown by a wine, particularly red, as it ages in bottle.

SEKT
German for sparkling wine. The wine will be entirely German only if it is called Deutscher Sekt or Sekt bA. The best wines are traditional-method made from 100% Riesling or from 100% Weissburgunder (Pinot Blanc).

SÉLECTION DE GRAINS NOBLES
A superripe category for sweet Alsace wines, now also being used by some producers of Coteaux du Layon in the Loire for the most concentrated wines. *See also* Vendange Tardive.

SMARAGD
The top of the three categories of wine from the Wachau in Austria, the lower two being Federspiel and Steinfeder. Made from very ripe and usually late-harvested grapes, the wines have a minimum of 12% alcohol, often 13–14%.

SOLERA
Traditional Spanish system of blending fortified wines, especially sherry and Montilla-Moriles.

SPÄTLESE
German for late-picked (therefore riper) grapes. Often moderately sweet, though there are dry versions.

SPUMANTE
Italian for sparkling. Bottle-fermented wines are often referred to as *metodo classico* or *metodo tradizionale*.

SUPÉRIEUR
French for a wine with a slightly higher alcohol content than the basic AC.

SUPERIORE
Italian DOC wines with higher alcohol or more aging potential.

SUR LIE
French for on the lees, meaning wine bottled direct from the cask/fermentation vat to gain extra flavour from the lees. Common with quality Muscadet, white Burgundy, similar barrel-aged whites and, increasingly, commercial bulk whites.

TAFELWEIN
German for table wine.

TANNIN
Harsh, bitter, mouth-puckering element in red wine, derived from grape skins and stems, and from oak barrels. Tannins soften with age and are essential for long-term development in red wines.

TERROIR
A French term used to denote the combination of soil, climate and exposure to the sun – that is, the natural physical environment of the vine.

TRADITIONAL METHOD
See Champagne method.

TROCKEN
German for dry. In most parts of Germany and Austria Trocken matches the standard EU definition of dryness – less than 9g per litre residual sugar.

TROCKENBEEREN-AUSLESE (TBA)
German for 'dry berry

selected', denoting grapes affected by noble rot (*Edelfäule* in German) – the wines will be lusciously sweet although low in alcohol.

VARIETAL
Wine made from, and named after, a single or dominant grape variety.

VDP
German organization recognizable on the label by a Prussian eagle bearing grapes. The quality of estates included is usually – but not always – high.

VDQS (VIN DÉLIMITÉ DE QUALITÉ SUPÉRIEURE)
The second-highest classification for French wines, behind AC.

VELHO
Portuguese for old. Legally applied only to wines with at least 3 years' aging for reds and 2 years for whites.

VENDANGE TARDIVE
French for late harvest. Grapes are left on the vines beyond the normal harvest time to concentrate flavours and sugars. The term is traditional in Alsace. The Italian term is *vendemmia tardiva*.

VIEILLES VIGNES
French term for a wine made from vines at least 20 years old. Should have greater concentration than wine from younger vines.

VIÑA
Spanish for vineyard.

VIN DE GARAGE
Wines made on so small a scale they could be made in one's garage. Such wines may be made from vineyards of a couple of hectares or less, and are often of extreme concentration.

VIN DE PAILLE Sweet wine found mainly in

the Jura region of France. Traditionally, the grapes are left for 2–3 months on straw (*paille*) mats before fermentation to dehydrate, thus concentrating the sugars. The wines are sweet but slightly nutty.

VIN DE PAYS
The term gives a regional identity to wine from the country districts of France. It is a particularly useful category for adventurous winemakers who want to use good-quality grapes not allowed under the frequently restrictive AC regulations. Many are labelled with the grape variety.

VIN DE TABLE
French for table wine, the lowest quality level.

VIN DOUX NATUREL (VDN)
French for a fortified wine, where fermentation has been stopped by the addition of alcohol, leaving the wine 'naturally' sweet, although you could argue that stopping fermentation with a slug of powerful spirit is distinctly unnatural.

VIN JAUNE
A speciality of the Jura region in France, made from the Savagnin grape. In Château-Chalon it is the only permitted style. Made in a similar way to fino sherry but not fortified. Unlike fino, *vin jaune* usually ages well.

VINIFICATION
The process of turning grapes into wine.

VINO DA TAVOLA
The Italian term for table wine, officially Italy's lowest level of production, is a catch-all that until recently applied to more than 80% of the nation's wine, with virtually no regulations controlling

quality. Yet this category also provided the arena in the 1970s for the biggest revolution in quality that Italy has ever seen, with the creation of innovative, DOC-busting Super-Tuscans in main A–Z.

VINTAGE
The year's grape harvest, also used to describe wines of a single year. 'Off-vintage' is a year not generally declared as vintage. *See* Port in main A–Z.

VITICULTURE
Vine-growing and vineyard management.

VITIS VINIFERA
Vine species, native to Europe and Central Asia, from which almost all the world's quality wine is made.

VQA (VINTNERS QUALITY ALLIANCE)
Canadian equivalent of France's AC system, defining quality standards and designated viticultural areas.

WEISSHERBST
German rosé wine, a speciality of Baden.

WO (WINE OF ORIGIN)
South African system of appellations which certifies area of origin, grape variety and vintage.

YIELD
The amount of fruit, and ultimately wine, produced from a vineyard. Measured in hectolitres per hectare (hl/ha) in most of Europe and in the New World as tons per acre or tonnes per hectare. Yield may vary from year to year, and depends on grape variety, age and density of the vines, and viticultural practices.

WHO OWNS WHAT

The world's major drinks companies are getting bigger and, frankly, I'm worried. As these vast wine conglomerates stride across continents, it seems highly likely that local traditions will – for purely business reasons – be pared away, along with individuality of flavour. It's not all bad news: in some cases wineries have benefited from the huge resources that come with corporate ownership, but I can't help feeling nervous knowing that the fate of a winery rests in the hands of distant institutional investors. Below I have listed some of the names that crop up again and again – and will no doubt continue to do so, as they aggressively pursue their grasp of market share.

Other wine companies – which bottle wines under their own names and feature in the main A–Z – are spreading their nets. GALLO has agreements with SIEUR D'ARQUES in southern France, Leonardo Da Vinci winery in Tuscany, MCWILLIAM'S of Australia and Whitehaven of New Zealand. The HESS COLLECTION in California owns Peter LEHMANN in Australia, GLEN CARLOU in South Africa and Colomé in Argentina. As well as Ch. MOUTON-ROTHSCHILD, the Rothschild family have other interests in France, co-own OPUS ONE and, in partnership with CONCHA Y TORO, produce ALMAVIVA in Chile.

The never-ending whirl of joint ventures, mergers and takeovers shows no signs of slowing down: the following can only be a snapshot at the time of going to press.

AXA-MILLESIMES
The French insurance giant AXA's subsidiary owns Bordeaux châteaux PETIT-VILLAGE, PICHON-LONGUEVILLE, Pibran and SUDUIRAUT, plus Dom. de l'Arlot in Burgundy, Ch. Belles Eaux in the Languedoc, TOKAJI producer Disznókö and port producer Quinta do NOVAL.

BEAM WINE ESTATES
A subsidiary of Fortune Brands and owner of California's GEYSER PEAK, Canyon Road and Wild Horse, in 2005 Beam acquired Allied Domecq's US wine brands, including ATLAS PEAK, CLOS DU BOIS, Buena Vista and Gary Farrell, as well as Harveys sherry. In 2006 Beam formed an agreement with New Zealand brewers Lion Nathan – owners of PETALUMA (with KNAPPSTEIN, Mitchelton and STONIER), St Hallett, Tatachilla and WITHER HILLS.

CONSTELLATION BRANDS
The world's largest wine company was created in 2003 by the merger of US-based wine, beer and spirits group Constellation Brands with Australia's BRL Hardy. In late 2004 Constellation paid out $1.36 billion for the prestigious Robert MONDAVI Winery and all its entities, including OPUS ONE (although it later surrendered Italian premium wines Luce della Vite and ORNELLAIA to FRESCOBALDI). Robert Mondavi Winery is now part of Constellation's Icon Estates division, along with FRANCISCAN Oakville Estate, Estancia, Mount Veeder Winery, RAVENSWOOD and SIMI in California, Columbia Winery in Washington and Veramonte in Chile. Other US brands include Almaden, Blackstone, Covey Run, Inglenook and Paul Masson. BRL Hardy had already looked outside Australia (where brands include Banrock Station, BAROSSA VALLEY ESTATE, HARDYS, HOUGHTON, LEASINGHAM, Moondah Brook, Reynell, Stonehaven, Yarra Burn) to New Zealand's NOBILO (Selaks, White Cloud) – and in 2003 launched Shamwari ('Friendship') wines, a joint venture with Stellenbosch Vineyards (now Omnia Wines) of South Africa. One of the UK's top-selling brands, Stowells, is part of Constellation,

which has also has a 40% stake in Italy's RUFFINO. Constellation recently bought Canada's Vincor in a hostile takeover. The Canadian company includes Kim Crawford in New Zealand, Kumala in South Africa, Australia's Amberley Estate and Goundrey, Toasted Head in California, Hogue Cellars in Washington State, as well as INNISKILLIN and other producers in Canada.

FOSTER'S GROUP

The wine division of Foster's, the Australian brewing giant, was founded on the twin pillars of Australia's Wolf BLASS and BERINGER in California. In May 2005 Foster's won control of Southcorp, Australia's biggest wine conglomerate. It currently controls around 60 different brands and producers. In California it owns, among others, Carmenet, CHATEAU ST JEAN, Chateau Souverain, Etude, Meridian, St Clement and Stags' Leap Winery. Australian brands include Annie's Lane, Baileys of Glenrowan, Leo Buring, COLDSTREAM HILLS, Devil's Lair, Jamiesons Run, LINDEMANS, Metala, Mildara, Greg Norman, PENFOLDS, ROSEMOUNT ESTATE, Rothbury Estate, Rouge Homme, Saltram (Mamre Brook), Seaview, SEPPELT, T'Gallant, Tollana, WYNNS, Yarra Ridge and Yellowglen. Foster's also owns Herrick in southern France, and MATUA VALLEY and Secret Stone in New Zealand.

FREIXENET

Owner of some of Spain's biggest names (including Castellblanch, Conde de Caralt, Segura Viudas, René Barbier) and companies in California, Mexico and Argentina. It also owns the Champagne house of Henri Abelé, Bordeaux négociant/producer Yvon Mau and Australia's Wingara Wine Group (Deakin Estate, KATNOOK ESTATE, Riddoch Estate).

JACKSON FAMILY WINES

Jess Jackson, founder of California's KENDALL-JACKSON, also owns a number of other wineries in California, including ARROWOOD, Atalon, Cambria, Cardinale, Edmeades, HARTFORD, La Crema, La Jota, MATANZAS CREEK, Pepi, Stonestreet and Vérité. Jackson also owns Calina (Chile), Yangarra Estate (Australia), Château Lassegue (ST-EMILION) and Villa Arceno (Tuscany).

LVMH

French luxury goods group Louis Vuitton-Moët Hennessy owns Champagne houses MOET & CHANDON (including Dom Pérignon), KRUG, Mercier, RUINART and VEUVE CLICQUOT, and has established DOMAINE CHANDON sparkling wine companies in California, Australia and Argentina. It also owns Ch. d'YQUEM, CAPE MENTELLE in Australia, CLOUDY BAY in New Zealand, NEWTON in California, and TERRAZAS DE LOS ANDES in Argentina.

PERNOD RICARD

The French spirits giant owns Australia's ORLANDO Wyndham Group, with its all-conquering Jacob's Creek brand. In 2005 it acquired the UK-based Allied Domecq group, but sold a number of wineries to Beam Wine Estates Pernod Ricard's empire encompasses New Zealand's mighty MONTANA (CHURCH ROAD, Corbans, Deutz, Lindauer, Stoneleigh), Champagne producers MUMM and PERRIER-JOUET, Californian fizz MUMM NAPA, Long Mountain in South Africa and a number of Argentinian producers, including Balbi, Etchart and Graffigna. In Spain it controls CAMPO VIEJO, Palacio de la Vega, Marqués de Arienzo, Siglo and Tarsus, among others, and in Georgia it has a 75% stake in Georgian Wines & Spirits.

INDEX OF PRODUCERS

Numbers in **bold** refer to main entries.

321

328

330

340

OLDER VINTAGE CHARTS *(top wines only)*

FRANCE										
Alsace (vendanges tardives)	96	95	90	89	88	85	83	81	76	71
	8◆	9◆	10◆	9◆	8◆	8◆	9◆	7◇	10◆	9◇
Champagne (vintage)	96	95	90	89	88	86	85	83	82	76
	9◇	8◆	9◆	8◆	9◆	7◆	8◆	7◇	10◆	9◇
Bordeaux	96	95	94	90	89	88	86	85	83	82
Margaux	8◆	8◆	6◇	10◆	8◆	7◆	8◆	8◆	9◇	8◆
St.-Jul., Pauillac, St-Est.	9◆	8◆	7◇	10◆	9◆	8◆	9◆	8◆	7◇	10◆
Graves/Pessac-L. (red)	8◆	8◆	6◇	8◆	8◆	8◆	6◆	8◆	8◇	9◆
St-Émilion, Pomerol	7◆	9◆	6◇	10◆	9◆	8◆	7◆	9◆	7◇	9◆
Bordeaux (cont.)	81	75	70	66	61	59	55	53	49	47
Margaux (cont.)	7◇	6◇	8◇	7◇	10◆	8◇	6◇	8◇	9◇	8◇
St.-Jul. etc. (cont.)	7◇	8◇	8◇	8◇	10◆	9◇	8◇	9◇	10◇	9◇
Graves etc. (R) (cont.)	7◇	6◇	8◇	8◇	10◆	9◇	8◇	8◇	10◇	9◇
St-Émilion etc. (cont.)	7◇	8◇	8◇	6◇	10◆	7◇	7◇	8◇	9◇	10◇
Sauternes	96	95	90	89	88	86	83	80	76	75
	9◆	7◆	10◆	9◆	9◆	9◆	9◆	7◇	8◇	8◇
Sauternes (cont.)	71	67	62	59	55	53	49	47	45	37
	8◇	9◇	8◇	9◇	8◇	8◇	10◇	10◇	9◇	10◇
Burgundy										
Chablis	96	95	92	90	89	88	86	85		
	9◆	8◆	7◇	10◆	8◇	8◇	7◇	9◇		
Côte de Beaune (wh.)	95	93	92	90	89	88	86	85	82	79
	9◇	7◇	8◇	7◇	9◇	6◇	8◇	8◇	7◇	8◇
Côte de Nuits (red)	96	95	93	90	89	88	85	83	80	78
	9◆	8◆	8◆	9◆	7◇	8◇	9◇	6◇	6◇	10◆